Key to the road maps
Pages 33-352

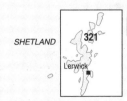

SHETLAND

321

Lerwick

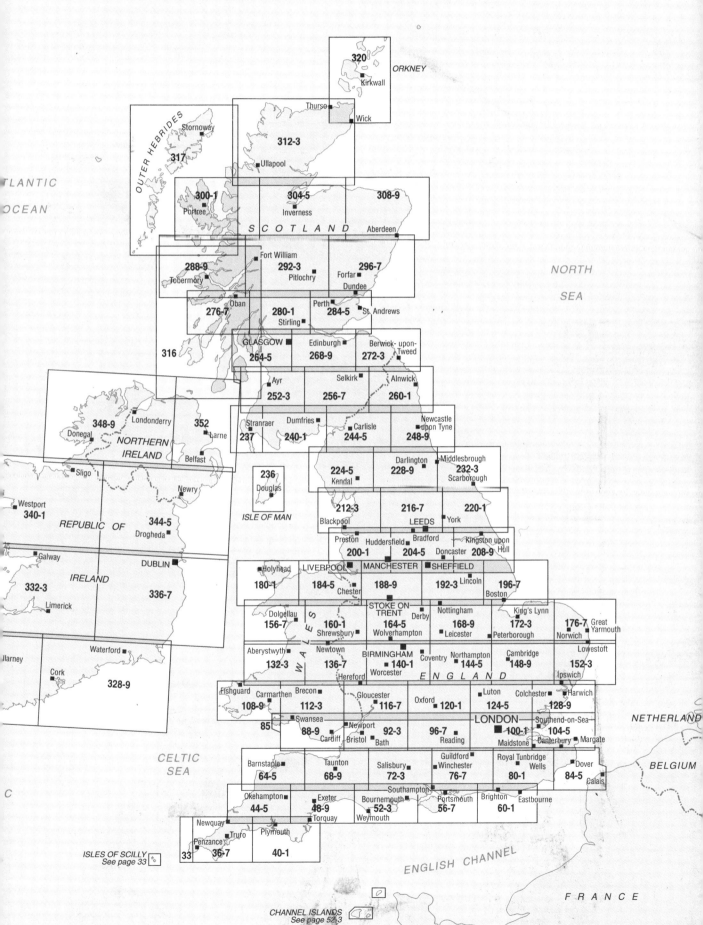

320

ORKNEY

Kirkwall

Thurso

Wick

312-3

Ullapool

OUTER HEBRIDES

Stornoway

317

ATLANTIC

OCEAN

300-1

Portree

304-5

Inverness

308-9

SCOTLAND

Aberdeen

NORTH

SEA

288-9

Tobermory

Fort William

292-3

Pitlochry

296-7

Forfar

Dundee

Oban

276-7

280-1

Stirling

Perth

284-5

St. Andrews

316

GLASGOW

264-5

Edinburgh

268-9

Berwick-upon-Tweed

272-3

Ayr

252-3

Selkirk

256-7

Alnwick

260-1

348-9

Donegal

Londonderry

352

Larne

NORTHERN
IRELAND

Belfast

Stranraer

237

Dumfries

240-1

Carlisle

244-5

Newcastle
upon Tyne

248-9

Sligo

Newry

236

Douglas

ISLE OF MAN

Kendal

224-5

Darlington

228-9

Middlesbrough

232-3

Scarborough

Westport

340-1

REPUBLIC OF

344-5

Drogheda

Blackpool

212-3

216-7

LEEDS

York

220-1

Galway

IRELAND

DUBLIN

Preston

Huddersfield

200-1

Bradford

204-5

Doncaster

Kingston upon Hull

208-9

332-3

Limerick

336-7

Holyhead

180-1

LIVERPOOL

184-5

Chester

MANCHESTER

188-9

SHEFFIELD

192-3

Lincoln

196-7

Boston

Killarney

Waterford

328-9

Dolgellau

156-7

WALES

160-1

Shrewsbury

STOKE ON
TRENT

164-5

Wolverhampton

Derby

Nottingham

168-9

Leicester

Peterborough

King's Lynn

172-3

Norwich

176-7

Great
Yarmouth

Cork

Aberystwyth

132-3

Newtown

136-7

Hereford

BIRMINGHAM

140-1

Worcester

Coventry

ENGLAND

Northampton

144-5

Cambridge

148-9

Lowestoft

152-3

Ipswich

Fishguard

108-9

Carmarthen

112-3

Brecon

Gloucester

116-7

Oxford

120-1

Luton

124-5

Colchester

128-9

Harwich

NETHERLAND

85

Swansea

88-9

Cardiff

Newport

Bristol

92-3

Bath

96-7

Reading

LONDON

100-1

Maidstone

Southend-on-Sea

104-5

Canterbury

Margate

CELTIC

SEA

Barnstaple

64-5

Taunton

68-9

Salisbury

72-3

Guildford
Winchester

76-7

Royal Tunbridge
Wells

80-1

Dover

84-5

Calais

BELGIUM

Okehampton

44-5

Exeter

48-9

Torquay

Bournemouth

52-3

Weymouth

Southampton

Portsmouth

56-7

Brighton

60-1

Eastbourne

Newquay

Penzance

Truro

36-7

Plymouth

40-1

33

ISLES OF SCILLY
See page 33

ENGLISH CHANNEL

FRANCE

CHANNEL ISLANDS
See page 52-3

READER'S DIGEST

BOOK *of the* ROAD

Published by The Reader's Digest Association Limited
LONDON • NEW YORK • SYDNEY • CAPE TOWN • MONTREAL

READER'S DIGEST BOOK OF THE ROAD
was edited and designed by
The Reader's Digest Association Limited, London.

First edition Copyright © 1996
The Reader's Digest Association Limited,
Berkeley Square House, Berkeley Square,
London W1X 6AB.

Copyright © 1996 Reader's Digest Association
Far East Limited.

Philippines Copyright © 1996 Reader's Digest
Association Far East Limited.

® Reader's Digest, The Digest and the Pegasus logo
are registered trademarks of The Reader's Digest
Association, Inc, of Pleasantville, New York, USA.

Printed by Venturini & C SpA,
San Martino in Rio (RE), Italy, and
BPC Hazell Books Ltd, Aylesbury, Bucks.
Bound by BPC Hazell Books Ltd, Aylesbury, Bucks.

Index processed by Barbers Ltd, Wrotham, Kent.

ISBN 0 276 42190 6

CONTENTS

EDITOR
Joyce Pendry

ART EDITOR
Julie Busby

CARTOGRAPHIC EDITOR
Alison Ewington

....

WRITERS
Russell Chamberlin
Anne Gatti
Charlie Hurt
Ron Mellor

ASSISTANT EDITORS
John Andrews
Alison Freegard
Peter Lawson
Tim Locke
Claire Monk

RESEARCHERS
Hilary Arafeh
Sally Bamber
Alison Knowles
Sarah Toynbee

EDITORIAL ASSISTANT
Stacey Mendoza

ASSISTANT CARTOGRAPHIC EDITOR
David Irvine

CARTOGRAPHIC RESEARCHERS
Sally Gable
Vanessa Gale

CARTOGRAPHIC CONTRIBUTORS
The Automobile Association
Colourmap Scanning Ltd
Map Data Management Ltd
Ordnance Survey, Dublin
Ordnance Survey, Southampton
Ordnance Survey of Northern Ireland,
Belfast

....

CONSULTANTS
Ted Clements MBE, Chief Examiner,
Institute of Advanced Motorists
PHH Vehicle Management Services
Jim Williams, British Red Cross

ASSISTANT DESIGNERS
Clare Marshall
David Oh

PICTURE RESEARCHER
Rosie Taylor

ILLUSTRATORS
Ian Atkinson

Peter Barrett
Graham Byfield
represented by Artists' Partners Ltd

Paul Guest
represented by Beint and Beint Ltd

Nicolas Hall
Jon Jackson
Kuo Kang Chen
Precision Illustration
Tim Pearce
Gill Tomblin
Paul Weston

PHOTOGRAPHER
Martin Cameron

....

READER'S DIGEST GENERAL BOOKS

EDITORIAL DIRECTOR
Robin Hosie

EXECUTIVE EDITOR
Michael Davison

MANAGING EDITOR
Paul Middleton

EDITORIAL GROUP HEADS
Julian Browne
Noel Buchanan
Cortina Butler
Jeremy Harwood

ART DIRECTOR
Bob Hook

RESEARCH EDITOR
Prue Grice

PICTURE RESEARCH EDITOR
Martin Smith

Planning your route

To decide on a route for your journey, first chart it in outline between starting and finishing points on the map of principal motorways below, then use the route-planning maps—scale about 25 miles to 1 inch—on pages 6-12 to fill in the overall picture. The distance charts inside the back cover give a general idea of mileages. For detailed plans of motorways, turn to pages 14-32; these show junctions and link roads. It is a good idea to note down the road numbers of your route, and turn-off points from one road to another, for reference during your journey.

Your route can be followed in detail on the larger-scale road maps beginning on page 33. There is even greater detail in the local routes that start on page 353; these provide street plans of major towns, ports and airports, as well as routes to guide you through and round some of the most crowded major city areas.

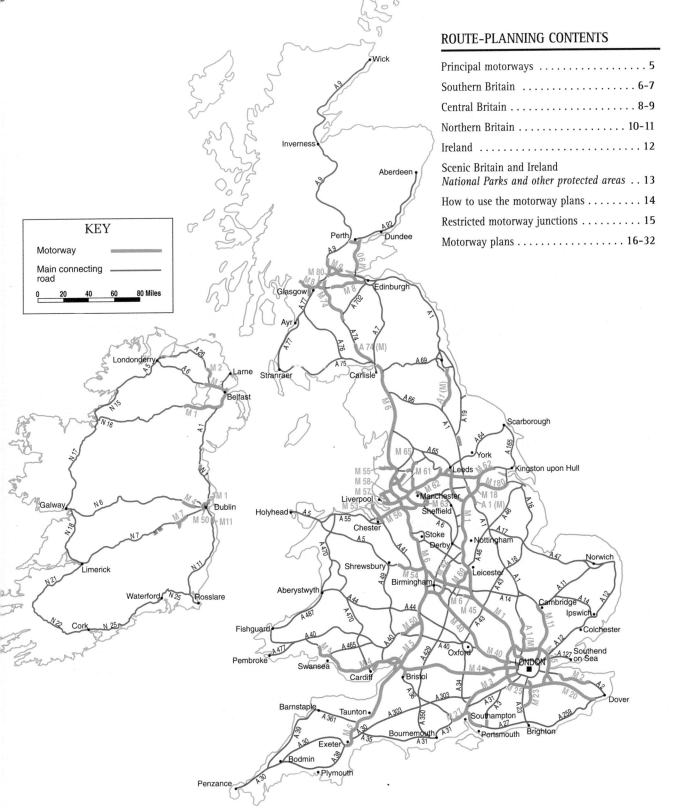

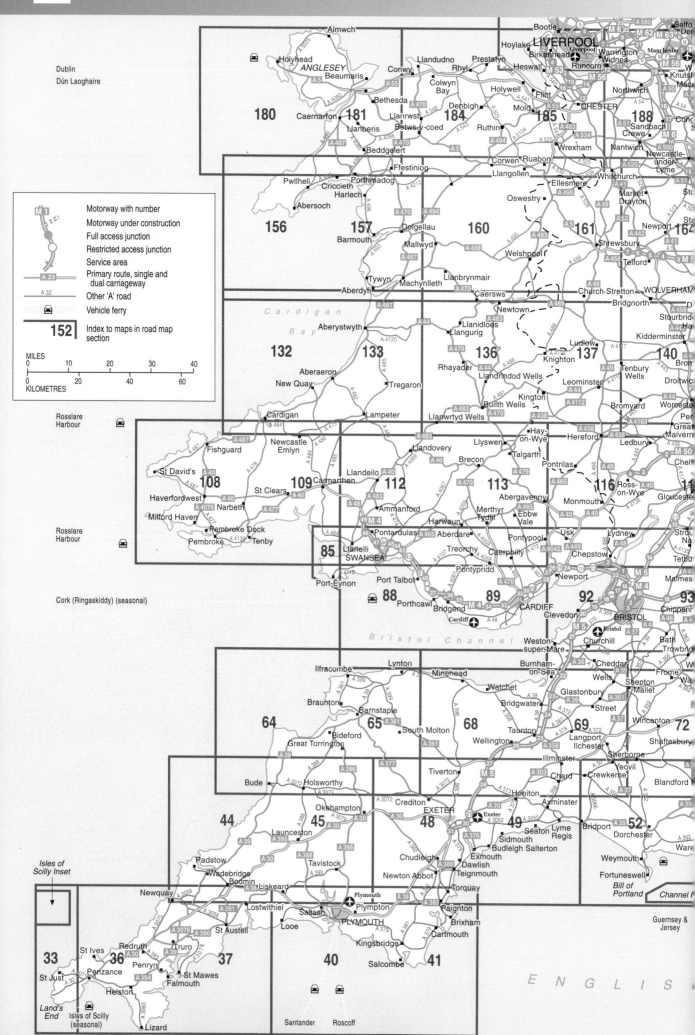

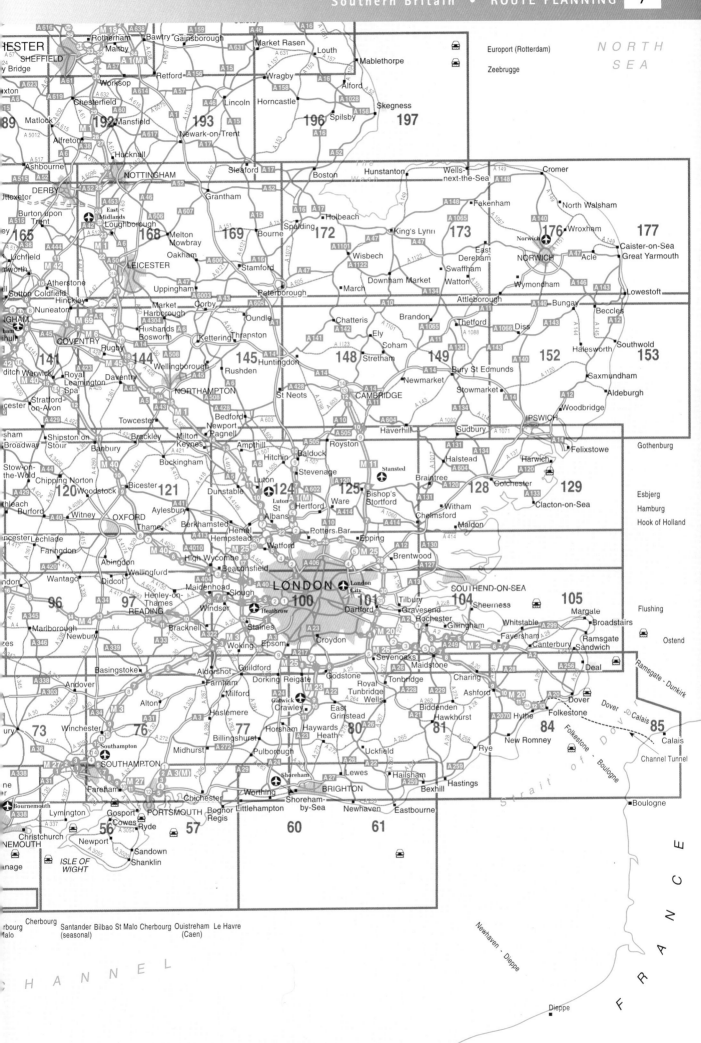

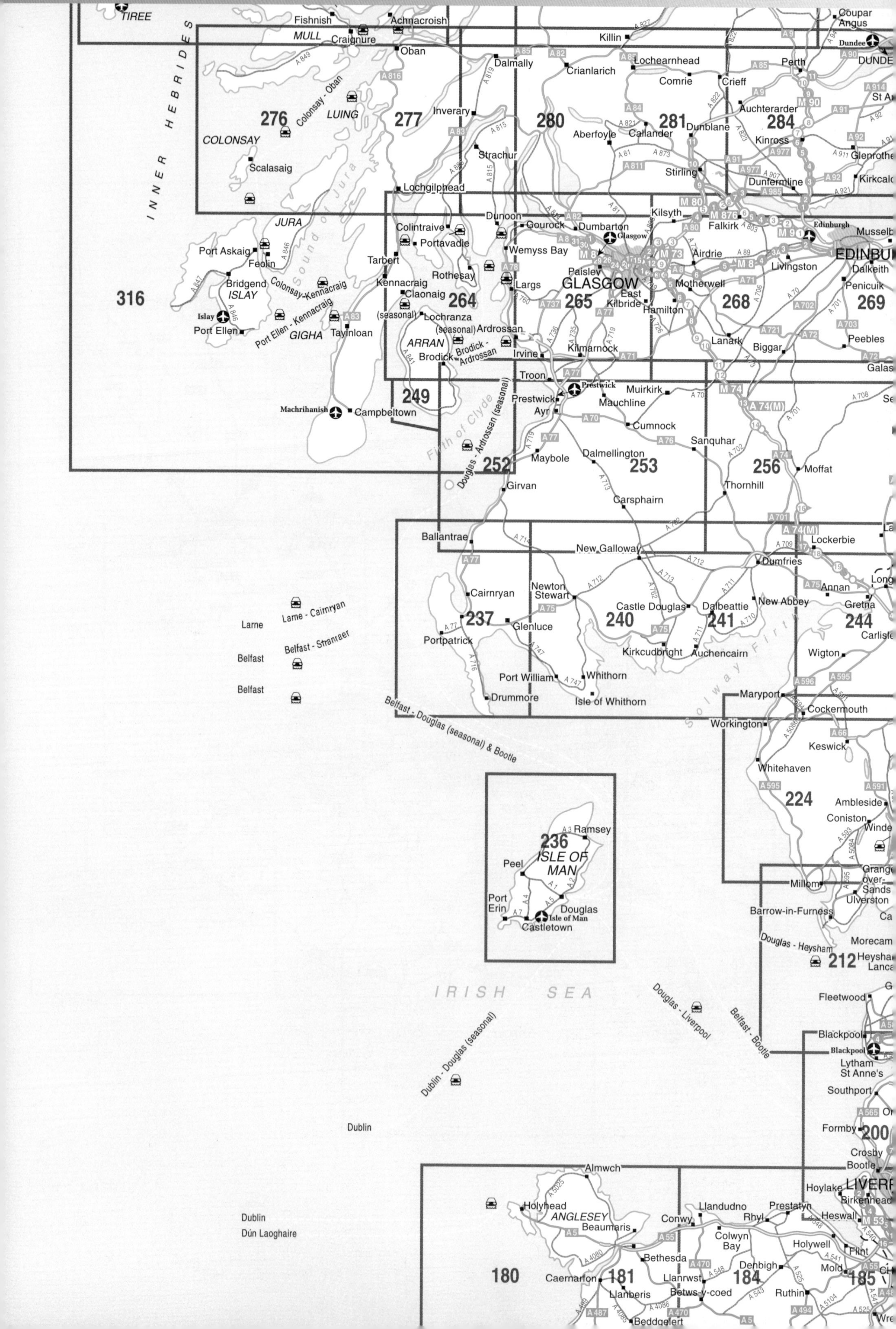

TIREE

INNER HEBRIDES

MULL
Fishnish
Achnacroish
Coupar Angus
Craignure
Oban
Killin
A 827
Dundee
DUNDE
St A
A 914

Dalmally
A 85
A 82
Lochearnhead
Perth
A 85
Crianlarich
Comrie
Crieff
Auchterarder
A 90
Inverary
A 821
Dunblane
Kinross
284
A 91
A 92
Gleprothe
Kirkcal

276 COLONSAY–Oban *LUING*
COLONSAY
Scalasaig
277
280
281
Aberfoyle
Callander
Stirling
A 977
A 907
Dunfermline
A 985
A 92
A 921

Lochgilphead
Strachur
A 811
M 80
M 90
M 91

JURA
Sound of Jura
Colintraive
Portavadie
Dunoon
Gourock
Kilsyth
Falkirk
Airdrie
Edinburgh
EDINBU
Mussel

Port Askaig
Feolin
Tarbert
Rothesay
Wemyss Bay
Paisley
Glasgow
Motherwell
Livingston
Dalkeith
Penicuik

Bridgend
ISLAY
Colonsay–Kennacraig
Kennacraig
Claonaig (seasonal)
264
Largs
265
East Kilbride
Hamilton
268
Lanark
Biggar
269
Peebles

316
Islay
Port Ellen
GIGHA
Tayinloan
Port Ellen–Kennacraig
Lochranza (seasonal)
ARRAN
Ardrossan
Irvine
Kilmarnock
A 71
A 721
A 72
A 703
Galas

Machrihanish
Campbeltown
249
Brodick
Brodick–Ardrossan
Troon
Prestwick
Prestwick
Ayr
Muirkirk
Mauchline
A 70
Cumnock
Sanquhar
M 74
A 74(M)
A 708
Se

Firth of Clyde
Douglas–Ardrossan (seasonal)
252
Maybole
Girvan
Dalmellington
A 76
Carsphairn
Thornhill
253
256
Moffat
A 701

Ballantrae
A 77
New Galloway
A 712
Dumfries
A 74(M)
Lockerbie
La

Larne
Larne–Cairnryan
Belfast
Belfast–Stranraer
Belfast
Cairnryan
Newton Stewart
Castle Douglas
Dalbeattie
New Abbey
Annan
Gretna
Long
Carlisle
237
Glenluce
A 75
240
A 75
241
244

Portpatrick
Kirkcudbright
Auchencairn
Wigton

Belfast–Douglas (seasonal) & Bootle
Port William
Whithorn
Drummore
Isle of Whithorn
Maryport
A 595
A 596
Cockermouth
Workington
A 66
Solway Firth
Keswick

Whitehaven
A 595
A 591
224
Ambleside
Coniston
Winde

IRISH SEA
236 *ISLE OF MAN*
Ramsey
Peel
Port Erin
Douglas
Isle of Man
Castletown
Millom
Grange-over-Sands
Ulverston
Ca
Barrow-in-Furness
Douglas–Heysham
212
Heysha
Lanca
Morecam

Douglas–Liverpool
Belfast–Bootle
Fleetwood
G
Douglas–Douglas (seasonal)
Blackpool
Blackpool
Lytham St Anne's
Southport
A 565
Or
Dublin
Formby
200
Crosby
Bootle

Almwch
Hoylake
Hoylake
Birkenhead
LIVERF
LIVER

Dublin
Dún Laoghaire
Holyhead
ANGLESEY
Beaumaris
Llandudno
Conwy
Rhyl
Prestatyn
Heswall
Holywell

A 55
Colwyn Bay
Denbigh
Holywell
Mold
Flint

180
Caernarfon
181
Bethesda
184
Llanrwst
185
Llanberis
Betws-y-coed
Ruthin
Beddgelert

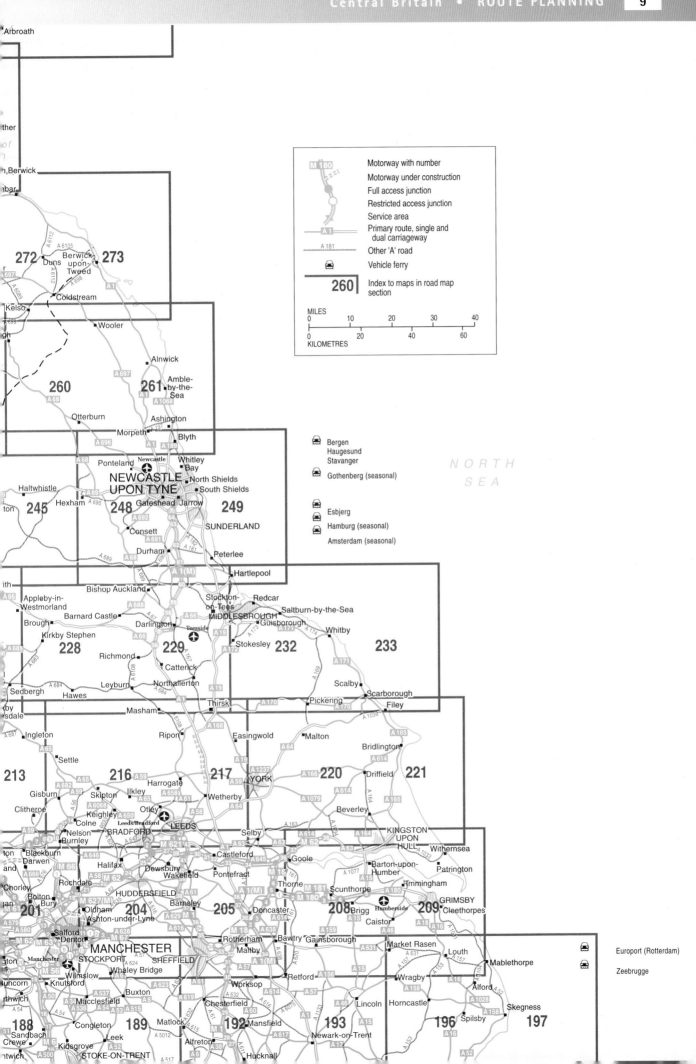

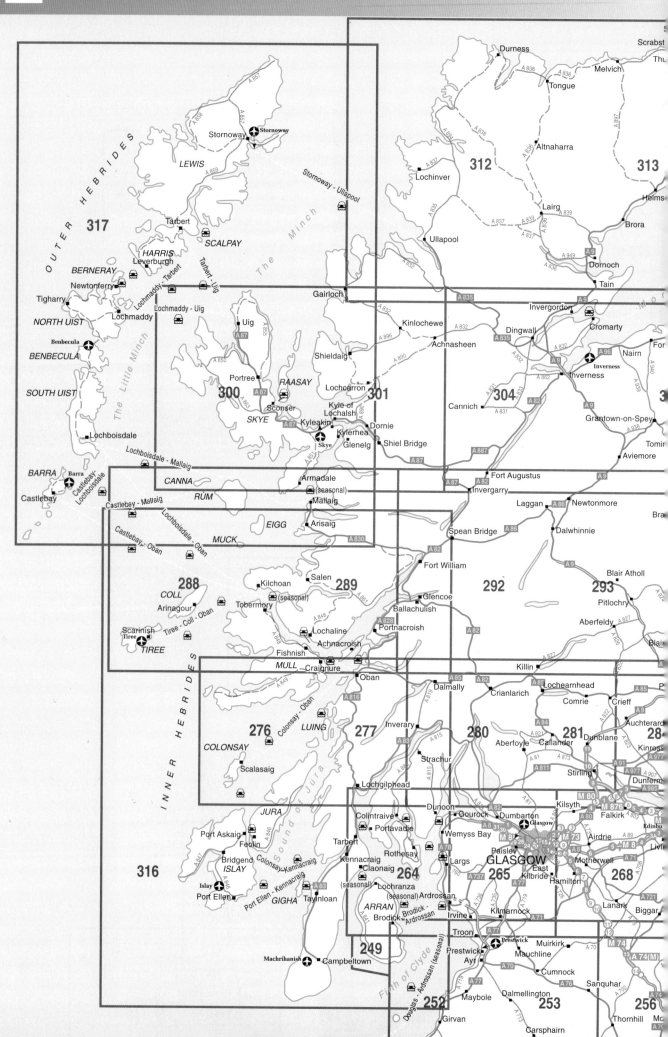

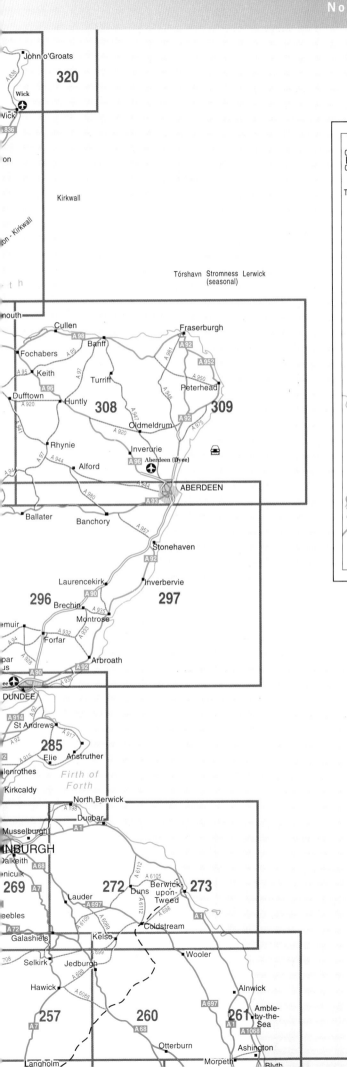

John o'Groats
320
Wick
Wick

Kirkwall

Cullen
Fochabers
Banff
Keith
Turriff
Dufftown
Huntly
308
Oldmeldrum
Rhynie
Inverurie
Alford
Aberdeen (Dyce)

Fraserburgh
Peterhead
309

Tórshavn Stromness Lerwick
(seasonal)

ABERDEEN

Ballater
Banchory
Stonehaven

Laurencekirk
296 Brechin
Montrose
muir
Forfar
Arbroath
297

Inverbervie

DUNDEE
St Andrews
285
Elie Anstruther
lenrothes
Kirkcaldy

*Firth of
Forth*

North Berwick
Dunbar
Musselburgh
NBURGH
alkeith
nicuik
269
Lauder
Duns
Berwick-upon-Tweed
272
273
eebles
Galashiels
Kelso
Coldstream
Selkirk
Jedburgh
Wooler
Hawick
Alnwick
257
260
261
Amble-by-the-Sea
Otterburn
Ashington
Langholm
Morpeth Blyth

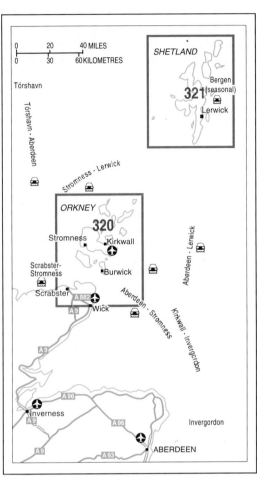

SHETLAND
321
Bergen
(seasonal)
Lerwick

Tórshavn

Tórshavn - Aberdeen

Stromness - Lerwick

ORKNEY
320
Stromness
Kirkwall

Aberdeen - Lerwick

Scrabster-Stromness
Burwick
Scrabster
Wick

Aberdeen - Stromness

Kirkwall - Invergordon

A9

Inverness
A96
Invergordon
A9
A96
ABERDEEN
A9
A93

NORTH   SEA

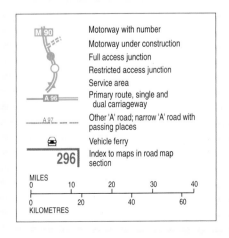

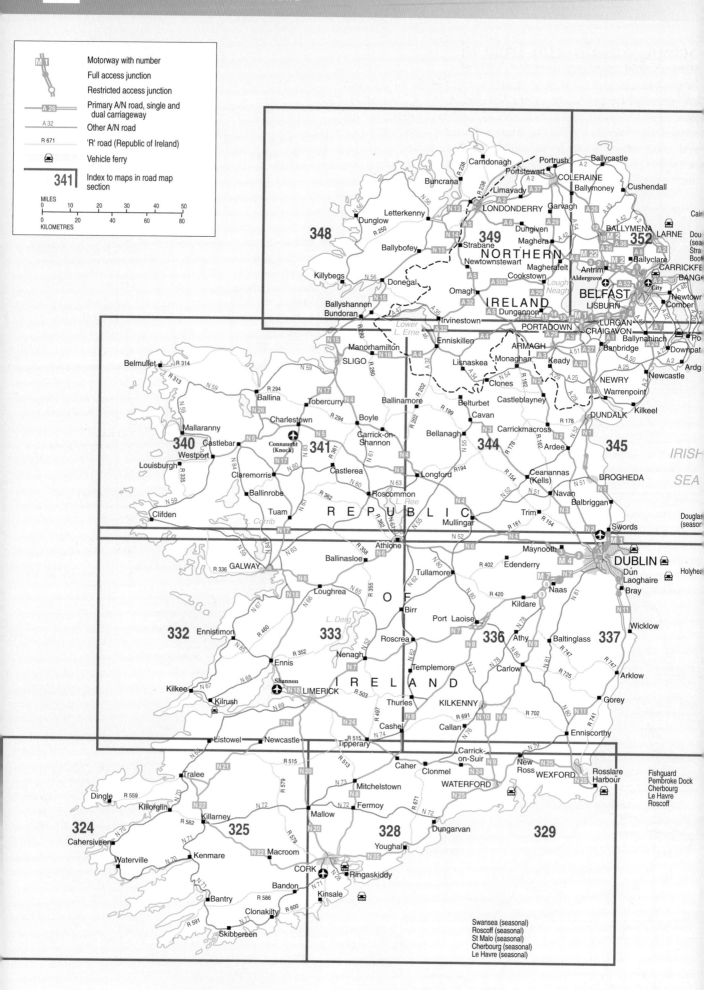

Scenic Britain and Ireland

Large stretches of the most spectacular scenery in the British Isles are protected for public use within National Parks or other designated areas. Walkers can enjoy a great deal of the scenery along the many waymarked long-distance paths, most of which are also open to cyclists and horse-riders; the routes are marked with an acorn motif in England and Wales, a thistle motif in Scotland and a 'walking man' symbol in Ireland.

KEY TO SCENIC AREAS

National Parks (including The Broads)
Protected areas of countryside in England and Wales, managed to preserve the landscape for recreation and conservation. Visitor centres have information about walks, talks and places to visit in the area

Irish National Parks
Protected areas of countryside in the Republic of Ireland

Areas of Outstanding Natural Beauty
Scenic areas in England, Wales and Northern Ireland where development is strictly controlled

National Scenic Areas
Areas of special scenic significance in Scotland

Forest Parks
Open expanses and forests in the United Kingdom, managed by the Forestry Commission. Many have picnic sites, visitor centres and waymarked walks

New Forest
A Special Protected Area. The forest is laced with paths that are open to walkers

World Heritage Sites
Natural treasures of exceptional interest

—— **Long-distance paths (official National Trails)**

---- **National Trails approved but not yet open**

Shetland (North)

Foula

Shetland (South)

Fair Isle

Hoy & West Mainland

North-west Sutherland

Kyle of Tongue

South Lewis, Harris & North Uist

Assynt-Coigach

St Kilda

Dornoch Firth

Wester Ross

Trotternish

Glen Strathfarrar

Speyside Way

Inverness

SCOTLAND

The Cuillin Hills

Glen Affric

Glenmore

Aberdeen

South Uist Machair

Kintail

Knoydart

The Cairngorm Mountains

Deeside & Lochnagar

The Small Isles

Loch Shiel

Loch Rannoch & Glen Lyon

Morar, Moidart & Ardnamurchan

Ben Nevis & Glen Coe

Loch Tummel

River Tay (Dunkeld)

Loch na Keal, Isle of Mull

Lynn of Lorn

West Highland Way

River Earn (Comrie to St Fillans)

Dundee

Scarba, Lunga & The Garvellachs

Argyll

The Trossachs

Jura

Kyles of Bute

Queen Elizabeth

Knapdale

Loch Lomond

Edinburgh

North Arran

Glasgow

Upper Tweeddale

Northumberland Coast

Giant's Causeway

Causeway Coast

Eildon & Leaderfoot

Glenveagh

Londonderry

North Derry

Antrim Coast and Glens

Southern Upland Way

Border Forest

Northumberland

Sperrin

Glenariff

Galloway

Nith Estuary

Hadrian's Wall Path

Gortin Glen

NORTHERN IRELAND

Fleet Valley

East Stewartry Coast

North Pennines

Newcastle-upon-Tyne

Drum Manor

Belfast

Whinlatter

Solway Coast

Florence Court

Ulster Way

Parkanaur

Lagan Valley

Strangford Lough

Lecale Coast

Lake District

Cleveland Way

North York Moors

Leitrim Way

Gosford

Mourne

Pennine Way

Yorkshire Dales

North Riding

Western Way

Cavan Way

Ring of Gullion

Tain Way

Castlewellan & Tollymore

Millennium Way

Grizedale

Nidderdale

Howardian Hills

Wolds Way

Douglas

REPUBLIC OF IRELAND

Forest of Bowland

Leeds

Connemara

Offaly Way

Royal Canal Way

Pennine Bridleway

Liverpool

Sheffield

Lincolnshire Wolds

Burren Way

Grand Canal Way

Manchester

Peak

Sherwood Pines

Aran Ways

The Burren

Lough Derg Way

Slieve Bloom Way

Dublin

Anglesey

Gwydyr

Clwydian Range

Delamere

The National Forest

Norfolk Coast

Peddars Way & Norfolk Coast Path

Norfolk & Suffolk Broads

Slieve Felim Way

Barrow Way

Wicklow Mountains

Snowdonia Coed-y-Brenin

Offa's Dyke Path

Cannock Chase

Dingle Way

Limerick

Wicklow Way

Lleyn

Shropshire Hills

Birmingham

Thetford

Suffolk Coast and Heaths

Ballyhoura Way

South Leinster Way

Aberystwyth

ENGLAND

Cambridge

Kerry Way

Killarney

Cork

WALES

Malvern Hills

Wye Valley

Cotswolds

Chilterns

Dedham Vale

Beara Way

Pembrokeshire Coast Path

Pembrokeshire Coast

Brecon Beacons

The Forest of Dean

Ridgeway

Thames Path

LONDON

Gower

Swansea

Cardiff

Mendip Hills

North Wessex Downs

North Downs Way

Surrey Hills

Kent Downs

Exmoor

Quantock Hills

Cranborne Chase & West Wiltshire Downs

East Hampshire

High Weald

North Devon

Blackdown Hills

South Hampshire Coast

Sussex Downs

Bodmin Moor

Exeter

Dorset

The New Forest

Chichester Harbour

South Downs Way

South West Coast Path

Cornwall

Tamar Valley

Dartmoor

East Devon

South West Coast Path

Isle of Wight

South Devon

Isles of Scilly

Miles
0   20   40   60   80

0   40   80   120
Kilometres

How to use the motorway plans

The principal motorways of Britain and Ireland are shown as strip plans giving details of junctions and interchanges. Each plan starts at the junction with the lowest number and reads from the base of the column to the top, then continues from the base of the adjacent strip on the right. Mileages between the first and last destinations of the strips on each page are given at the foot; where a plan continues on the next page, a separate mileage is given.

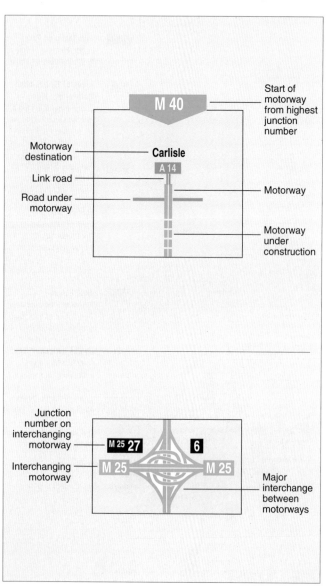

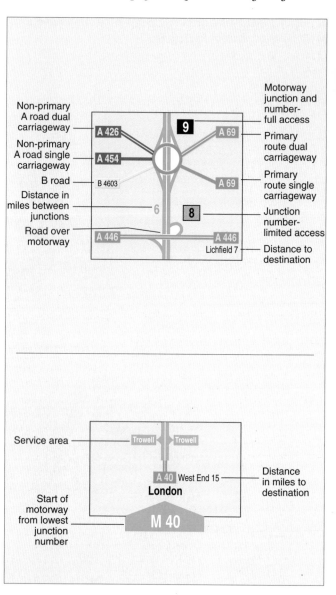

CONTENTS—PRINCIPAL MOTORWAYS IN BRITAIN AND IRELAND

Junction	Driving Northwards	Driving Southwards
M1		
2	Access only from A1 northbound	Exit only to A1 southbound
4	Access only from A41 northbound	Exit only to A41 southbound
6A	No exit to M25	No access from M25
7	Access only from M10	Exit only to M10
17	Exit only to M45	Access only from M45
19	Exit only to M6	Access only from M6
21A	Exit only	Access only
23A	No access from A453	No exit to A453
35A	Exit only	Access only
44	Access only	Exit only
45	Exit only	Access only
46	Unrestricted	Exit only
A1(M)		
2&3	Unrestricted	Unrestricted
5	Access only	No exit or access
57	Exit to A66(M) only	Access from A66(M) only
65	No exit to A1231 or B1288; no access from A194(M)	Access from A1 and A194(M) only
M5		
10	Access only from A4019 westbound	Exit only to A4019 eastbound
11A	No access from A417 eastbound	No exit to A417 westbound
12	Exit only	Access only
18A	Exit only to M49	No exit to M49; access from M49 only
29	Exit only to A30	Access only from A30
M6		
4	Exit to M42 and A446 only, unrestricted access	Exit to A446 only, unrestricted access
4A	Access only from M42 southbound	Exit only to M42
5	Exit only	Access only
10A	Exit only to M54	Access only from M54
20	No direct exit to M56 eastbound	Unrestricted
24	Access only from A58	Exit only to A58
25	Exit only to A49	Access only from A49
30	Access only from M61	Exit only to M61
M11		
4	Access only from A406 eastbound	Exit only to A406 westbound
5	Exit only to A1168	Access only from A1168
9	Exit only	Access only
13	Exit only to A1303	Access only from A1303
14	Exit only to A14 northbound	Access only from A14 southbound
M23		
7	Exit only to A23 northbound	Access only from A23 southbound
M40		
3	Exit only	Access only
7	Exit only	Access only
8	No direct exit to A418	Unrestricted
13&14	Unrestricted	Unrestricted
16	Access only from A3400	Exit only to A3400
M42		
1	Access only	Exit only
7	Exit only to M6 northbound	Access only from M6 northbound
7A	Exit only to M6 southbound	No exit–no access
8	Access only from M6 northbound	Exit to M6 northbound only; access from M6 southbound only
M53		
11	Exit to M56 eastbound only; access from M56 westbound only	Exit to M56 eastbound only; access from M56 westbound only
M61		
1&2	No access from A580 eastbound	Exit to A580 eastbound and M62 only
3	Exit only	Unrestricted
9	Exit only	Access only
M66		
1	No exit or access	Access only from A56
12	Unrestricted	Exit only
M74 and A74(M)		
2	Exit only	Access only
3	Access only	Exit only
4	Access from M73 only	Unrestricted
7	Access only from A72	Exit only to A72
9&10	Unrestricted	Unrestricted
11	Access only from B7078	Exit only; no access
12	Exit only	Access only
18	Exit only	Access only
19	Unrestricted	Exit only
M90		
7	Access only from A91	Exit only to A91
8	Exit only	Access only
10	No access from A912	No exit to A912

Junction	Driving Westwards	Driving Eastwards
M2		
1	Exit only to A2 westbound	Unrestricted
M3		
8	Exit only to A303	Access only from A303
10	Access only	Exit only
13	Exit only	Unrestricted
14	Exit only	Access only
M4		
1&2	Access and exit from A4 westbound only	Access and exit from A4 eastbound only
23	Access only from M48	Exit only to M48
25	Exit only	Access only
25A	Exit only to A4042	Access only from A4042
29	Exit only to A48(M)	Access only from A48(M)
38&39	Unrestricted	Unrestricted
41&42	Unrestricted	Unrestricted
46	Access only–no exit	Exit only–no access
M8		
8	No access from M73 southbound or from A8 and A89 eastbound	No access from A89; no exit to A8 or M73 northbound
9	Access only	Exit only
13	Exit only	Exit to M80 only
14	Access only	Exit only
16	Exit only	Access only
17/18	Unrestricted	No exit to A81
19	No access from A814 westbound	No exit to A814 eastbound
20	Exit only	Access only
21	Access only	Exit only
22	No access from M77	No exit to M77
23	Exit only to B768	Access only from B768
25	Unrestricted	No access from A739 northbound

Junction	Driving Northwards	Driving Southwards
28	Exit only	Access only
M9		
1	Exit only	Access only
2	Access only	Exit only
3	Exit only	Access only
6	Access only	Exit only
8	Exit only to M876	Access only from M876
M20		
2&3	Unrestricted	Unrestricted
5&6	Unrestricted	Unrestricted
11A	Access only	Exit only
M27		
4	Access and exit to M3 only	Access and exit to M3 only
10	Exit only to A32 northbound	Access only from A32 southbound
12	Exit to M275 only	Exit only; no access
M56		
1	No access from M63 westbound or A34 southbound	No exit to M63 westbound or A34 southbound
2&3	Unrestricted	Unrestricted
3	Access only	Exit only
4	Exit only	Access only
7	Exit only	Unrestricted
8	Access only	No exit or access
9	No direct exit to M6 southbound	Unrestricted
15	Exit only to M53	Access only
M62		
14	Access from M61 only; exit to M61 and A580 westbound only	Access from M61 and A580 eastbound only; exit to M61
15	Exit only to A666	Access only from A666
23	Access only	Exit only
M63		
7	Exit only to A56 southbound	Access only from A56 southbound
9	Exit to A5103 northbound only; access from A5103 northbound only	Exit to A5103 southbound only; access from A5103 southbound only
10	No exit to A34 northbound; no access from M56	No exit to A34 northbound or to M56 in either direction
11	Access only from A560	Exit only to A560
13	Access only	Exit only
14	Unrestricted	No access or exit
15	Access from M66 southbound only	Exit only
M65		
9	Access only	Exit only
11	Exit only	Access only
M180		
1	Access only	Exit only

Junction	Driving Clockwise	Driving Anticlockwise
M25		
1B	Exit only	Access only
5	No exit to M26	Unrestricted
19	Exit only	Access only
21	Access from M1 southbound only; exit to M1 northbound only	Access from M1 southbound only; exit to M1 northbound only
21A	No exit from M1	No access to M1
31	Access only	Exit only

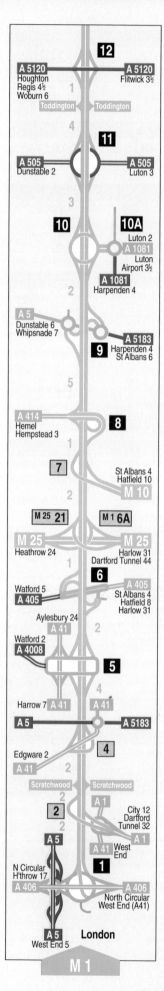
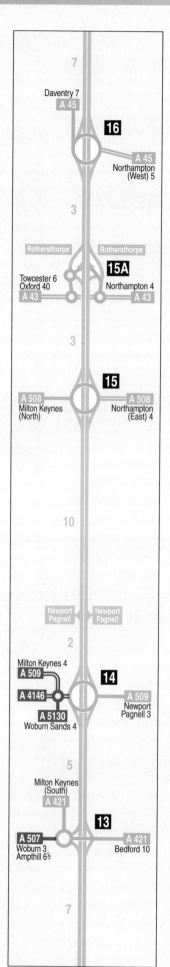
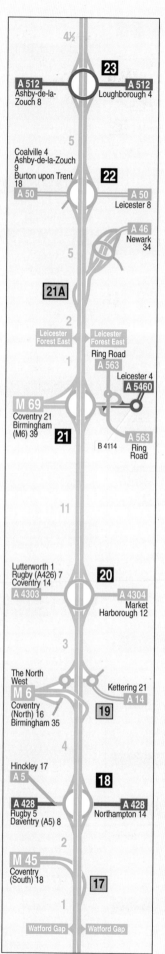
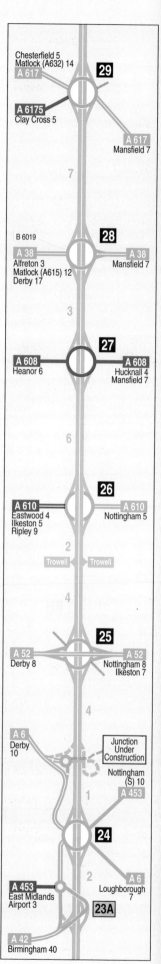

M1 London–Chesterfield 138 miles

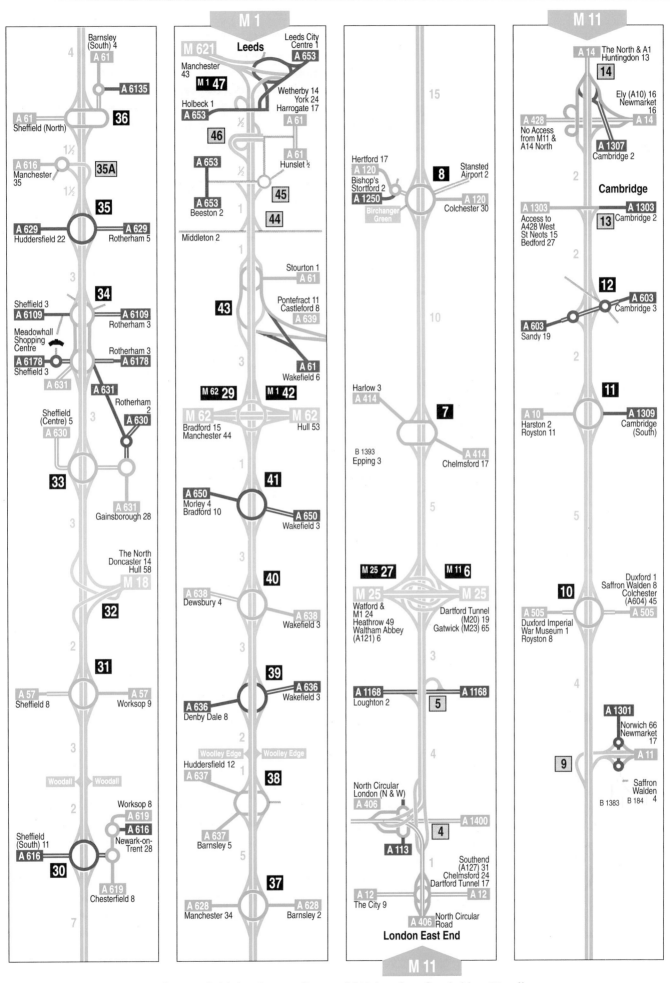

M1 Chesterfield-Leeds 51 miles • M11 London-Cambridge 61 miles

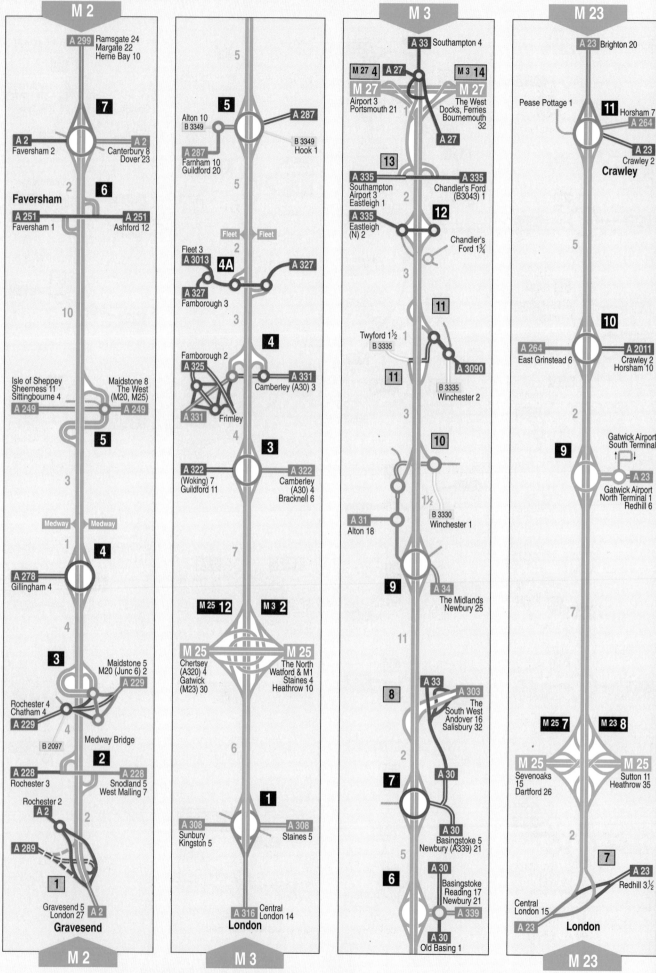

M 2

A 299 — Ramsgate 24 / Margate 22 / Herne Bay 10

7

A 2 — Faversham 2
A 2 — Canterbury 8 / Dover 23

6

Faversham

A 251 — Faversham 1
A 251 — Ashford 12

10

Isle of Sheppey / Sheerness 11 / Sittingbourne 4
A 249
A 249
Maidstone 8 / The West (M20, M25)

5

3

Medway — Medway

1

4

A 278 — Gillingham 4

4

3

Maidstone 5 / M20 (Junc 6) 2
A 229
Rochester 4 / Chatham 4
A 229
4
B 2097 — Medway Bridge

2

A 228 — Rochester 3
A 228 — Snodland 5 / West Malling 7

2

Rochester 2
A 2
A 289

1

Gravesend 5 / London 27 — A 2

Gravesend

M 2

M 3

5

5

Alton 10 / B 3349
A 287
B 3349 — Hook 1
A 287 — Farnham 10 / Guildford 20

2

Fleet — Fleet

Fleet 3 / A 3013
4A
A 327
A 327 — Farnborough 3

3

4

Farnborough 2
A 325
A 331
A 331 — Camberley (A30) 3
A 331 — Frimley

4

3

A 322 — (Woking) 7 / Guildford 11
A 322 — Camberley (A30) 4 / Bracknell 6

7

M 25 12   **M 3 2**

M 25   M 25
Chertsey (A320) 4 / Gatwick (M23) 30
The North / Watford & M1 / Staines 4 / Heathrow 10

6

1

A 308 — Sunbury / Kingston 5
A 308 — Staines 5

A 316 — Central London 14

London

M 3

M 3

A 33 — Southampton 4

M 27 4   A 27   **M 3 14**
M 27
Airport 3 / Portsmouth 21
M 27
The West / Docks, Ferries / Bournemouth 32
A 27

1

13

A 335 — Southampton Airport 3 / Eastleigh 1
A 335 — Chandler's Ford (B3043) 1

2

12

A 335 — Eastleigh (N) 2
Chandler's Ford 1¾

3

11

Twyford 1½ / B 3335
A 3090

11

B 3335 — Winchester 2

3

10

B 3330 — Winchester 1

A 31 — Alton 18

1½

9

A 34 — The Midlands / Newbury 25

11

8

A 33
A 303 — The South West / Andover 16 / Salisbury 32

2

7

A 30
A 30 — Basingstoke 5 / Newbury (A339) 21

5

6

A 30 — Basingstoke / Reading 17 / Newbury 21
A 339
A 30 — Old Basing 1

M 23

A 23 — Brighton 20

Pease Pottage 1
11
Horsham 7
A 264
A 23 — Crawley 2

Crawley

5

10

A 264 — East Grinstead 6
A 2011 — Crawley 2 / Horsham 10

2

Gatwick Airport South Terminal

9

A 23 — Gatwick Airport North Terminal 1 / Redhill 6

7

M 25 7   **M 23 8**

M 25   M 25
Sevenoaks 15 / Dartford 26
Sutton 11 / Heathrow 35

2

7

A 23 — Redhill 3½
Central London 15
A 23

London

M 23

M2 Gravesend–Faversham 33 miles • M3 London–Southampton 80 miles
M23 London–Crawley 28 miles

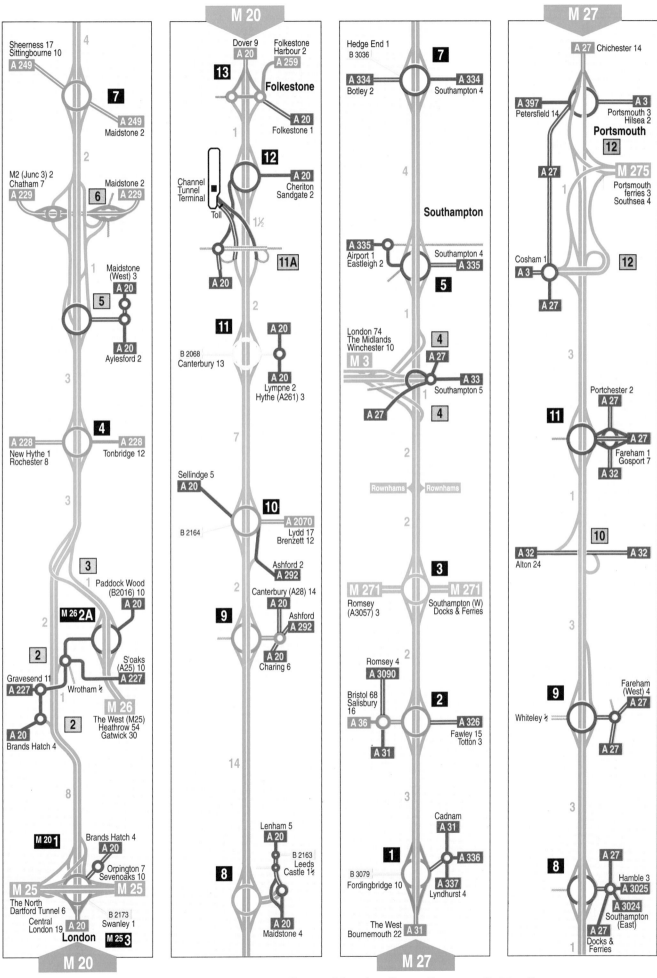

M 20

Sheerness 17
Sittingbourne 10
A 249

7

A 249
Maidstone 2

M2 (Junc 3) 2
Chatham 7
A 229

6   A 229
Maidstone 2

Maidstone
(West) 3
A 20

5

A 20
Aylesford 2

4

A 228
New Hythe 1
Rochester 8

A 228
Tonbridge 12

3

Paddock Wood
(B2016) 10
A 20

M 26 2A

2

S'oaks
(A25) 10
A 227

Gravesend 11
A 227

Wrotham ½

M 26

The West (M25)
Heathrow 54
Gatwick 30

2

A 20
Brands Hatch 4

M 20 1

Brands Hatch 4
A 20

Orpington 7
Sevenoaks 10

M 25   M 25

The North
Dartford Tunnel 6

Central
London 19
A 20

B 2173
Swanley 1

London

M 25 3

M 20

M 20

Dover 9
A 20

Folkestone
Harbour 2
A 259

13

Folkestone

A 20
Folkestone 1

12

A 20
Cheriton
Sandgate 2

Channel
Tunnel
Terminal
Toll

1½

11A

A 20

11

B 2068
Canterbury 13

A 20

A 20
Lympne 2
Hythe (A261) 3

Sellindge 5
A 20

10

A 2070
Lydd 17
Brenzett 12

B 2164

Ashford 2
A 292

Canterbury (A28) 14
A 20

Ashford
A 292

9

A 20
Charing 6

Lenham 5
A 20

B 2163
Leeds
Castle 1½

8

A 20
Maidstone 4

M 27

Hedge End 1
B 3036

7

A 334
Botley 2

A 334
Southampton 4

Southampton

A 335
Airport 1
Eastleigh 2

Southampton 4
A 335

5

London 74
The Midlands
Winchester 10

M 3

4

A 27

A 33
Southampton 5

A 27

4

Rownhams   Rownhams

3

M 271   M 271

Romsey
(A3057) 3

Southampton (W)
Docks & Ferries

Romsey 4
A 3090

Bristol 68
Salisbury
16
A 36

2

A 326
Fawley 15
Totton 3

A 31

Cadnam
A 31

1

A 336

B 3079
Fordingbridge 10

A 337
Lyndhurst 4

The West
Bournemouth 22   A 31

M 27

M 27

A 27 Chichester 14

7

A 397
Petersfield 14

A 3
Portsmouth 3
Hilsea 2

Portsmouth

12

A 27

M 275
Portsmouth
ferries 3
Southsea 4

Cosham 1
A 3

12

A 27

3

Portchester 2
A 27

11

A 27
Fareham 1
Gosport 7

A 32

1

10

A 32
Alton 24

A 32

3

Fareham
(West) 4
A 27

9

Whiteley ½

A 27

8

A 27
Hamble 3
A 3025

A 3024
Southampton
(East)

A 27
Docks &
Ferries

M20 London-Folkestone 73 miles • M27 Lyndhurst-Portsmouth 34 miles

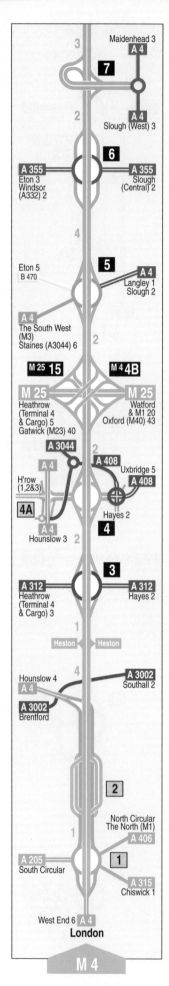
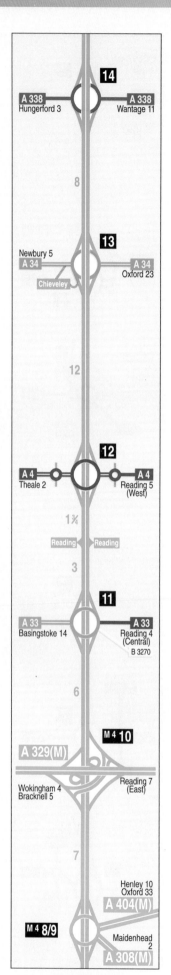
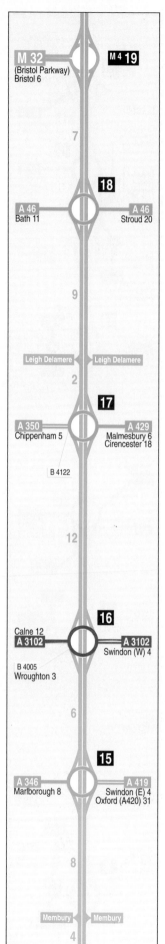

M4 London–Newport 138 miles

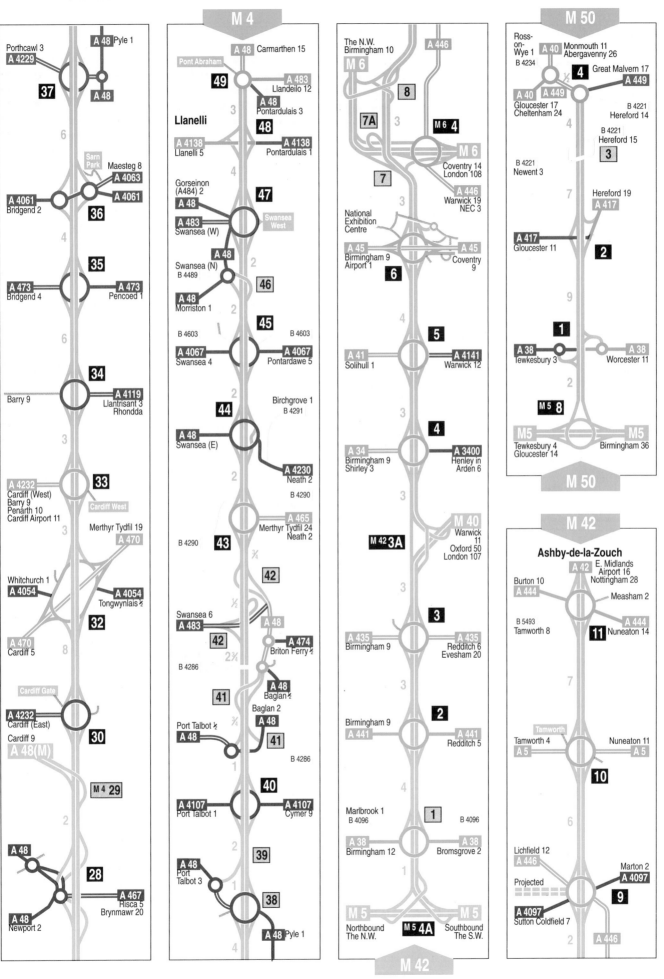

**M4 Newport-Llanelli 64 miles • M42 Bromsgrove-Ashby-de-la-Zouch 49 miles
M50 Strensham-Ross-on-Wye 22 miles**

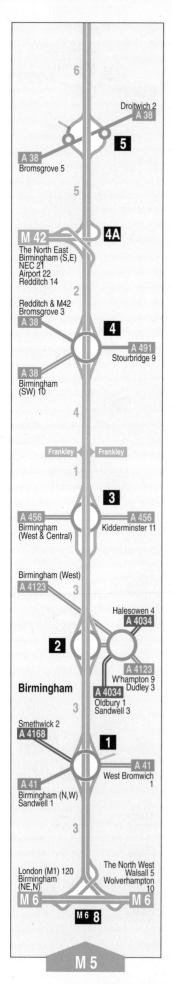

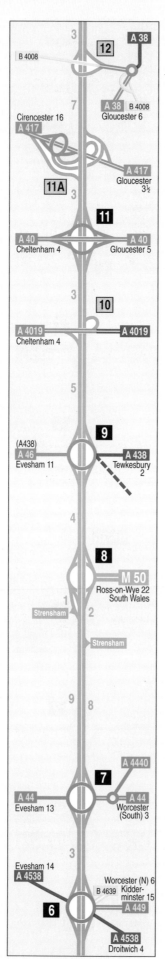

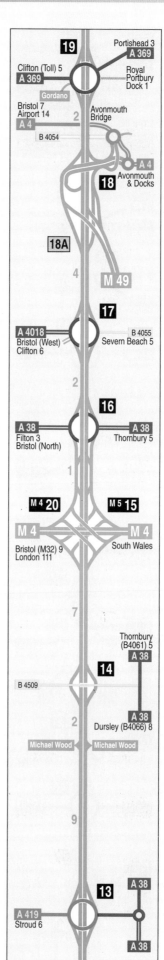

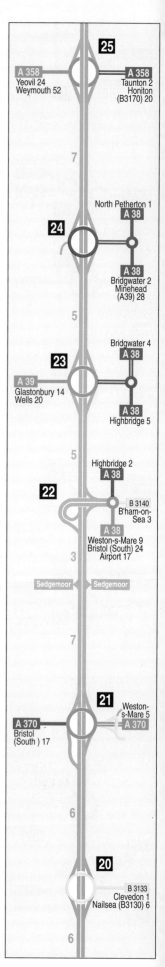

M5 Birmingham–Taunton 130 miles

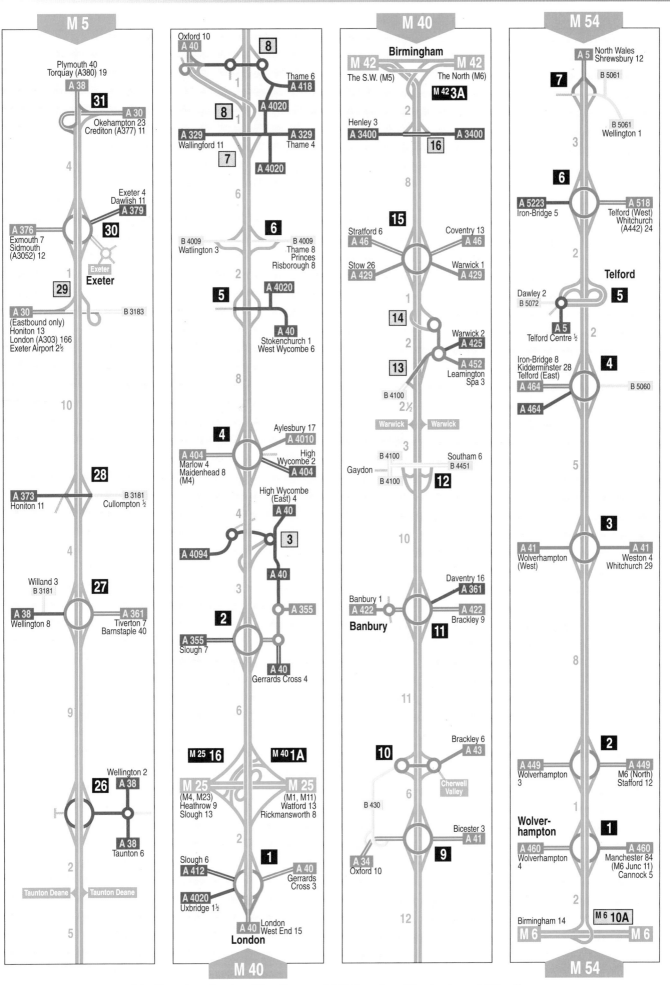

M5 Taunton–Exeter 35 miles • M40 London–Birmingham 120 miles
M54 Wolverhampton–Telford 23 miles

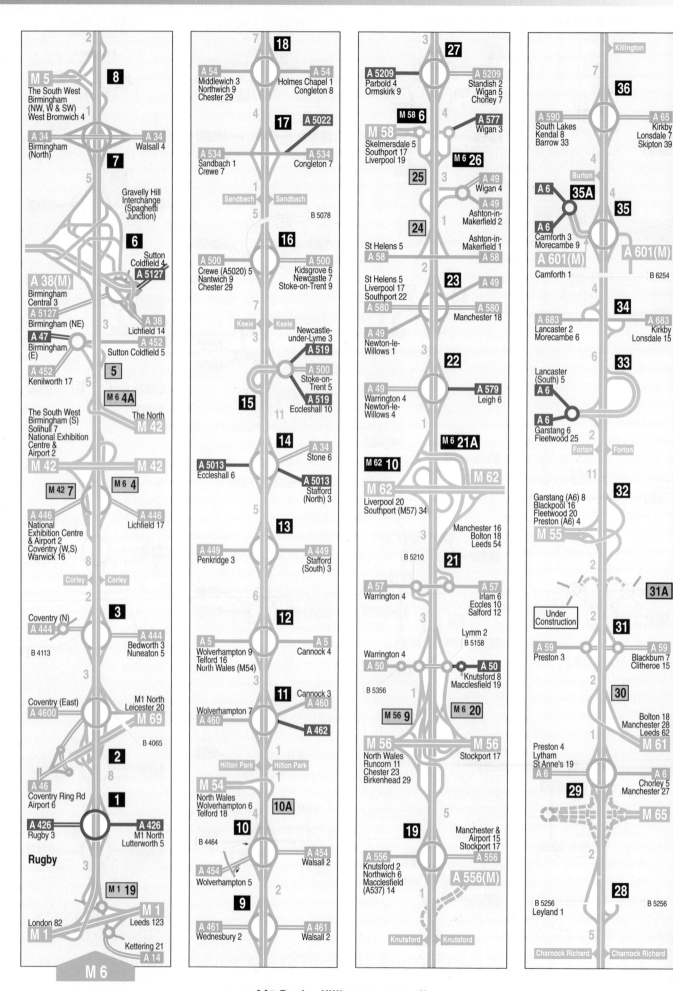

M6 Rugby–Killington 162 miles

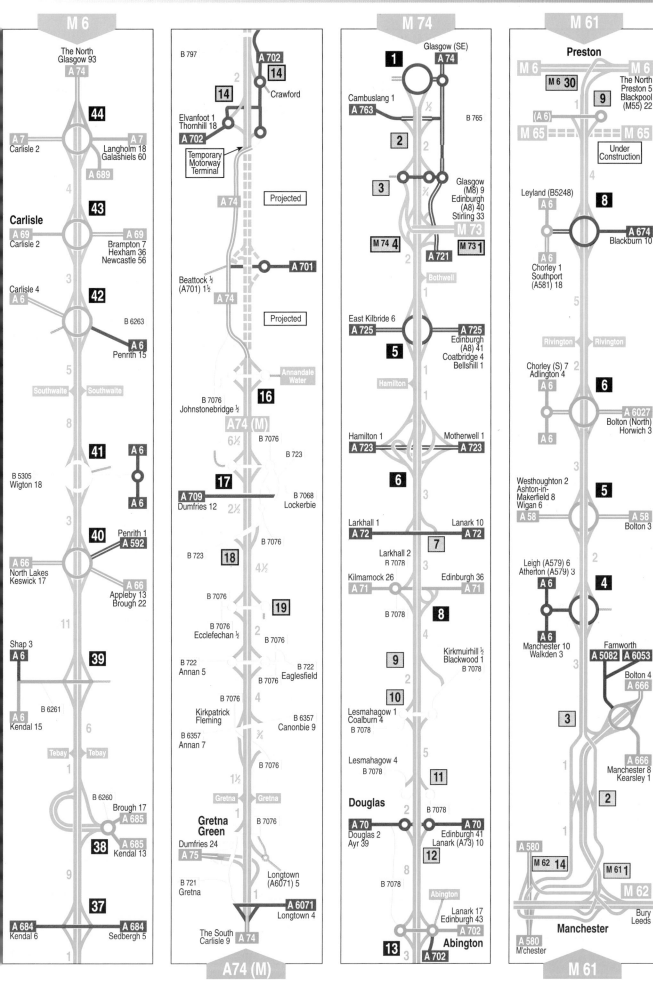

M6

The North
Glasgow 93
A 74

44

A 7
Carlisle 2
A 7
Langholm 18
Galashiels 60

A 689

43

Carlisle

A 69
Carlisle 2
A 69
Brampton 7
Hexham 36
Newcastle 56

Carlisle 4
A 6

42

B 6263

A 6
Penrith 15

Southwaite   Southwaite

41

A 6

B 5305
Wigton 18

A 6

40
Penrith 1
A 592

A 66
North Lakes
Keswick 17

A 66
Appleby 13
Brough 22

Shap 3
A 6

39

A 6
Kendal 15

B 6261

Tebay   Tebay

B 6260

Brough 17
A 685

38
A 685
Kendal 13

37

A 684
Kendal 6
A 684
Sedbergh 5

A74(M)

B 797

A 702
14

14
Crawford

Elvanfoot 1
Thornhill 18
A 702

Temporary
Motorway
Terminal

A 74

Projected

A 701

Beattock ½
(A701) 1½
A 74

Projected

Annandale
Water

B 7076
Johnstonebridge ½
16

A74(M)

6½
B 7076

B 723

A 709
Dumfries 12
17
B 7068
Lockerbie

2½

B 723
18
B 7076

4½

B 7076
19

B 7076
Ecclefechan ½
B 7076

B 722
Annan 5
B 722
Eaglesfield
B 7076

B 7076

Kirkpatrick
Fleming
B 6357
Canonbie 9

B 6357
Annan 7

B 7076

1½

Gretna   Gretna

**Gretna
Green**
Dumfries 24
A 75

B 721
Gretna

B 7076

Longtown
(A6071) 5

A 6071
Longtown 4

The South
Carlisle 9   A 74

M74

1
Glasgow (SE)
A 74

Cambuslang 1
A 763
½
B 765

2
2

3
¾
Glasgow
(M8) 9
Edinburgh
(A8) 40
Stirling 33
M 73

M 74 **4**
A 721
M 73 1

Bothwell
1

East Kilbride 6
A 725
A 725
Edinburgh
(A8) 41
Coatbridge 4
Bellshill 1

5
1

Hamilton
1

Hamilton 1
A 723
A 723
Motherwell 1

6
3

Larkhall 1
A 72
A 72
Lanark 10

7
Larkhall 2
B 7078
3

Kilmarnock 26
A 71
A 71
Edinburgh 36

B 7078
8

9
Kirkmuirhill ½
Blackwood 1
B 7078

10
4

Lesmahagow 1
Coalburn 4
B 7078

5

Lesmahagow 4
B 7078

11
2

Douglas
B 7078

A 70
Douglas 2
Ayr 39
A 70
Edinburgh 41
Lanark (A73) 10

12
8

B 7078

Abington
Lanark 17
Edinburgh 43
A 702

13
3
Abington
A 702

M61

Preston

M 6   M 6
M 6 **30**
The North
Preston 5
Blackpool
(M55) 22
(A 6)
9

M 65 ===   === M 65

Under
Construction

Leyland (B5248)
A 6
8

A 674
Blackburn 10

Chorley 1
Southport
(A581) 18
A 6

5

Rivington   Rivington

Chorley (S) 7
Adlington 4
A 6
2
6

A 6027
Bolton (North)
Horwich 3
A 6

3

Westhoughton 2
Ashton-in-
Makerfield 8
Wigan 6
A 58
5
A 58
Bolton 3

2

Leigh (A579) 6
Atherton (A579) 3
A 6
4

Manchester 10
Walkden 3
A 6
Farnworth
A 5082   A 6053
Bolton 4
A 666

3

A 666
Manchester 8
Kearsley 1

1
2

A 580
M 62 **14**
M 61 **1**

M 62

A 580
M'chester
Manchester

M 61

**M6 A74(M) M74 Killington–Glasgow 156 miles
M61 Manchester–Preston 31 miles**

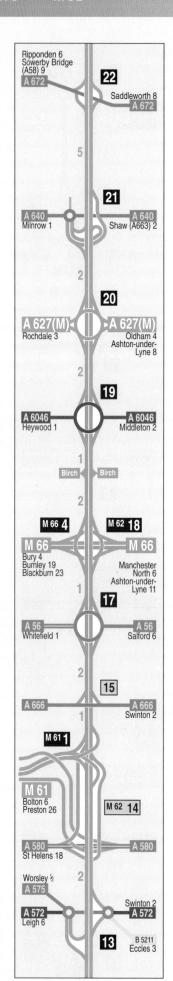

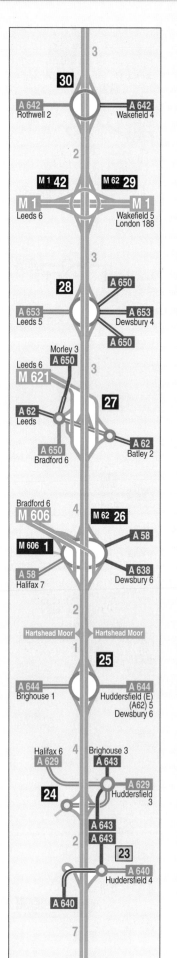

M62 Liverpool–Kingston upon Hull 128 miles

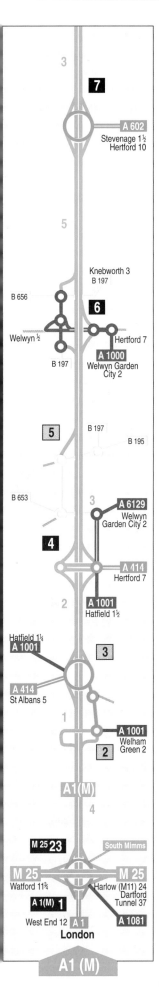

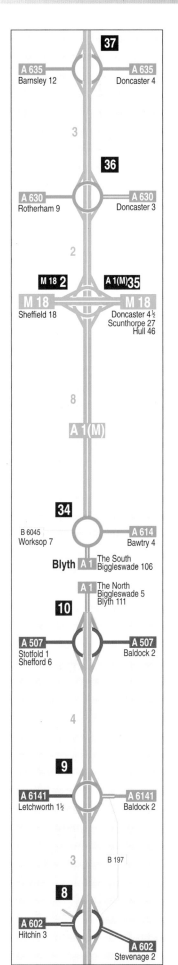

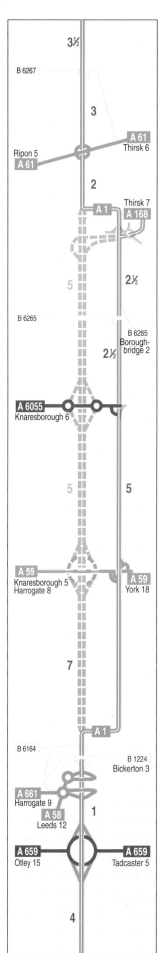

A1(M) London–Biggleswade 25 miles, Blyth–Ripon 65 miles

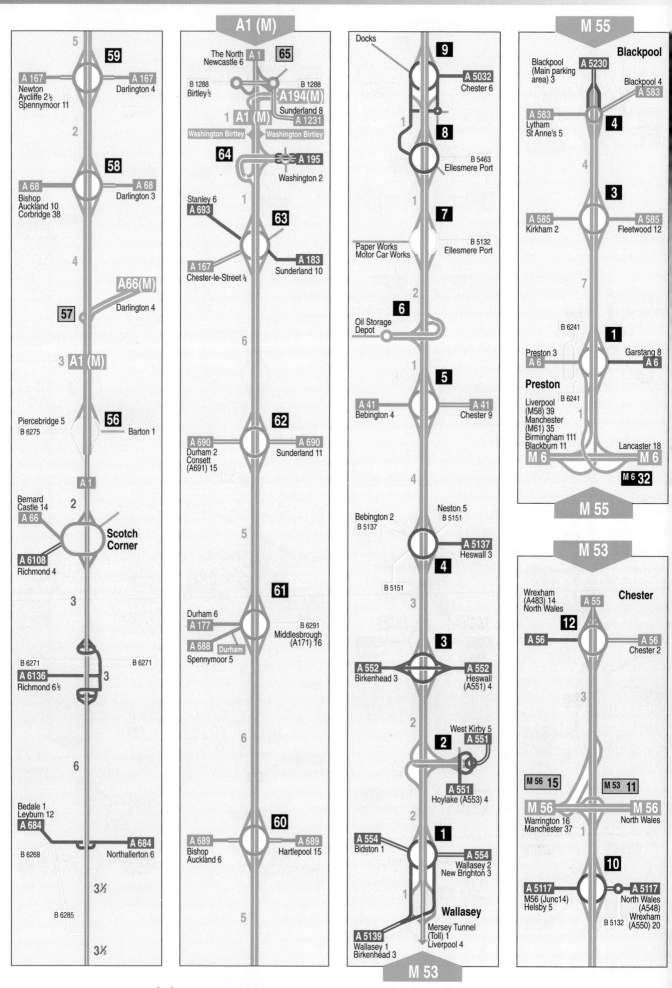

A1(M) Ripon–Newcastle 53 miles • M53 Wallasey–Chester 24 miles
M55 Preston–Blackpool 18 miles

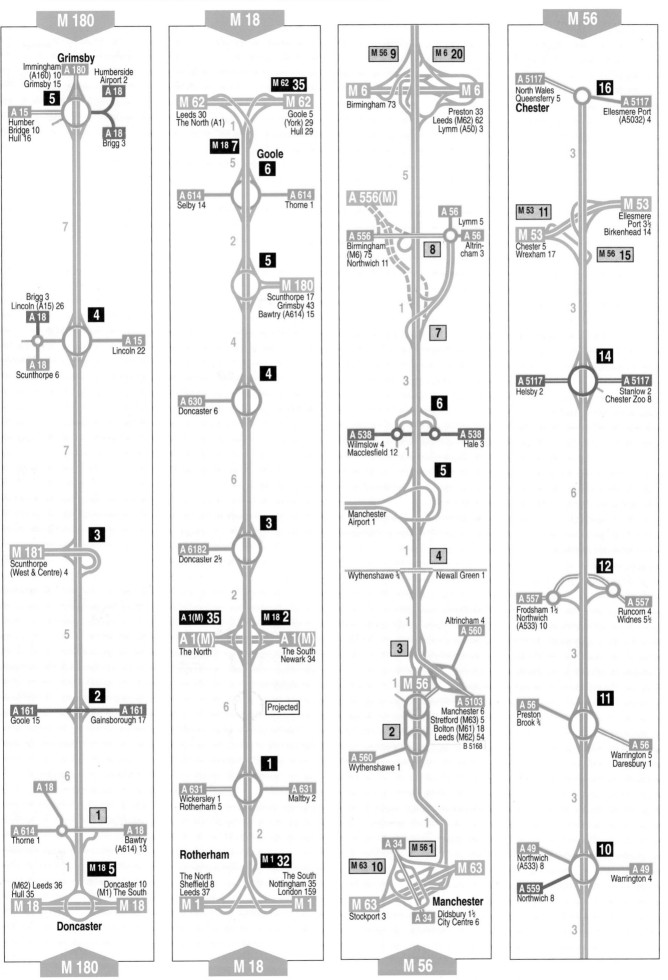

M 180

Grimsby

Immingham (A160) 10
Grimsby 15
A 180
Humberside Airport 2
A 18

5

A 15
Humber Bridge 10
Hull 16

A 18
Brigg 3

7

Brigg 3
Lincoln (A15) 26
A 18
4
A 15
Lincoln 22

A 18
Scunthorpe 6

7

3
M 181
Scunthorpe (West & Centre) 4

5

2
A 161
Goole 15
A 161
Gainsborough 17

6

A 18
1
A 614
Thorne 1
A 18
Bawtry (A614) 13

1
M 18 **5**
(M62) Leeds 36
Hull 35
Doncaster 10
(M1) The South
M 18
M 18

Doncaster

M 180

M 18

M 62 **35**
M 62
Leeds 30
The North (A1)
M 62
Goole 5
(York) 29
Hull 29

M 18 **7**
Goole
6

5

A 614
Selby 14
A 614
Thorne 1

2

5
M 180
Scunthorpe 17
Grimsby 43
Bawtry (A614) 15

4

4

A 630
Doncaster 6

6

3

A 6182
Doncaster 2½

2

A 1(M) **35**
M 18 **2**
A 1(M)
The North
A 1(M)
The South
Newark 34

6   Projected

1

A 631
Wickersley 1
Rotherham 5
A 631
Maltby 2

2

Rotherham
M 1 **32**
The North
Sheffield 8
Leeds 37
The South
Nottingham 35
London 159
M 1
M 1

M 18

M 56

M 56 **9**
M 6 **20**
M 6
Birmingham 73
M 6
Preston 33
Leeds (M62) 62
Lymm (A50) 3

5

A 556(M)

A 556
Birmingham (M6) 75
Northwich 11
A 56
Lymm 5
A 56
Altrin-cham 3

8

1

7

3

6

A 538
Wilmslow 4
Macclesfield 12
A 538
Hale 3

1

5

Manchester Airport 1

1

4

Wythenshawe ¾   Newall Green 1

1

Altrincham 4
A 560

3

1   M 56
Manchester 6
Stretford (M63) 5
Bolton (M61) 18
Leeds (M62) 54
A 5103

2
A 560
Wythenshawe 1
B 5168

1

A 34
M 56 **1**
M 63 **10**
M 63
M 63
Stockport 3
A 34
Didsbury 1½
City Centre 6
Manchester

M 56

M 56

A 5117
North Wales
Queensferry 5
16
A 5117
Ellesmere Port
(A5032) 4
Chester

3

M 53 **11**
M 53
M 53
Chester 5
Wrexham 17
M 53
Ellesmere Port 3½
Birkenhead 14
M 56 **15**

3

14

A 5117
Helsby 2
A 5117
Stanlow 2
Chester Zoo 8

6

12
A 557
Frodsham 1½
Northwich (A533) 10
A 557
Runcorn 4
Widnes 5½

3

11
A 56
Preston Brook ¾
A 56
Warrington 5
Daresbury 1

3

A 49
Northwich (A533) 8
10
A 49
Warrington 4
A 559
Northwich 8

3

M 56

M180 Doncaster–Grimsby 51 miles • M18 Rotherham–Goole 35 miles
M56 Manchester–Chester 24 miles

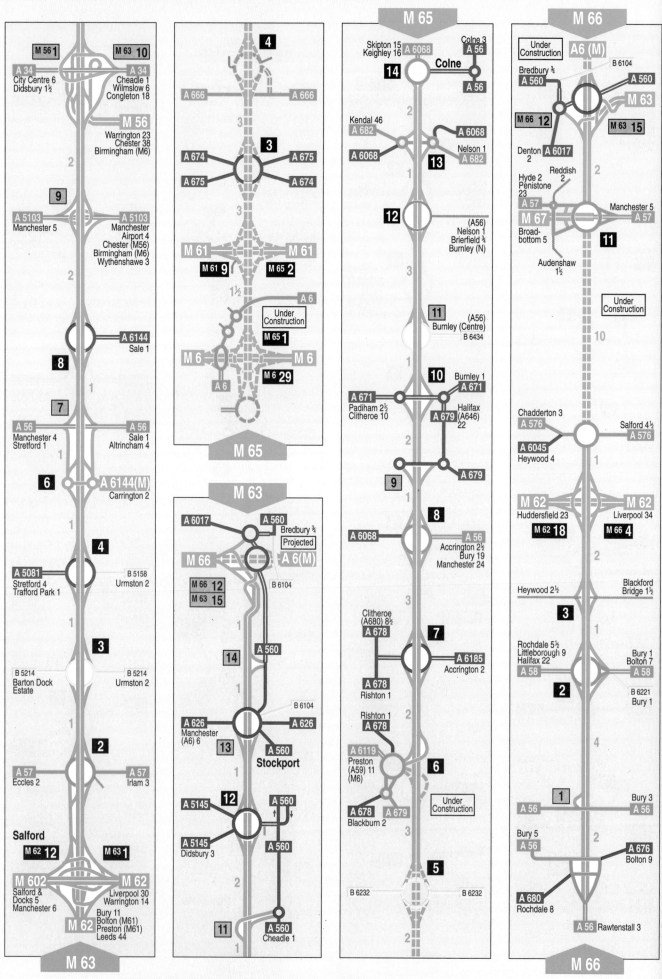

M63 Salford–Stockport 20 miles • **M65** Bamber Bridge–Colne 28 miles
M66 Ramsbottom–Stockport 22 miles

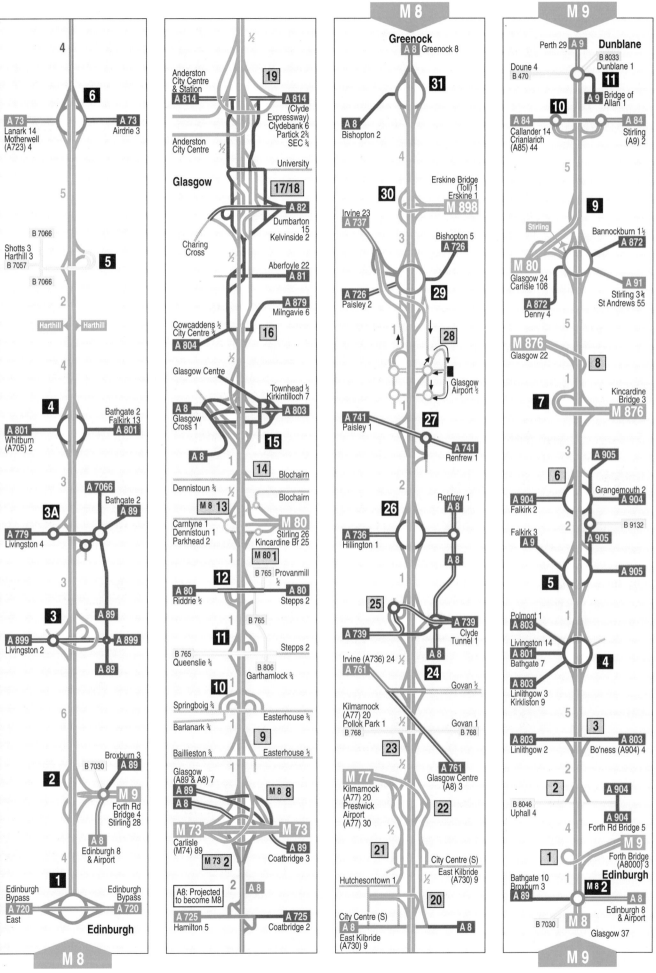

M8 Edinburgh–Greenock 68 miles • M9 Edinburgh–Dunblane 40 miles

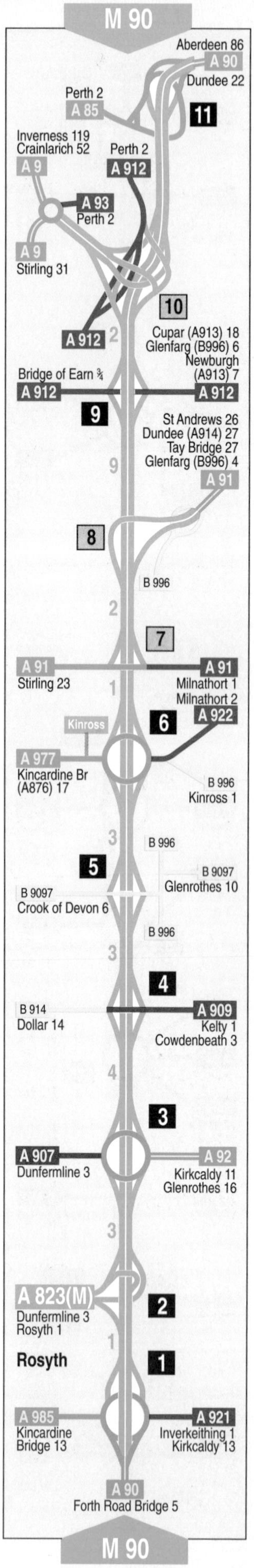

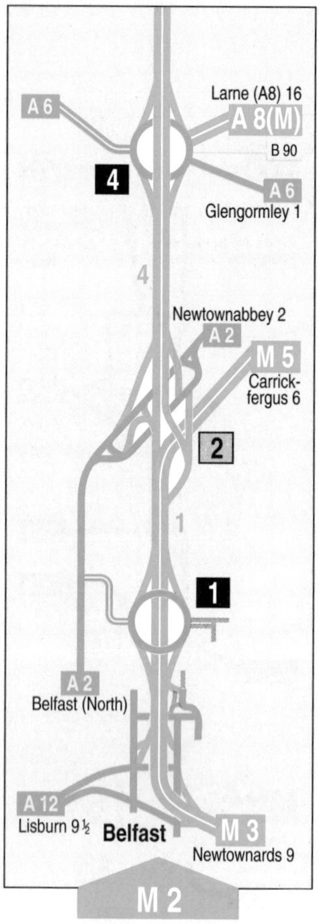

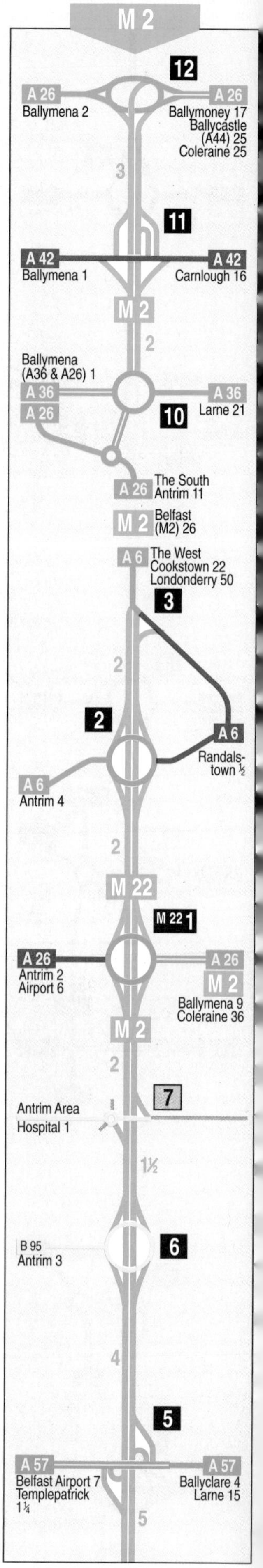

M 90

Aberdeen 86
A 90
Dundee 22
11

Perth 2
A 85
Inverness 119
Crainlarich 52
A 9
Perth 2
A 912
Perth 2

A 93
Perth 2

A 9
Stirling 31

10

A 912
2
Cupar (A913) 18
Glenfarg (B996) 6
Newburgh
(A913) 7
A 912

Bridge of Earn ¾
A 912
9

St Andrews 26
Dundee (A914) 27
Tay Bridge 27
Glenfarg (B996) 4
A 91

9

8

B 996

2

7

A 91
Stirling 23
1
A 91
Milnathort 1
Milnathort 2

Kinross
6
A 922

A 977
Kincardine Br
(A876) 17
B 996
Kinross 1

3
B 996

5
B 9097
Glenrothes 10
B 9097
Crook of Devon 6
3
B 996

4
A 909
Kelty 1
Cowdenbeath 3
B 914
Dollar 14
4

3
A 907
Dunfermline 3
A 92
Kirkcaldy 11
Glenrothes 16

3

A 823(M)
Dunfermline 3
Rosyth 1
2

1

Rosyth
1

A 985
Kincardine
Bridge 13
A 921
Inverkeithing 1
Kirkcaldy 13

A 90
Forth Road Bridge 5

M 90

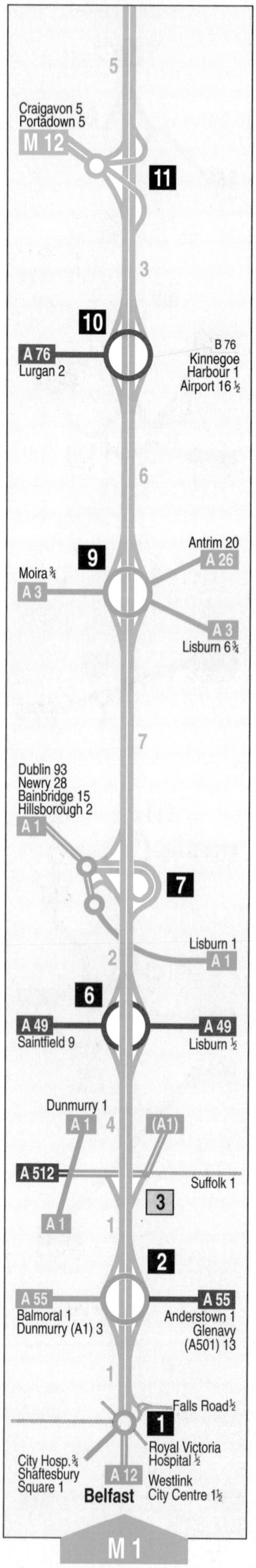

M 1

Craigavon 5
Portadown 5
M 12
11

10
A 76
Lurgan 2
B 76
Kinnegoe
Harbour 1
Airport 16 ½

5

3

6

Antrim 20
A 26
9
Moira ¾
A 3
A 3
Lisburn 6 ¾

Dublin 93
Newry 28
Bainbridge 15
Hillsborough 2
A 1

7

7

Lisburn 1
A 1

2

6
A 49
Saintfield 9
A 49
Lisburn ½

Dunmurry 1
A 1
4
(A1)
A 512
Suffolk 1
A 1
1
3

2
A 55
Balmoral 1
Dunmurry (A1) 3
A 55
Anderstown 1
Glenavy
(A501) 13

1

Falls Road ½
1
City Hosp. ¾
Shaftesbury
Square 1
Royal Victoria
Hospital ½
A 12
Westlink
City Centre 1½
Belfast

M 1

M 2

A 6
Larne (A8) 16
A 8(M)
B 90

4
A 6
Glengormley 1

Newtownabbey 2
A 2
M 5
Carrick-
fergus 6

2

1

A 2
Belfast (North)

A 12
Lisburn 9 ½
Belfast
M 3
Newtownards 9

M 2

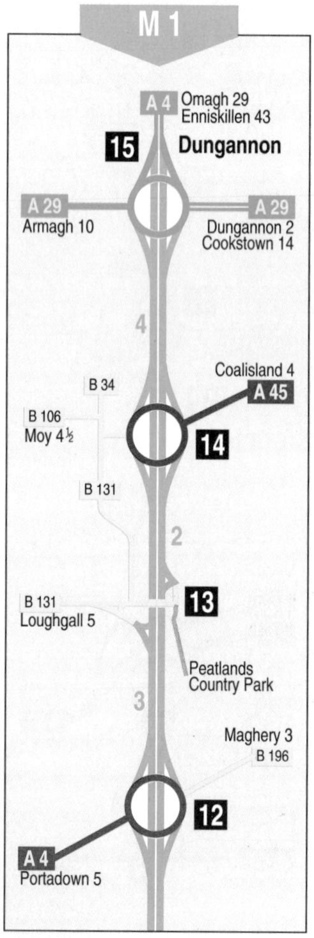

M 1

A 4
Omagh 29
Enniskillen 43

15 **Dungannon**

A 29
Armagh 10
A 29
Dungannon 2
Cookstown 14

4

Coalisland 4
A 45
B 34
B 106
Moy 4 ½
14

B 131

B 131
Loughgall 5
13

2

Peatlands
Country Park

3

Maghery 3
B 196

A 4
Portadown 5
12

M 2

12
A 26
Ballymena 2
A 26
Ballymoney 17
Ballycastle
(A44) 25
Coleraine 25

3

11
A 42
Ballymena 1
A 42
Carnlough 16

M 2

2

Ballymena
(A36 & A26) 1
A 36
A 36
A 26
10
Larne 21

A 26
The South
Antrim 11
M 2
Belfast
(M2) 26

A 6
The West
Cookstown 22
Londonderry 50
3

2

2
A 6
Randals-
town ½
A 6
Antrim 4

2

M 22

M 22 **1**
A 26
Antrim 2
Airport 6
A 26
M 2
Ballymena 9
Coleraine 36

M 2

Antrim Area
Hospital 1
7

1½

B 95
Antrim 3
6

4

5

A 57
Belfast Airport 7
Templepatrick
1¼
A 57
Ballyclare 4
Larne 15

5

**M90 Rosyth–Perth 30 miles • M1 Belfast–Dungannon 41 miles
M2 Belfast–Ballymena 26 miles**

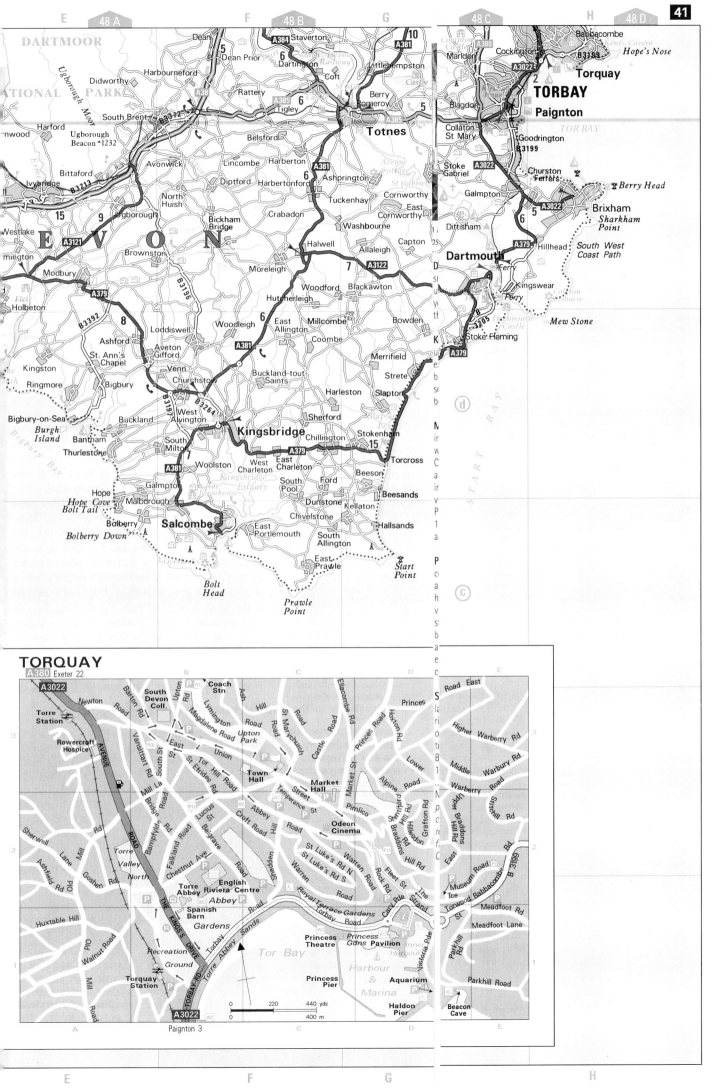

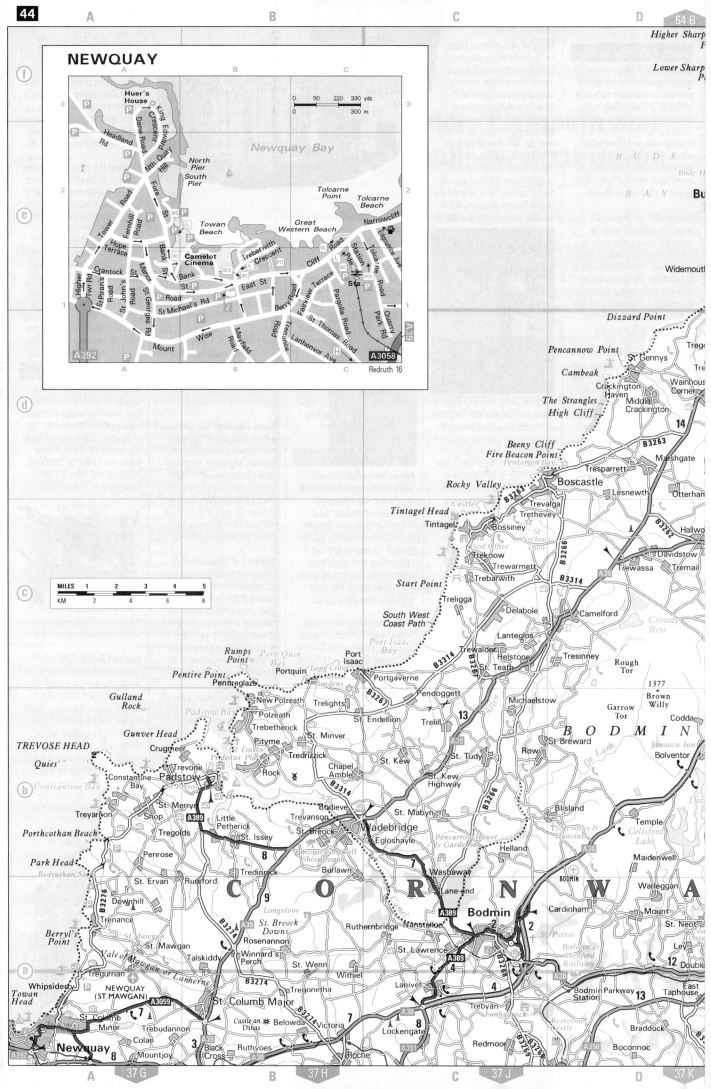

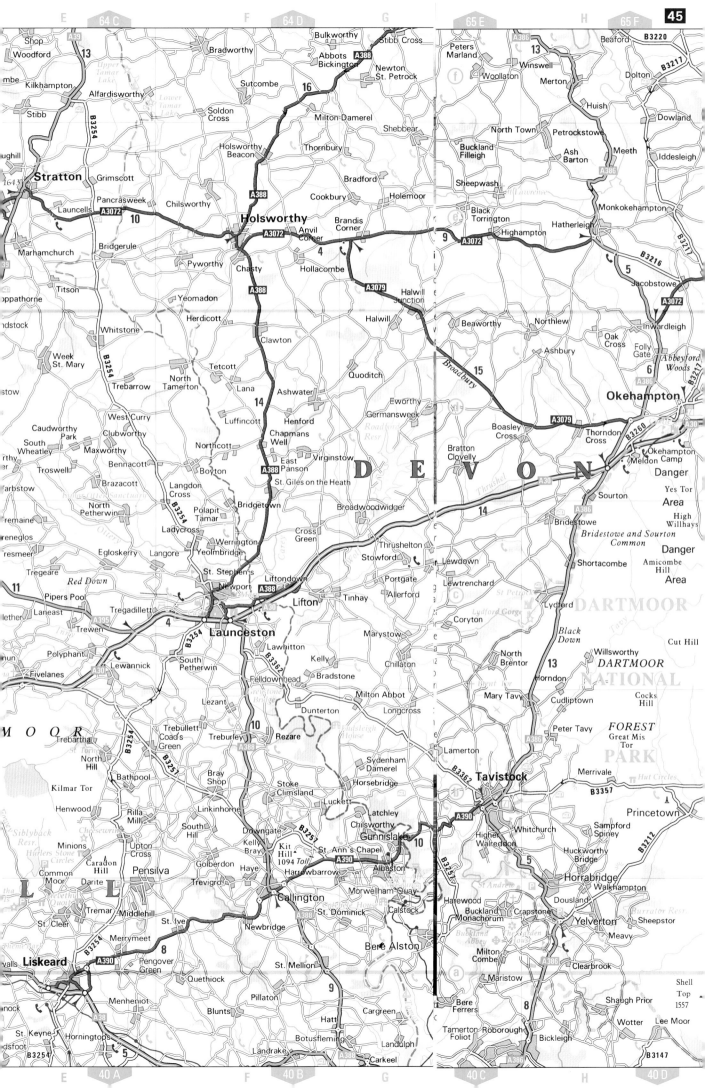

EXETER
Barnstaple 40

Okehampton 23 A30—A38 Plymouth 44

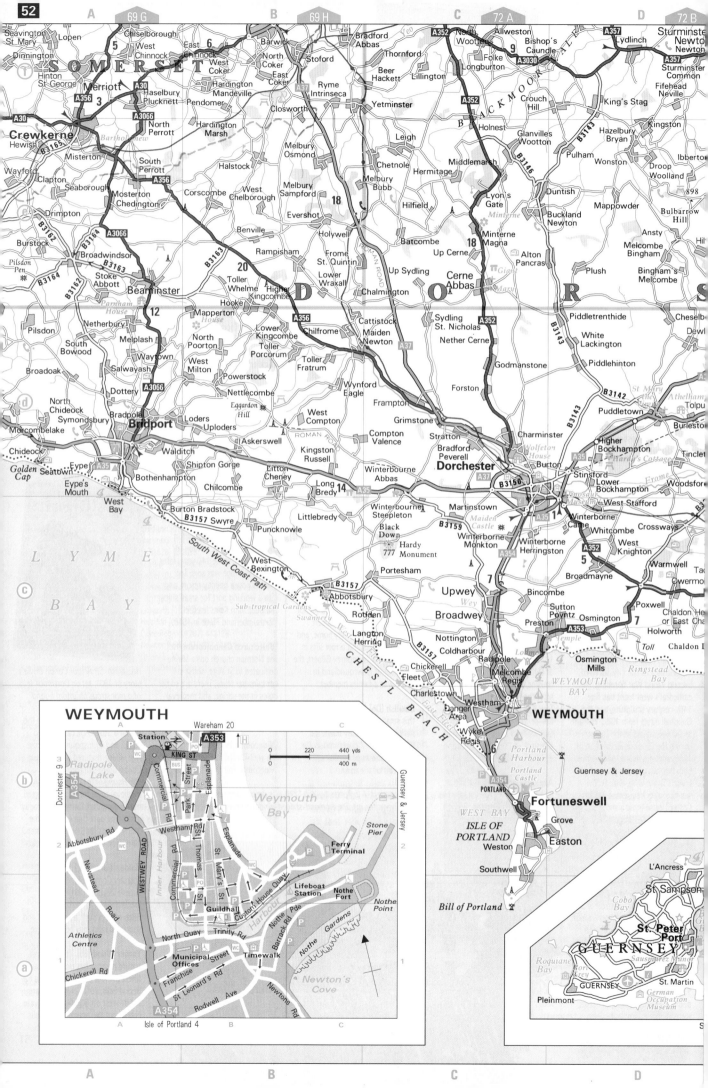

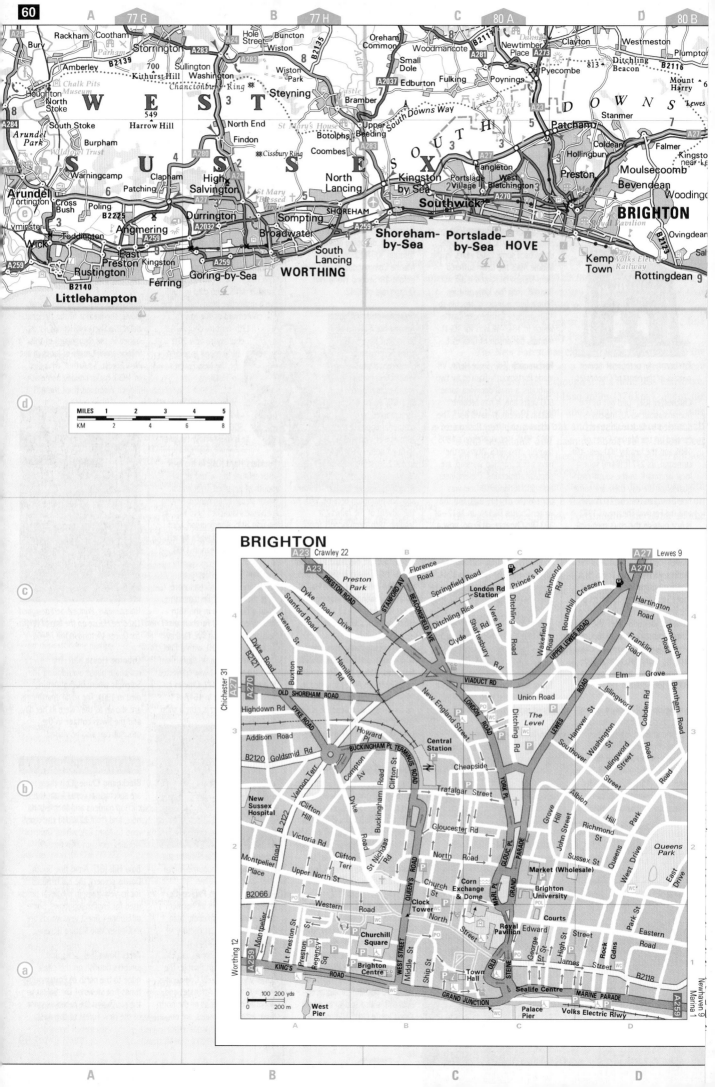

77 G   77 H   80 A   80 B

A   B   C   D

WEST

Rackham   Cootham
Bury
Storrington
Amberley
B2139
Kithurst Hill   Sullington
700   Washington
Chalk Pits   Chanctonbury Ring
Museum
Houghton
North
Stoke

Hole
Street
Buncton
Wiston
Wiston
Park
B2135
Steyning
Bramber

Oreham
Common
Woodmancote
Small
Dole
Edburton
Fulking
Poynings

Newtimber
Place
Clayton
Ditchling
Beacon
813
Westmeston
Plumpton

A283
A283
A24
Castle
South Downs Way
A2037
Upper
Beeding
St Mary's House
Devil's
Dyke
A273
A281
Pyecombe
A23
Mount
Harry
Lewes
B2116

SUSSEX

South Stoke
Burpham
Harrow Hill
549
South
North End
Findon
Botolphs
Coombes
North
Lancing
Kingston
by Sea
Portslade
Village
West
Blatchington
Patcham
Coldean
Hollingbury
Preston
Falmer
Stanmer
near
DOWNS
Moulsecoomb
Bevendean
Woodingdean

Arundel
Park
Wildfowl
Trust
Warningcamp
Clapham
Patching
High
Salvington
St Mary
Blessed
Virgin
A280
A24
SHOREHAM
Southwick
BRIGHTON
Royal Pavilion

Arundel
Tortington
Cross
Bush
Poling
Durrington
A2032
Sompting
Broadwater
Shoreham-
by-Sea
Portslade-
by-Sea
HOVE
Ovingdean

Wick
Teddington
Angmering
A259
A27
A2225
Kingston
Goring-by-Sea
South
Lancing
WORTHING
Kemp
Town
Volks Electric
Railway
Rottingdean

Littlehampton
B2140
Rustington
Ferring
B2120

MILES 1   2   3   4   5
KM   2   4   6   8

BRIGHTON

A23 Crawley 22   A27 Lewes 9

A   B   C   D

A23
Preston
Park
Florence
Road
Springfield Road
London Rd
Station
Prince's Rd
Richmond
Rd
Roundhill Crescent
A270
Hartington
Road

Dyke   Road   Drive
Stanford Road
Beaconsfield Ave
Ditchling Rise
Vere Rd
Ditchling
Road
Wakefield
Upper Lewes Road
Elm   Grove
Bonchurch
Road
Franklin
Road

Dyke Road
Exeter St
Stanford Road
Clyde
Shaftesbury Rd
Viaduct Rd
Union Road
The
Level
Islingword
Cobden Rd
Bentham
Road

B2121
A27
A270
Hamilton Rd
Buxton Rd
Old Shoreham Road
New England Street
London Road
Ditchling Rd
Lewes   Road
Hanover St
Southover
Washington
St
Islingword
Street

Highdown Rd
Howard
Pl
Central
Station
Cheapside
Road
Albion
Grove
Hill
John Street
Richmond
St

Addison Road
Buckingham Pl
Terminus Road
Trafalgar Street
York Pl
Grand   Parade
Hill
Sussex St
Queens
Park

B2120 Goldsmid Rd
Compton
Av
Dyke
Clifton St
Gloucester Rd
North   Road
Grove
West Drive
East
Drive

New
Sussex
Hospital
Vernon Terr
Clifton
Hill
Buckingham   Road
St Nicholas
Rd
Church
St
Corn
Exchange
& Dome
Brighton
University
Richmond
St
Park St

B2122
Victoria Rd
Montpelier
Place
Upper North St
Clifton
Terr
St Nicholas   Rd
North
Market (Wholesale)

B2066
Montpelier
Road
Western   Road
Church
St
Royal
Pavilion
Edward
George
Street
Eastern
Road

Worthing 12
A259
Preston St
Regency
Sq
Churchill
Square
Brighton
Centre
Clock
Tower
North
Street
Town
Hall
Courts
High St
James   Street
Rock
Gdns
B2118

Chichester 31
KING'S   ROAD
West
Pier
Brighton
Centre
West
Street
Middle St
Ship St
Sealife Centre
MARINE PARADE
A259

0 100 200 yds
0   200 m
West
Pier
GRAND JUNCTION
Palace
Pier
Volks Electric Rlwy
Newhaven 9
Marina 1

A   B   C   D

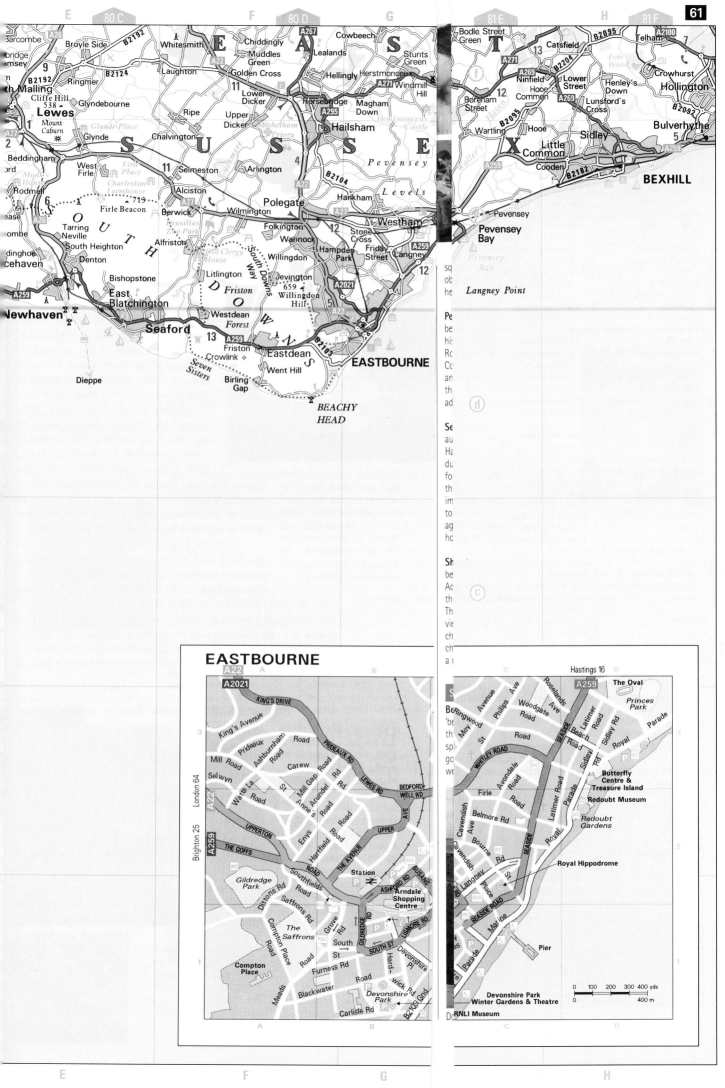

EASTBOURNE

A   B   C   D

B R I S T O L   C H A N N E L

f

Northwest Point ✳

LUNDY

e

✳ *The Landing Beach*
Rat Island
Great Shutter Rock ✳

BARNSTAPLE

Lynton 18

Ilfracombe 13   A361   ROLLE ST   A39

Mill Road   North Walk

Green Lanes Shopping Centre

Coronation St

INNER

St

Civic Centre

Castle Mound

Athenaeum Library

High St

Boutport St

Bear St

Vicarage Lawn

Vicarage Street

RELIEF

Guildhall

Joy St

Pannier Mkt

Queen's Theatre

Cross St

Q Anne's Walk

St Anne's Chapel

Silver St

Queen Street

ROAD

River Taw

Long Br

North Devon Mus

Litchdon Street

Taw Vale

A361 / A377

Leisure Centre

B.3233

0   220 yds
0   200 m

A   B

---

d

B A R N S T A P L E

O R

B I D E F O R D   B A

HARTLAND POINT ✳

Titchberry   *Windbury Point*

St Nectan

Hartland Abbey

c

Hartland Quay   Stoke   Hartland   B3248   Clovelly

B3237   Dyke   Buck's Mills   14

Milford   Philham   Buck's Cross   Goldwor

Clovelly Dykes   A39   Cranford

Edistone   Parkhar

Elmscott   Tosberr   Woolfardisworthy   Parkham Ash

South Hole   Alminstone Cross   Melb

Welcombe   Ashmansworthy

Meddon   A39

Gooseham   Youlstone   **D**   East

St Morwenna

b

Vicarage Cliff   Morwenstow   Eastcott   Dinworthy   West Putford

Higher Sharpnose Point   Shop   Bulkw

Woodford   Bradworthy

Lower Sharpnose Point   Upper Tamar Lake   Abb Bickin

Kilkhampton   13   Lower Tamar Lake   Sutcombe

Coombe   Alfardisworthy   Soldon Cross   Milton Damere

B U D E   Stibb   B3254

CORNWALL   Holsworthy Beacon

B A Y   Poughill

Flexbury   Grimscott   Holsworthy

a

Stratton   Pancrasweek   Chilsworthy   A388

Bude   Launcells   10   An Cor

A3072   A3072

Marhamchurch   Bridgerule   Pyworthy   Chasty   Hollacc

A39   18   Widemouth Bay   Yeomadon   A388

Coppathorne   Titson   14

MILES   1   2   3   4   5
KM   2   4   6   8

A   B   44 D   C   45 E   D   45 F

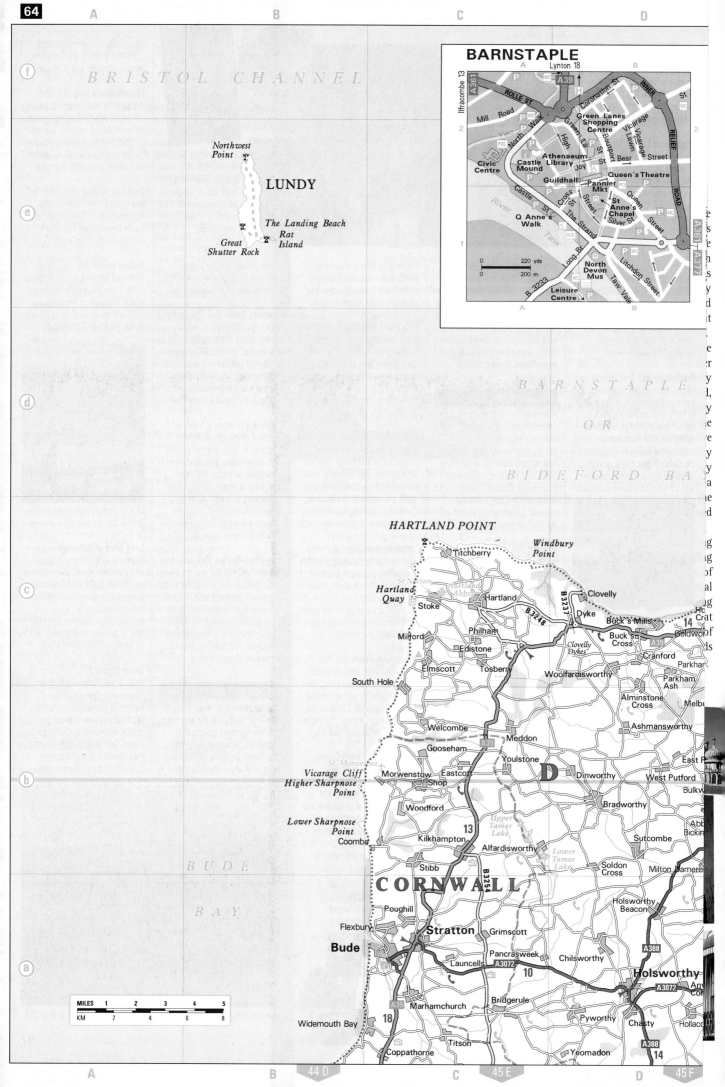

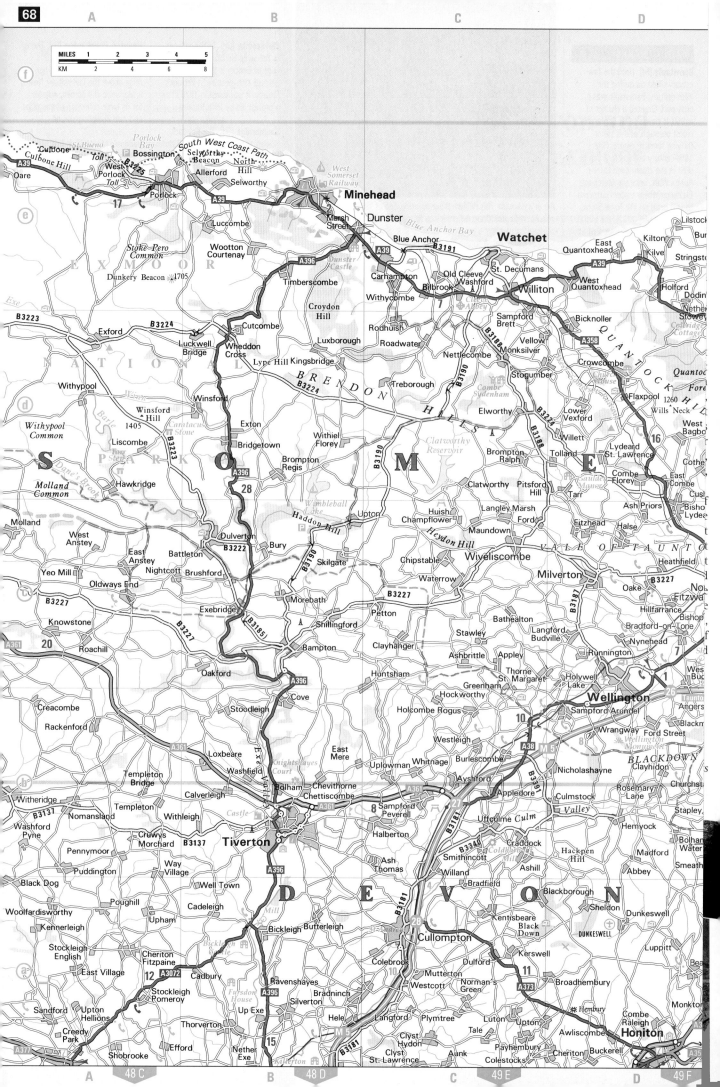

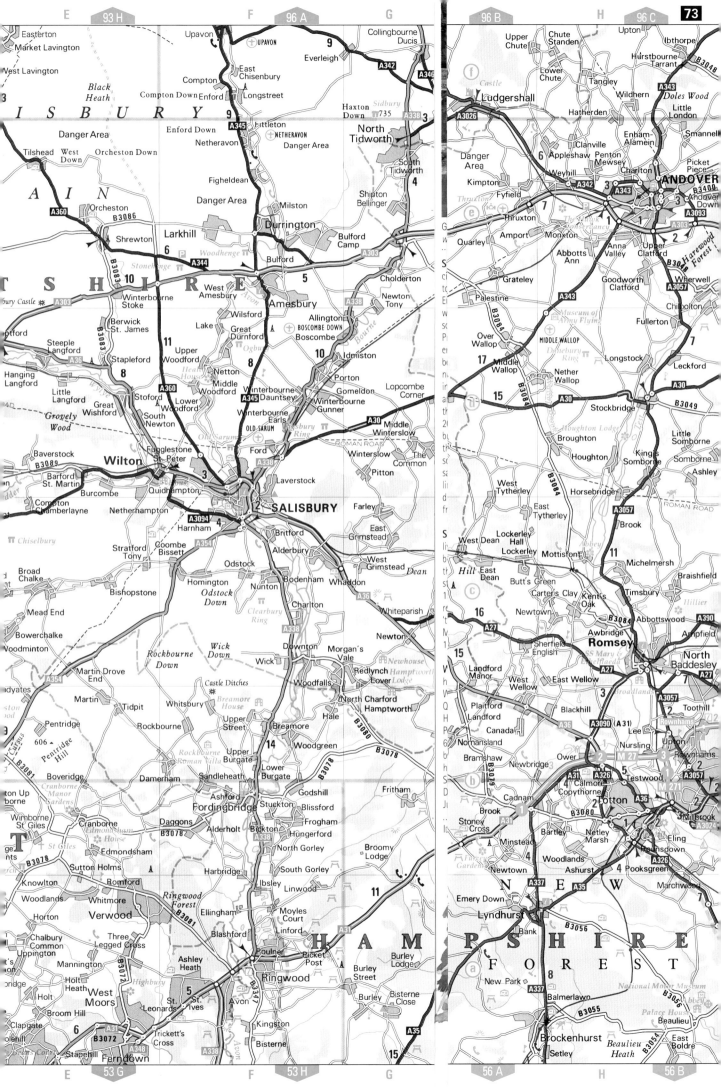

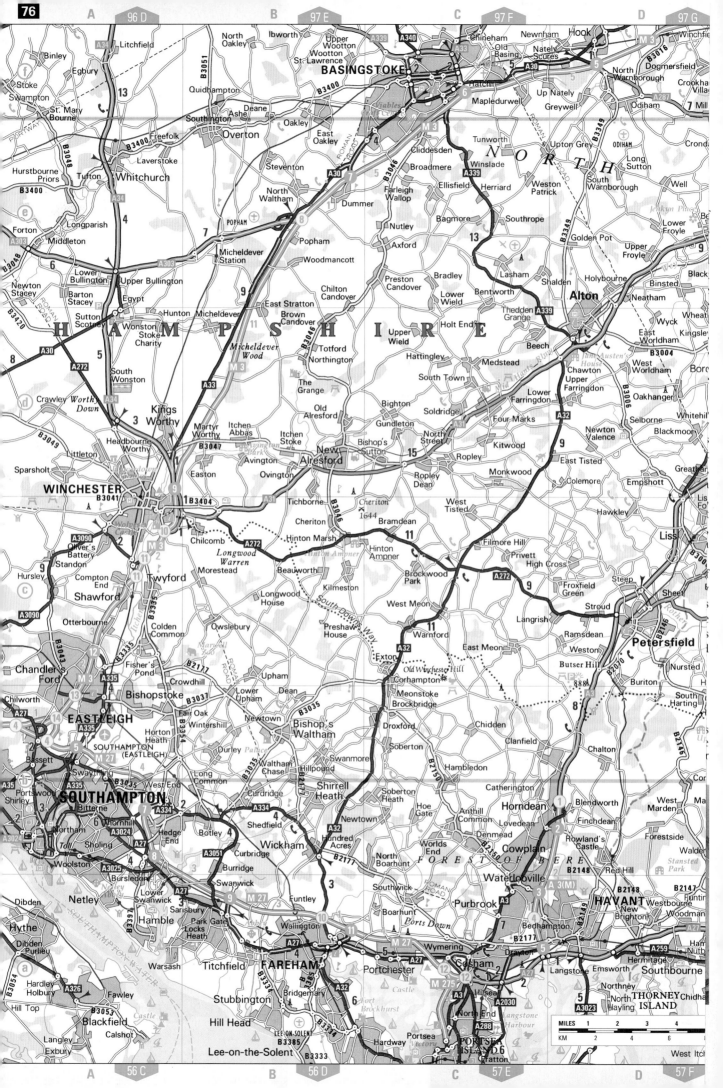

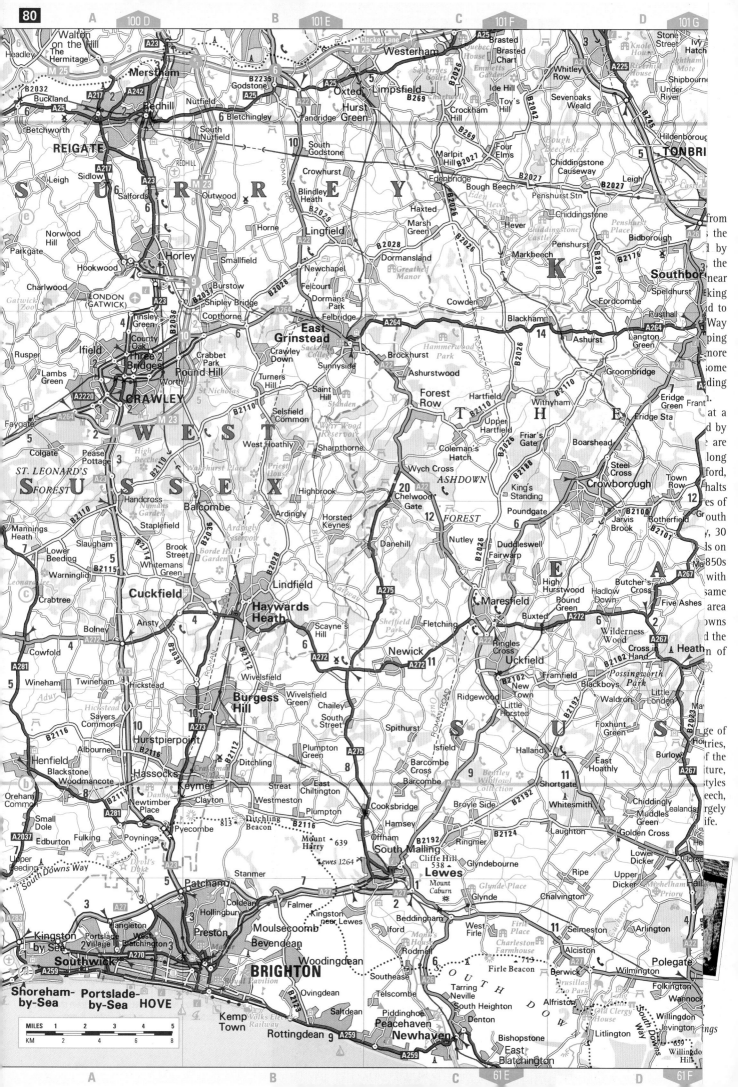

FOLKESTONE

Ashford 15 **A20** — **A20** Dover 7

Royal Victoria Hospital

Radnor Park

Radnor Park West

Radnor Avenue

Radnor Park

RADNOR PARK ROAD

Ashford 14

A2034

A20

Bournemouth Road

Broadmead

BLACK BULL RD

Linden Crescent

Archer Rd

Canterbury Rd

B2067

A259

A2033

Hythe 5 **M20**

A259

CHERITON RD

Folkestone Central Station

Brockman Road

Coolinge Road

Castle Hill Ave

FOORD ROAD

Guildhall St

GRACE HILL

DOVER ROAD

St Michaels St

Harvey St

Harbour Way

THE TRAM ROAD

DOVER ROAD

Civic Centre

Christ Church

Castle Hill

CHERITON GDNS

Manor Road

CHERITON

Mill Field

Victoria Gr

MIDDELBURG RD

SQ

High St

TONTINE ST

The Stade

Courts

BOUVERIE RD W

Church St

Road

The Parade

Church Street

WC

East Pier

Harbour

Boulogne

Clifton Gdns

SANDGATE ROAD

Sandgate

Lower Sandgate Rd

Manne Terr

Marine Parade

Harbour Station

The Lower Leas

The Leas Cliff Hall

Leas Sandgate

Cliff Lift Road

Toll Gate

Marine Parade

Car Ferry Terminal

Harbour Pier

0 — 330 yds
0 — 300 m

CARMARTHEN

109 G · 109 H

Pembrey Circuit

Waun y Clyn

Trimsaran

A484

B4311

Burry Port

Pembrey

19

B4308

Pwll

B4311

Cefn Padrig

Whiteford Point

Llanrhidian Sands

Llanmadoc

Cheriton

Landimore

Llangennith

Oldwalls

Llanrhidian

Webley Castle

Fairyhill

Burry Holms

St Cennydd

Rhossili Down

Cefn Bryn

Reynoldston

Llanddewi

Rhossili Bay

St Mary

Rhossili

B4247

Knelston

Penrice

WORMS HEAD

Middleton

Pilton Green

Horton

Oxwich

Oxwich Green

Gower Coast

Overton

Port-Eynon

Culver Hole

Port-Eynon Bay

Port-Eynon Point

CHANNEL TUNNEL

For additional information, see page 370

Channel Tunnel

CALAIS

D 119

CALAIS DUNKIRK

Marck

N1

N1

R940

Sangatte

Coquelles

13 14

15 16 17 18 19

A16 E402

Lille 110 miles

Cap Blanc-Nez

D243E

12

Channel Tunnel Terminal

Coulogne

D127

Paris 170 miles

A26 E15

N43

Escalles

11

A16 E402

Fréthun

Les Attaques

R940

10

D215

Guînes

D231

Wissant

D238

9

St-Inglevert

Hames Boucres

D231

D127

TGV Line

D215

Brèmes

D224

Cap Gris-Nez

8

Leubringhen

P A S - D E - C A L A I S

Audinghen

7

Ferques

Rety

Hardinghen

Licques

D127

D217

Audresselles

D231

Marquise

D791

Rinxent

6

Ambleteuse

5

D217

Le Wast

Colembert

D224

Wimereux

4

A16 E402

Wimille

Boulogne 2 miles

R940

3

E · F · G · H

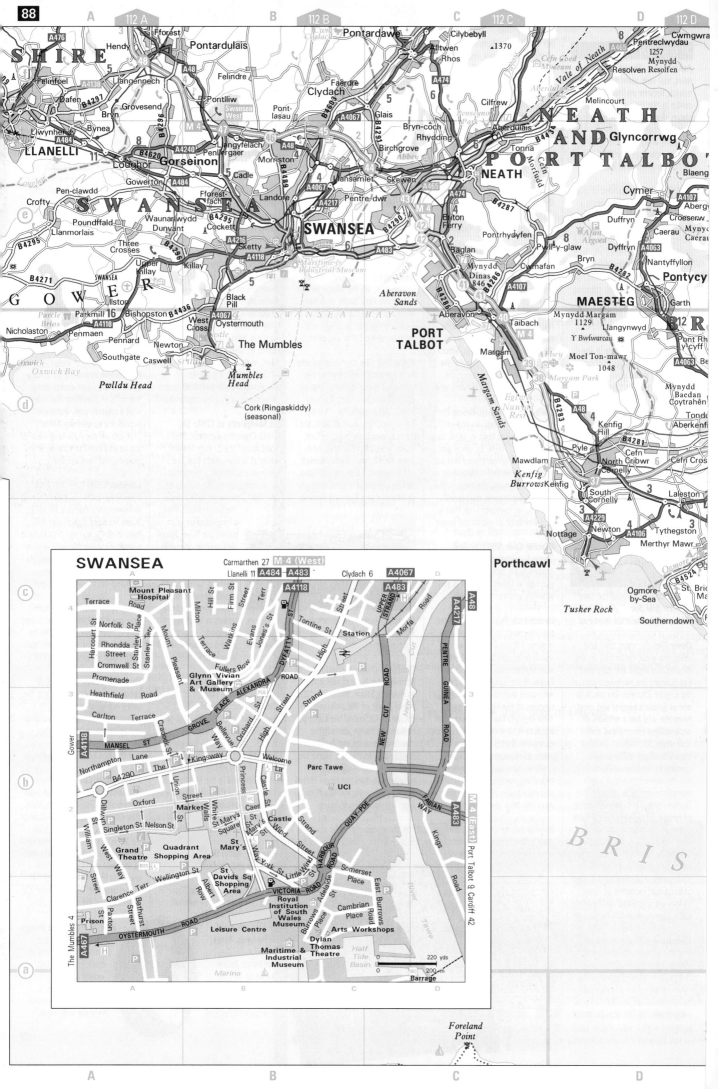

MONMOUTHSHIRE

VALE OF BERKELEY

MOUTH OF THE SEVERN

NEWPORT
Caerleon
Usk
Chepstow
Thornbury
BRISTOL
Kingswood
Keynsham
Clevedon
Portishead
Yatton
WESTON-SUPER-MARE
Cheddar
Midsomer Norton
Radstock
Lydney

Kemeys Commander, Penperlleni, Croes y pant, Little Mill, Monkswood, Glascoed, Cwm, New Inn, Coed-y-paen, Llanllowell, Llanbadoc, Llancayo, Gwehelog, Llandenny, Llandegveth, Llanishen, Llansoy, Llandogo, St. Briavels, Purton, Parkhouse, Trelleck Grange, Hewelsfield Common, Hewelsfield, Aylburton, Llanvihangel, Gwernesney, Llangwm-isaf, Llangwm, New Inn, Wolvesnewton, Devauden, Tintern Parva, Brockweir, Netherend, Alvington, Woolaston, Plusterwine, Shepperdine, Berkeley, Ham, Stone

Pontrhydyrun, Croesyceiliog, Llangybi, Llandegveth, Tredunnock, Newbridge-on-Usk, Pen-y-cae-mawr, Earlswood, Kilwrrwg Common, Newchurch, Chepstow Park Wood, St. Arvans, Itton, Tintern Abbey, Tutshill, Woodcroft, Boughspring, Tidenham, Wibdon, Bevington, Hill, Rockhampton, Whitfield, Falfield

Malpas, Christchurch, Langstone, Llanbeder, Penhow, Caerwent, Crick, Mathern, Beachley, Severn Road Bridge, Littleton-upon-Severn, Morton, Milbury Heath, Cromhall, Llanmartin, Wilcrick, Bishton, Llanwern, Magor, Rogiet, Undy, Caldicot, Portskewett, Sudbrook, Severn Tunnel, Aust, Ingst, Northwick, Redwick, Elberton, Alveston, Olveston, Rudgeway, Tockington, Rangeworthy, Latteridge, Iron Acton

Pye Corner, Broadstreet Common, Summerleaze, Redwick, Whitson, Goldcliff, Nash, Power Stn, Second Severn Bridge (Due open Summer 1996), Severn Beach, Pilning, Easter Compton, Almondsbury, Awkley, Over, Patchway, Frampton Cotterell, Winterbourne, Works, Hallen, Filton, Catbrain, Stoke Gifford, Hambrook, Downend, Frenchay, Mangotsfield

Porton Grounds, Welsh Grounds, Caldicot Level, Avonmouth, Battery Point, Shirehampton, Henbury, Westbury, Stapleton, Redland, Clifton, Hanham, Brislington, Oldland, Upton Cheyney

Middle Grounds, Portishead, Redcliffe Bay, West Hill, Sheepway, Pill, Ham Green, Easton-in-Gordano, Portbury, Abbots Leigh, Leigh Woods, Long Ashton, Knowle, Bishopsworth, Whitchurch, Queen Charlton, Saltford

Clevedon, Walton-in-Gordano, Clapton-in-Gordano, Weston-in-Gordano, Wraxall, Failand, Flax Bourton, Barrow Gurney, Dundry, North Wick, Chewton Keynsham, Compton Dando, Burnett

Sand Point, Wick St. Lawrence, Kingston Seymour, Tickenham, Nailsea, West End, St. Mary's Grove, Kenn, Chelvey, North End, East End, Farleigh, Backwell, West Town, Lulsgate Bottom, Upper Town, Dundry Hill, Norton Hawkfield, Norton Malreward, Belluton, Chewton Keynsham

Sand Bay, Kewstoke, Bourton, Hewish, Brockley, Cleeve, Downside, Claverham, Congresbury, Puxton, East Rolstone, Wrington, Redhill, Felton, Winford, Chew Magna, Stanton Drew, Stanton Wick, Pensford, Hunstrete, Chelwood, Marksbury

Worle, West Wick, Banwell, Sandford, Star, Churchill, Rickford, Burrington, Blagdon, Butcombe, Nempnett Thrubwell, Chew Stoke, Ridgehill, Bishop Sutton, Stowey, Clutton, High Littleton, Farmborough, Timsbury, Carlingcott

Hutton, Locking, Bleadon, Bleadon Hill, Christon, Loxton, Winscombe, Sidcot, Shipham, Rowberrow, Compton Bishop Cross, Axbridge, Charterhouse, Cheddar, Black Down, Compton Martin, West Harptree, East Harptree, Hinton Blewett, Farrington Gurney, Hallatrow, Paulton, Litton, Chewton Mendip, Ston Easton, Chilcompton

Uphill, Lympsham, Berrow, Brent Knoll, East Brent, Biddisham, Badgworth, Weare, Lower Weare, Stone Allerton, Chapel Allerton, Clewer, Nyland, Nyland Hill 251, Draycott, Rodney Stoke, Priddy, Green Ore, Emborough, Downside, Stratton-on-the-Fosse, Chilcompton

MENDIP HILLS, MENDIP FOREST, Cheddar Gorge, Cheddar Reservoir, Blagdon Lake, Chew Valley Lake, Danger Area

A48, A449, A472, A466, A4042, A4058, M4, M48, M49, M5, M32, A38, A370, A371, A368, A369, A4018, A4054, A4057, A4059, A4174, A4320, A4175, A432, A431, A420, B4293, B4235, B4245, B4228, B4461, B3128, B3130, B3129, B3133, B3134, B3135, B3114, B3116, B3139, B3140, B3151

Toll, Works, Roman Road, Olio's Dyke Path, Wentwood, Oldbury Sands, Oldbury-on-Severn, Severn View, Cheddar Caves, Mendip Forest

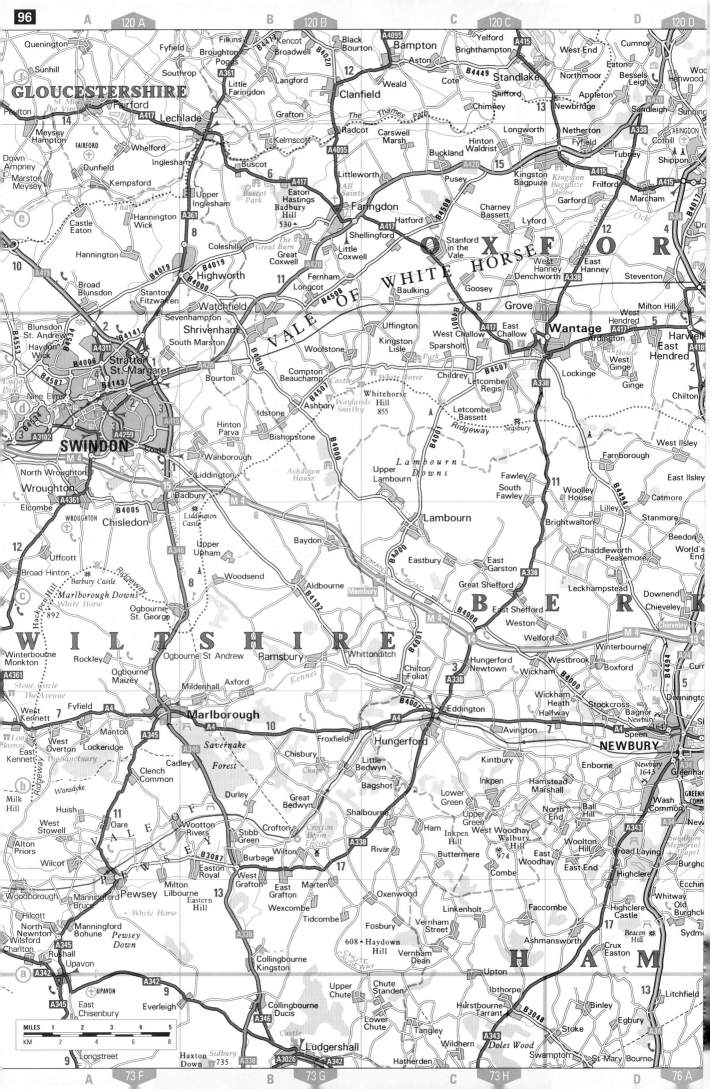

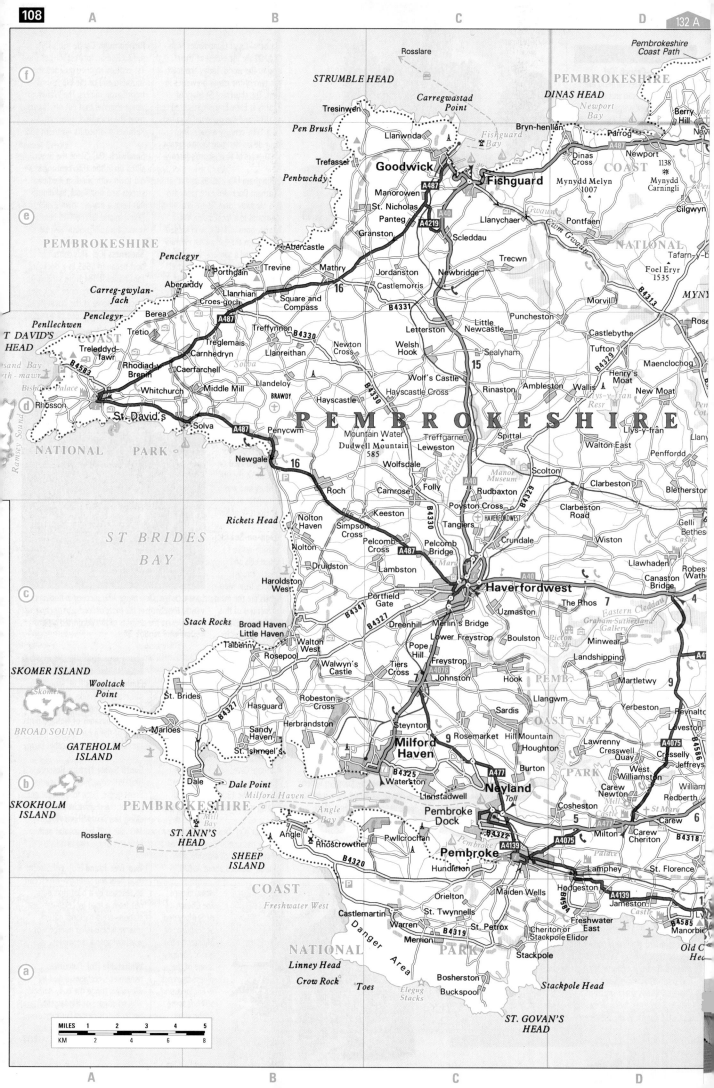

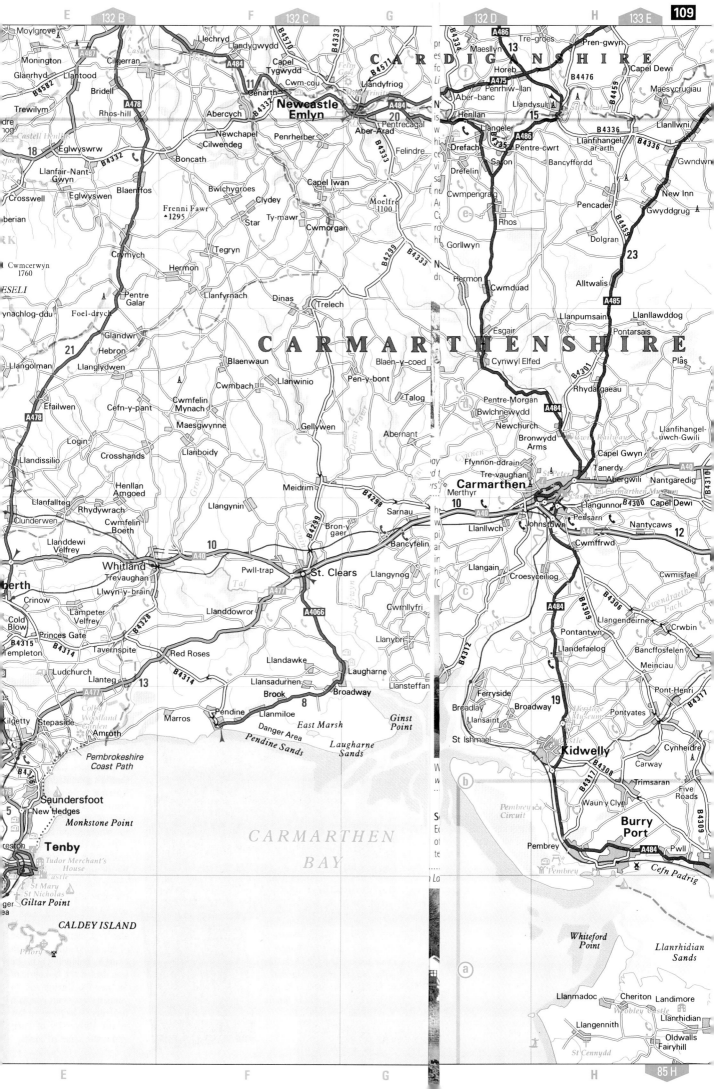

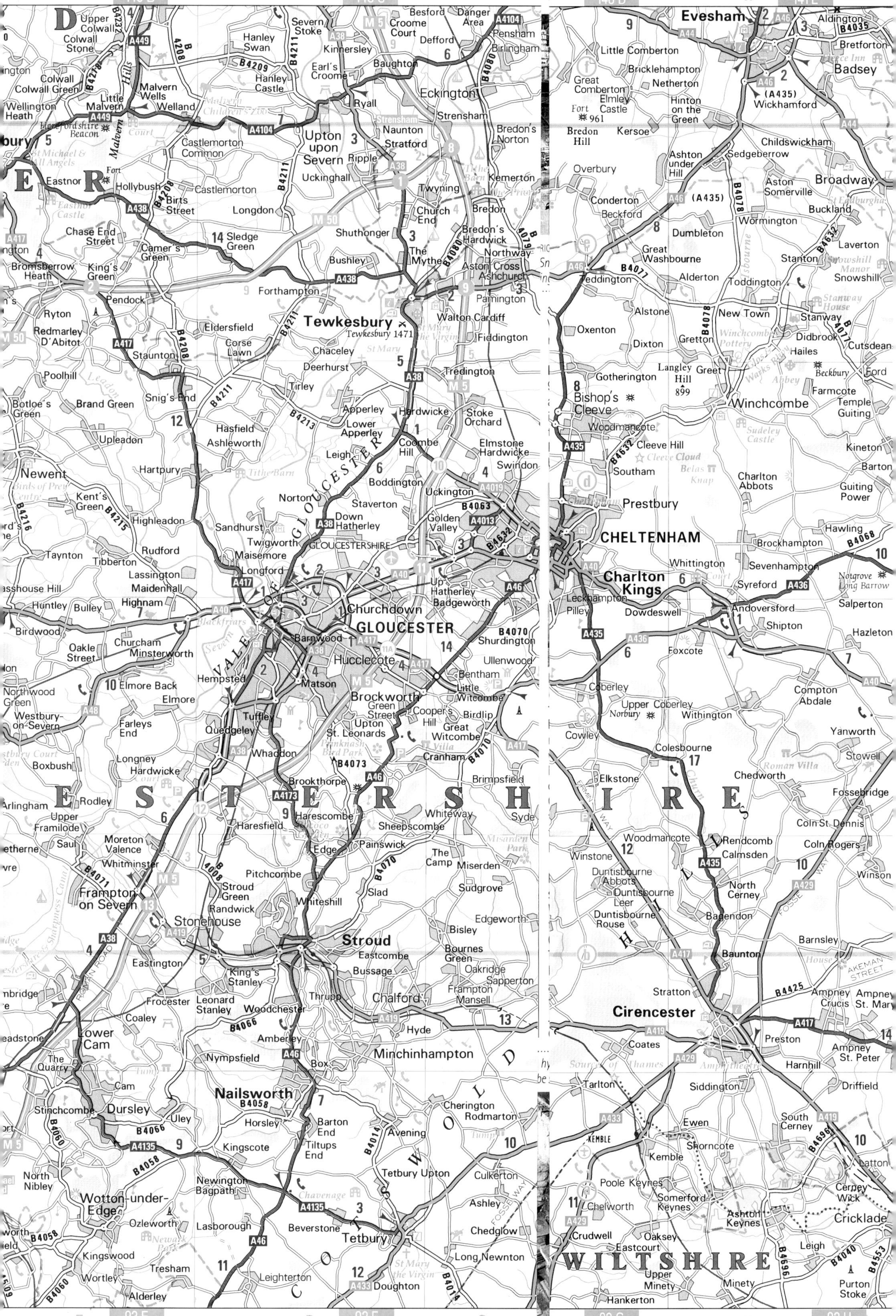
Evesham
Aldington
Bretforton
Badsey
Wickhamford
Little Comberton
Bricklehampton
Netherton
Great Comberton
Elmley Castle
Hinton on the Green
Bredon Hill
Kersoe
Childswickham
Sedgeberrow
Ashton under Hill
Broadway
Aston Somerville
Overbury
Conderton
Beckford
Buckland
Wormington
Dumbleton
Laverton
Great Washbourne
Stanton
Snowshill Manor
Snowshill
Alderton
Toddington
Teddington
Stanway House
Stanway
Alstone
New Town
Didbrook
Oxenton
Dixton
Gretton
Winchcombe Pottery
Hailes
Cutsdean
Gotherington
Langley Hill
Greet
Beckbury
Ford
Farmcote
Bishop's Cleeve
Winchcombe
Temple Guiting
Woodmancote
Sudeley Castle
Cleeve Hill
Kineton
Southam
Cleeve Cloud
Belas Knap
Barton
Charlton Abbots
Guiting Power
Prestbury
CHELTENHAM
Hawling
Brockhampton
Whittington
Sevenhampton
Notgrove Long Barrow
Charlton Kings
Syreford
Leckhampton
Pilley
Dowdeswell
Andoversford
Salperton
Shipton
Hazleton
Foxcote
Coberley
Compton Abdale
Upper Coberley
Norbury
Withington
Yanworth
Cowley
Colesbourne
Stowell
Roman Villa
Chedworth
Elkstone
Fossebridge
Coln St. Dennis
Woodmancote
Rendcomb
Coln Rogers
Winstone
Calmsden
Winson
Duntisbourne Abbots
North Cerney
Duntisbourne Leer
Duntisbourne Rouse
Bagendon
Barnsley
Baunton
Stratton
Ampney Crucis
Ampney St. Mary
Cirencester
Preston
Coates
Ampney St. Peter
Harnhill
Tarlton
Siddington
Driffield
Ewen
South Cerney
Kemble
Shorncote
Latton
Poole Keynes
Somerford Keynes
Cerney Wick
Chelworth
Ashton Keynes
Cricklade
Crudwell
Oakley
Eastcourt
Leigh
WILTSHIRE
Upper Minety
Minety
Purton Stoke
Hankerton
Upper Colwall
Colwall Stone
Colwall
Colwall Green
Malvern Wells
Little Malvern
Welland
Wellington Heath
Herefordshire Beacon
Eastnor
Hollybush
Eastnor Castle
Castlemorton Common
Castlemorton
Birts Street
Chase End Street
Camer's Green
Sledge Green
Bromsberrow Heath
King's Green
Hanley Swan
Hanley Castle
Severn Stoke
Kinnersley
Earl's Croome
Croome Court
Besford
Danger Area
Defford
Pensham
Birlingham
Baughton
Eckington
Ryall
Strensham
Naunton
Upton upon Severn
Stratford
Ripple
Uckinghall
Bredon's Norton
Kemerton
Twyning
Church End
Longdon
Bredon
Bredon's Hardwick
Northway
Shuthonger
The Mythe
Bushley
Aston Cross
Ashchurch
Forthampton
Pamington
Pendock
Ryton
Redmarley D'Abitot
Eldersfield
Corse Lawn
Tewkesbury
Walton Cardiff
Fiddington
Staunton
Chaceley
Deerhurst
Tredington
Poolhill
Tirley
Botloe's Green
Brand Green
Snig's End
Apperley
Hardwicke
Stoke Orchard
Lower Apperley
Hasfield
Ashleworth
Upleadon
Coombe Hill
Leigh
Elmstone Hardwicke
Newent
Hartpury
Swindon
Boddington
Norton
Kent's Green
Staverton
Uckington
Highleadon
Sandhurst
Down Hatherley
Golden Valley
Twigworth
Taynton
Tibberton
Rudford
Maisemore
Lassington
Longford
Maidenhall
Highnam
Huntley
Bulley
Up Hatherley
Badgeworth
Churchdown
Birdwood
GLOUCESTER
Churcham
Minsterworth
Barnwood
Shurdington
Oakle Street
Hucclecote
Ullenwood
Hempsted
Matson
Bentham
Northwood Green
Elmore Back
Elmore
Brockworth
Little Witcombe
Westbury-on-Severn
Farleys End
Cooper's Hill
Birdlip
Green Street
Great Witcombe
Quedgeley
Tuffley
Upton St. Leonards
Whaddon
Prinknash Bird Park
Cranham
Boxbush
Longney
Hardwicke
Brookthorpe
Brimpsfield
Arlingham
Rodley
Upper Framilode
Harescombe
Whiteway
Haresfield
Sheepscombe
Syde
Saul
Moreton Valence
Edge
Painswick
Miserden Park
Whitminster
The Camp
Miserden
Frampton on Severn
Pitchcombe
Stroud Green
Randwick
Slad
Sudgrove
Whiteshill
Stonehouse
Edgeworth
Bisley
Stroud
Eastcombe
Bournes Green
Eastington
Oakridge
Sapperton
King's Stanley
Bussage
Frampton Mansell
Frocester
Leonard Stanley
Thrupp
Chalford
Coaley
Woodchester
Hyde
Lower Cam
Amberley
Nympsfield
Minchinhampton
The Quarry
Box
Cam
Nailsworth
Dursley
Stinchcombe
Cherington
Rodmarton
Uley
Horsley
Barton End
Avening
Kingscote
Tiltups End
North Nibley
Newington Bagpath
Tetbury Upton
Culkerton
Wotton-under-Edge
Chavenage
Ashley
Ozleworth
Lasborough
Beverstone
Tetbury
Chedglow
Kingswood
Newark Park
Long Newnton
Tresham
Wortley
Leighterton
Doughton
Alderley
COTSWOLD
ESTERSHIRE
VALE OF GLOUCESTER

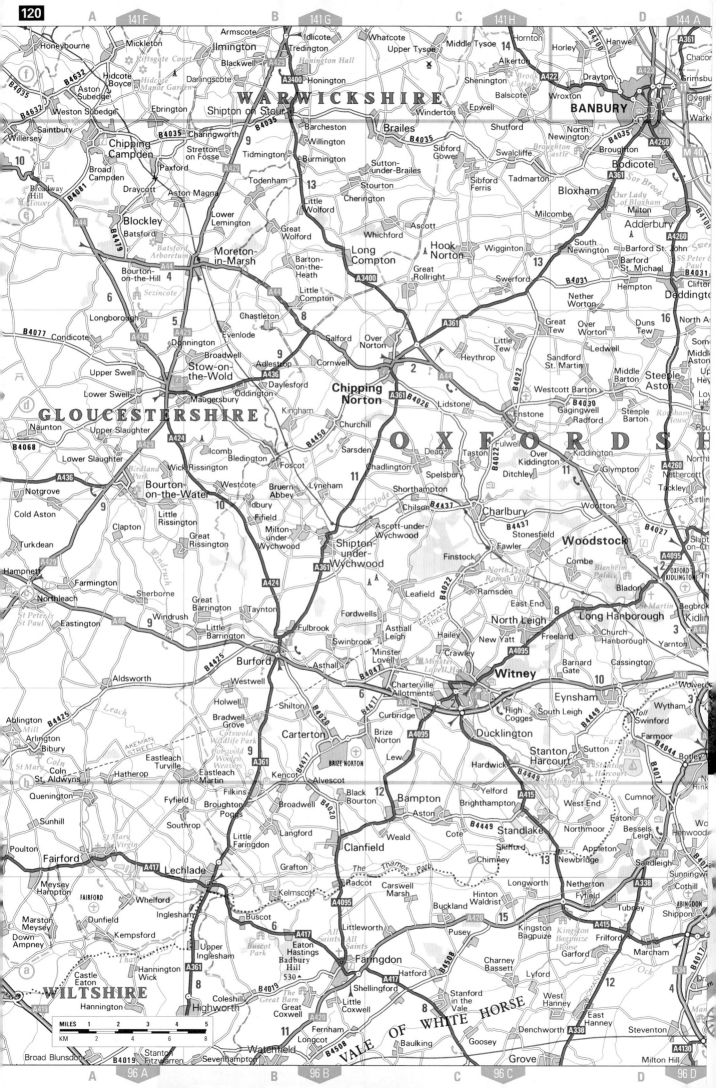

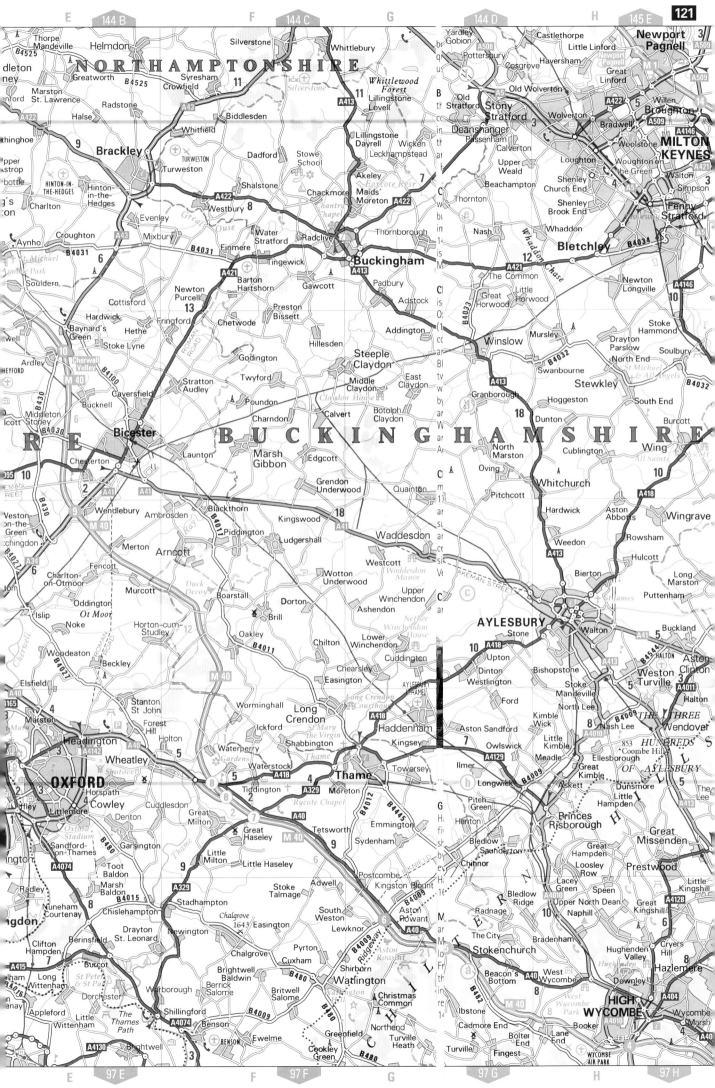

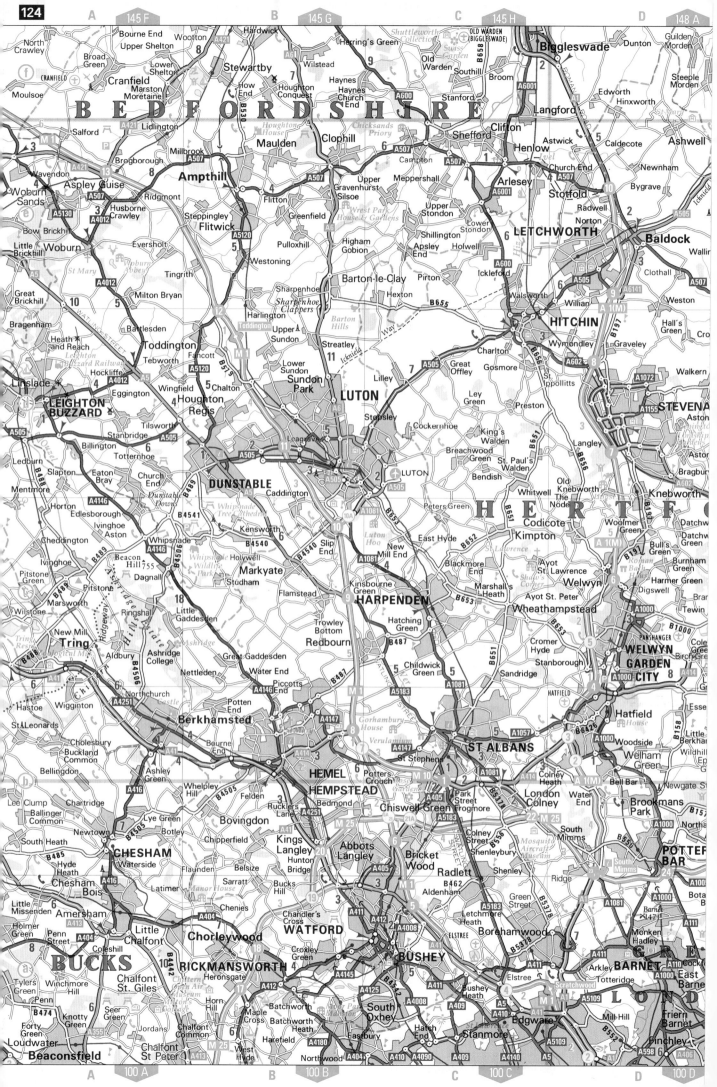

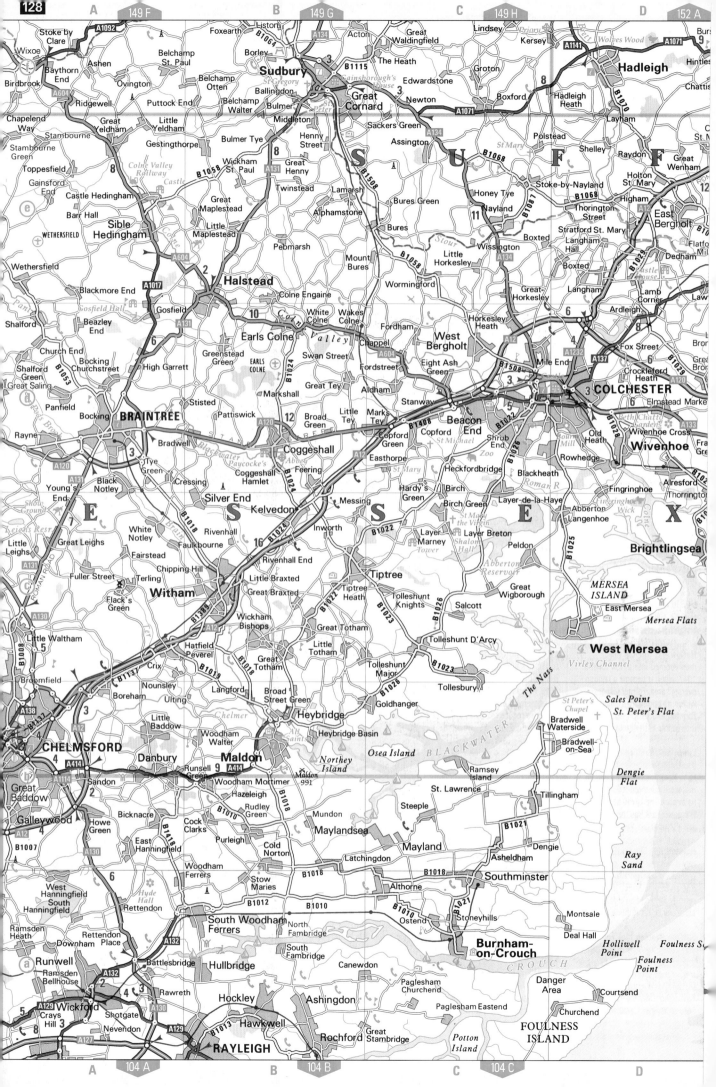

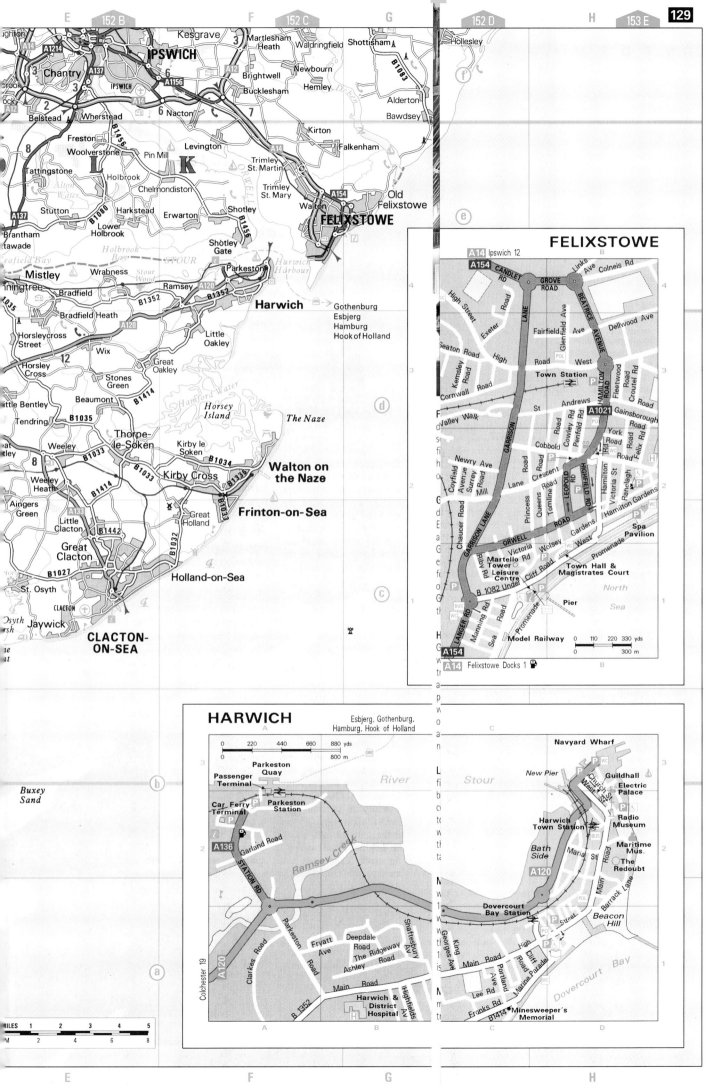

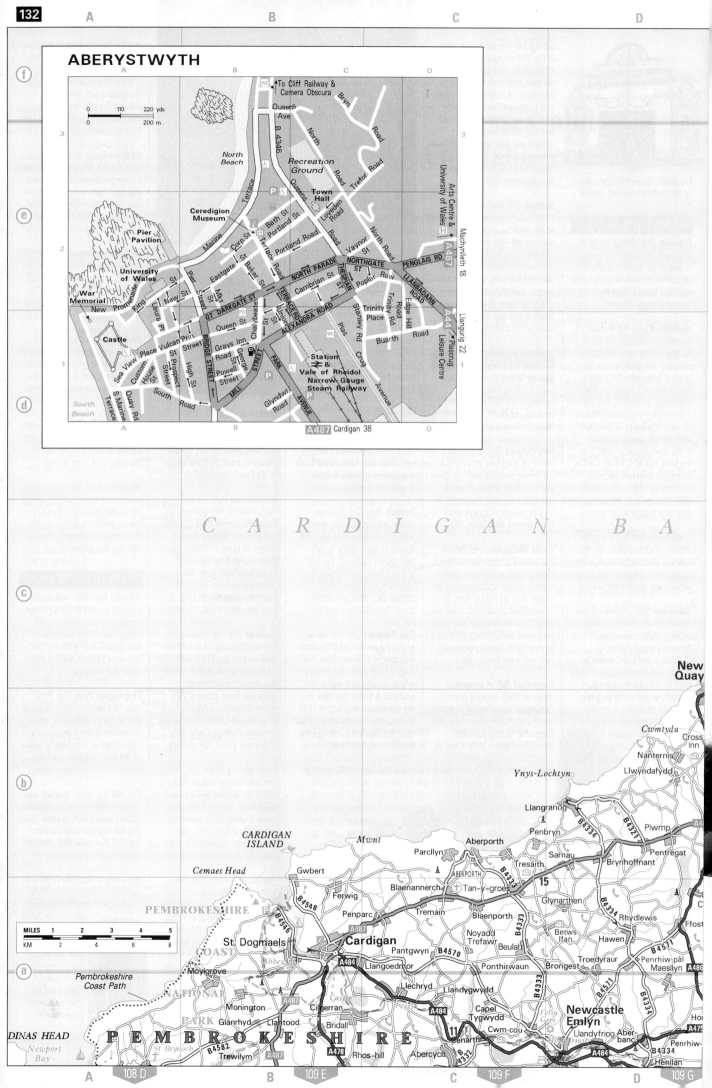

ABERYSTWYTH

To Cliff Railway & Camera Obscura

Queens Ave

North Beach

Recreation Ground

Ceredigion Museum

Pier Pavilion

University of Wales

War Memorial

Castle

Sea View Place

South Beach

Town Hall

Bath St
Portland St
Portland Road

Corp St

Marine Terrace

Eastgate St

Baker St

North Road
Trefor Road

Loveden Road

North Parade

Cambrian St

Thespian St

Vavnor St
Poplar Row

Northgate St

Llanbadarn Road

Penglais Rd

Arts Centre & University of Wales

A487 Machynlleth 18

A44 Llangurig 22

Plascrug Leisure Centre

Trinity Place

Stanley Rd
Trinity Rd
Edge Hill Road

Buarth

Terracerd Road

Alexandra Road

Union St
Chalybeate

Gt Darkgate St

Queen St

Grays Inn Road

Powell St
George St

Prin. Street

Vulcan Street

Prospect Street

Custom House

King St

New St

Laura Pl

Mkt St

Pier Street

Bridge Street

High St

South Road

S Marine Terrace

Quay Rd

Glyndwr Road

Mill Street

Park Avenue

Plas Crug Avenue

Station & Vale of Rheidol Narrow Gauge Steam Railway

A487 Cardigan 38

CARDIGAN BAY

New Quay

Cwmtydu

Cross Inn

Nanternis

Llwyndafydd

Ynys-Lochtyn

Llangranog

Penbryn

Plwmp

Pentregat

Aberporth

Parcllyn

Sarnau

Brynhoffnant

Mwnt

Tresaith

Glynarthen

Rhydlewis

CARDIGAN ISLAND

Gwbert

Blaenannerch

Tan-y-groes

15

Cemaes Head

Ferwig

Penparc

Tremain

Blaenporth

Betws Ifan

Hawen

Troedyraur

Penrhiw-pâl

Maesllyn

PEMBROKESHIRE

St Dogmaels

Cardigan

Pantgwyn

Noyadd Trefawr

Beulah

Brongest

Pembrokeshire Coast Path

Moylgrove

Llangoedmor

Ponthirwaun

Glanrhyd

Llechryd

Llandygwydd

Capel Tygwydd

Newcastle Emlyn

DINAS HEAD

Monington

Cilgerran

Bridall

Cwm-cou

Llandyfriog

Aberbanc

Penrhiw-

Newport Bay

St Brynach

PEMBROKESHIRE

Trewilym

B4582

A487

Rhos-hill

Abercych

A478

11

Cenarth

A484

Henllan

B4334

108 D

109 E

109 F

109 G

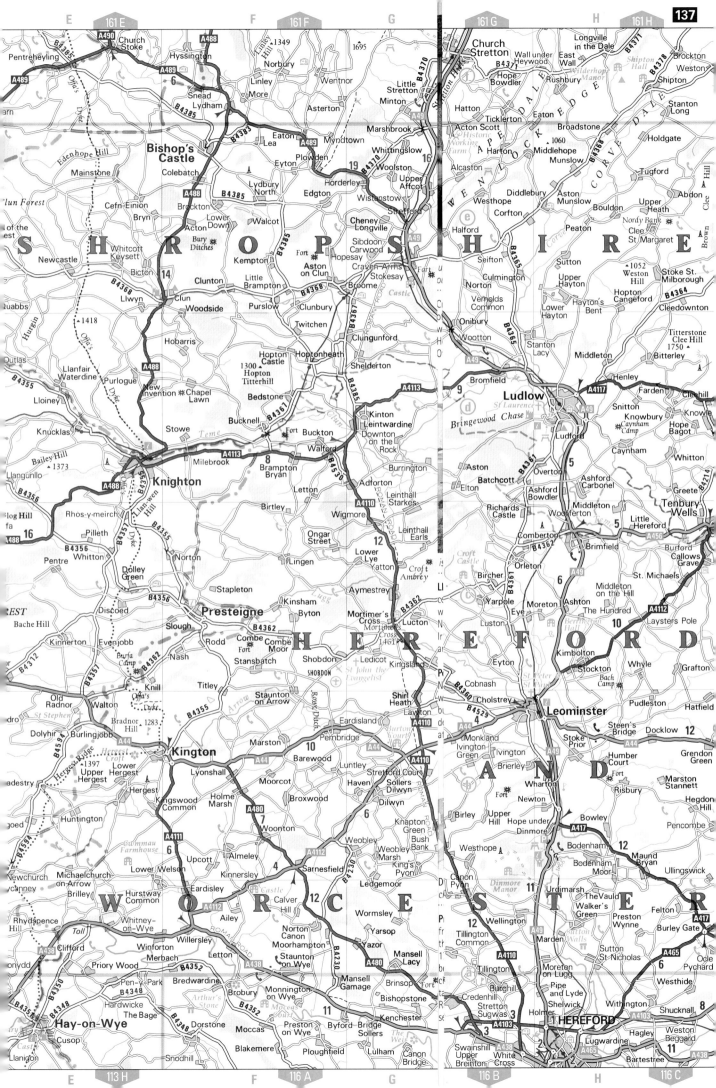

Ordnance Survey / road atlas map — page 140

Counties: SHROPSHIRE, STAFFS (WEST), HEREFORD AND WORCESTER

Major towns and places:
BRIDGNORTH, DUDLEY, WEST BROMWICH, STOURBRIDGE, HALESOWEN, KIDDERMINSTER, BROMSGROVE, Stourport-on-Severn, Bewdley, Droitwich, WORCESTER, GREAT MALVERN, Bromyard, Cleobury Mortimer, Sedgley, Wombourne, Kingswinford, Wordsley, Brierley Hill, Rowley Regis, Blackheath, Cradley, Pedmore, Hagley, Romsley, Belbroughton, Chaddesley Corbett, Ombersley, West Malvern, Malvern Link, Malvern Wells, Kempsey, Pershore, Eckington

Other place names (selection):
Aston Eyre, Morville, Tasley, Monkhopton, Upton Cressett, Middleton Priors, Chetton, Ditton Priors, Oldbury, Quatford, Eardington, Glazeley, Chelmarsh, Quatt, Tuckhill, Six Ashes, Sutton, Hampton, Billingsley, Woodhill, Alveley, Birdsgreen, Romsley, Sidbury, Chorley, Highley, Kinver, Enville, Wolverley, Kingsford, Shatterford, Trimpley, Low Habberley, Franche, Blakebrook, Wribbenhall, Upper Arley, Buttonoak, WYRE FOREST, Callow Hill, Ribbesford, Areley Kings, Wilden, Hartlebury, Stone, Harvington, Mustow Green, Shenstone, Rushock, Dodford, Bournheath, Elmley Lovett, Cutnall Green, Elmbridge, Hampton Lovett, Stoke Prior, Aston Fields, Finstall

SHROPSHIRE places: Aston Botterell, Loughton, Wheathill, Farlow, Silvington, Cleeton St Mary, Doddington, Hopton Wafers, Hints, Coreley, Milson, Neen Sollars, Nash, Boraston, Frith Common, Lindridge, Newnham Bridge, Rochford, Eardiston, Orleton, Stockton on Teme, Stanford on Teme, Hanley William, Hanley Childe, Broadheath, Kyre Park, Stoke Bliss, Upper Sapey, Sapey Common, Stanford Bridge, Shelsley Walsh, Shelsley Beauchamp, Clifton upon Teme, Lower Sapey

WORCESTER area: Astley Cross, Lincomb, Dunley, Abberley, Great Witley, Little Witley, Holt Fleet, Shrawley, Uphampton, Oldfield, Salwarpe, Hadzor, Martin Hussingtree, Fernhill Heath, Claines, Hindlip, Warndon, St Johns, Whittington, Powick, Norton, Littleworth, Stoulton, Spetchley, Bredicot, Crowle, Broughton Hackett, Upton Snodsbury, Grafton Flyford, Naunton Beauchamp, Peopleton, Pinvin, Throckmorton, Wyre Piddle, Wadborough, Pirton, Besford, Defford, Birlingham, Great Comberton, Little Comberton, Bricklehampton

Bromyard / Hereford area: Bredenbury, Edwyn Ralph, Bromyard Downs, Pencombe, Little Cowarne, Much Cowarne, Lower Egleton, Stretton Grandison, Yarkhill, Tarrington, Canon Frome, Ashperton, Coddington, Colwall, Colwall Stone, Colwall Green, Wellington Heath, Munderfield Row, Munderfield Stocks, Stoke Lacy, Moreton Jeffries, Five Bridges, Bishop's Frome, Evesbatch, Cradley, Storridge, Suckley, Leigh, Leigh Sinton, Alfrick, Bransford, Rushwick, Broadwas, Knightwick, Lulsley, Broad Green, Hallow, Lower Broadheath, Upper Broadheath, Martley, Wichenford, Moseley, Horsham, Whitbourne, Tedstone Delamere, Tedstone Wafre, Collington, Thornbury, Wall Hills, Edvin Loach, Bank Street, Wolferlow, High Lane, Harpley, Garmsley Camp

Motorways and roads: M5, M42, A456, A458, A442, A449, A451, A443, A44, A38, A4103, A4104, A417, A465, A4117, B4368, B4364, B4363, B4555, B4194, B4201, B4202, B4203, B4204, B4214, B4219, B4220, B4197, B4196, B4189, B4188, B4193, A4025, A4133, A4538, A4440, A422, A4103, B4082, B4084

Grid references: A 164, B 164, C 164, D 164 (top); A 116 D, B 117 E, C 117 F, D 117 G (bottom)

MILES scale: 1 2 3 4 5
KM scale: 2 4 6 8

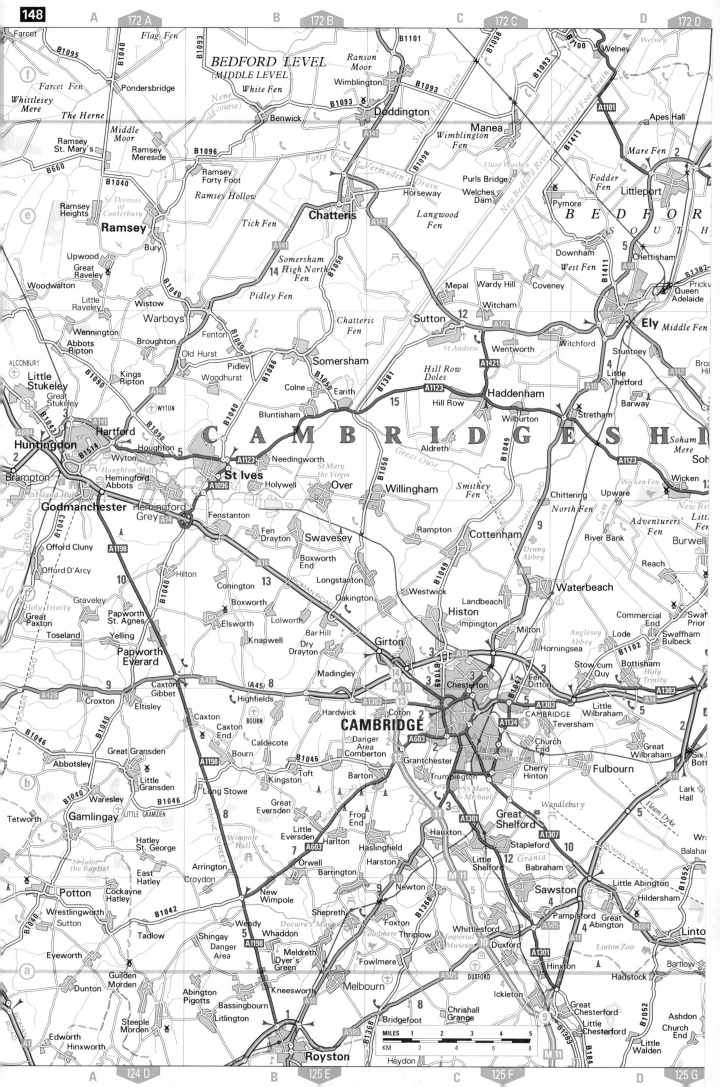

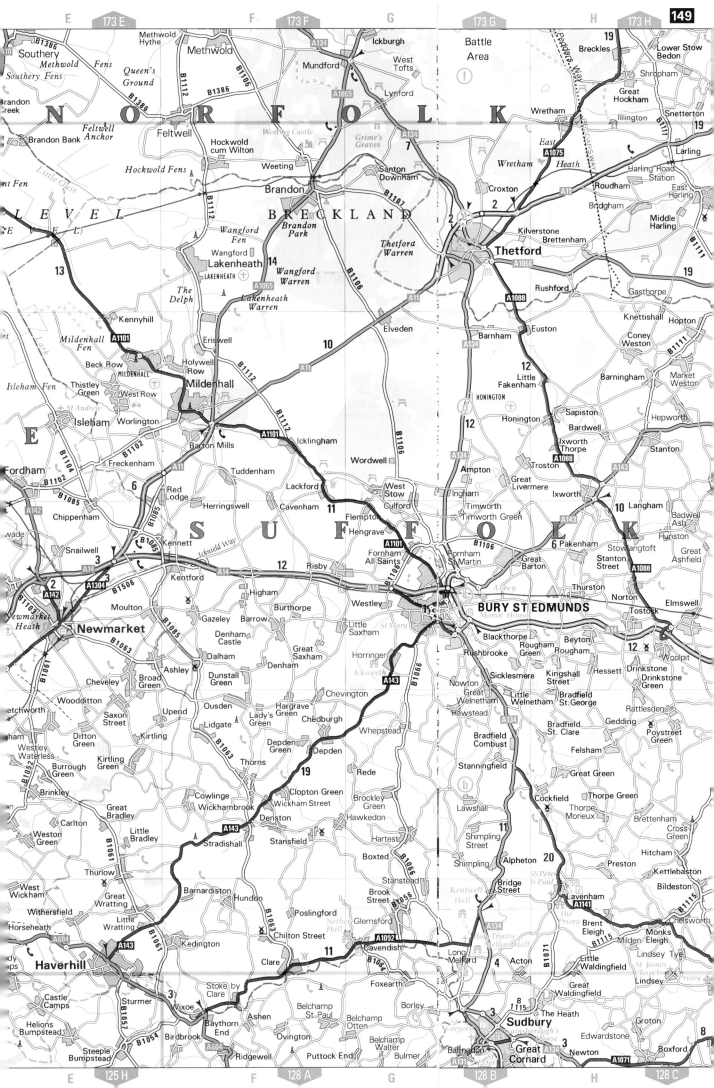

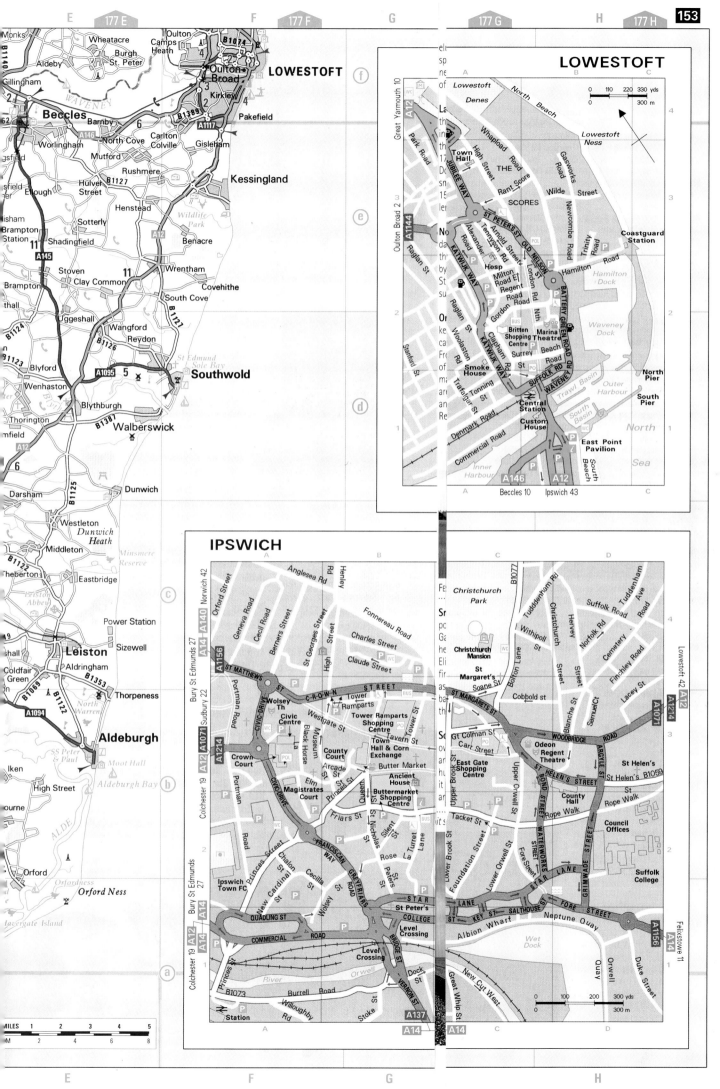

LOWESTOFT

Lowestoft Denes

Lowestoft Ness

Beccles 10   Ipswich 43

Great Yarmouth 10
Oulton Broad 2

Town Hall
THE SCORES
Whapload Road
North Beach
Gasworks Road
Wilde Street
Newcombe Road
Trinity Road
Coastguard Station
Park Road
High Street
Rant Score
JUBILEE WAY
ST PETER'S ST OLD NELSON
Alexandra Road
Tennyson Rd
Arnold Street
London Rd
Hamilton Road
Hamilton Dock
KATWIJK WAY
Hosp
Milton Road E
Regent Road
Gordon Road
Raglan St
Waveney Dock
BATTERY GREEN ROAD
Britten Shopping Centre
Marina Theatre
Woodaston Rd
Clapham Rd
Surrey St
Beach Road
Trawl Basin
Stamford St
Smoke House
Trafalgar St
Tonning St
SUFFOLK RD
WAVENEY DR
North Pier
South Pier
Central Station
Custom House
South Basin
Outer Harbour
Denmark Road
East Point Pavilion
North Sea
Commercial Road
Inner Harbour
South Beach
A146   A12

IPSWICH

Norwich 42
A14—A140
A1156
ST MATTHEWS
Bury St Edmunds 27
A12 A1071 Sudbury 22
A12 A1071
A1214
Colchester 19
A12 A14
Bury St Edmunds 27
A12 A14
Colchester 19

Christchurch Park
Christchurch Mansion
St Margaret's
Tuddenham Rd
Christchurch St
Suffolk Road
Tuddenham Ave
Hervey St
Withipoll St
Norfolk Rd
Cemetery
Finchley Road
Lowestoft 42
A1214 A12
Lacey St
Bolton Lane
Soane St
Cobbold st
Blanche St
SamuelCt
A1071
WOODBRIDGE ROAD
ST MARGARETS ST
Gt Colman St
Carr Street
Odeon Regent Theatre
St Helen's
ARCHLE STREET
St Helen's B1059
Orford Street
Geneva Road
Cecil Road
Berners Street
St Georges Street
High Street
Anglesea Rd
Henley Rd
Fonnereau Road
Charles Street
Claude Street
CROWN STREET
Tower Ramparts
Wolsey Th
Westgate St
Museum
Tower Ramparts Shopping Centre
Civic Centre
Black Horse
County Court
Town Hall & Corn Exchange
Tavern St
Butter Market
East Gate Shopping Centre
Upper Brook St
County Hall
Rope Walk
Council Offices
Suffolk College
Crown Court
CIVIC DRIVE
Portman Road
Elm St
Arcade St
Ancient House
Magistrates Court
Buttermarket Shopping Centre
Princes St
Queen St
Friars St
St Nicholas St
Silent St
Turret Lane
Rose La
Gt Colman St
Upper Orwell St
Tacket St
Lower Orwell St
Foundation Street
Fore Street
WATERWORKS STREET
BOND STREET
ST HELEN'S STREET
Rope Walk
GRIMWADE STREET
FRANCISCAN WAY
GREYFRIARS ROAD
Chalon St
Cecilia St
Wolsey St
New Cardinal St
Ipswich Town FC
QUADLING ST
COMMERCIAL ROAD
St Peter's
St Peter's St
COLLEGE
STAR LANE
KEY ST
SALTHOUSE ST
STAR LANE
FORE STREET
Albion Wharf
Neptune Quay
Wet Dock
A1156 A14
Felixstowe 11
BRIDGE ST
Level Crossing
VERNON ST
Dock St
Great Whip St
New Cut West
Orwell Quay
Duke Street
Bramford Road
River Orwell
Burrell Road
Willoughby Rd
Station
B1073
Stoke Rd
A137
A14   A14

(West Suffolk coast and towns)

Monks
Wheatacre
Oulton Camps Heath
B1074
LOWESTOFT
Burgh St. Peter
Aldeby
Gillingham
WAVENEY
Oulton Broad
Kirkley
Pakefield
Beccles
Barnby
North Cove
Carlton Colville
Gisleham
B1389
A1117
A146
Worlingham
Mutford
Kessingland
Hulver Street
Rushmere
B1127
Henstead
Wildlife Park
A12
Benacre
Shadingfield
Brampton Station
Stoven
Clay Common
Wrentham
A145
Covehithe
South Cove
Ellough
Uggeshall
B1127
Wangford
B1126
Reydon
B1124
St Edmund Sole Bay
Southwold
Blyford
A1095
Wenhaston
B1123
Walberswick
Thorington
Blythburgh
B1387
A12
Dunwich
B1125
Darsham
Westleton
Dunwich Heath
Middleton
Minsmere Reserve
Eastbridge
Leiston Abbey
Theberton
Power Station
Leiston
Sizewell
Aldringham
B1353
Coldfair Green
B1069
Thorpeness
B1122
A1094
North Warren
Aldeburgh
SS Peter & Paul
Moot Hall
Aldeburgh Bay
High Street
ALDE
Orford
Orfordness
Orford Ness
Havergate Island

MILES 1 2 3 4 5

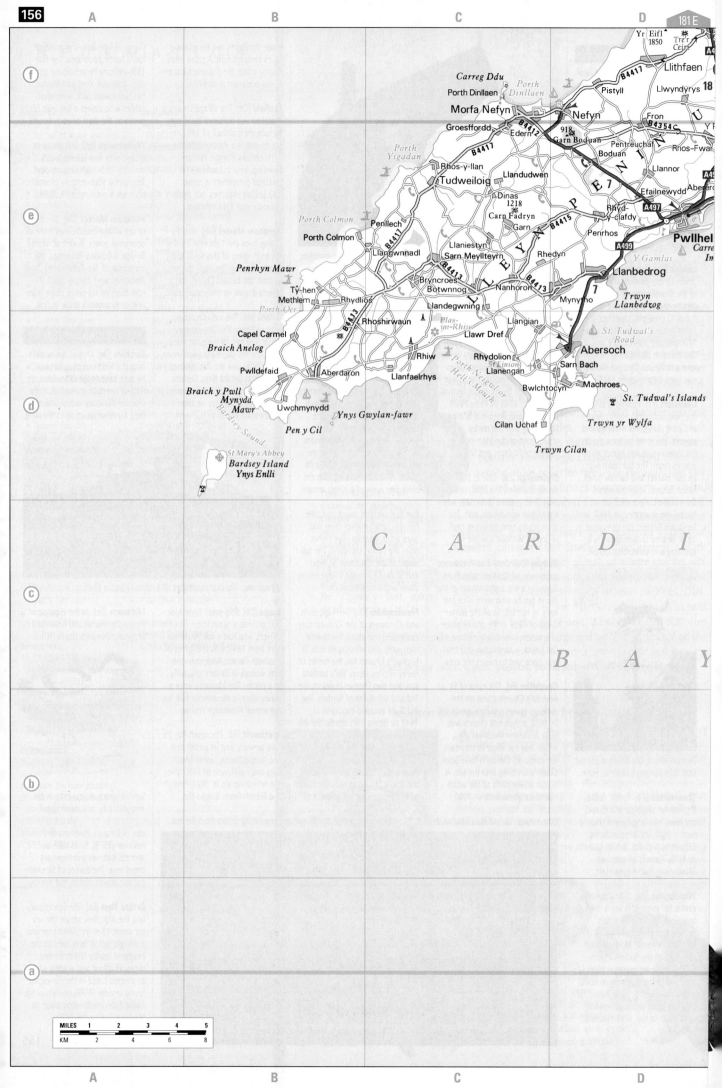

A   B   C   D

f

Yr Eifl 1850
Trer Ceiri
Llithfaen
B4417
Pistyll
Llwyndyrys
18
Carreg Ddu
Porth Dinllaen
Porth Dinllaen
Fron
Morfa Nefyn
Nefyn
B4354
Groesffordd
Edern
918
Garn Boduan
Pentreuchaf
Boduan
Rhos-Fwar

e

Porth Ysgadan
B4417
Rhos-y-llan
Llandudwen
Llannor
Tudweiliog
Dinas 1218
Carn Fadryn
Efailnewydd
Aberer
Porth Colmon
Penllech
Llaniestyn
Garn
B4415
Rhyd-y-clafdy
A497
Porth Colmon
Sarn Meyllteyrn
Penrhos
Pwllhel
Llangwnnadl
Rhedyn
Carre
In
Penrhyn Mawr
B4413
Bryncroes
Nanhoron
B4413
Llanbedrog
Tŷ-hen
Botwnnog
Mynytho
Trwyn Llanbedrog
Methlem
Rhydlios
Llandegwning
Y Gamlas
Porth Oer
B4413
Rhoshirwaun
Llangian
St. Tudwal's Road
Plas-yn-Rhiw
Capel Carmel
Llawr Dref
Braich Anelog
Rhiw
Rhydolion
Abersoch
Pwlldefaid
Aberdaron
St Einion
Llanengan
Sarn Bach
Braich y Pwll
Llanfaelrhys
Machroes
Mynydd Mawr
Uwchmynydd
Bwlchtocyn
St. Tudwal's Islands
Ynys Gwylan-fawr
Cilan Uchaf
Pen y Cil
Trwyn yr Wylfa
Bardsey Sound
Trwyn Cilan
St Mary's Abbey
Bardsey Island
Ynys Enlli

d

C A R D I

c

B A Y

b

a

MILES 1   2   3   4   5
KM   2   4   6   8

A   B   C   D

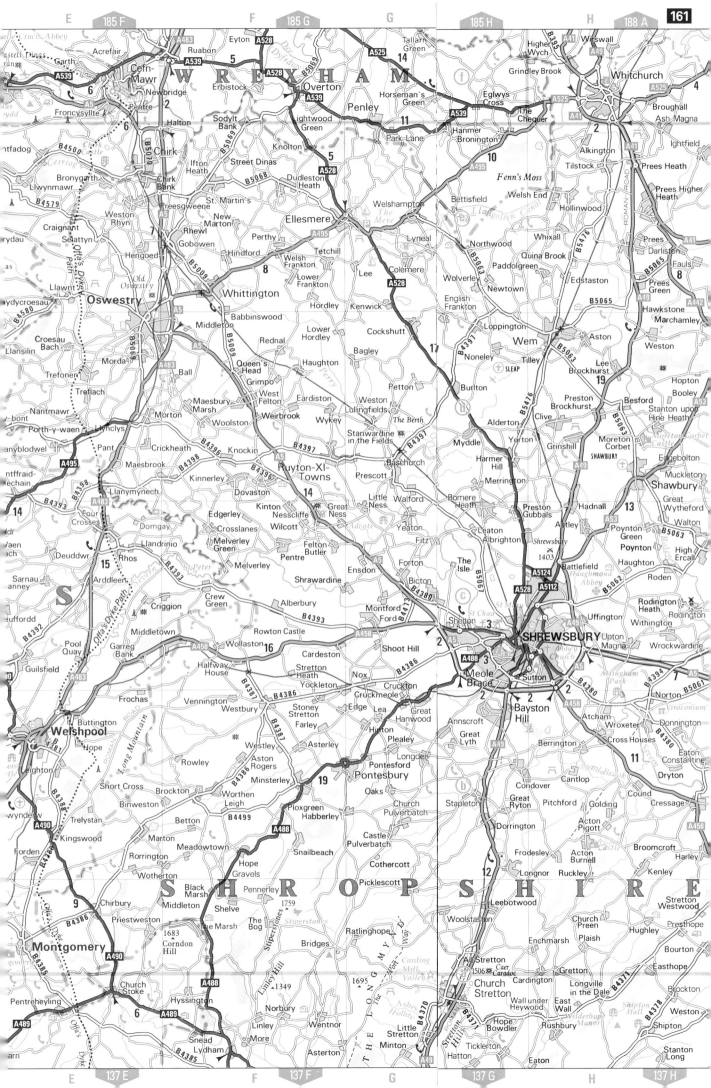

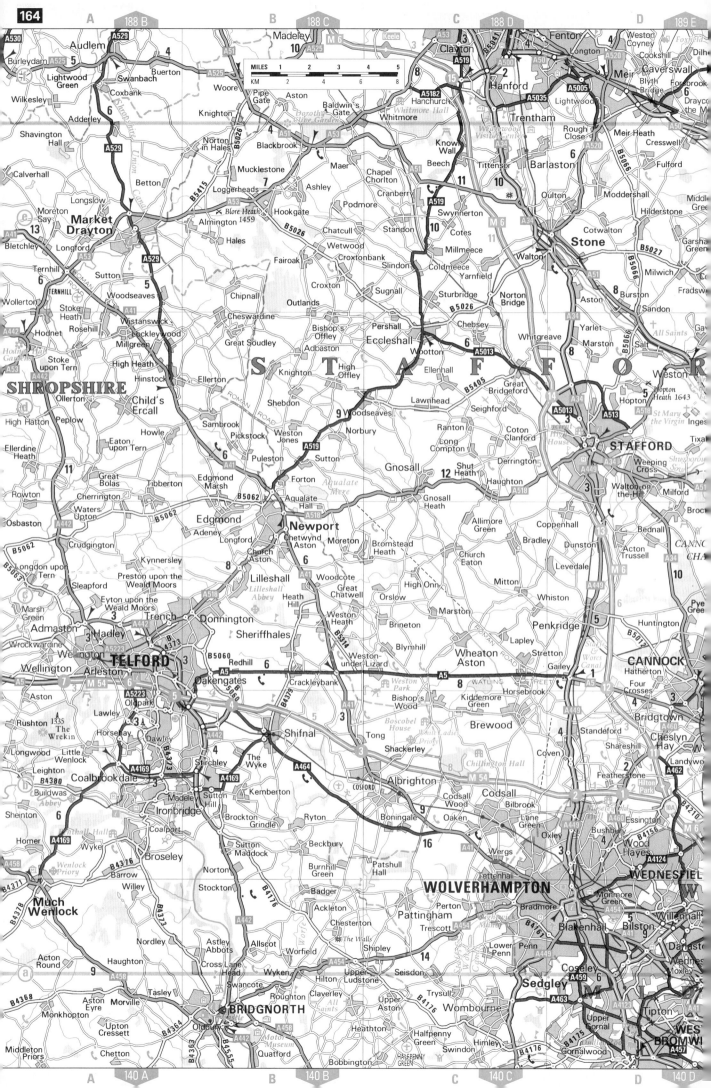

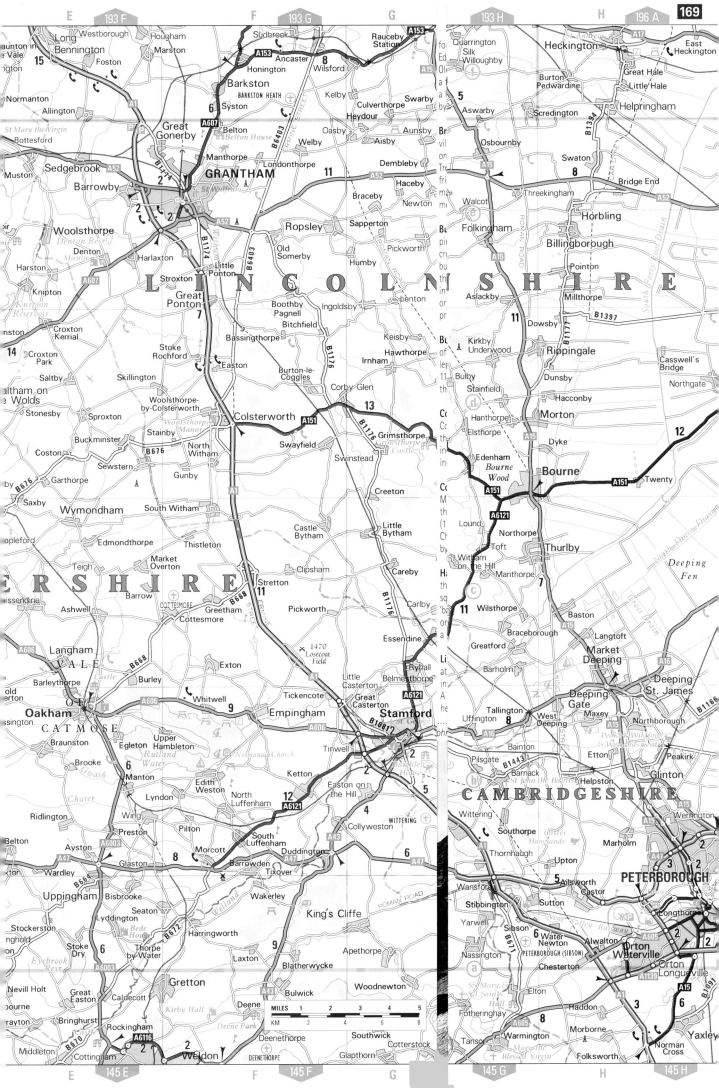

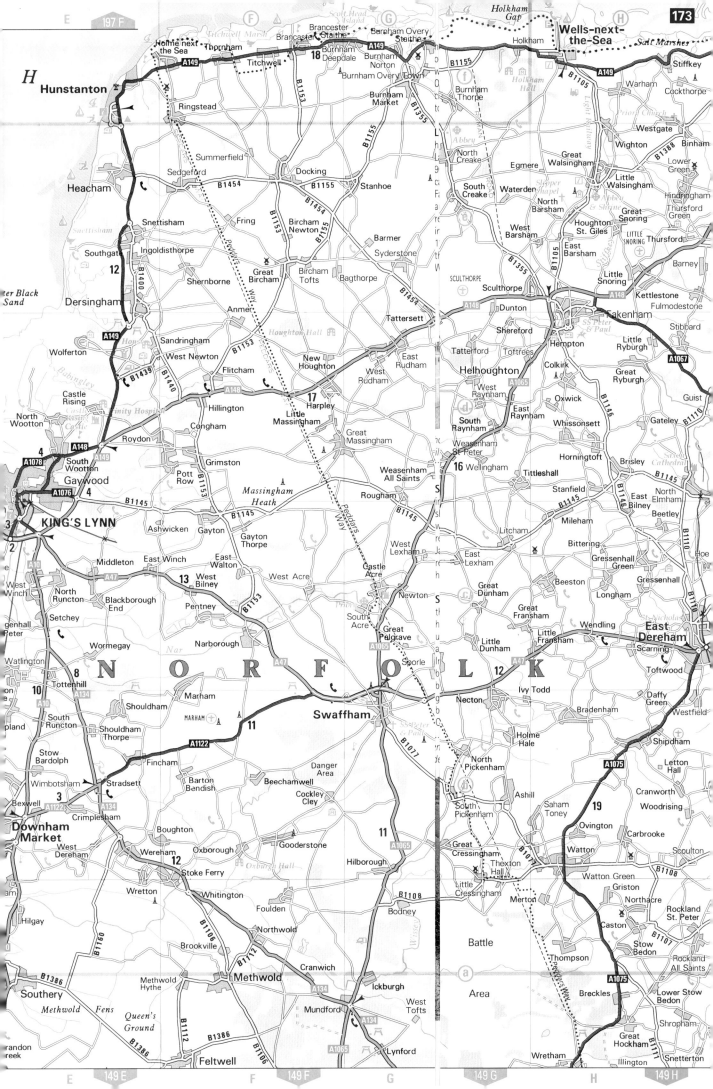

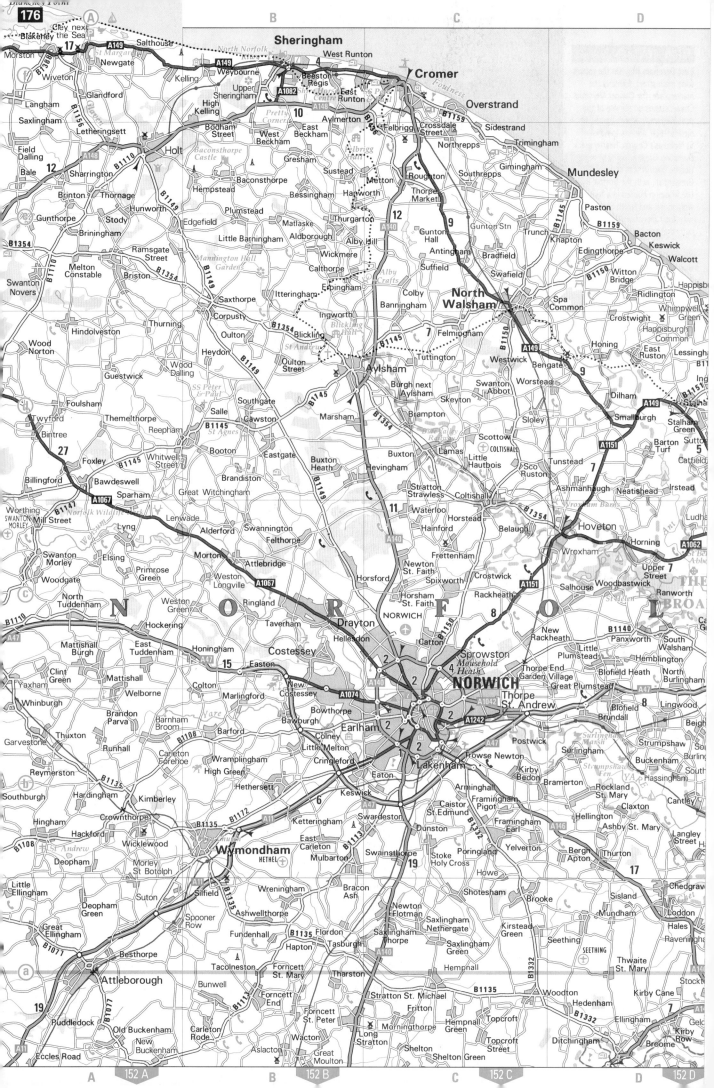

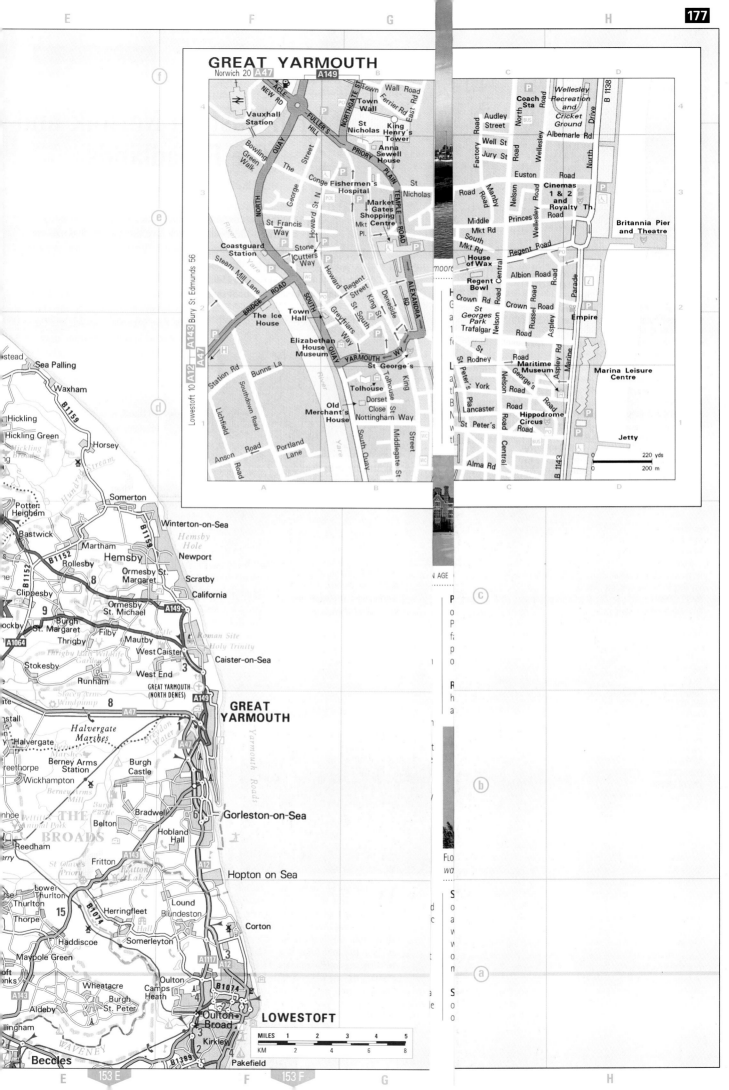

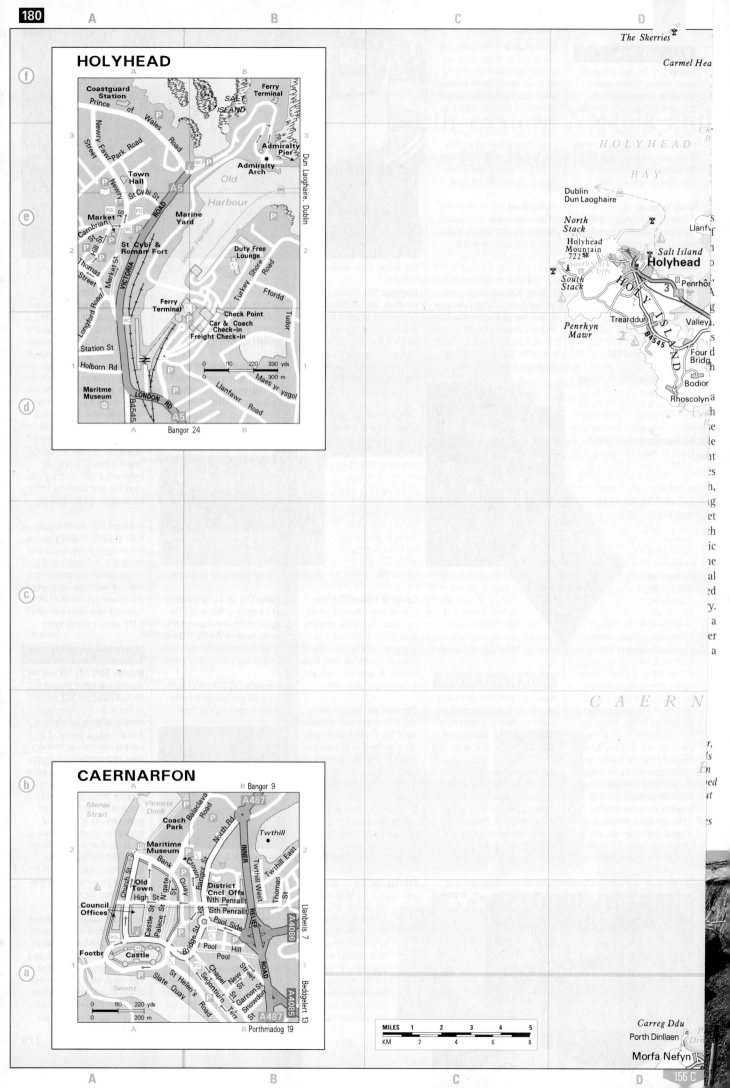

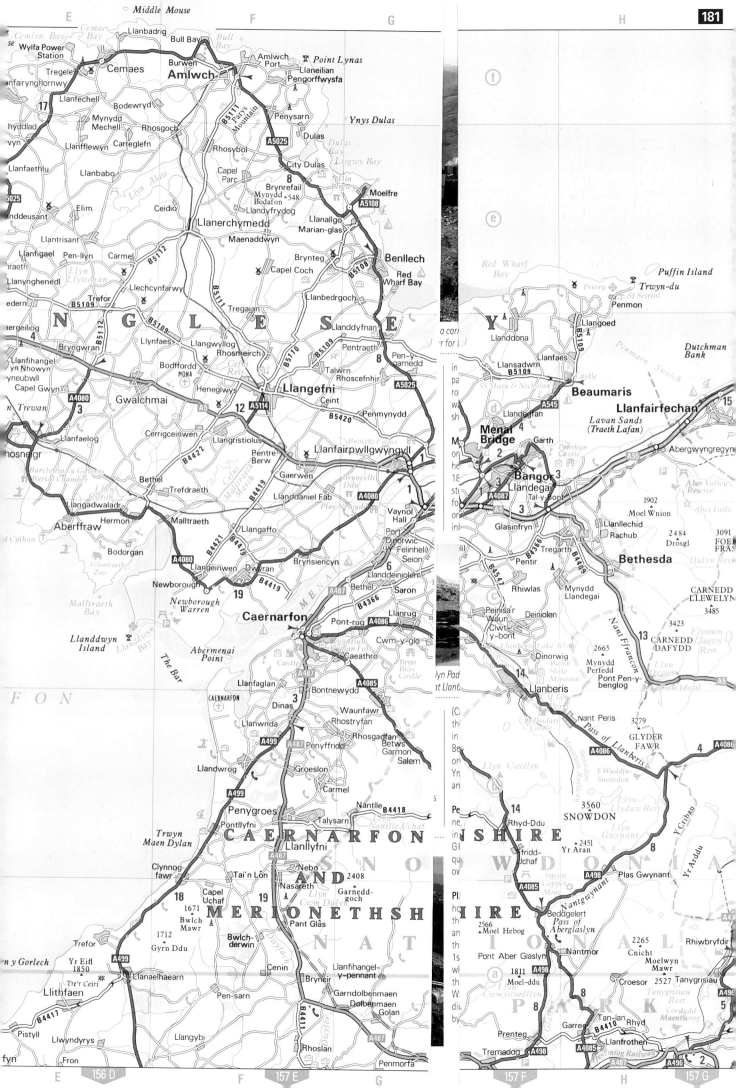

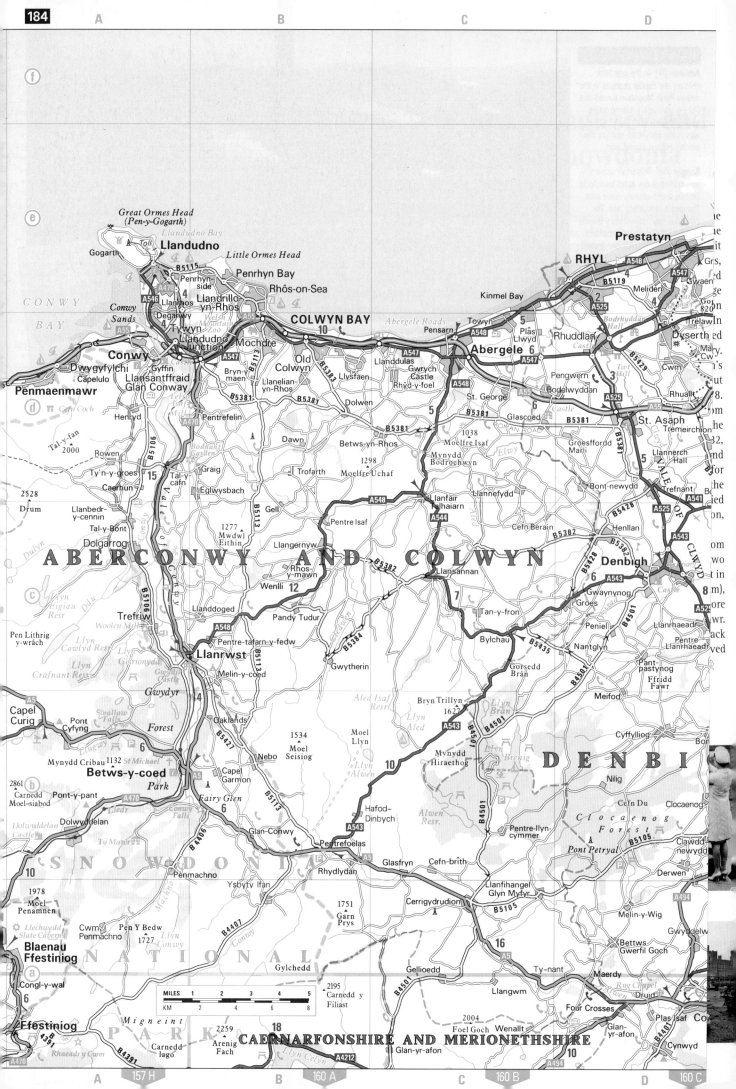

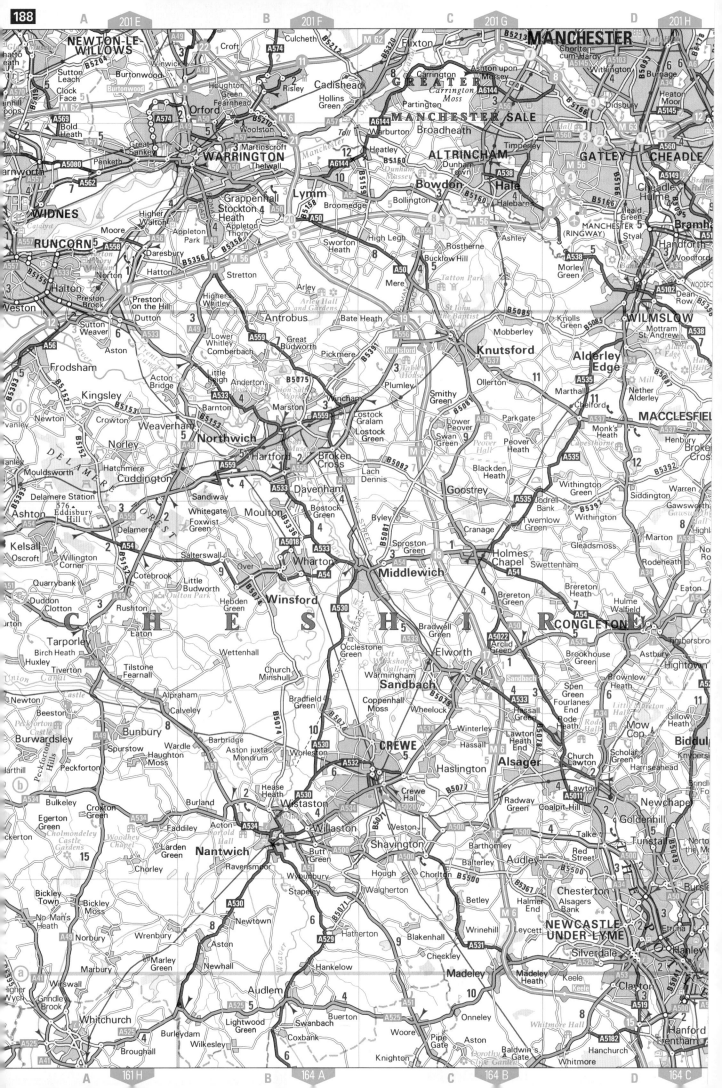

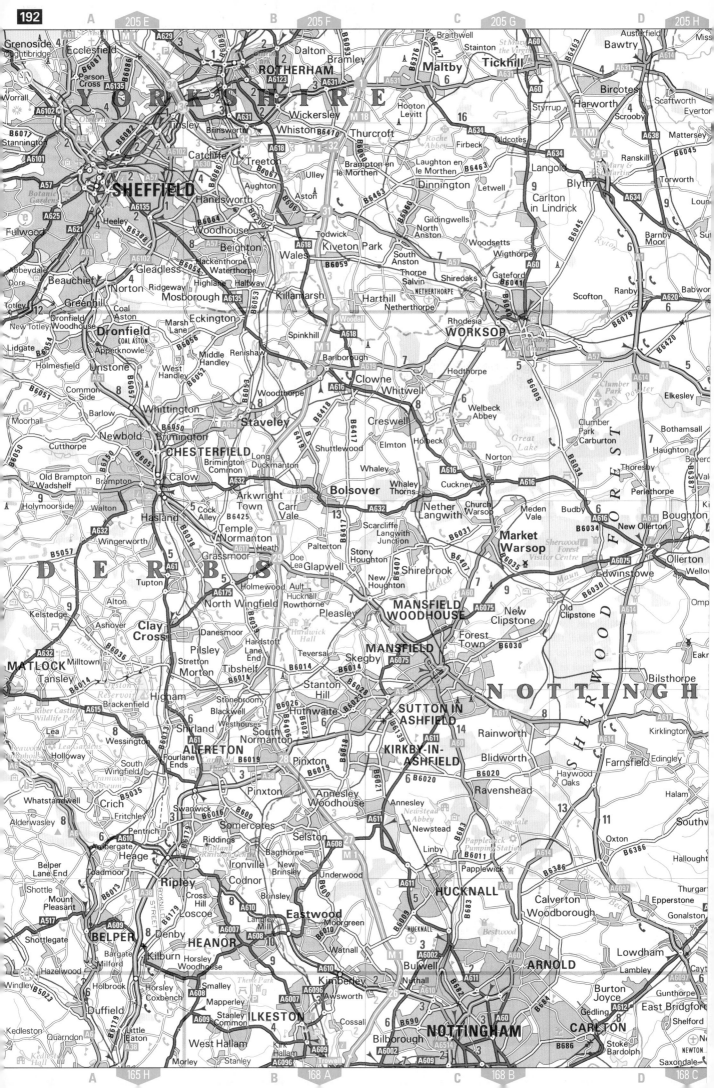

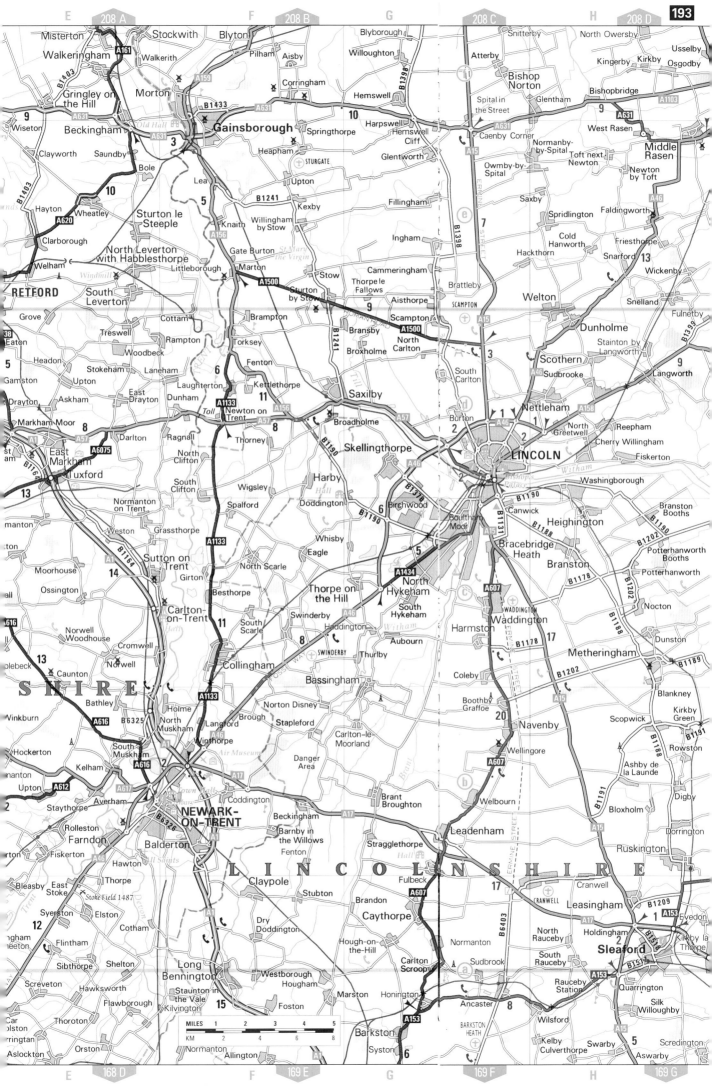

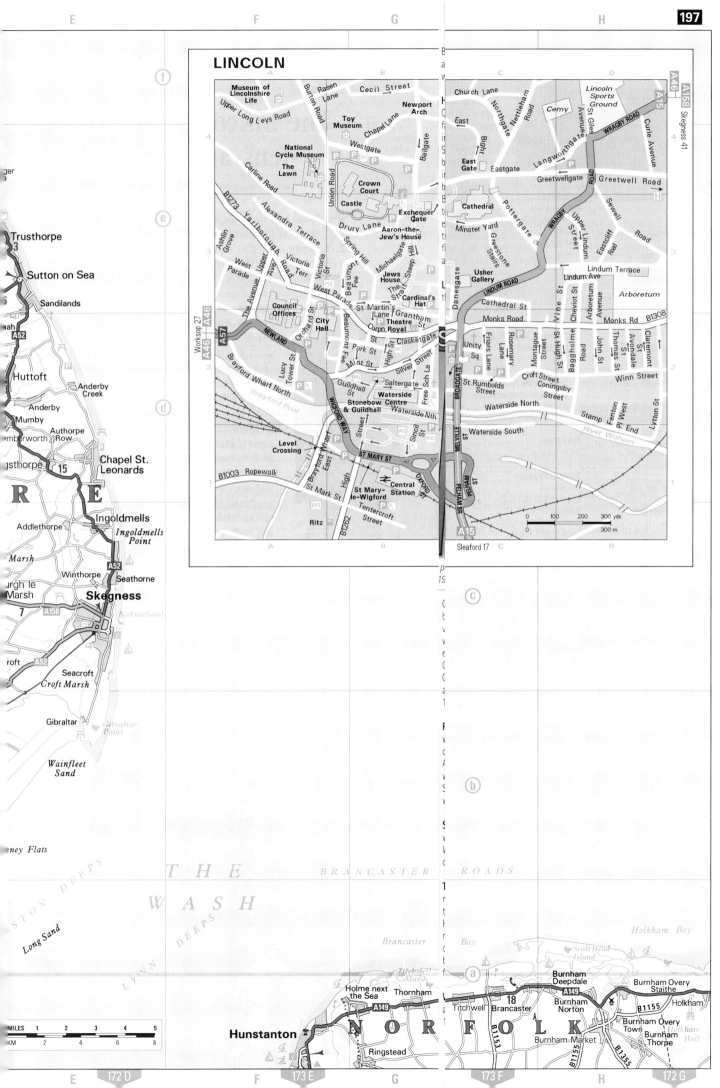

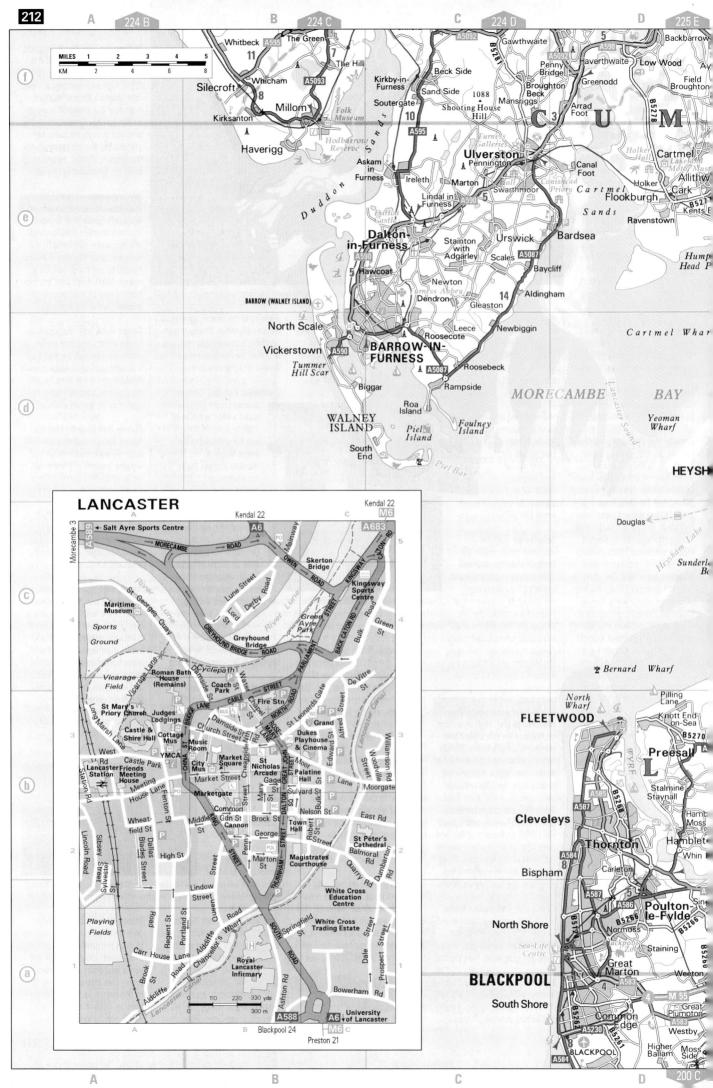

LANCASTER

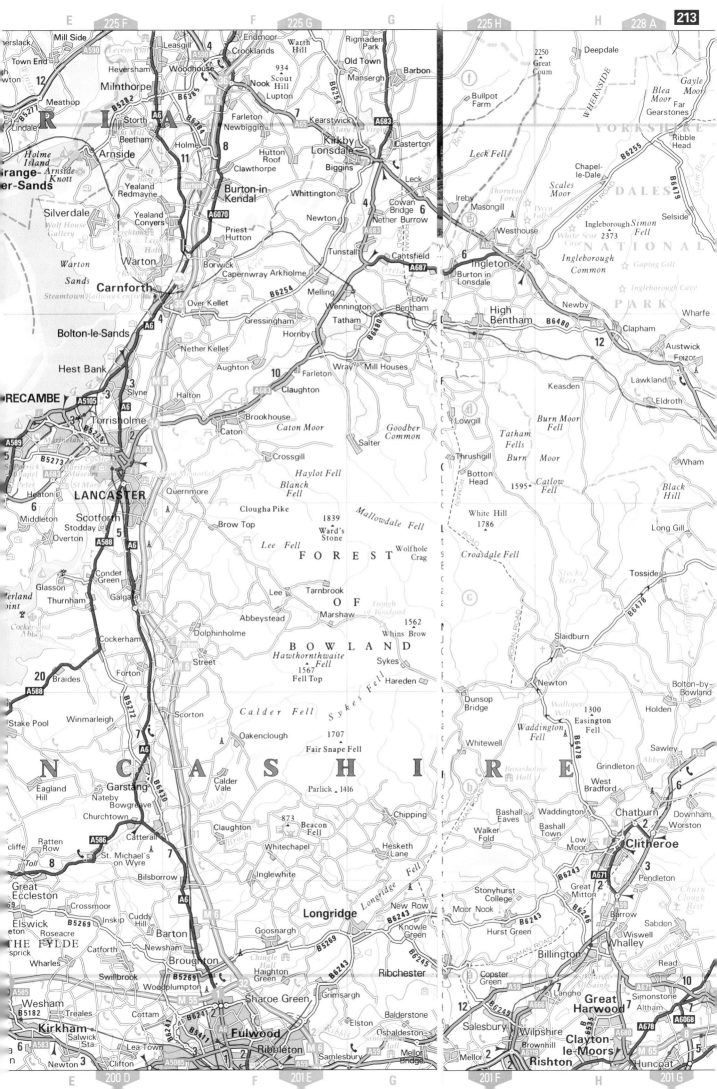

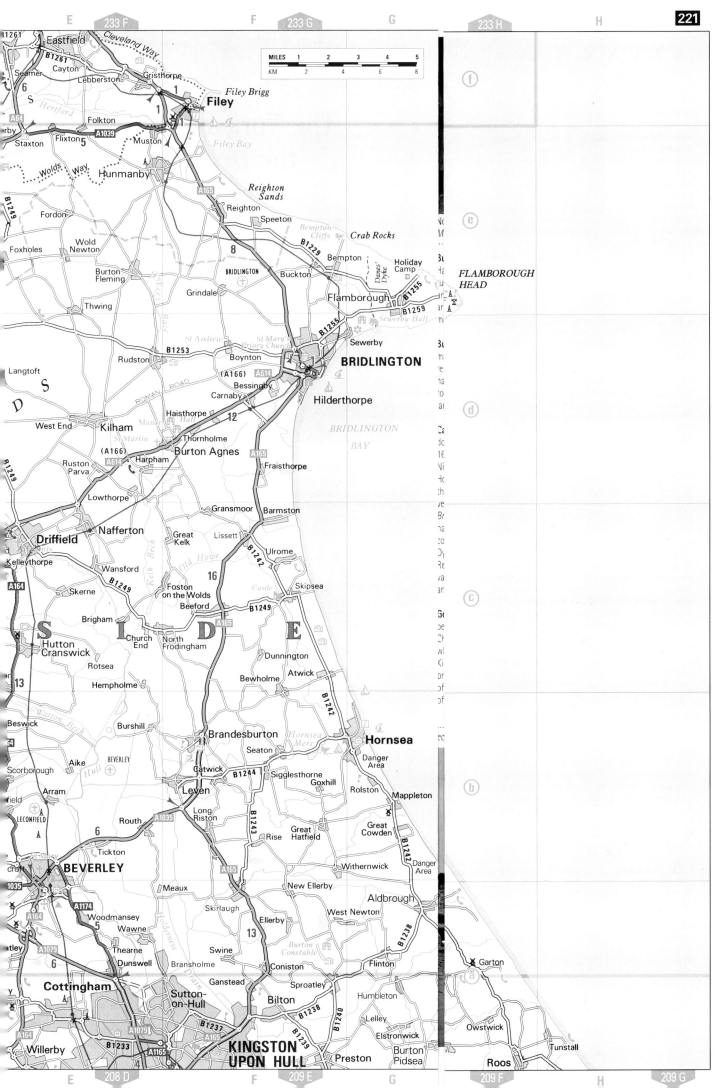

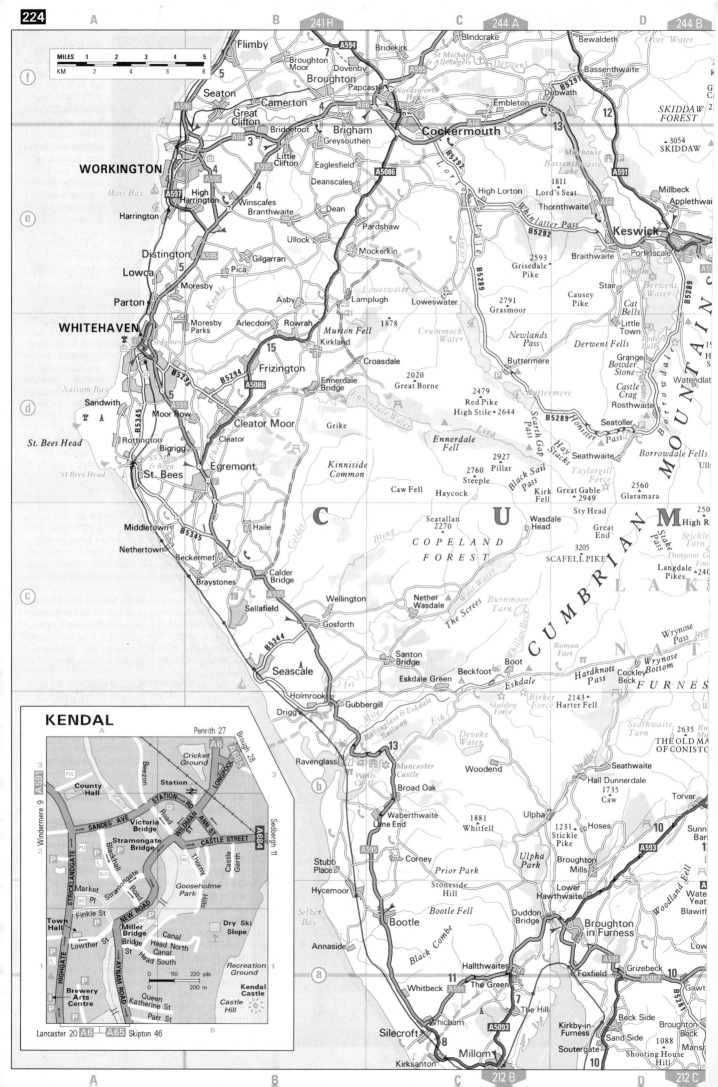

MILES 1 2 3 4 5
KM 2 4 6 8

Flimby
A594
Broughton Moor
Dovenby
Broughton
Papcastle
Seaton
Camerton
Great Clifton
A596
Bridgefoot
Brigham
Greysouthen
A66
Little Clifton
Eaglesfield
Deanscales
WORKINGTON
A596
A595
Dean
High Harrington
Winscales
Branthwaite
Harrington
A597
Distington
Moss Bay
Ullock
Pardshaw
Mockerkin
Lowca
Gilgarran
Pica
Moresby
Parton
A595
Moresby Parks
Arlecdon
Asby
Lamplugh
Loweswater
WHITEHAVEN
St. James
B5345
B5345
Rowrah
Murton Fell
1878
Kirkland
Frizington
B5294
A5086
Croasdale
Ennerdale Bridge
Grike
Moor Row
Cleator Moor
Cleator
Sandwith
St. Bees Head
Rottington
Bigrigg
Egremont
Haile
St Bees Head
SS Maria
& Bega
St. Bees
Kinniside Common
Middletown
B5345
Nethertown
Beckermet
Braystones
Calder Bridge
A595
Sellafield
Wellington
B5344
Gosforth
Santon Bridge
Seascale
Eskdale Green
Holmrook
Gubbergill
Drigg
Ravenglass
Ravenglass & Eskdale Railway
Muncaster Castle
Woodend
Broad Oak
Waberthwaite
Lane End
A595
Stubb Place
Corney
Hycemoor
Bootle
Annaside
Selker Bay
Black Combe
Hallthwaites
Whitbeck
A595
The Green
Silecroft
A5093
Millom
Kirksanton
Whicham

A66 Cockermouth
Bridekirk
St Michael & All Angels
Wordsworth House
Blindcrake
Bewaldeth
Over Water
Bassenthwaite
B5291
Dubwath
Embleton
A66
12
SKIDDAW FOREST
Bassenthwaite Lake
1811
Lord's Seat
Thornthwaite
Millbeck
Applethwaite
3054
SKIDDAW
A591
13
High Lorton
Whinlatter Pass
B5292
Keswick
Portinscale
B5289
2593
Grisedale Pike
Braithwaite
Stair
Lingholm
Derwent Water
Causey Pike
2791
Grasmoor
Newlands Pass
Cat Bells
Little Town
Lodore Falls
Loweswater
Crummock Water
Derwent Fells
Grange
Bowder Stone
Watendlath
Buttermere
Buttermere
2020
Great Borne
2479
Red Pike
High Stile 2644
Castle Crag
Rosthwaite
Scarth Gap Pass
B5289
Honister Pass
Seatoller
Hay Stacks
Seathwaite
Borrowdale Fells
Ennerdale Fell
Liza
2927
Pillar
2760
Steeple
Black Sail Pass
Kirk Fell
Great Gable
2949
Taylorgill Force
Ull
Caw Fell
Haycock
Seatallan
2270
Sty Head
2560
Glaramara
Wasdale Head
Great End
2500
High R
COPELAND FOREST
3205
SCAFELL PIKE
Great Langdale Pass
Stickle Tarn
Dungeon G
Langdale Pikes
2400
Nether Wasdale
The Screes
Wast Water
Burnmoor Tarn
CUMBRIAN
Roman Fort
Wrynose Pass
Wrynose Bottom
Hardknott Pass
Cockley Beck
FURNES
NAT
Beckfoot
Boot
Eskdale
Eskdale Green
Stanley Force
Birker Force
Harter Fell
2143
Devoke Water
Seathwaite Tarn
2635
THE OLD MAN OF CONIST
Duddon
Seathwaite
Hall Dunnerdale
1735
Caw
Torver
1881
Whitfell
Ulpha
1231
Hoses
Stickle Pike
A593
10
Sunny Ban
Ulpha Park
Broughton Mills
Prior Park
Lower Hawthwaite
Stoneside Hill
Duddon Bridge
A595
Broughton in Furness
Woodland Fell
Water Yeat
Blawith
Low
Grizebeck
Foxfield
A5092
10
B5281
11
7
The Hill
8
Kirkby-in-Furness
Sand Side
Soutergate
1088
Mansr
Shooting House Hill
Beck Side
Broughton Beck
10
Gawt

212 B   212 C
241 H   244 A   244 B

KENDAL

Penrith 27
A6
Brough 28
A685
LONGPOOL
Cricket Ground
Sedbergh 11
A684
Windermere 9
A591
County Hall
POL
Station
STATION
WILDMAN ST
MAIN ST
CASTLE STREET
A684
Beezon
Sandes Ave
Victoria Bridge
Blackhall
River Kent
Stramongate Bridge
Thorny Hills
Castle Garth
Castle Street
Market Pl
BUS
Stramongate Road
Gooseholme Park
Dry Ski Slope
Town Hall
Finkle St
New Road
Miller Bridge
Canal Head North Canal
St Head South
Recreation Ground
Kendal Castle
Castle Hill
Brewery Arts Centre
Highgate
Stricklandgate
Lowther St
Aynam Road
Queen Katherine St
Parr St
0 110 220 yds
0 200 m

Lancaster 20   A6   A65   Skipton 46

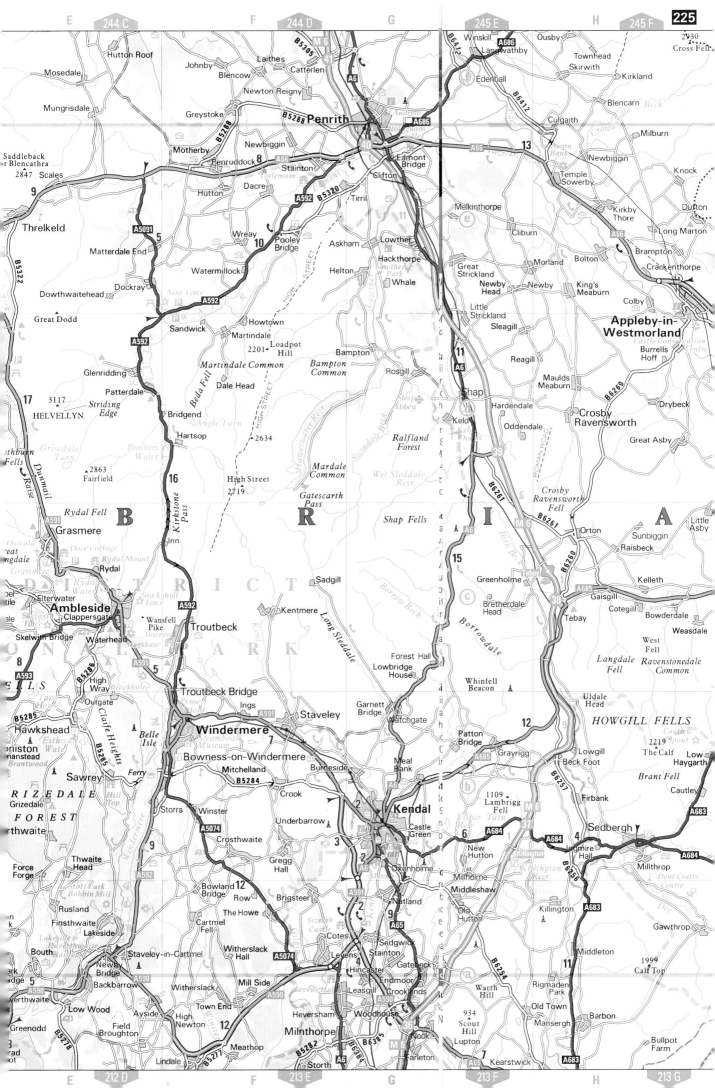

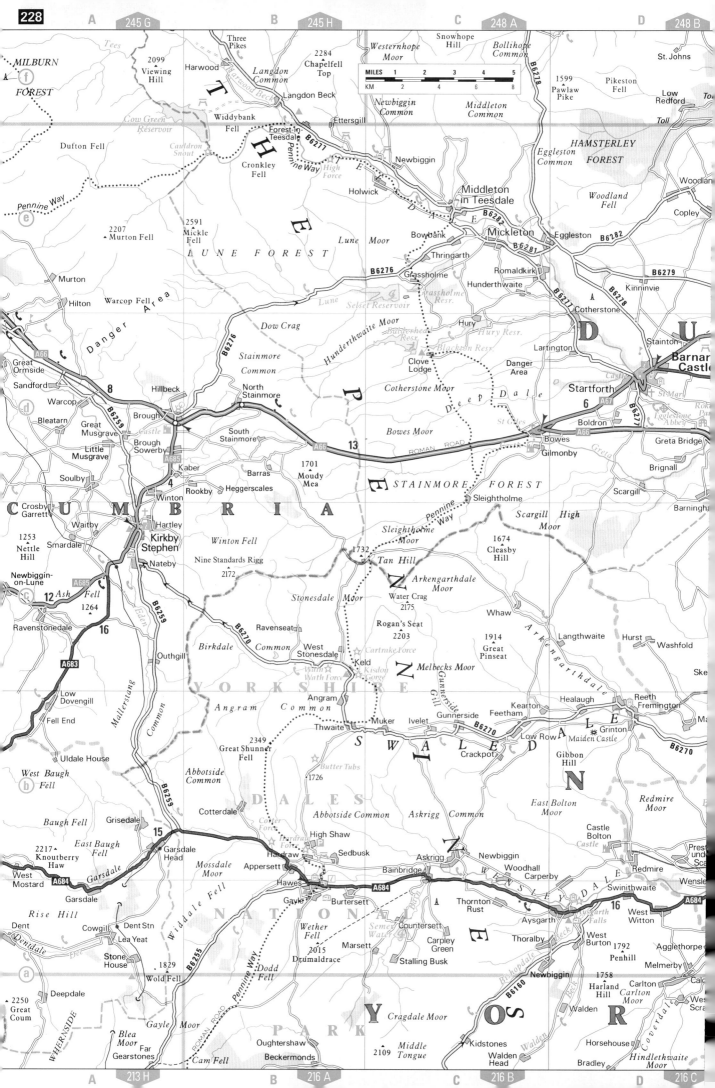

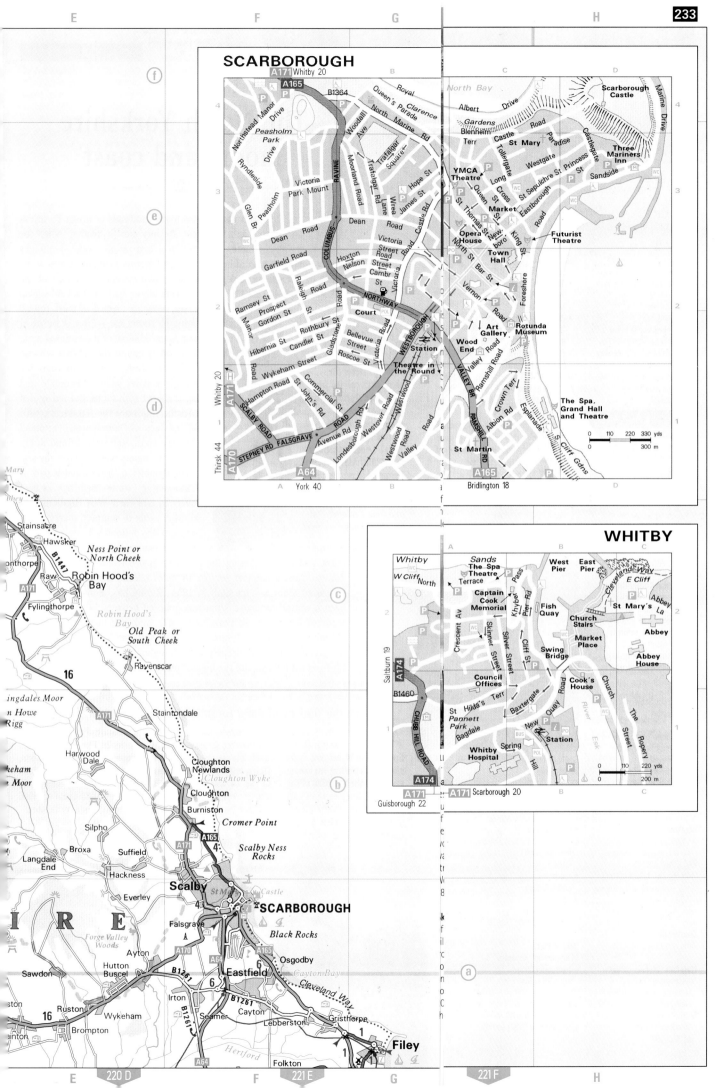

SCARBOROUGH

WHITBY

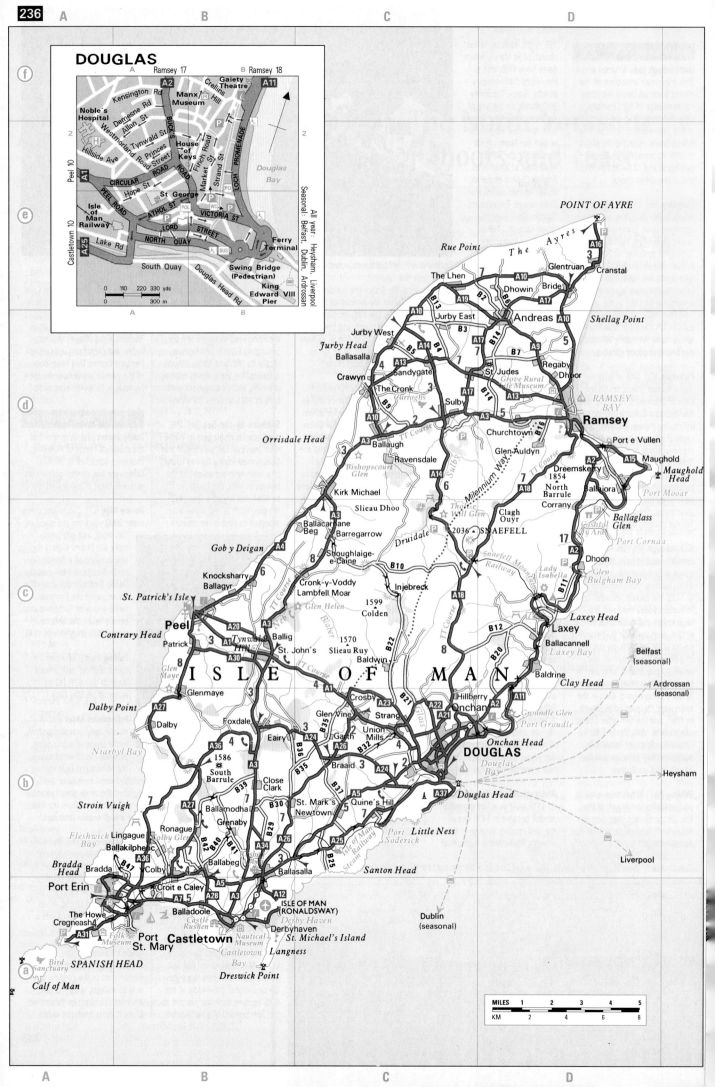

DOUGLAS

Ramsey 17
Ramsey 18

Noble's Hospital
Manx Museum
Gaiety Theatre
A2
A11
Crellins Hill
Kensington Rd
Demesne Rd
Allan St
Westmorland Road
Tynwald St
Hillside Ave
Princes Street
BUCK'S ROAD
House of Keys
Finch Road
Market St
Strand St
ROAD
St George
Hope St
CIRCULAR
Peel 10
A1
ATHOL ST
POL
WC
Victoria St
Isle of Man Railway
Castletown 10
A25
LORD
STREET
NORTH QUAY
Lake Rd
Ferry Terminal
South Quay
Douglas Head Rd
Swing Bridge (Pedestrian)
King Edward VIII Pier
Douglas Bay
PROMENADE
LOCH
PO
BUS
P

All year: Heysham, Liverpool
Seasonal: Belfast, Dublin, Ardrossan

0 110 220 330 yds
0   300 m

POINT OF AYRE
Rue Point
The Ayres
A16
3
Glentruan
Cranstal
The Lhen
Dhowin
Bride
A10
Shellag Point
A13
B13
A19
B2
B6
A17
Jurby East
Andreas
A10
Jurby West
B5
A14
B4
B3
A17
B14
5
Jurby Head
Ballasalla
B3
St Judes
B7
Regaby
Dhoor
Crawyn
4
A13
Sandygate
3
A17
B14
Grove Rural Life Museum
RAMSEY BAY
The Cronk
Curraghs
B9
Sulby
A3
A13
Ramsey
Orrisdale Head
A10
2
5
Port e Vullen
A2
A15
Maughold
Ballaugh
Churchtown
Glen Auldyn
Maughold Head
Bishopscourt Glen
Ravensdale
A14
6
Dreemskerry
North Barrule
Corrany
Ballajora
Port Mooar
Kirk Michael
Slieau Dhoo
1854
Clagh Ouyr
A18
A2
Ballaglass Glen
Ballacarnane Beg
A3
Druidale
2036
SNAEFELL
17
Dhoon
Port Cornaa
Gob y Deigan
A4
Barregarrow
B10
Injebreck
Snaefell Mountain Railway
Lady Isabella
Glen Bulgham Bay
Knocksharry
6
Shoughlaige-e-Caine
8
A18
B11
Laxey Head
Ballagyr
Cronk-y-Voddy
Lambfell Moar
1599
Colden
B22
B12
Laxey
St Patrick's Isle
Glen Helen
Blaber
1570
Slieau Ruy
Ballacannell
Laxey Bay
Contrary Head
Peel
A20
A3
Ballig
Baldwin
8
Belfast (seasonal)
Patrick
3
Tynwald Hill
St John's
B20
Baldrine
Ardrossan (seasonal)
A30
Clay Head
ISLE
OF
MAN
B21
Crosby
A23
Strang
A22
Hillberry
A11
Onchan
Clay Head
Glen Maye
4
A1
Glenmaye
3
Glen Vine
Groundle Glen
Port Groundle
Dalby Point
A27
Foxdale
Garth
Union Mills
A21
Onchan Head
Dalby
A36
Eairy
A24
B35
B32
4
DOUGLAS
Heysham
Niarbyl Bay
1586
South Barrule
A3
A26
Braaid
3
A24
2
Douglas Bay
Stroin Vuigh
7
B39
Close Clark
B36
B37
St Mark's
A5
Quine's Hill
A37
Douglas Head
Ronague
A27
Ballamodha
Grenaby
B30
Newtown
5
Little Ness
Lingague
B40
B29
B26
A25
Port Soderick
Ballakilpheric
B42
B41
A34
Ballabeg
3
Isle of Man Steam Railway
Santon Head
Bradda Head
B47
A36
Colby
Ballasalla
Liverpool
Bradda
Port Erin
A5
A12
The Howe
A28
A3
ISLE OF MAN (RONALDSWAY)
Cregneash
Croit e Caley
A7
Derby Haven
Dublin (seasonal)
A31
Folk Museum
Balladoole
Castle Rushen
Derbyhaven
St Michael's Island
Bird Sanctuary
Port St Mary
Castletown
Nautical Museum
Castletown Bay
Langness
SPANISH HEAD
Dreswick Point
Calf of Man

MILES 1 2 3 4 5
KM   2   4   6   8

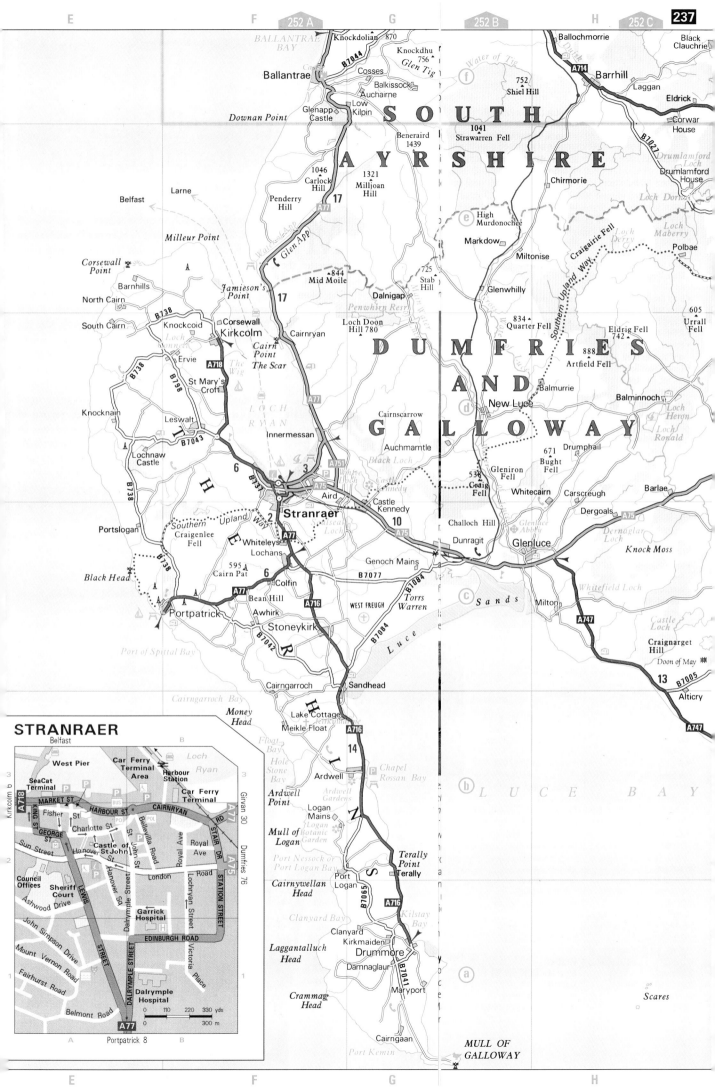

252 A   252 B   252 C

SOUTH

AYRSHIRE

DUMFRIES

AND

GALLOWAY

Ballantrae
Knockdolian 870
Cosses
Balkissock
Auchairne
Low Kilpin
Glenapp Castle
Downan Point
Knockdhu 756
Glen Tig
Ballochmorrie
Black Clauchrie
Barrhill
Laggan
Eldrick
Corwar House
Beneraird 1439
Strawarren Fell
Shiel Hill 752
Drumlamford Loch
Drumlamford House
1046 Carlock Hill
Penderry Hill
1321 Milljoan Hill
Chirmorie
Larne
Belfast
Milleur Point
Glen App
High Murdonochee
Markdow
Miltonise
Loch Maberry
Polbae
Corsewall Point
Jamieson's Point
Mid Moile 844
725 Stab Hill
Glenwhilly
605 Urrall Fell
Barnhills
North Cairn
Penwhirn Resr
Dalnigap
Craigairie Fell
Southern Upland Way
834 Quarter Fell
Eldrig Fell 742
South Cairn
Knockcoid
Kirkcolm
Loch Connell
Ervie
Cairnryan
Loch Doon Hill 780
888 Artfield Fell
Cairn Point The Scar
St Mary's Croft
The Wig
Cairnscarrow
Balmurrie
Loch Heron
Loch Ronald
Balminnoch
Knocknain
Leswalt
LOCH RYAN
Innermessan
Auchmamtle
New Luce
671 Bught Fell
Drumphail
Barlae
Lochnaw Castle
6
Aird
Auchmamtle
Geniron Fell
538 Craig Fell
Whitecairn
Carscreugh
Dergoals
Portslogan
3
Stranraer
Castle Kennedy
Black Loch
Castle Kennedy
Challoch Hill
Glenluce Abbey
Glenluce
Knock Moss
Dernaglar Loch
Southern Craigenlee Fell
Upland Way
2
Whiteleys
Lochans
10
Dunragit
Southern Craigenlee Fell
595 Cairn Pat
6
Colfin
Genoch Mains
Torrs Warren
SANDS
Milton
Whitefield Loch
Black Head
Bean Hill
A716
B7077
WEST FREUGH
A747
Castle Loch
Portpatrick
Awhirk
Stoneykirk
B7084
Luce
Craignarget Hill
Doon of May
Port of Spittal Bay
B7042
13
B7005
Cairngarroch
Sandhead
Alticry
A747
Cairngarroch Bay
Money Head
Lake Cottage
Meikle Float
Kirkmabreck
LUCE BAY
Float Bay
Hole Stone Bay
14
Chapel Rossan Bay
Ardwell
Ardwell Point
Ardwell Gardens
Logan Mains
Mull of Logan
Logan Botanic Garden
Port Nessock or Port Logan Bay
Cairnywellan Head
Port Logan
Terally Point
Terally
B7065
A716
Clanyard Bay
Kilstay Bay
Clanyard
Kirkmaiden
Laggantalluch Head
Drummore
B7041
Damnaglaur
Maryport
Scares
Crammag Head
Cairngaan
Port Kemin
MULL OF GALLOWAY

STRANRAER

Belfast

West Pier
Car Ferry Terminal Area
Harbour Station
SeaCat Terminal
Car Ferry Terminal
Loch Ryan
MARKET ST
KING ST
HARBOUR ST
CAIRNRYAN
Fisher St
Charlotte St
GEORGE ST
Castle of St John
Hanover St
St John St
Bellevilla Road
Royal Ave
Royal Ave
Girvan 30
STAIR DR
RD
Dumfries 76
Sun Street
London Road
A75
STATION STREET
Council Offices
Sheriff Court
Ashwood Drive
LEWIS STREET
Hanover Sq
Dalrymple Street
Lochryan Street
Garrick Hospital
John Simpson Drive
Mount Vernon Road
EDINBURGH ROAD
Victoria Place
Fairhurst Road
Belmont Road
Dalrymple Hospital

0   110   220   330 yds
0   300 m

A77

Portpatrick 8

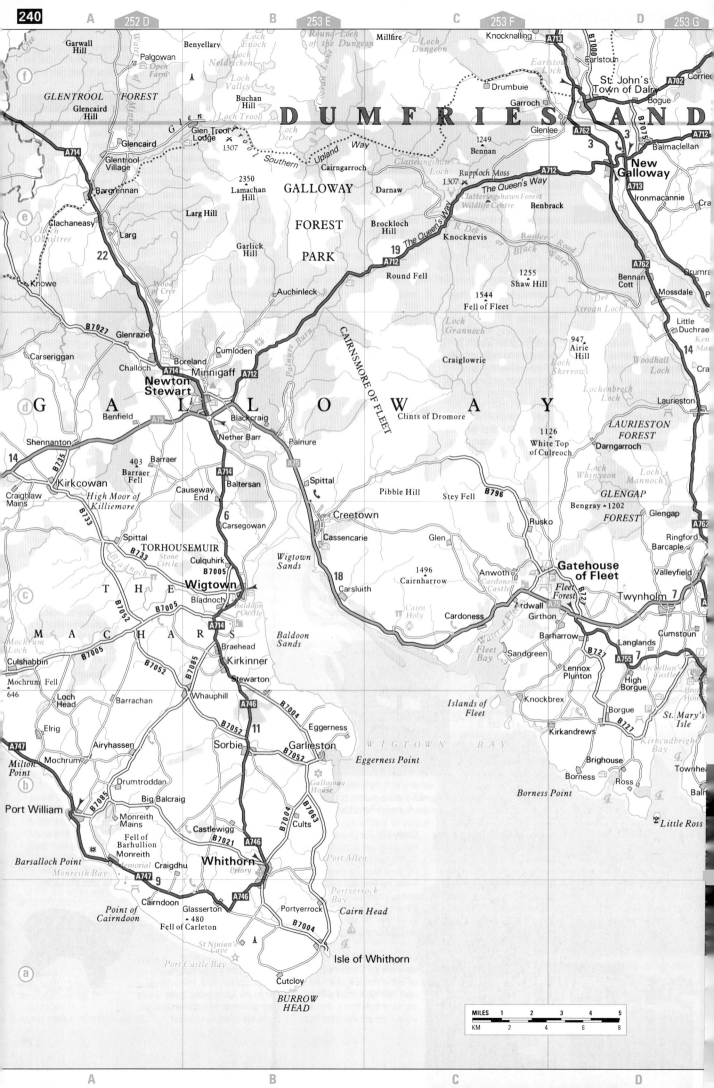

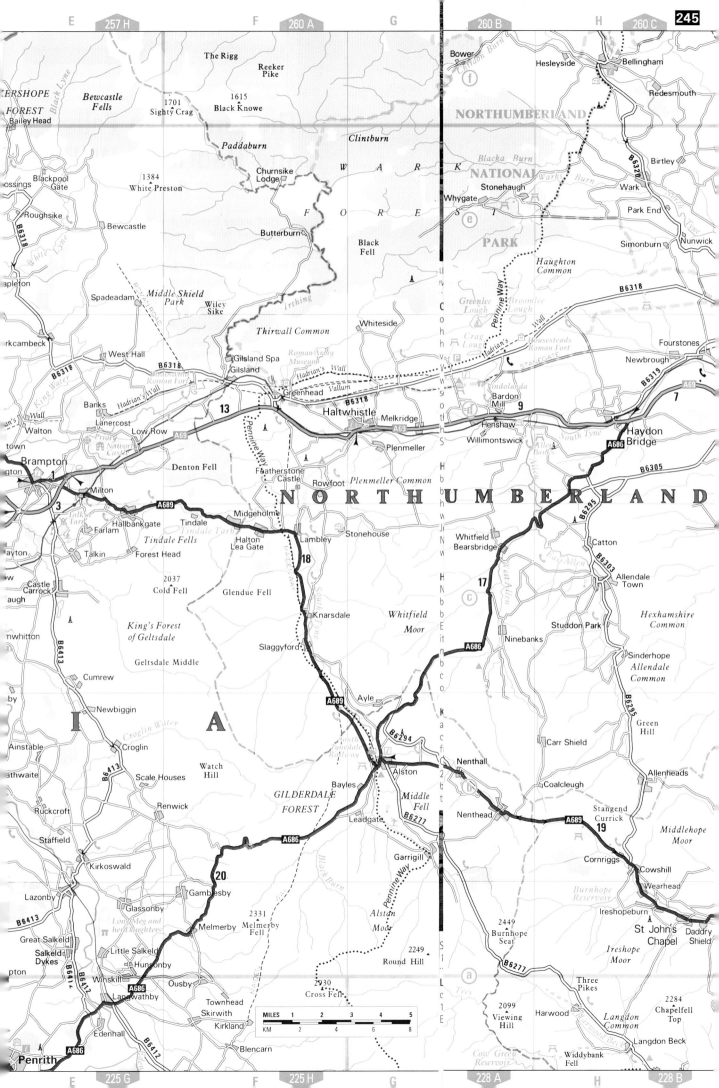

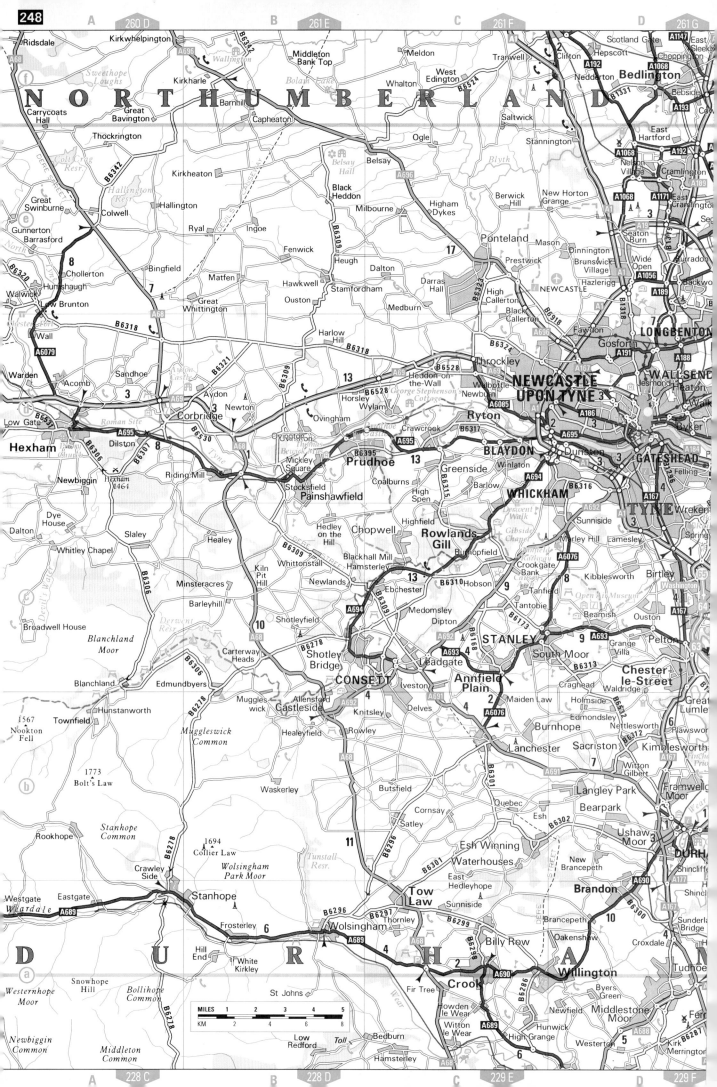

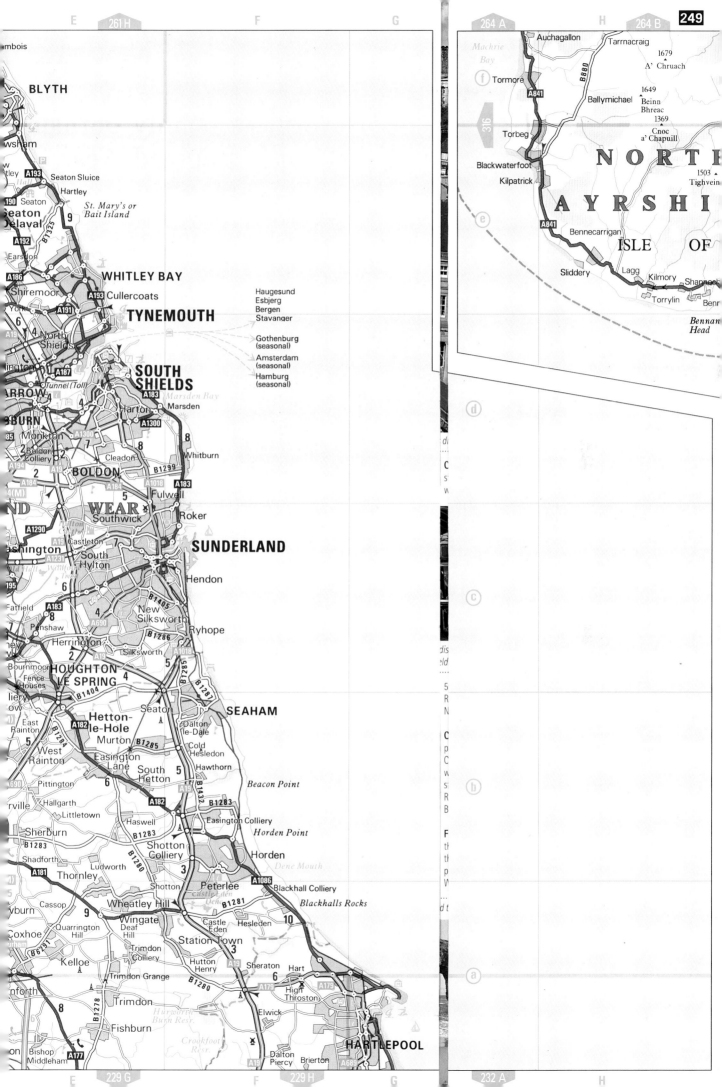

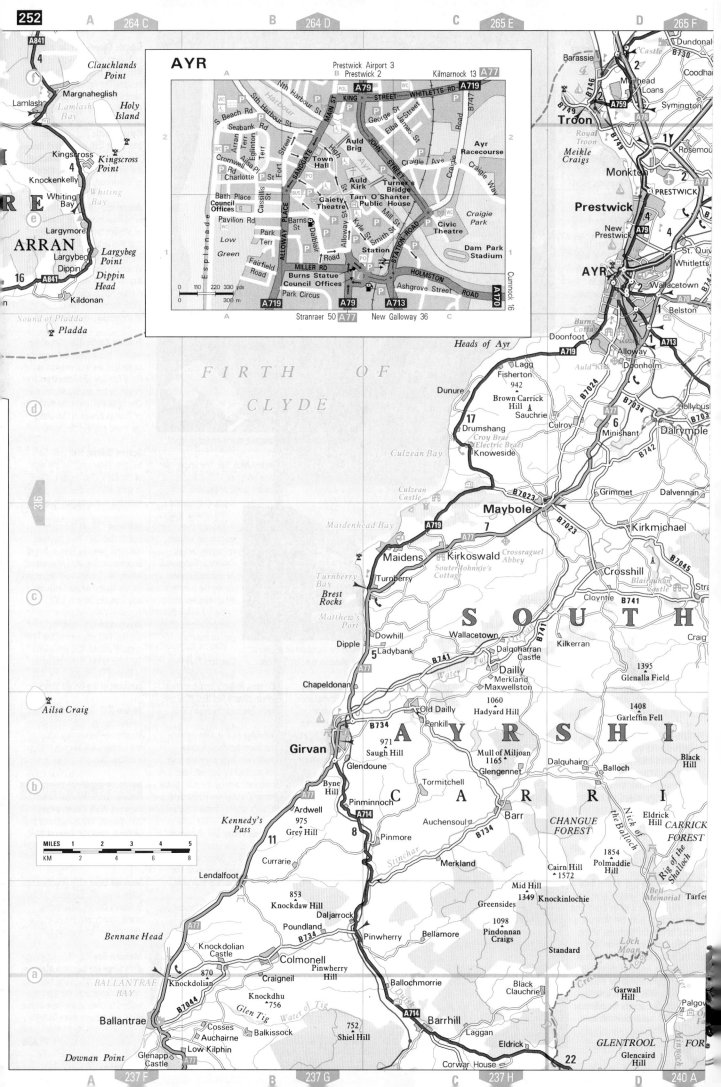

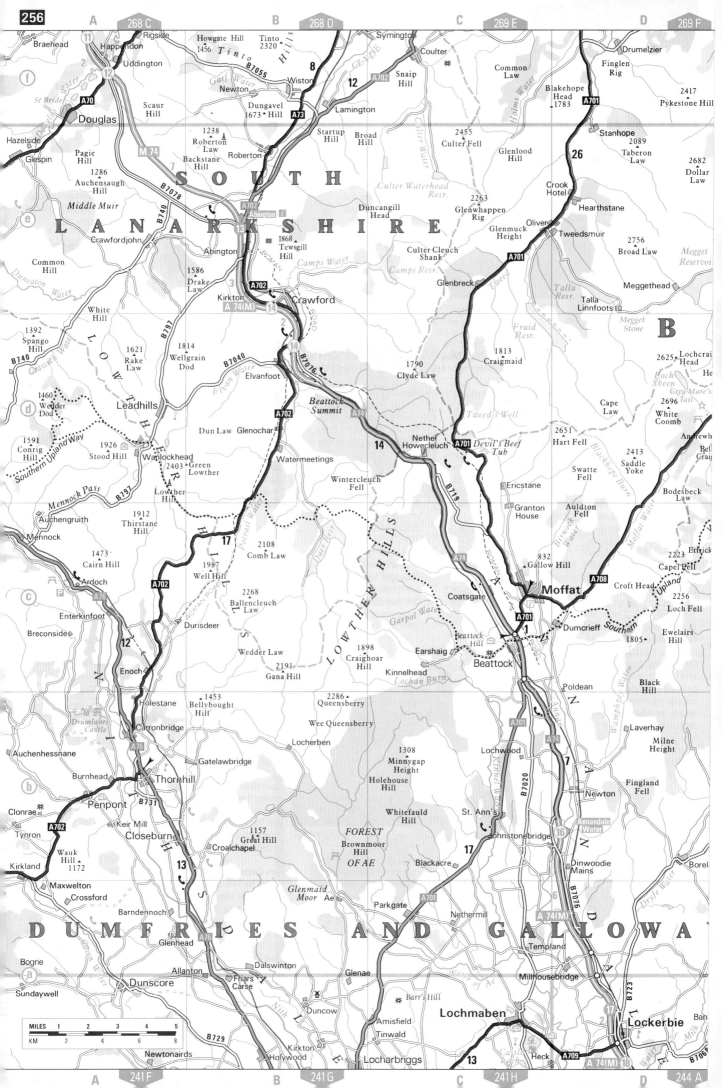

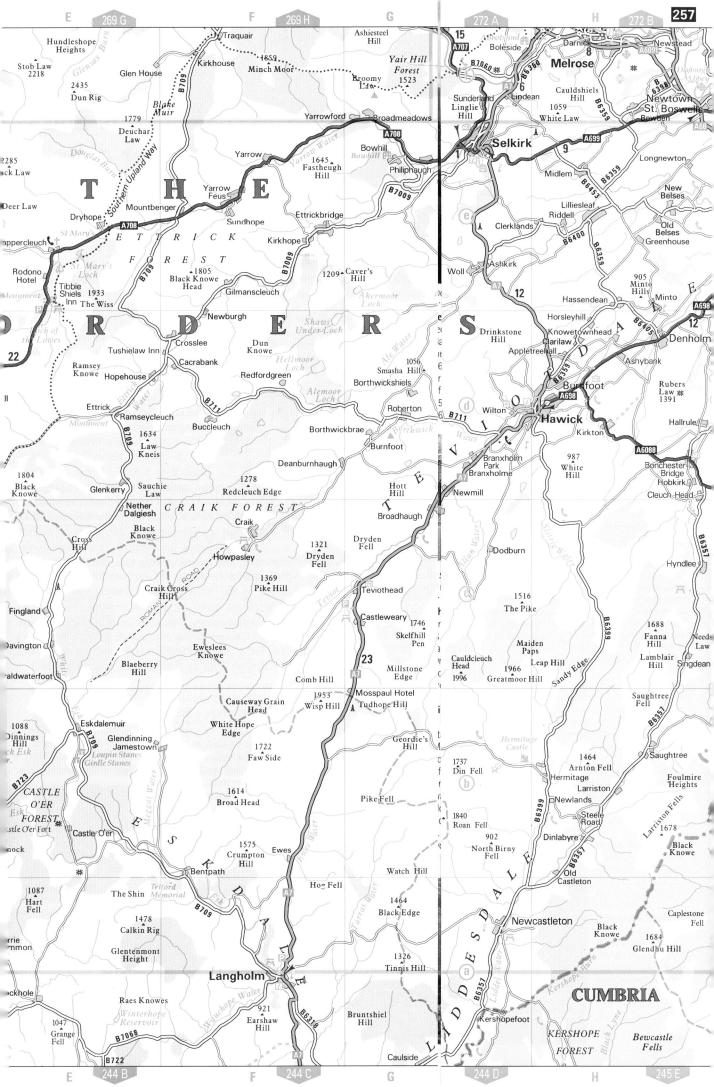

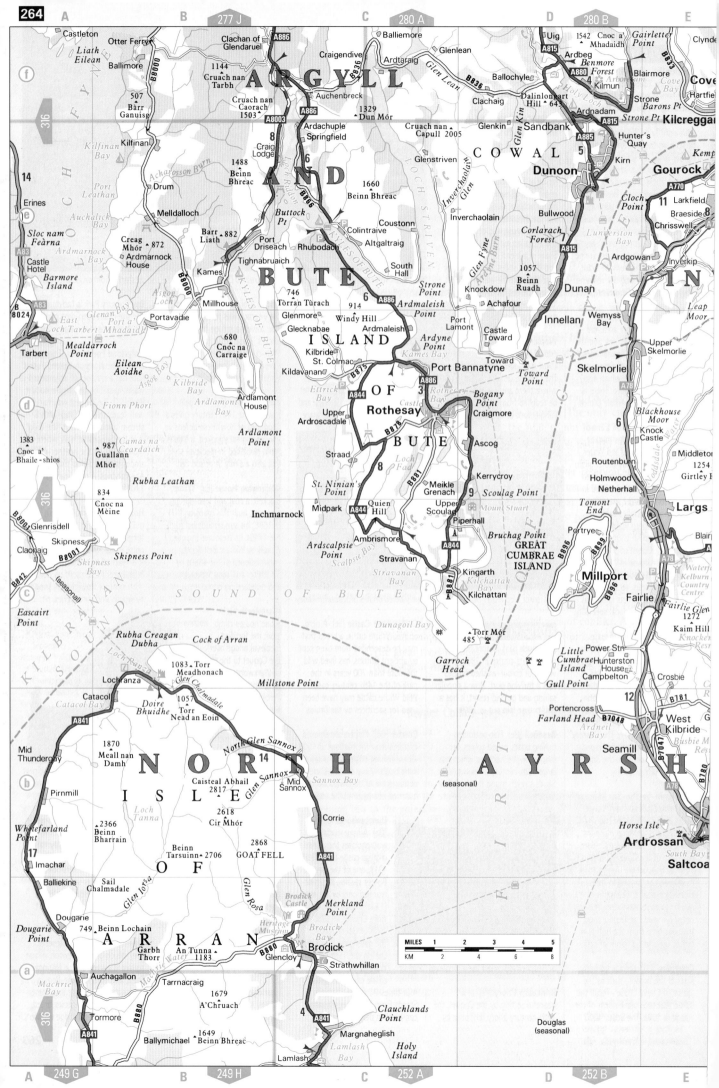

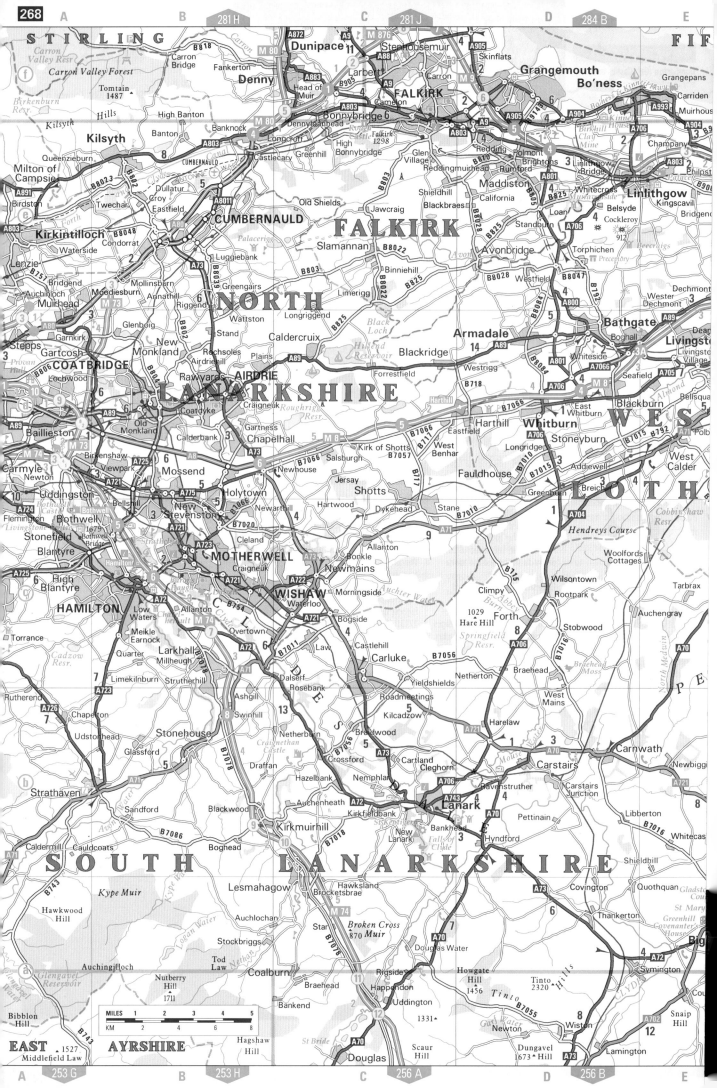

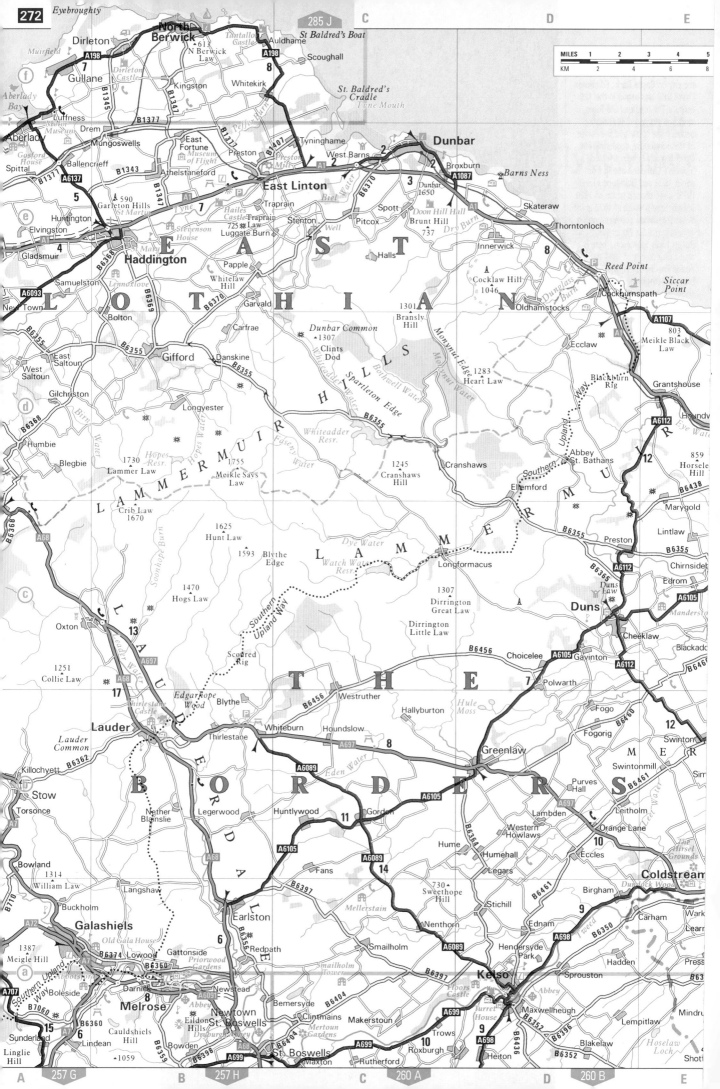

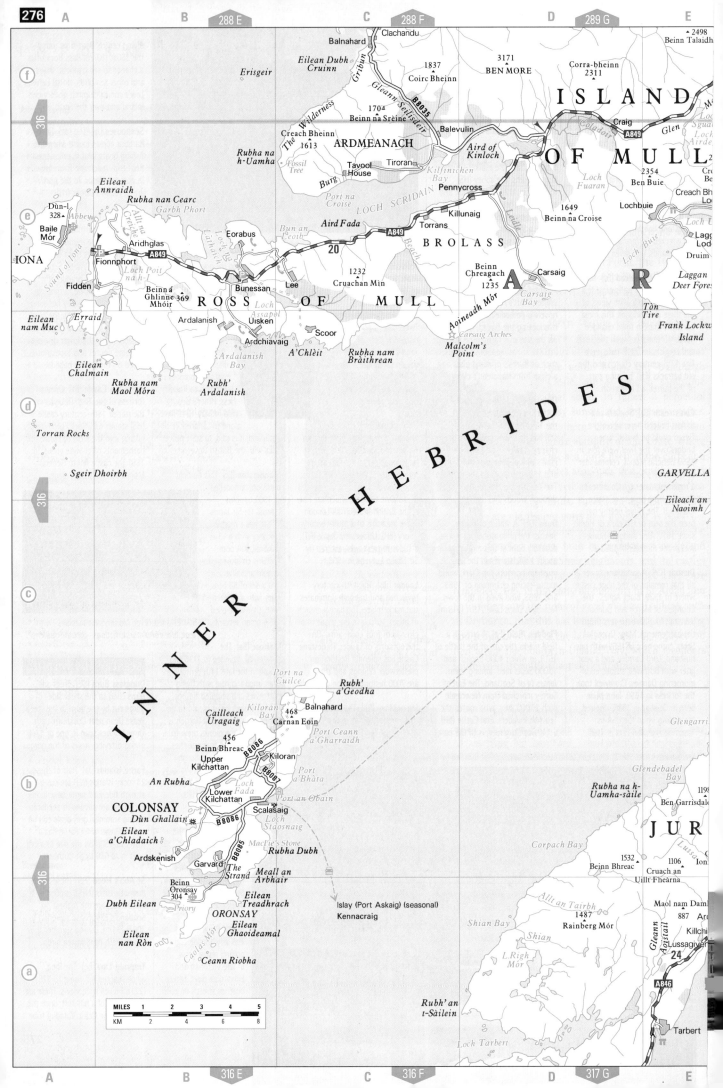

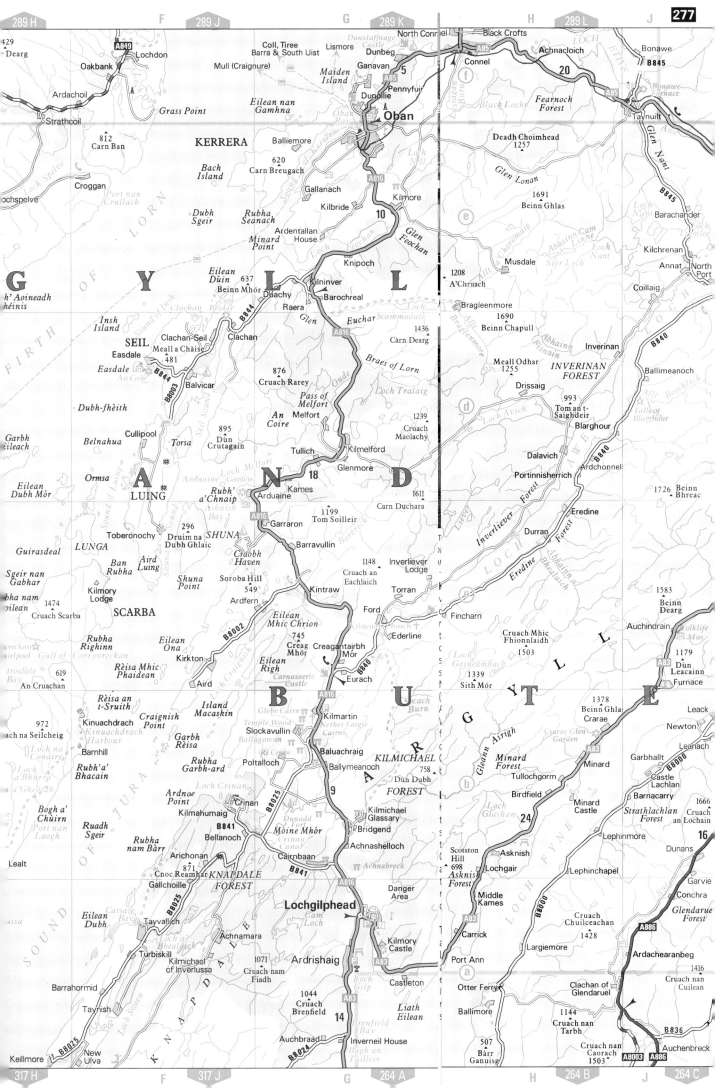

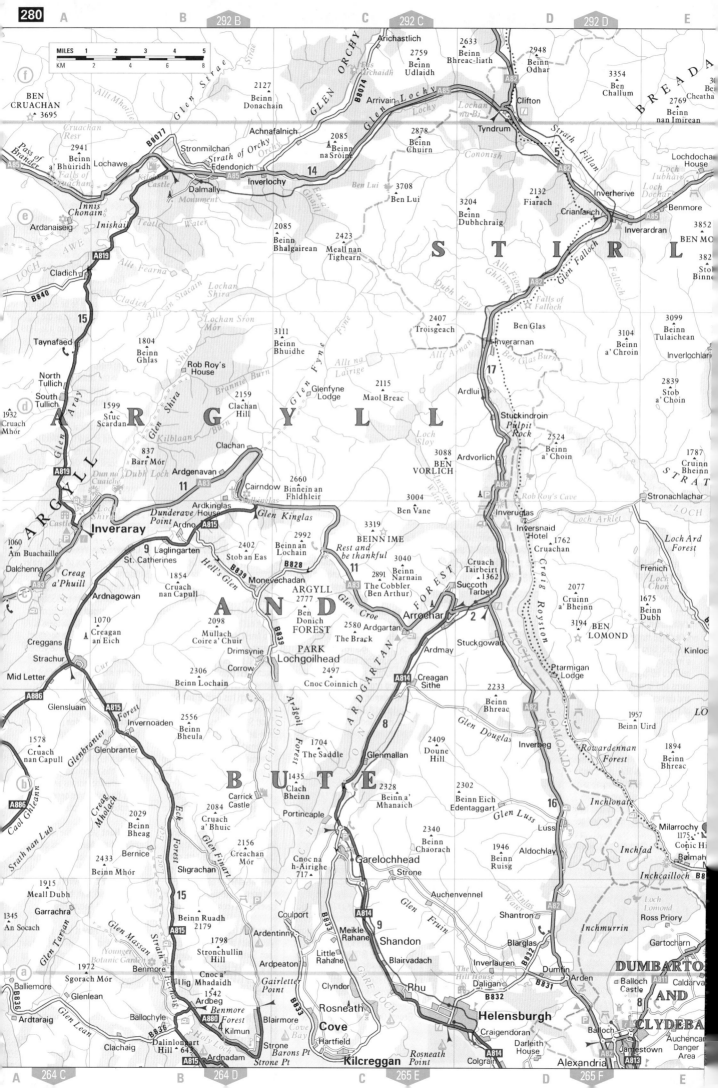

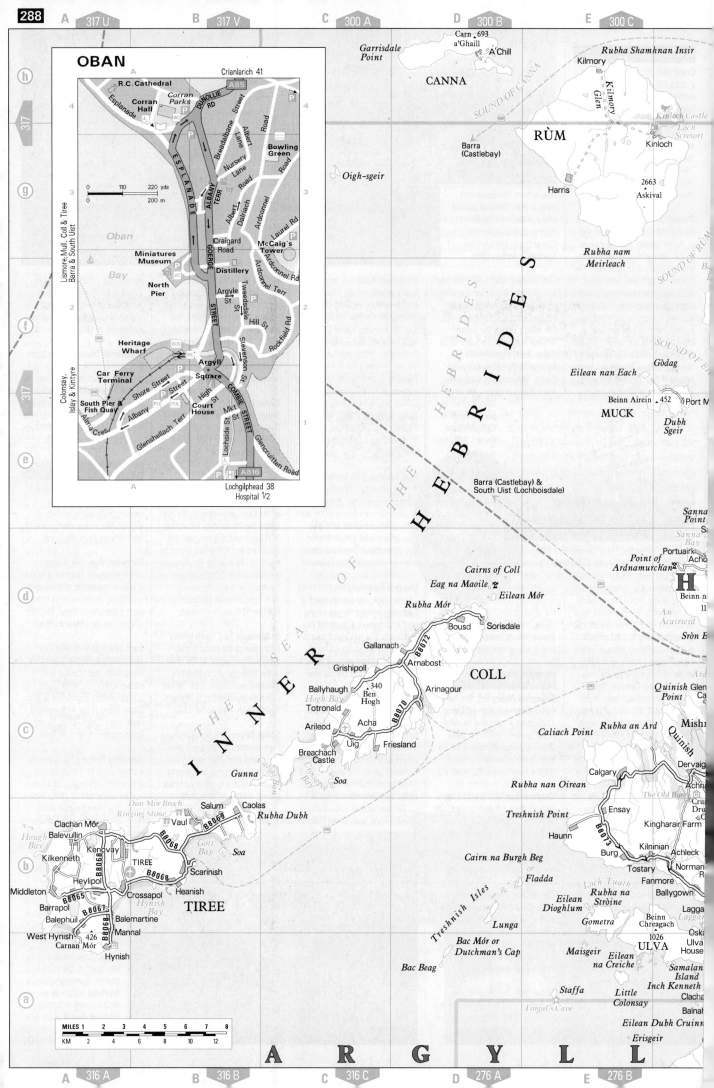

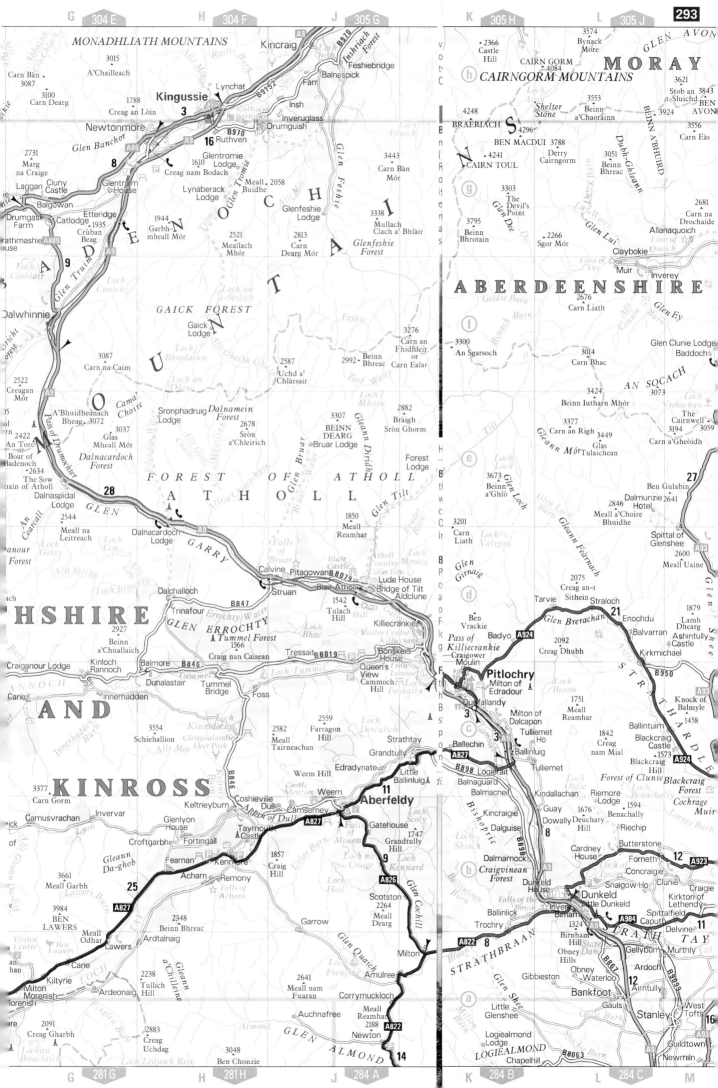

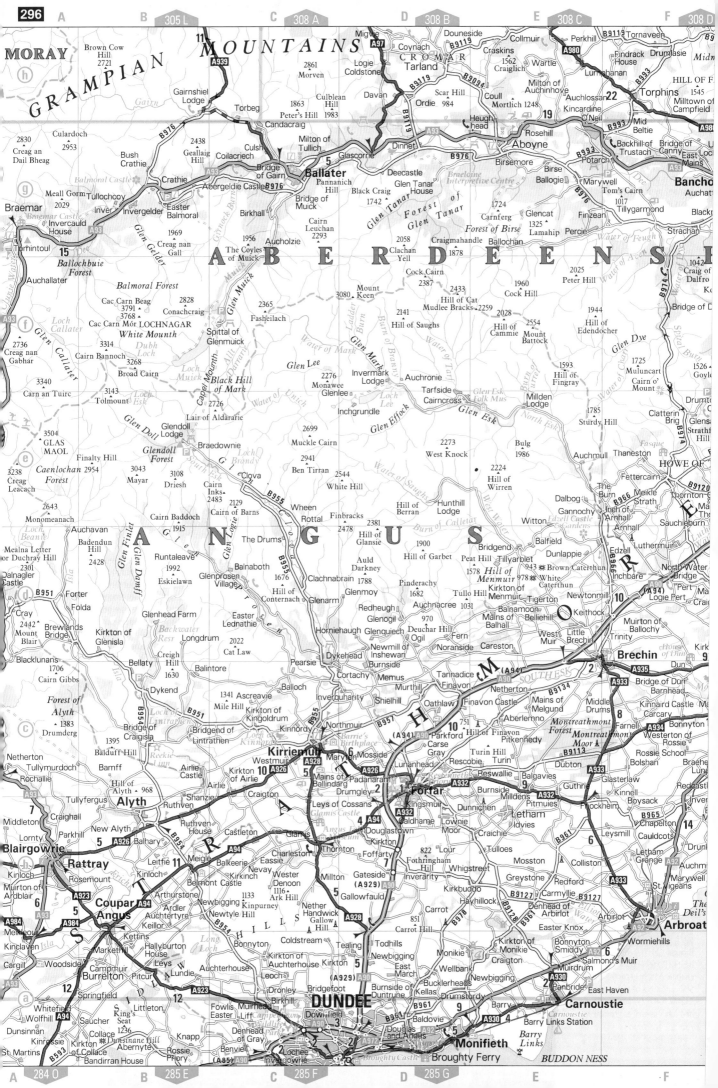

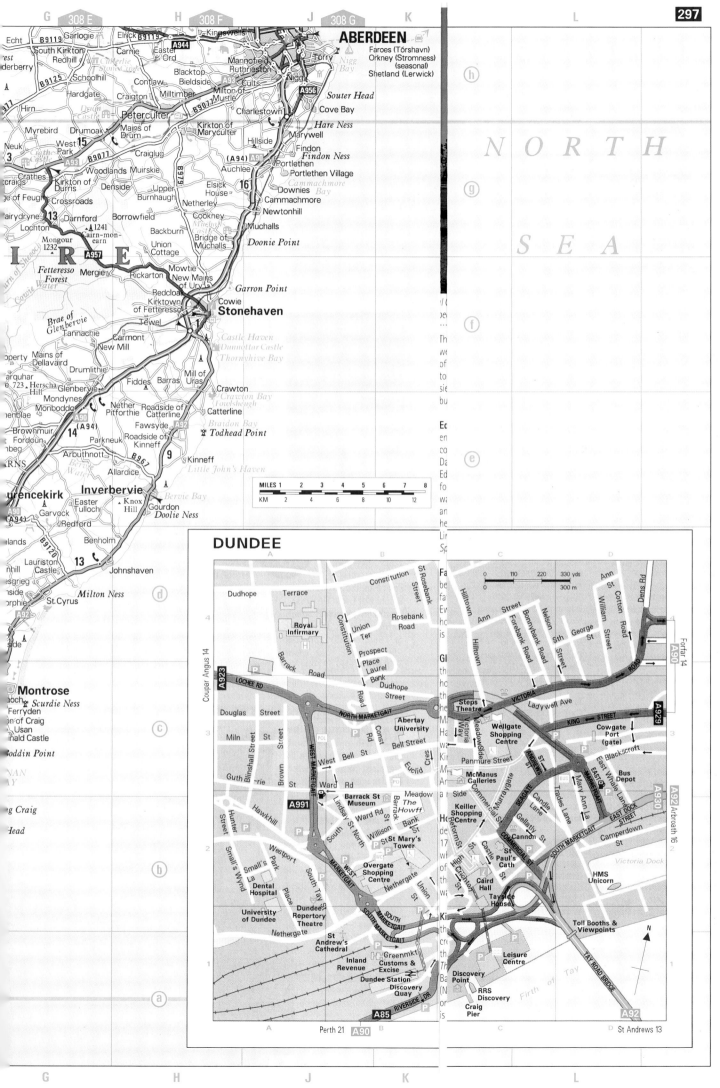

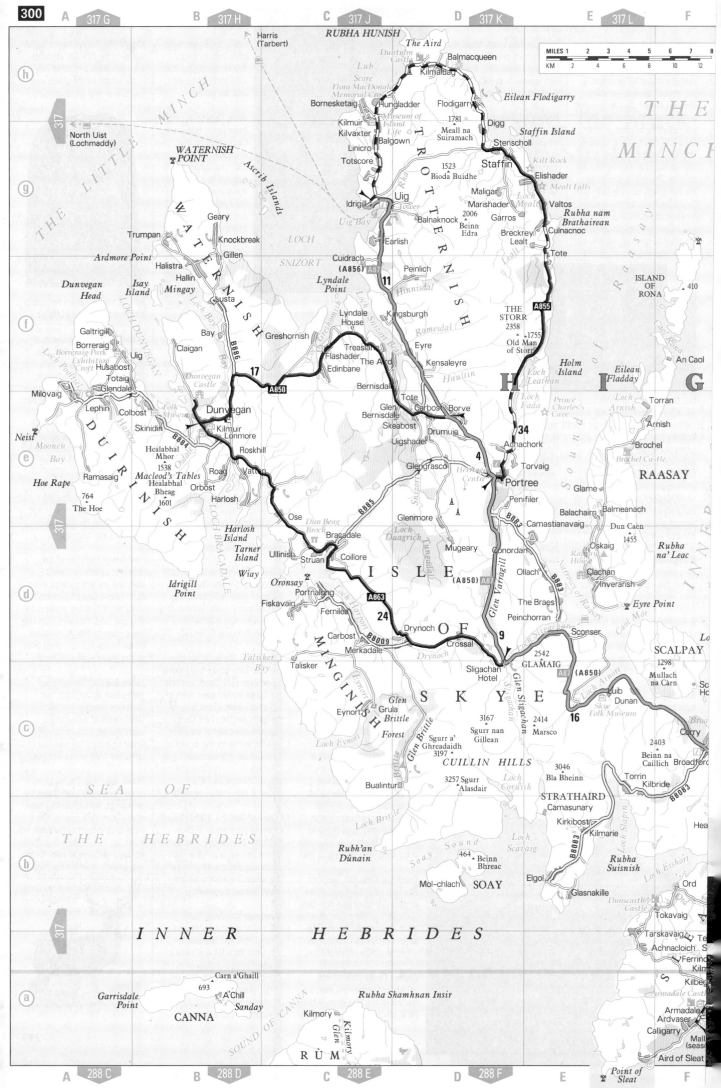

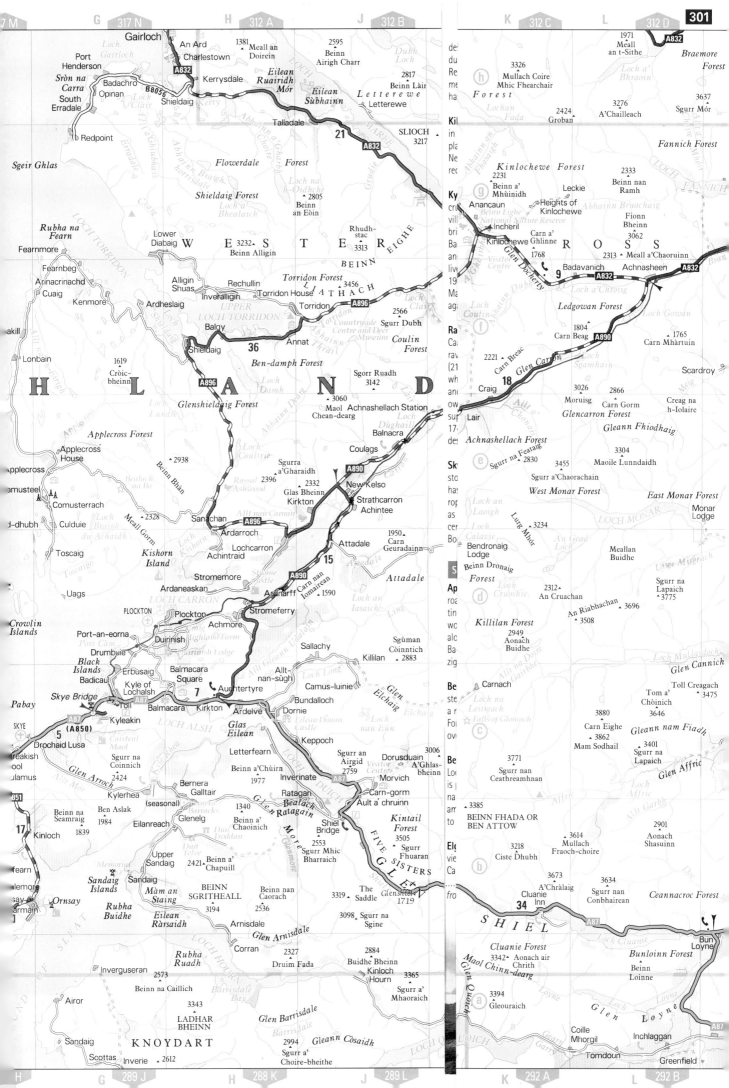

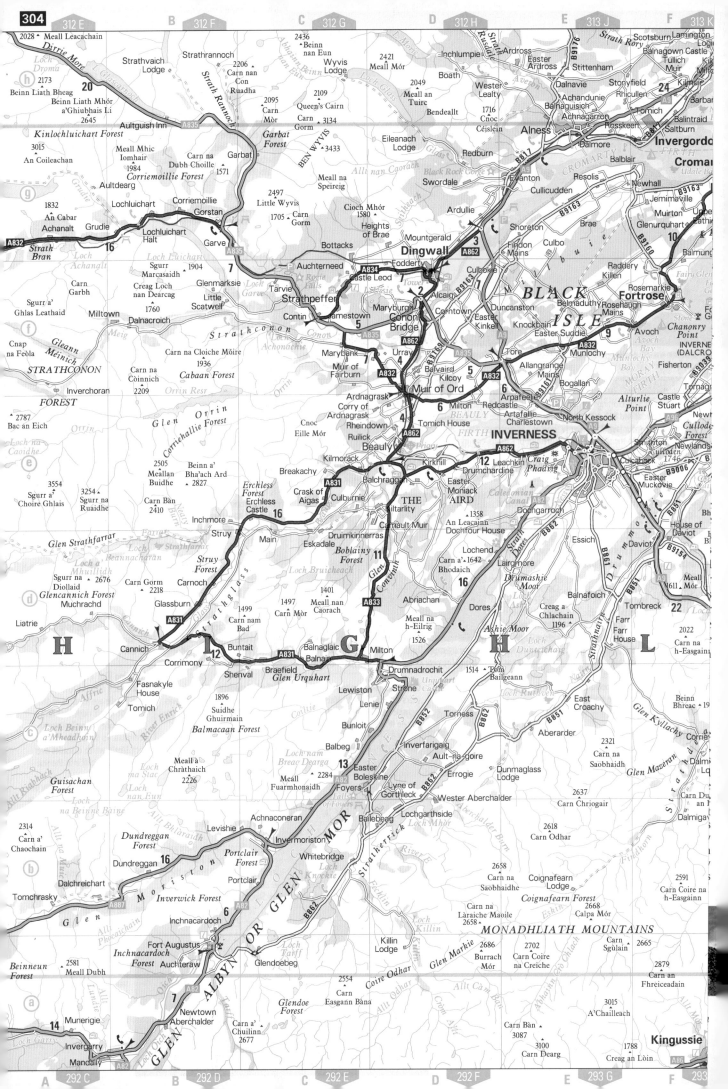

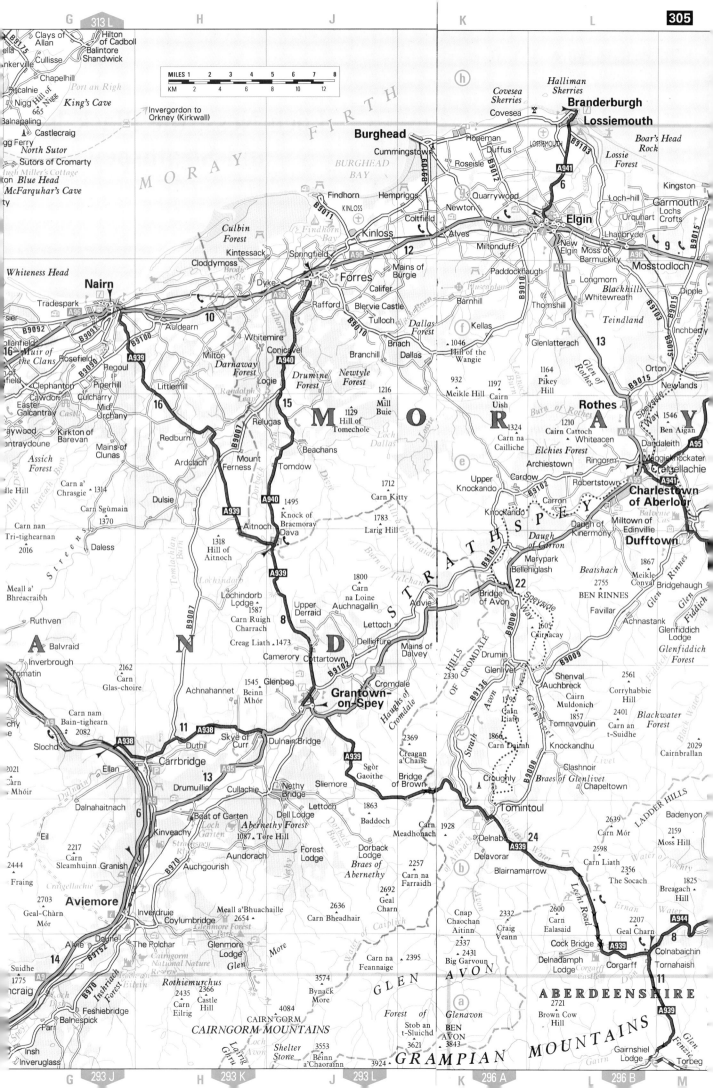

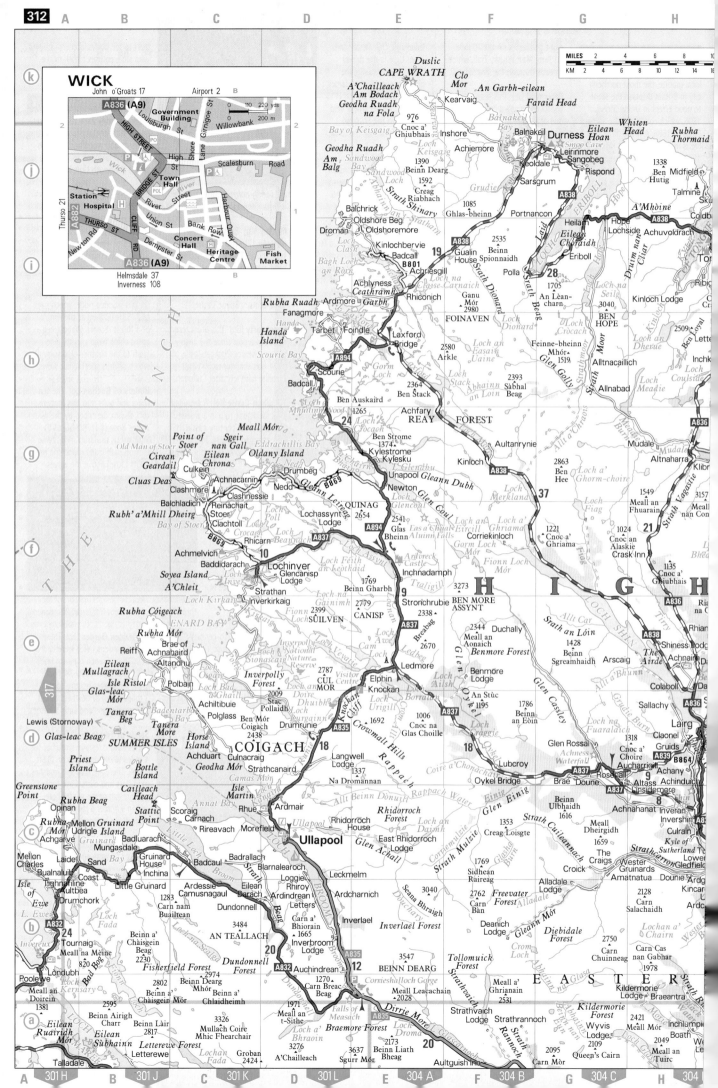

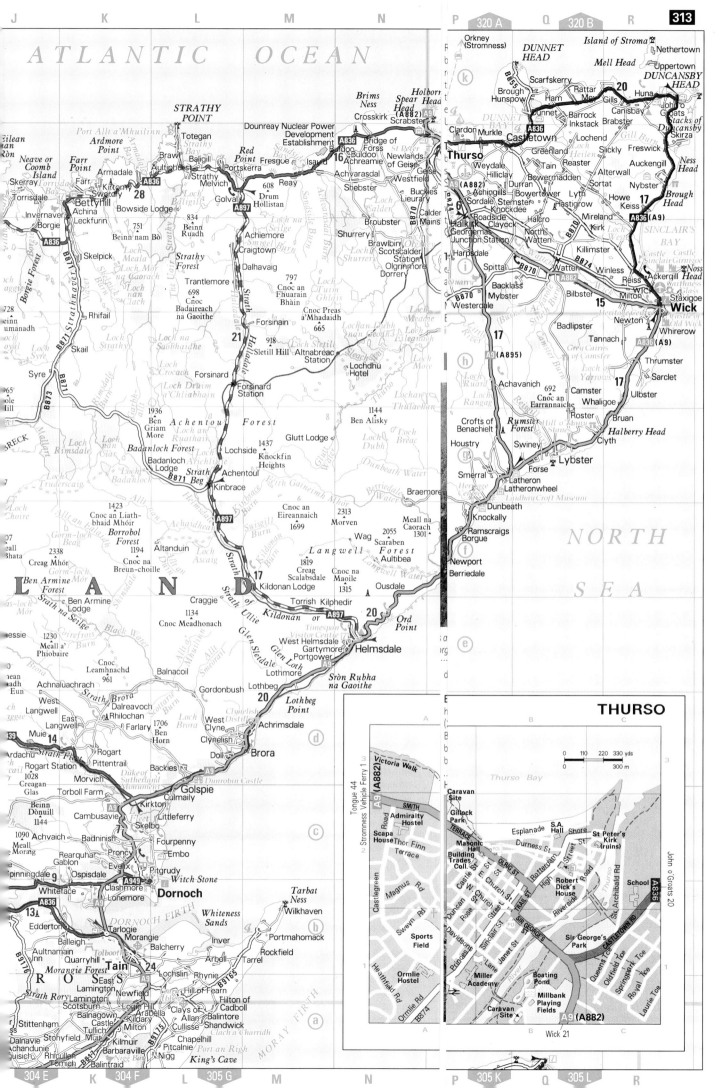

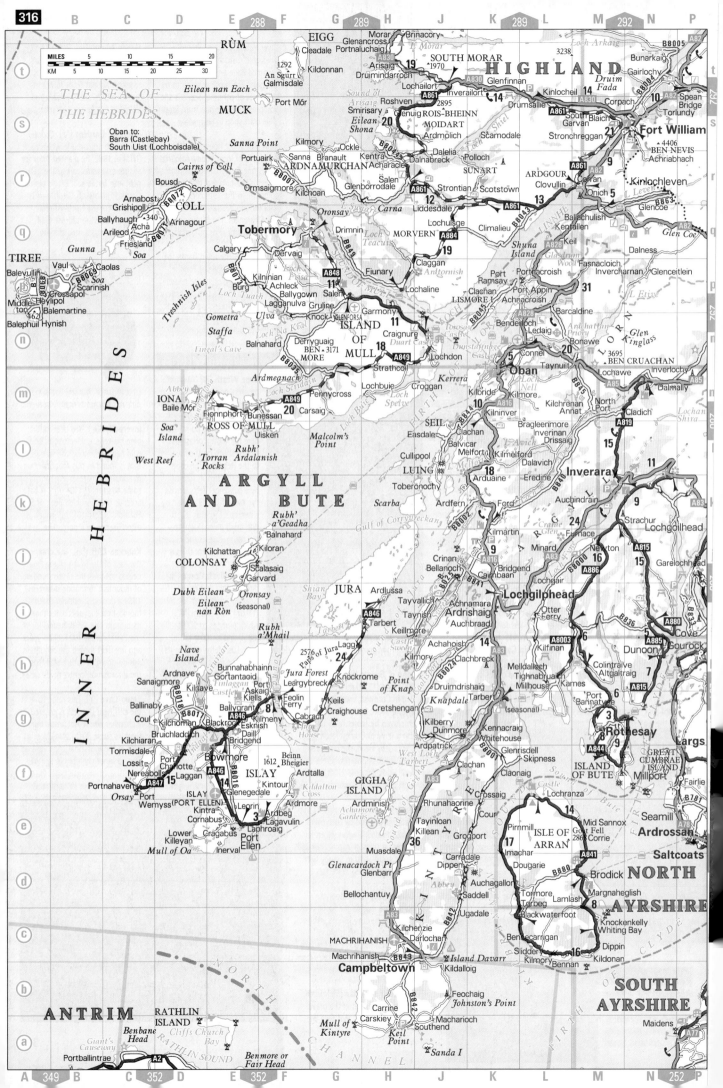

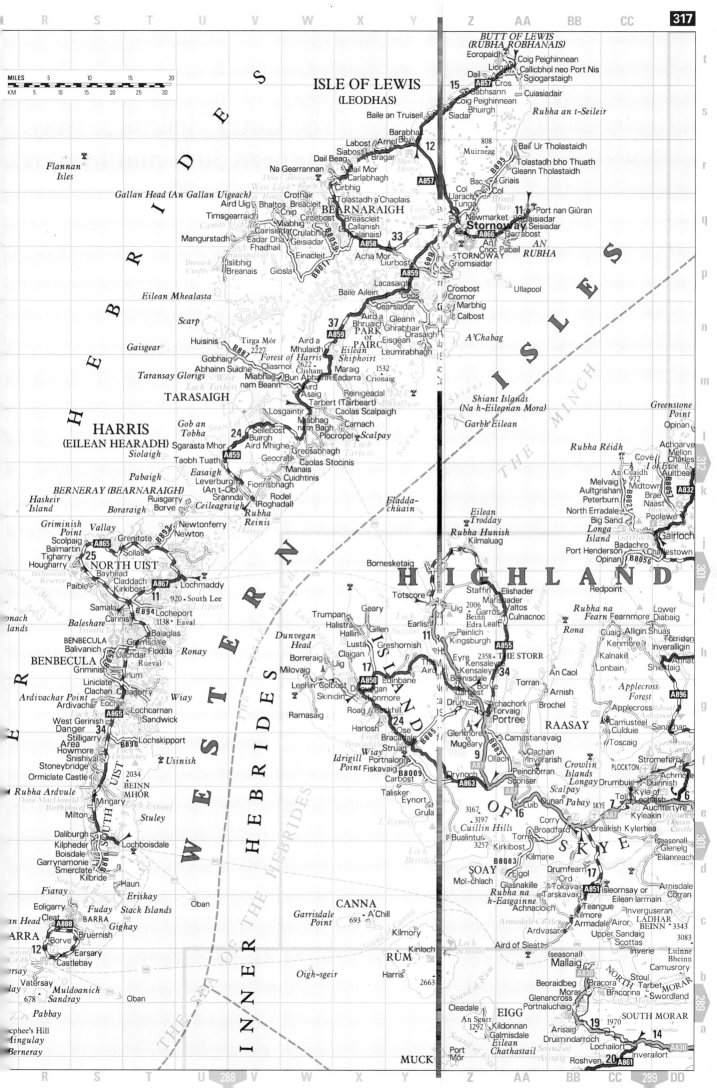

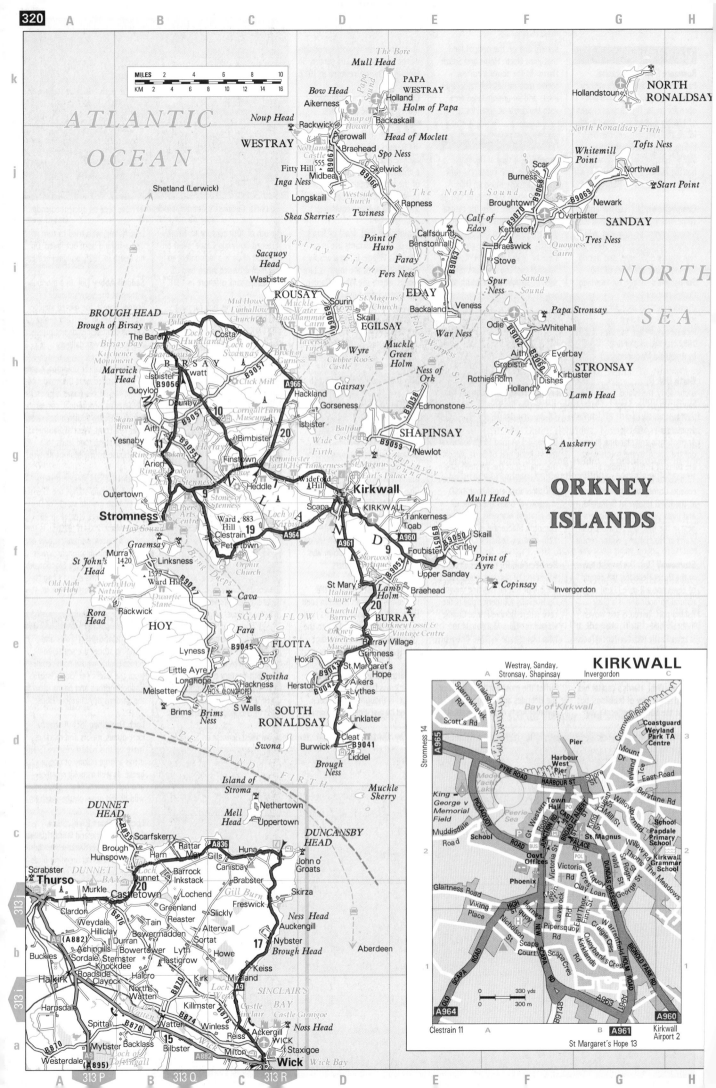

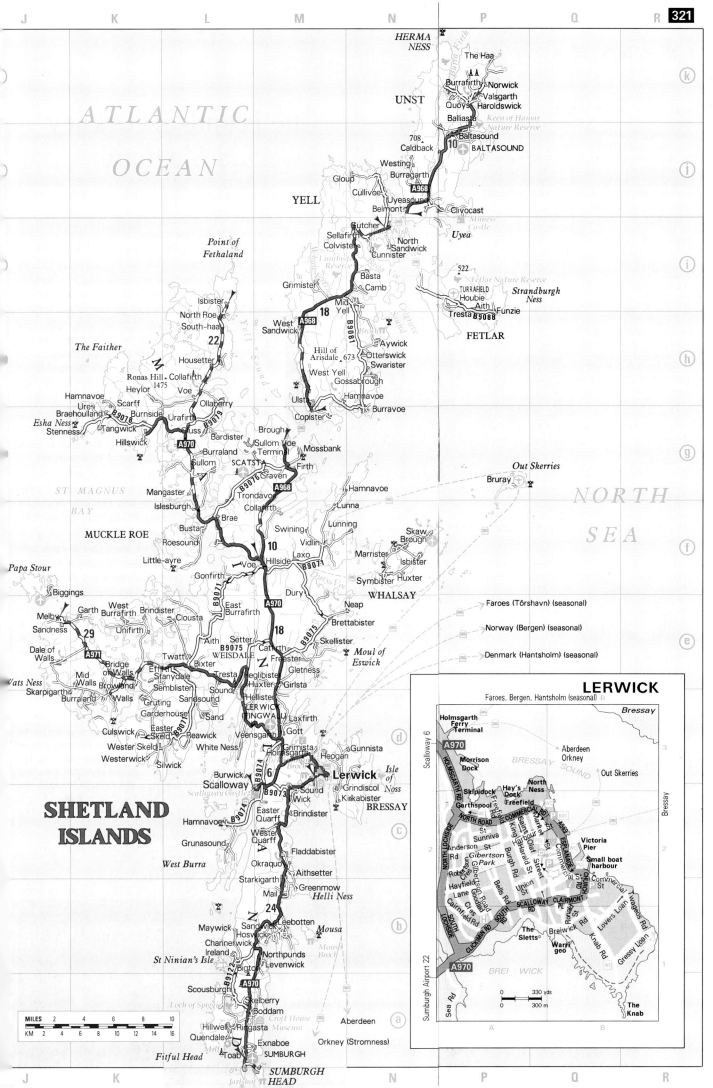

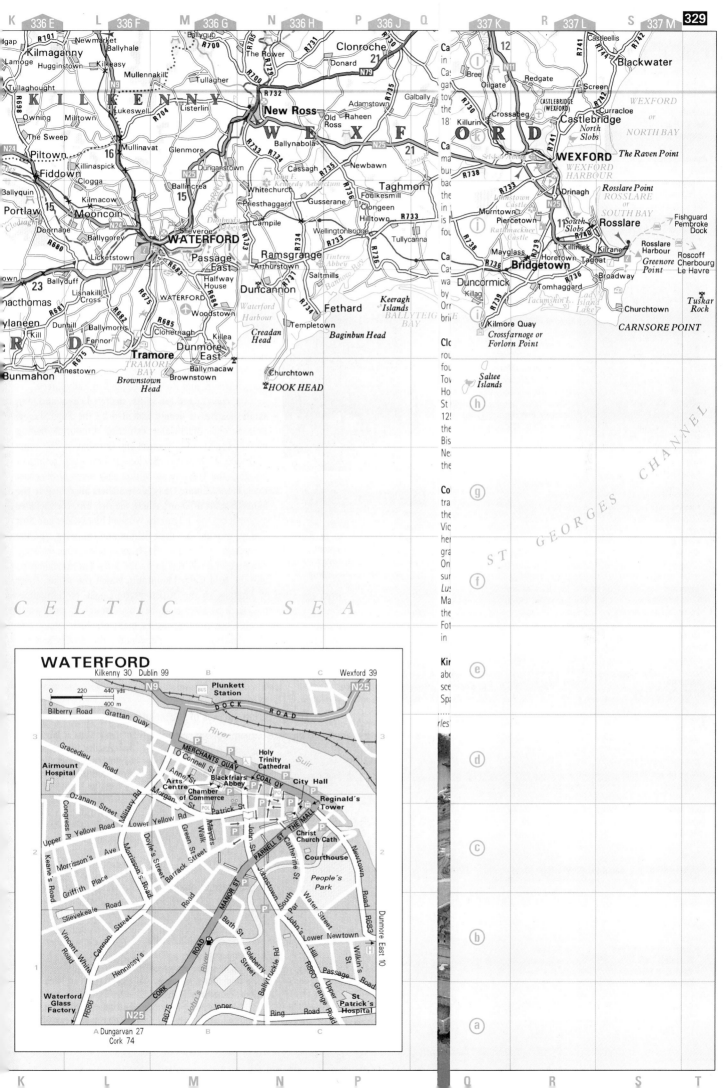

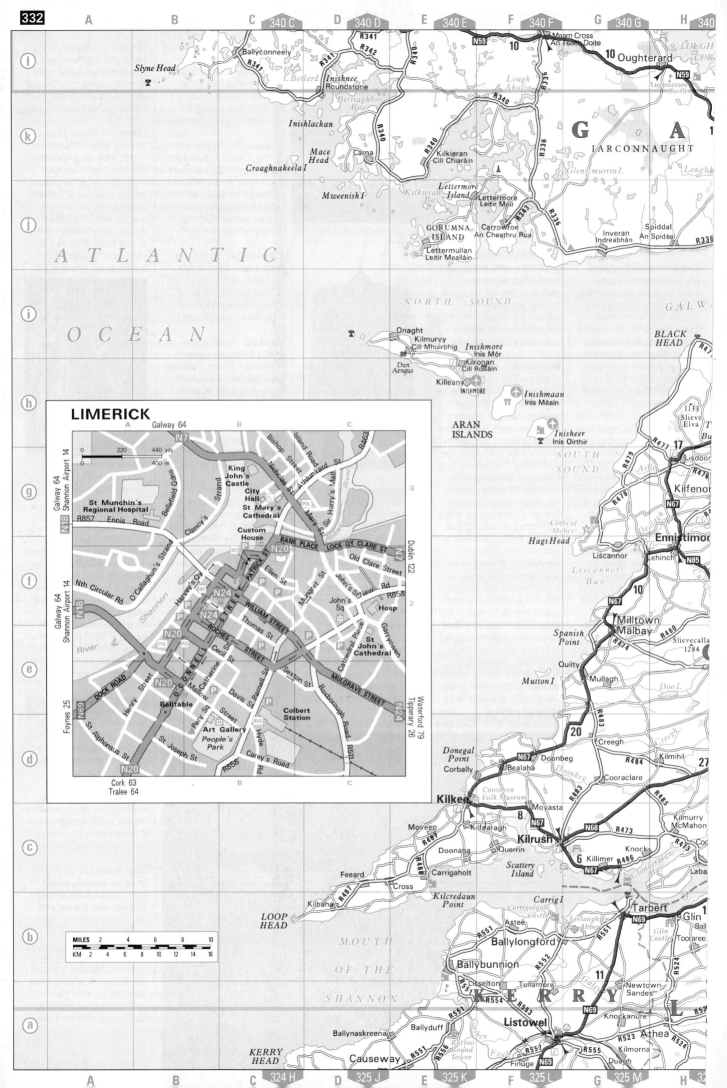

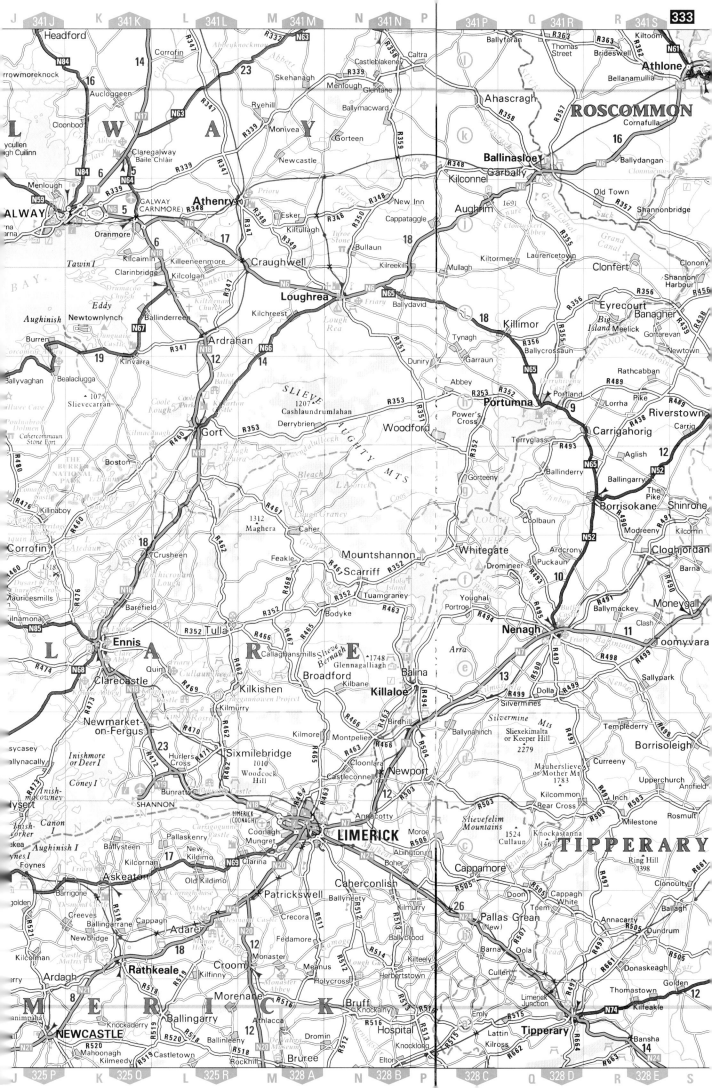

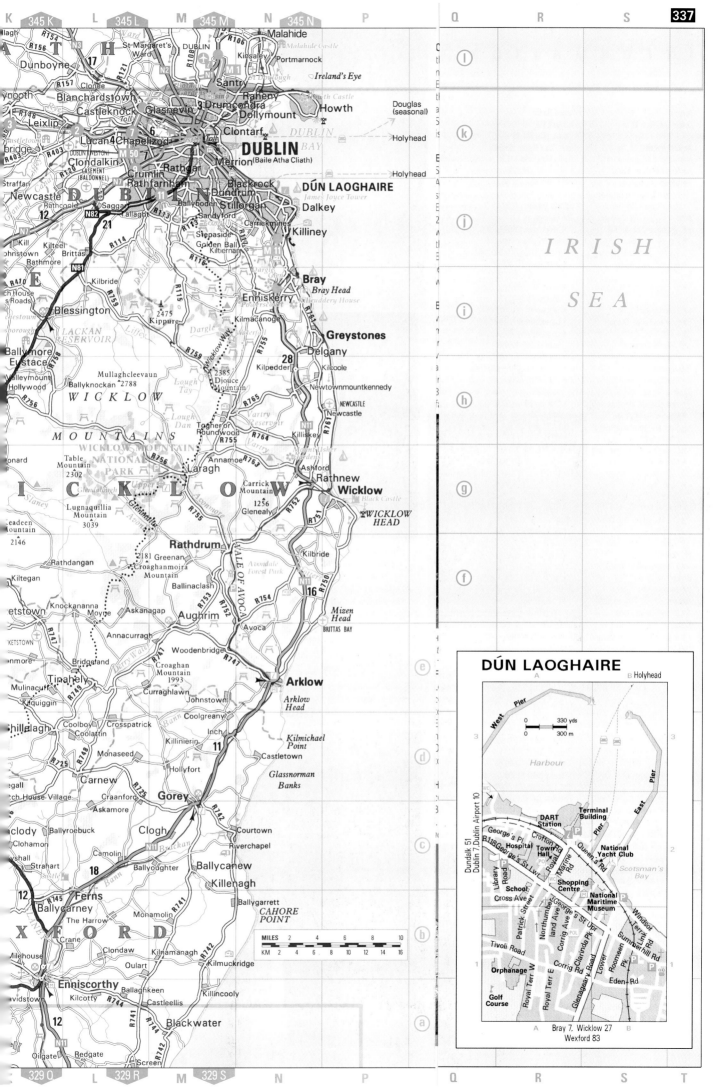

345 K 345 L M 345 M N 345 N P Q R S

R154 R156 N3 T H
Dunboyne 17 St Margaret's Ward DUBLIN
R157 Clonee R121 R106 Malahide
Blanchardstown R108 Kinsaley Malahide Castle Portmarnock
Castleknock Glasnevin Drumcondra Santry Ireland's Eye
Leixlip Toll Chapelizod Dollymount Raheny Howth
R148 Lucan Toll Clontarf Howth Castle
Clondalkin Rathgar DUBLIN BAY
Crumlin Merrion (Baile Atha Cliath)
Newcastle Rathfarnham Blackrock DÚN LAOGHAIRE
Rathcoole Saggart Dundrum Stillorgan James Joyce Tower
Tallaght Ballyboden Sandyford Dalkey
Kill Kilteel Stepaside Carrickmines Killiney
Johnstown Rathmore Golden Ball Kiltiernan M 11
Kilbride R116 Dargle

Douglas (seasonal)
Holyhead
Holyhead

IRISH SEA

Blessington Bray
Enniskerry Bray Head
Kilmacanoge Killruddery House
2475 Kippure Greystones
Ballymore Eustace Mullaghcleevaun 2788 Delgany
Valleymount Ballyknockan Kilpedder 28 Kilcoole
Hollywood R756 Lough Tay 2385 Djouce Mountain
WICKLOW Newtownmountkennedy
Table Mountain 2302 MOUNTAINS NEWCASTLE Newcastle
WICKLOW MOUNTAINS NATIONAL PARK Lough Dan Vartry Reservoir Killiskey
Lugnaquillia Mountain 3039 Togher or Roundwood Annamoe Ashford Mount Usher Gardens
Glendalough Upper Laragh Rathnew
Leaden Mountain 2146 Carrick Mountain 1256 Glenealy Wicklow
Slaney Glenmalure Black Castle
WICKLOW HEAD
Rathdangan Rathdrum
2181 Greenan Croaghanmoira Mountain Kilbride
Kiltegan Ballinaclash VALE OF AVOCA
Knockananna Moyne Askanagap Aughrim Avoca 16 Mizen Head
Annacurragh BRITTAS BAY
Bridgeland Woodenbridge
Tinahely Croaghan Mountain 1993 Arklow
Curraghlawn Johnstown Arklow Head
Mulinacuff Coolgreany
Kilquiggin Coolboy Killinierin Inch Kilmichael Point
Shillelagh Coolattin Monaseed Hollyfort 11 Castletown
Carnew Craanford Glassnorman Banks
Church House Village Askamore Gorey
Ballyroebuck Clogh Courtown
Clohamon Camolin Riverchapel
Strahart Ballyoughter Ballycanew
18 Killenagh
Ferns Ballygarrett CAHORE POINT
Ballycarney Monamolin
The Harrow
Crane Clondaw Kilnamanagh
Milehouse Oulart Kilmuckridge
Enniscorthy Ballaghkeen
Kilcotty Killincooly
12 Blackwater Castleellis
Oilgate Redgate Screen

MILES 2 4 6 8 10
KM 2 4 6 8 10 12 14 16

DÚN LAOGHAIRE

A   B Holyhead
West Pier
0   330 yds
0   300 m
Harbour
East Pier
Dundalk 51
Dublin 7, Dublin Airport 10
Terminal Building
DART Station
George's Pl
Crofton Rd
Hospital Town Hall
Library Marine Rd National Yacht Club
Cross Ave George's St Lwr Pier Queen's Rd Scotsman's Bay
Patrick Street School Shopping Centre
Northumberland Ave George's St Upr National Maritime Museum
Corrig Ave Clarinda Pk Windsor Terr Link Rd
Tivoli Road Corrig Rd Roomeen Sumberhill Rd
Orphanage Royal Terr W Royal Terr E Corrig Rd Lower Glenageary Road Eden Rd
Golf Course

A Bray 7, Wicklow 27 B
Wexford 83

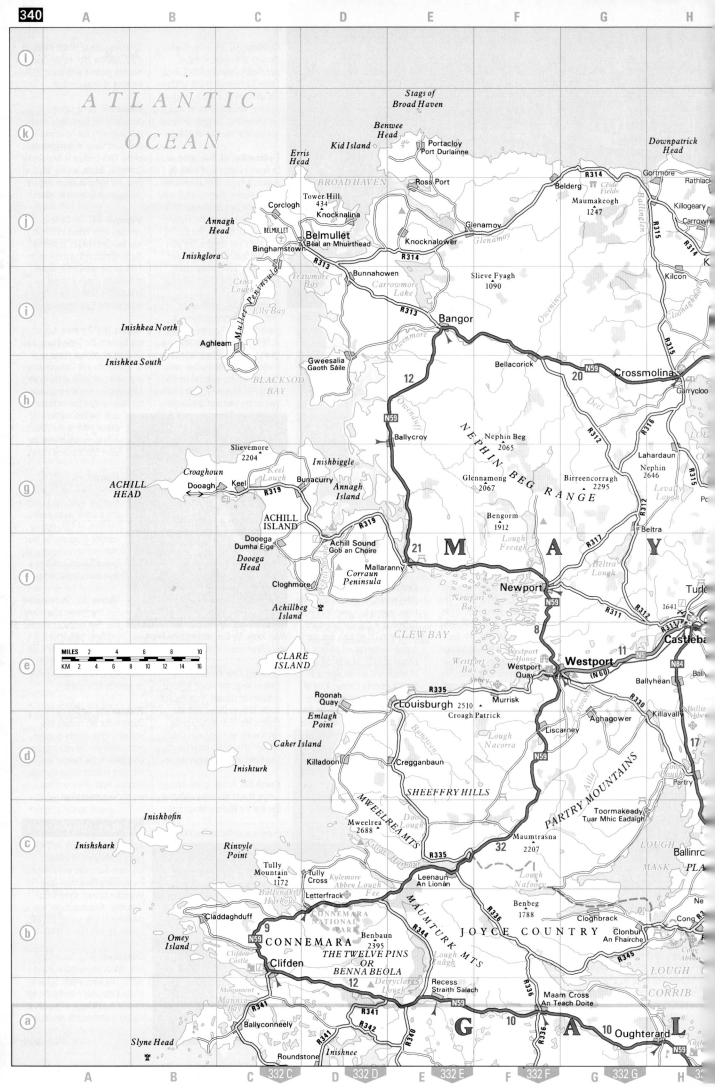

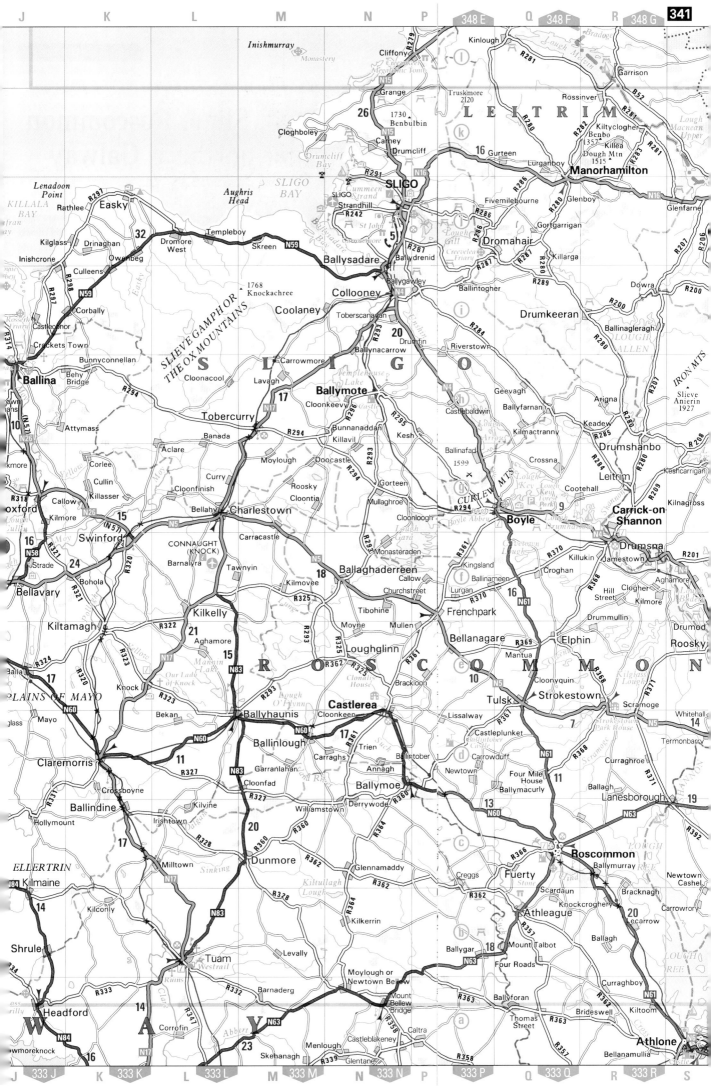

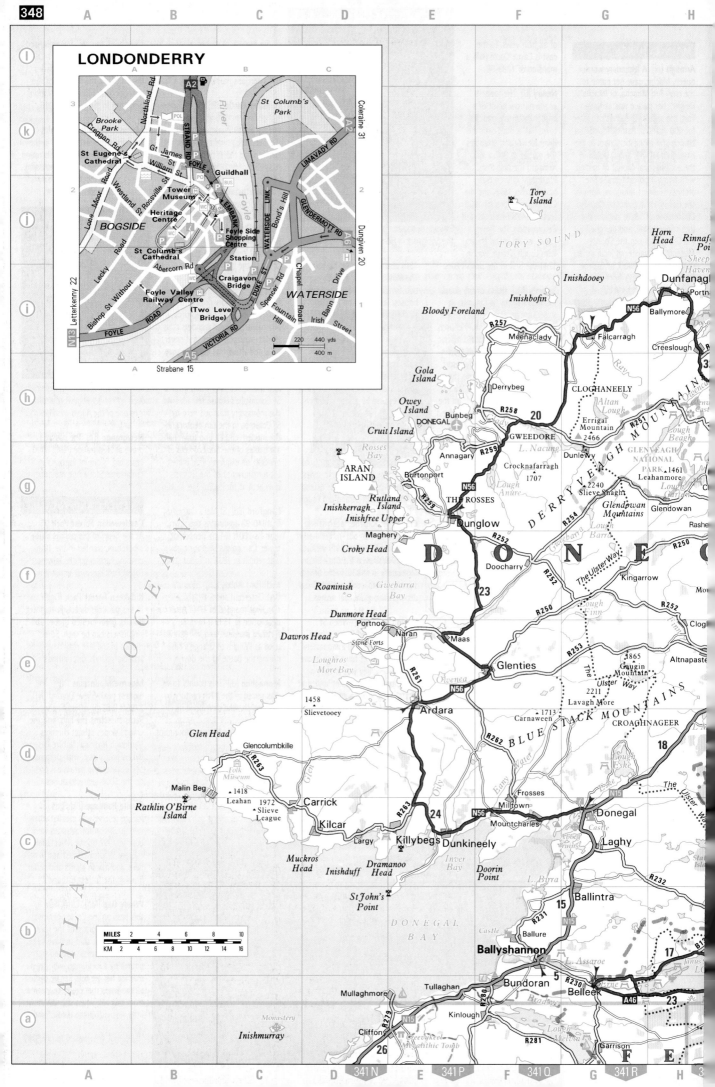

LONDONDERRY

Brooke Park
St Eugene's Cathedral
BOGSIDE
Gt James St
William St
Tower Museum
Heritage Centre
Guildhall
St Columb's Cathedral
Abercorn Rd
Station
Foyle Side Shopping Centre
Craigavon Bridge
Foyle Valley Railway Centre
(Two Level Bridge)
WATERSIDE
POL
St Columb's Park
Creggan Rd
Northland Rd
STRAND RD
FOYLE
River
Foyle
Limavady Rd
Coleraine 31
Dungiven 20
A6
Glendermott Rd
Bond's Hill
Waterside Link
Duke St
Spencer Rd
Chapel Rd
Bann Rd
Irish Street
Fountain Hill
Victoria Rd
Foyle Rd
Bishop St Without
Westland St
Rossville St
Lone Moor Road
Lecky Road
N13 Letterkenny 22
A5 Strabane 15
A2

0 220 440 yds
0   400 m

Tory Island
Horn Head
Rinnafa Poi
TORY SOUND
Inishdooey
Dunfanagh
Inishbofin
Portna
Bloody Foreland
R257
Meenaclady
Falcarragh
Creeslough
N56
Ballymore
Gola Island
Derrybeg
CLOGHANEELY
DERRYVEAGH MOUNTAIN
Owey Island
DONEGAL
R258
20
Errigal Mountain 2466
Altan Lough
Lough Beagh
Cruit Island
Bunbeg
GWEEDORE
L. Nacung
Dunlewy
GLENVEAGH NATIONAL PARK 1461
Rosses Bay
Annagary
R259
Crocknafarragh 1707
Slieve Snaght 2240
Glendowan Mountains
Glendowan
ARAN ISLAND
Burtonport
Lough Anure
R259
N56
THE ROSSES
Dunglow
R254
Lough Barra
The Ulster Way
Rashe
Inishkerragh Island
Rutland Island
Inishfree Upper
Maghery
R252
Doocharry
R252
Kingarrow
R250
Crohy Head
DONE
Roaninish
Gweebarra Bay
R252
Lough Finn
Clog
23
R250
Dunmore Head
Portnoo
Naran
Maas
R253
1865 Gaugin Mountain
Altnapaste
Dawros Head
Stone Forts
Owenea
Glenties
The Ulster Way
Loughros More Bay
R261
N56
2211 Lavagh More
1458 Slievetooey
Ardara
1713 Carnaween
BLUE STACK MOUNTAINS
CROAGHNAGEER
Glen Head
R262
18
Glencolumbkille
R263
Folk Museum
Lough Eske
The Ulster
Malin Beg
1418 Leahan
1972 Slieve League
Carrick
R263
Eany Water
Frosses
N15
Kilcar
Largy
24
Milltown
Donegal
Killybegs
Dunkineely
N56
Mountcharles
Castle
Laghy
Muckros Head
Inishduff
Dramanoo Head
Inver Bay
Doorin Point
Abbey
R232
St John's Point
L. Birra
Ballintra
DONEGAL BAY
15
Castle
Ballure
N15
R231
Mullaghmore
Bundoran
Ballyshannon
L. Assaroe
5
R230
Belleek
17
Tullaghan
Brodoe
A46
23
Inishmurray
Kinlough
Cliffony
R279
N15
Greevykeel Megalithic Tomb
Lough Melvin
Garrison
R281
26
F E

MILES 2 4 6 8 10
KM 2 4 6 8 10 12 14 16

ATLANTIC OCEAN

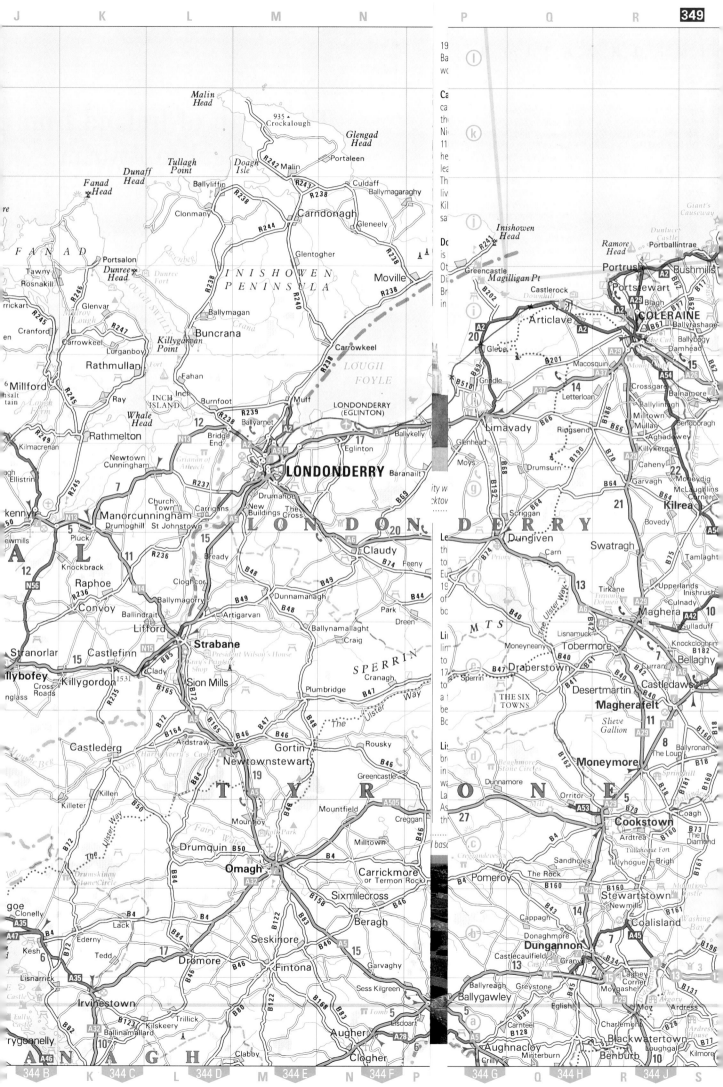

LARNE

Carnlough 14

Carnfunnock
Country Park

Town
Park

The Roddens

Lower Glenarm Rd

A2

Chaine
Memorial
Tower

Dixon
Park

Laharna Ave

Lower Cairncastle Rd

Moyle
Hospital

Victoria Road

Tower

Road

Road

Town
Hall

Pound St

Main St

Regal

CURRAN

ROAD

Bay Road

Mill Brae

Belfast 22

A8

Larne F.C.

Mill

Road

Inver

Road

HARBOUR

POL

Station

Harbour
Road

CIRCULAR ROAD

Cairnryan

Island Magee

Whitla's

Brae

Glynn Rd

Carrickfergus Road

BANK

ROAD

HIGHWAY

Station
& Ferry
Terminal

Larne
Lough

Harbour
Industrial
Area

Redlands Rd

Olderfleet
Castle

A2

Curran
Point

0   440   880 yds

0   800 m

Carrickfergus 14

MILES 2   4   6   8   10
KM 2 4 6 8 10 12 14 16

NORTH CHANNEL

Bull Point

Kebble

Church
Bay

Bruce's Cave

RATHLIN
ISLAND

Rue Point

RATHLIN
SOUND

Benbane
Head

White Park
Bay

Carrickarade
Island

Rope
Bridge

Kinbane or
White Head

Ballycastle
Bay

Benmore or
Fair Head

Murlough Bay

B146

26

Dunseverick
Castle

A2

B15

B11

Ballyvoy

Torr Head

Castlecat

B17

B147

B67

Ballycastle

Bonamargy
Friary

Moss-side

B147

A44

Cape
Castle

B15

Carnanmore
1253

Runabay Head

B61

Derrykeighan

B86

B141

Stranocum

Armoy

B15

Knocklayd
1695

Ballypatrick
Cairn

Cushendun

Dervock

B66

Kirkhills

B16

Ossian's
Grave

B141

Fayd
Old Church

Cushendall

Ballymoney

A44

Kilraghts

Loughguile

Trostan
1817

Glenariff or
Waterfoot

11

Red Bay

Garron
Point

B62

Knockaholet

Corkey

A43

A2

B62

B16

Finvoy

Dunloy

Clogh
Mills

Newtown-
Crommelin

20

Glenarm

Dooey's
Cairn

B93

Glenvale

Cloghy

B64

McGregor's
Corner

The
Sheddings

Carnlough

Glenarm

12

A2

Rasharkin

B96

B64

Carncormick
1431

Martinstown

16

A42

Buckha

The Maidens or
Hulin Rocks

B62

B93

Craigs

12

Quarrytown

Carnalbanagh
Sheddings

Carncastle

B62

B94

Broughshane

Ballygalley

IRISH

Cullybackey

12

M2

B94

Slemish Mt
1437

B148

Larne

Cairnryan

Portglenone

A26

Galgorm

BALLYMENA

Agnews Hill
1565

Ballylumford

A42

Ahoghill

Gracehill

Kilwaughter

Glynn

ISLAND MAGEE

SEA

A54

9

Moorfields

21

A36

B99

Glenoe

A54

8

Newferry
Chesney's
Corner

B18

Kells

B53

Connor

A8

8

Beltoy

Ballycarry

Black Head

Moneyglass

B52

B93

Caddy

B53

B59

Ballynure

Ballycarry

B149

B90

Whitehead

Randalstown

Woodgreen

Ballyclare

B58

Straid

Kilroot

11

3

M22

Doagh

6

Woodburn

Eden

Stranraer
Douglas (seasonal)

Toomes

Shane's
Castle

Parkgate

6

B90

Carrickfergus

Staffordstown

5

Muckamore

Mossley

Greenisland

Mew Island

Cranfield
Church

Antrim

Dunadry

B95

Monkstown

Helen's
Bay

BANGOR

Groomsport

Copeland
Island

A26

Killead

A6

B56

5

BELFAST
LOUGH

Foreland Point

BELFAST
(ALDERGROVE)

Killealy

Mallusk

Newtownabbey

A48

Donaghadee

The Diamond

Aldergrove

A57

B39

Hyde
Park

Crawfordsburn

Conlig

Millisle

Ardmore Pt

Loanends

11

Holy-
wood

Ulster Folk
Transport Mus

A21

B172

Crumlin

Killead

A52

A52

Legoniel

B110

Abbey

8

NEWTOWNARDS

Gartree
Pt

Dundrod

B154

Stormont

10

B172

Glenavy

B38

B101

Dunmurry

Castlereagh

Dundonald

A20

Mount
Stewart

Ballyferis Point

Rams I

Stonyford

B154

Giant's
Ring

Comber

Carrowdore

Ardboe Point

Lennymore
Bay

Lambeg

Ballylesson

Moneyreagh

A21

Greyabbey

A2

Hog Park Pt

Aghalee

B104

A30

Carryduff

Ballygowan

A22

STRANGFORD

Ballywalter

Ardmore
Point

B156

Maghaberry

B178

11

Balligan

Oxford I

Aghagallon

A26

Drumbo

10

Ballyhalbert

Charlestown
or Bannfoot

B2

Mazetown

Ravernet

B178

Balloo

Kircubbin

18

Lady Bay

LISBURN

Boardmills

Killinchy

Glastry

Rubane

ARDS
PENINSULA

Moira

14

The
Temple

A21

Sketrick Castle

Portavogie

Lurgan

Magheralin

5

A24

B6

Saintfield

B7

Kirkistown

CRAIGAVON

Dollingstown

B178

21

Raffrey

Ardkeen

Cloghy

Scotch
Street

Kilntown

Hillsborough

B177

Derryboye

A20

A28

Waringstown

Donaghcloone

Ballykeel

The Cock

Shrigley

Audley's
Castle

A2

Portadown

Dromore

A26

DOWN

A1

Crossgar

B7

Killyleagh

Kearney Point

A50

B77

Ballynahinch

A24

Kilmore

A7

Castle Ward

Portaferry

TOWN PLANS AND LOCAL ROUTES

Roads and amenities for London and 134 cities, towns and ports in the British Isles

STREET PLANS FOR CITIES, *towns and ports show you where to find car parks, services and amenities, and indicate routes avoiding the centres. Most town plans follow alphabetically from page 378, but some appear alongside the relevant road maps between pages 33 and 352. Page numbers for all are listed below. For London*

and some major city areas there are local route maps in addition to street plans. There are also 11 plans of French, Belgian and Dutch ferry ports showing the distances to other major towns, and 10 plans of the major British airports with the most passenger traffic. All distances given in the margins of plans are in miles.

SYMBOLS USED ON PLANS AND LONDON ROUTE MAPS

P	Car park
WC	Public convenience
&	Public convenience with facilities for the disabled
i	Tourist information
P	24-hour petrol station
BUS	Bus station
POL	Police station
PO	Post office
⌂	Museum or art gallery
H	Hospital with casualty department
⊞	Swimming pool
☞	Theatre
⌘	Cinema
▭	Library

M 8	Motorway and number
limited access 22 / 22 full access	Motorway junction number
	Motorway under construction
A 7	Primary route
A 7	A road (non-primary)
	B road
	Minor road
←	One-way traffic
	Road with restricted access
	Road in tunnel
	Road under construction
	Ferry: vehicle; passengers only
	Railway and station
	Important building
	Park

SYMBOLS—ROUTE MAPS OUTSIDE LONDON

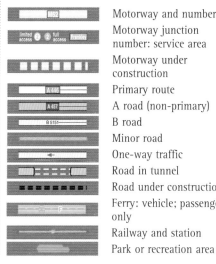

M62	Motorway and number
limited access 2 / 2 full access Frankley	Motorway junction number: service area
	Motorway under construction
A 446	Primary route
A 457	A road (non-primary)
B 5151	B road
	Minor road
←	One-way traffic
	Road in tunnel
	Road under construction
	Ferry: vehicle; passenger only
	Railway and station
	Park or recreation area

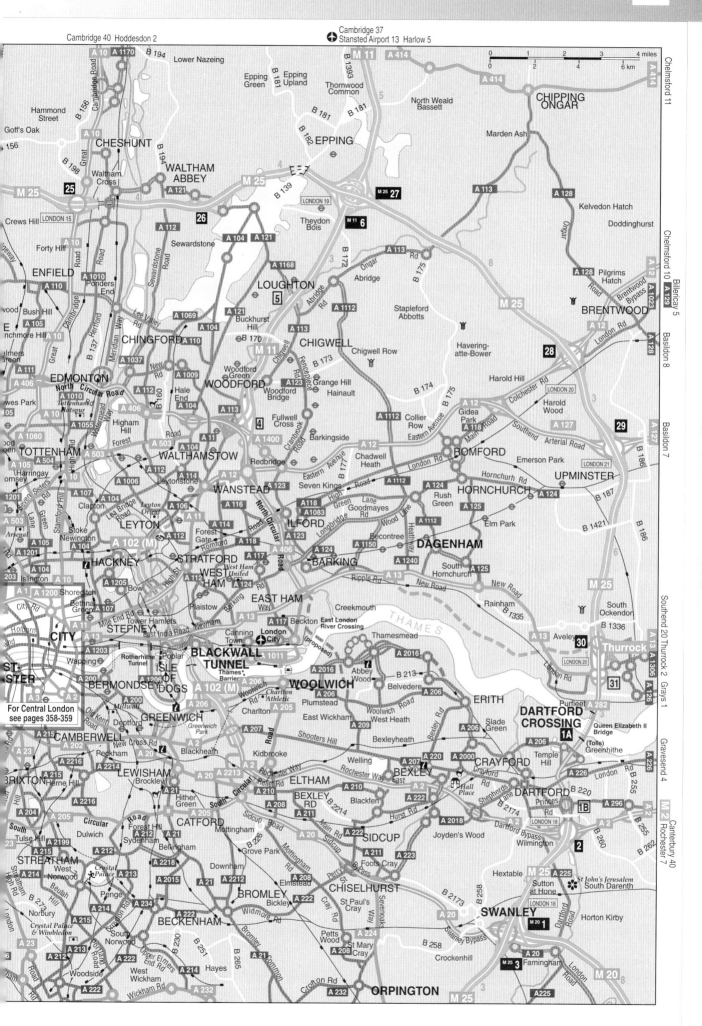

Harefield Northwood Hills PINNER Wealdstone KENTON HENDON Golders Green Highgate Archway A 504 A 1 A 1000
Chalfont Bypass Oxford 37 High Wycombe 13 Beaconsfield 5 South Harefield HARROW Harrow on the Hill Preston Brent Cross Shopping Centre Hendon Way Kenwood Hampstead Heath Tufnell
Denham Green RUISLIP Eastcote Rayners Lane Roxeth Sudbury WEMBLEY Wembley Stadium Neasden Cricklewood HAMPSTEAD Kentish Town Swiss Cottage
Gerrards Cross Denham Ickenham South Ruislip NORTHOLT Harlesden Kensal Green WILLESDEN KILBURN Maida Vale Regent's Park
UXBRIDGE HILLINGDON GREENFORD Perivale Alperton Park Royal Harrow Rd Maida Vale Notting Hill WESTWAY
Iver Heath Yeading EALING Hanger Lane Acton Rd HAMMERSMITH Bayswater Rd Hyde Park
Iver Wood End HAYES SOUTHALL Hanwell Uxbridge Road QPR CHISWICK Great West Rd FULHAM
Langley Yiewsley West Drayton Heston Cranford Osterley Park BRENTFORD Kew Syon House Mortlake BARNES WANDSWORTH Kings Road
Datchet Colnbrook Poyle Harmondsworth Bath Road Harlington Hounslow West Isleworth HOUNSLOW Syon House Fulham Palace Upper Richmond Rd South Circular Road PUTNEY
Heathrow Airport Terminals 1, 2 & 3 Cargo Terminal Terminal 4 East Bedfont Twickenham RICHMOND UPON THAMES Marble Hill East Sheen Roehampton Southfields Wimbledon
Horton Sunnymeads Wraysbury Southern Perimeter Rd Stanwell FELTHAM TWICKENHAM Ham Richmond Park Roehampton Vale Wimbledon Common Wimbledon
Windsor 3 Runnymede Stanwell Moor Rd ASHFORD Hanworth TEDDINGTON Ham House Strawberry Hill KINGSTON UPON THAMES WIMBLEDON MERTON MITCH
EGHAM Englefield Green STAINES Knowle Green Kingston Road Staines Road West Kempton Park Hampton Bushy Park Norbiton New Malden MITCHAM
Camberley 9 Thorpe Park Laleham Littleton SUNBURY Staines Rd East Hurst Road Hampton Court Palace SURBITON Morden Park St Helier CARSHALTON
Virginia Water CHERTSEY Shepperton West Molesey East Molesey Thames Ditton Long Ditton Worcester Park Stoneleigh SUTTON Cheam
Southampton 56 Basingstoke 25 Addlestone WALTON-ON-THAMES Sandown Park Chessington Kingston Bypass Hook EWELL Banstead
Chobham 1 WEYBRIDGE Hersham ESHER Claygate Chessington World of Adventures EPSOM Woodman Chipste
Row Town St George's Hill Claremont Fairmile Oxshott Ashtead Burgh Heath Kingswood
Woodham Byfleet Cobham Stoke D'Abernon Epsom Tadworth Kingswood
West Byfleet Sheerwater Pyrford RHS Wisley Garden Stoke Road LEATHERHEAD Fetcham Walton on the Hill Lower Kingswood
Horsell WOKING Kingfield Ockham Effingham East Horsley Mickleham Headley
Aldershot 11 Mayford Ripley Send Burntcommon Great Bookham Polesden Lacey Westhumble REIGATE
West Clandon Hatchlands West Horsley Guildford Road Buckland Betchworth
Portsmouth 53 Bellfields Jacobs Well Clandon Park Merrow Epson Road West St RED
GUILDFORD DORKING

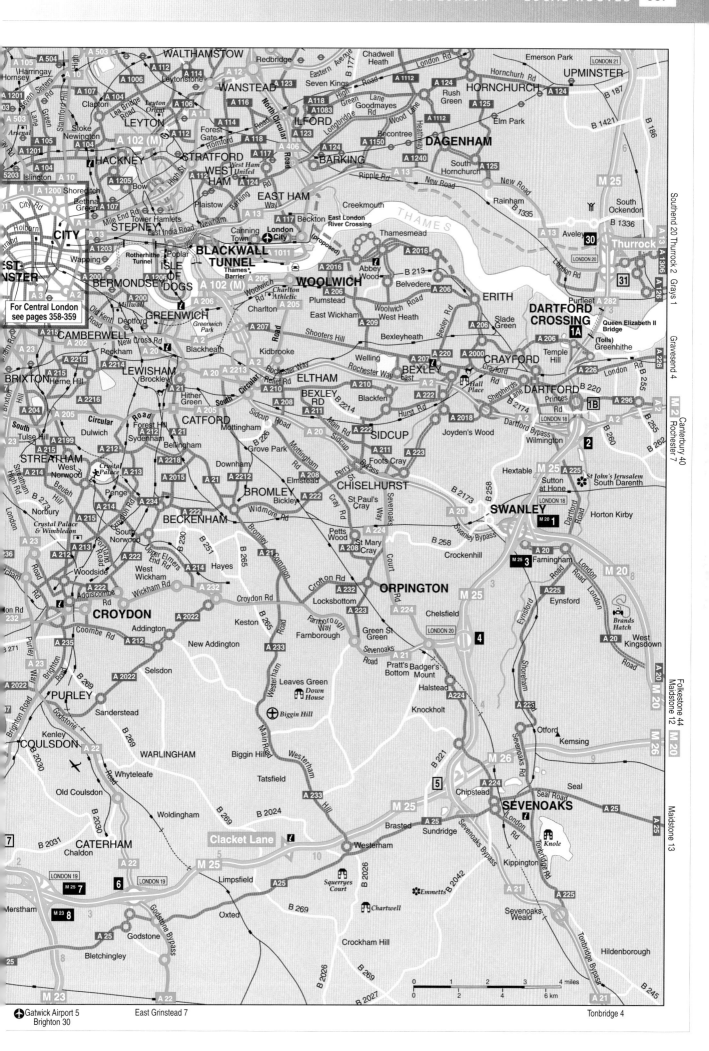

For Central London
see pages 358-359

Clacket Lane

Gatwick Airport 5
Brighton 30

East Grinstead 7

Tonbridge 4

N E London A 503 A 1(M) Hatfield A 1(M) Hatfield A 1(M) Hatfield A 1 Cambridge

A 5200 A 5203 M 1 A 1200 A 10

Goods Way KING'S CROSS HOXTON Geffrye Museum Hackney 1½ A 107

King's Cross Station Scala PENTONVILLE Pitfield St Hoxton Street Falkirk St Cremer A 1208

King's Cross Thameslink Sadlers Wells SHOREDITCH Columbia Rd A 107 Bethnal Green ½ A 1209

Camden Town Hall FINSBURY City University Moorfields Eye Hospital OLD STREET GREAT EASTERN STREET Westley's House BETHNAL GREEN RD A 1202 Cambridge M 11 A 12 A 11 A 13 Tilbury

Jewish Museum A 5200 Hol of Detention Lever Street Bath Street Luke St Worship Street Shoreditch SPITALFIELDS

Mount Pleasant Sorting Office A 5201 CLERKENWELL St John's Gate Exhibition Halls Tabernacle St Curtain Rd Broadgate Liverpool Street Stn Brushfield St Fashion St Brick Lane

Coram's Fields A 401 Farringdon Smithfield Mkt Long Lane Beech St Barbican Centre Broadgate COMMERCIAL STREET A 1202

Nat Hosp for Sick Children THEOBALD'S ROAD Gray's Inn Charterhouse St St Bartholomew's Hospital The Barbican Mus of London Moorgate Liverpool HOUNDSDITCH ALDGATE Aldgate East WHITECHAPEL HIGH ST

RUSSELL SQUARE BLOOMSBURY Cochrane A 401 Hatton Garden Holborn Circus City Thameslink Postal Mus Guildhall CITY Nat West Tower A 1202 MANSELL ST PRESCOT ST

British Museum HOLBORN Staple Inn Patent Office NEWGATE ST Central Criminal Court St Paul's Cathedral Cheapside Bank of England Stock Exchange Royal Exchange Leadenhall MINORIES ROYAL MINT ST

NEW OXFORD ST Chancery Lane Ludgate Hill St-Mary-le-Bow Bank Cornhill Lloyd's Fenchurch St Stn EAST SMITHFIELD A 1203

GILES HIGH ST KINGSWAY FLEET STREET St Bride's Queen Victoria Mansion House Fenchurch The Monument London Docklands

Royal Courts of Justice Temple Ave Blackfriars Cannon St Stn Eastcheap Tower Hill TOWER HILL St Katharine Docks

CHARING CROSS ROAD ALDWYCH STRAND The Temple Unilever Ho Mermaid UPPER THAMES ST Cannon St Stn Tower Hill Pageant Tower of London TOWER BRIDGE

Leicester Square Covent Garden Drury Lane Somerset House EMBANKMENT Blackfriars Stn Bankside Jetty Globe Clink Museum London Bridge Pool of London Tower Bridge Museum

National Portrait Gallery National Gallery TRAFALGAR Charing Cross Stn Royal National Theatre Upper Ground Bankside Power Stn (Disused) Shakespeare's Globe Exhibition Southwark Cathedral Hay's Galleria HMS Belfast Design Museum

NORTHUMBERLAND AVE WATERLOO BRIDGE Royal Festival Hall STAMFORD STREET A 3200 SOUTHWARK STREET A 300 Sumner St London Bridge Stn Britain at War Mus La Bramah Tea & Coffee Museum

WHITEHALL Jubilee Gardens YORK ROAD Cornwall Rd Roupell St A 201 Lavington St London Dungeon TOOLEY STREET Jamaica Rd A 100

Waterloo East Stn Young Vic Union Redcross Way Guy's Hospital ST THOMAS STREET DRUID ST A 200 Woolwich

VICTORIA Waterloo International Waterloo Station The Cut Suffolk Borough Snowsfields Weston BERMONDSEY JAMAICA RD

WESTMINSTER BRIDGE Westminster SOUTHWARK Webber Street LONG LANE Tanner Abbey Street

Houses of Parliament St Thomas's Hospital BOROUGH ROAD A 3202 Trinity St GREAT DOVER ST A 100 Grange Road Spa Road Deptford A 2206

Westminster Abbey A 3212 Broad Sanctuary WESTMINSTER BRIDGE ROAD ST GEORGE'S ROAD LONDON RD D.O.H. Harper Falmouth Rd DOVER ST Willow Walk

A 3036 Archbishop's Park South Bank University A 302 Elephant & Castle A 201 Southwark Park Rd

Victoria Tower Gardens Lambeth Palace KENNINGTON ROAD Imperial War Museum London College of Printing & Distributive Trades Elephant & Castle Stn NEW KENT ROAD OLD KENT ROAD

LAMBETH BRIDGE Mus of Garden History A 3203 Brook Drive NEWINGTON BUTTS Cuming Museum Rodney Road Mandela Way A 2206

Horseferry Rd LAMBETH NEWINGTON Heygate St WALWORTH Southwark Park Rd

Tate Gallery ALBERT EMBANKMENT Black Prince Rd A 23 KENNINGTON PARK ROAD A 3204 A 3 Thurlow Street Rolls Road

WESTMINSTER VAUXHALL Sancroft Street A 3204 A 23 Kennington Manor Place East Street

A 202 Glasshouse Walk A 3 A 215

A 3212 VAUXHALL BRIDGE Fitzalan St Wincott St A 3 Clayton St Canterbury Dover A 2

A 3036 A 203 HARLEYFORD RD KENNINGTON Cooks Rd Albany Road A 215

A 3 Guildford A 3 A 23 The Oval Kennington Park Oval A 202

A 3 Guildford Guildford A 3 A 23 A 20 A 2 Folkestone, Dover Camberwell Green ½ S E London A 2 Canterbury Dover

Scale:
0 220 440 660 880 yds
0 200 400 600 800 m

Oxford Street where marked is closed, except for buses and taxis, between 7am and 7pm, Monday-Saturday

□ Car park

For London route maps see pages 354-355 (North) and 356-357 (South)
For London West End map see pages 362-363
For London Docklands map see pages 366-367

For West End & South Bank see pages 362-363

A guide to places in Central London

COVERING AN AREA OF JUST 1 square mile (3 km²) north of the river, the City of London is the capital's legal and commercial hub. Ravaged by the Great Fire of 1666 and bombing in the Second World War, it still has many streets that follow medieval courses, and although remains of the walls, which date back to Roman times, are scant, their gateways live on in street names such as Moorgate and Ludgate. Christopher Wren (1632-1723) graced the City skyline with St Paul's Cathedral and dozens of distinctive churches, such as Fleet Street's St Bride's, with its 'wedding-cake' spire. Modern landmarks include the 600 ft (183 m) National Westminster Tower, the glass and aluminium Lloyd's Building and, outside the City area, the slender 619 ft (189 m) BT Tower. During the 18th and 19th centuries, elegant residential areas such as Bloomsbury, Belgravia and Marylebone, some with graceful squares, spread north and west of the City. The green expanses of Hyde Park, Kensington Gardens and Regent's Park provide spacious playgrounds for Londoners; the more compact Primrose Hill has a fine view over the capital.

PLACES OF INTEREST

Apsley House [C2] When the 'Iron Duke'—the first Duke of Wellington—lived in this mansion, built in 1771-8 by Robert Adam, it was known simply as 'Number One, London'. The house is now the Wellington Museum, and has personal relics of the Duke.

Bank of England [F3] Known as the 'Old Lady of Threadneedle Street', the Bank was founded in 1694 and is the central bank of the United Kingdom. Its role includes maintaining the value of the nation's currency and the stability of the financial system. It has in its museum a collection of banknotes spanning more than 300 years. Nearby is the Mansion House of 1739-53, the residence of the Lord Mayor of London.

The Barbican [E3] On the site of one of the city's ancient gates, the high-rise residential complex, with two towers more than 40 storeys high, was begun in 1963 on an area destroyed by Second World War bombing. It includes an arts centre—the home of the London Symphony Orchestra—as well as a conference centre and exhibition halls. Nearby are the Museum of London, overlooking a ruined Roman fort once on London's wall, and 16th-century St Giles Cripplegate church.

Bloomsbury [D3] The leafy squares and imposing terraces, many laid out by dukes of Bedford in the 18th and 19th centuries, have long been a haunt of London's intelligentsia. At the area's heart are London University and the British Museum, with its superb collections. Among former residents were the writer Virginia Woolf and the economist John Maynard Keynes; Charles Dickens once lived in Doughty Street—his house is now a museum.

Chelsea [B1] Blue plaques record the district's many famous past residents, among them artists Dante Gabriel Rossetti, Whistler and J M W Turner, writers Oscar Wilde and George Eliot, and the historian Thomas Carlyle. South of fashionable King's Road, with its boutiques and designer shops, is the Royal Hospital built by Christopher Wren in 1682-92; its 400 or so 'In-Pensioners', retired soldiers, wear long blue coats and tricorn hats—or scarlet coats on official occasions. Nearby are the National Army Museum and the Chelsea Physic Garden, set up in 1673 by the Worshipful Society of Apothecaries for the study and collection of medicinal plants.

Clerkenwell [E3] A maze of narrow streets is interrupted by the iron arcades of Smithfield meat market of 1868, and also the secluded churchyard of St Bartholomew the Great; within the church is the tomb of its founder, Rahere, who died in 1144. Spanning St John's Lane is the gatehouse of the former St John's Priory; it now houses the Museum of the Order of St John. Clerkenwell Green has been paved over for some 300 years but retains a village-like seclusion.

Geffrye Museum [F4] Housed in 14 single-storey almshouses of 1715, the museum has displays of English domestic interiors from Tudor times to the 20th century.

HMS Belfast [F2] Europe's largest surviving Second World War warship, the cruiser *Belfast* was launched in 1938. Now it is a floating museum permanently moored on the Thames. From the ship and adjacent Queen's Walk, there are fine views of Tower Bridge and the Tower of London.

Hyde Park and Kensington Gardens [AB2] Split almost in half by the Serpentine boating and swimming lake, these parks merge into one green expanse. At Speakers' Corner, anyone is free to hold forth on almost any subject—it is usually liveliest on Sunday mornings. Nearby stands Marble Arch, originally erected in front of Buckingham Palace in 1828. In Kensington Gardens, the Albert Memorial commemorates Queen Victoria's consort, Prince Albert. Kensington Palace was bought by William III as a royal residence in 1689; he wanted to get away from the damp riverside air of Whitehall Palace—at that time the official residence—most of which burned down in 1698.

Imperial War Museum [E2] Britain's involvement in the two 20th-century world wars forms the bulk of a large display within the museum—formerly the site of Bedlam asylum. The days of the Blitz and life in the trenches are re-created, and there are vivid paintings by war artists.

Lambeth Palace [D2] The official residence of archbishops of Canterbury for 800 years, the palace is sometimes open for tours. Nearby is the Church of St Mary Lambeth, now housing the Museum of Garden History.

Little Venice [A3] Poets Lord Byron and Robert Browning named this peaceful meeting point of the Regent and Grand Union canals. Narrowboat cruises run between here and Camden Lock, passing London Zoo.

London Dungeon [F2] Grisly sights and ghoulish tales await at this museum beneath London Bridge Station—London's oldest railway terminus. The Dungeon features instruments of torture and famous murders. Nearby is Winston Churchill's Britain at War, including re-creations of wartime shops and an air raid.

Madame Tussaud's [B3] Life-size wax figures at this museum, opened in 1802, include royalty, statesmen, sports stars and murderers. The Spirit of London is a fantasy 'taxi ride' through London's history. Nearby, the London Planetarium projects the night sky onto a dome.

The Monument [F3] Capped by a gilt urn, this slender column was built by Christopher Wren in 1671-7. Its height, 202 ft (62 m), equals its distance from the point in Pudding Lane where the Great Fire started in 1666, destroying much of London. Inside, 311 steps lead to a balcony that gives a splendid panorama of the City.

Regent's Park [B4] John Nash, the Regency architect, laid out the park, and the curving terrace of stucco-fronted houses that look onto it, in the early 19th century. The park has a boating lake and a summer open-air theatre. On its northern side it is bounded by Regent's Canal and London Zoo, founded in 1825.

St Paul's Cathedral [E3] Sir Christopher Wren's masterpiece, the domed Renaissance cathedral, 555 ft (169 m) long, was built after the Great Fire of 1666 had destroyed most of the city, including an earlier cathedral on the site. Grinling Gibbons carved the ornate choir stalls. In the Whispering Gallery, whispers carry across the 40 yd (37 m) width of the dome. The crypt has the tombs of Wren, Lord Nelson and the painter J M W Turner.

Shakespeare Globe Centre [E2] A replica of the thatched, and half-timbered Globe Theatre where Shakespeare's plays were performed in his lifetime stands near the original site. Built from traditional materials, it is the heart of an international theatre, education and exhibition centre planned for completion in 1999. The original Globe burnt down in 1613 after a stage cannon was fired during a performance of *Henry VIII*. A later theatre on the site was demolished in 1644.

South Kensington [A1] The Victorians' thirst for knowledge is reflected in the great museums founded here in the 19th century. The Science Museum has lively exhibits on power, space travel and British innovation, and the Natural History Museum explores all aspects of the natural world from insects to dinosaurs. A worldwide collection of art and applied arts can be seen at the Victoria and Albert Museum. The nearby Royal Albert Hall hosts the summer 'Proms', one of Europe's biggest classical music festivals.

Southwark Cathedral [F2] This imposing Gothic church, made a cathedral in 1905, dates mostly from the 13th century and has a superb 15th-century altar screen. Memorials include an oak effigy of a 13th-century knight, and there is a chapel to John Harvard, founder of Harvard University in the USA, who was baptised here.

Tate Gallery [D1] British and modern art is exhibited in this museum founded by the sugar merchant and philanthropist Henry Tate in 1897. Its collections include works by Turner, Hogarth, Reynolds, Rénoir and Degas.

Tower Bridge [F2] London's best-known Thames bridge was built in 1894. Its two neo-Gothic towers house the original machinery for raising the bridge for large shipping. Electric motors took over in 1976, but the old machinery is on display in the south tower; visitors can enjoy views from the high, windowed walkway between the towers.

Tower of London [F3] This magnificently preserved castle has guarded the Thames since William the Conqueror began it in the 11th century, and has been a palace as well as an execution site. The ancient White Tower is at its heart, and the Crown Jewels are in the modern Jewel House. The yeomen warders, or 'beefeaters', wear a uniform of the time of Henry VIII, and legend has it that if the resident ravens leave, the Tower will fall. Nearby is the church of All Hallows by the Tower, which is mainly of 12th-15th century date; a model of Roman London is on show in the undercroft. A more modern neighbour is Tower Hill Pageant museum, which offers a ride through 2000 years of London's history, depicted in tableaux.

Wallace Collection [B3] The 1st Marquess of Hertford began this collection of European art in the 18th century. Now in Hertford House, it was added to by later generations, among them Sir Richard Wallace, who brought his art treasures from France. The house has superb 18th-century French furniture and paintings, as well as *The Laughing Cavalier* painted in 1624 by Frans Hals.

Westminster Cathedral [C1] Red brick and stripes of white Portland stone distinguish the Byzantine exterior of this Roman Catholic cathedral of 1895-1903. In its Italianate bell tower, 284 ft (87 m) high, there is a lift to a viewing point. In the cathedral interior there are marble facings, dazzling mosaics and stone carvings of 1913-18 by Eric Gill.

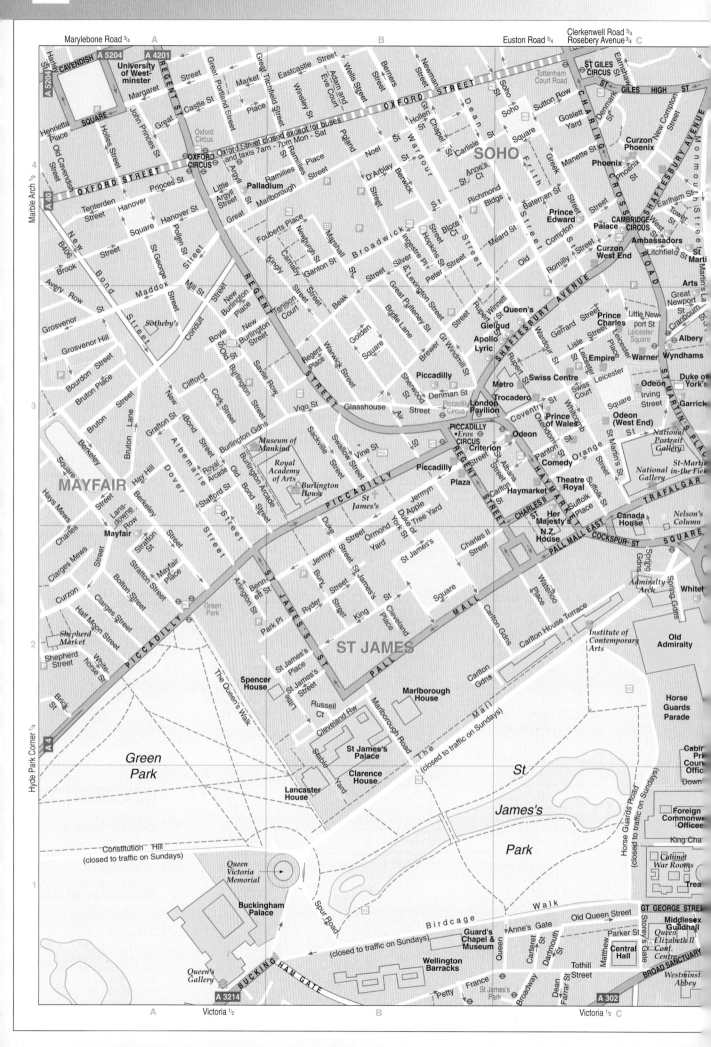

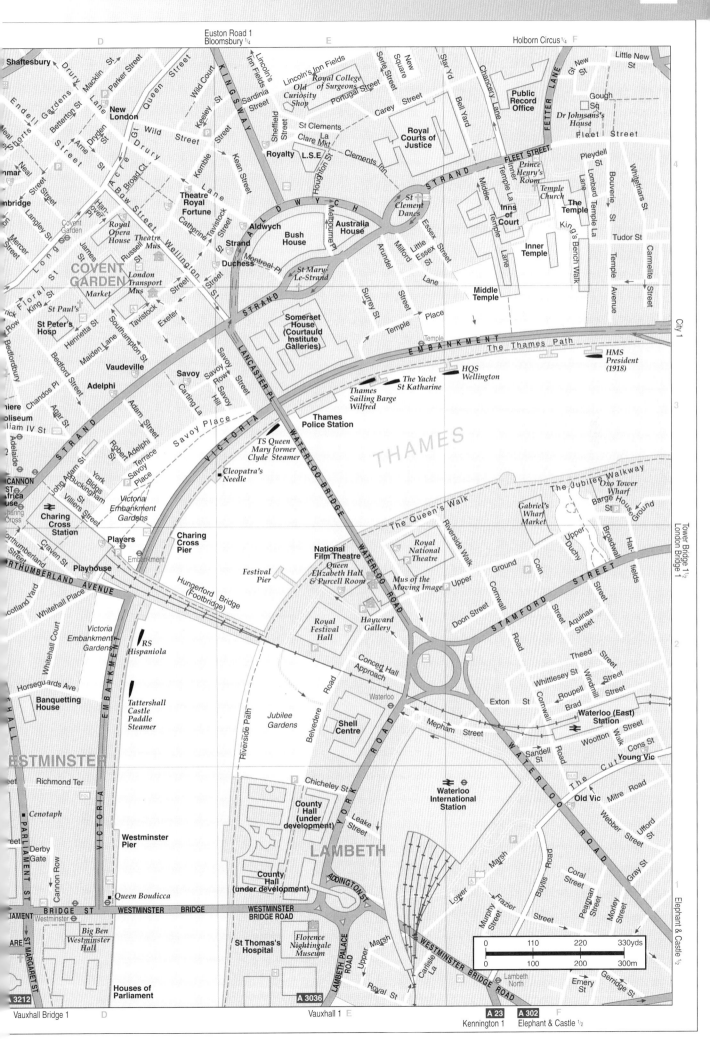

Euston Road 1
Bloomsbury ¼

Holborn Circus ¼

Shaftesbury
Drury Lane
Macklin St.
Parker Street
Wild Court
Queen Street
Wild Street

Lincoln's Inn Fields
Lincoln's Inn
Sardinia Street
Portugal Street
Old Curiosity Shop
Royal College of Surgeons
New Square
Serle Street
Star Yd
Carey Street
Bell Yard
Chancery Lane
Public Record Office
Fetter Lane
Gough Sq
Gt New St
Little New St
Dr Johnsan's House
Fleet Street

New London
Betterton St.
Endell Gardens
Shorts
Neal
St
Street
mbridge Street
Dryden St.
Arne Street
Kemble
Kean Street
Sheffield Street
St Clements La
Clare Mkt
Clements Inn
Carey Street

Royalty
L.S.E.
Clements Inn

Royal Courts of Justice
Temple La
Inner Temple La
Prince Henry's Room
Pleydell St
Bouverie St
Whitefriars St
Temple Church
The Temple

Fleet Street
Strand
Inner Temple
King's Bench Walk
Tudor St
Carmelite Street

Theatre Royal Fortune
Catherine
Tavistock St
Wellington
Aldwych
Bush House
Australia House
St Clement Danes
Essex Street
Middle Temple La
Inns of Court

Covent Garden
Royal Opera House
Theatre Mus
Russell Street
Strand
Duchess
Melbourne Pl
Montreal Pl
Arundel St
Millord
Little Essex St
Essex Street
Inner Temple
Temple Avenue

COVENT GARDEN
London Transport Mus
Tavistock St
Exeter St
Duchess
St Mary Le-Strand
Surrey St
Middle Temple
Temple Avenue

Floral St
King St
St Paul's
Southampton St
Wellington St
Strand
Temple Place
Temple

St Peter's Hosp
Henrietta St
Maiden Lane
Somerset House (Courtauld Institute Galleries)
Temple Place

Vaudeville
Adam Street
Savoy
Savoy Row
Savoy Hill
Carting La
EMBANKMENT
The Thames Path
HMS President (1918)

Adelphi
Robert Adelphi
Savoy Place
Savoy Place
HQS Wellington

Chandos Pl
niere
oliseum
iliam IV St
Adelaide
John Adam St
Villiers Street
York Bldgs
Victoria Embankment Gardens
VICTORIA
WATERLOO BRIDGE
The Yacht St Katharine
Thames Sailing Barge Wilfred
Thames Police Station

CANNON ST
Africa use
aring oss
Charing Cross Station
Buckingham
Craven St
Players
Charing Cross Pier
TS Queen Mary former Clyde Steamer
Cleopatra's Needle

RTHUMBERLAND AVENUE
Northumberland Street
Playhouse
Hungerford Bridge (Footbridge)
Festival Pier
National Film Theatre
Queen Elizabeth Hall & Purcell Room
Mus of the Moving Image
Royal National Theatre
Riverside Walk
THAMES
The Jubilee Walkway
Oxo Tower Wharf
Barge House Ground

The Queen's Walk
Gabriel's Wharf Market
Upper Ground
Broadwall
Hatfields

cotland Yard
Whitehall Place
Victoria Embankment Gardens
RS Hispaniola
Royal Festival Hall
Hayward Gallery
Upper Ground
Coin Street
Cornwall Road
STAMFORD STREET
Aquinas Street

Horseguards Ave
Banquetting House
EMBANKMENT
Tattershall Castle Paddle Steamer
WATERLOO ROAD
Concert Hall Approach
Doon Street
Theed Street

ESTMINSTER
Victoria Embankment Gardens
Riverside Path
Jubilee Gardens
Shell Centre
Waterloo
Whittlesey St
Roupell St
Windmill
Cornwall
Waterloo (East) Station
Exton St
Brad
Sandell
Wootton
Cons St
Young Vic

Richmond Ter
Cenotaph
Belvedere Road
Chicheley St
County Hall (under development)
Waterloo International Station
Old Vic
Mitre Road
Webber Street
Ufford St

PARLIAMENT ST
Derby Gate
VICTORIA EMBANKMENT
Westminster Pier
Queen Boudicca
County Hall (under development)
LAMBETH
YORK ROAD
Leake Street
ADDINGTON ST
Lower Marsh
Frazier Street
Baylis Road
Coral Street
Gray St

BRIDGE ST
WESTMINSTER BRIDGE
WESTMINSTER BRIDGE ROAD
Big Ben
Westminster Hall
Florence Nightingale Museum
LAMBETH PALACE ROAD
Lambeth North
Peagram Street
Morley Street
Gerridge St

ST MARGARET ST
3212
Houses of Parliament
St Thomas's Hospital
Upper Marsh
Royal St
Carlisle La
WESTMINSTER BRIDGE ROAD
Emery St

Vauxhall Bridge 1
Vauxhall 1
A 3036
A 23 Kennington 1
A 302 Elephant & Castle ½

City 1
Tower Bridge 1½
London Bridge 1
Elephant & Castle ½

| 0 | 110 | 220 | 330yds |
| 0 | 100 | 200 | 300m |

A guide to the West End and South Bank

SEVERAL DISTINCT AREAS make up London's West End. Theatres, cinemas and restaurants radiate from the grandeur of Trafalgar Square and Nelson's Column along Haymarket and Shaftesbury Avenue, and round Leicester Square and Piccadilly Circus. Piccadilly, home of Burlington Arcade and the Ritz, is flanked to the south by exclusive St James, with gentlemen's clubs, foreign embassies and St James's Palace, and to the north by prosperous Mayfair round Curzon Street and Berkeley Square. Soho lies north of Shaftesbury Avenue and Chinatown south; east is the shopping and recreational area of Covent Garden, where entertainment ranges from grand opera to street performers in its elegant piazza.

From Admiralty Arch, The Mall leads beside St James's Park to the Queen's London home, Buckingham Palace. Britain's Parliament building, the Palace of Westminster, with its clock tower and the bell known as Big Ben, rises in majestic splendour by the Thames. Across the Thames at Waterloo is the South Bank Arts Centre, where places of entertainment include the Royal Festival Hall and the Royal National Theatre.

PLACES OF INTEREST

Buckingham Palace [A1]
The Queen's residence, where the ceremony of Changing the Guard can be seen daily, was originally a house built in 1703 for the Duke of Buckingham. Bought in 1762 by George III, it was transformed into a palace by John Nash in the 1820s and Edward Blore in 1847. The Portland stone façade was added in 1913. Most of the state apartments are open to visitors in August and September, including the throne room and the superb picture gallery, which includes paintings by Dürer, Rubens, Canaletto and Rembrandt.

Cabinet War Rooms [C1] In a basement beneath the Cabinet Office, 21 rooms survive of 100 or more used as a central planning headquarters during the Second World War. The rooms on view include the Cabinet Room, the Transatlantic Telephone Room, from which Churchill spoke to President Roosevelt in the White House, and Churchill's bedroom.

Cleopatra's Needle [E3] A granite obelisk of about 1475 BC, brought from Egypt and erected in 1878, the 60 ft (18 m) Needle is flanked by two bronze Victorian sphinxes of 1882. It stands on the Victoria Embankment of 1870, which runs alongside the River Thames between Westminster and Blackfriars bridges. The statue on the north end of Westminster Bridge is of Queen Boudicca.

Courtauld Institute Galleries [E3] Housed in the neoclassical Somerset House of 1777-86 is a fine collection of paintings, with many French Impressionists and post-Impressionists among them. The house's splendid frontage stretches beside the Thames for some 200 yd (183 m), and it has two immense wings added in the 19th century. To the west is the luxurious Savoy Hotel of 1889, which includes the Savoy Theatre with a superb Art Deco interior.

Covent Garden [D4] Fashionable shops and restaurants line the restored neoclassical piazza, opened in 1980. There has been an opera house on the site of the Royal Opera House since 1732, but the present building dates from 1860. A market for 300 years until 1974, the central market building of 1830 replaced a 17th-century design by Inigo Jones. The Palladian St Paul's Church—also by Jones—is known as 'the actors' church' and has memorials to artists and actors. A Theatre Museum and the Theatre Royal, Drury Lane, are nearby.

Lincoln's Inn Fields [E4] This square laid out in 1618 by Inigo Jones has a park-like atmosphere. A plaque in the central pavilion marks the place where William, Lord Russell was beheaded in 1683 for plotting to assassinate Charles II. The fine Royal College of Surgeons of 1813-37 is on the south side. Sir John Soane's Museum, an eccentric private

collection of 1813, is on the north side. On the east is Lincoln's Inn, one of four Inns of Court where barristers have worked since the 14th century—the others are the Middle Temple, Inner Temple and Gray's Inn. Close by are the Royal Courts of Justice of 1882.

Mayfair [A2/3] A May Fair held here annually from 1688 until the mid 18th century gives this area its name. The site of the fair is now Shepherd Market of 1735, a charming maze of streets with 19th-century shops and houses. One of the finest of Mayfair's elegant 18th century squares and streets is Berkeley Square; Queen Elizabeth II was born in 1926 just off the square at 17 Bruton Street, now part of Berkeley Square House. Prime Minister Benjamin Disraeli died nearby at 19 Curzon Street in 1881.

Piccadilly Circus [B3] At the heart of the West End, the circus is famed for its statue of 1893, known as Eros, and its dazzle of neon signs. Branching off are Haymarket and Shaftesbury Avenue with their theatres and Piccadilly with its clubs, hotels and splendid shops, including Fortnum and Mason's grocery store and Hatchard's bookshop, both of the 18th century. The Quadrant—the elegant curve of Regent Street leading to Oxford Circus—was designed by John Nash in the 1820s, and rebuilt 1898-1928. East from the circus is the Trocadero entertainment complex of 1984 and Leicester Square, flanked by cinemas.

Royal Academy [B3] Burlington House has been the home of the Royal Academy of Arts, founded in 1768 by Sir Joshua Reynolds, since 1869, when the original 17th-century house was enlarged. New galleries were added in 1991. Regular exhibitions are held, and the annual Summer Exhibition is devoted to new art not previously displayed in public.

St Clement Danes [E4] Famous in song for its bells–'Oranges and lemons, say the bells of St Clement's'–this Wren church of 1682 on an island flanked on both sides by the Strand is now the headquarters church of the Royal Air Force. Eastwards lies Temple Bar, a boundary between the cities of Westminster and London, and Fleet Street—the home of national newspapers from 1702 to the 1980s.

St James's Palace [B2] Of the palace built by Henry VIII in 1532, only parts remain, including the Chapel Royal in the Ambassadors' Court. Nearby are Clarence House, a mansion of 1825-8 that is the

residence of the Queen Mother, and Marlborough House of 1711, now housing the Commonwealth Secretariat. Nearby are Pall Mall, which takes its name from a type of croquet, 'pall-mall', played there in the 17th century, and The Athenaeum club founded in 1830.

Savile Row [AB3] Fine tailors have worked in Savile Row since the 1850s–Henry Poole was tailor to Napoleon III. In 1969 the Beatles gave a concert from the roof of 3 Savile Row; this concert appeared in the film *Let It Be*. In adjoining Burlington Gardens, a splendid Italianate building of 1867 is the home of the Museum of Mankind–the ethnographic collection of the British Museum.

Soho [BC4] Cosmopolitan Soho is known for its many restaurants of all nationalities and its clubs, delicatessen shops and fruit and vegetable markets such as Rupert Street and Berwick Street. Soho Square, which was laid out in 1681, is a centre of the British music industry; music venues include Ronnie Scott's Jazz Club. Wardour Street and Golden Square are home to several major film companies. On the eastern border lies Charing Cross Road, with its many bookshops, among them Foyles, founded in 1904. The Chinese quarter lies to the south, centred on Gerrard Street.

South Bank Arts Centre [E2] Developed on the site of the Festival of Britain in 1951, the South Bank has three concert halls–including the Royal Festival Hall–and also the Royal National Theatre, the National Film Theatre, the Museum of the Moving Image and the Hayward Gallery, all linked by a riverside path. Close by is County Hall of 1932, the former headquarters of the Greater London Council.

Strand [D3-F4] Linking the City with Westminster, the Strand, one of London's busiest streets, ran right beside the Thames until the Victoria Embankment was built in 1864-70. At its west end is the fine neo-Gothic Charing Cross Station of 1864; the cross in its forecourt is a replica of one of 12 crosses erected by Edward I in the 13th century in memory of his wife, Eleanor of Castile. The splendid neoclassical Church of St Mary-le-Strand of 1714 by James Gibbs, with its graceful steeple, stands on a traffic island.

Trafalgar Square [C2/3] At the centre of the square is Nelson's Column of 1843, 187 ft (57 m) high. At its base are four bronze lions of 1867 by Edwin Landseer, and fountains constructed in 1939. Grand buildings include

South Africa House and Canada House, as well as the National Gallery of 1838, with a wing of 1991, and the National Portrait Gallery. St Martin-in-the-Fields, a church of 1726 by James Gibbs, in 1924 held the first religious service to be broadcast on radio.

Westminster [CD1/2] Rising above the neo-Gothic Houses of Parliament of 1860 is the 320 ft (98 m) clock tower housing the bell Big Ben. Nearby Westminster Abbey, 13th-16th century, is the scene of coronations–the oak Coronation Chair, with the Stone of Scone, dates from about 1300. There are more than 600 tombs and monuments, and among those buried in Poets' Corner is Geoffrey Chaucer (1343-1400).

Whitehall [CD2] An archway guarded by mounted sentries leads to Horse Guards Parade. Opposite is the fine Banqueting House of 1619-22 by Inigo Jones, a relic of Whitehall Palace where Charles I was executed in 1649.

STREET INDEX

The map reference in bold after each entry identifies the grid square in which it appears on pages 362-3

Broadwall **F2**
Broadway **C1**
Broadwick Street **B4**
Brook Street **A4**
Bruton Lane **A3**
Bruton Place **A3**
Bruton Street **A3**
Buckingham Gate **A1-B1**
Buckingham Street **D3**
Burlington Arcade **A3-B3**
Burlington Gardens **A3-B3**
Bury Street **B2**
Cambridge Circus **C4**
Cannon Row **D1**
Carey Street **E4**
Carlisle Lane **E1**
Carlisle Street **B4**
Carlton Gardens **B2**
Carlton House Terrace **C2**
Carlton Street **C3**
Carmelite Street **F4**
Carnaby Street **B3-B4**
Carteret Street **C1**
Carting Lane **D3**
Catherine Street **D4**
Cavendish Square **A4**
Chancery Lane **F4**
Chandos Place **D3**
Charing Cross Road **C4**
Charles II Street **B2**
Charles Street **A2-A3**
Chicheley Street **E1**
Clare Market **E4**
Clarges Mews **A2**
Clarges Street **A2**
Clements Inn **E4**
Cleveland Place **B2**
Cleveland Row **B2**
Clifford Street **A3**
Cockspur Street **C2**
Coin Street **F2**
Concert Hall Approach **E2**
Conduit Street **A3-A4**
Cons Street **F2**
Constitution Hill **A1**
Coral Street **F1**
Cork Street **A3**
Cornwall Road **F2**
Coventry Street **C3**
Cranbourn Street **C3**
Craven Street **D2**
Curzon Street **A2**
D'Arblay Street **B4**
Dartmouth Street **C1**
Dean Farrar Street **C1**
Dean Street **B4-C4**
Denman Street **B3**
Denmark Street **C4**
Derby Gate **D1**
Doon Street **F2**
Dover Street **A2-A3**
Downing Street **C1-D1**
Drury Lane **D4**
Dryden Street **D4**
Duchy Street **F2**
Duke of York Street **B2-B3**
Duke Street St James's **B2-B3**
Duncannon Street **D3**
Earlham Street **C4**
Earnshaw Street **C4**
Eastcastle Street **B4**
Emery Street **F1**
Endell Street **D4**
Essex Street **E4**
Exeter Street **D3-D4**
Exton Street **F2**
Fetter Lane **F4**
Fleet Street **F4**
Floral Street **D3-D4**
Foubert's Place **A4-B4**
Frazier Street **F1**
Frith Street **C4**
Ganton Street **B4**

Garrick Street **D3**
Gerrard Street **C3**
Gerridge Street **F1**
Glasshouse Street **B3**
Golden Square **B3**
Goslett Yard **C4**
Gough Square **F4**
Grafton Street **A3**
Gray Street **F1**
Great Castle Street **A4**
Great Chapel Street **B4**
Great George Street **C1**
Great Marlborough Street **A4-B4**
Great Newport Street **C3**
Great New Street **F4**
Great Portland Street **A4**
Great Pulteney Street **B3-B4**
Great Queen Street **D4**
Great Scotland Yard **D2**
Great Titchfield Street **A4-B4**
Great Windmill Street **B3**
Greek Street **C4**
Grosvenor Hill **A3**
Grosvenor Street **A3**
Half Moon Street **A2**
Hanover Place **D4**
Hanover Square **A4**
Hanover Street **A4**
Harley Street **A5**
Hatfields **F2**
Hay Hill **A3**
Haymarket **C3**
Hays Mews **A3**
Henrietta Place **A4**
Henrietta Street **D3**
Hollen Street **B4**
Holles Street **A4**
Hopkins Street **B4**
Horseguards Avenue **D2**
Horse Guards Road **C1**
Houghton Street **E4**
Hungerford Bridge **D2-E2**
Ingestre Place **B4**
Inner Temple Lane **F4**
Irving Street **C3**
James Street **D4**
Jermyn Street **B2-B3**
John Adam Street **D3**
John Princes Street **A4**
Kean Street **E4**
Keeley Street **D4-E4**
Kemble Street **D4-E4**
King Charles Street **C1-D1**
Kingly Street **A4-B3**
King Street, Covent Garden **D3**
King Street, St James **B2**
King's Bench Walk **F4**
Kingsway **E4**
Lambeth Palace Road **E1**
Lancaster Place **E3**
Langley Street **D4**
Lansdowne Row **A3**
Leake Street **E1**
Leicester Place **C3**
Leicester Square **C3**
Leicester Street **C3**
Lexington Street **B3-B4**
Lichfield Street **C4**
Lincoln's Inn Fields **E4**
Lisle Street **C3**
Little Argyle Street **A4**
Little Essex Street **E4**
Little Newport Street **C3**
Little New Street **F4**
Little St James's Street **B2**
Lombard Lane **F4**
Long Acre **D4**
Lower Marsh **E1-F1**
Macklin Street **D4**
Maddox Street **A3-A4**
Maiden Lane **D3**
Manette Street **C4**
Margaret Street **A4**

Market Place **A4**
Marlborough Road **B2**
Marshall Street **B4**
Mathew Parker Street **C1**
Mayfair Place **A2**
Meard Street **C4**
Melbourne Place **E4**
Mepham Street **E2-F2**
Mercer Street **C4-D4**
Middle Temple Lane **F4**
Milford Lane **E4**
Mill Street **A3**
Mitre Road **F1**
Monmouth Street **C4**
Montreal Place **E4**
Morley Street **F1**
Murphy Street **F1**
Neal Street **C4-D4**
New Bond Street **A3**
Newburgh Street **B4**
New Burlington Place **A3**
New Burlington Street **A3**
New Compton Street **C4**
Newman Street **B4**
New Row **D3**
New Square **E4**
Noel Street **B4**
Northumberland Ave **C2-D2**
Northumberland Street **D2**
Old Bond Street **A3**
Old Burlington Street **A3**
Old Cavendish Street **A4**
Old Compton Street **C4**
Old Queen Street **C1**
Orange Street **C3**
Ormond Yard **B2**
Oxendon Street **C3**
Oxford Circus **A4**
Oxford Street **A4-C4**
Pall Mall **B2-C2**
Pall Mall East **C2-C3**
Panton Street **C3**
Parker Street **D4**
Park Place **A2-B2**
Parliament Square **C1-D1**
Parliament Street **D1**
Pearman Street **F1**
Peter Street **B4**
Petty France **B1**
Phoenix Street **C4**
Piccadilly **A2-B3**
Piccadilly Circus **B3**
Pleydell Street **F4**
Poland Street **B4**
Pollen Street **A4**
Portugal Street **E4**
Princes Street **A4**
Queen Anne's Gate **C1**
Ramillies Place **B4**
Ramillies Street **B4**
Regent Place **B3**
Regent Street **A4-B3**
Richmond Buildings **B4-C4**
Richmond Terrace **D1**
Robert Street **D3**
Romilly Street **C4**
Roupell Street **F2**
Royal Arcade **A3**
Royal Street **E1**
Rupert Street **B3-C3**
Russell Court **B2**
Russell Street **D4**
Ryder Street **B2**
Sackville Street **B3**
Sardinia Street **E4**
St Alban's Street **C3**
St Anne's Court **B4**
St Clement's Lane **E4**
St George Street **A3-A4**
St Giles Circus **C4**
St Giles High Street **C4**
St James's Place **B2**
St James's Square **B2**

St James's Street **A2-B2**
St Margaret Street **D1**
St Martin's Lane **C3**
St Martin's Place **C3-C4**
St Martin's Street **C3**
Sandell Street **F2**
Sardinia Street **E5**
Saville Row **A3-B3**
Savoy Hill **D3-E3**
Savoy Place **D3-E3**
Savoy Row **D3-E3**
Savoy Street **D3-E3**
Searle Street **E4**
Shaftesbury Avenue **B3-C4**
Sheffield Street **E4**
Shelton Street **C4-D4**
Shepherd Street **A2**
Sherwood Street **B3**
Shorts Gardens **C4-D4**
Silver Place **B4**
Soho Square **C4**
Soho Street **C4**
Southampton Street **D3**
Spring Gardens **C2**
Spur Road **B1**
Stable Yard **B1-B2**
Stafford Street **A3**
Stamford Street **F2**
Star Yard **E4-F4**
Storey's Gate **C1**
Strand **D3-E3**
Stratton Street **A2**
Suffolk Place **C3**
Surrey Street **E3-E4**
Sutton Row **C4**
Swallow Street **B3**
Swiss Court **C3**
Tavistock Street **D3-D4**
Temple Avenue **F3-F4**
Temple Lane **F4**
Temple Place **E3-F3**
Tenison Court **B3**
Tenterden Street **A4**

Theed Street **F2**
The Cut **F1-F2**
The Mall **B1-C2**
The Queen's Walk **A2-B1**
Tothill Street **C1**
Tower Street **C4**
Trafalgar Square **C2-C3**
Tudor Street **F4**
Ufford Street **F1**
Upper Ground **E2-F2**
Upper Marsh **E1**
Upper St Martin's Lane **C3-C4**
Victoria Embankment **D1-F3**
Vigo Street **B3**
Villiers Street **D2-D3**
Vine Street **B3**
Wardour Street **B4-C3**
Warwick Street **B3**
Waterloo Bridge **E3**
Waterloo Place **C2**
Waterloo Road **E2**
Webber Street **F1**
Wellington Street **D4-E3**
Wells Street **B4**
Westminster Bridge **D1**
Westminster Bridge Road **E1**
West Street **C4**
Whitcombe Street **C3**
Whitefriars Street **F4**
Whitehall **C2-D2**
Whitehall Court **D2**
Whitehall Place **D2**
Whitehorse Street **A2**
Whittlesey Street **F2**
Wild Court **D4**
Wild Street **D4**
William IV Street **C3-D3**
Windmill Walk **F2**
Winnet Street **B3-C3**
Winsley Street **B4**
Wooton Street **F2**
York Buildings **D3**
York Road **E1-E2**

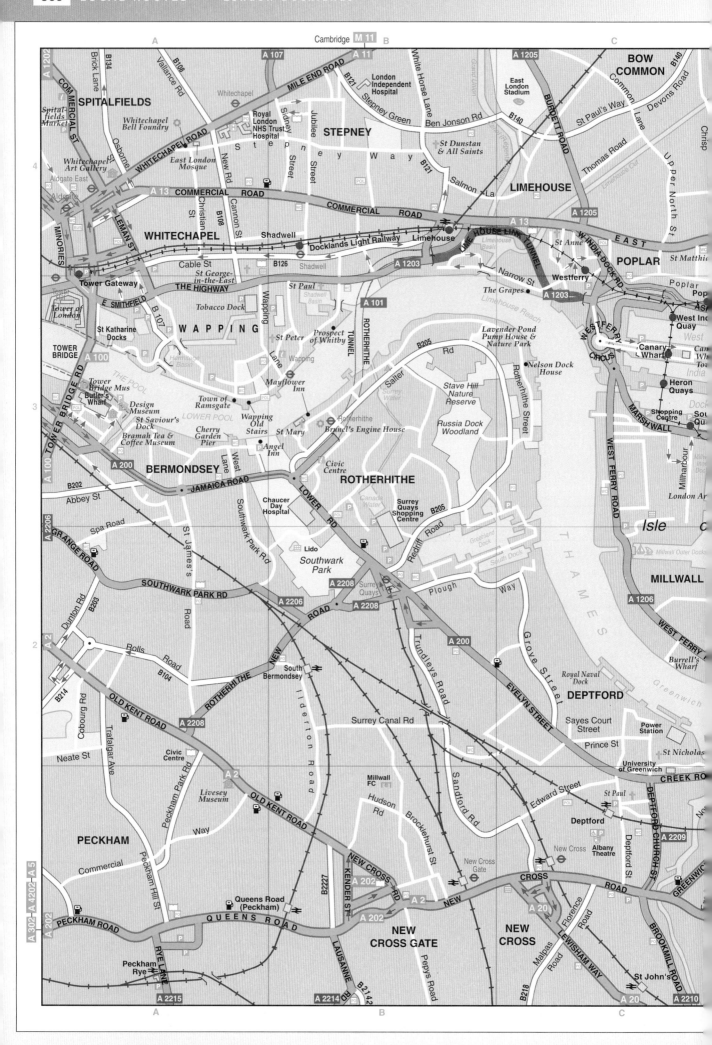

A 102(M) A 12 Chelmsford

Tilbury
Dagenham

A 102

BLACKWALL TUNNEL NORTHERN APPROACH

B164 Stephenson St

MANOR ROAD

A 1011

BARKING ROAD

A 124

New Barn St

Cumberland Rd

Pulpit Pl

A 112

Tilbury
Dagenham

A 13

NEWHAM WAY

Tollgate Road

Terrance McMillan Stadium

Lido

CUSTOM HOUSE

Stansfield

King George V Park

Road

Abbott Rd

Canning Town

A 13

DOCK ROAD

LEAMOUTH ROAD

SILVERTOWN

Docklands Light Railway

Financial Times Building

SOUTH BROMLEY

LOWER LEA CROSSING

East India Dock

CANNING TOWN

Freemasons Road

PRINCE REGENT LANE

All Saints

East India

Blackwall

A 1261

LEAMOUTH

A 1020

Victoria Dock Road

Royal Victoria

Custom House

Prince Regent

A 1020

Royal Albert

gh St

Blackwall Reach

WAY

A 112

Royal Albert Dock

Royal Victoria Dock

London City Airport

llingsgate sh Market

PRESTON'S ROAD

BLACKWALL TUNNEL

Blackwall Basin

Poplar Dock

A 1011

NORTH WOOLWICH ROAD

ALBERT RD

Tilbury Dagenham

A 1011

A 13

Coldharbour

The Gun

THAMES

Pontoon Dock

SILVERTOWN

Silvertown & London City Airport

Storm Water Pumping Station

A 102

Tunnel Avenue

Lyle Park

THAMES BARRIER

RSH WALL

East Ferry Rd

A 1206

Docklands Visitor Centre

Crossharbour

CUBBITT TOWN

MANCHESTER ROAD

Bugsby's Reach

A 206

A 282

M 25

Dogs

Superstore

Mudchute Farm

Tunnel Avenue

BLACKWALL LANE

BUGSBY'S WAY

Anchor and Hope Lane

Lombard Wall

La

NEW CHARLTON

Eastmoor St

WOOLWICH ROAD

Charlton Lane

Thornttree Rd

Mudchute

Dockands Light Railway

Millwall Park

BLACKWALL TUNNEL

A 102(M)

BUGSBY'S WAY

Superstore

A 206

Horn

Island Gardens

A 2203

Tunnel Ave

Charlton

Charlton Athletic FC

Charlton Church La

Pelton Road

WOOLWICH ROAD

Yacht Tavern

Cutty Sark Tavern

Ballast Quay

Trafalgar Tavern

Greenwich Foot Tunnel

Greenwich Pier

Greenwich District Hospital

East Greenwich Pleasaunce

Westcombe Park

SOUTHERN APPROACH

The Village

CHARLTON

Charlton Park Rd

Reach

Gipsy Moth IV

Royal Naval College

Cutty Sark

TRAFALGAR ROAD

Vanbrugh Hill

Charlton House

Canberra Road

Greenwich Market

ROMNEY RD

Maze Hill

Maze Hill

Hornfair Rd

Charlton Park La

A 200

St Alfege with St Peter

National Maritime Museum

Park Vista

Vanbrugh Castle

Westcombe Road

Charlton Road

reenwich

Fan Museum

Dreadnought Seamen's Hospital

Greenwich Theatre

GREENWICH

Old Royal Observatory

The Avenue

Greenwich Park

Old Dover Rd

GH

06

Crooms Hill

Hyde Vale

Ranger's House

The Wilderness

Charlton Way

Strathden Road

A 2

SHOOTERS HILL ROAD

A 207

A 2

SHOOTERS

Chesterfield Walk

Blackheath Gate

HILL

Prince Charles Road

Long Pond Road

Prince of Wales Road

St Germans's Place

Kidbrooke Gdns

KIDBROOKE

ROCHESTER WAY RELIEF ROAD

Blackheath

Hare and Billet Road

Wat Tyler Road

ROAD

B212

South Row

Morden College

KIDBROOKE PARK RD

A 2213

LEWISHAM ROAD

BLACKHEATH

A 2211 A 20 M 20 Channel Tunnel, Folkstone

M 25

A 2 M 2 Canterbury Dover

0	220	440	660	880 yds
0	200	400	600	800 m

Docklands Light Railway Station

A guide to London's Docklands

B RITAIN'S TALLEST BUILDING—the Canary Wharf tower, also known as One Canada Square—looms to a height of 800 ft (244 m) above part of a huge system of docks that in the 19th century made London the world's largest port. After the 1960s the quays and wharves fell into disuse, but they took on a new life in the 1980s as a business and leisure centre. Warehouses were restored, marinas opened and offices and houses built. Billingsgate Fish Market moved from the City to West India Docks in 1982, the Thames Barrier—London's flood shield—was completed in 1983, the Docklands Light Railway opened in 1987; and the London Arena concert hall seating 12 500 opened in 1989.

From the railway terminus at Island Gardens there are views across the Thames to Greenwich, London's historic maritime centre, which can be reached by a foot tunnel under the Thames. Here the Royal Naval College, the National Maritime Museum, the tea clipper *Cutty Sark* and the Old Royal Observatory form an impressive group. At weekends Greenwich's antiques and arts and crafts markets add a lively bustle.

PLACES OF INTEREST

Billingsgate Fish Market [D3] The UK's largest inland wholesale fish market, Billingsgate was originally established in the City of London in 1699. The clock at its centre is a copy of the one that stood in the old market. It is still owned by the Corporation of London; every year the Lord Mayor ceremonially donates fish to the Mayor of Tower Hamlets.

Blackheath [D1] James I is said to have chosen this grassy heath to introduce the game of golf to England in 1608. It was here in 1381 that the peasant army led by Wat Tyler gathered to march on London, as did the Kentish army of Jack Cade in 1450. Once a haunt of highwaymen, the heath is now a place for flying kites and sailing model boats on its pond. The nearby suburb of Blackheath has elegant Georgian houses, including The Paragon, a crescent of 14 villas dating from 1794-1807. Nearby is Morden College of 1695, designed by Sir Christopher Wren and founded by Sir John Morden as almshouses for 'decayed Turkey merchants who had fallen on hard times'.

Bramah Tea and Coffee Museum [A3] The world's largest teapot is among more than 1000 displayed in the museum, along with old advertisements and 1950s coffee machines. Tea and coffee were imported to local warehouses for some 350 years.

Burrell's Wharf [C2] The *Great Eastern*, a huge steamship designed by Isambard Kingdom Brunel and John Scott Russell, was launched from a shipyard here (now a residential area) in 1858. A passenger vessel for the Eastern Steam Navigation Company, the 688 ft (210 m) long ship could carry 4000 passengers to India round the Cape of Good Hope without refuelling, but was too slow. It was used to lay Atlantic cables before being broken up in 1888.

Canary Wharf [C3] The most prominent landmark on London's skyline, Britain's tallest building towers above West India Docks. Built in 1991, it was designed by Cesar Pelli, the architect of New York's World Financial Center. It houses offices, restaurants and shops, and includes a piazza.

Charlton House [F2] Bombing in the Second World War destroyed the north wing of this red-brick house, completed in 1612 for the tutor of James I's eldest son Henry (who died the same year). The orangery, stables and park survived, and the north wing has been rebuilt. The house is now a library and community centre.

Crooms Hill [D1] Some of the finest 17th-18th-century houses in London line this street along the west side of Greenwich Park. At number 12 there is a Fan Museum with some 2000 fans from all parts of the world.

Cutty Sark [D2] Now in dry dock, the *Cutty Sark*—launched in 1869 and the last clipper to be built—was the fastest sailing ship of its day; on April 11, 1872, it covered 363 miles (584 km) in 24 hours on the way from London to Shanghai. Close by is the 53 ft (16 m) ketch *Gipsy Moth IV*, in which Francis Chichester sailed round the world single-handed in 226 days in 1966-7, at the age of 66. Beyond Greenwich Pier to the east are Trinity Hospital, with 17th-century almshouses, and the bow-windowed Cutty Sark Tavern of 1804, which was renamed in honour of the clipper.

Deptford [C2] The playwright Christopher Marlowe was killed in a tavern brawl here in 1593; he is buried in the 17th-century Church of St Nicholas, which has an oak panel carved by Grinling Gibbons. Henry VIII founded the Royal Naval Dockyard in Deptford in 1513. In 1581 Francis Drake arrived in the *Golden Hind* from his round-the-world trip and was knighted here by Elizabeth I. The dockyard closed in 1869. St Paul's Church of 1712-30 by Thomas Archer is in baroque style.

Design Museum [A3] Restored Victorian warehouses line Shad Thames, the narrow street from Tower Bridge to the Design Museum, which is housed in a restored 1950s warehouse on Butler's Wharf. Displays explore the relationship between how things look and how they work.

East London Mosque [A4] A crescent moon caps the tallest of three minarets of this 1985 mosque. Some 3000 followers of Islam attend the Friday service.

Financial Times Building [A4] Erected in 1987-8 to the design of Nicholas Grimshaw, this building with 320 ft (98 m) long glass walls, through which a printing press can be seen, has won several architectural awards.

The Grapes [C3] Charles Dickens collected material for *Our Mutual Friend* at this old riverside pub. It is entered from Narrow Street, which has a handsome terrace of 18th-century merchants' houses.

Greenland Dock [B2] Leisure boats are moored in this rebuilt 1697-9 dock, the largest area of water still left of the old Surrey Docks, now mostly filled in. The Entrance Lock still has its original hydraulic capstans and rams. Part of the former Surrey Docks now forms the Russia Dock Woodland and Ecological Park, which has a 65 ft (20 m) high mound with a relief map of the docks as they were; it affords extensive views.

Greenwich Park [D1] Enclosed as a hunting ground in 1433, the park is one of London's ten royal parks. It was laid out in the 1660s for Charles II by the French gardener Le Nôtre, who designed the gardens at Versailles for Louis XIV of France. In the avenue leading from Blackheath Gate there is a statue of General James Wolfe, the hero of the Battle of Quebec in 1759, who lived nearby. The Wilderness (not open) is a woodland bird sanctuary and the home of a herd of fallow deer. Views extend across to the Isle of Dogs and the City of London.

Island Gardens [D2] Considered by Sir Christoper Wren to be the best place to view Greenwich Hospital, now the Royal Naval College, this small garden at the southern tip of the Isle of Dogs looks across the Thames to the historic heart of Greenwich. To its north there is a spectacular high-level section of the 1987 Docklands Light Railway.

Millwall Docks [C2/3] Ships transporting grain from the Baltic brought their cargoes to these docks, built in 1868. Beside the docks is an area known as the Mudchute, which was created from silted mud dredged from the docks; it includes a farm and a riding school, and is open to visitors. Nearby is the Docklands Visitor Centre, which has an exhibition about the area.

National Maritime Museum [D1] England's earliest example of neoclassical architecture, the Queen's House is the centrepiece of the museum. Begun in 1616 by Inigo Jones in Palladian style, it was built for Anne of Denmark, wife of James I. Inside is the spiral Tulip Staircase, with tulip motifs in its wrought-iron balustrade. Museum displays cover Britain's seafaring history from Tudor to Victorian times, and include seascapes by J M W Turner and Nelson's uniform from the Battle of Trafalgar (1805).

Old Royal Observatory [D1] Designed by Sir Christopher Wren in 1675 for John Flamsteed, the first Astronomer Royal, this building in Greenwich Park is no longer an observatory; however, daily at 1pm Greenwich Mean Time, a red ball of 1833 on the rooftop mast is still lowered as a guide for river shipping. On display are historic telescopes and clocks, and in the courtyard there is a brass strip marking the Greenwich Meridian, which divides Earth's western and eastern hemispheres at 0 degrees longitude. At night, the meridian is marked by a laser beam pointing across the river.

Prospect of Whitby [B3] This pub dating from 1520 is said to be London's oldest Thames-side tavern. Its name recalls Yorkshire coal ships, which used to anchor here. There are fine river views.

Ranger's House [D1] Built for Vice-Admiral Francis Hosier in 1700-20, this red-brick villa (EH) later passed to the Stanhope family; Philip Stanhope, Earl of Chesterfield, wrote a celebrated set of letters of advice to his son. The house became the Greenwich Park Ranger's residence in 1815, and in 1902 was bought by London County Council. Displays include musical instruments and portraits, some by William Larkin (died 1619) with rich details of early 17th-century costumes. In the former coach house, an Architectural Study Centre has a collection of 17th-19th-century London domestic architecture.

Rotherhithe [B3] St Mary's Church, begun in 1714 on the site of a medieval church, is the burial place of Christopher Jones, the master of the *Mayflower*, the ship in which in 1620 the Pilgrim Fathers sailed to settle in the New World. The Mayflower Inn, partly of 16th-century date, is nearby. Brunel's Engine House has a restored steam engine that powered the pump used to drain the first tunnel under the Thames, built by Marc Brunel in 1825-43. The 400 yd (366 m) foot tunnel ran between Rotherhithe and Wapping, and in 1865 became an Underground Railway tunnel.

Royal Naval College [D2] Begun by John Webb in 1667 as a palace for Charles II, the building was continued by Sir Christopher Wren for William and Mary in 1695 as the Royal Hospital for Seamen, and was completed in 1705 by Wren's pupil Nicholas Hawksmoor. It includes a splendid chapel, rebuilt in 1779-90, and the Painted Hall, which has a fine decorated ceiling painted by Sir James Thornhill. The building became the Royal Naval College in 1873. The palace where Henry VIII and Elizabeth I were born once stood on the site.

Royal Victoria Dock [E/F3] Opened in 1855, this was the first of London's docks to be built for iron steamships. Today it is a playground for windsurfers, canoeists and small-boat sailors. To the east are Royal Albert Dock and King George V Dock, which could accommodate the liner *Mauretania*, and the City Airport serving several European cities.

St Alfege with St Peter [D1] Nicholas Hawksmoor and John James designed this neoclassical church of 1711-14, restored after Second World War damage, which has a galleried interior and an altarpiece by Sir James Thornhill. The composer Thomas Tallis, who died in 1585, is buried here, as is General James Wolfe. Henry VIII was baptised in an earlier church that stood on the site–the place where in 1012, Alphege, the Archbishop of Canterbury, was killed by Vikings.

St Anne's Church [C4] With its distinctive stepped tower, this Nicholas Hawksmoor church of 1712-30 is a Limehouse landmark. The splendid organ was built for the Great Exhibition of 1851.

St Katharine Docks [A3] This site by the Tower was a trading centre on land donated by King Edgar 1000 years ago. Designed by Thomas Telford, the docks opened in 1828, named after a 12th-century hospital on the site. They closed down in 1968, and the warehouses designed by Philip Hardwick became offices, shops and restaurants. Traditional Thames sailing barges can be seen moored here.

Storm Water Pumping Station [D3] This notable building of 1988 (not open) was designed by John Outram and has won a number of design awards.

Thames Barrier [F3] Opened by the Queen in 1984, the year after its completion, the barrier was built across the river to protect London from tidal floods. It spans 568 yd (520 m), and ships can pass between its eight huge steel shells. The curved floodgates resting on the river bed can be raised in less than an hour. A visitor centre explains the barrier's operation. One of the branches of the Green Chain Walk, a long-distance route through some of the woods and open spaces of south London, starts and ends beside the barrier.

Vanbrugh Castle [E1] Sir John Vanbrugh, the architect of Castle Howard in North Yorkshire and Blenheim Palace in Oxfordshire, designed this house of 1718-26 in the style of a medieval castle for his own use. Now converted into flats, it is the only survivor of a number of houses he built for members of his family.

Wapping [A3] A busy dock area in the 19th century, Wapping was badly damaged by Second World War bombing. Several newspapers moved here from Fleet Street in the 1980s, among them *The Times* and *The Sun*. Next to the Town of Ramsgate, a 17th-century tavern, are Wapping Old Stairs, where once pirates and thieves were

chained for the duration of three tides. Nearby is Execution Dock where the privateer Captain William Kidd was hanged in 1701.

West India Docks [C3] Designed by William Jessop for the West India Company, the docks opened in 1802 and were the first to be enclosed beside the river. They closed in 1980 and are now at the heart of a commercial centre. In Coldharbour, the street where many company officials once lived, is The Gun public house; its name marks the firing of a gun by *The Henry Aldington*, the first ship to enter Import Dock.

Whitechapel Art Gallery [A4] With its square corner towers and huge arched doorway, the gallery of 1897-9 by C H Townsend is one of London's most striking Art Nouveau buildings. Whitechapel Bell Foundry nearby dates from 1738. Bow bells (for the church of St Mary-le-Bow) and Big Ben, 13½ tons, were cast here.

STREET INDEX

The map reference in bold after each entry identifies the grid square in which it appears on pages 366-7

THE CHANNEL TUNNEL TERMINALS

Fast access routes to and from the terminals at Folkestone and Calais
Details of terminal layouts showing departure and arrival areas

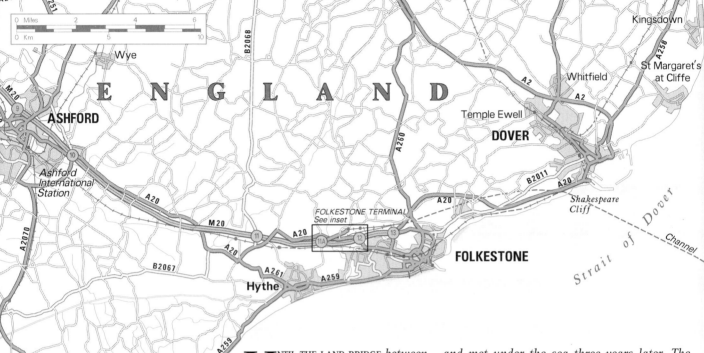

U NTIL THE LAND BRIDGE *between England and France sank into the sea about 10 000 years ago, the two were joined. It was this knowledge brought to light in 1750 that sparked off the idea of building a link across the English Channel. Various plans were put forward over the years, and tunnels were actually begun and abandoned in 1880 and 1960. The idea of a link was relaunched in 1981, and in 1985 four schemes considered included a 230 ft (70 m) high 'Eurobridge'. The favoured option was a railway tunnel. Borings began from both shores on December 1, 1987,*

and met under the sea three years later. The culmination of this engineering feat was the opening in 1994 of the world's second longest undersea tunnel after Japan's Seikan tunnel.

With terminals at Folkestone and Calais, the Channel Tunnel is 31 miles (50 km) long, with 23 miles (38 km) under the sea. It is in fact three tunnels—two one-way rail tunnels and a central service tunnel. The train service, Le Shuttle, carries motor vehicles 2-4 times an hour daily all year, and every 75 minutes at night. The journey takes 35 minutes—or about an hour from England's M20 to France's autoroutes A26 and A16.

FOLKESTONE TERMINAL

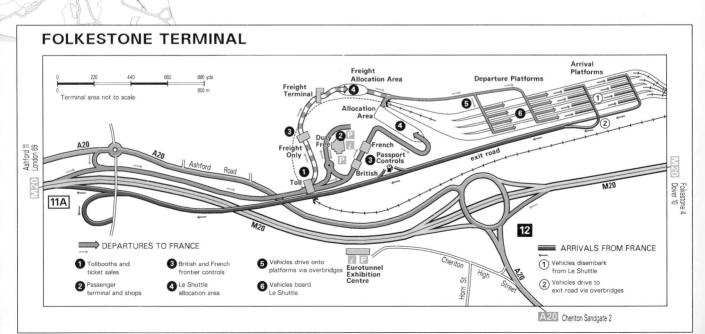

➡ DEPARTURES TO FRANCE

❶ Tollbooths and ticket sales
❷ Passenger terminal and shops
❸ British and French frontier controls
❹ Le Shuttle allocation area
❺ Vehicles drive onto platforms via overbridges
❻ Vehicles board Le Shuttle

Eurotunnel Exhibition Centre

━━ ARRIVALS FROM FRANCE

① Vehicles disembark from Le Shuttle
② Vehicles drive to exit road via overbridges

A20 Cheriton Sandgate 2

The French end

The terminal The French shuttle terminal is near the village of Coquélles, just outside Calais, and is well signposted from the A16 (E402) and A26 (E15) motorways. There is an information centre with displays explaining the tunnel's construction and operation. Cité Europe, opposite the terminal, has shops and restaurants. For enquiries about the shuttle service telephone (0033) 21 00 61 00.

The town Calais is a popular day trip for British visitors. Outside its Flemish-style town hall is Auguste Rodin's 1895 bronze sculpture, 'The Burghers of Calais', recalling the six men who in 1347 offered their lives to Edward III of England to save the town from destruction after a siege of almost a year—they were saved by Queen Philippa's intercession. Calais remained English until 1558. A former German blockhouse is now a museum of Nazi occupation in the Second World War, when much of the town was razed by bombing.

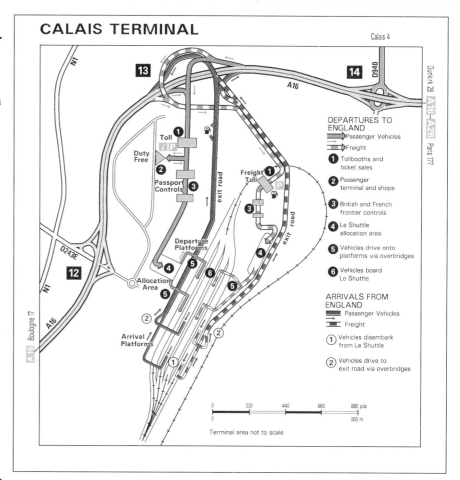

The English end

To reach the Folkestone terminal, leave the M20 eastbound at junction 11A, westbound at junction 12. The terminal has a duty-free shop, bureau de change, automatic cash dispensers, restaurants and shops.

In Cheriton High Street, near the tunnel terminal, is the Eurotunnel Exhibition Centre, where displays include an idea of what it is like to go through the tunnel, construction models and a large model railway layout.

Tickets and enquiries UK passengers must have a valid passport; there are passport controls and random Customs checks. Tickets can be bought just before the journey or booked in advance. Booked tickets are posted, or for bookings within seven days of travel must be collected from the Customer Service Centre off M20 junction 12, open 7am-7pm daily. For enquiries telephone (0990) 353535; disabled passengers (01303) 273747; freight sales (01303) 273300. ABTA travel agents can also arrange bookings.

Travelling without a car Passengers on foot can travel by Eurostar service from London Waterloo to Brussels in 3¼ hours or to Paris in 3 hours; there is a station at Ashford, Kent, and some trains stop at Lille and Fréthun near Calais. For enquiries phone (0345) 881881 or (01233) 617575.

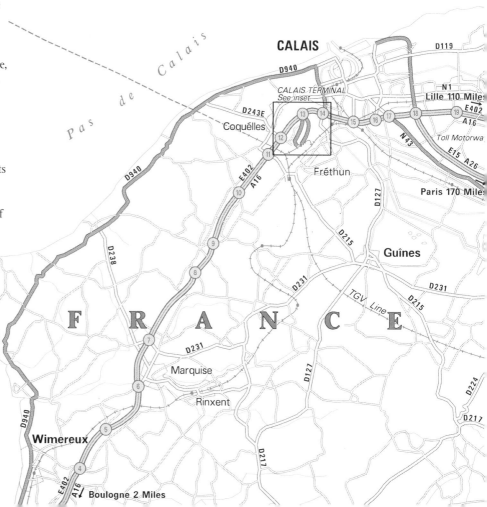

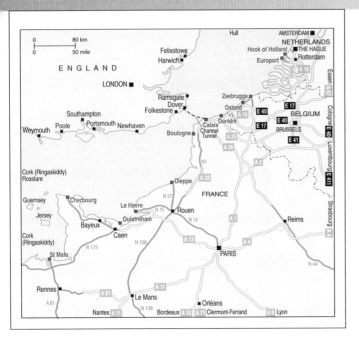

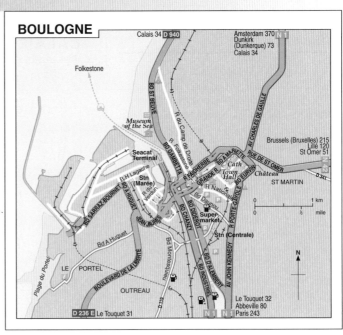

BOULOGNE

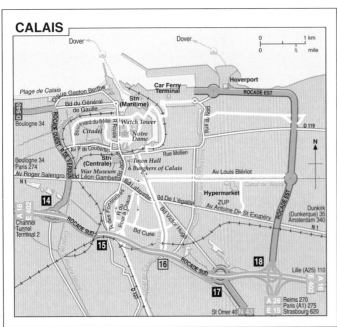

CALAIS

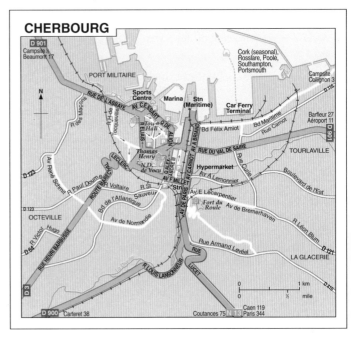

CHERBOURG

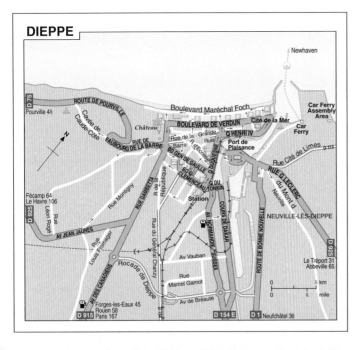

DIEPPE

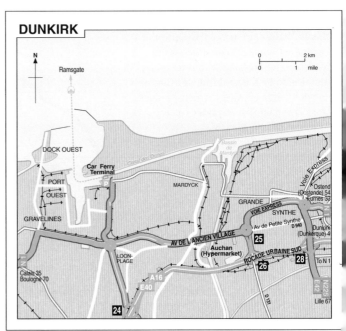

DUNKIRK

HOOK OF HOLLAND & EUROPORT

LE HAVRE

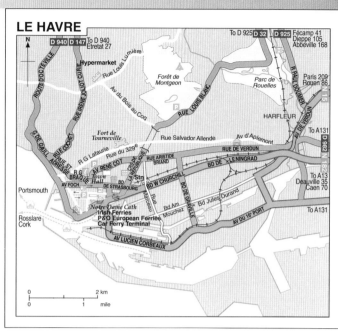

OSTEND

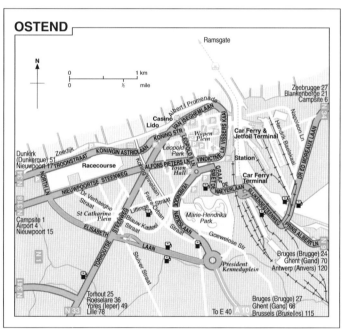

OUISTREHAM (CAEN)

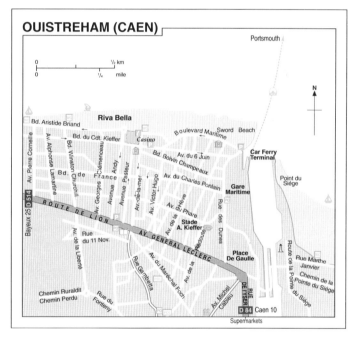

ST MALO

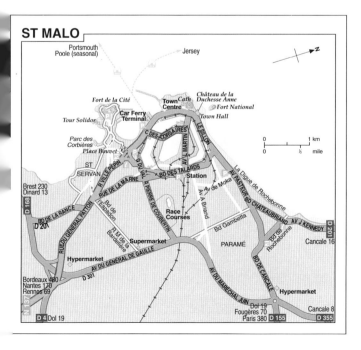

ZEEBRUGGE

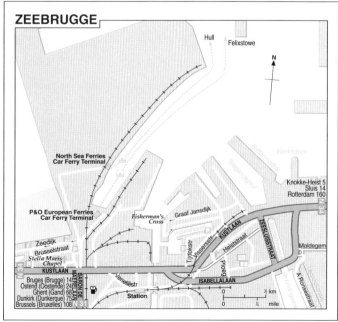

ABERDEEN (DYCE) (01224) 722 331

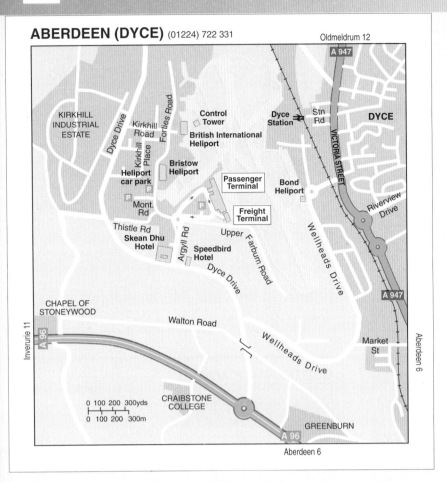

BIRMINGHAM INTERNATIONAL (0121) 767 7145

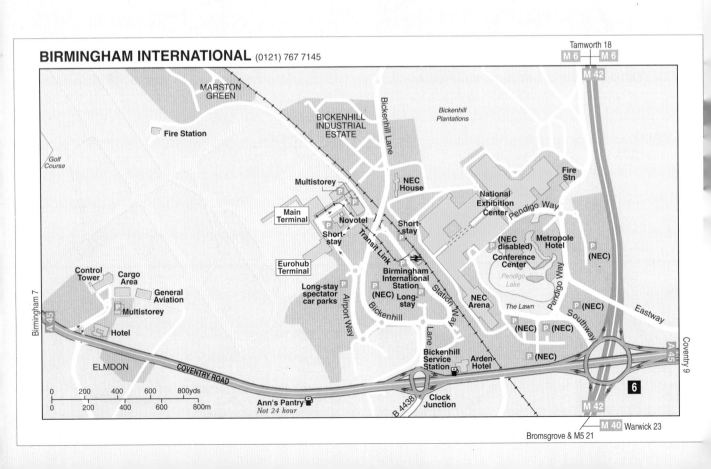

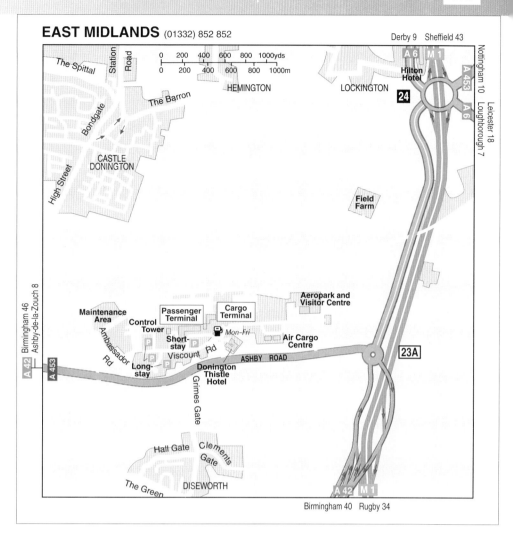

EAST MIDLANDS (01332) 852 852

Derby 9   Sheffield 43

Nottingham 10   Loughborough 7

Leicester 18

Birmingham 46   Ashby-de-la-Zouch 8

The Spittal
Station Road
Bondgate
The Barron
HEMINGTON
LOCKINGTON
Hilton Hotel
24
CASTLE DONINGTON
High Street
Field Farm
Aeropark and Visitor Centre
Maintenance Area
Passenger Terminal
Cargo Terminal
Control Tower
Short-stay
Air Cargo Centre
Ambassador Rd
Viscount Rd
Mon–Fri
Long-stay
Donington Thistle Hotel
ASHBY ROAD
23A
Grimes Gate
Hall Gate
Clements Gate
The Green
DISEWORTH
A 42   M 1

Birmingham 40   Rugby 34

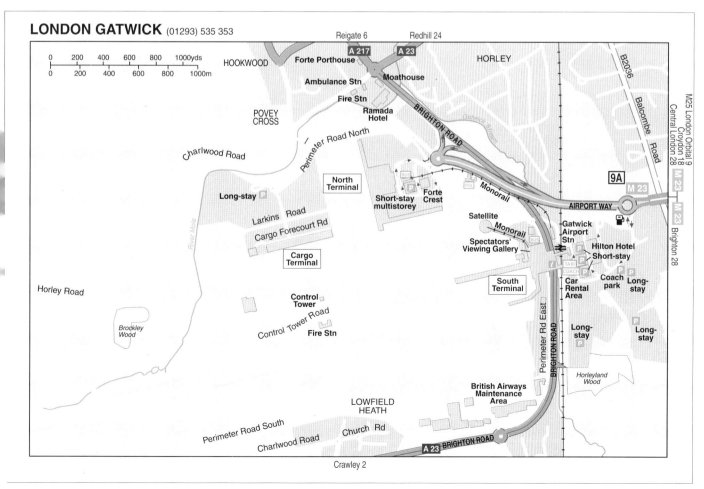

LONDON GATWICK (01293) 535 353

Reigate 6   Redhill 24

A 217   A 23

HOOKWOOD   Forte Porthouse   HORLEY
Ambulance Stn
Moathouse
Fire Stn
Ramada Hotel
POVEY CROSS
BRIGHTON ROAD
Gatwick Stream
B2036
Balcombe Road
Charlwood Road
Perimeter Road North
North Terminal
M25 London Orbital 9
Croydon 18
Central London 28
9A   M 23
Long-stay
Short-stay multistorey
Forte Crest
Larkins Road
Cargo Forecourt Rd
River Mole
Satellite
Monorail
AIRPORT WAY
M 23   Brighton 28
Cargo Terminal
Spectators' Viewing Gallery
Gatwick Airport Stn
Hilton Hotel
Short-stay
Horley Road
Control Tower
South Terminal
Car Rental Area
Coach park
Long-stay
Brockley Wood
Control Tower Road
Fire Stn
Perimeter Rd East
BRIGHTON ROAD
Long-stay
Long-stay
British Airways Maintenance Area
Horleyland Wood
LOWFIELD HEATH
Perimeter Road South
Charlwood Road
Church Rd
A 23   BRIGHTON ROAD

Crawley 2

EDINBURGH (0131) 331 1000

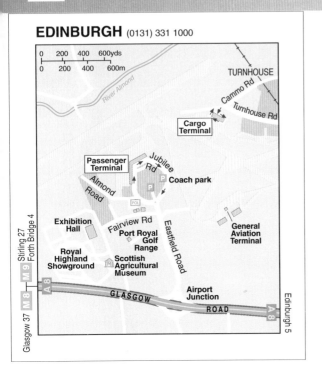

GLASGOW (0141) 887 1111

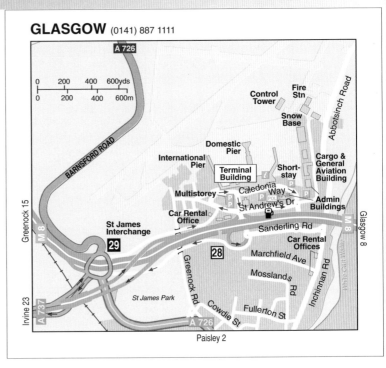

LONDON HEATHROW (0181) 759 4321

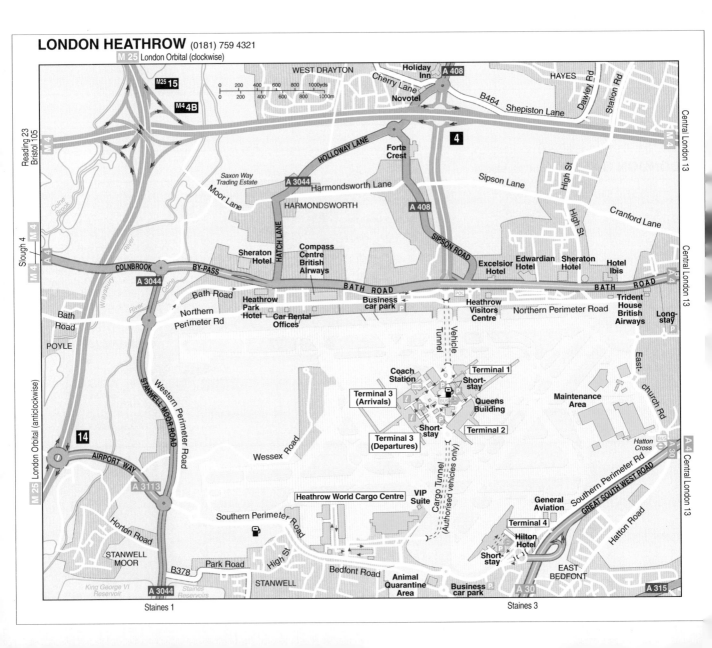

LUTON (01582) 405 100

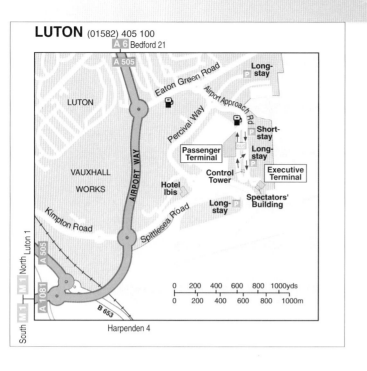

A 6 Bedford 21
A 505
LUTON
Eaton Green Road
Long-stay
Airport Approach Rd
Percival Way
Short-stay
Long-stay
Passenger Terminal
AIRPORT WAY
VAUXHALL WORKS
Control Tower
Executive Terminal
Hotel Ibis
Long-stay
Spectators' Building
Spittlesea Road
Kimpton Road
M1 A 505
North Luton 1
A 1081
South M1
B 653
Harpenden 4

| 0 | 200 | 400 | 600 | 800 | 1000yds |
| 0 | 200 | 400 | 600 | 800 | 1000m |

MANCHESTER (RINGWAY) (0161) 489 3000

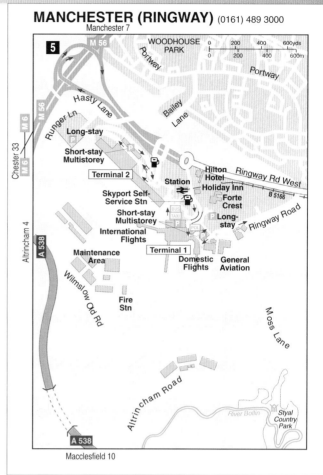

Manchester 7
5
M 56
WOODHOUSE PARK
Portway
Portway
Hasty Lane
Bailey Lane
Chester 33 M6 M56
Runger Ln
Long-stay
Short-stay Multistorey
Terminal 2
Station
Hilton Hotel
Ringway Rd West
Holiday Inn
Skyport Self-Service Stn
Forte Crest
B 5166
Short-stay Multistorey
Long-stay
Ringway Road
Altrincham 4
International Flights
Terminal 1
A 538
Maintenance Area
Domestic Flights
General Aviation
Wilmslow Old Rd
Fire Stn
Moss Lane
Altrincham Road
River Bollin
Styal Country Park
A 538
Macclesfield 10

| 0 | 200 | 400 | 600yds |
| 0 | 200 | 400 | 600m |

LONDON STANSTED (01279) 662 520

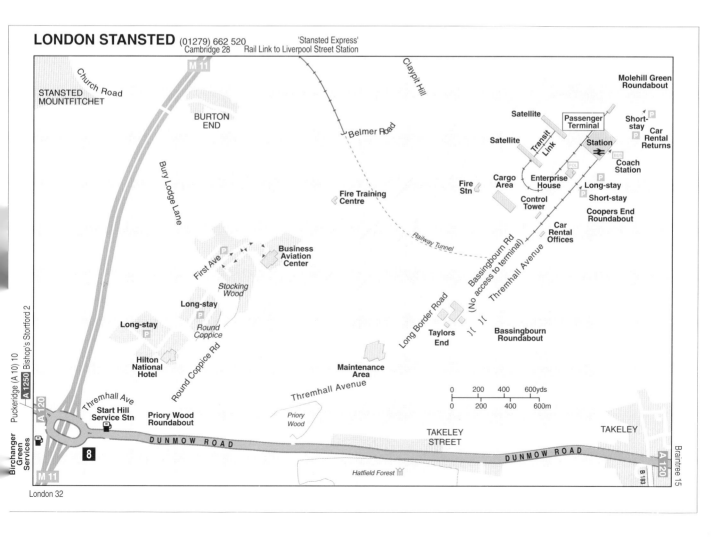

Cambridge 28
'Stansted Express'
Rail Link to Liverpool Street Station
M 11
Church Road
STANSTED MOUNTFITCHET
BURTON END
Claypit Hill
Molehill Green Roundabout
Belmer Road
Satellite
Passenger Terminal
Short-stay
Bury Lodge Lane
Satellite
Transit Link
Station
Car Rental Returns
Coach Station
Fire Training Centre
Railway Tunnel
Fire Stn
Cargo Area
Enterprise House
Long-stay
Short-stay
Business Aviation Center
Control Tower
Coopers End Roundabout
First Ave
Bassingbourn Rd (No access to terminal)
Car Rental Offices
Stocking Wood
Long-stay
Thremhall Avenue
Round Coppice
Long Border Road
Long-stay
Round Coppice Rd
Taylors End
Bassingbourn Roundabout
Bishop's Stortford 2
Hilton National Hotel
Maintenance Area
Puckeridge (A 10) 10
A 1250
Thremhall Avenue
A 120
Thremhall Ave
Priory Wood Roundabout
Priory Wood
Start Hill Service Stn
M 11
Birchanger Green Services
8
DUNMOW ROAD
TAKELEY STREET
DUNMOW ROAD
TAKELEY
London 32
Hatfield Forest
B 183
Braintree 15

| 0 | 200 | 400 | 600yds |
| 0 | 200 | 400 | 600m |

BATH

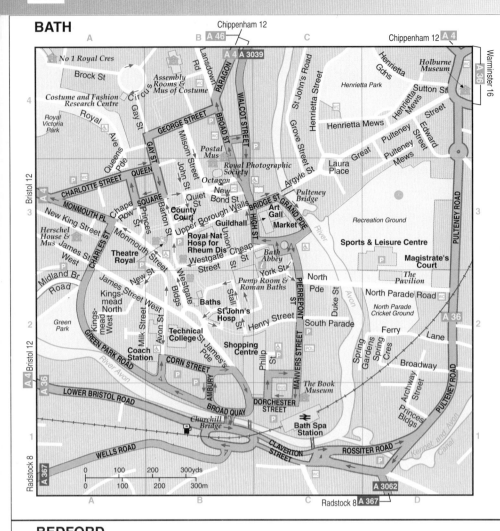

Ambury	B1–B2
Argyle Street	C3
Bridge Street	C3
Broad Quay	B1
Broad Street	B4
Charles Street	A3
Charlotte Street	A3
Cheap Street	B3
Claverton Street	C1
Corn Street	B2
Dorchester Street	C1
Gay Street	A4–B3
George Street	B4
Grand Parade	C3
Great Pulteney Street	D4
Green Park Road	A2
High Street	B3–C3
James Street West	A2
Landsown Road	B4
Laura Place	C3
Lower Bristol Road	A1
Manvers Street	C2
Milsom Street	B4–B3
Monmouth Place	A3
Monmouth Street	A3–B3
North Parade	C2
North Parade Road	D2
Paragon	B4
Pierrepont Street	C2
Pulteney Road	D1–D3
Queen Square	A3–B3
Rossiter Road	C1–D1
St James's Parade	B2
Upper Borough Walls	B3
Walcot Street	B4
Wells Road	A1
Westgate Buildings	B2
Westgate Street	B3

BEDFORD

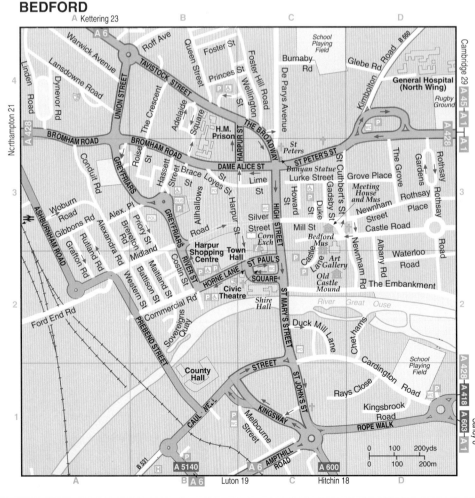

Adelaide Square	B4
Allhallows	B3
Ampthill Road	C1
Ashburnham Road	A3
Bromham Road	B3
Cardington Road	D1
Castle Road	D3
Cauldwell Street	B1–C2
Commercial Road	B2
Costin Street	B2
Dame Alice Street	B3–C3
De Parys Avenue	C4
Ford End Road	A2
Greyfriars	A3–B3
Harpur Street	B3
Harpur Street	C3–C4
Hassett Street	B3
High Street	C3
Horne Lane	B2
Kimbolton Road	D4
Kingsway	C1
Lurke Street	C3
Midland Road	B2–B3
Mill Street	C3
Prebend Street	B2
River Street	B2
Roff Avenue	B4
Rope Walk	D1
St John's Street	C1
St Mary's Street	C2
St Paul's Square	C2
St Peter's Street	C3
Silver Street	C3
Tavistock Street	B4
The Broadway	C4–C3
The Embankment	D2
Union Street	A4
Waterloo Road	D2

BELFAST

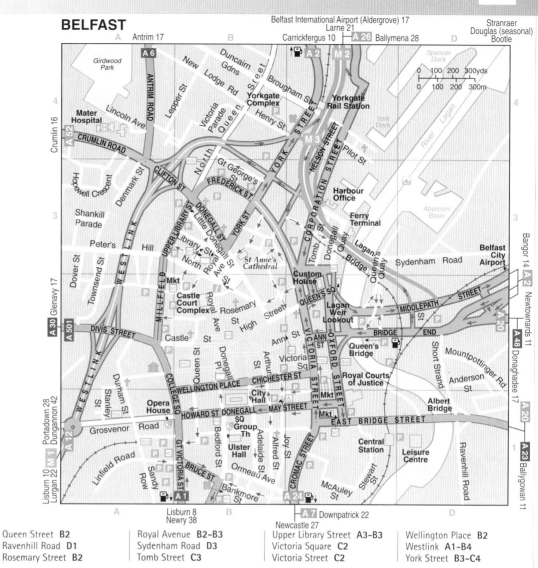

BLACKBURN

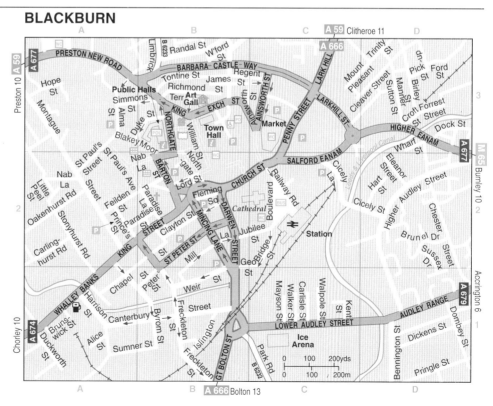

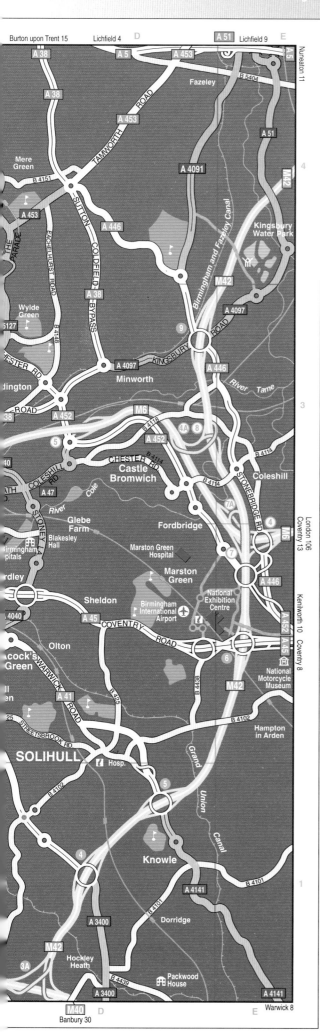

Around Birmingham and Wolverhampton

Birmingham, at the heart of England, is a major centre for art and music and one of Britain's foremost convention and exhibition centres. Birmingham Museum and Art Gallery and the Barber Institute of Fine Arts at the University of Birmingham are among the country's best, and music includes the City of Birmingham Symphony Orchestra at the Symphony Hall, the D'Oyly Carte Opera at the Alexandra Theatre and a yearly Jazz Festival. Legacies of the city's industrial and commercial past include the Jewellery Quarter, with its Discovery Centre, and an extensive network of canals that linked factories to rivers and seaports; there are towpath walks in the city centre and the leafy suburbs.

Wolverhampton lies at the heart of what was once the Black Country—a sprawl of towns that became large industrial centres during the 19th century. Surrounding towns such as West Bromwich, Dudley, Stourbridge and Walsall also developed during this era through the exploitation of local coal and iron deposits. Some developed specific industries, including leather in Walsall, locks in Willenhall and glass in Stourbridge. Past industries are recalled at Kingswinford's Broadfield House Glass Museum and Walsall's Leather Museum.

PLACES OF INTEREST

Aston Hall [C3] A riot of turrets, gables and octagonal chimneys surmount this ornate Jacobean country house of 1618-35. Its elaborate interior includes a 135 ft (41 m) oak-panelled long gallery, a cantilevered oak staircase and fine plasterwork ceilings.

Black Country Museum [A3] Victorian workshops, homes, a pub, a chapel and a small colliery recreate life from the region's industrial past. Workshops include a chainmaker's and a glasscutter's. An electric tram provides transport. Nearby, there are narrowboat canal trips through Dudley Tunnel, with spectacular limestone caverns.

Blakesley Hall [D2] A half-timbered house of 1590, the hall is furnished according to an inventory of 1684. The Painted Chamber is adorned with 16th-century wall paintings.

Bournville [C2] George and Richard Cadbury built this garden village in 1894 for the workers at their chocolate factory. Cadbury's World visitor centre tells how the Quaker firm began chocolate-making to find a non-alcoholic substitute for beer.

Dudley Zoo [A3] On Castle Hill stands a partly medieval but mainly 16th-century castle with a well-preserved great hall. The zoo, begun in the 1930s, is in the wooded grounds, with animals in natural settings.

Jerome K Jerome Museum [B4] The author of *Three Men In A Boat*, Jerome was born in Walsall in 1859; his birthplace in Bradford Street is now a museum.

Leather Museum [B4] Saddles, bridles, belts and satchels are among the variety of leather goods on display at this museum in Walsall, a leather centre of high standing for nearly two centuries. Demonstrations show skilled workers crafting leather goods.

Museum of Science and Industry [p 382 A4] The Smethwick Engine of about 1799, the world's oldest working steam engine, is among the Birmingham industry on display in this converted factory. Light on Science is a 'hands-on' exhibition.

St Chad's Cathedral [p 382 C5] Augustus Pugin designed this red-brick, twin-spired building of 1841—the first Roman Catholic cathedral to be built in Britain since the 16th-century Reformation. The ornate neo-Gothic interior has fine 15th-century statues and a 16th-century French pulpit.

St Philip's Cathedral [p 382 C3] Four stained-glass windows of the 1890s by Edward Burne-Jones, born in the city, adorn this elegant English baroque building of 1715. Churchyard monuments include one to Colonel Frederick Burnaby (1842-85), war correspondent and balloonist.

Sarehole Mill [C2] Birmingham's only surviving water mill, this 18th-century building inspired J R R Tolkien, who spent his boyhood in the area, to write his fantasy novel of 1937, *The Hobbit*.

Sutton Park [C4] An ancient royal hunting ground, Sutton has been a public park since the time of Henry VIII. It includes a 1½ mile (2 km) stretch of the Roman Ryknild Street.

Town Hall [p 382 B3] Joseph Hansom, designer of the Hansom cab, is said to have modelled Birmingham's neoclassical town hall of 1834-49 on the Temple of Castor and Pollux in Rome. Across the square is the Renaissance-style Council House of 1879.

Walsall Museum and Art Gallery [B4] The 20th-century art collection at the Central Library has many works by the sculptor Jacob Epstein, given by his widow.

See also pages 142-143 and 167

BIRMINGHAM

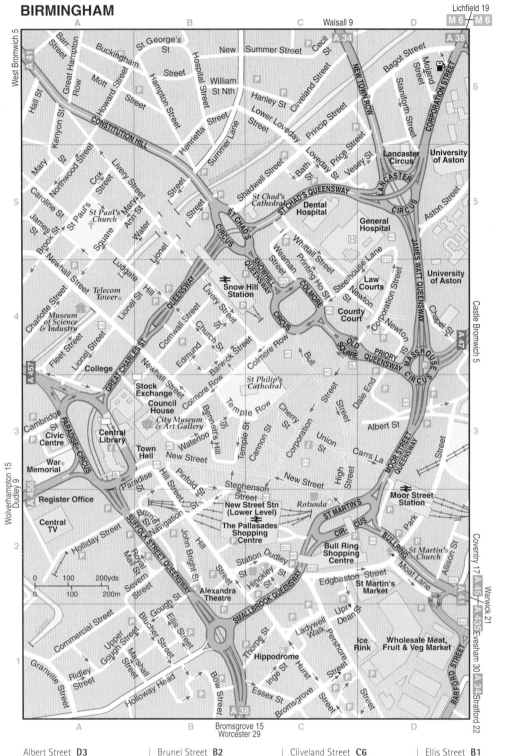

West Bromwich 5
Wolverhampton 15
Dudley 9
Lichfield 19
Walsall 9
Bromsgrove 15
Worcester 29
Castle Bromwich 5
Coventry 17
Warwick 21
Evesham 30
Stratford 22

BLACKPOOL

Abingdon Street **A3**
Adelaide Street **A3–B3**
Albert Road **B3**
Ashton Road **B2**
Banks Street **A4**
Bonny Street **A2**
Buchanan Street **B4**
Caunce Street **C4**
Central Drive **B1–B2**
Chapel Street **A2**
Charnley Road **B3**
Church Street **A3**
Church Street **B3–C3**
Clifton Street **A3**
Cocker Street **A4**
Coleridge Road **C4**
Condor Grove **C1**
Cookson Street **B4–B3**
Coop Street **A2**
Coronation Street **B3–B2**
Cumberland Avenue **C2**
Deansgate **A4–B4**
Devonshire Road **C4**
Dickson Road **A4**
Edward Street **B3**
Elizabeth Street **B4**
George Street **B4–C4**
Gloucester Avenue **C2**
Gorton Street **B4–C4**
Granville Road **C4**
Grasmere Road **B1**
Grosvenor Street **B4–B3**
High Street **A4–B4**
Hornby Road **B3–C3**
Hull Road **A2–A3**
Kent Road **B2**
Keswick Road **B2–C2**
King Street **B4–B3**
Leamington Road **C3**

Leeds Road **C3**
Leicester Road **C3**
Levens Grove **C1**
Lincoln Road **C3**
London Road **C4**
Lonsdale Road **A1–B1**
Lord Street **A4**
Lune Grove **B1–C1**
Lytham Road **A1**
Manchester Road **C4**
Milbourne Street **B4**
North Promenade **A4**
Oxford Road **C4**
Palatine Road **B2–C3**
Park Road **B3–C2**
Peter Street **C4**
Princess Street **A1–B2**
Promenade **A1–A3**
Queen Street **A4**
Queen Victoria Road **B1–C1**
Raikes Parade **B3**
Reads Avenue **B2–C3**
Regent Road **B3**
Ribble Road **B2**
Rigby Road **A1–B1**
Selbourne Road **C4**
Sharow Grove **C1**
South King Street **B3**
Springfield Road **A4**
Talbot Road **A4–B4**
Thornber Grove **C1**
Tyldesley Road **A1**
Victoria Street **A3**
Victory Road **B4–C4**
Westmorland Avenue **B1–C2**
Whitegate Drive **C3**
Woolman Road **B2**
Yorkshire Street **A2**
York Street **A2**

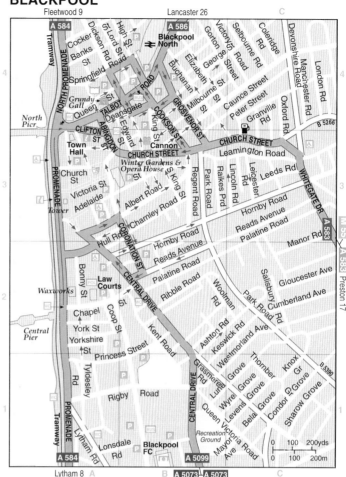

BOLTON

Ashburner Street **B2**
Bank Street **C3**
Bark Street **A3–B4**
Blackhorse Street **B3–B2**
Bow Street **C4**
Breightmet Street **C2–D2**
Bridgeman Place **D2**
Bridge Street **C4–C3**
Broadshaw Gate **C2**
Bury New Road **D4–D3**
Castle Street **D3**
Church Bank **D3**
Church Gate **C3**
Clive Street **C2**
Crown Street **C3**
Deane Road **A1**
Deansgate **B3–C3**
Derby Street **A1**
Folds Road **C4–D4**
Great Moor Street **B2–C2**
Higher Bridge Street **C4**
Knowsley Street **B4–B3**
Manor Street **C3**
Marsden Road **B3**
Moor Lane **B2**
Nelson Square **C2**
Newport Street **C2**
Ormrod Street **B2**
Oxford Street **B3**
River Street **D2**
St George's Road **A4**
St George's Street **C4**
St Peter's Way **D3–D1**
Salop Street **D2**
Shiffnall Street **C2–D2**
Silverwell Street **C3**
Spa Road **A3**
Topp Way **B4**
Trinity Street **B1–C1**

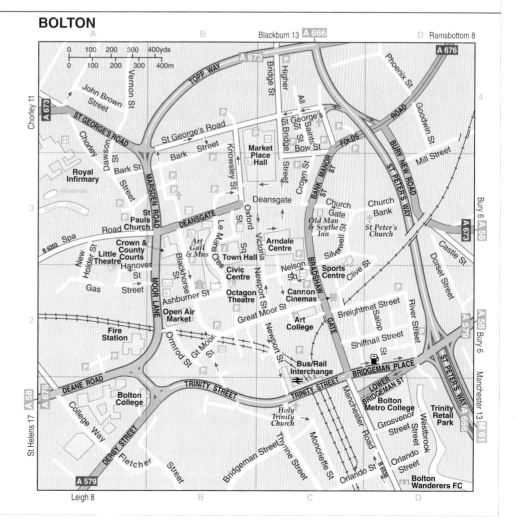

BOURNEMOUTH

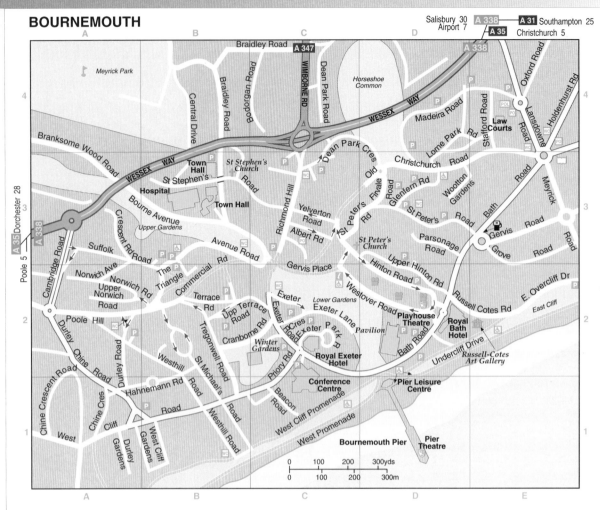

Salisbury 30 · A 338 · A 31 Southampton 25
Airport 7 · A 35 · Christchurch 5

Albert Road **C3**
Bath Road **D2-E3**
Beacon Road **C1**
Bourne Avenue **B3**
Braidley Road **B4**
Cambridge Road **A2**
Central Drive **B4**
Christchurch Road **D3**
Commercial Road **B2**
Cranborne Road **B2**
Durley Chine Road **A2**
Durley Gardens **A1**
East Overcliff Road **E2**
Exeter Lane **C2**
Exeter Road **C2**
Firvale Road **D3**
Gervis Place **C2**
Gervis Road **E3**
Hinton Road **D2**
Holdenhurst Road **E4**
Lansdowne Road **E4**
Madeira Road **D4**
Meyrick Road **E3**
Oxford Road **E4**
Poole Hill **A2**
Priory Road **C2**
Richmond Hill **C3**
Russell Cotes Road **D2**
St Stephen's Road **B3**
Suffolk Road **A3**
Terrace Road **B2**
The Triangle **B2**
Tregonwell Road **B2**
Wessex Way **A3-E4**
West Cliff Road **A1**
Westover Road **D2**
Wimborne Road **C4**
Wootton Gardens **D3**

BRADFORD

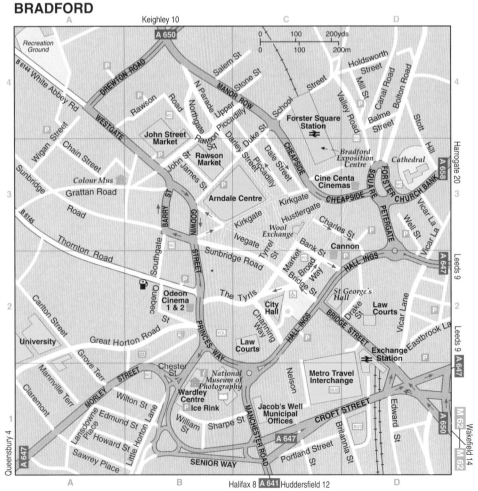

Keighley 10 · A 650

Bank Street **C3-C2**
Barry Street **B3**
Bolton Road **D4**
Bridge Street **C2-D1**
Broad Way **C2**
Channing Way **C2**
Charles Street **C3**
Cheapside **C3**
Chester Street **B1**
Church Bank **D3**
Croft Street **C1-D1**
Darley Street **B4-C3**
Drake Street **D2**
Drewton Road **A4-B4**
Duke Street **C3-C4**
Foster Square **D3**
Godwin Street **B3-B2**
Great Horton Road **A1-B2**
Hall Ings **C2-D2**
Ivegate **C3**
John Street **B3**
Kirkgate **C3**
Manchester Road **C1**
Manor Row **B4-C4**
Morley Street **A1-B1**
Northgate **B4**
North Parade **B4**
Petergate **D3**
Princes Way **B2**
Rawson Square **B4**
Senior Way **B1**
Sunbridge Road **B3-C2**
The Tyris **B2-C2**
Thornton Road **A3-B2**
Upper Piccadilly **B4**
Valley Road **D4**
Vicar Lane **D2**
Westgate **A4**

Halifax 8 · A 641 Huddersfield 12

BRISTOL

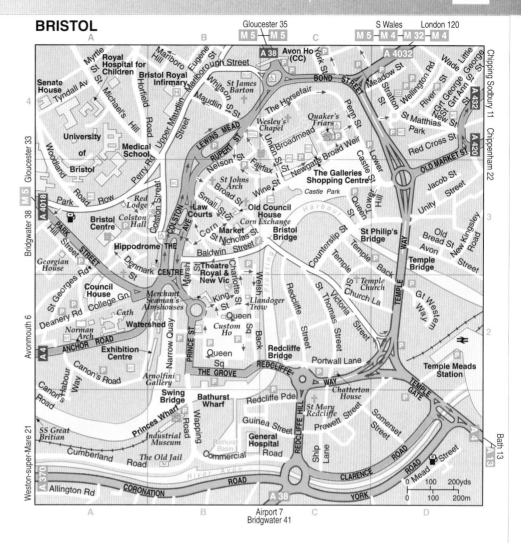

CANTERBURY

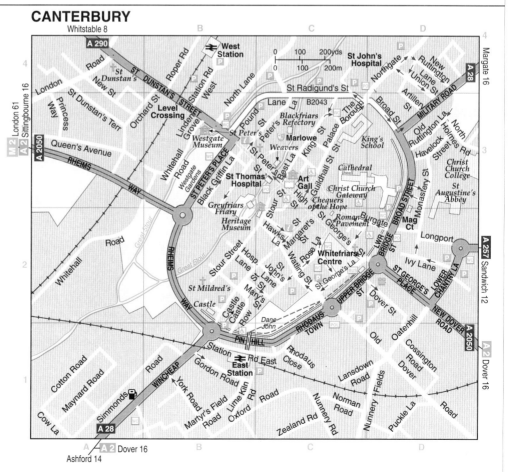

CAMBRIDGE

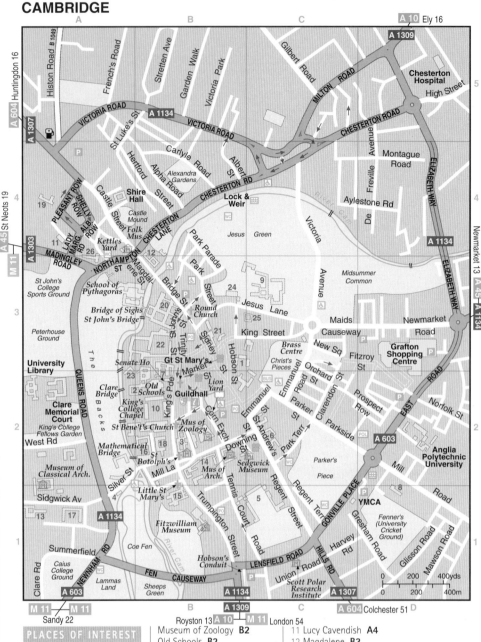

Albert Street **B4**
Alpha Road **B4**
Aylestone Road **D4**
Bridge Street **B3**
Carlyle Road **B4**
Castle Street **A4**
Chesterton Lane **B4**
Chesterton Road **B4–D5**
Clare Road **A1**
Clarendon Street **C2**
Corn Exchange **B2**
De Freville Avenue **D4**
Downing Street **B2**
East Road **D2**
Elizabeth Way **D4–D3**
Emmanuel Road **C2**
Emmanuel Street **C2**
Fen Causeway **B1**
Fitzroy Street **D3**
French's Road **A5**
Garden Walk **B5**
Gilbert Road **C5**
Glisson Road **D1**
Gonville Place **C1**
Gresham Road **D1**
Harvey Road **C1**
Hertford Street **B4**
High Street **D5**
Hills Road **C1**
Histon Road **A5**
Hobson Street **B3**
Jesus Lane **C3**
King Street **C3**
King's Parade **B2**
Lady Margaret Road **A4**
Lensfield Road **C1**
Madingley Road **A3**
Magdalene Street **B3**
Maids Causeway **C3**
Market Street **B2**
Mawson Road **D1**
Mill Lane **B2**
Mill Road **D2–D1**
Milton Road **C5**
Montague Road **D4**
New Square **C3**
Newmarket Road **D3**
Newnham Road **A1**
Norfolk Street **D2**
Northampton Street **A3**
Orchard Street **C2**
Park Parade **B4**
Park Street **B3**
Park Terrace **C2**
Parker St **C2**
Parkside **C2**
Pleasant Row **A4**
Prospect Row **D2**
Queens Road **A2**
Regent Street **C1**
St Andrew's Street **C2**
St John's Street **B3**
St Luke's Street **A5**
Shelly Row **A4**
Sidgewick Avenue **A1**
Sidney Street **B3**
Silver Street **A2**
Stretten Avenue **B5**
Summerfield **A1**
Tennis Court Road **B1–C1**
Trinity Street **B3**
Trumpington Street **B1**
Union Road **C1**
Victoria Avenue **C4–C3**
Victoria Park **B5**
Victoria Road **A5–B5**
West Road **A2**

PLACES OF INTEREST

Arts Cinema **B3**
Arts Theatre **B2**
Brass Rubbing Centre **C3**
Bridge of Sighs **B3**
Cannon Cinema **C2**
Fitzwilliam Museum **B1**
Folk Museum **A4**
Grafton shopping Centre **D3**
Great St Mary's Church **B2**
Guildhall **B2**
Hobson's Conduit **B1**
Holy Sepulchre, Round
  Church **B3**
Kettles Yard Art Gallery **A4**
King's College Chapel **B2**
Lion Yard shopping
  centre **B2**
Little St Mary's Church **B2**
Mathematical Bridge **A2**
Mus of Arch and
  Anthropology **B2**
Mus of Classical
  Archaeology **A1**

Museum of Zoology **B2**
Old Schools **B2**
St Bene't's Church **B2**
St Botolph's Church **B2**
School of Pythagoras **A3**
Scott Polar Research Inst **C1**
Sedgwick Mus of Geology **B2**
Senate House **B2**
Victoria Cinema **B2**
Whipple Science Museum **B2**

CAMBRIDGE UNIVERSITY COLLEGES

1 Christ's **B3**
2 Clare **B2**
3 Corpus Christi **B2**
4 Darwin **A1**
5 Downing **C1**
6 Emmanuel **C2**
7 Gonville and Caius **B2**
8 Hughes Hall **D1**
9 Jesus **C3**
10 King's **B2**

11 Lucy Cavendish **A4**
12 Magdalene **B3**
13 Newnham **A1**
14 Pembroke **B2**
15 Peterhouse **B1**
16 Queen's **B2**
17 Ridley Hall **A1**
18 St Catherine's **B2**
19 St Edmund's House **A4**
20 St John's **B3**
21 Sidney Sussex **B3**
22 Trinity **B3**
23 Trinity Hall **A2**
24 Wesley House **B3**
25 Westcott House **C3**
26 Westminster **A4**

Colleges outside map area

Churchill college is on
Madingley Road. Clare Hall,
Robinson and Selwyn are on
Grange Road. Fitzwilliam,
Girton and New Hall are on
Huntingdon Road.

CARDIFF

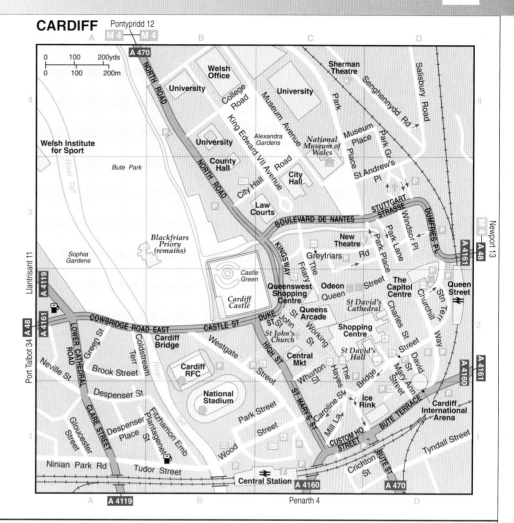

CARLISLE

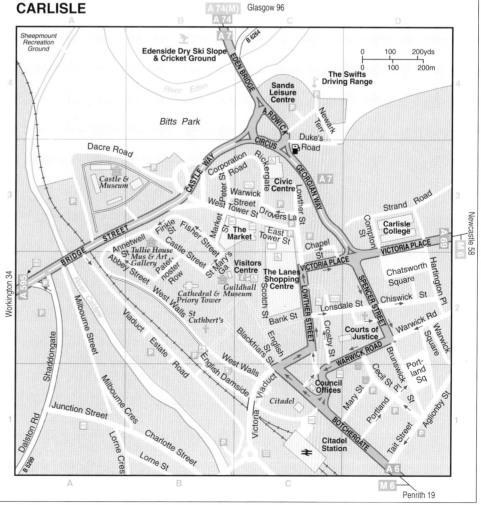

CHELTENHAM

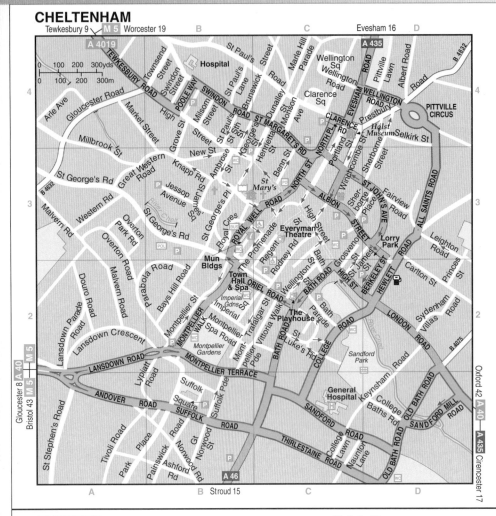

Albion Street **C3**
All Saints Road **D3**
Andover Road **A1**
Bath Road **C2**
Berkeley Street **D2**
Clarence Road **C4**
College Road **C2**
Evesham Road **C4-D4**
Gloucester Road **A4**
Hewlett Road **D2-D3**
High Street **C3-C2**
Lansdown Road **A2**
London Road **D2**
Montpellier Terrace **B2-C1**
Montpellier Walk **B2**
North Place **C4**
North Street **C3**
Old Bath Road **D1**
Oriel Road **B2-C2**
Park Place **A1-B1**
Pittville Circus **D4**
Poole Way **B4**
Prestbury Road **D4**
Regent Street **C3**
Rodney Road **C2-C3**
Royal Well Road **B3-C3**
St George's Road **A3-B3**
St John's Avenue **D3**
St Margaret's Road **C4**
St Paul's Road **B4-C4**
Sandford Mill Road **D1**
Sandford Road **C1**
Suffolk Road **B1**
Swindon Road **B4**
Tewkesbury Road **A4-B4**
Thirlestaine Road **C1**
Wellington Road **D4**
Winchcombe Street **C3-C4**

CHESTER

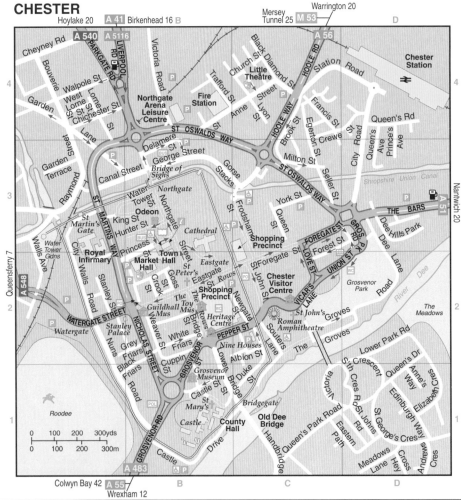

Bridge Street **B2**
Canal Street **A3-B3**
Cheyne Road **A4**
City Road **D3-D4**
City Walls Road **A3-A2**
Eastgate **B2**
Foregate Street **C2-C3**
Garden Lane **A4-A3**
George Street **B3**
Gorse Stacks **B3-C3**
Grosvenor Park **D3**
Grosvenor Road **B1**
Grosvenor Street **B1-B2**
Handbridge **C1**
Hoole Road **C4**
Hoole Way **C3-C4**
Hunter Street **A3-B3**
Liverpool Road **A4**
Love Street **C2-C3**
Lower Bridge **B2-C1**
Newgate Street **C2**
Nicholas Street **B2-B1**
Northgate Street **B3-B2**
Nuns Road **A2-A1**
Parkgate Road **A4**
Pepper Street **B2-C2**
Princess Street **A2-B3**
Raymond Street **A3-A4**
St Anne Street **B4-C4**
St John Street **C2**
St Martin's Way **A3-A2**
St Oswalds Way **B4-C3**
Station Road **C4-D4**
The Bars **D3**
Union Street **C2-D2**
Vicar's Lane **C2**
Watergate Street **A2**
White Friars **B2**

CHICHESTER

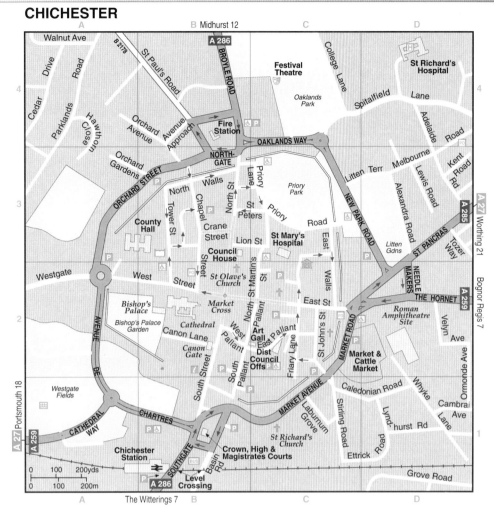

COLCHESTER

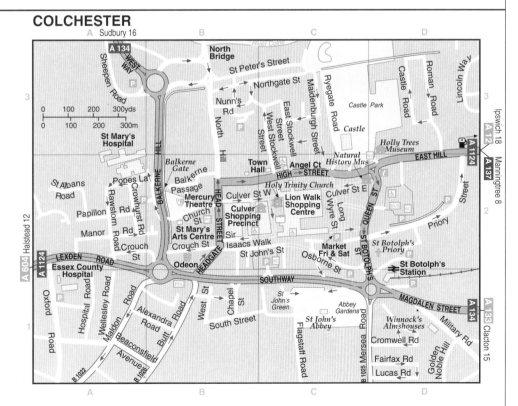

COVENTRY

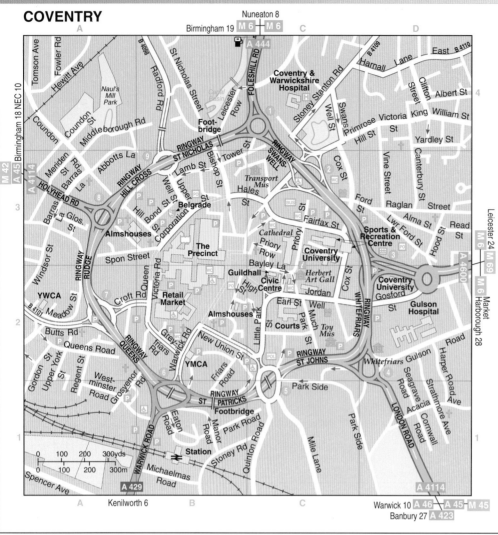

Barras Lane **A3**
Bishop Street **B3**
Butts Road **A2**
Corporation Street **B3**
Coundon Road **A4–A3**
Cox Street **C2**
Croft Road **A2–B2**
Earl Street **C2**
Fairfax Street **C3**
Foleshill Road **C4**
Gosford Street **D2**
Greyfriars Road **B2**
Gulson Road **D2**
Hales Street **B3–C3**
Harnal Lane East **D4**
Holyhead Road **A3**
Jordan Well **C2**
Little Park Street **C2**
London Road **D1**
Mile Lane **C1**
New Union Street **B2**
Primrose Hill Street **C4–D4**
Queen Victoria Road **B2**
Quinton Road **C1**
Radford Road **B4**
Ringway Hill Cross **A3–B3**
Ringway Queens **A2**
Ringway Rudge **A2–A3**
Ringway St Johns **C2**
Ringway St Nicholas **B4**
Ringway St Patricks **B1**
Ringway Swanswell **C4–C3**
Ringway Whitefriars **D2**
Spencer Avenue **A1**
Stoney Stanton Road **C4**
Swans Well Street **C4**
Upper Well Street **B3**
Warwick Road **B1**
Warwick Road **B2**

CROYDON

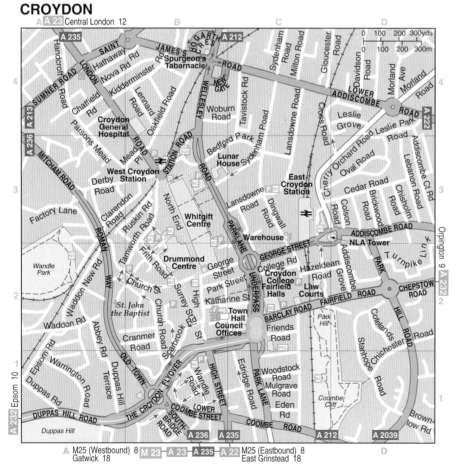

Addiscombe Grove **D2**
Addiscombe Road **D3**
Barclay Road **C3**
Chepstow Road **D2**
Cherry Orchard Road **C3–D4**
Coombe Road **C1**
Duppas Hill Road **A1**
Fairfield Road **D2**
Frith Road **B2**
George Street **B2–C2**
High Street **B2**
Hogarth Crescent **B4**
Lansdowne Road **C3–C4**
London Road **A4–B3**
Lower Addiscombe Road **D4**
Lower Coombe Street **B1**
Mitcham Road **A3**
Morland Road **D4**
North End **B3**
Oakfield Road **B4**
Old Town **B1**
Park Hill Road **D2**
Park Lane **C1**
Parkland Underpass **C3–C2**
Park Street **B2–C2**
Roman Way **A3–A2**
Saint James's Road **A4–C4**
Southbridge Road **B1**
Station Road **B3**
Sumner Road **A4**
Sydenham Road **C3–C4**
Tamworth Road **B2–B3**
The Croydon Flyover **B1**
Turnpike Link **D2**
Wellesley Road **B4–B3**

DARLINGTON

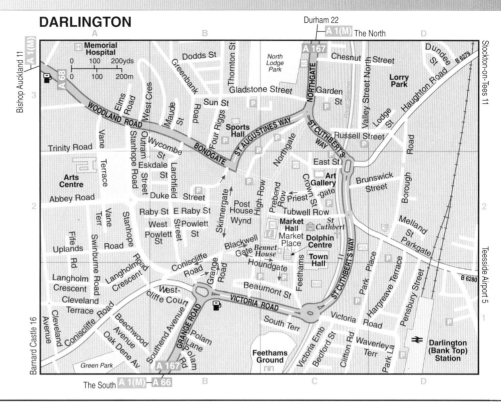

DERBY

Matlock 19

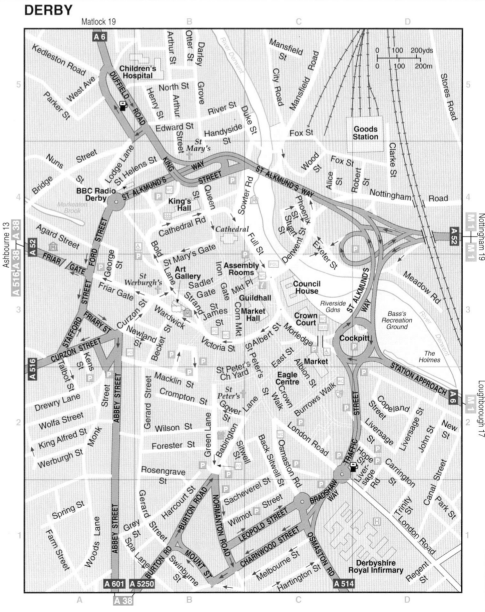

DONCASTER

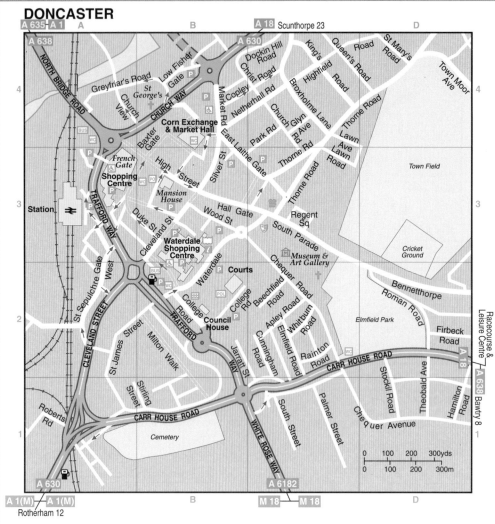

Apley Road **C2**
Beechfield Road **C2**
Bennetthorpe **D2**
Broxholme Lane **C4**
Carr House Road **A1-D2**
Chequer Avenue **D1**
Chequer Road **C2**
Church Road **C4**
Church Way **B4**
Cleveland Street **A2**
Cleveland Street **B3**
College Road **B2**
Cunningham Road **C2**
Duke Street **B3**
East Laithe Gate **B4-C3**
Firbeck Road **D2**
Greyfriar's Road **A4-B4**
Hall Gate **B3-C3**
Highfield Road **C4-D4**
High Street **B3**
Jarratt Street **B2**
King's Road **C4**
Lawn Road **C3**
Market Road **B4**
Milton Walk **B2**
Netherhall Road **B4-C4**
North Bridge Road **A4**
Regent Square **C3**
St James Street **A1-B2**
St Sepulchre Gate
   West **A2-A3**
Silver Street **B3**
South Parade **C3**
Thorne Road **C3-D4**
Town Moor Avenue **D4**
Trafford Way **A3-B2**
Waterdale **B2-B3**
White Rose Way **C1**
Wood Street **B3**

DUNFERMLINE

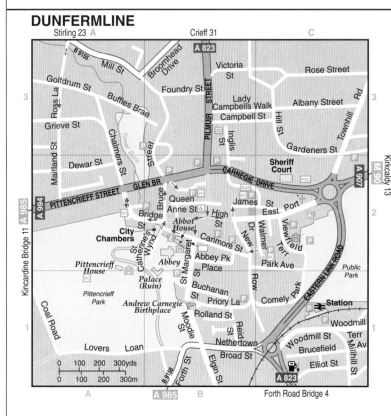

Abbey Park Place **B2**
Albany Street **C3**
Bridge Street **A2-B2**
Broomhead Drive **B3**
Bruce Street **B2-B3**
Brucefield Avenue **C1**
Buchanan Street **B1**
Buffies Brae **A3-B3**
Campbell Street **B3-C3**
Canmore Street **B2**
Carnegie Drive **B2-C2**
Chalmers Street **A3-A2**
Coal Road **A1**
Comely Park **C1**
Dewar Street **A2**
Eastport **C2**
Elgin Street **B1**
Elliot Street **C1**
Forth Street **B1**
Foundry Street **B3**
Gardeners Street **C3**
Glen Bridge **A2-B2**
Golfdrum Street **A3**
Grieve Street **A3**
High Street **B2**
Hill Street **C3**
Inglis Street **B3-B2**

James Street **B2-C2**
Lady Campbells Walk **B3-C3**
Lovers Loan **A1**
Maitland Street **A2-A3**
Mill Street **A3**
Millhill Street **C1**
Moodie Street **B1**
Nethertown Broad Street **B1**
New Row **B2-B1**
Park Avenue **C2**
Pilmuir Street **B3**
Pittencrieff Street **A2**
Priory Lane **B1**
Queen Anne Street **B2**
Reid Street **B1**
Rolland Street **B1**
Ross Lane **A3**
Rose Street **C3**
St Catherine's Wynd **B2**
St Margaret Street **B1-B2**
St Margaret's Drive **C1-C2**
Townhill Road **C3**
Victoria Street **B3**
Viewfield Terrace **C2**
Walmer Drive **C2**
Woodmill Street **C1**
Woodmill Terrace **C1**

DUBLIN

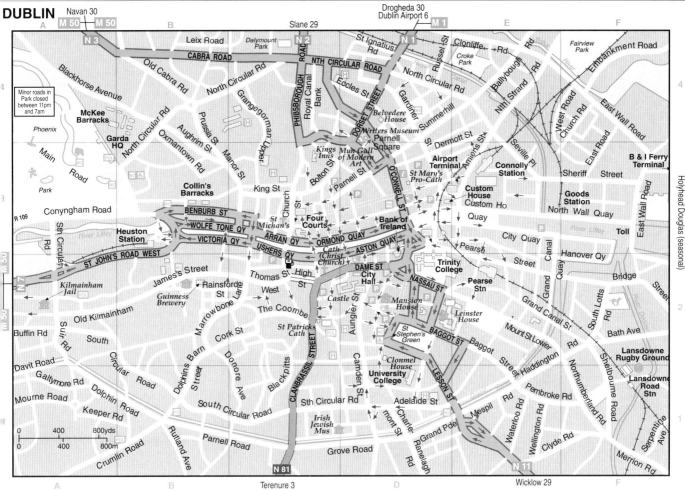

DURHAM

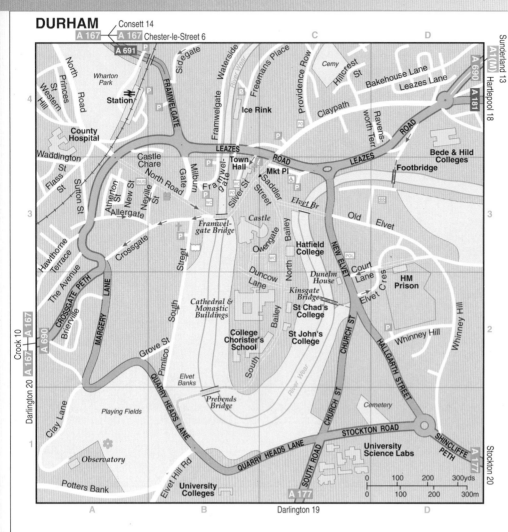

FALMOUTH

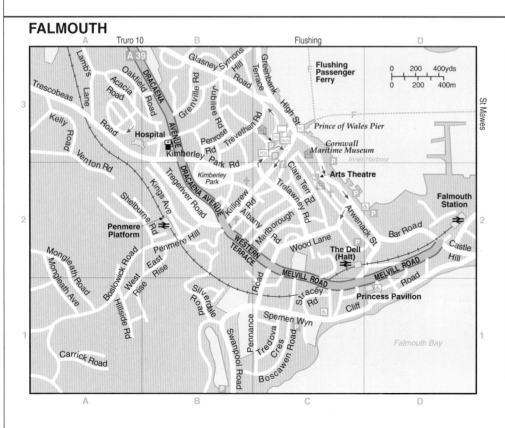

EDINBURGH

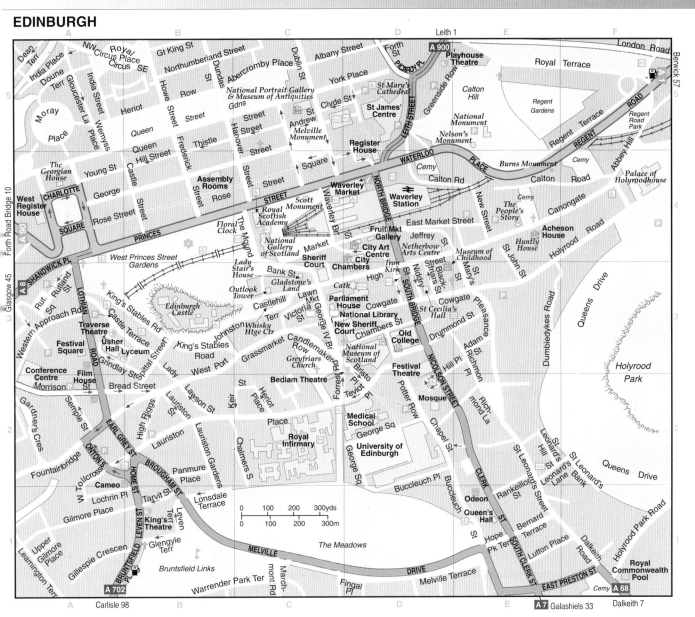

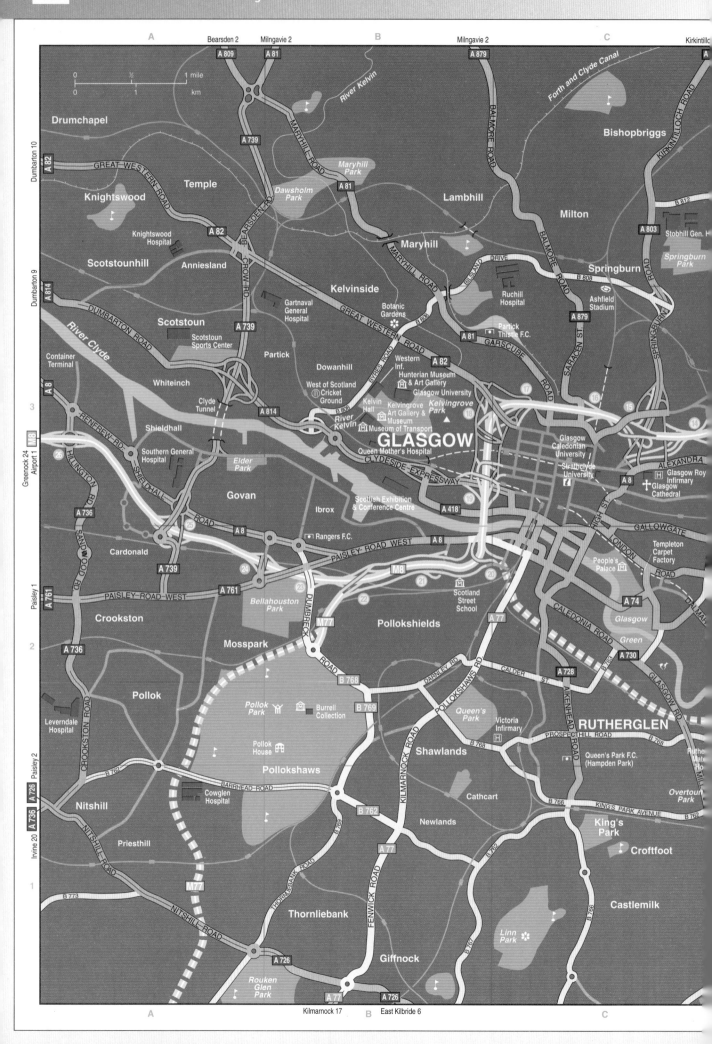

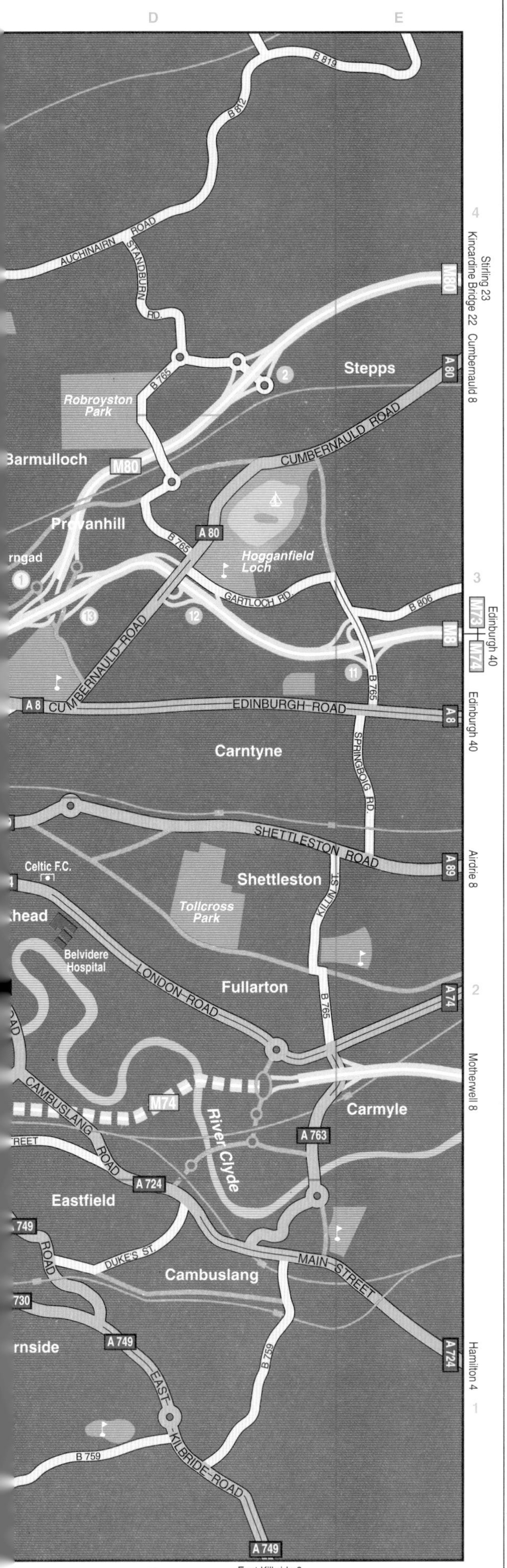

The map on the left shows areas including:

- B 818
- B 812
- Stirling 23
- Kincardine Bridge 22 / Cumbernauld 8
- M80
- A 80
- Stepps
- AUCHINAIRN ROAD / STANDBURN RD
- Robroyston Park
- B 765
- Barmulloch
- M80
- CUMBERNAULD ROAD
- Provanhill
- A 80
- Hogganfield Loch
- rngad
- GARTLOCH RD
- B 806
- 13
- 12
- 11
- B 765
- Edinburgh 40
- M73 / M74 / M8
- A 8
- CUMBERNAULD ROAD
- EDINBURGH ROAD
- A 8
- Edinburgh 40
- Carntyne
- SPRINGBOIG RD
- SHETTLESTON ROAD
- A 89
- Airdrie 8
- Celtic F.C.
- Shettleston
- Tollcross Park
- KILLIN ST
- head
- Belvidere Hospital
- LONDON ROAD
- Fullarton
- B 765
- A 74
- Motherwell 8
- Carmyle
- M74
- CAMBUSLANG ROAD
- River Clyde
- A 763
- REET
- A 724
- Eastfield
- 749
- DUKES ST
- MAIN STREET
- Cambuslang
- 730
- A 749
- B 759
- rnside
- A 749
- B 759
- A 74
- Hamilton 4
- EAST KILBRIDE ROAD
- B 759
- A 749
- East Kilbride 2

Places to see in Glasgow

❧

MUSIC, ART AND ARCHITECTURE play a large part in Glasgow life. The Royal Scottish National Orchestra, the Scottish Opera and the Scottish Ballet are based there, and the Kelvingrove Art Gallery and the Hunterian Museum and Art Gallery are outstanding, as is Charles Rennie Mackintosh's turn-of-the-century Glasgow School of Art. Clustered round the cathedral at the city's east end is the tiny survival of the medieval city, where Provand's Lordship of 1471 is Glasgow's oldest house. Glasgow Cross, a 1929 replica of a medieval cross, and Tolbooth Steeple of 1629 mark what was the city's main crossroads before the railway brought a new focus in the mid 19th century.

The true centre of Glasgow is now farther west in a grid of streets developed in the 18th-19th centuries, with opulent architecture such as the Merchant's House in George Square and the decorative façades of St Vincent Place. Other buildings include Robert Adam's Trades Hall of 1794 and the Royal Exchange of 1780, once a tobacco lord's mansion and now the Gallery of Modern Art. The late 20th century has added St Enoch's Square shopping centre, with Europe's largest glass roof—nearly 7 acres (2.8 ha) in extent. A walk through Glasgow Green gives views across the Clyde to the Gorbals district, its 1960s high-rise blocks contrasting with the leafy West End, where the Botanic Gardens and Kelvingrove Park flank the River Kelvin and are overlooked by Glasgow University and the elegant Victorian houses of Woodlands Terrace and Park Circus.

PLACES OF INTEREST

Botanic Gardens [B3] Noted for their orchids and begonias, the gardens, founded in 1817, are dominated by the Kibble Palace, a Victorian conservatory where white statues stand out amid the luxuriant tree ferns. Skirting the gardens is the Kelvin Walkway, leading through a wooded gorge.

City Chambers [p 398 D2] A symbol of the city's former wealth, this spectacular Italianate building of 1888 stands on the east side of George Square. Its interior reveals marble staircases, lavish mosaics, granite columns and an opulent banqueting hall, where murals depict Glasgow's growth.

Glasgow Cathedral [p 398 F2] Part of medieval Glasgow, the Gothic cathedral dates mainly from the 13th century. It is believed to stand on the site of a church built by Glasgow's founder, St Mungo, in the 6th century, and has the saint's tomb in the crypt. Close by are the St Mungo Museum of Religious Life and Art, and the Necropolis, with imposing tombs of city magnates.

Hunterian Museum and Art Gallery [B3] Within the vast 19th-century neo-Gothic buildings of Glasgow University, Scotland's oldest museum was opened in 1807, and includes one of the world's finest collections of coins and medals, assembled by the physician William Hunter (1718-83). The art gallery includes many paintings by James McNeill Whistler (1834-1903), and works by 19th and 20th-century Scottish artists.

Kelvingrove Art Gallery and Museum [B3] A red sandstone building of 1902 houses the city's principal art gallery and museum, which has a fine collection of British and European paintings, including works by the Pre-Raphaelites and French Impressionists. The gallery stands in Kelvingrove Park, laid out in 1852 by Sir Joseph Paxton, who designed London's Crystal Palace.

Museum of Transport [B3] Glasgow trams, models of Clyde ships, Scottish locomotives and a reconstruction of a Glasgow street of 1938, with a cinema and underground station, can be seen in this museum in twin-towered Kelvin Hall.

People's Palace [C2] Opened in 1898 as a cultural centre for Glasgow's East End, the 'palace' museum tells the city's history from 1175 and includes Winter Gardens and a fine Victorian conservatory. It stands on Glasgow Green, a public space since the 12th century. A memorial celebrates James Watt's improvement to the steam engine, an idea that came to him while walking here in 1767. Nearby, the former Templeton Carpet Factory of 1889 was modelled in bricks and tiles on the Doge's Palace in Venice.

Scotland Street School [B2] Charles Rennie Mackintosh designed this 1904 school. It houses a museum of education from Victorian times to the late 1960s.

Tenement House [p 398 A4] Life in a typical gaslit Glasgow tenement in the early 20th century is evoked in the former home (NTS) of Miss Agnes Toward, a typist in a shipping firm, who lived here from 1911 to 1965. She changed nothing and threw little away. Jam pots stand in a cupboard, a table is laid for tea and a fire glows in the grate.

See also pages 266-267

GLASGOW

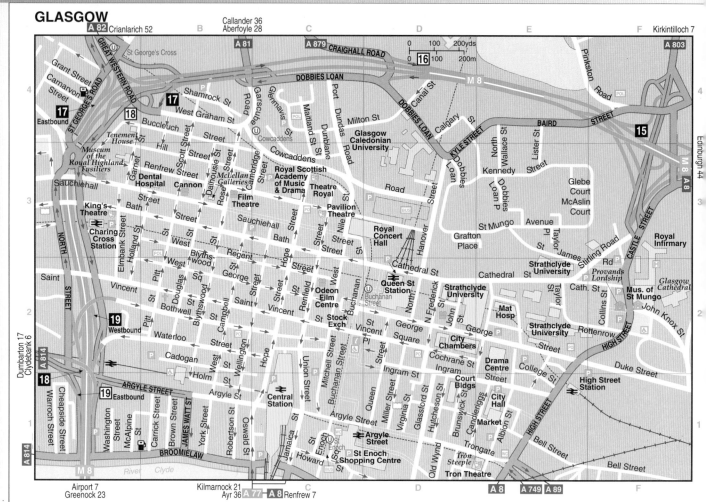

GLOUCESTER

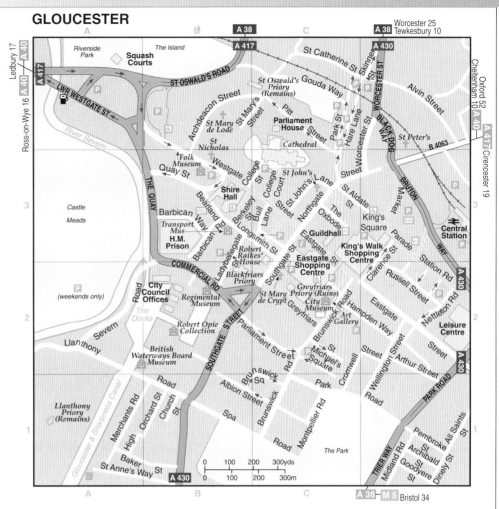

GUILDFORD

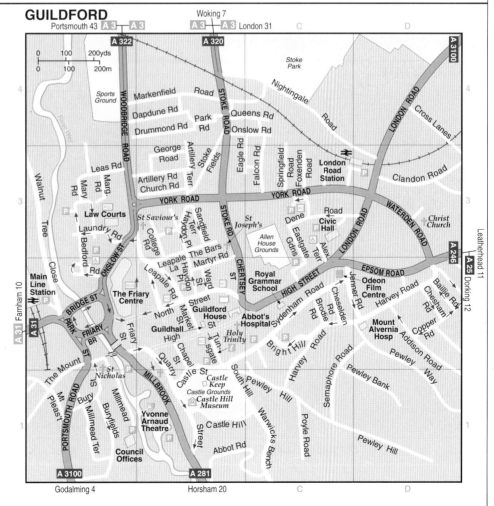

HALIFAX

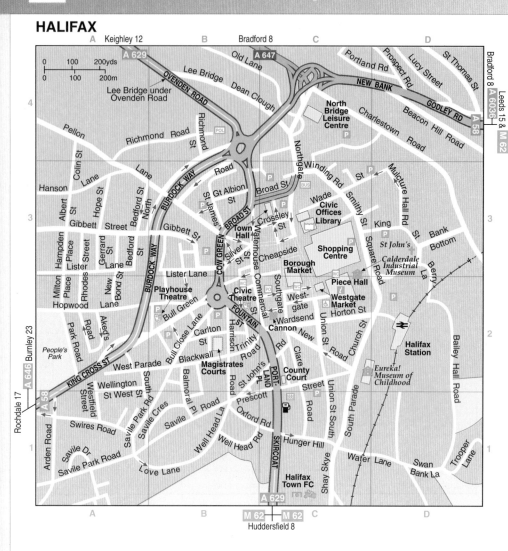

Beacon Hill Road **D4**
Broad Street **B3-C3**
Bull Close Lane **B2**
Bull Green **B2**
Burdock Way **A2-B3**
Charlestown Road **C4-D4**
Church Street **C2**
Clare Road **C2-C1**
Cow Green **B3**
Crossley Street **C3**
Dean Clough **B4-C4**
Fountain Street **B2**
Gibbett Street **B3**
Godley Road **D4**
Great Albion Street **B3**
Horton Street **C2**
King Cross Street **A2**
Lee Bridge **B4**
Lister Lane **B3**
New Bank **C4-D4**
New Road **C2**
Northgate **C4-C3**
Ovenden Road **B4**
Pellon Lane **A4-A3**
Portland Place **C2**
St Thomas Street **D4**
Savile Road **B1**
Shay Skye **C1**
Skircoat **C1**
Smithy Street **C3**
South Parade **C1**
Southgate **C2**
Square Road **C3-D2**
Trinity Road **B2**
Union Street **C2**
Wardsend **C2**
Waterhouse Commercial
 Street **B3-C2**
Winding Road **C3**

HARROGATE

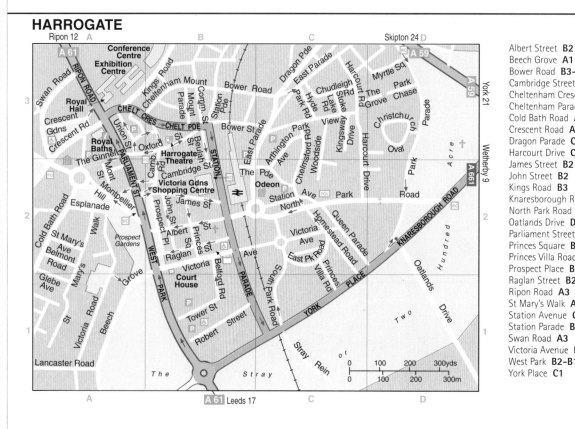

Albert Street **B2**
Beech Grove **A1**
Bower Road **B3-C3**
Cambridge Street **B2**
Cheltenham Crescent **A3-B3**
Cheltenham Parade **B3**
Cold Bath Road **A2**
Crescent Road **A3**
Dragon Parade **C3**
Harcourt Drive **C3-C2**
James Street **B2**
John Street **B2**
Kings Road **B3**
Knaresborough Road **D2**
North Park Road **C2-D2**
Oatlands Drive **D2-D1**
Parliament Street **A3-A2**
Princes Square **B2**
Princes Villa Road **C2-C1**
Prospect Place **B2**
Raglan Street **B2**
Ripon Road **A3**
St Mary's Walk **A1-A2**
Station Avenue **C2**
Station Parade **B3-B1**
Swan Road **A3**
Victoria Avenue **B2**
West Park **B2-B1**
York Place **C1**

HEREFORD

Aubrey Street **A3**
Barrs Court Road **C4**
Barton Road **A2**
Bath Street **C3**
Bewell Street **A3–B3**
Blackfriars Street **B4**
Blue School Street **B3**
Bridge Street **A2**
Broad Street **B3**
Cannonmoor Street **A4**
Cantilupe Street **B2–C2**
Castle Street **B2**
Catherine Street **B3**
Commercial Road **C3**
Conningsby Street **B4**
East Street **B3**
Edgar Street **B4–A4**
Eign Street **A3**
Friar Street **A3**
Gaol Street **C3–C2**
Green Street **C2–C1**
Greyfriars Bridge **A2**
Grove Road **C2**
Gwynne Street **A2–B2**

Harold Street **C1**
Hinton Road **A1–B1**
King Street **A2**
Kyrle Street **C3**
Mill Street **C2**
Moorfield Street **A4**
Nelson Street **C1**
New Market Street **B3**
Park Street **C1**
Portland Street **A4–A3**
Quay Street **B2**
St Guthlac Street **C3–C2**
St James Road **C2**
St Martin's Avenue **A1–B1**
St Martin's Street **A1–A2**
St Owen Street **B3–C2**
Station Approach **C4**
Stonebow Road **C3**
Symonds Street **C3**
Turner Street **C2**
Union Street **B3**
Victoria Street **A3–A2**
West Street **A3**
Widemarsh Street **B4–B3**

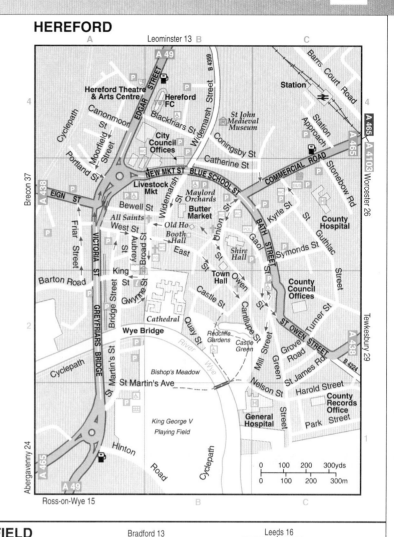

HUDDERSFIELD

Albion Street **B1**
Byram Street **C3–C2**
Castlegate **B1–B4**
Cross Church Street **C2**
Firth Street **D1**
Fitzwilliam Street **A3–B3**
Half Moon Street **B2**
High Street **B2**
John William Street **B3–C2**
King Street **C2**
King's Mill Lane **D1**
Kirkgate **C2**
Leeds Road **C3–C4**
Lord Street **C3–C2**
Manchester Road **A1–B1**
Market Street **B2**
Merton Street **A1–B1**
New North Road **A3**
New Street **B1–B2**
Northumberland Street **C3**
Outcote Bank **B1**
Princess Street **B1–C1**
Queen Street **C2**
Queen Street South **C1**
Queensgate **C1**
Railway Street **B3–B2**
Ramsden Street **C1–B1**
St Andrew's Road **D4–D2**
St John's Road **B4–B3**
St Peter's Street **C3**
Southgate **C3–C2**
Springwood Avenue **A1**
Trinity Street **A3–A2**
Venn Street **C2**
Viaduct Street **B3**
Victoria Lane **C2**
Wakefield Road **D2–D1**
Westgate **B2**
Zetland Street **C2**

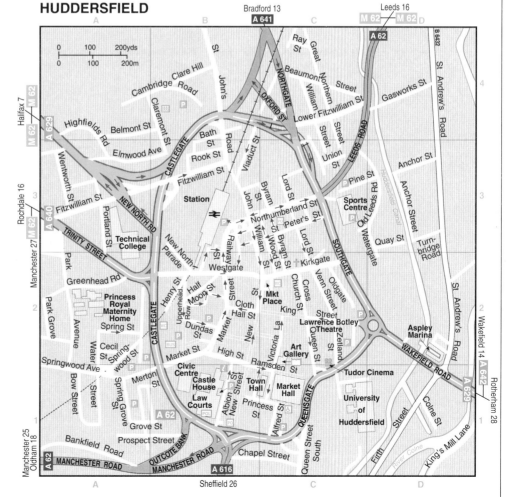

INVERNESS

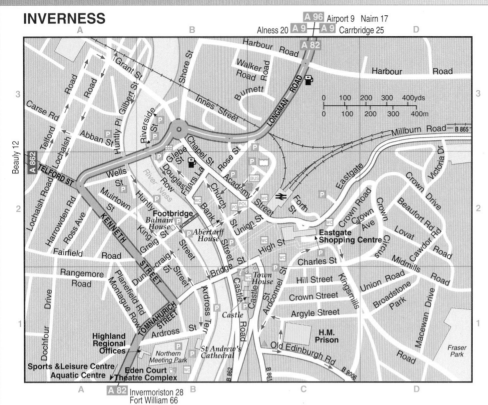

Abban Street **A3**	Bank Street **B2**	Chapel Street **B3–B2**	Crown Road **C2–D2**
Academy Street **B2–C2**	Bridge Street **B1–B2**	Charles Street **C2**	Crown Street **C1**
Ardconnel Street **C1**	Burnett Road **B3–C3**	Church Street **B2**	Dochfour Drive **A1**
Ardross Street **B1**	Carse Road **A3**	Crown Avenue **C2–D2**	Douglas Row **B2**
Ardross Terrace **B1**	Castle Road **B1**	Crown Circus **D2**	Duncraig Street **B1–B2**
Argyle Street **C1**	Castle Street **C1**	Crown Drive **D2**	Eastgate **C2**

Fairfield Road **A2**
Forth Street **C2**
Friars Lane **B2**
Gilbert Street **A3**
Glebe Street **B2–B3**
Grant Street **A3**
Greig Street **B2**
Harbour Road **C3–D3**
High Street **C2**
Hill St **C1**
Huntly Place **A3**
Huntly Street **B2**
Innes Street **B3**
Kenneth Street **A2–B1**
King St **B2–B1**
Kingsmills Rd **C1–D1**
Lochalsh Road **A2–A3**
Longman Road **C3**
Lovat Road **D2**
Midmills Road **D2–D1**
Millburn Road **D3**
Montague Row **A1**
Muirtown Street **A2**
Old Edinburgh Road **C1**
Planefield Road **A1**
Rangemore Road **A1**
Riverside Street **B3**
Rose Street **B2**
Ross Avenue **A2**
Shore Street **B3**
Telford Road **A3**
Telford Street **A3**
Tomnahurich Street **B1**
Union Road **D1**
Union Street **B2–C2**
Walker Road **B3–C3**
Wells Street **A2**

KING'S LYNN

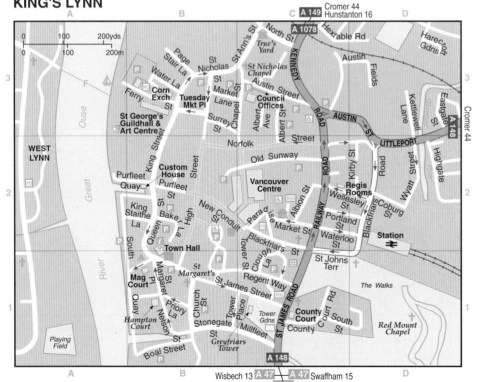

Albert Avenue **C3**	Baker Lane **B2**	Church Street **B1**	Ferry Street **B3**
Albert Street **C3**	Blackfriars Road **D2**	Clough Lane **C1**	Harecroft Gardens **D3**
Albion Street **C2**	Blackfriars Street **C2**	Coburg Street **D2**	Hextable Road **C3**
Austin Fields **D3**	Boal Street **B1**	County Court Road **C1**	Highgate **D2**
Austin Street **C3–D3**	Chapel Street **C3**	Eastgate Street **D3**	High Street **B2**

Kennedy Road **C3**
Kettlewell Lane **D3**
King Staithe Lane **B2**
King Street **B2**
Littleport **D2**
Market Lane **B3**
Market Street **C2**
Millfleet **C1**
Nelson Street **B1**
New Conduit Street **B2**
Norfolk Street **B2–C2**
North Street **C3**
Old Sunway **C2**
Paradise **C2**
Portland Street **C2**
Priory Lane **B1**
Purfleet Quay **B2**
Purfleet Street **B2**
Queen Street **B2**
Railway Road **C2**
Regent Way **C1**
St Ann's Street **C3**
St James Road **C1**
St James Street **B1–C1**
St Johns Terrace **C1**
St Margaret Place **B1**
St Nicholas Street **B3**
South Quay **A2–B1**
South Street **C1**
Stonegate Street **B1**
Surrey Street **B3**
Tower Place **B1**
Tower Street **C2–C1**
Water Lane **B3**
Waterloo Street **C2**
Wellesley Street **C2**
Wyatt Street **D2**

KINGSTON UPON HULL

Alfred Gelder Street B2-C2
Anlaby Road A2
Beverley Road A3
Bond Street B2
Carr Lane A2
Castle Street B1
Charles Street B3
Dagger Lane B1
Dock Office Row C3-C2
Dock Street B2
Ferensway A3-A1
Freetown Way A3-B3
Garrison Road D1-D2
George Street B2-B3
Great Union Street C3-D2
Grimston Steet B3-B2
Guildhall Road B2
Hessle Road A1
High Street C1-C2
Jameson Street A2-B2
Jarratt Street B3
King Edward Street B2
Lowgate C2
Manor Street C2
Myton Bridge C1
New Cleveland Street C3
Osborne Street A1
Percy Street A3
Posterngate B1
Prospect Street A3
Waterhouse Lane B1
West Street A2
Whitefriargate B2
Witham D3

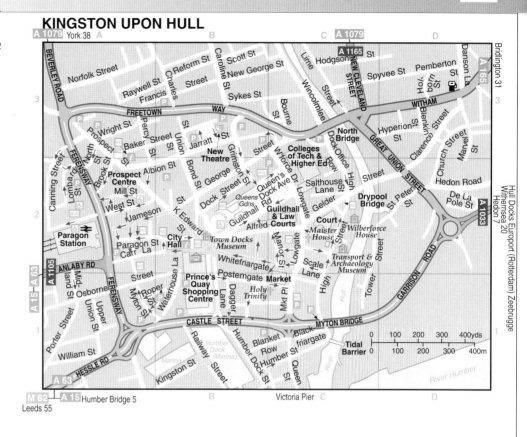

LEICESTER

Abbey Street C4
Bedford Street South C3-C4
Belgrave Gate C4
Belvoir Street C2
Burleys Way B4-C4
Carlton Street B1
Charles Street C3-C2
Church Gate B3
Clyde Street D3
Conduit Street D1
Duke Street C1
Duns Lane A2
Eastbond Street B3
Granby Street C2
Haymarket C3
High Cross Street A3
High Street B3
Humberstone Gate C3
Lee Street C3
London Road D1
Market Street B2
Newarke Street B2
Northgate Street A4
Oxford Street B1
Peacock Lane B2
Pocklingtons Walk B2
Queen Street D2
Regent Road C1
Rutland Street C2-D3
St George's Way D2-D3
St Margarets Way B4
St Matthews Way D4
St Nicholas Circle A2
St Peter's Lane B3
Sanvey Gate A4-B4
Southgates A2-B2
Swain Street D2
Vaughan Way B3
Waterloo Way C1-D1
Welford Road B1
Western Boulevard A2-A1
Wharf Street South C4-C3
Yeoman Street C3

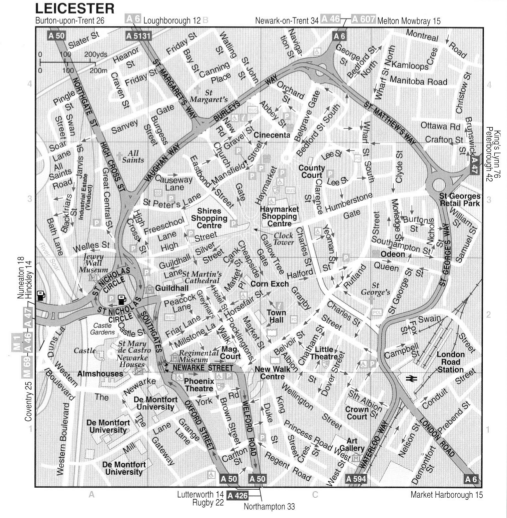

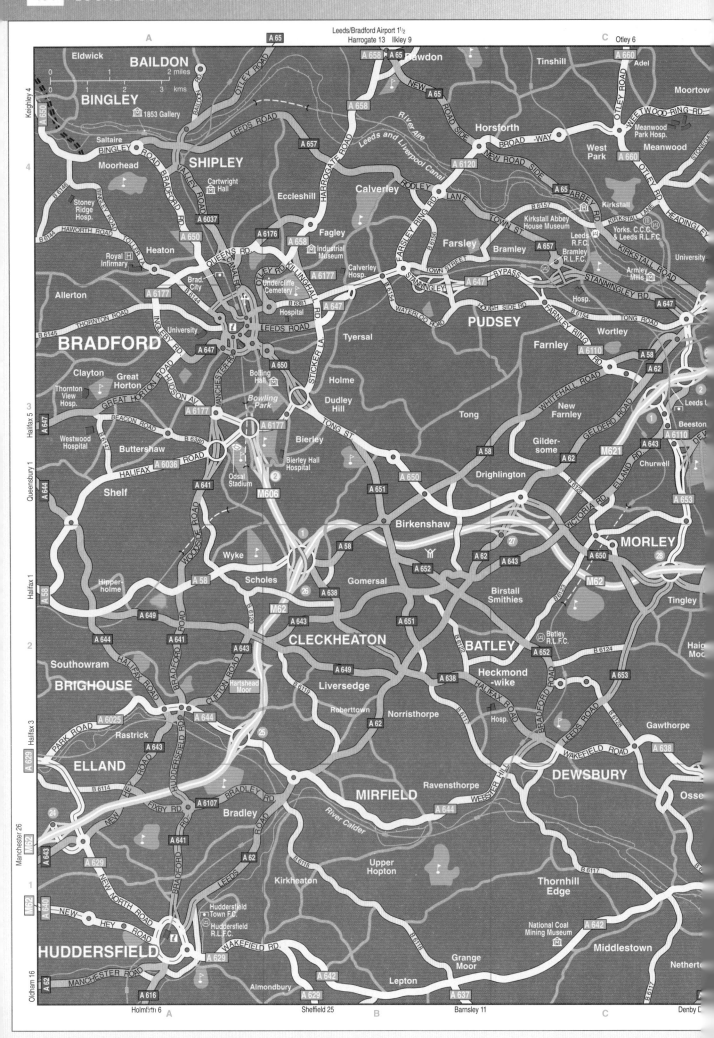

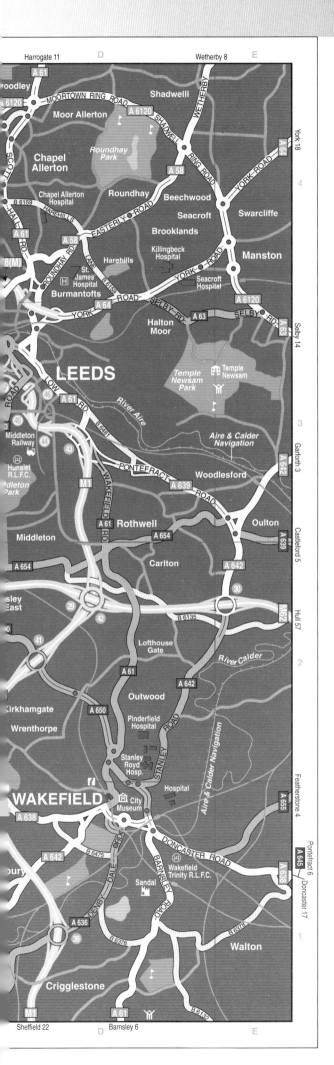

Places to see in Leeds and Bradford

BOTH LEEDS AND BRADFORD HAVE EMERGED as business and cultural centres in recent years, and have made new use of the industrial and civic buildings that date largely from their heyday as giant textile producers in the 19th century. Leeds has restored its Edwardian Kirkgate Market–the largest market in the north of England–and its ornate Victorian shopping arcades, and has converted the old grain mills and warehouses by the Aire into offices, hotels and restaurants. Opera North has its home in the city's Grand Theatre, and its opulent town hall is the setting for an international piano competition every three years.

Bradford's Venetian-style Wool Exchange of the 1860s is becoming a shopping centre, and its 1914 Alhambra Theatre has been restored to its former splendour. But there are still working textile mills in the area, some of which offer tours and have mill-shops. Bradford's Moorside Mills and Leeds's Armley Mills have been revived as industrial museums, and Bradford's National Museum of Photography, Film and Television is the most visited museum outside London. Works by artist David Hockney, born in Bradford in 1937, can be seen at the 1853 Gallery in Salt's Mill, an Italianate building in the factory village of Saltaire to the north.

PLACES OF INTEREST

Armley Mills Museum [C4] Once the world's largest mill, this former woollen mill on an island in the River Aire now tells the industrial history of Leeds. The mill was in operation between 1806 and 1967.

Bingley [A4] An impressive flight of five locks carries the Leeds and Liverpool Canal up 59 ft (18 m) at this medieval wool town, which has a 16th-century church. John Braine, who was born in Bradford, wrote his best-selling novel *Room at the Top* (1957) while working at the library in 1940-51.

Bolling Hall Museum [B3] Built onto a medieval pele tower in the 16th-18th centuries, this is a good example of a former West Yorkshire country residence. It has fine panelling and oak furniture; a stained-glass window depicts 24 coats of arms.

Bradford Cathedral [p 384 D3] Until 1919, the 14th-15th-century cathedral was a parish church. Its Chapter House and Lady Chapel were added in 1951-63, and stained glass of 1862 from the studios of William Morris was transferred to the Lady Chapel. The nearby merchant quarter of Little Germany has 19th-century warehouses.

Bradford Industrial Museum [B4] Moorside Mills, where raw wool was converted into high-quality cloth, has been restored to its original state. Visitors can see inside the former homes of the mill owner and his workers, and there are horse-drawn tram and bus rides round the site.

Cartwright Hall Art Gallery [A4] A Bradford mill owner, Samuel Cunliffe Lister, financed the building of this baroque-revival art gallery in 1904. Its collections of British paintings of the 19th and 20th centuries include works by Dante Gabriel Rossetti (1828-82) and David Hockney.

Colour Museum [p 384 A3] Britain's only museum devoted to colour includes displays that vary from the world as seen through the eyes of a dog to the making of dyes. You may also have the chance to try your hand at computer-aided interior design.

Kirkstall Abbey House Museum [C4] Once Abbey House was a manor converted from the gatehouse of a 12th-century Cistercian abbey–of which the impressive remains include the abbey church, with a finely carved west doorway. Today the former gatehouse is home to a museum that includes reconstructed Victorian streets with cottages, shops and an inn.

Leeds City Art Gallery [p 406 C3] The sculptors Henry Moore and Barbara Hepworth both studied at Leeds College of Art, and some of their works are on display. The gallery has a fine collection of Victorian paintings and early English watercolours. Nearby, the City Museum has displays including natural history and coins.

National Museum of Photography, Film and Television [p 384 B1] Lively exhibits give the opportunity to read the news on camera and to 'ride' on a flying carpet with scenery projected behind. There are also photographs, vintage televisions and cameras, and a magic lantern show.

Tetley's Brewery Wharf [p 406 E2] English pub life through the ages can be studied at this theme museum, which celebrates Leeds's place as a brewing centre. There are also tours round Tetley's brewery.

Undercliffe Cemetery [B4] The ornate and monumental tombs of many of Bradford's wealthy Victorians can be viewed in this hillside cemetery of 1854, which received a BBC tourism award in 1989.

See also pages 206-207 and 218-219

LEEDS

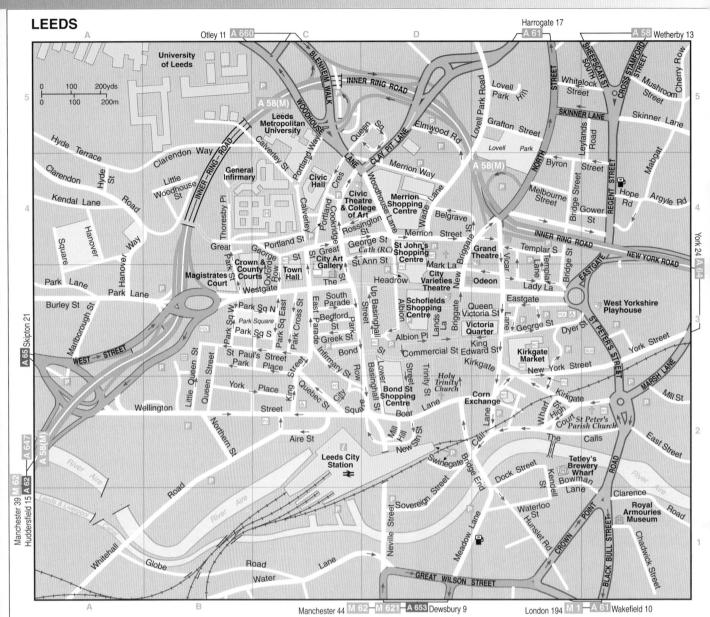

LIVERPOOL

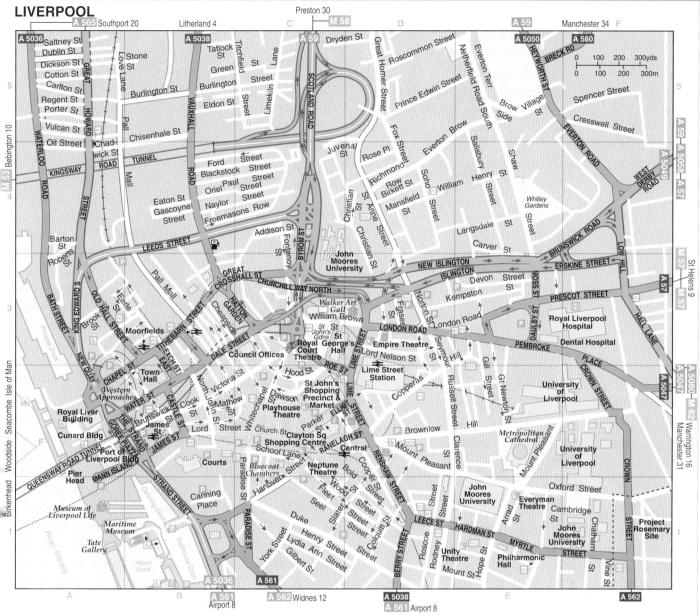

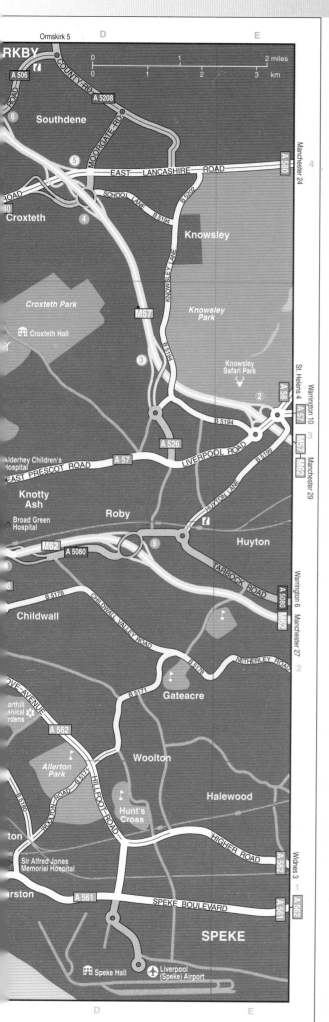

A guide to Liverpool and Birkenhead

WILLIAM BROWN STREET has some of Liverpool's finest buildings, including the Walker Art Gallery–one of Europe's foremost art galleries–the Central Libraries, the Liverpool Museum and neoclassical St George's Hall, all legacies of the city's days as a great Victorian port on the River Mersey. On Pier Head, the Royal Liver Building, the Cunard Building and the Port of Liverpool Building are the city's best-known landmarks, and its two huge 20th-century cathedrals are in contrasting styles. Although shipbuilding and passenger liners no longer enliven the river front, the Victorian Albert Dock now has a new lease of life as a family entertainment centre; fans of the Liverpool-born pop group The Beatles can find a reconstruction of The Cavern club where they played in the 1960s, and visit The Beatles Story.

Birkenhead across the Mersey can be reached by one of Europe's oldest ferries. Also a 19th-century port and shipbuilding centre, it now harbours two 1982 Falklands War ships, the submarine HMS *Onyx*–built at nearby Cammell Laird shipyard–and the frigate HMS *Plymouth*, both open to visitors. Hamilton Square has fine Victorian architecture, and Birkenhead Park–which was laid out in 1847 by Sir Joseph Paxton–was Britain's first public park and the model for Central Park in New York.

PLACES OF INTEREST

Albert Dock [B2] Once at the hub of Liverpool's prosperous sea trade, the dock, opened in 1846, declined with the coming of steamships, for which it was too shallow. It closed in 1972, but in the 1980s the colonnaded five-storey warehouses were restored to become a large tourist and shopping centre. Attractions include the Tate Gallery, with collections of modern art, and the Merseyside Maritime Museum, recalling Liverpool's great days as a port.

Anglican Cathedral [B2] Britain's largest cathedral, 636 ft (194 m) long, this red sandstone Gothic Revival building was designed by Giles Gilbert Scott at the age of 21. Begun in 1904, it was not completed until 1978–18 years after Scott's death. From the central tower, 331 ft (101 m) high, Blackpool and the Welsh hills can be seen.

Birkenhead Priory [B2] Founded in 1150 by Benedictine monks, the Priory of St James is now a ruin. The Benedictines ran the first Mersey ferry some 800 years ago.

Croxteth Hall and Country Park [D3] Once part of the country estate of the Earl of Sefton, the Jacobean hall has furnishings and costumes of Edwardian times, and there is a Victorian walled garden, a home farm, and extensive woods and parkland.

Knowsley Safari Park [E3] In the early 1800s the 13th Earl of Derby set up a fine private menagerie here. Today, lions, zebras, tigers and elephants are among the animals to be seen in the safari park, which has sea lion shows and a miniature railway.

Lady Lever Art Gallery [B1] Lord Leverhulme built the gallery in 1922 in memory of his wife. It has a fine collection of English paintings and furniture.

Metropolitan Cathedral [C2] A spiked lantern tower tops the circular nave of this ultramodern Roman Catholic cathedral of 1967, designed by Sir Frederick Gibberd. Inside, 13 chapels radiate from the nave, which is 194 ft (59 m) in diameter. The crypt is the only completed part of Sir Edwin Lutyens's immense 1930s design, abandoned after the Second World War; had his cathedral been built, it would have had a larger dome than St Peter's, Rome.

Museum of Liverpool Life [p 407 A1] The story of Merseyside life and culture is told, including its sporting events such as the Grand National and the working lives of cotton graders, dockers and shipbuilders.

Pier Head [B2] Three early 20th-century office buildings overlook the sweep of the Mersey. Topping the twin towers of the Royal Liver Building of 1911 are statues of the Liver Birds–which probably take their name from the seaweed, or laver, in their beaks. The neighbouring Cunard Building dates from 1916, and next to it is the Port of Liverpool Building of 1907, with a green dome and globes supported by dolphins.

St George's Hall [p 407 C3] One of the finest neoclassical buildings in Britain, the hall of 1854 designed by Londsale Elmes has a portico of 60 ft (18 m) high Corinthian columns facing Lime Street.

Sudley Art Gallery [C2] Victorian shipping magnate George Holt lived here. His 18th and 19th-century art collection includes works by Landseer and the Pre-Raphaelites.

Williamson Art Gallery and Museum [A2] Watercolours by Gainsborough and Turner are on view, also Liverpool porcelain and Birkenhead's maritime history.

See also pages 202-203

LUTON

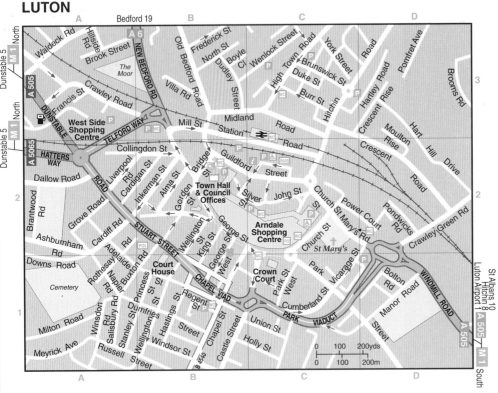

Alma Street **B2**	Brunswick Street **C3**
Ashburnham Road **A2**	Burr Street **C3**
Boyle Close **B3**	Buxton Road **A1**
Bridge Street **B2**	Cardiff Road **A2**
Brook Street **A3**	Cardigan Street **A2–B2**
Brooms Road **D3**	Castle Street **B1**

Chapel Street **B1**	Crescent Rise **D3**
Chapel Viaduct **B1**	Cumberland Street **C1**
Church Street **C2**	Dallow Road **A2**
Collingdon Street **A2–B2**	Dudley Street **B3**
Crawley Green Road **D2**	Dunstable Road **A3–A2**
Crawley Road **A3**	Francis Street **A3**

Frederick Street **B3**	Park Street West **C1**
George Street **B2**	Park Viaduct **C1**
George Street West **B1–B2**	Pomfret Avenue **D3**
Gordon Street **B2**	Power Court **C2–D2**
Guildford Street **B2–C2**	Princess Street **B1**
Hartley Road **D3**	Regent Street **B1**
Hatters Way **A2**	St Mary's Road **C2**
High Town Road **C3**	Silver Street **B2–C2**
Hillside Road **A3**	Station Road **B3–C3**
Hitchin Road **C3–D3**	Stuart Street **B2**
Inkerman Street **B2**	Telford Way **A3**
John Street **C2**	Vicarage Street **C1**
King Street **B2**	Villa Road **B3**
Liverpool Road **A2**	Waldeck Road **A3**
Manor Road **D1**	Wellington Street **B2**
Midland Road **B3–C3**	Wenlock Street **C3**
Mill Street **B3**	Windmill Road **D1**
New Bedford Road **B3**	York Street **C3**
Old Bedford Road **B3**	
Park Street **C1–D1**	

MAIDSTONE

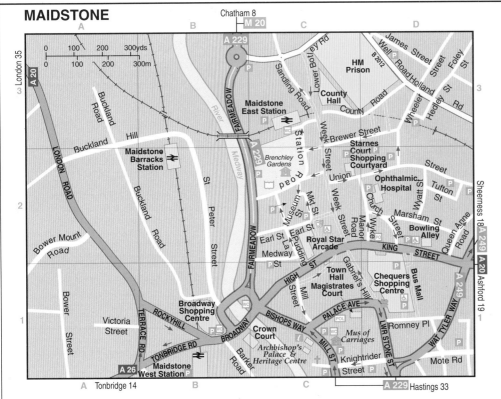

Barker Road **B1**	Bower Street **A1**
Bishops Way **C1**	Brewer Street **C3–D3**
Bower Mount Road **A2**	Broadway **B1**

Buckland Hill **A3**	County Road **C3–D3**
Buckland Road **A3–B2**	Earl Street **C2**
Church Street **D2**	Fairmeadow **C2–B3**

Foley Street **D3**	Palace Avenue **C1**
Gabriel's Hill **C1**	Pudding Lane **C2**
Hedley Street **D3**	Queen Anne Road **D2**
High Street **C1**	Rockyhill **B1**
Holland Road **D3**	Romney Place **D1**
King Street **D2**	St Peter Street **B2**
Knightrider Street **C1–D1**	Sandling Road **C3**
London Road **A2**	Station Road **C3–C2**
Lower Botley Road **C3**	Terrace Road **B1**
Lower Stone Street **D1**	Tonbridge Road **B1**
Market Street **C2**	Tufton Street **D2**
Marsham Street **D2**	Union Street **C2–D2**
Medway Street **C2**	Victoria Street **A1**
Mill Street **C1**	Wat Tyler Road **D1**
Mote Road **D1**	Week Street **C3–C2**
Museum Street **C2**	Well Road **D3**
	Wheeler Street **D3**
	Wyatt Street **D2**
	Wyke Manor Road **D2**

MANCHESTER

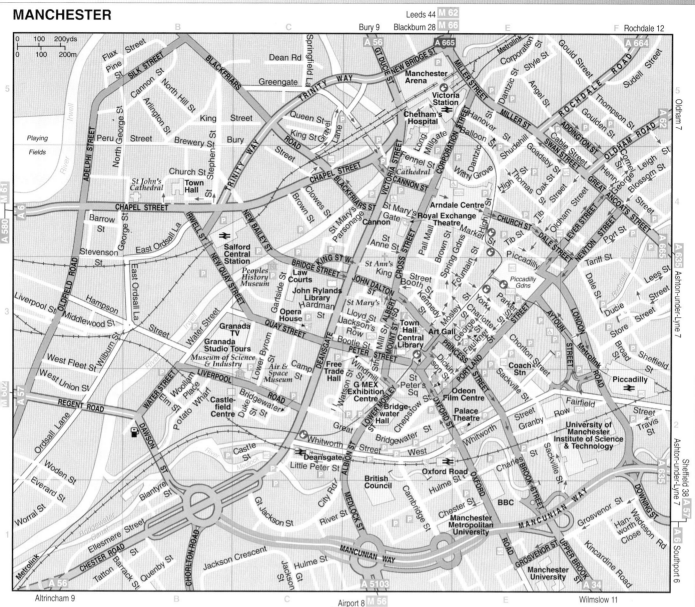

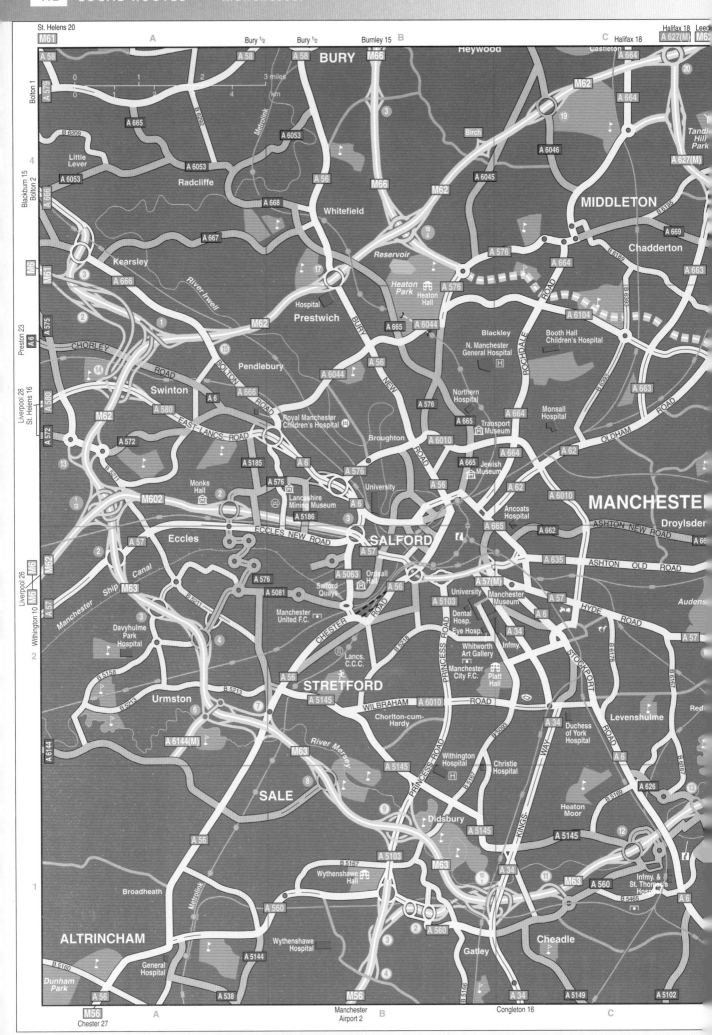

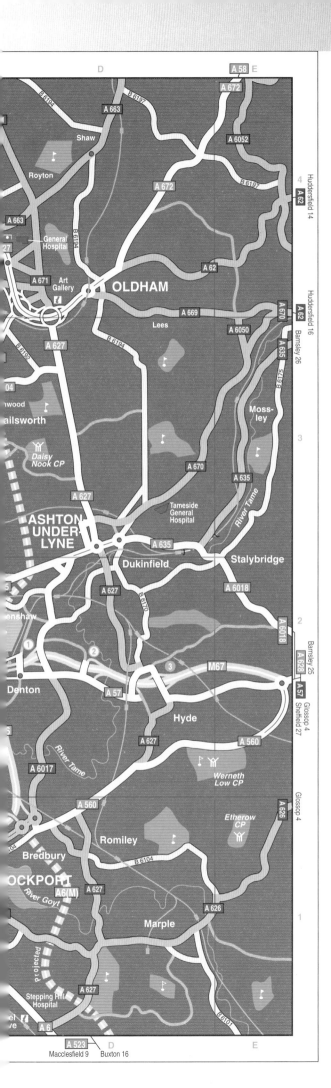

Places to see in Manchester

ONE OF EUROPE'S LARGEST covered shopping centres, Manchester's Arndale Centre covers some 26 acres (11 ha) and serves around one million customers a year. It is on the route of Metrolink, the modern tram system that crosses the city. Side by side with its modern developments, the city has many impressive 19th-century monuments of its days as a major centre for the Lancashire cotton industry, such as the galleried, glass-domed Barton Arcade of 1871, also a shopping centre, the grandiose town hall, the Italianate Free Trade Hall of 1856 close by and the fine neo-Gothic John Rylands Library built between 1890 and 1900. The circular Central Library was opened in 1934. Some older buildings have been put to new uses—for example, the Royal Exchange of 1921, one of the city's several former cotton exchanges, now houses the country's largest theatre-in-the-round, and the former Central Station is today the G-Mex International Exhibition and Events Centre.

Castlefield, an area near the city centre, is now a heritage park linking the city's past and future; it has a visitor centre, and its places of interest include the Castlefield Canal Basin on the once-busy Bridgewater Canal, with boat trips and towpath walks, the Museum of Science and Industry, Granada Studios Tour and a replica of the north gate of the Roman fort of Mancunium, the remains of which were demolished during the 19th century to make way for a railway viaduct.

PLACES OF INTEREST

Albert Square [p 411 D3] Overlooking the pedestrianised square is the neo-Gothic town hall of 1877 by Alfred Waterhouse, with a 281 ft (86 m) clock tower; its great hall has murals by Ford Madox Brown recounting Manchester's history. The Albert Memorial of 1862 is the largest statue in the square, and in the cobbles round it are mosaics depicting roses, thistles, leeks and shamrocks; outside the town hall are cotton flowers—a source of the city's wealth.

City Art Gallery [p 411 D3] One of the country's finest collections of Pre-Raphaelite and other Victorian paintings is housed in Sir Charles Barry's classical building of 1829. Nearby stands the Princess Street Gallery of 1839, which was also designed by Barry.

Granada Studios Tour [p 411 BC3] There are backstage tours of the TV studios; sets on view include those for *Coronation Street.*

Heaton Hall [B3] Set amid parkland, the classical mansion of 1772 has a domed central block flanked by colonnaded wings. Its Cupola Room is styled on Pompeii, the buried Roman city revealed in the 18th century. A boulder in the park marks the spot where Pope John Paul celebrated Mass during his visit to Manchester in 1982.

Lancashire Mining Museum [B3] A 1930s drift mine, with coal seams near the surface, is reconstructed on the ground floor of Buile Hill Park, a neoclassical mansion of 1827, and scenes from 19th-century coal mines are recreated in the basement. Sir Thomas Potter, the mansion's original owner, was one of the 11 men who launched the *Manchester Guardian* newspaper in 1821.

Manchester Cathedral [p 411 D4] Dark red stone distinguishes this Perpendicular, mainly 15th-16th-century church made a cathedral in 1847. Carved misericords of animals grace the choir. To the north is Chetham's Hospital of 1421, built to house collegiate church members and now a music school. Chetham's Library of 1653 is one of England's oldest free public libraries.

Manchester Jewish Museum [B3] A former Spanish and Portuguese synagogue of 1874 tells of 250 years of local Jewish history in its Ladies' Gallery. The lower floor has been restored to its original condition.

Museum of Science and Industry [p 411 BC3] Housed in Liverpool Road Station of 1830—the oldest passenger railway station in the world—the museum has working exhibits and includes a Power Hall and Air and Space, Gas, and Electricity galleries, as well as a reconstruction of a Victorian sewer, complete with smells.

Platt Hall [BC2] Fashionable and everyday clothes from Tudor times until the 20th century are on display in this hall of 1762, built for a wealthy textile merchant. There is a boating lake in the surrounding park.

Shambles Square [p 411 D4] The Old Wellington Inn of about 1550 was once the home of John Byrom (1692-1763), who wrote the hymn 'Christians Awake' as a Christmas present for his daughter.

Wythenshawe Hall [B1] A half-timbered 16th-century manor house with Georgian additions, the hall has 16th-17th-century paintings and furniture on display.

See also pages 83-84

MARGATE

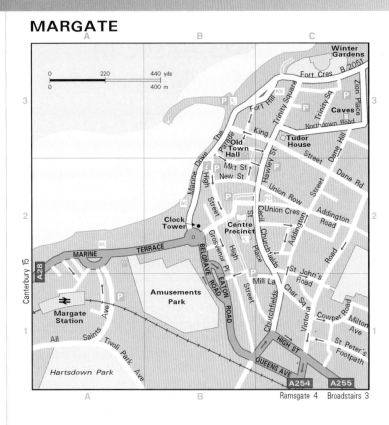

Addington Road **C2**
Addington Street **C2**
All Saints Avenue **A1**
Belgrave Road **B2-B1**
Cecil Street **C2**
Char Square **C1**
Churchfields **C1**
Churchfields Place **C2**
Cowper Road **C1**
Dane Hill **C3**
Dane Road **C2**
Eaton Road **B1**
Fort Crescent **C3**
Fort Hill **C3**
Grosvenor Place **B2**
Hawley Street **C2**
High Street **C1-B2**
King Street **C3**
Marine Drive **B2**
Marine Terrace **A2**
Market Street **A2**
Mill Lane **C1**
Milton Avenue **C1**
New Street **B2**
Northdown Road **C3**
Queens Avenue **C1**
St Peter's Footpath **C1**
The Parade **B3**
Tivoli Park Avenue **A1**
Trinity Square **C3**
Union Crescent **C2**
Union Row **C2**
Victoria Road **C1-C2**
Zion Place **C3**

MIDDLESBROUGH

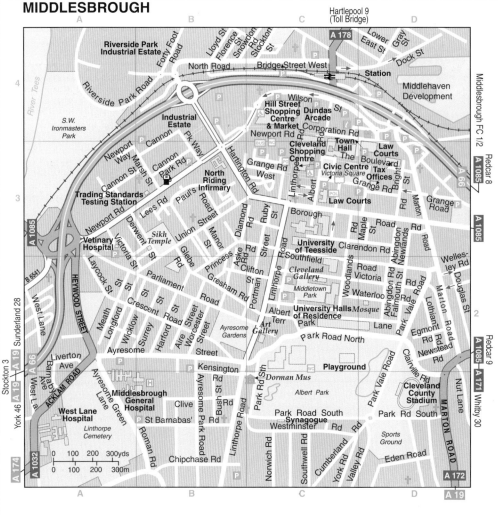

Acklam Road **A1**
Albert Road **C3-C4**
Albert Terrace **C2**
Ayresome Green Lane **A1**
Ayresome Park Road **B1**
Ayresome Street **A2-B2**
Borough Road **C3-D3**
Bridge Street West **C4**
Chipchase Road **B1**
Clairville Road **D2-D1**
Clarendon Road **C3-D3**
Clive Road **B1**
Corporation Road **C4**
Crescent Road **B2**
Derwent Street **B3**
Diamond Road **B3**
Dock Street **D4**
Eden Road **D1**
Grange Road **C3-D3**
Gresham Road **B2**
Hartington Road **B3**
Heywood Street **A2**
Linthorpe Road **B1-C4**
Marsh Street **B3**
Marton Road **D1-D3**
Newport Road **A3**
North Road **B4**
Park Lane **C2-D2**
Park Road North **C2**
Park Road South **C1-D1**
Park Vale Road **D1-D2**
Parliament Road **B2**
Princess Road **B2-C3**
Riverside Park Road **A4-B4**
Roman Road **B1**
Southfield Road **C3-D2**
The Boulevard **C3-D3**
Union Street **B3**
West Lane **A2**
Westminster Road **C1**
Wilson Street **C4**
Woodlands Road **C2-C3**
Worcester Street **B2**

MILTON KEYNES

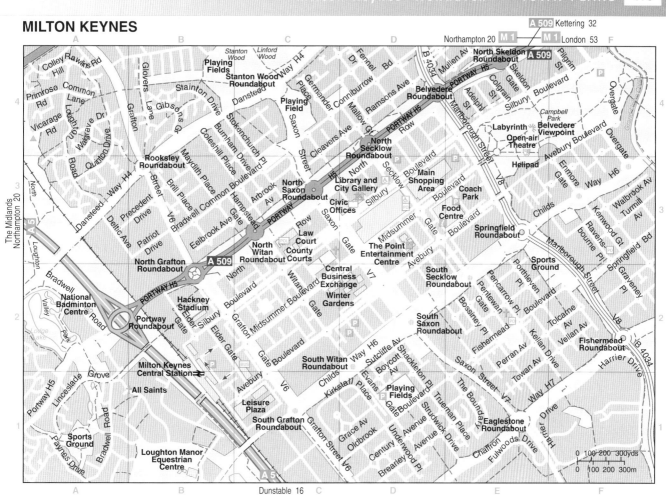

NEWHAVEN

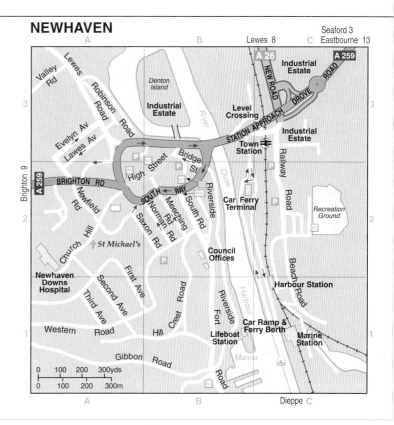

NEWCASTLE UPON TYNE

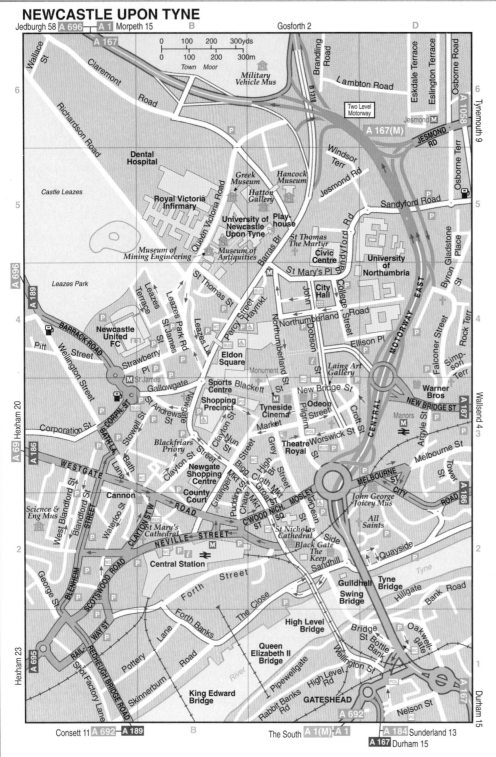

NEWPORT

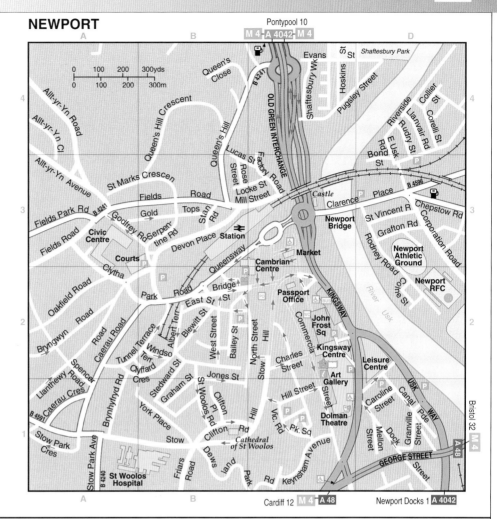

NORTHAMPTON

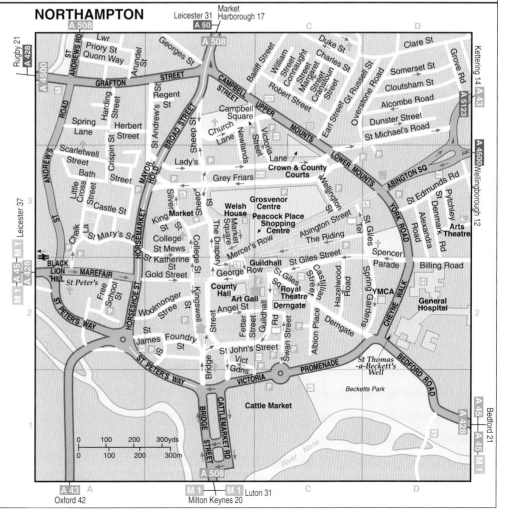

NORWICH

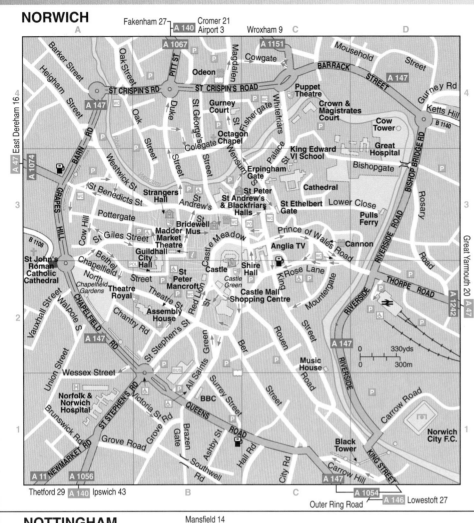

All Saints Green **B1–B2**
Barn Road **A3–A4**
Barrack Street **C4–D4**
Ber Street **C2–C1**
Bishop Bridge Road **D3–D4**
Carrow Hill **C1–D1**
Castle Meadow **B3**
Chapelfield North **A2**
Chapelfield Road **A2**
Colegate **B3–B4**
Duke Street **B4–B3**
Earlham Road **A3**
Fishergate **C4**
Grapes Hill **A3**
Ketts Hill **D4**
King Street **D1**
Magdalen Street **B4**
Mountergate **C2**
Newmarket Road **A1**
Oak Street **A4–B3**
Palace Street **C3**
Pitt Street **B4**
Prince of Wales Road **C3**
Queens Road **B1**
Red Lion Street **B2**
Riverside **C2**
Riverside Road **D3**
Rosary Road **D3**
Rose Lane **C2**
Rouen Road **C2–C1**
St Andrew's Street **B3**
St Benedicts Street **A3**
St Crispin's Road **A4–C4**
St Giles Street **A3–B3**
St Stephen's Road **A1–B2**
Theatre Street **B2**
Thorpe Road **D2**
Whitefriars **C4**

NOTTINGHAM

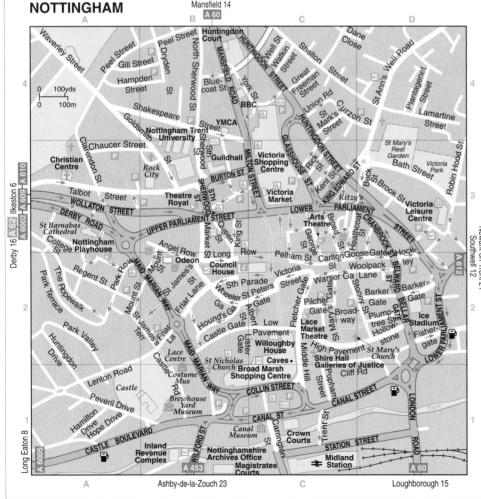

Angel Row **B3–B2**
Barker Gate **D2**
Bellar Gate **D2**
Belward Street **D2**
Burton Street **B3**
Canal Street **C1–D1**
Carrington Street **C1**
Castle Boulevard **A1**
Collin Street **C1**
Cranbrook Street **D3**
Derby Road **A3**
Fletcher Gate **C2**
Friar Lane **B2**
Glasshouse Street **C3**
Goldsmith Street **A4–C3**
High Pavement **C2**
Hollowstone **D2**
Huntingdon Street **C4–C3**
King Edward Street **C3**
London Road **D1**
Lower Parliament
  Street **C3–D2**
Maid Marian Way **B2–B1**
Mansfield Road **B5–B4**
Market Street **B3**
Middle Hill **C2–C1**
Milton Street **C3**
St Ann's Well Road **D4**
St Peters Gate **C2**
Shakespeare Street **B4**
South Sherwood Street **B3**
Station Street **C1–D1**
Upper Parliament Street **B3**
Victoria Street **C2**
Waverley Street **A4**
Wheeler Gate **B2**
Wilford Street **B1**
Woollaton Street **A3**

OXFORD

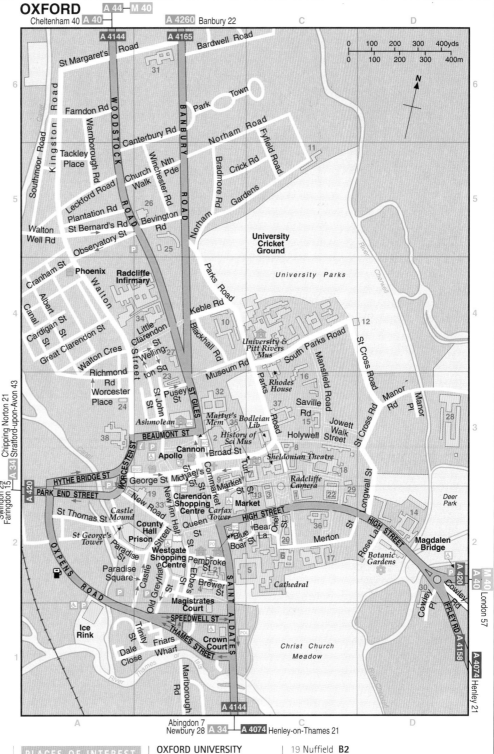

PERTH

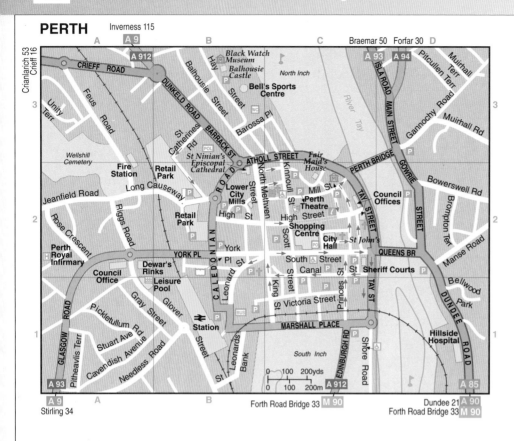

Atholl Street **B3–C3**
Bowerswell Road **D2**
Caledonian Road **B1–B2**
Crieff Road **A3**
Dundee Road **D1**
Edinburgh Road **C1**
Feus road **A3**
Gannochy Road **D3**
Glasgow Road **A1**
Glover Street **B1**
Gowrie Street **D2**
High Street **B2–C2**
Jeanfield Road **A2**
King Street **C1**
Kinnoull Street **C2**
Leonard Street **B1–B2**
Long Causeway **A2–B2**
Main Street **D3**
Manse Road **D2**
Marshall Place **C1**
Muirhall Road **D3**
Needless Road **A1**
North Methven Street **B2**
Princes Street **C1**
Riggs Road **A2**
Rose Crescent **A2**
St Leonards Bank **B1**
South Street **C2**
Tay Street **C2–C1**
York Place **B2**

PETERBOROUGH

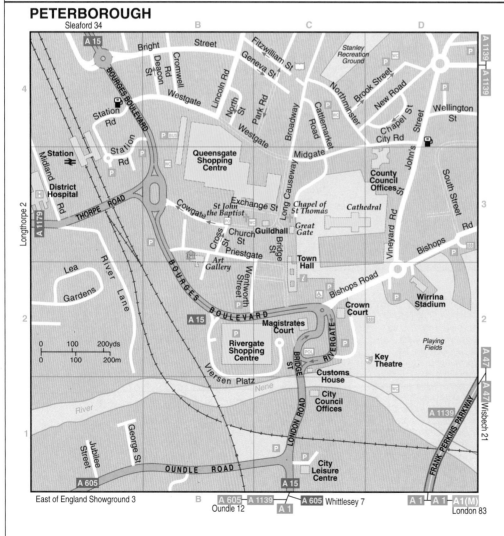

Bishops Road **C2–D3**
Bourges Boulevard **A4–C2**
Bridge Street **C2–C3**
Bright Street **B4**
Broadway **C4**
Brook Street **D4**
Cattlemarket Road **C4**
Chapel Street **D4**
City Road **D4**
Cromwell Road **B4**
Cross Street **B3**
Deacon Street **B4**
Exchange Street **B3**
Fitzwilliam Street **C4**
Frank Perkins Parkway **D1**
Geneva Street **C4**
George Street **A1**
Jubilee Street **A1**
Lea Gardens **A2**
Lincoln Road **B4**
London Road **C1**
Long Causeway **C3**
Midgate **C3**
Midland Road **A3**
New Road **D4**
North Street **B4**
Northminster **C4**
Oundle Road **B1**
Park Road **C4**
Priestgate **B3**
River Lane **A2**
Rivergate **C2**
St John's Street **D3–D4**
South Street **D3**
Station Road **A4**
Thorpe Road **A3**
Viersen Platz **B1–B2**
Vineyard Road **D3**
Wellington Street **D4**
Wentworth Street **B2**
Westgate **B4–C3**

POOLE

Ballard Road **B1**
Catalina Drive **C1**
Church Street **A1**
Dear Hay Lane **B2**
Denmark Lane **C3**
Denmark Road **C3**
East Street **B1**
Elizabeth Road **C3**
Emerson Road **B2-B1**
Esplanade **B3**
Furnell Road **C1**
Green Road **B1**
Green Gardens **C1**
Heckford Road **C3**
High Street **A1-B2**
Holes Bay
　Road **A3-B3**
Kingland Road **C2**
Kingston Road **C3**
Lagland Street **B1**
Longfleet Road **C3**
Maple Road **C3**

Mount Pleasant Road **C2**
New Orchard **A2-A1**
Newfoundland Drive **C1**
North Street **B2**
Old Orchard **B1**
Parkstone Road **C3**
Perry Gardens **B1**
Quay Road **B1**
St Johns Road **C3**
St Mary's Road **C3**
Seldown Bridge **C1-C2**
Seldown Lane **C2**
Shaftesbury Road **C3**
Skinner Street **B1**
South Road **B2**
Stanley Road **B1**
Sterte Road **B3**
Strand Street **A1**
The Quay **A1-B1**
Towngate Bridge **B2**
West Street **A2**
Wimborne Road **B3-C3**

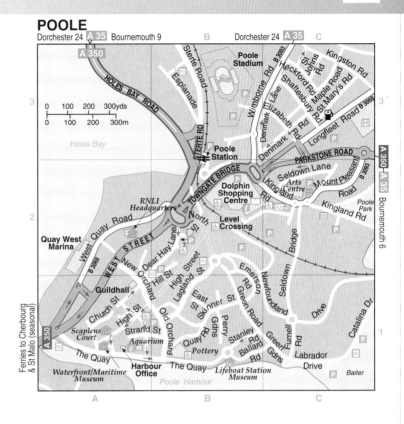

PRESTON

Adelphi Street **A4**
Avenham Lane **C1**
Birley Street **B2**
Bolton's Court **C2-C1**
Butler Street **A1**
Carlisle Street **C3**
Church Street **C2-D2**
Corporation Street **A3-A2**
Deepdale Road **D4-D3**
Derby Street **C2**
Elizabeth Street **B3**
Fishergate **A2-B2**
Fleet Street **B2**
Friargate **A3-B2**
Fylde Road **A3**
Fylde Street **A3**
Grimshaw Street **D2**
Lancaster Road **C3-C2**
Lancaster Road North **B4**
Larkhill Road **D1**
Lawson Street **B3**
Lune Street **B2**
Manchester Road **D2-D1**
Market Street **B2**
Marsh Lane **A3**
Meadow Street **C3-D4**
North Road **B4-C3**
Orchard Street **B2**
Ormskirk Road **C3**
Oxford Street **C1**
Pitt Street **A2**
Pole Street **D2**
Queen Street **D2**
Ringway **A2-D3**
St Paul's Road **C4**
Sedgwick Street **C4**
Titheburn Street **C3-C2**
Victoria Street **A4**
Walker Street **A3-B3**
Winckley Square **B1**

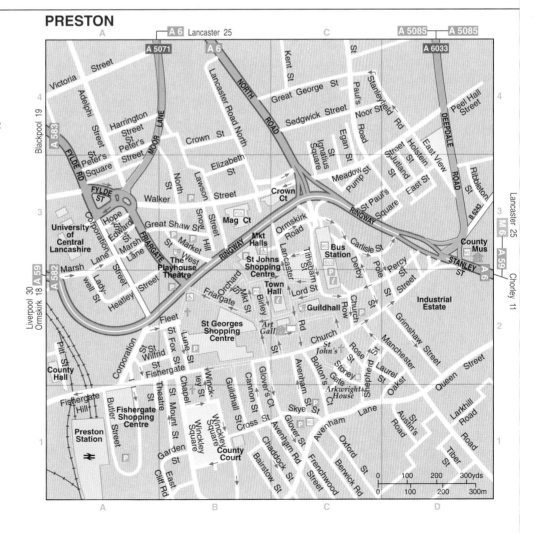

READING

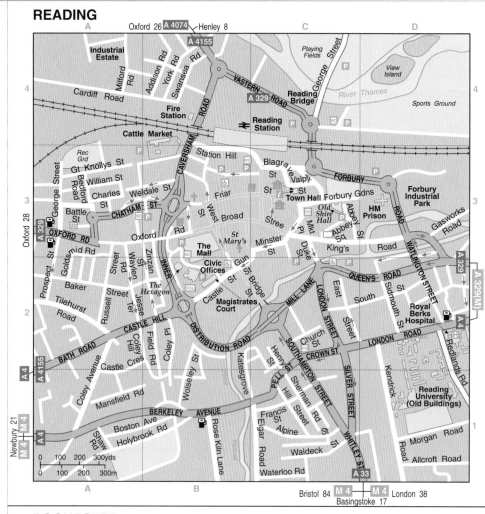

Bath Road **A2**
Battle Street **A3**
Berkeley Avenue **B2**
Blagrave Street **C3**
Bridge Street **C2**
Broad Street **B3–C3**
Castle Hill **A2–B2**
Castle Street **B2**
Caversham Road **B3–B4**
Chatham Street **A3**
Coley Avenue **A1**
Crown Street **C2**
Duke Street **C3**
Forbury Road **C3–D3**
Friar Street **B3–C3**
George Street **A3**
George Street **C4**
Gun Street **B2**
Inner Distribution Road **B2**
Kendrick Road **D1**
Kings Road **C3–D3**
London Road **D2**
Mill Lane **C2**
Minister Street **C3**
Oxford Road **A3–B3**
Pell Street **C1**
Rose Kiln Lane **B1**
Russell Street **A2**
Silver Street **C1**
South Street **D2**
Southampton Street **C2–C1**
Station Hill **B3**
Tilehurst Road **A2**
Valpy Street **C3**
Vastern Road **B4–C4**
Watlington Street **D2**
West Street **B3**
Whitley Street **C1**
Zinzan Street **B2**

ROCHESTER

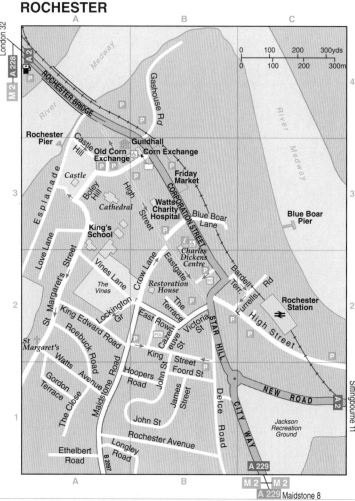

Bardell Terrace **C2**
Blue Boar Lane **B3**
Boley Hill **A3**
Castle Hill **A3**
Cazeneuve Street **B2**
City Way **C1**
Corporation Street **B3**
Crow Lane **B2**
East Row **B2**
Eastgate **B2**
Esplanade **A3**
Ethelbert Road **A1**
Foord Street **B1**
Furrells Road **C2**
Glasshouse Road **B4**
Gordon Terrace **A1**
High Street **A3–C2**
Hoopers Road **B1**
James Street **B1**
John Street **B1**
King Edward Road **A2**
King Street **B2**
Lockington Grove **A2**
Longley Road **A1**
Love Lane **A2–A3**
Maidstone Road **A1**
New Road **C1**
Rochester Avenue **B1**
Rochester Bridge **A4**
Roebuck Road **A2**
St Margaret's Street **A2**
Star Hill **B2**
The Close **A1**
The Terrace **B2**
Victoria Street **B2**
Vines Lane **A2**
Watts Avenue **A1**

ST ALBANS

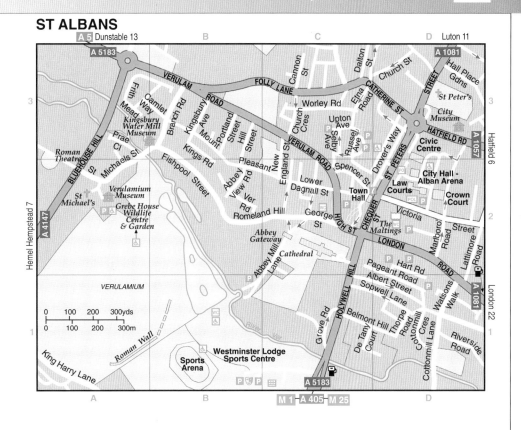

SALISBURY

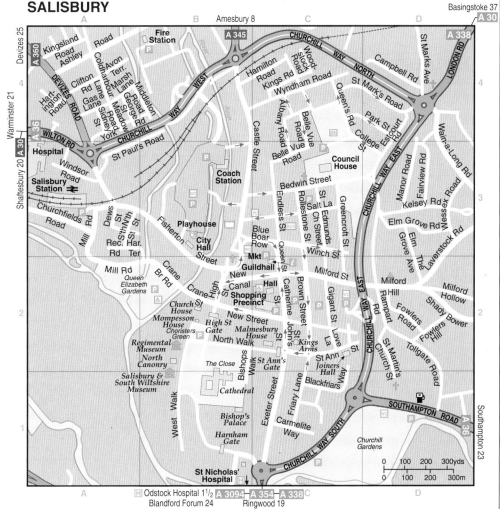

SHREWSBURY

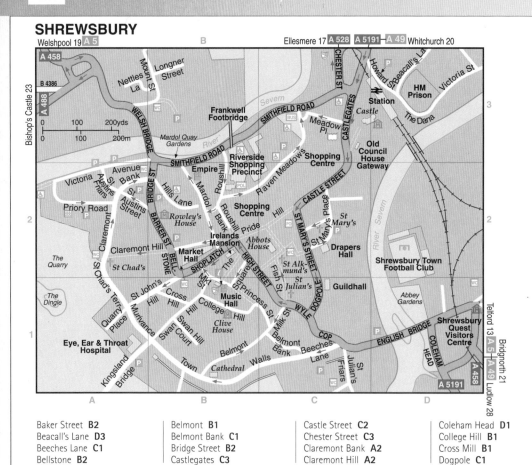

Welshpool 19 A 5   Ellesmere 17 A 528 A 5191 A 49 Whitchurch 20

Baker Street **B2**
Beacall's Lane **D3**
Beeches Lane **C1**
Bellstone **B2**

Belmont **B1**
Belmont Bank **C1**
Bridge Street **B2**
Castlegates **C3**

Castle Street **C2**
Chester Street **C3**
Claremont Bank **A2**
Claremont Hill **A2**

Coleham Head **D1**
College Hill **B1**
Cross Mill **B1**
Dogpole **C1**

English Bridge **D1**
Fish Street **C2**
High Street **B2-C1**
Hills Lane **B2**
Howard Street **D3**
Kingsland Bridge **A1**
Longner Street **B3**
Mardol **B2**
Market Street **B1**
Meadow Place **C3**
Milk Street **C1**
Mount Street **B3**
Murivance Town Walls **A1-C1**
Pride Hill **B2**
Princess Street **B1**
Priory Road **A2**
Quarry Place **A1**
Raven Meadows **C2**
Roushill **B2**
Roushill Bank **B2**
St Austins Friars **A2**
St Austins Street **A2**
St Chad's Terrace **A2-A1**
St John's Hill **A1-B1**
St Julian's Friars **C1**
St Mary's Place **C2**
St Mary's Street **C2**
Shoplatch **B2**
Smithfield Road **B3-C3**
Swan Hill **B1**
Swan Hill Court **B1**
The Dana **D3**
Victoria Avenue **A2**
Victoria Street **D3**
Welsh Bridge **A3**
Wyle Cop **C1**

SOUTHEND-ON-SEA

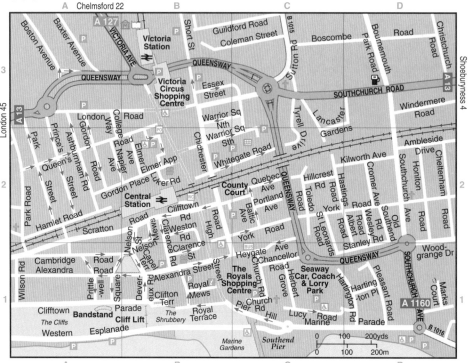

Alexandra Street **B1**
Ashburnham Road **A2**
Baxter Avenue **A3**
Boscombe Road **C3-D3**
Boston Avenue **A3**
Bournemouth Park Road **D3**

Cambridge Road **A1**
Capel Terrace **B1**
Chancellor Road **C1**
Cheltenham Road **D2**
Chichester Road **B2**
Christchurch Road **D3**

Church Road **C1**
Clarence Street **B1**
Clifftown Parade **A1**
Clifftown Road **B2**
Clifton Terrace **B1**
Coleman Street **C3**

College Way **A3**
Devereux Road **B1**
Elmer Approach **B2**
Elmer Avenue **B2**
Essex Street **B3**
Gordon Place **A2-B2**

Gordon Road **A2**
Guildford Road **B3**
Hamlet Road **A2**
Honiton Road **D2**
Kilworth Avenue **D2**
Lancaster Gardens **C3**
London Road **A3**
Lucy Road **C1**
Luker Road **B2**
Marine Parade **C1-D1**
Napier Avenue **A2**
Nelson Street **B1-B2**
Park Road **A2**
Park Street **A2**
Pier Hill **C1**
Pleasant Road **D1**
Portland Avenue **C2**
Prince's Street **A2**
Prittlewell Square **A1**
Quebec Avenue **C2**
Queen's Road **A2**
Queensway **A3-D1**
Royal Mews **B1**
Scratton Road **A2-B2**
Short Street **B3**
Southchurch Avenue **D1-D2**
Southchurch Road **D3**
Sutton Road **C3**
Toledo Road **C2**
Tyler's Avenue **C2**
Tyrell Drive **C3-C2**
Victoria Avenue **A3-B3**
Warrior Square North **B3**
Western Esplanade **A1**
Weston Road **B2**
Whitegate Road **B2-C2**
Windermere Road **D3**
York Road **C2-D2**

SHEFFIELD

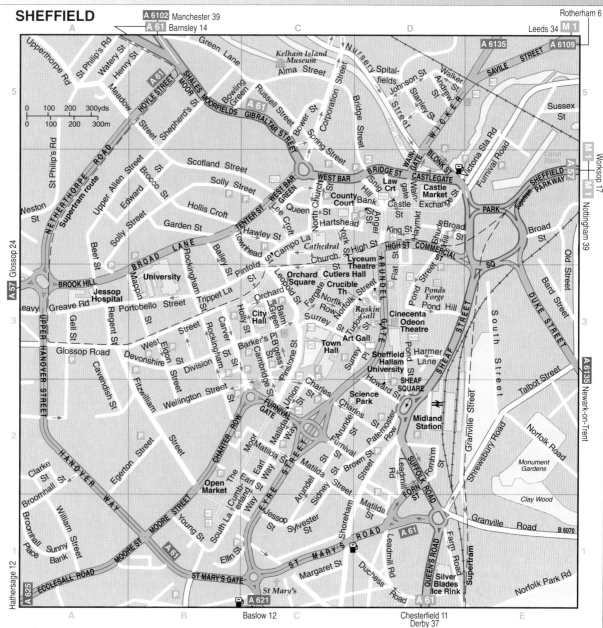

SOUTHAMPTON

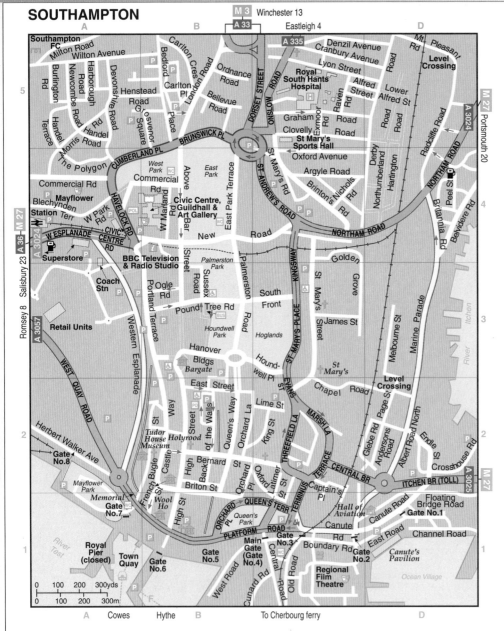

SOUTHPORT

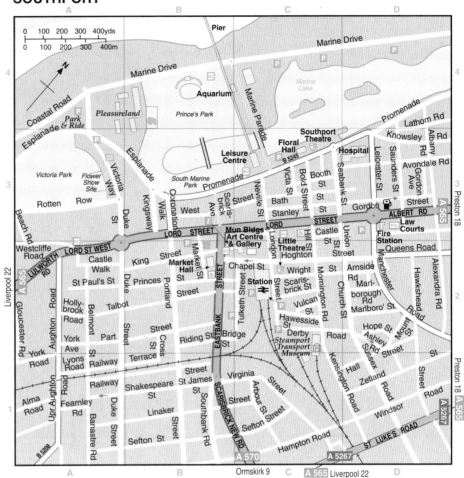

STIRLING

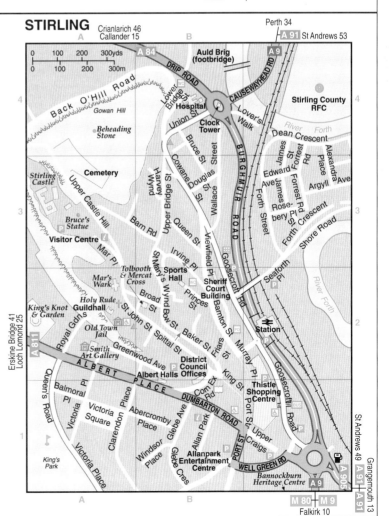

HANLEY

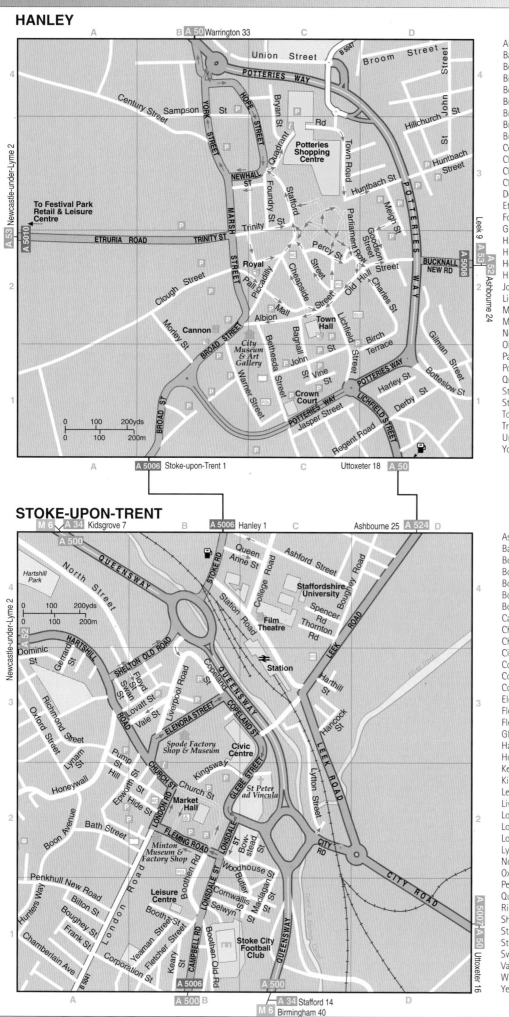

Albion Street **C2**
Bagnall Street **C2-C1**
Bethesda Street **C1**
Birch Terrace **D1-D2**
Botteslow Street **D1**
Broad Street **B1-B2**
Broom Street **D4**
Bryan Street **C4-C3**
Bucknall New Road **D2**
Century Street **A4-B3**
Charles Street **D2**
Cheapside **C2**
Clough Street **B2**
Derby Street **D1**
Etruria Road **A2-B2**
Foundry Street **C3**
Gilman Street **D2-D1**
Harley Street **D1**
Hillchurch Street **D3-D4**
Hope Street **B4-C3**
Huntbach Street **C3-D3**
John Street **C1**
Lichfield Street **C2-D1**
Marsh Street **B3-B2**
Morley Street **B2**
Newhall Street **B3-C3**
Old Hall Street **C2-D2**
Pall Mall **C2**
Potteries Way **C4-C1**
Quadrant Road **C3**
St John Street **D3-D4**
Stafford Street **C3-C2**
Town Road **C3**
Trinity Street **B2-C3**
Union Street **C4**
York Street **B4-B3**

STOKE-UPON-TRENT

Ashford Street **C4**
Bath Street **A2**
Boon Avenue **A2**
Booth Street **B1**
Boothen Old Road **B1**
Boothen Road **B1-B2**
Bowstead Street **C2**
Campbell Road **B1**
Chamberlain Avenue **A1**
Church Street **B2**
City Road **C2-D1**
College Road **C4**
Copeland Street **B3-C3**
Corporation Street **A1-B1**
Elenora Street **B3**
Fleming Road **B2**
Fletcher Street **B1**
Glebe Street **B2-C2**
Hartshill Road **A4-A3**
Honeywall **A2**
Keary Street **B1**
Kingsway **B2**
Leek Road **C2-D4**
Liverpool Road **B3**
London Road **A1-B2**
Lonsdale Street **B1-B2**
Lovatt Street **B3**
Lytton Street **C2**
North Street **A4**
Oxford Street **A3**
Penkhull New Road **A1**
Queensway **A4-C1**
Richmond Street **A3**
Shelton Old Road **A3-C4**
Station Road **B4-C4**
Stoke Road **B4**
Swan Street **A3**
Vale Street **B3**
Woodhouse Street **B2-C2**
Yeaman Street **B1**

STRATFORD-UPON-AVON

Albany Road **A2**
Alcester Road **A3**
Arden Street **A3**
Arthur Road **B4**
Avenue Road **C4**
Birmingham Road **A4-B3**
Bridge Street **B2**
Bridgefoot **C2**
Bridgeway **C2**
Broad Street **A1**
Bull Street **A1**
Chapel Lane **B2-B1**
Chapel Street **B2**
Chestnut Walk **A1**
Clopton Road **B4**
College Lane **A1**
College Street **A1**
Ely Street **A2-B2**
Great William Street **B3**
Greenhill Street **A3-A2**
Grove Road **A2**
Guild Street **B3**
Henley Street **B3-B2**
High Street **B2**
John Street **B3**
Kendall Avenue **B4**
Maidenhead Road **C4**
Manswell Street **A3**
Market Place **A2-B2**

Meer Street **B2**
Mulberry Street **B3**
Myfield Avenue **B4**
Old Town **A1**
Percy Street **B4**
Regal Road **A4-B4**
Rother Street **A2**
Rowley Crescent **C4**
St Gregory's Road **C3**
St Mary's Road **B4S**
Sanctus Street **A1**
Scholars Lane **A2**
Shakespeare Street **B3**
Sheep Street **B2**
Shipston Road **C1**
Southern Lane **B1**
Tamway Walk **C1**
Tyler Street **B3**
Union Street **B2**
Vincent Avenue **B4**
Warwick Crescent **C3**
Warwick Road **C3**
Waterside **B2**
Welcombe Road **C3-C4**
Wellesbourne Grove **A2**
West Street **A1**
Western Road **A4**
Windsor Street **B3**
Wood Street **B2**

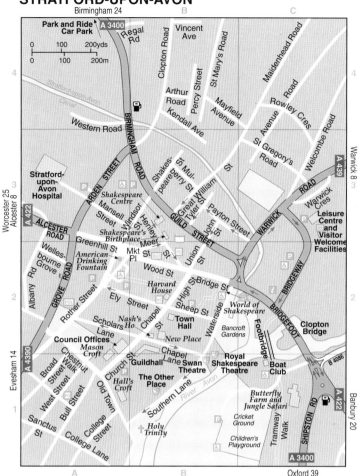

SUNDERLAND

Bedford Street **C3**
Belvedere Road **B1-C1**
Bridge Street **C3**
Brougham Street **C2-D3**
Brougham Street **C2-D3**
Burdon Road **C2-C1**
Burn Park Road **A1**
Chester Road **A2-B2**
Coronation Street **D3**
Derwent Street **B2-C2**
Durham Road **A1**
Fawcett Street **C3-C2**
High Street **D3**
High Street West **C3**
Holmeside **C2**
Hylton Road **A3**
John Street **C3-C2**
Livingstone Road **B3**
Low Row **B3-B2**
New Durham Road **A2-B2**
Norfolk Street **D3**
North Bridge Street **C4**
Olive Street **C2**
Park Lane **C2**
Park Road **C1-D1**
St Mary's Way **C3**
St Michael's Way **B3-C2**
Silksworth Row **A3-B3**
Stockton Road **C2-C1**
Tatham Street **D2**
The Royalty **A2**
Thornholme Road **B1**
Toward Road **D1**
Toward Road **D2-D1**
Trimdon Street **A4-A3**
Tunstall Road **B1**
Vine Place **B2**
West Wear Street **C3-D3**

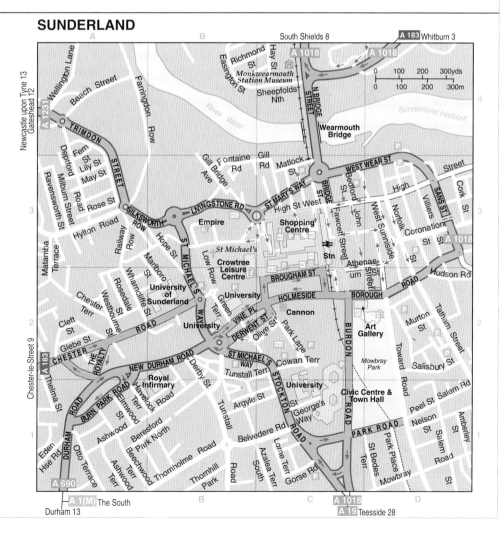

SWINDON

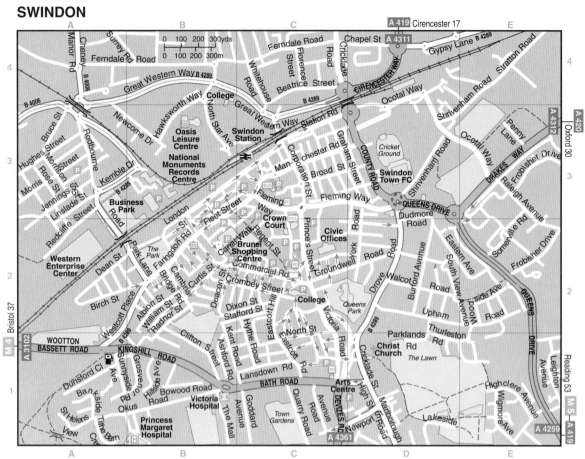

Bath Road **C1**
Broad Street **C3**
Cheney Manor Road **A4**
Cirencester Way **D4**
Commercial Road **C2**
County Road **D3**
Crickdale Street **D1**
Cricklade Road **C4**
Crombey Street **C2**
Deacon Street **B2**
Devizes Road **C1**
Drakes Way **E3**
Drove Road **D2**
Faringdon Road **B2**
Fleet Street **B3**
Fleming Way **C3-D3**
Graham Street **C3-D3**
Great Western Way **B4–**
Gypsy Lane **D4-E4**
High Street **D1**
Kemble Drive **A3**
Kingshill Road **B1**
London Street **B2-B3**
Manchester Road **D1**
Marlborough Road **D1**
Newport Street **D1**
Ocotal Way **D4-E3**
Prince's Street **C2**
Queens Drive **D3-E1**
Rodbourne Road **A3**
Shrivenham Road **D3**
Station Road **C3**
Victoria Road **C2-C1**
William Street **B2**
Wootton Bassett Road **A**

TUNBRIDGE WELLS

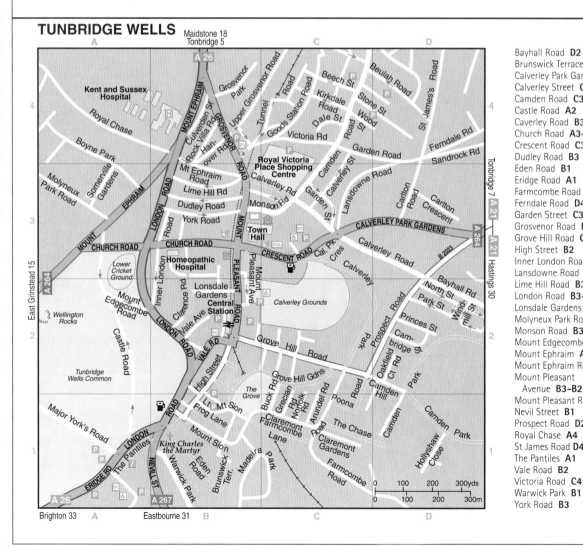

Bayhall Road **D2**
Brunswick Terrace **B1**
Calverley Park Gardens **D3**
Calverley Street **C3**
Camden Road **C3-C4**
Castle Road **A2**
Caverley Road **B3-D3**
Church Road **A3-B3**
Crescent Road **C3**
Dudley Road **B3**
Eden Road **B1**
Eridge Road **A1**
Farmcombe Road **C1**
Ferndale Road **D4**
Garden Street **C3**
Grosvenor Road **B4**
Grove Hill Road **C2**
High Street **B2**
Inner London Road **B2-B3**
Lansdowne Road **C3-D3**
Lime Hill Road **B3**
London Road **B3-A1**
Lonsdale Gardens **B2**
Molyneux Park Road **A3**
Monson Road **B3-C3**
Mount Edgecombe Road **A2**
Mount Ephraim **A3-B4**
Mount Ephraim Road **B3**
Mount Pleasant
  Avenue **B3-B2**
Mount Pleasant Road **B2-B3**
Nevil Street **B1**
Prospect Road **D2**
Royal Chase **A4**
St James Road **D4**
The Pantiles **A1**
Vale Road **B2**
Victoria Road **C4**
Warwick Park **B1**
York Road **B3**

WARRINGTON

Academy Street **B2**
Academy Way **B2**
Allen Street **A3**
Arpley Street **A2**
Arthur Street **A3**
Ashton Street **B3**
Austins Lane **B2**
Bank Street **B2**
Battersby Lane **C4**
Bewsey Road **A4**
Bridge Street **B2**
Buckley Street **B4**
Buttermarket Street **C3**
Cairo Street **B2**
Catherine Street **A4**
Chester Road **B1**
Church Street **C3**
Clegge Street **C4**
Cobden Street **C4**
Cockhedge Lane **C3**
Crosfield Street **A3**
Crown Street **B3**
Dallam Lane **B4–B3**
Ellesmere Street **C2**
Ellison Street **C3**
Eustace Street **A3**
Forshaw Street **C4**
Foundry Street **B3**
Fountain Street **C1**
Frog Hall Lane **A3**
Golborne Street **B3**
Hall Street **C2**
Haydock Street **B4**
Horse Market **B3**
John Street **B3**
Kendrick Street **A3**
Knutsford Road **C1**
Lakeside Drive **A1**

Leigh Street **A3**
Lilford Street **A4**
Marbury Street **C1**
Mersey Street **C2**
Museum Street **A2**
Napier Street **C2**
Nelson Street **C2**
Nicholson Street **A3**
Norman Street **B4–C4**
Oliver Street **B4**
Orchard Street **C3**
Orford Lane **B4–C4**
Owen Street **B4**
Palmyra Square **B2**
Park Boulevard **B1**
Parker Street **A2**
Parr Street **C2**
Paul Street **A3**
Pinners Brow **B4**
Pitt Street **A4**
St Mary's Street **C1**
St Peters Way **C4**
Sankey Street **A2**
Scotland Road **B3**
Scott Street **C4**
Sharp Street **C4**
Slutchers Lane **A1**
Suez Street **B2**
Sutton Street **C2**
Tanners Lane **B3**
Thynne Street **A2**
Vernon Street **C2**
Wellington Street **C2**
Wharf Street **C2**
Wilderspool Causeway **B1**
Wilson Patten Street **A2–B2**
Winwick Road **B4**
Winwick Street **B3**

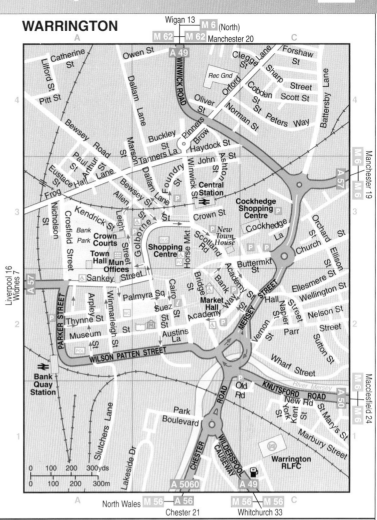

WARWICK

Albert Street **A4**
Banbury Road **C2–C1**
Barrack Street **A3**
Bowling Green Street **A2**
Bridge End **C1**
Brook Street **A2**
Cape Road **A4**
Castle Close **A1**
Castle Hill **B2**
Castle Lane **A2–B2**
Castle Street **B2**
Chapel Street **B3**
Church Street **A2–B2**
Coten End **C3**
Coventry Road **C3–C4**
Deerpark Drive **A4**
Edward Street **A3**
Gerrard Street **B3–B2**
Guy Street **C4–C3**
High Street **A2**
Jury Street **B2**
Lakin Road **C4**
Market Place **A3**
Market Street **A2**
Mill Street **B2**
New Street **A2–A3**
Northgate Street **A3**
Old Square **A3**
Paradise Street **C4**
Priory Road **B3**
St Johns **C3**
St Nicholas Church
Street **C2–C3**
Smith Street **B3**
Station Road **C4**
Swan Street **A2**
The Butts **B3**
Theatre Street **A3**
West Street **A2**

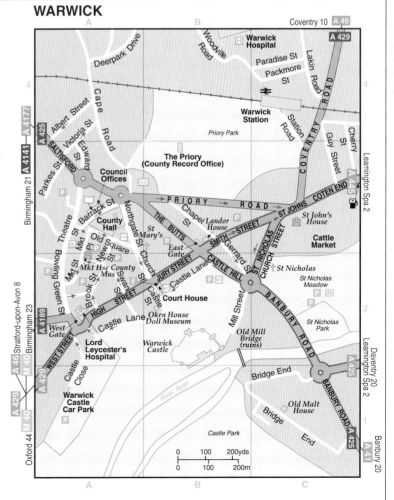

WESTON-SUPER-MARE

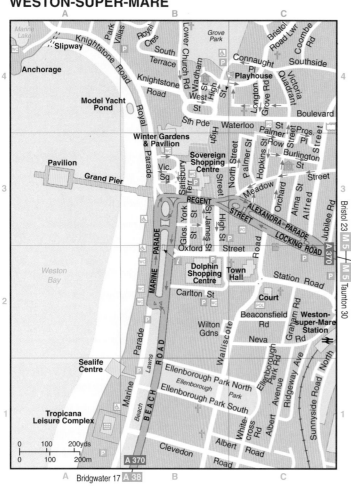

Albert Avenue **C1**
Albert Road **B1–C1**
Alexandra Parade **C3**
Alfred Street **C3**
Alma Street **C3**
Beach Road **B1**
Beaconsfield Road **C2**
Boulevard **C4**
Bristol Road Lower **C4**
Burlington Street **C3**
Carlton Street **B2**
Clevedon Road **B1**
Connaught Place **C4**
Coombe Road **C4**
Ellenborough Park North **B1–C1**
Ellenborough Park Road **C1–C2**
Ellenborough Park South **B1–C1**
Gloucester Street **B3**
Graham Road **C2**
High Street **B3**
High Street **B4**
Hopkins Street **C3**
Jubilee Road **C3**
Knightstone Road **A4–B4**
Locking Road **C3–C2**
Longton Grove Road **C4**

Lower Church Road **B4**
Marine Parade **B1–B3**
Meadow Street **C3**
Neva Road **C2**
North Street **C3**
Orchard Street **C3**
Oxford Street **B2**
Palmer Street **C3**
Park Villas **A4**
Prospect Place **C4–C3**
Regent Street **B3–C3**
Ridgeway Avenue **C1**
Royal Crescent **B4**
Royal Parade **B4–B3**
St James Street **B3**
Salisbury Terrace **B3**
South Parade **B4**
South Terrace **B4**
Southside **C4**
Station Road **C2**
Victoria Quadrant **C4**
Victoria Square **B3**
Wadham Street **B4**
Walliscote Road **B1–C3**
Waterloo Street **C4**
West Street **B4**
Whitecross Road **C1**
Wilton Gardens **B2**
York Street **B3**

WINCHESTER

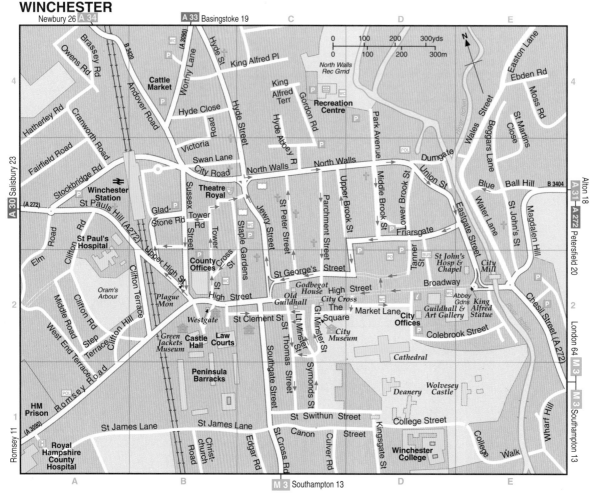

Andover Road **B4**
Broadway **D2**
Chesil Street **E2**
City Road **B3**
College Walk **E1**
Culver Road **C1**
Eastgate Street **E3**
Easton Lane **E4**
Ebden Road **E4**
Elm Road **A2–A3**
Friarsgate **D3**
Gladstone Road **B3**
Gordon Road **C4**
High Street **B2**
Hyde Close **B4**
Hyde Street **B4**
Jewry Street **C3**
Magdalen Hill **E3**
Moss Road **E4**
North Walls **C3**
Owens Road **A4**
Parchment Street **C3**
Romsey Road **A1**
St Cross Road **C1**
St George's St **C2**
St Pauls Hill **A3**
Southgate Street **C1**
Stockbridge Road **A3**
Sussex Street **B3**
Swan Lane **B3**
Tanner Street **D2**
Tower Road **B3**
Union Street **D3**
Upper High St **B2**
Wales Street **E4**
Water Lane **E3**
Wharf Hill **E1**
Worthy Lane **B4**

WINDSOR

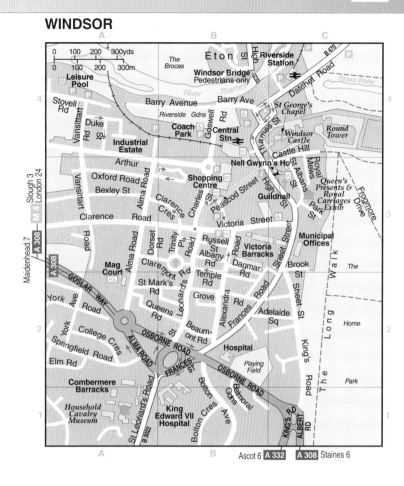

WOLVERHAMPTON

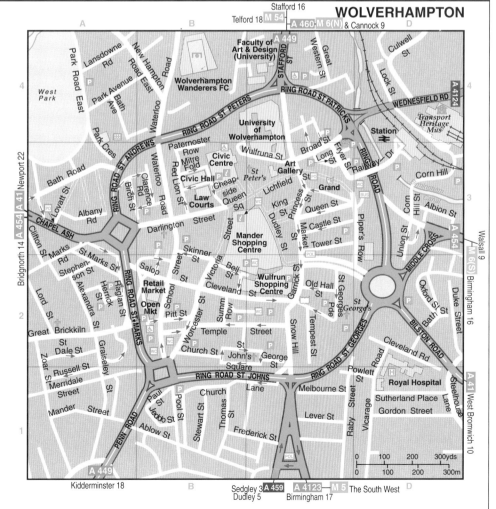

WORCESTER

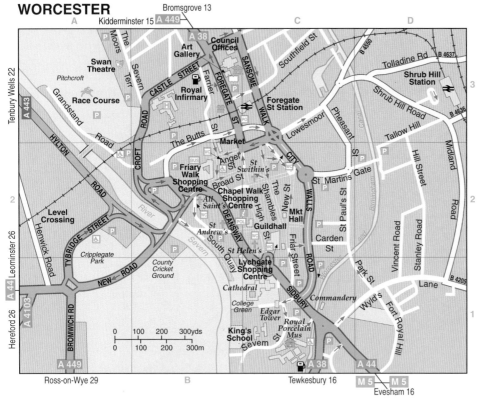

New Street **C2**
Pheasant Street **C3**
St Martins Gate **C2–D2**
St Paul's Street **C2**
Sansome Walk **C3**
Severn Street **C1**
Severn Terrace **B3**
Shrub Hill Road **D3**
Sidbury **C1**
South Quay **B2**
Stanley Road **D2**
Tallow Hill **D3**
The Butts **B2–B3**
The Moors **A3**
The Shambles **C2**
Tolladine Road **D3**
Tybridge Street **A2**
Wyld's Lane **D1**

Angel Street **B2**
Broad Street **B2**
Bromwich Road **A1**
Carden Street **C2**
Castle Street **B3**

City Walls Road **C2**
Croft Road **B2**
Deansway **B2**
Farrier Street **B3**
Foregate Street **B3**

Fort Royal Hill **D1**
Friar Street **C2–C1**
Grandstand Road **A3**
Henwick Road **A2**
High Street **C2**

Hill Street **D2**
Hylton Road **A2**
Lowesmoor **C3**
Midland Road **D2**
New Road **A1**

WORTHING

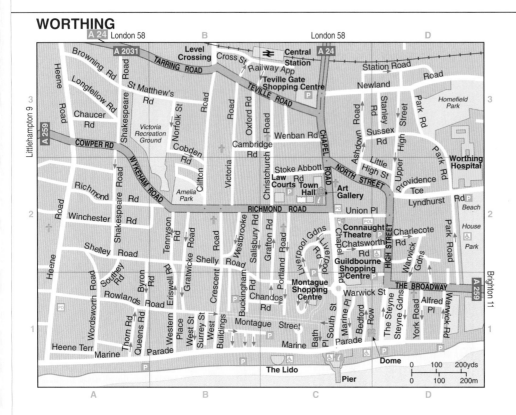

Lyndhurst Road **D2**
Marine Parade **A1–D1**
Marine Place **C1**
Montague Street **B1–C1**
Newland Road **C3–D3**
Norfolk Street **B3**
North Street **C2**
Oxford Road **B3**
Park Road **D3–D2**
Portland Road **C1–C2**
Queens Road **A1**
Railway Approach **C3**
Richmond Road **A2–C2**
St Matthew's Road **A3–B3**
Salisbury Road **B2**
Shakespeare Road **A2–A3**
Shelley Road **A2–B2**
South Street **C1**
Stanley Road **D3**
Station Road **D3**
Sussex Road **D3**
Tarring Road **B3**
Tennyson Road **B2**
Teville Road **B3–C3**
The Broadway **D1**
The Steyne **D1**
Thorn Road **A1**
Upper High Street **D2–D3**
Victoria Road **B2–B3**
Warwick Gardens **D2**
Warwick Street **C1**
Wenban Road **C3**
Westbrooke **B2**
Western Place **B1**
West Street **B1**
Winchester Road **A2**
Wordsworth Road **A1**
Wykeham Road **A2**

Ashdown Road **C3**
Bath Place **C1**
Bedford Row **C1**
Browning Road **A3**
Buckingham Road **B1**
Byron Road **A1**

Cambridge Road **B3**
Chandos Road **C1**
Chapel Road **C3–C2**
Chaucer Road **A3**
Christchurch Road **C2–C3**
Clifton Road **B2–B3**

Cobden Road **B3**
Cowper Road **A3**
Crescent Road **B1–B2**
Cross Street **B3**
Grafton Road **C2**
Gratwicke Road **B1–B2**

Heene Road **A3–A1**
Heene Terrace **A1**
High Street **D2**
Liverpool Gardens **C2**
Liverpool Road **C2**
Longfellow Road **A3**

YORK

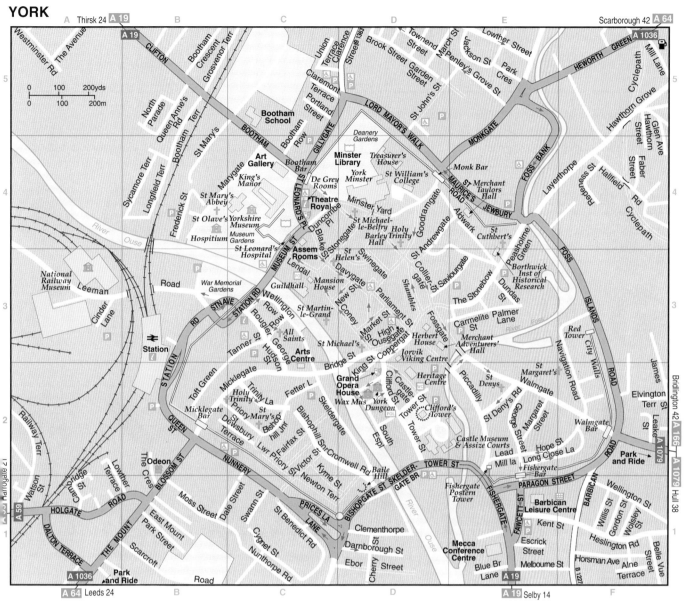

Thirsk 24 A 19   Scarborough 42 A 64

A 19

A 64 Leeds 24   A 19 Selby 14

A 1036

Bridlington 42 A 166 A 1079 Hull 38

Harrogate 21

READING ROAD SIGNS

THE SHAPES AND COLOURS of British road signs are related to their function. In general, circular signs give orders, triangular signs give warnings and rectangular signs give information. Direction signs on motorways are blue and on primary routes they are green. Some Irish signs differ; those giving warnings are yellow and diamond-shaped.

Signs that give orders

BLUE DISCS *mostly give positive instructions. Red discs and white discs with red borders are mostly prohibitive. Give Way and Stop signs stand out by their distinctive shapes.*

Turn left ahead

Turn left ahead onto one-way street

Turn left ahead onto dual carriageway

Trams only

Keep left

Pass either side to reach same destination

Pedal cycles only

Mini roundabout

One-way traffic

Follow direction indicated by arrow

Minimum speed

End of minimum speed

SIGNALS THAT GIVE ORDERS

Traffic lights
- RED means stop and wait behind the stop line on the carriageway
- RED and AMBER together also means stop. Do not pass the stop line until GREEN shows
- GREEN means you may go if the way is clear
- AMBER means stop. You may go on only if the AMBER appears after you have crossed the line, or if you are so close to the line that to pull up might cause an accident

Filter light
A green arrow with the traffic signals allows movement in the direction shown before the main green phase occurs. Signs may appear alongside green lights to qualify the direction—such as no left turn, or left turn only

Pelican lights
Pedestrians use a push-button to control the traffic signals. RED and AMBER do not appear together. Instead flashing AMBER means give way to pedestrians; go on only if the crossing is clear

Waiting restrictions apply

No stopping (clearway)

National speed limit applies

Maximum speed

No cycling

No pedestrians

All motor vehicles prohibited

No vehicles except bicycles being pushed by hand

Stop and give way

Give way (Ireland)

Give way to traffic on major road

School crossing patrol. Vehicles must stop

Lane control signals
On some busy roads, signals are used at certain times of day to give priority to the main traffic flow by varying the number of lanes available in each direction. A red cross means the lane is closed to approaching traffic, a green downward-pointing arrow that the lane is open to approaching traffic; a white arrow pointing diagonally means the lane is closed ahead—traffic should move into the next left-hand lane

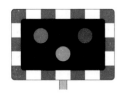

Alternately flashing red lights
This signal means STOP. It is used at places such as railway level crossings, swing bridges and entrances to fire or ambulance stations, where traffic has to be stopped occasionally. A steady amber light means stop at the crossing—go on only if you are so close to the line that to pull up might cause an accident

No entry

No vehicles except motorcycles without sidecars

No U turns

Overtaking prohibited

Give priority to vehicles coming from the opposite direction

No right turn (no left turn if reversed)

No goods vehicles over maximum gross weight shown in tonnes

No vehicles over the maximum gross weight shown

Signs giving warning

THE SYMBOL INSIDE *a red triangle (or in the Republic of Ireland on a yellow diamond) denotes the kind of danger ahead. There may be a plate attached giving more details.*

Crossroads

Side road

Staggered junction

T-junction

A thickened line indicates the priority through the junction

Road narrows on right (left if reversed)

Road narrows on both sides

Dual carriageway ends

Two-way traffic crosses route

Road tunnel

Available width of headroom indicated in feet and metres

Bend to right (left if reversed)

Junction on bend (may be reversed)

Double bend (may be reversed)

Two-way traffic

Roundabout

Side winds

Road works

Hump bridge

Risk of falling or fallen rocks

Quayside or river bank

Opening or swing bridge

Low-flying aircraft

Migratory toad crossing

Horse riders likely to be in road

Cattle likely to be crossing road

Uneven road

Loose chippings

Slippery road

Traffic signals (may warn of a pelican crossing)

Pedestrian crossing

Steep hill upwards with 1 in 5 gradient

Slow-moving vehicles

STOP 100 yds
Distance to STOP line ahead

GIVE WAY 50 yds
Distance to GIVE WAY line

School
Children going to and from school

Patrol
School crossing patrol

Soft verges for 2 miles
Soft verges

Farm traffic
Farm traffic on road

Ice
Ice (often seasonal)

Humps for ½ mile
Road humps for distance shown

Safe height 16'-6"
Overhead electric cables. Plate gives maximum safe height for vehicles

Accident
Other danger! Plate indicates nature of danger

SIGNS AT LEVEL CROSSINGS

Level crossing without gate or barrier

Level crossing with gate or barrier

STOP when lights show
Light signals ahead—used with triangular warning sign

Level crossing without gate or barrier (Ireland)

Countdown markers approaching level crossing round bend

St Andrew's Cross used at crossings without gates or barriers

DRIVERS OF LONG LOW VEHICLES phone before crossing
Risk of grounding. Long low vehicles must obtain permission to drive over crossing

OTHER WARNING SIGNS

Sharp deviation off route to left (or to right if the chevrons are reversed)

Temporary sharp deviation of route to left (or the right if the chevrons are reversed)

Barrier indicating the boundary of an area of highway closed to vehicular and pedestrian traffic

Junction with lesser road (Ireland)

Road bends (Ireland)

Major road ahead (Ireland)

Light signals have failed

Escape lane ahead
Escape lane ahead for vehicles unable to stop on steep hill

Signs giving information

IN BRITAIN, *information signs are rectangular. Primary route signs are green and those on lesser routes are white with black borders. Motorway signs are blue. For tourist attractions and facilities, brown rectangular signs are used.*

Vehicles may park partially on the verge or footway

Priority over oncoming vehicles

You have right of way over vehicles coming from the opposite direction

Distance to parking place ahead

Use the appropriate traffic lane for the junction ahead

No through road

Parking place for towed caravans

Parking available (Ireland)

Hospital: a blue sign means Accident and Emergency facilities are not available, a red sign that they are; restrictions are shown

Number of traffic lanes reduced ahead (for permanent signs the background colour is green on primary routes and blue on motorways)

ROAD WORKS AND DIVERSIONS

Where the flow of traffic has to be restricted to allow road maintenance or improvements, one or more lanes of the carriageway may be closed. Yellow signs indicate lane diversions, sometimes onto the opposite carriageway in a contraflow arrangement

Courtesy sign informing of delays

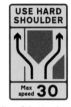

Symbols used along diverted routes to aid following the required route

Diversion from a motorway or other main road

Restrictions ahead on motorway because of road works

Diversion of the two lanes open to traffic; the left-hand lane uses the hard shoulder, the right-hand lane uses the other carriageway

ROUTE DIRECTION SIGNS

PRIMARY ROUTES

Primary road and lesser route in white

Ring road

For primary routes (usually allowing faster travel than ordinary roads), direction signs have green backgrounds. Ring roads that bypass town centres are shown by an R sign. Where a ring road is a not a primary route, the R sign is black on a white background

A gantry sign over the road before a junction directs traffic into the correct lane for the destination required. The name of the junction may be shown at the top of the sign

OTHER (NON-PRIMARY) ROUTES

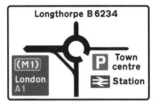

Roundabout ahead with a primary route to the left and other routes ahead and to the right. The primary route leads to a motorway, and for traffic turning onto the primary route there is a dedicated lane (slip road) avoiding the roundabout

A confirmation sign giving the number of the road being followed; a road number in brackets is a road that can be joined farther on

TOURIST SIGNS

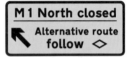

Signs with a brown background give directions to various named tourist attractions, and may also show a symbol indicating the type of attraction. At junctions, repeat signs may show the symbol alone

The examples shown are:

1 English Heritage
2 National Trust
3 Information centre
4 Country park
5 Castle
6 House of historical or architectural interest
7 Wildlife park
8 Zoo
9 Flower garden
10 Museum or art gallery
11 Air museum
12 Picnic area
13 English Tourist Board recognised attraction
14 Scottish Tourist Board recognised attraction
15 Welsh Tourist Board recognised attraction

Markings on the carriageway and the kerb

WHITE LINES *marked on the carriageway are used to separate traffic lanes or to indicate restrictions or hazards. Yellow or red lines along the edge of the road and on the kerb indicate that there are waiting, parking or loading restrictions.*

DOUBLE WHITE LINES IN THE CENTRE OF THE ROAD

If the line nearest to you is unbroken, you must not cross or straddle it—except to get into or out of a property or a side road, to avoid a stationary vehicle blocking your lane, or to overtake a pedal cyclist, horse or road works vehicle moving at not more than 10 mph (16 km/h). Where both lines are unbroken, drivers in both directions are similarly restricted. A white arrow indicates the direction in which traffic should pass double white lines. If you have moved out to overtake, you must return to the left-hand lane before the start of the continuous white line

SINGLE WHITE LINES ON THE CARRIAGEWAY

Short broken white lines
Short broken lines mark the edges of a traffic lane. Keep within them. There may be reflecting road studs in the gaps between the lines

Long broken white lines
Long broken lane lines are warnings of a hazard. Do not cross the lane line unless the road is clear for a long way ahead

Longer broken white lines
Longer broken lines with shorter gaps between are more emphatic warnings of a greater hazard in crossing them to overtake

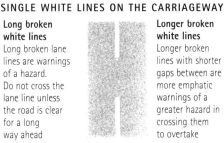

White diagonal lines or hatched markings
These are used to separate traffic lanes, to protect traffic turning right, or to keep traffic away from the carriageway edge. If the border line is unbroken, do not enter except in an emergency. If the border line is broken, do not enter unless it is safe to do so

WHITE LINES ALONG THE EDGE OF THE CARRIAGEWAY

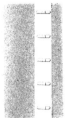

Unbroken white lines with raised ribs
These mark the edge of the carriageway on motorways and on all-purpose roads with hard shoulders or strips. They give drivers a warning that can be both heard and felt

Broken white lines with short gaps
These mark the carriageway edge at junctions and the exits from private drives and lay-bys, also the division between a main carriageway and a lane that leaves it to join a junction ahead. If set diagonally, they mark the start of a traffic lane

Short broken white lines with small gaps
These mark the edge of the carriageway at a junction and an exit from a private drive or lay-by. If set diagonally across part of a carriageway, they indicate the start of a cycle lane

Unbroken white lines
These mark the carriageway edge at places other than junctions and exits from private drives and lay-bys

YELLOW LINES AT THE ROAD EDGE OR ON THE KERB

WAITING RESTRICTIONS

Yellow lines on the carriageway, pavement and verge are a guide only to the waiting restrictions in force—generally, two yellow lines are an indication of more stringent restrictions than a single line. For full information on the restrictions, consult the plates posted nearby, or the entry signs to controlled parking zones. Where waiting is restricted, you may stop to load or unload bulky items, or while passengers board or alight, unless there are also loading restrictions as shown below

Two unbroken yellow lines
No waiting, except for loading and unloading, during the times indicated on the nearby plates. If no days or dates are given, waiting is not allowed at any time, including Sundays and Bank Holidays

At any time

No waiting

No waiting between dates given

At any time 1 May - 30 Sept

One unbroken yellow line
No waiting—except for loading and unloading—during the times indicated on the nearby plates

8 am - 6 pm →

No waiting between times shown. Arrow gives direction of restricted area

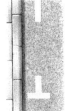

One broken yellow line
Waiting limited to, or prohibited at times, on blue or yellow plates. These are being phased out. Bays marked by broken white lines and with white plates nearby will replace some

Limited waiting in a bay

P	Mon - Sat 8 am - 7 pm 20 mins No return within 40 mins

LOADING RESTRICTIONS

Yellow marks on the kerb or carriageway edge are a guide to the loading restrictions in force, as indicated on nearby black and white plates—in general, the more lines, the greater the restriction. If plates give no dates, the restrictions are in force every day including Sundays and Bank Holidays. Where a loading restriction is in force, you must not park unless you are loading or unloading

No loading at any time
Double lines (or triple lines until 1999) indicate no loading at all

No loading Mon - Fri 11 am - 3 pm
A single line indicates no loading or unloading at certain times

Loading only
Reserved for loading

CONTROLLED PARKING ZONES

Meter ZONE
Mon - Fri 8.30 am - 6.30 pm Saturday 8.30 am - 1.30 pm

The details of the restrictions in force and the times at which they operate are given at the zone entrance. Within the zones, <u>yellow lines only</u> are used to indicate where no waiting is allowed, and there are <u>no accompanying signs</u>. Places where parking is allowed are shown by white bay markings, accompanied by signs or parking meters

Zone ENDS

CLEARWAYS

Bus stop clearway
The clearway sign is accompanied by a thick yellow line and BUS STOP marked on the carriageway. In the marked area, no vehicle other than a bus may stop, even to allow passengers to get in or out, between the times shown on the sign

No stopping 7 am - 7 pm except buses

Urban clearway
Where these signs appear, no stopping is allowed on the carriageway or verges—except briefly to set down or pick up passengers—during the times shown. Waiting restrictions may apply at other times. The yellow lines on the carriageway used with these signs are to be phased out by 1999

URBAN CLEARWAY Monday to Friday	
am 8.00 - 9.30	pm 4.30 - 6.30

OTHER LINES ACROSS OR BESIDE THE ROAD

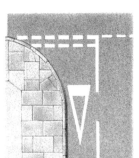

Broken white lines at junctions
Double broken lines across the carriageway mean that drivers must give way to traffic on the major road. There may be a triangular Give Way sign beside the road and a triangle on the road to give advance warning

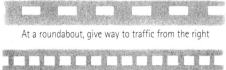

At a roundabout, give way to traffic from the right

At a mini roundabout, give way to traffic from the right

Unbroken white lines at junctions
A single unbroken white line across the carriageway, accompanied by the word STOP, means that drivers must stop—as required by a hexagonal Stop sign beside the road—and must ensure that the way is clear before entering the major road

Thin unbroken STOP line at signals or police control

Crossed diagonal yellow lines
These lines mark a box junction. You must not enter the box until your exit is clear, unless you intend to turn right and are waiting for oncoming traffic to stop, or unless vehicles within the box are stationary and waiting to turn right

Zigzag lines Do not park or wait where these lines are marked

Zigzag lines along the road edge
On the approach to a zebra or pelican crossing, you must not park or wait within the area bounded by zigzag lines, except to give way to pedestrians on the crossing or in circumstances beyond your control. When giving way to pedestrians, stop at the broken white line about 3 ft (1 m) before the crossing. Where there are zigzag lines, do not overtake vehicles in front of you, either moving or stationary. Yellow zigzag lines mark school areas. Do not stop, even to pick up or set down children or other passengers

BUS AND CYCLIST LANES

Special lanes for buses or bicycles, or both These are in use in some areas, and are shown by both signs and road markings. They may be in operation for 24 hours a day, or for shorter periods indicated on roadside plates. The signs give details of the vehicles that may use the lane. Outside the period of operation, all vehicles may use a bus lane and, unless the lane is physically separated from the rest of the carriageway by an island, may enter to stop for loading or unloading—but only at times when there is no restriction on loading

Red road markings
Roads edged with double or single red lines are designated as Red Routes, and are also marked by signs. Traffic must not stop on red routes during specified times

Lane reserved for buses, cyclists and taxis ahead

Lane reserved for buses

Lane reserved for cyclists

Lane for cycling in traffic direction

Contraflow cycle lane

Red Route sign

Lines indicate Red Route

Understanding motorway signs

ON MOTORWAYS, *the blue and white signs are designed to be clearly seen and easily understood while driving at speed. All exits are numbered; this simplifies route-planning.*

Start of motorway
The sign marks where motorway regulations come into operation, and identifies the motorway by number

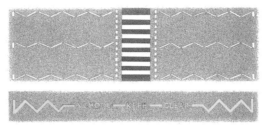

Route confirmation sign
Beyond a junction, a route sign gives main destinations ahead, with distances to those destinations shown in miles

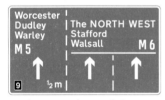

Increase or decrease in lanes
Traffic in the left lane is leaving the main carriageway

Junction sign
Warning of a junction ahead is first given usually 1 mile (1.6 km) before the exit slip road, then again ½ mile later. The sign gives the number of the road being joined, the main destinations and, in a black panel, the number of the junction

Countdown markers
These indicate the distance to the start of a junction deceleration lane. Each bar represents about 100 yd (90 m)

Junction direction sign
A direction sign is usually sited where the deceleration lane leaves the main carriageway

End of motorway
The sign is at the motorway end or on its slip road. Here motorway regulations cease

Motorway slip road
On a motorway slip road, a sign may show the destinations reached along a primary route on a green panel, or along a non-primary route on a white panel

HAZARD SIGNALS

Signals are sited on gantries over the road or on posts beside the carriageway. At most times they are blank, and are switched on by the police only if road, traffic or weather conditions are abnormal. Hazard signals tell drivers what action to take—reduce speed to 50 mph (80 km/h) or leave the motorway, for example. Amber lights flashing alternately above and below a signal are warnings to draw attention to the signal itself

Leave motorway at next exit

Gantry signals
These each concern only the drivers in the lane beneath. A flashing red signal means that vehicles in the lane must stop if they are prevented from joining another lane

Do not proceed in this lane

End of restriction

Carriageway signals
Signals on the far edge of the hard shoulder and on the central reservation concern drivers in all lanes. The reason for the restriction signalled, such as a speed limit or a lane closure, may not be apparent at first, but there may be an accident ahead, for instance, or a belt of fog, and traffic approaching must be warned and controlled

Temporary maximum speed limit advised

Lane closed ahead (right-hand lane)

EMERGENCY TELEPHONES

Marker post
Pointer at every 100 yd (90 m) to nearest phone

SOS telephones
Telephones about 1 mile (1.6 km) apart on the hard shoulder are linked to a police switchboard

GETTING THE BEST FROM YOUR JOURNEY

Safe and skilful driving—an A-Z guide

SKILL AND SAFETY *go hand in hand. A good driver 'reads the road' and is ready to react to any situation. Skilful driving calls for alertness, patience, courtesy to other road users and, above all, knowledge of the best way to deal with problems or hazards—from those met every day, such as overtaking, to those less often encountered, such as floods or a shattered windscreen.*

ANIMALS ON THE ROAD

- Slow down if you see a dog or cat by the roadside—it may dart into the road. Watch for road signs warning that animals such as deer or cattle may stray onto the road.
- If cattle or sheep are blocking the road, stop and wait until the animals have gone. Don't sound your horn or rev the engine, as this may frighten them and make them blunder into your car.

If there are horses ahead, slow down. Keep well behind until it is clear to overtake. As you pass, allow plenty of room. Don't sound your horn or accelerate hard, as the horses may shy or bolt.

- Be very careful if you come upon a group of riders—possibly a riding school—in case an inexperienced rider loses control of a horse. Stop if one of the group signals you to do so, and turn off your engine.

If you accidentally hit an animal, stop. If the animal is in the road, switch on the hazard lights and, if you have one, put out a warning triangle to alert other drivers. By law, you must stop if you hit a dog, cow, bull, bullock, pig, goat, horse or donkey, but not if you hit a cat or a wild animal. Report the accident to the police as soon as possible.

- If the animal is small enough to handle, gently wrap it in a car rug, but keep away from its teeth, as it may bite—tie a belt or something similar round a dog's muzzle to prevent it biting. Take the animal to a vet, who may charge you for treatment.
- If you hit a pet or farmyard animal, go to the nearest house or farm and try to find the owner. Don't attempt to move or deal with the wounds of a large animal.

BENDS OR CORNERS

As you approach a bend, look out for signs telling you its nature—if it is sharp and whether it is one of a series.

- Slow down by decelerating and using your footbrake to warn those behind you.
- Before a sharp bend or corner, change to a lower gear appropriate to your road speed—third, or second if necessary. Your speed should be at its lowest as you enter. Don't go in too fast—braking hard on a bend quickly wears out your tyres.
- On acute blind bends and very narrow roads, consider sounding your horn before you enter to alert oncoming drivers—but not in a built-up area at night.

On the bend itself, decelerate smoothly and keep both hands on the steering wheel. Don't brake unless going downhill.

- On a right-hand bend keep well to the left to get a good view ahead. Watch for driveways or blind side roads and pedestrians close to the road.
- If the road slopes towards the outer edge, keep speed down—centrifugal force pushes a car outwards on a bend, and a high speed may force it off the road.

- On a left-hand bend, position the car towards the centre line of the road so you get a good view ahead, but don't veer too far right—there may be an oncoming vehicle in the middle of the road.
- Accelerate as you drive out of the bend and can see ahead clearly.
- Extra loads, such as a roof rack, increase the risk of skidding at a bend. Make sure that a heavy load is evenly distributed, and increase tyre pressures to the level recommended in the car handbook.

At night, dip your headlights as you approach a bend. Don't look directly at oncoming headlights; if you are dazzled, slow down or stop to rest your eyes.

- For forewarning of a bend, keep an eye on the brake lights of a vehicle ahead of you. The sweep of its headlights will also reveal the severity of the bend.

BLIND SPOTS

All cars have blind spots caused by the bodywork interfering with the driver's view of the road behind in the wing and rear-view mirrors. Vehicle accessory shops sell small convex mirrors that can be stuck onto side-view mirrors to open up a wider field of vision.

- Before moving off, look over your right shoulder to check the area of a blind spot.

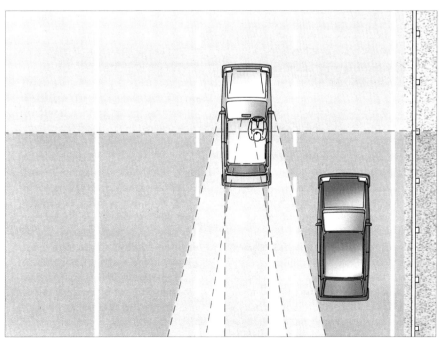

CAUGHT IN THE BLIND SPOT *The areas of light shading show the centre-lane driver's view ahead and through the rear and side-view mirrors. The red car is in the blind spot—the dark shading.*

- On the move, check your car mirrors frequently to keep up to date with what is happening around you.
- Don't cover your windows with stickers as this creates unnecessary blind spots.

Before you change lanes, especially on a motorway, glance quickly over your right shoulder to check whether a vehicle that has just disappeared from your mirror is coming up beside you. Take great care, especially at high speed.

- Don't linger alongside another vehicle as you overtake it—you could be in the other motorist's blind spot.

BRAKE FAILURE

If the footbrake fails, don't switch the engine off—without it you can't control the car.

- Apply the handbrake smoothly and pump the footbrake to restore brake pressure.
- Hold the steering wheel firmly, because the rear wheels are likely to lock and cause the car to skid.
- As the handbrake slows the car, steadily change down through the gears—if you do it too fast, the car will be thrown about.
- With automatic transmission, move the gear lever into L (low lock) or 2 (second gear) at about 20 mph (30 km/h).
- If you can't slow down or stop in time to avoid a collision, try to run the car up a slope or bank, or—where it is safe to do so—slow down by mounting a kerb or scraping the car along a hedge or fence.

If the handbrake fails as you go to pull away on a hill, try to 'heel and toe'. Put the toes of your right foot on the footbrake and the heel on the accelerator. As you release the clutch, ease your toes off the footbrake and press the heel down on the accelerator. Once you move forwards, release the footbrake.

- If the car rolls backwards, turn the steering wheel so that the rear wheels back against the kerb or verge.

BURST TYRE

- Don't change gear to slow down.
- If a front tyre has burst, the car will pull towards the side with the damage. Avoid braking. Turn the steering wheel smoothly in the opposite direction to the sideways pull, and hold a straight course.
- If a rear tyre has burst, the back end of the car may slide to one side. Brake very gently and grip the steering wheel firmly to keep the car steady.
- Signal left, and if possible steer the car to the side of the road and roll to a stop.
- If a tyre bursts in the outside lane of a motorway and you can't safely move across to the hard shoulder, pull into the central reservation, if possible. Turn on the hazard lights and wait for assistance.
- Never change a wheel on a motorway or hard shoulder—call for assistance.

CROSSWINDS

In windy conditions, keep a firm grip on the steering wheel to avoid being pulled out of your lane, particularly on exposed stretches of road such as motorways, bridges and viaducts.

- When you move from a sheltered area into an exposed section of road, be prepared for sudden crosswinds.
- Watch out for cyclists or motorcyclists who may be blown into your path. Allow them extra room when overtaking.
- Be careful when overtaking a high-sided vehicle. Adjust your steering to allow for being pulled towards the other vehicle as you pass, and pushed away beyond it.

When towing a caravan or trailer, listen for radio forecasts of strong winds. Avoid high bridges and high, exposed routes.

FATIGUE AT THE WHEEL

- Bright sunlight puts strain on the eyes and increases fatigue. Wear sunglasses with polarised lenses, which cut out dazzling reflected light.
- Don't eat a heavy meal before a long journey as this may make you sleepy. Do eat something light, however—an empty stomach makes concentration difficult.
- Don't drive for more than three hours without a break. On a long journey, alternate the driving with someone else.
- To keep alert at the wheel, play the radio, a lively tape or CD, or get passengers to chat to you. Wind down the window to let in fresh air, but on motorways and busy roads for short periods only, because traffic noise increases fatigue.

If you feel drowsy, direct cold air from the fan onto your face. If necessary, lick your finger and dampen your forehead and eyelids—particularly at the inner corner of each eye. Take deep breaths, purse your lips, and exhale slowly.

- If you feel particularly tired, slow down, pull off the road and park safely. Don't stop on a motorway hard shoulder—turn into the next service station, or first leave the motorway and then stop.

When you have stopped, a short nap or a hot drink will help to revive you. Get out of the car and walk around to exercise your limbs and to get the circulation going.

- Take off your shoes and socks for a while, as this will cool and relax your feet.

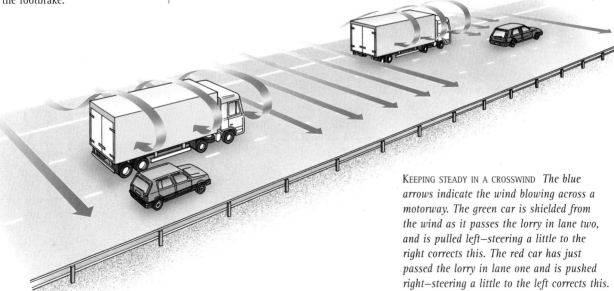

KEEPING STEADY IN A CROSSWIND *The blue arrows indicate the wind blowing across a motorway. The green car is shielded from the wind as it passes the lorry in lane two, and is pulled left—steering a little to the right corrects this. The red car has just passed the lorry in lane one and is pushed right—steering a little to the left corrects this.*

FIRE IN THE CAR

If you see smoke or flames coming from under the bonnet as you drive, switch off the engine; leave the key in the ignition so that the steering wheel stays unlocked.

- Coast to the side of the road and stop.
- Get all passengers out and well away from the car and from traffic.
- If flames spread towards the fuel tank, get well away and phone the fire brigade.
- Otherwise, lift the bonnet a little way and disconnect the wires from the battery terminals–tug them off if necessary. Don't open the bonnet wide–letting in air will increase the flames.
- Smother flames with a blanket, car rug or any thick material.
- If you have a fire extinguisher, direct the foam at the base of the flames and work from side to side, covering the whole area of the fire. If the fire is in the engine, lift the bonnet a little and direct the foam through the gap.
- If you can't quickly put out the fire, phone the fire brigade.

FLOODS

Slow down if the road ahead is flooded, and stop if you are uncertain of the water's depth. Ford crossings usually have a gauge showing the depth of the water; check it before driving your car across.

- Avoid drenching passers-by at the side of the road. Give them plenty of room.
- Don't drive through water higher than the centre of the car's road wheels–a depth of about 10-12 in (250-300 mm)–because the spray may damage the engine. If the water seems too deep, take another road to avoid the flood.

If the water appears shallow–cars ahead may be getting through without a problem, for example–then drive through slowly, entering at the shallowest point, which is where the road camber is highest.

- To avoid stalling, slip the clutch–that is, hold down both the accelerator and clutch pedals about half way. Drive slowly in first or second gear–on an automatic car L (low lock) or 1 (first gear)–to limit the water splashed onto the engine.
- Don't change gear–the change of engine speed may cause water to be sucked up the exhaust; this can damage the engine.

Once out of the water, drive slowly, pressing lightly on the brake pedal for 100 yd (90 m) or so. This will dry the brakes. Test the brakes several times before you pick up speed, to make sure they are pulling evenly on all wheels.

FOG

- Drive with dipped headlights–sidelights are insufficient. Don't use full beam, as the light reflects from fog particles and may dazzle or confuse you.
- Keep the screen clear inside and out by using windscreen wipers and the demister.
- Use front fog lamps, if you have them. Switch on rear fog lamps only where visibility ahead is less than about 100 yd (90 m); switch them off when fog clears, as it is then an offence to use them.
- As a guide, use the nearside kerb or verge–if possible, get a passenger to tell you how close you are. Reflective studs, or Catseyes, in the middle of the road are also a guide, but don't drive too near to the centre line, risking collision with cars coming from the opposite direction.
- So that you can hear other vehicles or horns, turn off a radio, cassette player or CD player and wind down your window.
- Drive slowly enough to stop within the distance clear ahead, taking into account that roads are more slippery in fog than in rain. Be prepared for patches of thicker fog, where visibility deteriorates suddenly.
- Keep well behind the vehicle in front, and don't blindly follow its rear lights as a guide–they may lead you into a collision.
- Don't speed up to get away from a vehicle that is driving close behind you.
- Avoid overtaking. If you have to pass another car, flash your headlights and sound your horn to give the driver plenty of warning–but not between 11.30 pm and 7 am in a built-up area.
- If you have to stop, pull off the road. If forced to stop on the carriageway or a hard shoulder, switch on hazard lights.

GEAR-CHANGING MANUALLY

- When you change gear, you temporarily disengage the engine from the driveshaft that turns the road wheels in order to engage a different set of toothed wheels in the gearbox. This changes the speed of the driveshaft.
- Lower gears produce more turning power at low speeds to get the car moving. An engine will judder or stall if the gear selected is too high for the road speed.
- Before changing gear, adjust your road speed by braking (to change down) or accelerating (to change up) so that it is suitable for a smooth change. Road/gear speeds are given in the car handbook–a good driver learns to judge them.
- When you change gear, press the clutch pedal down fully, move the gear lever smoothly into the new gear position and release the clutch gently and steadily.

- During normal driving, take your foot off the clutch pedal–'riding' the clutch increases wear on the mechanism. But for slow driving, as in a traffic queue, it is often necessary to 'slip' the clutch in low gear–that is, drive with the clutch pedal partly held down.

HIGHWAY SECURITY

- Don't keep valuables where they can be seen when you are driving or parked. In built-up areas, keep windows and the sun-roof closed and doors locked, especially where you have to stop–at traffic lights, for example–in case someone tries to enter your vehicle.
- Beware of giving lifts to strangers. If a hitchhiker threatens you with a weapon, do as you are told and drive on. Hand over items demanded, and don't struggle. If you reach a place full of people, make as much noise as you can to attract their attention–this may scare off the attacker. If you think you are in danger, stop the car and get out as fast as you can.
- If, as a male driver, you give a woman a lift and she threatens to accuse you of assaulting her unless you hand over money, keep calm, don't give any money and contact the police immediately.
- Beware of someone flagging you down for help–this could be a trap. Slow down and change to a low gear so that you can accelerate away if necessary. If you stop, make sure your doors are locked, keep the engine running and be ready to drive off quickly. If you are uncertain whether the situation is genuine, drive on until it is safe to contact the police.
- If another driver is trying to ram your car or force you off the road, don't retaliate. Keep calm and drive to a well-lit, busy place, or directly to a police station.

ICE AND SNOW

- Make sure tyres are at the recommended pressures (see your car handbook), so that they give the best grip possible.
- On ice, braking distances can be ten times longer than in normal, dry conditions, so keep your speed down and leave plenty of space between your car and other vehicles (see 'Stopping distances' on page 448).
- Drive in a high gear–no lower than third, or D (drive) on an automatic–to reduce the chances of wheelspin.
- Brake and accelerate gently, and don't brake and steer at the same time–on icy roads, anti-lock (ABS) brakes may not be effective against wheel lock.

GETTING OUT OF SNOW
When car tyres lose their grip on a snowy surface, put pieces of sacking in front of the two driving wheels—the front wheels on a front-wheel-drive car, or otherwise the rear wheels. Hold the front wheels straight and accelerate ahead gently in second gear, then keep going slowly in as high a gear as you can until the road surface again offers a firm grip.

- To slow the car, use 'cadence braking', that is, brake with a pumping action to avoid the wheels locking; flashing brake lights will also warn drivers behind.
- Don't change down through the gears any more than you have to, as you lose traction with each gear change.
- Approach corners and bends on icy roads at a gentle, steady speed in high gear. Avoid braking or touching the clutch, and steer smoothly.

On an icy hill, don't stop or change gear when you ascend, as you may lose tyre grip and slide. If you stop it is difficult to start again. Try to keep going in third gear. In an automatic, select second gear.
- Descend slowly in a low gear, using the brakes very lightly.

In falling snow, use dipped headlights and stop regularly to clear windows and lights. Take extra care on hard-packed snow or ice hidden beneath fresh snow.
- Where snow is particularly deep, you may fit snow chains round tyres to increase grip. Remove chains as soon as you are clear of ice and snow—they may damage your tyres and the road surface.

If heavy snow is forecast, carry in the car a spade, some sacking, Wellington boots, and a torch and spare batteries, in case you get stuck. If you have to make a long journey, especially at night, take a flask of hot drink, rugs and blankets, and high-energy rations such as chocolate.
- If the car gets stuck in snow or ice, don't accelerate hard, because the wheels will spin, compacting the snow and packing it into the tyre treads. This reduces grip.
- To get out of snow, put sacking, twigs, sand or grit immediately in front of the driving wheels. Make sure the front wheels are straight, select second gear, and accelerate gently while letting the clutch out slowly to avoid wheel spin.

- If necessary, ask passengers or passers-by to help to push the car. Make sure they stand at the side so that the car doesn't roll or slide into them, but away from the driving wheels or they will be sprayed with dirt and snow.
- Once the car is moving, drive until you are on a firmer, more level surface.

If you are stuck in deep snow, try to build up a solid surface of piled up snow under the wheels by moving the car backwards and forwards a short way. Select first gear and edge ahead, revving gently and slipping the clutch to avoid stalling. When the car is as far forward as it can go, engage reverse and move slowly backwards. Repeat the action until you can drive out of the trough over the piled up snow. If this fails, dig the snow out from round the wheels and resort to putting sacking in front of them as described above.

If you are stranded in a blizzard and can't drive on, stay in the car. If you get out to seek shelter or help, you could get lost in falling snow, or stumble into a snowdrift.
- Keep awake—if you fall asleep you could suffer hypothermia. Turn the ignition key to its first position so that you can play the radio or a tape, but not for too long at a time or you will drain the battery.
- Keep warm by wrapping yourself in rugs, clothing or newspapers, especially your head, from which most body heat is lost.
- Don't drink alcohol to keep warm, as it in fact encourages loss of body heat, and will make you sleepy.
- Don't switch on the engine to use the heater unless you have been able to clear snow from round the exhaust, otherwise poisonous fumes could enter the car.
- Run the engine and heater for about 10 minutes every hour—not longer, or you will use up fuel, and may become drowsy.
- Open a window occasionally—on the side away from drifting snow—to let in air.

LEVEL CROSSINGS

- Approach guarded or unguarded level crossings with caution—don't speed up in an attempt to beat the lights. If you have already crossed the white line when the warnings start, keep going.
- At crossings with automatic barriers but no warning signals, stop as soon as the barriers start to come down. Never zigzag round barriers that fall only half-way across the road.
- While waiting at a crossing, save fuel and cut down exhaust emissions by turning off the engine until the train has passed.
- Drive across only when the road on the other side is clear. Don't drive across nose to tail with other cars.

If your car stalls or breaks down on a level crossing, abandon it and get yourself and passengers out and away from the crossing as fast as possible. If there is a railway telephone, call the signalman and follow his instructions.
- If there is time to move the car before the next train is due, release the handbrake, put the gear lever into neutral and push the car away from the crossing. Then call the signalman, if there is a railway telephone. But if warning bells ring or lights flash while you are on the crossing, leave the car and get well away.

MOTORWAYS

When joining a motorway, signal a right turn as you approach along the slip road, adjust your speed to take advantage of a gap in the traffic on lane one, check that there is nothing in your blind spot and accelerate carefully into a gap. Traffic already on the motorway has right of way—don't try to force your way in, or drive along the hard shoulder.

Once on the motorway, adjust your speed to that of the other traffic in the lane. The maximum speed allowed in any lane is 70 mph (112.5 km/h).
- Drive steadily in the centre of the lane, and far enough from the car ahead to allow you to stop in an emergency—see 'Stopping distances' on page 448.
- Change lanes only if you want to overtake, to follow directions where a motorway divides, or to allow traffic from a slip road to merge into lane one. Signal in plenty of time to warn other cars.
- On a two-lane motorway, use lane two for overtaking only, not as a fast lane.
- On a three or four-lane motorway, keep to lane one unless overtaking slower cars. Don't sit in lane two if lane one is clear.

- If another car sits on your tail in lane two, don't accelerate away; move over to the left as soon as there is a safe gap.
- At junctions where other vehicles are joining, adjust your speed as necessary to allow them to merge into lane one. If you can, move to lane two to make room.
- If you see flashing hazard signals, slow down and obey their directions, changing into other lanes in plenty of time. Don't increase speed until you see signs that the restriction is at an end.
- To rejoin the motorway after a necessary stop on the hard shoulder, build up speed on the hard shoulder and merge into lane one when it is safe to do so.

When leaving a motorway, move across into lane one well before your exit. Signal left from lane one into the deceleration lane leading to the exit slip road.
- While on the slip road, reduce your speed to suit normal driving conditions for other roads, and mentally readjust to the different pace and demands of traffic.

NIGHT DRIVING

- Keep all lights clean, particularly headlights, and check that they are all in working order. Carry spare bulbs.
- In built-up areas, always use dipped headlights. Don't let yourself be distracted by lights from shops, houses and other cars. Watch out for obstacles or pedestrian crossings that are not well lit.
- Don't sound your horn between 11.30 pm and 7 am; warn other road users of your presence by flashing your headlights.
- On unlighted roads, use full-beam headlights, but dip them for oncoming traffic. Before you dip, check for hazards such as parked cars or cyclists.
- Watch your speed. You are driving too fast if you could not stop safely within the range of your headlights.
- Dip your headlights when driving behind another vehicle—full beam dazzles the driver. If you are overtaken, dip your headlights as soon as the other vehicle starts to move past.
- Don't get too close to the vehicle in front—your headlight beam, whether on full or dipped, should fall short of its rear.
- Overtake with care—at night, junctions, bends and road hazards can be difficult to spot. If in doubt, don't overtake.
- When waiting at junctions and traffic lights, use your handbrake; don't keep your foot on the brake pedal as this can distract the driver behind.
- If you are dazzled by the lights of an oncoming vehicle, slow down or stop safely and allow your eyes to readjust.

Don't retaliate by switching on your own headlights to full beam.
- Avoid using interior lights in the car. They reflect against the windscreen and reduce the clarity of your view.

OVERTAKING

- Never overtake where your visibility is restricted—for example, when approaching a junction, on a bend, or on the brow of a hill. Obey markings or road signs that prohibit overtaking; don't take risks.
- Signal a right turn *before* you overtake, not during the manoeuvre. Indicate left before you pull in again, then make sure your indicator is cancelled.
- Don't hug the rear of the vehicle you wish to overtake—keep a safe stopping distance between you, and a clear view ahead.
- On a two-way road that has a central

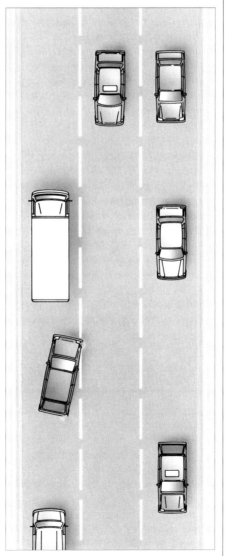

HAZARDOUS OVERTAKING *The red car pulling out into the central overtaking lane is too close to the lorry to get a clear view ahead. The oncoming green car will have little chance of pulling back to the inside lane.*

overtaking lane, don't pull out unless the lane is clear. If an approaching vehicle moves out, wait until it has passed.

On a motorway, look ahead and behind for other vehicles on, or about to move into, your overtaking lane. Indicate right, but before pulling out glance over your shoulder to check the blind spot.
- Move out smoothly and accelerate past slower vehicles. Pull in as soon as a safe gap opens up, but check that no other vehicle is about to move into that gap.
- Never overtake on the left, except in slow traffic when the queue on your right is travelling more slowly.
- Don't use the motorway hard shoulder for overtaking unless directed to do so by the police or by traffic signs at road works.
- If a vehicle wants to overtake, pull to the left as soon as you can and let it pass.

PARKING

- Whenever possible, park off the road or in a car park or parking place.

If you park on the road, keep well away from pedestrian crossings, school entrances and road junctions. Never park where your car would obstruct emergency vehicles.
- Take notice of parking and waiting restrictions—putting on hazard warning lights isn't an excuse to stop anywhere.
- Park on the left of the road as close to the kerb as you can. Avoid brushing against or mounting a kerb—this weakens tyres.
- If you are forced to park on the right in a two-way road, be extra careful as you pull out in the face of oncoming traffic. At night, it is illegal to park on the right, except in one-way streets.
- In a line of parked cars, find a space at least 1½ times your car's length—the smallest you can comfortably get into. Pull alongside the vehicle in front of the space, and slowly and carefully reverse in.
- Allow room for cars in front of or behind your vehicle to pull out. Leave plenty of room for a car with a disabled driver's badge—the driver may need space in which to manoeuvre a wheelchair.
- Never park on the pavement, unless a sign is displayed permitting it.

When parking on a slope, if on the left and facing uphill, turn the wheels to the right so that the kerb will stop the car if it rolls backwards; put the car in first gear with the handbrake on. If on the left facing downhill, turn the wheels to the left and put the car in reverse with the handbrake on. With an automatic, put the handbrake on before selecting the park setting, P.

PEDESTRIANS

- When turning left or right into another road, give way to pedestrians crossing.
- In built-up areas particularly, watch out for children dashing into the road. On a road lined with parked cars, a child could dash out unseen. Be especially alert, and keep your speed to no more than 20 mph (32 km/h) where this is likely, such as near school buses and ice-cream vans.
- On country roads, keep a lookout for pedestrians walking in the road, especially in poor visibility or at night. Slow down and give them plenty of room.

On the approach to a zebra crossing, slow down and check whether anyone is about to cross. You must stop once someone has set foot on the crossing. Never wave people across—a car behind may overtake, or an oncoming car may not stop.

- In a queue of traffic, leave a pedestrian crossing clear.

CEDING RIGHT OF WAY *When you pull out of a driveway—or turn into one—always give way to pedestrians using the pavement. If your view is blocked by a hedge, wall or other obstruction, edge out slowly until you can see clearly to both the left and the right.*

RAIN AND SPRAY

- In wet weather, slow down—braking takes longer on a wet road—and turn on dipped headlights so that you can be seen clearly.
- If the windows mist up, obscuring your view of the road, turn on the demisters and, if there is one, the rear-window heater. Don't wipe the windscreen with your hand—this makes the surface greasy.
- If your car aquaplanes—slides on water not channelled away by the tyres—don't brake or steer sharply; ease pressure on the accelerator until the tyres regain grip.
- On motorways in driving rain, avoid overtaking heavy goods vehicles, as their spray can completely obscure your vision.
- Be prepared—keep the windscreen clean and the washer bottle filled with water.

BEWARE OF PEDESTRIANS *In the busy streets of a built-up area, keep your speed down and watch for children who may dart suddenly into the road from behind or between parked vehicles.*

REVERSING

- Before you get into the car, make sure there is nothing behind, such as a small child or a cat, that would not be visible through the mirrors or rear window.
- In the car, check mirrors, and turn slightly to look over your right shoulder through the rear window. Undo your seat belt if necessary (remember to refasten it before you drive off).
- Reverse slowly, slipping the clutch if necessary. To change direction, turn the steering wheel in the direction that you want the rear of the car to turn.
- Look out through the side window if necessary, but don't lean your elbow on it. Keep your hands on the wheel.
- If you get confused about which way to turn the steering, get out and see which way your front wheels are facing.
- If you are reversing a trailer to the right or the left, turn the steering the *opposite* way from the direction in which you want the trailer to turn.

ROUNDABOUTS

On the approach to a roundabout, slow down and get into a suitable lane for your turn right or left. When going straight on, approach in the left-hand lane or, if it is occupied, the next lane.

- You must give way to traffic coming from the right, but if the road is clear move out smoothly without stopping, keeping to your chosen lane.
- After passing the exit before your turn-off, signal a left turn.
- On mini roundabouts, wait for other vehicles to exit before you join—beware of drivers who are using the roundabout to make a U-turn.

- At a double mini roundabout, don't enter the first until you are sure you can enter and leave the second without stopping or interfering with other traffic.

DRIVING ON THE RIGHT ABROAD

- When driving on the right in a car with righthand drive, the trickiest manoeuvres are turning left and overtaking. Make sure your car has a left-hand wing mirror to show up following traffic.
- You will need to adjust your headlight beam to the right. You can buy a kit with adhesive masking tape for the purpose.
- Until you feel confident, keep your speed down and carefully check in all mirrors before manoeuvring.
- To overtake, ease out gradually until you have a clear view. A front-seat passenger can help by letting you know about oncoming traffic.
- When turning left, you have to cross the path of oncoming traffic. As you turn into the new road, remember to go into the right-hand lane.
- The rule of the road is to give way on the right. Not all main roads have priority over side roads—watch for traffic coming from the right.
- Give way to trams and to people getting on or off them.
- Be careful at roundabouts. Traffic flows anticlockwise—don't try to go round in the familiar way.
- If hiring a left-hand drive vehicle, take time to familiarise yourself with the different control layout, and get used to changing gear with your right hand.

CLEARING A SHATTERED SCREEN *Stop in a safe place before you remove any glass. Cover up the dashboard with a sheet or blanket to collect the glass fragments. Protecting the demister slots stops pieces of glass being blown into your face later by the fan. Wrap padding round the whole of the hand you use to push out the glass.*

SHATTERED WINDSCREEN

Most cars have laminated windscreens—with a layer of plastic sandwiched between glass. This will crack or chip but should not shatter.

If your windscreen does shatter, don't punch out an area of glass—you could cut your arm and eyes.

- Lean forward to get a better view, and quickly signal and move left to stop.
- Cover the demister slots on top of the dashboard and spread newspaper or a blanket over the bonnet. Pad your hand with a glove or cloth, get back inside the car and push out as much glass as you can onto the paper.
- Dust any fragments off the dashboard and wrap all the glass in the newspaper or blanket. Don't leave glass by the roadside, dispose of it safely.
- If glass has fallen through the heater vents, don't use the demister until the system has been cleaned, or the fan will blow fragments of glass into the car.

As a roadside repair, fit a temporary windscreen if you have one. It is normally wrapped round the front door jambs and held in place by the closed doors.

- Otherwise, either cover the grooved rubber flange that held the screen with adhesive tape or masking tape to stop fragments flying out, remove the rubber flange completely, or protect your eyes with sunglasses.
- Drive carefully to the nearest service station, or telephone to arrange for an emergency windscreen to be fitted.

SINGLE-TRACK ROADS

- Country roads wide enough for only one car usually have passing places at intervals to allow one vehicle to pull in and stop while the other passes.
- If you meet an oncoming vehicle, either pull into a passing place near at hand on

PASSING ON SINGLE-TRACK ROADS *When you meet a car coming the opposite way and there is a passing place on your left, pull in, stop and let the other car continue.*

your side, or stop and let the other vehicle pull into a convenient place so that you can then drive on.

- Give way where possible to vehicles coming uphill, so that they are not forced to make an awkward hill start.
- Keep a note of passing places on your side as you drive. If you know there is one only a short distance behind you, reverse into it to let the other car pass.
- Never park in a passing place.

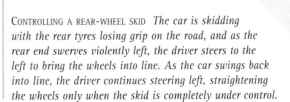

CONTROLLING A REAR-WHEEL SKID *The car is skidding with the rear tyres losing grip on the road, and as the rear end swerves violently left, the driver steers to the left to bring the wheels into line. As the car swings back into line, the driver continues steering left, straightening the wheels only when the skid is completely under control.*

SKIDDING

Avoid skidding by adjusting your driving to the road conditions so that you never have to change speed or direction suddenly, or brake violently.

- Skids occur when tyres lose their grip on the road surface, and are most likely to happen during slowing down or speeding up, or on corners or hills.
- Be particularly careful in conditions of the greatest risk—on slippery roads wet with rain, snow or ice, or where there are patches of loose shale, oil or wet leaves.
- Even on a dry road, never brake violently. The car is likely to skid because its weight is pitched to the front, and with a loss of weight to the rear, the rear wheels tend to lock and the body swings.
- Avoid driving in shoes or boots with very thick soles, which make control of the brake, clutch and accelerator difficult.

To control a skid, don't press the brake pedal or the accelerator.

- For a slight slide, turn the steering in the direction of the skid and ease off the accelerator until tyre grip is regained.
- If the skid is more violent, take your feet right off the brake and accelerator, and steer sharply in the direction of the skid. If the rear of the car swings left, turn the steering left to bring front and rear wheels into line. If the car rear swings right, turn the steering to the right.
- Once the skid is controlled, straighten the steering, and don't accelerate or brake until all four wheels are in line.

SPEED

- Fast driving is not necessarily skilful. The skill lies in adjusting your speed to suit road and traffic conditions—being able to hold to a steady 30 mph (48 km/h) in a built-up area, and maintain a steady, safe and fuel-saving speed on a motorway, at the same time respecting the limits of your vehicle.

- Don't be intimidated into exceeding speed limits by drivers sitting on your tail.
- In built-up areas where your view is obscured by parked vehicles, watch for likely hazards and keep to a safe speed. A child that darts into the road from between parked cars is unlikely to survive being hit at 30 mph (48 km/h).
- Don't race away from traffic lights. The time saved in accelerating so fast that the tyres squeal is offset by the cost of wasted fuel and tyres soon worn out.
- Driving too slowly can also be dangerous. Dawdling—on motorways and A roads particularly—causes traffic queues and irritation. Don't frustrate other drivers by driving slowly near the centre of the road.

STOPPING DISTANCES

- Your speed, reaction time and the road conditions all affect the distance in which you can bring your car to a halt.
- Most people need at least 0.7 seconds thinking time before they start to brake or take evasive action.
- The faster the speed, the farther the car will travel while you are reacting, and the longer it will take to brake to a halt.
- Keep to a speed that allows you to stop within the distance between you and the car in front. Never drive closer than the stopping distances that are shown in the diagram below.

- To judge a safe distance, use the two-second rule. Pick a stationary object at the side of the road, such as a lamppost, and begin counting seconds as soon as the car in front has passed it. You are too close if you pass the same object before you have counted two seconds—or can say 'Only a fool breaks the two-second rule'.
- In ice, snow and rain, braking takes longer. Double the safety gap.

TRAFFIC JAMS

In a slow-moving traffic jam, keep calm. Don't sound your horn. Relax and listen to the radio, or to relieve tension and boredom and to stimulate circulation, do simple exercises, such as curling your toes, flexing your wrists and stretching your shoulders and neck.
- Don't let your attention wander. Keep your eyes on the road and traffic ahead.
- Leave space at junctions for vehicles to pull out or cross.

If traffic is at a standstill, switch off the engine to conserve fuel and reduce emissions. Set your fan to recirculate the air inside the car rather than take in air and fumes from outside.
- Stay in the car, as the traffic may move forward at any time. If the other drivers have to wait for you to return to the car, they will be even more frustrated.

TURNING RIGHT OR LEFT

- Check the traffic behind in your mirror and signal your direction well before you brake and change down.

TURNING RIGHT AT A JUNCTION *Two drivers turning right (above) get the best view ahead if they pass behind each other. At a small or staggered junction (below), turning in front may be easier, but it restricts vision—drivers must watch carefully for oncoming traffic.*

- To turn right, position your car near the centre line. To turn left, keep well into the left as you slow down.
- At a junction, if an oncoming car also wants to turn right, normally pass it on the offside so that both drivers can see oncoming traffic.
- At small or staggered junctions, offside passing may be impractical; if you have to pass nearside to nearside, take great care to watch for oncoming traffic.
- In fog, signal in plenty of time and put your head a little way out of the window to watch and listen for oncoming traffic. Warn other drivers by keeping your foot on the brake before you turn, and sounding the horn—but not between 11.30 pm and 7 am in a built-up area.

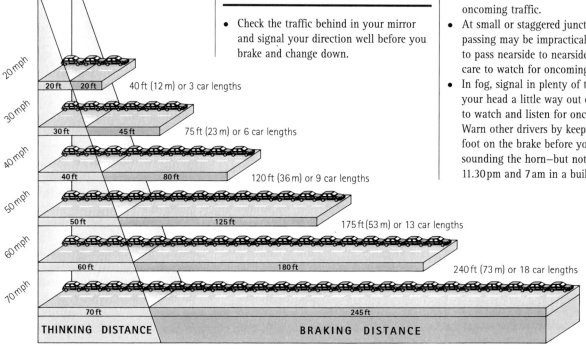

20 mph — 20 ft | 20 ft — 40 ft (12 m) or 3 car lengths
30 mph — 30 ft | 45 ft — 75 ft (23 m) or 6 car lengths
40 mph — 40 ft | 80 ft — 120 ft (36 m) or 9 car lengths
50 mph — 50 ft | 125 ft — 175 ft (53 m) or 13 car lengths
60 mph — 60 ft | 180 ft — 240 ft (73 m) or 18 car lengths
70 mph — 70 ft | 245 ft — 315 ft (96 m) or 24 car lengths

THINKING DISTANCE BRAKING DISTANCE

WHAT IT TAKES TO STOP *The shortest distance in which a car can come to a halt increases dramatically with speed. Even with an alert driver, good brakes and tyres and perfect road conditions, a car about 13 ft (4 m) long doing 70 mph (112.5 km/h) will travel 24 times its own length.*

How driving technique can save fuel

BUYING FUEL *is likely to be your highest running cost, and how much fuel you use depends not only on the type of car but also on the way you drive. Think ahead, drive smoothly and safely and make sure your car is well maintained.*

PLAN YOUR JOURNEY

- Hold-ups at road works and in traffic jams increase fuel consumption. Before you start a journey, work out a route avoiding city and town centres, poor or tortuous roads and rush-hour traffic.
- Listen to local radio traffic reports and plan alternative routes, avoiding hold-ups.
- Avoid short trips. When you start from cold, fuel consumption during the first 3 miles (5km) can be twice the normal overall average. Where you can, walk or use public transport to save fuel and cut down air pollution from engine emissions.

STARTING UP

- Don't run the engine to let it warm up. This wastes fuel, increases wear and causes unnecessary exhaust emissions.
- If your car has a manual choke, pull the control out fully when starting from cold; push it in progressively as the engine warms up on the move–the sooner it is closed the better, but don't do it too quickly or the engine may misfire or stall.
- With an automatic choke, make sure the engine isn't racing at a high rate of revs. A quick touch on the accelerator with the clutch down or the gear in neutral helps to close the choke and bring the engine back to normal tick-over speed.

ON THE MOVE

- Violent acceleration and hard braking increase fuel consumption dramatically. Use a light touch on the accelerator, don't continually depress and release it.
- Avoid too much stopping and starting. Look ahead to anticipate road and traffic conditions, and slow down by easing off on the accelerator rather than by braking. Keep up with the traffic flow, however, and don't frustrate or delay other drivers.
- When approaching a red traffic light, slow down gradually so that when it turns to green you can either cruise through in top gear or engage a lower gear to drive through without stopping.
- As you slow down at a roundabout, try to time your arrival so that you enter a gap in the traffic from the right, in a lower gear if necessary, without having to stop.
- Keep a constant speed where possible,

particularly on motorways. Constantly varying your speed not only confuses and irritates other drivers, it wastes fuel through excessive use of the accelerator.

- A car engine is at its most efficient when the vehicle is travelling steadily at 50-60 mph (80-100km/h). The more you put your foot down, the faster fuel is used up. At 70mph (113km/h) costs and toxic emissions increase by at least 25 per cent.
- Change gears smoothly so that the engine doesn't surge or labour. Avoid excessive use of first, second and third gears. Move into top as soon as possible, accelerating steadily–but don't race the engine.
- If you have a fifth gear, use it as much as possible at speeds above 50mph (80km/h) on open roads.
- With an automatic, drive on the D setting and apply the accelerator gradually to move smoothly through the gears. Don't kick down on the accelerator unless you need to overtake or avoid danger.
- Never coast in neutral with the engine off. This may save fuel but reduces control of the car–the brakes may be less efficient, for example, and the steering may lock.

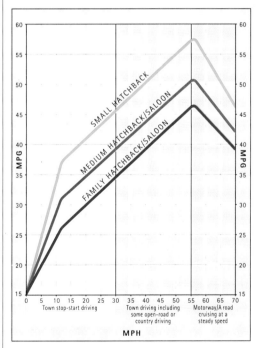

HOW A CAR CONSUMES FUEL *This is a guide to the average consumption of three types of car: 1300cc, 1600cc and 2000cc, based on figures quoted by manufacturers for town driving and constant-speed tests. Trips can rarely be made at a constant speed, but the figures show clearly how stop-start driving and speed affect consumption.*

- When climbing a hill, don't stay in top gear too long or you will lose speed and have to accelerate hard. As soon as you notice the slightest loss of speed, change down and accelerate gently.
- If you are stuck in a traffic jam or have to wait at a level crossing, switch off your engine to save fuel and cut emissions.
- At a journey's end, reverse into a garage or parking space if you can, so that any manoeuvring is done with the engine hot. When you start again from cold, the easy pull forward will save fuel.

EXTRA LOADS

- Extra weight increases fuel consumption. Make sure your car has no unnecessary loads, such as superfluous tools.
- A roof rack increases wind resistance and therefore fuel consumption. Bad packing can reduce maximum speed by 15mph (25km/h), and at 20mph (32km/h) can increase fuel consumption by about 12 per cent–or at 70mph (113km/h) by up to 25 per cent. Good packing cuts these figures by almost half.
- For the least wind resistance, place large cases flat on the bottom of the rack and pile smaller cases stepped towards the back of the car; don't put them upright or on edge facing the direction of travel, where they will present a solid wall to the airstream, slow the car and increase fuel consumption.
  - Cover the load with a tarpaulin and tuck in the sides. Secure it with a rope or a 'spider'–a braided elastic with eight hooked arms.
  - Remove a roof rack not in use. Even when it has no load, it increases wind resistance.

MAINTENANCE

- A car that is well maintained is the most economical on fuel. Get it serviced at the manufacturer's recommended intervals.
- When tyres are under-inflated or worn, more power is needed to drive the car, increasing wear and fuel consumption. Keep tyres in good condition and inflated to the recommended pressure.
- Don't drive with the fuel tank almost empty, as dirt and sediment at the bottom of the tank enter the engine and damage it. Fill up at just under a quarter full.
- Don't overfill the fuel tank, as some fuel will rapidly evaporate and go to waste.

Driving within the law

ROAD TRAFFIC LAW *is designed to protect road users; those who break it are likely to be endangering or inconveniencing others. A conviction may result in higher insurance premiums; serious breaches of the law may be punished by a fine, a driving ban or even imprisonment and forfeiture of the vehicle. The information here is for guidance only; seek a solicitor's advice if you have a legal problem.*

OBSERVING SPEED LIMITS

Driving too fast could lead to serious charges such as dangerous driving, or causing death. It is an offence to drive a private car:

- Faster than the speed displayed on signs on the road, whatever the type of road.
- Faster than 30 mph (48 km/h) in a built-up area—where street lights are spaced less than 600 ft (183 m) apart.
- Faster than 60 mph (96.5 km/h) on roads other than dual carriageways and motorways, or 50 mph (80 km/h) if towing a caravan or trailer.
- Faster than 70 mph (112.5 km/h) on a motorway or a dual carriageway in Britain, or 60 mph (96.5 km/h) if towing a caravan or trailer.
- Faster than 70 mph (112.5 km/h) on a motorway in the Irish Republic, or 50 mph (80 km/h) with a caravan or trailer.
- Lower limits may apply to goods vehicles and coaches.

Police checks Your speed may be checked by a speed pad set into the road, roadside radar, a laser-operated camera or a police car following you over a given distance. If you skid or have an accident, the police may use factors such as the length of tyre marks and the extent of damage to estimate your speed.

- If stopped for speeding, ask the speed alleged. If you dispute it, make sure the officer records your reply. Get a qualified engineer to check your speedometer and supply a written statement of its accuracy.

Penalties You may receive a fixed penalty or a summons. If you contest a fixed penalty in court and lose, or do not pay it within 28 days, the fine increases by 50 per cent.

- If you are summoned, you face a fine of up to £2500, depending on how much you exceeded the limit. You may also be banned, even for a first offence.
- Also, your licence will be endorsed with 3-6 penalty points. If these, with points from previous endorsements, amount to 12 or more over a three-year period, you will be banned for six months or more.

PARKING RESPONSIBLY

Always park in such a way that your vehicle (or trailer) is not likely to be an obstruction or cause danger to other road users. Examples of irresponsible, illegal or dangerous parking are:

- On the approach to a level crossing; on the brow of a hill; on a bend; too near a junction—legally, within 32 ft (10 m) unless in an authorised space; double parking.
- Near a school entrance, at or near a bus stop or taxi rank, or on the zigzag lines on the approach to a pedestrian crossing.
- Where the kerb has been lowered for prams, pushchairs or wheelchair users, or in front of the entrance to a property.
- At night, against the direction of traffic flow; this confuses oncoming drivers. Vehicles with projecting loads or trailers, or those more than 1½ tons (1525 kg) unladen, must have sidelights on.
- More than 15 yd (14 m) from the road on private land, without the owner's consent. You are trespassing if you park or turn round on private land without the owner's consent; the owner can insist that you leave, and can sue for damage costs.

Parking restrictions and meters

Parking illegally or exceeding the time paid for at a meter or with a parking disc can result in a parking ticket—a fixed-penalty fine issued by the police or traffic wardens.

- You must pay the amount asked within 28 days, or the penalty is increased. You can elect to go to court and dispute the charge, but you then risk a heavier penalty. For fines paid within 14 days, the penalty may be reduced.
- The police sometimes remove illegally parked vehicles, especially in cities or towns. To check if this has happened, ask at the nearest police station. To recover a vehicle from a police pound you have to pay a release fee and the parking fine.

Wheel clamps

If you park illegally, you may find a police wheel clamp on your vehicle. Do not damage the clamp or try to take it off. Instructions on where to pay to get the clamp removed will be posted on your windscreen.

Private clamping In England and Wales, wheel clamps are sometimes used on private land to restrict parking. The clamp will not be removed until you have paid the fee, which in some cases may be exorbitant.

- Whether or not private clamping is legal has still to be resolved. If you do get clamped in this way, do not try to remove the clamp, or you may be committing criminal damage.
- If you can prove that the place where you parked did not have an adequately displayed warning notice at the time, you may be able to recover the clamping fee from the clamping company, either through a small-claims court or by settlement out of court.

Parking for the disabled

Those with an official Orange Badge may park free of charge at meters and at on-street 'pay and display' parking, as well as at other places where signs indicate there are concessions.

- As long as the vehicle is not in any way hindering others, a disabled driver can, in England and Wales, park on single or double yellow lines for up to three hours (or in Scotland indefinitely) unless there is a loading restriction. The same applies to cars carrying passengers who hold disabled badges. But the concessions do not apply on clearways, red routes (see page 440), in central London and some other city or town centres.
- In the Republic of Ireland, holders of Orange Badges may park without charge by meters, in parking disc zones and on single yellow lines.

DRINKING AND DRIVING

Driving a vehicle after you have been drinking is risking your driving licence, your vehicle, and human life—including your own. A drink-driving conviction makes insurance cover difficult to get, and considerably increases premiums. It is also an offence to drive while unfit through taking drugs.

Eating before or while you are drinking may slow down the rate at which you absorb alcohol, but age, weight, size, fitness and the speed at which you drink are also relevant. In the same person, the same quantity of alcohol can produce different results at different times. If you drink in the evening, you may still be over the limit next morning.

If alcohol is proved to be impairing your ability, making you unfit to drive, or the level in your breath, blood or urine is above the legally defined limits, you could end up with one or more of the following penalties:

- *Being in charge of a motor vehicle:* disqualification, licence endorsement of 10 penalty points, a fine of up to £2500 and up to three months' imprisonment.
- *Driving or attempting to drive:* at least 12 months' disqualification, a 3-11 penalty points endorsement, a fine of up to £5000 and up to six months' imprisonment.
- *Causing death by careless driving, or for any dangerous driving:* disqualification for at least two years, an endorsement of

3-11 penalty points, an unlimited fine and up to ten years' imprisonment.

- *Refusing a roadside breath test without reasonable excuse:* disqualification, 4 penalty points and a fine of up to £1000.
- *Refusal to give a subsequent breath, blood or urine sample at a police station or hospital:* the same penalties as given above for driving or attempting to drive. If disqualified from driving, you may have to produce medical evidence that you are fit to drive before you can regain your licence, and you may have to take a driving test again.

Testing for alcohol levels

Legal limits for alcohol are measured in microgrammes per 100 millilitres. The alcohol level above which, according to law, your driving ability is impaired is:

In breath, 35 mg per 100 ml
In blood, 80 mg per 100 ml
In urine, 107 mg per 100 ml

- You must give a police officer who has reason to suspect you of being over the legal limit a sample of breath, blood or urine if asked. The officer will normally ask you to take a roadside breath test. If there has been an accident, the officer can ask you to give a sample at a police station. An officer may also ask for a breath test if you have been stopped for another traffic offence.
- Chronic asthmatics may be excused a breath test, and haemophiliacs a blood test. Say if you have a valid excuse. *Breath test* Ask the police officer why the test is required, and say when you last drank alcohol. For an accurate reading, the test must not be taken until 20 minutes after drinking alcohol, or until 10 minutes after smoking.
- To give a breath test, the officer may use a tester with an electronic meter, or an older type that has a bag with crystals that change colour. Before blowing, wipe your lips to remove any alcohol. Avoid half-hearted blows, which could be construed as refusing to give a sample. If a bag-and-tube is used and the officer says the result is positive—in which case the crystals should have changed from clear to green—ask to see it in good light.
- *If the test is positive*, you must go to a police station for more tests. The lower reading of two breath tests may be used in evidence against you. If the reading is between 35 and 50 mg per 100 ml, the police must give you the opportunity to give a blood or urine sample, usually done at a hospital or police station. A blood sample will be taken by a doctor from a finger or a vein in the arm. If the reading is more than 50 mg per 100 ml, you can be arrested and charged.

- Irregularities in a roadside test or an arrest do not affect the legality of later tests; leave arguments to a solicitor. You can be detained until the police consider there is no likelihood of you driving, or that driving or attempting to drive will not involve an offence.
- If you escape after refusing a test or giving a positive test, an officer can enter premises to arrest you. An officer can also enter premises, by force if need be, to give a breath test to a driver believed to have been involved in an accident involving injury to another person.

Contesting the charge Drink-driving laws are precise and have few loopholes. If you are threatened with prosecution and do not accept that you are guilty, get a solicitor's advice. Keep a blood or urine sample required for use as evidence in a cooled, sealed container; pass it to a qualified analyst as soon as possible.

- Even if you have passed an alcohol test, the prosecution can call scientific evidence to estimate the alcohol level that existed at the time you were driving. If this satisfies a court that you would have been above the limit at that time, you can be convicted.

RULES OF THE ROAD

Traffic signs, signals and road markings are intended to control traffic for everyone's benefit. You must comply with them.

Eyesight Watching traffic and road signs demands good eyesight. In good daylight, you must be able to read a vehicle number plate from a distance of 67 ft (20.5 m)—using spectacles or contact lenses if you wear them.

Offences Inattention while driving, such as reading a map or using a hand-held phone, or any failure to comply with the *Highway Code*, could lead to prosecution for driving without due care and attention, or without consideration for other road users. A 3-9 points endorsement is the penalty, or possible disqualification, and a fine of up to £2500.

- You must stop if involved in an accident resulting in injury to people or damage to property or vehicles. If cattle, horses, donkeys, pigs, sheep, goats or dogs have been injured, take reasonable steps to contact the owner, or report the incident to the police as soon as possible—in any case within 24 hours. You are not obliged to stop if a cat is involved.

Motorway regulations

Special regulations apply on motorways, because of the high speeds that are possible and the differences from other roads:

- Learner drivers, motorcycles under 50 cc and invalid carriages not exceeding 5 cwt (254 kg) unladen weight are forbidden.

- Stopping on the carriageway, a slip road, the hard shoulder (except in an emergency), the central reservation, or the verge is forbidden.
- Where a motorway has three lanes, the right-hand lane is barred to vehicles drawing trailers, goods vehicles of more than 7.4 tons when loaded, or buses or coaches longer than 40 ft (12 m).
- On slip roads and carriageways, U-turns, reversing, and driving against the traffic flow (that is, head-on towards other traffic) are forbidden.

Learners and beginners

- A vehicle driven by a learner must have red on white L plates visible on front and rear. L plates must be removed when the learner is not driving.
- A learner must have a valid provisional licence, be supervised by a driver in the front passenger seat who is at least 21 years old and has held a full licence for at least three years, and must not drive a vehicle towing a trailer.
- In Northern Ireland, drivers must display orange R plates for one year after passing the test, and must not drive faster than 45 mph (72 km/h) during this period.
- In the rest of the United Kingdom, drivers who have recently passed their test may drive with green L plates to warn other road users of their inexperience. These plates are not a legal requirement.
- Newly qualified drivers may, within a year of their test, take a special series of training sessions known as 'pass plus'. These give experience of different driving conditions, including motorway and night driving; those who pass the course may get up to 30 per cent off their initial insurance premium.

Seat belts

Wearing a seat belt greatly reduces the risk of death or serious injury in the event of an accident. By failing to wear one, you not only break the law but any compensation payable to you is likely to be reduced.

- The driver and passengers in a car or a small minibus—with an unladen weight of less than 2½ tons (2540 kg)—must wear a seat belt in the front and, if fitted, in the rear of the vehicle.
- The driver is legally responsible for ensuring that front-seat passengers and children under 14 comply with the law.
- Where a car has rear seat belts, any passenger aged 12 and over is legally required to wear one. All cars are now made with rear seat belts fitted, but there is no legal obligation to have them fitted to older cars without them.
- Children under 3 travelling in the front seat must be carried in a child restraint;

this must also be used in a rear seat if there is no other appropriate restraint.

- Children aged 3-11 and less than 5 ft (1.5 m) tall must travel in a child restraint if one is available; otherwise they must use a seat belt. Approved child restraints bear the British Standards Kitemark or international 'E' mark.
- Exemption from wearing a seat belt may be granted to a woman who is heavily pregnant or to someone to whom wearing a belt would cause pain. If you may be entitled to exemption on medical grounds, consult your doctor.

Motorcycles

- The rider and a pillion passenger must each wear an approved protective helmet, which must be fastened securely; the passenger must travel astride, with both feet on the footrests.
- A learner driver must not ride a machine of more than 125 cc or 12 bhp engine rating, must not carry a pillion passenger or tow a trailer, and before riding on a public road must undergo training with an approved training body. The local Road Safety Officer has details.
- A fully licensed car driver may ride a motorcycle up to 50 cc and carry a pillion passenger without taking a test. However, riding a motorcycle demands different techniques from car driving, and it is best to take lessons with a qualified instructor. A licensed car driver can also ride a motorcycle up to 125 cc or 12 bhp with L plates for an unlimited time.
- A provisional motorcycle licence issued before December 1, 1990, is valid indefinitely. A provisional licence issued after that date is valid for two years; after it expires, you must wait a year before applying for another.
- Those who take the test after July 1, 1996, and are at least 21 years old, can choose which size of machine on which to take their test. Riders aged 17-20 are restricted to driving motorcycles of 33 bhp (25 kW) for two years. For details of the regulations contact the Driving Standards Agency, telephone (0115) 955 7600.

KEEPING YOUR VEHICLE SAFE

You are endangering your life, as well as the lives of other road users, if your vehicle is not in a roadworthy condition.

- Ensure that brakes, steering, lights, speedometer, exhaust, suspension, seat belts and horn are all in working order.
- Check that tyres have a tread depth of at least 0.06 in (1.6 mm) across their whole width all the way round.
- Keep the windscreen, rear window, lamps,

wing mirrors and number plates clean.
- Window stickers and car mascots should be positioned so that they do not in any way obstruct the driver's view. Exterior mascots or attachments may be dangerous to other road users and could render your vehicle unroadworthy.
- A vehicle more than three years old must pass a test covering aspects such as lights, brakes, tyres, exhaust emissions and windscreen condition at a vehicle testing centre. A test ('MOT') certificate is valid for 12 months, and cannot be transferred to another vehicle.

Unsafe vehicle If your vehicle has been in an accident and is considered by a police officer to be unsafe, the officer can demand an immediate safety check or that you abandon it, upon which it will be towed away.

- Otherwise you can ask for a safety check to be deferred for up to 30 days, and can choose where it is to be done, as long as the vehicle is available for checking in the seven days before the 30 days expire.
- The police can enter private premises to check a vehicle if they believe it has been involved in an accident within the last 48 hours. Otherwise they can test it only if the owner of the premises consents, or they have a magistrate's warrant and the vehicle owner has been given at least 48 hours' notice.

YOUR DRIVING DOCUMENTS

Keep your driving licence, motor insurance certificate and vehicle test certificate (if required) with you when you drive. A police officer can demand to see them; if you do not have them you can be told to produce them at a police station named by you within seven days. A traffic warden can ask to see documents only at a car pound.

Driving licence It is against the law to drive without a valid full or provisional licence. If you change your name or address, you must complete the details on your driving licence and send it to DVLA, Swansea SA99 1BN.

- If you are aged 70 or over, the DVLA will automatically send you a licence renewal form every three years asking you to sign a medical declaration that you are still fit to drive. A doctor's certificate is not required, unless you are a resident of the Republic of Ireland.
- UK nationals may drive in the Republic of Ireland on a UK driving licence.
- Visitors to the UK may drive on their current licence for up to a year. New UK residents from EC countries should exchange their licences with the DVLA within a year; residents from outside the EC and intending to reside in the UK must take a driving test as soon as possible.

- If, within two years of passing the test, a driver has 6 or more penalty points endorsed on the licence, it reverts to provisional status and the driving test must be taken again.

Insurance certificate For driving without insurance the penalty is an endorsement of 6-8 penalty points on your licence and possible disqualification. If charged with driving while uninsured, you have a defence only if you can show that your employer was responsible for insuring the vehicle at the time of the offence, and that you believed it to be insured. You do not have this excuse if a borrowed vehicle proves to be uninsured.

Vehicle excise licence Every vehicle on the road must display a valid licence (or tax disc). A vehicle without one may be given a fixed-penalty notice by the police or a traffic warden, or be wheel-clamped.

Vehicle test certificate A vehicle more than three years old must have a current vehicle test certificate. Driving without one is illegal, and invalidates your motor vehicle insurance.

- You can have your vehicle tested up to one month before your current certificate expires; the new certificate is valid for a year from the expiry date of the old one.
- If your certificate expires before you get the vehicle tested, you may not drive it on a public road, except to take it to a booked test at a vehicle testing station.
- Test certificates are being introduced for private vehicles in the Republic of Ireland.

HOW THE LAW IS ENFORCED

The sheer number of minor breaches of the road traffic law make it impractical for the police to take every offender to court. A police officer has discretion merely to give a verbal warning. Many minor road traffic offences, including failure to wear seat belts and failing to stop at a red traffic light, are dealt with by fixed-penalty notices.

A police officer can arrest you on the spot for an alleged offence carrying a prison sentence, such as dangerous driving. The officer must say why you are being arrested. An officer can also enter premises, by force if need be, to arrest you. Resisting arrest is also an offence; leave arguments to a lawyer.

- If you receive a summons, it will state where and when you must attend court, and what offence you are alleged to have committed. Often there will also be a 'statement of facts', outlining the nature of the alleged incident. If your summons does not have a statement, ask for further information from the police.
- For most motoring offences, you will have the option of sending by post a plea of guilty, and your case can be heard and sentence given in your absence. You may,

however, wish to go to court to explain any mitigating circumstances that may be taken into account.

- Most cases are dealt with in a magistrates' court, but serious charges such as causing death by dangerous driving are heard before a judge in a Crown Court. In Scotland most cases are heard in a district court; the superior court is the High Court of Justiciary. In the Irish Republic the lower court is known as the district court; appeals are made to the circuit court.
- Magistrates, except for stipendiaries, are not legally qualified but have the aid of a legal adviser. You can engage a solicitor to represent you, but it is not essential.
- If found guilty of a road traffic offence, you are likely to be ordered to pay the costs of the prosecution. Costs are reduced if you inform the court in advance that you intend to plead guilty. Serious penalties such as imprisonment may also be reduced if you plead guilty.
- If you wish to plead not guilty, take legal advice. The date of your trial can be adjourned if you tell the court in writing. Legal aid is not usually available, but you may be eligible if you are to be tried for a serious charge that threatens your liberty, such as causing death by dangerous driving, or if you stand to lose your livelihood through disqualification.
- As the costs of legal representation are high, you may prefer to defend yourself; a member of a motoring organisation may be entitled to free legal representation by the organisation.
- If you have witnesses, get them to write down and sign what they believe occurred; their statements may help in presenting your case. You can ask the court to issue a summons for a witness to attend court. You may use diagrams or photos to explain your version of events.

Penalty points When a licence is endorsed with a road traffic offence, the driver is given penalty points; the number is mostly fixed according to the offence, but offences where the number is, within a given range, at the court's discretion include: causing death by careless or inconsiderate driving under the influence of drink or drugs; careless driving; failing to stop, report or give particulars after an accident; using or permitting the use of an uninsured vehicle; speeding; and driving after failing to notify a disability or after a licence has been refused or revoked.

- If within three years another offence takes your score to 12 or above, you will be disqualified for at least six months.
- Endorsements may usually be removed after four years, or after 11 years for drink-driving offences. After a period of disqualification is over, all reference to the penalty points is removed.

INSURING YOUR VEHICLE

Traffic accidents occur every day; not every driver has the means to pay for damage or injury caused to others, so the law requires every driver to be insured. If your vehicle is damaged or stolen, claiming compensation can take a long time. Adequate insurance provides support and funds to deal with it.

Types of insurance cover

- *Third party* The minimum insurance cover legally required, it covers anyone whom you accidentally injure or kill, including passengers in your vehicle, or any damage you might accidentally cause to property. It does not cover damage to your vehicle or property, or injury to you.
- *Third party, fire and theft* Such insurance gives third-party cover, and also covers your own vehicle against theft or damage by fire. It may also cover the contents of your vehicle against fire or theft.
- *Comprehensive* This insures not only third parties, but also damage to your own vehicle, even through your own negligence. A policy may specify other areas of cover, such as medical expenses and personal accident benefits. It is the most expensive type of cover. If you buy a vehicle on hire purchase, you may have to have it comprehensively insured until you have paid the debt.

Driving a vehicle other than your own Some policies give the policyholder third-party cover while driving other people's vehicles. Some cover anyone, or anyone over a certain age, driving the insured vehicle. If you plan to drive someone else's vehicle, including a hired one, check whether you are covered.

Excess Most policies include an 'excess'–the amount of a claim that the insured person must pay. With an excess of £100, for instance, insurers pay £50 for a £150 claim.

Uninsured loss You can recover losses not covered by your insurance, such as excesses and personal injury claims, by taking out a separate 'uninsured-loss policy'.

Driving abroad If you are insured in the UK and plan to drive abroad or in the Irish Republic, or if you are insured in the Irish Republic and plan to drive in the UK, tell your insurers. They may want an extra premium to extend the cover, and may issue a 'green card', or international insurance certificate. In the Irish Republic, caravans and trailers need separate insurance.

Insurance costs

What you pay varies according to age, driving experience, where you live, your job, your vehicle and your record of claims, accidents and road traffic offences. Drivers under 25 usually have to pay higher premiums than older drivers, and some

professions–journalism, for example–are regarded as high risks. You may be charged higher premiums if your vehicle is normally parked on the road, not in a garage.

- *No-claims bonus* If you do not make any claims on your policy, you benefit from a no-claims bonus, which gives you a lower premium; the bonus usually increases yearly, often up to 60 per cent after four years. It is reduced if you make a claim, so if the amount of a repair is small, it may be cheaper to pay for it yourself.
- Losing a no-claims bonus usually puts you back two years on the scale by which premiums are calculated; a four-year 60 per cent bonus would, typically, be put back to a two-year 40 per cent bonus.
- In the event of another party making a claim against you, your no-claims bonus is not at risk unless you are found to have been at least partly at fault, or if the loss cannot be fully recovered from the other party–an uninsured driver, for example.
- *Protected no-claims bonus* Many insurers operate a 'protected no-claims' scheme. Under this you pay higher premiums, but you keep part of your no-claims bonus even if you make up to a given number of claims during a certain period, normally three or four years.

If you are involved in an accident

You must stop after an accident that involves damage or injury to another person or other vehicle. The same applies to a collision with an animal such as a dog, horse, cow, goat or sheep, or roadside property such as a fence.

- Record the registration numbers of vehicles involved and exchange names and addresses, and insurance company names and addresses, with the other driver or drivers. You must also give your own name and address, and the vehicle owner's if different, and your vehicle's registration number to anyone who has reason to require them. If you are unable to give all the information required at the time report the details to the police as soon as reasonably practicable, but certainly within 24 hours.
- Do not admit liability for the accident, or get involved in discussions about the cause, especially if you think the fault is yours. If you admit blame, your insurers may refuse you cover. Do not apologise, even as an act of courtesy; an apology may be used as evidence against you in both civil and criminal proceedings.
- Make a sketch-map showing the final positions of all the vehicles involved, the length of any skid marks and where there is broken glass on the road. Record weather, road conditions at the time and the estimated speeds of the vehicles. If you have a camera with you, take

photos of the scene from different angles.

- If details have been exchanged, there is no need to report a damage-only collision to the police unless another driver cannot be traced or refuses details. Call the police if anyone is hurt, including you, or if you think another driver has committed an offence. You have no right to detain anyone until the police arrive. An officer may ask to see your driving licence, insurance certificate and MOT certificate; if you don't have them, you may have to produce them within seven days.
- *Making a statement* You are not obliged to make a statement to the police. Be aware that you may regret making one in haste, and that your own words may be given in evidence against you. On the other hand, if you have a valid excuse you would be wise to make a statement carefully and in detail. If, when the police question you, you fail to say something in your favour and try to bring it up at a later hearing, the court may infer that you concocted that evidence. If you do make a statement, you can write it out yourself or have an officer write it for you; read it carefully and make any necessary corrections before signing. Otherwise just give your name, address and insurance particulars, and get the help of a solicitor as soon as possible.

Collisions with parked vehicles If a parked vehicle is involved in an accident, you are not obliged to search for the owner. But it may be easier in the long run if you enquire at nearby buildings, and if necessary wait a short time for the owner to return.

- Record the vehicle's make, model, colour and registration number, the damage caused, and if there is any other damage not caused by the accident. Report the matter to the police and your insurers. If you decide to leave a note on the parked vehicle, beware of admitting liability.

How to make a claim

Your insurance policy will give details about making a claim. Report a theft or an accident to your insurance company or broker as soon as possible, regardless of who is at fault and even if you do not intend to claim. Failure to inform them may invalidate your policy. In most cases they will send a claim form and ask for a written quotation for repair costs.

- *Repair costs* Many insurers will direct you to an approved repairer. If not, get a detailed estimate of the repair costs from a garage. You will need this for claiming from your own insurers or from a third party. The insurers may want their own engineer to inspect the damage before confirming that repairs can go ahead. Before signing a garage's satisfaction note, ask an independent engineer to

check the work has been fully carried out.
- Many insurers recommend an approved repairer who will lend you a car to use while your vehicle is being repaired. It is rare for a policy to allow car-hire costs.
- *Betterment* Insurers will pay only for the repairs necessary to return a vehicle to its condition before the accident. If repairs remedy pre-existing defects, they may ask you to pay part of the bill as 'betterment'.
- *Knock for knock* Where two parties claim against each other, insurers may settle matters 'knock for knock', although this is becoming rare. Rather than spend time deciding who is to blame, each company pays for its own insured vehicle. Both parties lose a no-claims bonus unless able to prove they were not responsible.
- *Write-offs* If the insurers decide that the cost of repairing a car is more than it is worth on the market, they will treat it as a write-off, and pay only the estimated cost of replacing it with an identical vehicle of similar age and condition–and that only if it is within the sum insured. Hire-purchase payments outstanding will be deducted and paid to the hire-purchase company–you will have to pay any balance. The insurers become the owners of the damaged vehicle and are entitled to sell it. You may be able to negotiate to retain the scrap yourself, but its value will be deducted from the settlement offer.
- *An uninsured driver* If the other driver is not insured and you are not covered by a comprehensive policy, you will have to go through the courts. You can recover costs for damage only if the person can be traced and has the means to pay you. If you can prove beyond the balance of probabilities that the other driver was liable, and that liability was within the legal requirements of compulsory insurance, you may be able to make a claim to the Motor Insurers Bureau, 152 Silbury Boulevard, Central Milton Keynes MK9 1NB, telephone (01908) 240000.

Uninsured losses

Even with comprehensive insurance, you may need to claim against the other party to recover an uninsured loss such as an excess. If you have an uninsured-loss policy, contact the insurer to activate it.

- Send a letter by recorded delivery to the other party, stating that you hold him or her responsible. Then send an estimate of repair costs; allow 14 days for inspection of the damage, and ask for payment by the person or his or her insurers.
- If after 14 days you have not received a satisfactory response, ask a solicitor if it is worth pursuing the matter through the courts. For claims up to £3000, you can go to a small-claims court; this allows

informal arbitration without lawyers, and legal costs are not awarded to the winner.
- If you are not to blame and think you have a good chance of winning your case, you can hire a vehicle and claim the fee from the other party. Reimbursements for car hire usually cover a period of up to three weeks, but you must keep the hiring costs to a minimum.
- *If your insurers go out of business* If this occurs at a time when you need to claim, contact the Policy Holders' Protection Board, 51 Gresham Street, London EC2V 7HQ, telephone 0171-600 3333. They may provide 100 per cent funding for claims for third-party injuries and damage to other vehicles, and 90 per cent funding for damage to your vehicle.

If a claim is made against you

It is safest to pass the claim to your insurers. By settling privately, even if the case is a minor one, you may lose their backing. Fault and partial fault are often technical matters; you may not be the best judge, particularly if a passenger in your vehicle has a claim because he or she has been injured.

- *Settling a claim privately* Beware of admitting liability. Head letters 'without prejudice', so that they cannot be used as evidence in legal proceedings. When you pay the other party, get a receipt stating that the payment is 'in full and final settlement' so that the matter rests there.

If your vehicle is stolen

Tell the police and insurance company or insurance agent immediately, even if you have since recovered the vehicle, because it may have been used in a crime or involved in an accident. The police will issue you with a crime number. Your insurance company will send a form for you to claim the cost of the vehicle and its contents; there may be two separate excesses for each of these.

- If your vehicle is not recovered after a given period, usually stated in your policy, your insurers may decide to reimburse, after which time the vehicle ceases to be your property.
- If your vehicle is recovered, inform your insurers immediately. Whether the vehicle is now yours or theirs depends on the insurance conditions. If it is still yours, you will need to arrange for collection.
- The police may ask you if you would like a recovered vehicle stored in a police pound. For such storage, you or your insurers may have to pay a fixed fee, plus a given fee per day, until collection.
- You can reclaim vehicle excise tax if your current tax had not expired. Forms can be had from vehicle registration offices. Refunds are given only for each complete month unexpired at the time of the claim.

DEALING WITH AN EMERGENCY

What to do when an accident happens

IF YOU ARE THE FIRST *at the scene of an accident there are three main actions you must take, in the following order:*

FIRST *Warn other traffic, to protect crashed vehicles from further damage*

SECOND *Make the vehicles involved safe*

THIRD *Attend to the injured*

MAKING A CAR SAFE *Turn off the engine, but leave the keys so the car can be moved later.*

ignition in all the crashed vehicles. Do not remove ignition keys–leave them in place in case the cars have to be moved later. Also put the handbrakes on.

- Do not smoke, and warn others at the scene not to do so.
- Keep well away from a vehicle on fire, as the petrol tank may explode.

THIRD Attending to the injured

WARN OTHER TRAFFIC *If you have a warning triangle, alert other traffic by placing it at least 55 yd (50 m) behind the crashed vehicles towards the nearside edge of the road. Wave down another driver to go for assistance, but stand well away from the edge of the road to do so.*

PULL TO SAFETY *If a person is in danger, hold them under the armpits and drag them away.*

FIRST Protecting the scene

- Turn on your hazard lights and park well clear of the vehicles involved. If necessary, position your car so that it protects a casualty in the road–but keep it at least 15 yd (14 m) away; turn it so that it cannot move forwards if pushed by another vehicle and put the front wheels on full steering lock. At night, position it so that the headlights light up the scene.
- Do not rush straight from the car to the injured, or you, too, may be hit by a vehicle–especially on a motorway. Before you act take a moment to assess the situation, and get out of your car on the side away from the traffic.
- Flag down another vehicle, keeping well to the side of the road. Ask the driver to dial 999 at the nearest telephone and call the police, giving them the exact location,

the type of accident and the number of vehicles and casualties involved.

- Warn other drivers by placing a warning triangle, if you have one, at least 55 yd (50 m) behind the crashed vehicles, towards the nearside edge.
- On a motorway or dual carriageway, if safe to do so, put the triangle on the hard shoulder about 165 yd (150 m) behind the crashed vehicles; weight it at the base.
- On a road other than a motorway or dual carriageway, ask someone to stop traffic coming from the other direction, and to place another warning triangle 55 yd (50 m) ahead of the accident, if possible.

SECOND Dealing with the vehicles

- Do not move any vehicles unless it is imperative, to avoid another accident.
- To cut down the risk of fire, switch off the

- Do not move injured people–whether they are inside or outside a vehicle–unless they are obviously in immediate danger from fire, spillage or oncoming traffic. If absolutely necessary, hold them under the armpits and drag them away.
- Give first aid to the injured in the following order:

FIRST   To those who are unconscious and not breathing
SECOND To those bleeding severely
THIRD   To those unconscious but breathing

First aid on the road

BEFORE ATTENDING TO THE INJURED, *make sure that the scene is safe and medical help is on the way. While awaiting expert aid, it is helpful to have some idea of what to do—and what not to do. Some guidelines are given below.*

AN UNCONSCIOUS CASUALTY

Remember the ABC rule:
- A = **AIRWAY**   Clear the airway
- B = **BREATHING** Check the breathing
- C = **CIRCULATION** Check the circulation

Clearing the airway

1 Tilt the head back by lifting the chin with two fingers; this lifts the tongue, which may be pressing on the back of the throat.

2 Clear an obstruction such as blood by turning the head to one side and sweeping inside the mouth with two fingers.

Removing a protective helmet

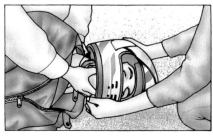

Never remove a helmet unless essential, but if breathing seems difficult, remove it so you can clear the airway. Ease your fingers under the base to support the neck and hold the jaw firmly with fingers spread. Get a helper to tilt the helmet first clear of the chin, then clear of the base of the skull, and lift it off.

Checking the breathing

1 Place your ear next to the person's mouth and nose and look along the chest. If it is rising and falling, there is breathing.

2 If the person is breathing, support the airway to prevent the tongue, blood or vomit from obstructing it. Put a person outside the car in the recovery position (see below).

Checking the circulation

1 If the person is not breathing, check the circulation by feeling for the pulse at the neck. If there is a pulse, start the kiss of life (see right).

2 If there is no pulse, get a person trained in the technique to apply chest compression; it can be lethal if performed incorrectly.

GIVING THE KISS OF LIFE

- Using the finger and thumb of one hand, close the person's nostrils and support the jaw with your other hand.

- Take a deep breath, seal your lips round the person's open mouth and then breathe out. Continue this procedure every six seconds until breathing is restored.

- Once breathing begins, maintain the airway. Put a person outside the car in the recovery position (see below).

3 When the pulse is restored, continue with the kiss of life (see above) until the person's breathing is restored; then place in the recovery position (see below).

HOW TO PUT SOMEONE IN THE RECOVERY POSITION

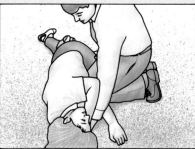

1 Kneel beside the person and raise the far leg to bend at the knee. Place the arm nearest to you at right angles to the body, with elbow bent and palm uppermost. Fold the other arm across the chest and rest the back of hand under the cheek.

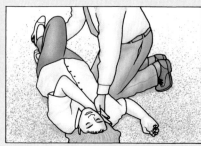

2 Put your hand on the far knee and pull it towards you, supporting the person's head as you do so. Use your knees as a support and control during the manoeuvre.

3 With the person now turned onto one side, align the bent knee so that it rests at right angles to the body, thus propping it in a secure and comfortable position.

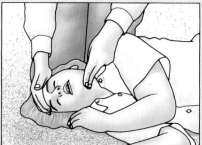

4 Tilt the chin up to straighten the throat and clear the airway, then rest the cheek on the back of the hand, as 3 above. Cover with a coat or rug to maintain body heat.

A CONSCIOUS CASUALTY

1 Speak reassuringly to an injured person, who may be suffering from shock. Do not give food, liquid, cigarettes or alcohol–this could interfere with an anaesthetic and delay hospital treatment, and might cause harm.

2 Do not move the person unless it is absolutely essential. Ask where the pain or numbness is, to help you to identify the injuries. Examine an injured area gently; ask the person to help to support it, if possible.

3 Apply a bandage or sling only if it is necessary. It will be removed at the hospital, and meanwhile ambulance personnel may have to put splints on a fractured limb.

MAKING RAISED PADS

Roll cotton wool or other absorbent material in clean cloth to make two curved pads that are higher than the foreign body projecting from the wound.

TREATING EXTERNAL BLEEDING

1 In general, lay the person down. Bleeding is slowest when lying down.

2 Carefully and gently remove or cut away clothing to expose the wound. Look for possible fractures–likely if there is swelling, pain or loss of use, or if the limb is in an unnatural position.

3 If there is no foreign object in the wound, and the limb is not fractured, make a pad of clean, absorbent material and press it down firmly over the wound to stem the bleeding. If nothing else is available, press paper tissues over the wound.

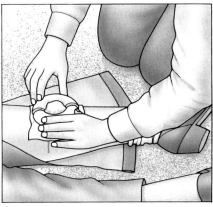

4 If there is a foreign object in the wound, don't remove it. Put raised pads round the object to prevent pressure on it.

5 Provided there is no fracture to an injured limb, raise it so that the wound is above the level of the heart to slow down the bleeding.

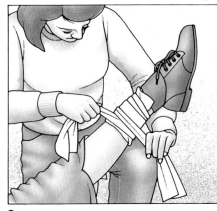

6 Bandage the wound firmly using a scarf or a strip of clean linen. Do not bandage directly over a foreign object in a wound. If blood seeps through, put another bandage on top. Do not apply a tourniquet to ease the bleeding–it can result in loss of limbs.

7 Get medical attention as soon as you can, but do not leave the person alone for more than a minute or two.

8 Keep an injured person warmly covered, reassured and as still as possible. Don't give anything to eat or drink–or to smoke.

TREATING INTERNAL BLEEDING

1 If an injured person is bleeding from the nose, mouth or ear, place in a half-sitting position with the head tilted towards the side from which the blood is coming.

2 Cover the bleeding point with a pad of clean material or cotton wool, but do not apply pressure. Call for an ambulance.

3 If the person loses consciousness before the ambulance arrives, put in the recovery position, injured side lowest (see page 456).

DEALING WITH BROKEN BONES

Do not move a fractured limb unless it is essential. Help the injured person into the position in which they are most comfortable, and support the fracture with a rolled-up blanket or coat while awaiting an ambulance.

If you have to move the person–to a better location in bad weather, for instance:

1 First protect any wound by covering it with a clean, non-fluffy cloth such as a handkerchief. If a bone is protruding, put a sterile pad such as a clean handkerchief round it as a protection.

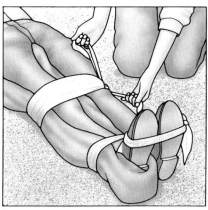

2 If a leg is broken, bandage over a protective pad first, and if another person is at hand ask them to support the leg as you do so. Don't tie the bandage tightly, as this can affect the person's blood circulation. Immobilise the injured leg by putting padding between the person's ankles and knees and then tying the legs together with bandages, as shown above–tie above and below the fracture, but not on it.

3 If an arm is broken, don't use force to bend it. Position it gently and strap it to the body, avoiding the injured part.

4 If the arm will bend easily, place it across the chest, putting some padding between it and the body, and secure it in a sling. Then strap the arm to the body with a piece of wide material round arm and chest. *[over*

5 Move the person very carefully to a more sheltered place. If necessary, get other people to help you to do this.

EYE INJURIES

1 If a person has an object embedded in the eye, do not attempt to remove it, as you may cause serious damage.

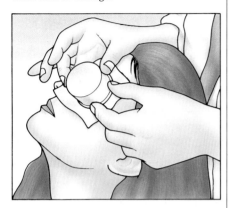

2 Cut a hole in a piece of clean cloth and put it over the eye. Place a paper or plastic cup over the cloth to protect the eye.

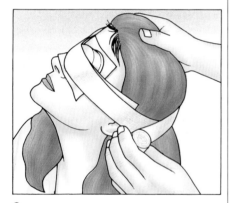

3 Hold the cup in place with a bandage. Bandage the sound eye as well, but tell the person why—it stops the sound eye moving, and consequently the injured eye also.

If chemicals get into the eye

1 Tilt the person's head with the injured eye downwards. With the eye open, gently wash it out with water for at least ten minutes.

2 When you have cleared the chemical from the eye, dry the face and put a clean dressing lightly over the eye. Get the person to a hospital as soon as possible.

BURNS AND SCALDS

1 Remove any tight clothing, rings or a wristwatch before the area begins to swell. Cool a superficial burn by applying clean, cold water for ten minutes or longer, until the pain has eased.

2 Cover the burn with clean, dry, non-fluffy material—a handkerchief, for example. Hold it in place with a soft towel or other material.

If the burn is widespread, lay the person down gently, speak reassuringly and cool with clean water. Call for an ambulance.

For a chemical burn, wash thoroughly with cold water and remove any contaminated clothing, taking care to protect yourself.

If the burned person is unconscious but breathing, place in the recovery position (see page 456).

If the mouth and throat are scalded or burned, speak reassuringly and give the person cold water, ice cubes or ice cream to suck in order to reduce the swelling.

If someone has clothing on fire

1 Hold a blanket or coat in front of you as you approach, then wrap it round the person to smother the flames. Lay the victim on the ground with the burnt side uppermost. Remove hot clothing that can be taken off easily, but don't take off any fragments that have stuck to the skin. Cool the burn by applying clean, cold water.

2 Don't apply lotions or ointments, as they may cause infection. Don't apply any plasters and don't prick any blisters.

INSECT AND ANIMAL BITES

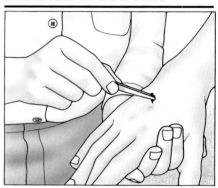

Stings **Remove a bee sting** with tweezers, taking care not to squeeze the poison bag and so pump more poison into the person's skin. No sting is left behind from a wasp or ant bite. Apply antihistamine cream to the bee, wasp or ant bite.

Bites **Wash a dog or cat bite** thoroughly with soap and warm water or a mild antiseptic and cover with a clean dressing. If the skin is broken, get the wound looked at by a doctor as soon as possible.

WHAT YOU NEED IN A BASIC FIRST AID KIT

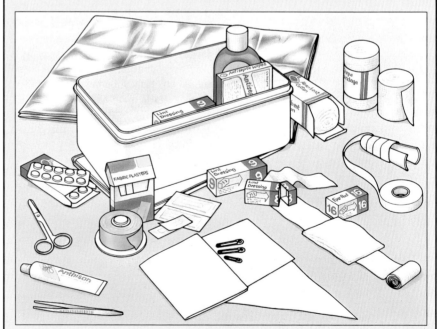

- Assorted adhesive plasters; roll of micropore tape; aspirin or paracetamol
- Blunt-ended scissors; antihistamine cream; tweezers
- Triangular bandages and several safety pins; sterile dressings of various sizes; sterile eye dressing with bandage attached
- Tubular gauze bandages for finger injuries; cotton wool; two or three conforming (flexible) bandages for wounds in awkward places—elbows, for instance; antiseptic lotion and antiseptic wipes
- Survival blanket for covering injured people, especially in cold or wet conditions

Breakdowns on the road

EVEN THE BEST-MAINTAINED CARS *may break down or fail to start. This section is designed to help you to find the cause and get you going again, or at least enable you to give a garage mechanic or breakdown service a good idea of what has gone wrong. The commonest causes of a breakdown are elementary problems such as a flat battery, a puncture or an empty fuel tank.*

Quick-reference contents

STOPPING SAFELY

SAFETY FIRST On any road, if the car breaks down, keep children away from the carriageway and leave pets in the car.

On a motorway

1 At the first sign of trouble, move into the inside lane and leave the motorway at the next exit, or pull into the first service area you reach. If you can't travel that far, move onto the hard shoulder and try to stop near an emergency telephone; they are sited at about 1 mile (1.6 km) intervals.

2 When stopping on the hard shoulder, put the car as far to the left as possible, well clear of traffic, and switch on your hazard lights. If it is dark or visibility is poor, keep the sidelights on. Get out by a left-side door and make sure passengers do too. If you are forced to get out of the car on the right side, wait for a clear space in the traffic—the rush of air from a fast-moving heavy vehicle can drag you off your feet.

3 If you have a warning triangle, put it about 165 yd (150 m) behind the car on the hard shoulder and weight it down, if you can, so that it isn't blown over by the slipstream of passing high-sided vehicles. Get away from the hard shoulder as soon as possible, particularly in dark, wet or windy conditions. Stay near the car but well away from the roadside—on the embankment, for example.

4 If you have no alternative but to stop in a driving lane, switch on your hazard lights. Leave the car only if you are certain you can get safely across the carriageway to the hard shoulder or the central reservation. If in doubt, stay in the car with your seat belt on until the emergency services arrive.

On a dual carriageway

1 Some dual carriageways have a hard shoulder and emergency telephones sited at regular intervals, but most don't. If you break down, get your car off the road onto a grass verge or a lay-by. If the car has a catalytic converter (part of the exhaust system under the car—all petrol-driven cars made after 1992 have one), avoid stopping on long grass, which could ignite from the heat.

2 Switch on the hazard lights; if you have a warning triangle, put it about 165 yd (150 m) behind the car on the same side of the road.

On other roads

1 Park off the road if possible—certainly away from approaching traffic. Switch on the hazard lights.

2 If you have a warning triangle, put it at least 55 yd (50 m) behind the car on the same side of the road. If the breakdown occurs just beyond a bend or the brow of a hill, put the triangle on the other side of the bend or hill to give drivers behind plenty of warning. On a very narrow road, place the triangle on the nearside verge or footpath.

3 Don't stand behind the car at night or in poor visibility, because you may obscure the rear lights.

GETTING HELP

SAFETY FIRST On any road, don't, in your anxiety, get out of the car until you have checked that it is safe to do so.

On a motorway

1 Never try to do a repair on a motorway. To find the nearest emergency telephone, follow the direction of the arrow on the marker posts set at about 100 yd (90 m) intervals on the hard shoulder.

2 Never cross the carriageway to use a telephone. Always face the traffic when you speak into the receiver, so that you can see any danger approaching.

3 Motorway telephones are linked to the police, who will ask for the telephone number—to pinpoint your location—the make, model and registration number of your car, and what you think is wrong. They will call the AA, RAC or Green Flag National Breakdown (if you are a member), or a local breakdown service, and tell you about how long you have to wait. The telephones are two-way, so the police can call you back.

4 Once you have finished the call, return to your car and wait nearby, but well away from the carriageway and hard shoulder.

5 When rejoining the carriageway after a repair, use the hard shoulder to build up speed before moving into a safe gap in the traffic. Switch off your hazard lights.

On other roads

1 Some dual carriageways have emergency roadside telephones linked to the police, AA or RAC. Otherwise, find the nearest telephone to call for assistance—most service stations and pubs have a payphone. If it is dark and you have some distance to walk, wear something light-coloured such as a white coat, or carry something light-coloured—a white plastic bag, for example—so that drivers can see you.

2 If your car is causing an obstruction, make sure you inform the police.

KEEPING IN TOUCH

If you do a lot of driving, consider installing a mobile telephone so that if you break down in a remote area, or don't want to leave your car, you can call for help without difficulty.

Lone drivers

1 If you are a woman whose car has broken down, tell the breakdown service you are on your own—women alone or with children are normally given priority.

2 Any lone driver who has called for breakdown assistance should wait away from the car and road—on an embankment or verge, for example. Leave the front passenger door unlocked so that you can get into the car and lock the doors if you feel threatened.

3 Be wary of accepting help from strangers. Tell anyone who approaches that the police know of your breakdown and that help is on its way. If a police car pulls up, ask to see the officers' identification.

Disabled drivers

1 If you can't get to a telephone, stay in the car, lock all the doors and switch on your hazard warning lights.

2 Hang a 'help' pennant, available from most motoring organisations, from your car.

DEALING WITH A FLAT TYRE

Change a wheel as soon as possible after a tyre deflates. A soft or flat tyre can affect the steering and may cause the car to slew off the road when braking. Driving even a short way on a soft tyre causes damage.

On a motorway

1 Pull onto the hard shoulder safely and call for assistance. Don't try to change the wheel. Switch on the hazard lights and place a warning triangle, if you have one, at least 165 yd (150 m) behind the car.

On other roads

1 Stop away from the road in a safe place—avoid changing a wheel on the carriageway. On a dual carriageway, use a lay-by, if possible. If you can't get right off the road, put a warning triangle, if you have one, at least 55 yd (50 m) behind the car to warn other drivers, particularly on a bend.

2 Try to position the car so that you don't have to work on the side near to fast-moving traffic.

Changing a wheel

1 First check the condition of your spare wheel. If it is badly in need of inflating and you have no foot pump, call for assistance.

Use a penknife or screwdriver to dig out stones or other obstructions from the tread. (Some cars have a slim and space-saving, temporary spare, allowing a driver to reach the nearest garage to get a flat tyre repaired.)

2 Make sure the handbrake is on securely.

3 Use the wheelbrace or a screwdriver to remove any wheel trim covering the wheel bolts (older cars may have wheel nuts). With the brace, slacken the bolts no more than one turn each. If they are tight, put a foot on the brace and use your weight to loosen them.

4 Locate a jacking point—usually under the edge of the bodywork near the front and rear wheels. Make sure the ground below is level and hard enough to support the jack.

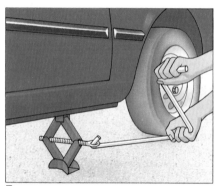

5 Fit the jack into the jacking point and slowly operate the handle to raise the car until the wheel is well clear of the ground.

6 Hold the wheel steady with one hand and unscrew the loosened bolts (or nuts). Put them to one side, keeping the threads clean. Take off the wheel, put it safely to one side and lift the spare into place.

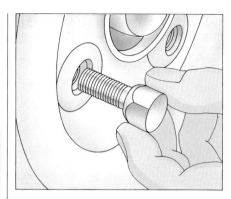

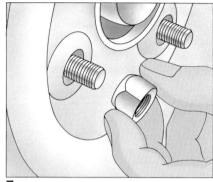

7 Hold the wheel securely in place with one hand so that the bolt holes align. Refit the bolts loosely with the other hand, making sure they all screw in straight. If the wheel is secured with nuts, lift the spare wheel onto the studs and refit the nuts with their bevelled sides towards the wheel.

8 Tighten the bolts (or nuts) diagonally, working from the top—top left then bottom right, top right then bottom left, for example. This ensures that the wheel isn't pulled to one side. Screw the bolts finger-tight, then tighten them with the wheelbrace.

9 Lower the jack until the full weight of the car is on the wheel. Remove the jack and use the wheelbrace to check that the bolts are tight. Refit any wheel trim.

10 Use a tyre pressure gauge (see page 470) to check that the air pressure in the newly fitted tyre is correct, according to the figure given in the car handbook. Driving with the tyre pressure either too low or too high can affect braking and steering. Get the damaged wheel repaired or replaced straight away—in case you soon need a spare.

TOWING AND BEING TOWED

A broken-down car should be moved by a breakdown recovery vehicle. If the car is in a dangerous position or is causing an obstruction, it may be towed to a safe place, from where it can be recovered.

AUTOMATICS Never tow an automatic car, because the gearbox, which is powered and lubricated only when the engine is running, may overheat and be damaged.

Attaching the towrope

1 Use a thick length of rope—preferably a purpose-made plastic rope with looped ends that is 9-15 ft (3-4.5 m) long. By law, the distance between a towing and a towed car should be no more than 15 ft (4.5 m).

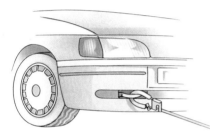

2 Fix the rope to the towing brackets or lugs at the front of the towed car and the rear of the towing car.

3 Tie a white marker, such as a piece of cloth, round the middle of the rope to make it easy for other drivers to see. On the rear of the towed car, place a sign saying 'On tow' and giving the registration number of the towing car.

Driving the towing car

1 Before setting off, make sure that the other driver agrees on the intended route and speed. Arrange signals for stopping, slowing down and changing gear; for gear changing, for example, hold up one, two, three or four fingers, as appropriate.

2 When you start to drive, take up slack gently to avoid breaking the rope or stalling. Outside built-up areas, drive at no more than 35-40 mph (55-65 km/h). Keep your dipped headlights on, even in daylight, to warn other drivers.

3 Signal in good time before turning, braking or changing gear, so that the towed driver can brake gently to prevent the car surging forward.

4 When changing gear, accelerate gently and slip the clutch slightly to keep the towrope taut.

The towed driver

1 Turn the ignition key to unlock the steering wheel. If possible, have the engine running so that the brake servo is operating; this makes braking easier.

2 Keep the hazard lights on. Use hand signals for turning or slowing down.

3 Keep the offside of the car near the centre of the road to give you a good view ahead.

4 While the towing car is slowing or going downhill, touch the brake pedal lightly to keep the rope taut. Be ready for the towing car to change gear—it will lose speed slightly and the rope will sag.

LIGHT FAILURE

Repair faulty lights as soon as possible. It is an offence not to have side and tail lights, headlights (main and dipped), indicators, stop lights and the rear number-plate light in working order.

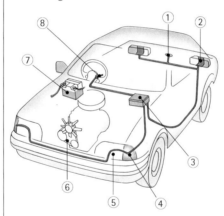

1 Rear number-plate light	5 Headlamp
2 Brake, reverse and rear indicator lights	6 Alternator belt
3 Fuse and relay box	7 Battery
4 Front indicator	8 Light switch

Possible causes

1 Blown bulb

2 Blown fuse—likely if both headlights have failed, or two or more lights on one side

3 Faulty wiring or switch, or connections poor or loose

4 Flat battery or poor connections—likely if all lights fail to work or are dim

5 Loose alternator belt (generally known as the fan belt)—likely if the lights go dim at speed or when the engine is idling

1 Checking a lamp bulb

• Most light units pull out from inside the car. Turn the bulb anticlockwise to get it out. If the unit is sealed, it will have to be replaced by a garage. On some older cars, bulbs are removed from outside the car after taking off the plastic lamp casing.

Single-filament bulb   Double-filament bulb

• If a filament inside the bulb (with either a single or double filament) is broken, or the glass is blackened or milky, fit a new bulb of the same rating.

• If the filament is unbroken but the bulb stem is corroded, use something abrasive such as sandpaper or a nail file to clean off all the corrosion, particularly from the contact end. The corrosion may result from a faulty seal at the back of the light unit; get it checked.

Halogen headlamp bulb

• If you have halogen headlamps, don't touch the glass envelope round the bulb, because oils from your skin may stain it; use a clean cloth.

• If you are not sure whether a bulb has blown, check by putting it into the holder of a bulb that is working. If the bulb then lights, check the inside of its holder to see whether the contacts are corroded. Clean them if they are.

2 Checking the fuses

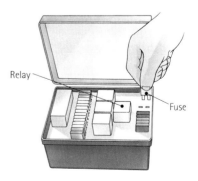

Relay

Fuse

• Find the fuse box; it is often under the dashboard or in a front knee-well. Fuses are usually numbered according to which circuit they protect or are identified by a symbol—check with your handbook. If there are no numbers or symbols, check each fuse in turn, replacing one before removing another.

Ceramic fuse with a shaped metal strip on one side that melts when overloaded

Plastic fuse with two metal push-in connectors linked by a visible fuse wire

- Examine the relevant fuse. If the wire or metal strip has broken, the fuse has blown. Replace it with a new fuse of the same rating.
- If the fuse looks all right, clean the metal contact points and the terminals in the fuse box, and refit the fuse.
- If the fuse blows again when the lights are switched on, there is a short circuit. Call for assistance.
- Some of the more powerful circuits are protected by relays—small square boxes generally alongside the fuses, sometimes with symbols on top to identify them. To test a relay, turn on the ignition and the relevant switch. Press the relay box with a finger. If it clicks, the relay is working; if not, the relay needs replacing.

SAFETY FIRST When carrying out checks under the bonnet, keep the car keys in your pocket, not in the ignition—unless the test needs the ignition or engine on.

3 Checking the wiring
- Reconnect any wires that have become disconnected.
- Clean any dirty or corroded connections.
- If the light still doesn't work, the switch may be faulty—call for assistance.
- If the indicators are not working, the flasher unit may be faulty. This is a sealed unit, so call for assistance or drive, using hand signals, to a garage.

4 Checking the battery

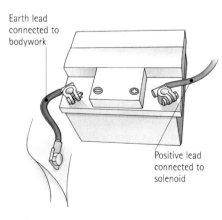

Earth lead connected to bodywork

Positive lead connected to solenoid

- Make sure that the battery leads and the earth connection on the car body have not been disconnected.

- If any of the leads are loose, unclamp them and clean the terminals with a wire brush or other abrasive surface, such as a nail file. Wipe with a cloth, refit and then tighten the terminal bolts or screws.
- Wait for 15 minutes with everything switched off to let the battery recover.

5 Checking the alternator belt

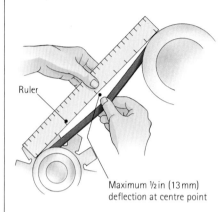

Ruler

Maximum ½in (13mm) deflection at centre point

- To check the tension of the alternator belt, find the mid point of its longest run and pull the belt inwards with finger and thumb. If you can move it more than ½in (13mm), it needs tightening.

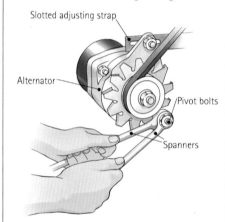

Slotted adjusting strap

Alternator

Pivot bolts

Spanners

- To tighten, loosen the pivot bolts and those on the slotted adjusting strap.

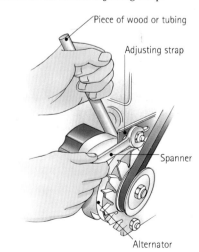

Piece of wood or tubing

Adjusting strap

Spanner

Alternator

- Use a piece of wood or tubing to lever the alternator away from the engine.

- When the tension is correct—measure as before—tighten the adjusting strap and pivot bolts.
- Check the tension after about 100 miles (160km), as it may slacken again.

HORN OR WIPER PROBLEMS

Finding a fault is a process of elimination, checking the fuse and electrical connections to the horn and the wiper motor, and making adjustments to the wipers.

Possible causes
1 Blown fuse
2 Dirty, rusted, loose or broken connections
3 Loose nuts on wiper arm
4 Worn wiper blades

1 Checking the fuse
- If the horn or both windscreen wipers fail to work, the fuse is probably blown. Unclip the relevant fuse from the fuse box (see page 461). If the wire or metal strip has broken, the fuse has blown. Replace it with a new fuse of the same rating.

2 Checking the electrical connections
- If the fuse hasn't blown, check inside the engine compartment that the connections from the horn push to the horn, and from the wiper switch to the wiper motor, are clean and secure. If the horn or wipers still don't work, the push or switch may be faulty; seek assistance.

3 Checking the wiper securing nut
- If one of the wipers doesn't work, switch off the wipers and use a screwdriver to lift off the cap at the base of the wiper arm. Tighten the nut with a spanner.

HORN WON'T STOP SOUNDING

- Look under the bonnet to find the horn, which is usually at the front of the engine.
- Pull off electrical connections.
- Get the horn repaired or replaced as soon as possible; it is an offence to drive without a horn in working order.

---

4 Worn wiper blades

- If the wiper blades judder as they sweep the windscreen, the rubbers are worn.

- Switch off the ignition with the blades vertical. Twist the wiper arm with your hands or pliers so that the less-worn edge of the rubber touches the screen.
- Replace the blades as soon as possible.

ENGINE CUTS OUT SUDDENLY

Finding the fault is by an elimination process—checking the path of the current via the battery, ignition coil, spark-plugs and distributor and looking for broken or faulty connections. For some checks, a helper is needed to turn on the ignition.

Possible causes

1 No current, or low current, from the battery
2 Faulty ignition coil
3 Faulty spark-plugs or incorrect plug gaps
4 Distributor with incorrect gap between contact-breaker points, or other faults

Electronic ignition Many modern cars, including all those with fuel injection, have an electronic ignition system. They may not have a distributor, or they may have a distributor that has no contact-breaker points. Leave fault-finding to a garage.

Computerised engine-management system If your car has one of these systems, don't attempt any fault-finding, or you may cause serious and expensive damage.

Diesel-powered cars These don't have spark-plugs or electronic ignition—the engine is fired by air compression in the cylinders. If you suspect a fault, call for assistance.

SAFETY FIRST When carrying out checks on the engine, keep the car keys in your pocket, not in the ignition—unless the test needs the ignition or the engine on.

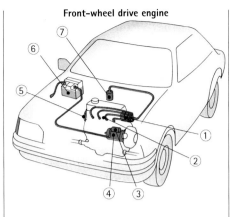

Front-wheel drive engine

Rear-wheel drive engine

1 Distributor
2 Spark-plugs and leads
3 Solenoid
4 Starter motor
5 Alternator belt
6 Battery
7 Coil

1 Checking the battery

- Switch on the headlights or windscreen wipers. If they don't work or are faint, the battery is disconnected, flat or in a low state of charge.

Bolt-and-clamp connector

Bolt-and-nut connector

- Check whether the leads, including the earth connection to the car body, are loose or disconnected. Twist them to see if they move.
- If they are loose, undo them—one at a time to avoid refixing wrongly—and clean the terminals with a wire brush or other abrasive surface, such as a coin's edge. Wipe clean with a dry cloth or tissue.
- Tighten refitted bolts or screws securely.
- If the lights now work, wait for 15 minutes then try to start the engine.
- If the engine still won't start, check the ignition system.

2 Checking the ignition coil

- If current is reaching the coil, there will be a spark between the high-tension (HT) lead and coil. To check this you need a helper. Stand clear of the bodywork and disconnect the HT lead (the thick one).

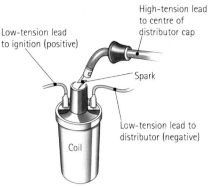

High-tension lead test

- Holding the lead with rubber-handled pliers, position it so that its metal contact is about ½ in (13 mm) from the top of the coil, then get your assistant to turn the key in the ignition. If the coil is working, a bright spark will jump across the gap.
- *If it sparks*, the spark-plugs may be at fault. Check their condition (see 3 below).

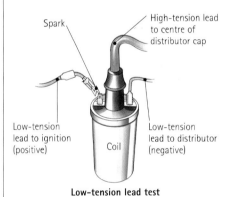

Low-tension lead test

- *If it doesn't spark*, the coil may be faulty or there may be no supply from the thin low-tension (LT) wires at the top of the coil. First, remove the distributor cap and make sure the contact-breaker points are closed (see 4 overleaf). Check the LT lead as for the HT lead. With a helper turning on the ignition while you stand clear of the bodywork, disconnect one of the LT wires and, holding it with rubber-handled pliers, touch it lightly against the coil terminal to see if there is a small spark.
- If there isn't, check the connections and clean the wires of the LT circuit—this includes the wires and terminals on the fuse box and starter solenoid (see pages 461 and 467). Then test the LT wire against the coil terminal again.
- If there is a small LT spark, current is flowing but the ignition coil is faulty and needs replacing.

3 Checking the spark-plugs

- Disconnect one spark-plug lead and clean its connector with a cloth and penknife.
- Into the lead connector wedge a nail, a small piece of metal or a roll of tinfoil such as a chocolate wrapping so that it protrudes beyond the cap.

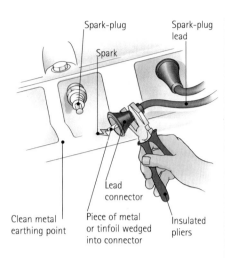

Spark-plug
Spark-plug lead
Spark
Lead connector
Clean metal earthing point
Piece of metal or tinfoil wedged into connector
Insulated pliers

- Stand clear of the car body and, using rubber-handled pliers, hold the connector so that the metal wedge is about ½ in (13 mm) from an earth—an area of clean metal. Any point on the car body except the rocker cover or carburettor will do.
- Turn on the ignition and look for a spark between the metal wedge and the earth.
- *If there is a spark*, the supply to the plugs is in order, but the plugs may be faulty, dirty or incorrectly adjusted. You cannot deal with them unless you have a plug spanner or a box or socket spanner with which to remove them.

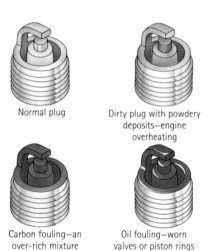

Normal plug

Dirty plug with powdery deposits—engine overheating

Carbon fouling—an over-rich mixture

Oil fouling—worn valves or piston rings

Heavy build-up of deposits—engine needs tuning

Both electrodes have burnt away or cracked—replace plug

Spark-plug condition

- Take off one plug lead and, using a suitable spanner, unscrew the plug. Wipe off any oil from the electrodes on the bottom of the plug, brush off any dirt with a paintbrush and remove carbon deposits using a nail file, the edge of a coin or abrasive paper.

- The gap between a plug's two electrodes may be incorrect. Use a feeler gauge, if you have one, to measure the gap; otherwise use a credit card, which is approximately the right thickness.

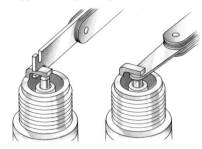

The gapping-tool attachment on a feeler gauge levers the spark-plug electrode to adjust the gap

The stiff feeler-gauge blades check the width of the spark-plug gaps

- Adjust the gap to the correct width by bending the outer electrode using the gapping tool on the feeler gauge or a pair of pliers.
- Repeat for the other spark-plugs, but reconnect each one before disconnecting another as incorrect connections will cause the engine to misfire.
- With all plugs refitted, start the car. If it still fails to start, there may be a problem with the fuel supply (see page 465) or call for assistance.
- *If there is no spark*, check the distributor.

4 Checking the distributor
- Remove the distributor cap by releasing the spring clips or undoing the screws.

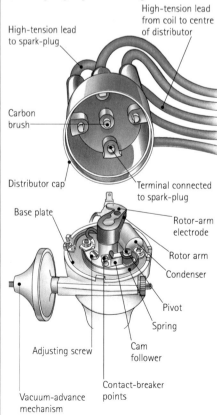

High-tension lead to spark-plug

High-tension lead from coil to centre of distributor

Carbon brush

Distributor cap

Base plate

Terminal connected to spark-plug

Rotor-arm electrode

Rotor arm

Condenser

Pivot

Spring

Cam follower

Adjusting screw

Vacuum-advance mechanism

Contact-breaker points

Lucas-type distributor

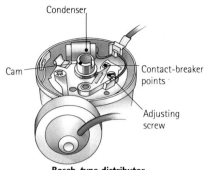

Condenser

Cam

Contact-breaker points

Adjusting screw

Bosch-type distributor (with rotor arm removed)

- Clean the inside of the cap with a dry cloth. (Spraying the inside with WD40 helps to prevent dampness, which causes corrosion.) Check that the spring-loaded carbon brush moves freely and can touch the rotor arm on top of the distributor.
- Turn the rotor arm. It should not move freely all the way round. If it does, the distributor drive or timing belt has broken and needs replacing—get assistance.

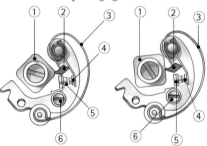

Points open   **Points closed**

1 Cam	5 Fixed contact point
2 Cam follower	6 Fixed-contact adjusting
3 Spring	screw
4 Movable contact point	

- If the rotor arm is in order, pull it off to reveal the contact-breaker points. Clean the faces of the points using something abrasive, such as a nail file, striker paper from a matchbox, or a penknife blade.

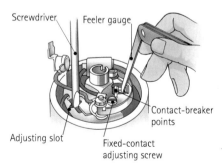

Screwdriver

Feeler gauge

Adjusting slot

Contact-breaker points

Fixed-contact adjusting screw

Measuring and adjusting the gap between contact-breaker points

- To check the points gap, turn the engine over slowly—with the ignition off—by selecting second gear and pushing the car backwards or forwards. On an automatic, use a spanner to turn the nut on the bottom alternator belt pulley.

- When the points are fully open, measure the gap, preferably with a feeler gauge. It should be about 0.02 in (0.5 mm)—see the car handbook—or a credit card's thickness.

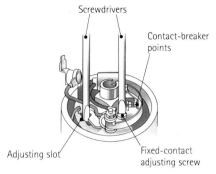

Tightening the fixed-contact adjusting screw

- To adjust the points gap, slacken the fixed-contact adjusting screw and move the plate with a screwdriver until the points just touch the faces of the feeler gauge (or credit card). Retighten the adjusting screw and recheck the gap.
- Refit the rotor arm and distributor cap and try to start the engine.
- *If it doesn't start*, remove the distributor cap and rotor arm. Turn the ignition and watch for a spark across the points every time they open.
- *If there is still no spark*, check that the wire from the points terminal makes good contact with the condenser—a cylinder screwed to the contact-breaker base plate, or a box mounted on the outside of the distributor. Try to start the engine.
- *If it fails to start*, and the points are burnt and discoloured, the condenser is probably faulty—call for assistance.

ENGINE SPLUTTERS AND DIES

Finding the fault is by an elimination process following the path of the fuel from the tank through the fuel pipe, filter and pump to the carburettor (there may be two in some cars), which delivers the right mixture of petrol and air to the engine.

Possible causes
1 No fuel in the tank
2 Leaks in the fuel system
3 Blockages in the fuel pipe or fuel-line filter, or a vapour lock
4 Faulty fuel pump
5 Dirty air filter or faulty carburettor

SAFETY FIRST Take great care during checking, especially when the engine is hot, as leaking fuel is a fire hazard. Don't smoke or use a naked flame near the car. Make sure also that hair and loose clothing are securely tucked away—they can get caught in moving parts.

Front or rear-wheel drive engine

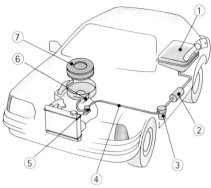

1 Fuel tank	5 Mechanical fuel pump
2 Fuel-line filter	6 Carburettor
3 Electric fuel pump	7 Air filter
4 Fuel pipe	

Fuel-injection engine

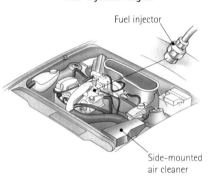

Fuel injector

Side-mounted air cleaner

Fuel injection Many cars, including all those fitted with an engine powered by diesel fuel, have a fuel-injection system instead of a carburettor; a fuel injector, which looks something like a spark-plug, enters each cylinder inlet duct at an angle. Cars with fuel injection often have an 'i' added to the model name, for example: 'GTi' or 'SRi'. Fuel injection is controlled electronically; don't attempt any fault-finding, because you may cause permanent damage—call for garage assistance.

1 Checking the fuel tank
- You may have run out of fuel. Even if the gauge registers that there is fuel in the tank, the gauge could be faulty. To check whether there is any fuel in the tank, remove the filler cap and rock the car from side to side. If there is no sloshing sound, fill up the tank. If you can hear fuel moving, leave the filler cap off for a few minutes, then replace tightly and try to start the car.
- *If it doesn't start*, check whether leaks in the system are preventing fuel from reaching the carburettor.

2 Checking for leaks
- Slacken the clip securing the fuel feed pipe to the carburettor or carburettors. (Some cars have factory-sealed clips that can be released only by a garage.)

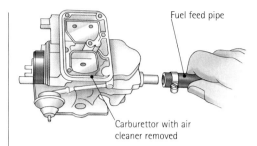

Fuel feed pipe

Carburettor with air cleaner removed

- Ease the pipe off. Fuel should spurt out for a moment. If fuel flows, the carburettor is faulty; seek assistance.
- If fuel doesn't flow, check the fuel pipe.
- Look under the car for leaks to the pipe and its connections, particularly its connections at the fuel pump. See if there are any patches of fuel on the ground, or patches of clean metal on the car where petrol has washed away dirt and oil.
- If any pipe connections are leaking, they can usually be sealed by tightening the screws or nuts. Soap rubbed on an area of pipe stops a leak temporarily. Don't try to stem a leak with tape or chewing gum, as petrol will wash them off.
- If the pipe is fractured, make a temporary repair by sliding a piece of plastic or rubber hose over the broken ends and securing it with wire or clips.
- For a small hole in the fuel tank, insert a self-tapping screw into the hole, or cover it with soap, as a temporary repair.
- If you are unable to stop the leak, call for breakdown assistance.
- If there are no leaks, there may be dirt blocking the fuel pipe.

3 Checking for blockages
- Disconnect the fuel pipe at the fuel-pump end and blow down it. If you can hear bubbling from the fuel tank, the pipe isn't blocked, or the blockage has been cleared.
- Try to start the engine. If it doesn't start, there may be a vapour lock in the fuel pipe. This can occur in hot weather when the engine has been idling for a long time—in a traffic jam, for example—and the fuel vaporises in the pipe rather than in the carburettor.
- Wait for the engine to cool, or wrap a cloth soaked in cold water round the fuel pipe until the pipe has cooled.
- Try to start the engine. If it doesn't start, the fuel pump may be faulty or, rarely, the fuel-line filter may be blocked and need replacing.

4 Checking the fuel pump
- The pump may be either mechanical or electric. A mechanical type is mounted on the engine. An electric type is usually fitted at the back of the car, near or inside the fuel tank, and makes a ticking noise when the ignition is on.

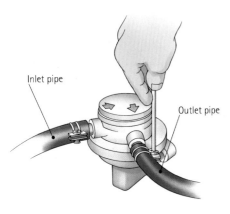

Mechanical fuel pump

- *To check a mechanical pump*, disconnect the outlet pipe, then get an assistant to switch on the ignition to operate the starter for a few seconds. Watch for fuel spurting from the pipe.
- If there is no fuel, the pump is faulty and you need breakdown assistance.
- If there is fuel, the pump is working. Reconnect the pipe and move to 5 below.

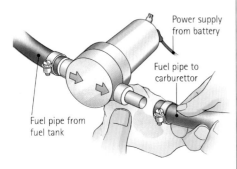

Electric fuel pump

WARNING Fuel spurts out fast from an electric pump. Wait—perhaps an hour—for the engine to cool before making any tests.

- *To check an electric pump*, ensure that the ignition is off, then slacken the clip on the outlet pipe to the carburettor.
- Hold a cloth under the connection to catch any fuel, and then pull the pipe away a little from the connection.
- Get a helper to switch the ignition on and then quickly off.
- If there is a ticking noise and fuel leaks out, the pump is working. Reconnect the pipe and move to 5 below.
- If no fuel flows, electric current may not be reaching the pump. Disconnect the supply wire coming from the battery, and the pump's earth wire (if fitted). Clean the terminals and refit the wires.
- If the pump still doesn't work, keep the ignition on and give the pump body a sharp tap with a screwdriver handle.
- If it works, the electrical points inside the pump are worn. Get a new pump fitted as soon as possible.
- If it doesn't work, call for assistance.

5 Checking the air filter
- A dirty air filter can cut off the air supply to the carburettor; this floods the engine with fuel and causes it to cut out. Some air cleaners are at the side of the engine.

Clip holding air-cleaner cover in place

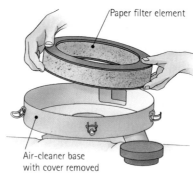

Paper filter element

Air-cleaner base with cover removed

- Undo the nuts or side clips holding the air-cleaner cover and remove the cover. Lift out the filter element inside.
- If the paper element is dusty, shake off the dust and refit it. If it is black and oily, throw it away. Refit the air-cleaner cover. You can run a car (except a fuel-injected car) with no filter for a short while, but fit a new filter as soon as possible.
- Try to start the engine. If it doesn't start, there is a problem with the carburettor and you need breakdown assistance.

USING THE CORRECT FUEL

When filling your car with fuel, make sure you are using the right pump. Putting petrol into a diesel-powered car damages the fuel injector pump. Putting diesel fuel into a car with a petrol-driven engine also upsets the fuel system. In both cases the car will quickly break down. If you do make this mistake, call for assistance—don't try to restart or drive the car. A garage will have to drain the system and check for any engine damage.

Using unleaded petrol in a car designed for leaded petrol will affect performance but won't cause damage on one fill-up. Using leaded instead of unleaded petrol doesn't damage the engine, but the exhaust gases may damage a catalytic converter.

ENGINE WILL NOT START

Finding the fault is by a process of elimination, following the starter and ignition system from the battery to the starter motor. More often than not, the problem is caused by a flat battery.

Possible causes
1 Damp or condensation in the ignition parts, especially in wet or foggy weather
2 Engine flooded with fuel
3 Flat battery
4 Faulty starter motor

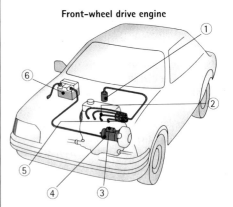

Front-wheel drive engine

Rear-wheel drive engine

1 Coil	4 Starter motor
2 Spark-plugs and leads	5 Distributor
3 Solenoid	6 Battery

WARNING If your car has electronic ignition, fuel injection or a computerised engine-management system, don't attempt any fault-finding—seek assistance.

SAFETY FIRST When carrying out checks under the bonnet, keep the car keys in your pocket, not in the ignition, unless the engine has to be turned over for a test.

1 Drying out the ignition
- Use a dry cloth to clean the spark-plug leads, distributor cap (inside and out), ignition coil and connecting wires. Or use a water-repellent spray such as WD40.
- If you have made repeated attempts to start the engine, switch off the ignition and any lights, and wait at least 15 minutes for the battery to recover power.
- Try to start the engine. If it won't start, the carburettor may be flooded with fuel.

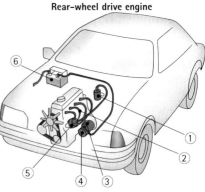

2 Starting a flooded engine

- *Manual choke* With a manual choke control on the dashboard, push it in all the way, depress the accelerator pedal fully and turn on the ignition.
- *Automatic choke* With an automatic choke (no dashboard choke control), take off the air cleaner to reveal the carburettor. Wedge open the choke flap in the top of the carburettor, press the accelerator pedal down fully and turn on the ignition.
- If the car doesn't start, there may be a problem with the battery.

WARNING If your car radio has a security code, it won't work again after the battery leads have been removed. A code has to be keyed in. If you don't know the code, the car or radio maker can supply it, upon proof that you are the owner.

3 Checking the battery

- Turn on the headlights. If they are bright and the starter motor turns over, then the battery is good and the fault may be at the spark-plugs (see 3 on page 463).
- If the headlights are dim and the starter motor doesn't turn, or turns slowly, disconnect the battery leads and clean both terminals with something abrasive, such as a nail file. Refit the leads.
- Check that the battery earth lead is secure and making good contact with the car bodywork, then try to start the engine. If it doesn't start, try a push or boost start.

Push starts If your car has an automatic gearbox, don't attempt a push start, as the gears are powered and lubricated from a pump that operates only when the engine is running. Also, don't push start a car fitted with a catalytic converter, as unburnt fuel will enter the system and cause damage.

- *To push start* Get one or two strong helpers to push the car. Depress the clutch pedal firmly, engage second gear, pull out the choke control (if there is one) and turn the ignition. When the car is moving at walking pace, release the clutch pedal sharply to turn the engine. As soon as the engine starts, depress the clutch fully.

Boost starts You need the battery of another car and jump leads with strong, clean clips and a rating of 50-70 amperes. Before using jump leads, check in your handbook that it is safe to do so, and ensure that the batteries on both cars are earthed from the negative terminal to the bodywork. Take care when boost starting, as any arcing of current could damage the alternator.
Don't boost start a car if it has fuel injection or electronic ignition, as surges of current could cause irreparable damage.

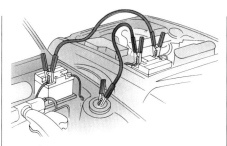

- *To boost start*, position the two cars with engines side by side but not touching, and with the batteries as close as possible. Switch off the ignition and all other electrical components on both cars.
- Make sure the jump lead connectors are not touching each other or the car bodywork. Connect the red (positive) lead first to the positive (+) terminal of the good battery, and then to the positive (+) terminal of the flat battery. Then connect the black (negative) lead to the negative (-) terminal of the good battery.
- Standing clear of both batteries, clip the other end of the black (negative) lead to a clean metal stud or part of the engine on the car with a flat battery, in a position at least 2 ft (60 cm) from its battery.
- Start the engine of the car with the good battery to begin charging the flat battery.
- Wait 20-30 seconds, then switch on the lights in the car being charged. If they are bright, there is some battery voltage. Turn off the lights and with the gear in neutral start the engine. To charge the battery, press the accelerator to take the engine speed to the equivalent of 30-40 mph (50-65 km/h) for 2 minutes.
- Stop the engine and remove the jump leads one at a time, avoiding any contact with the car bodywork. Never take both jump lead clips off one car at the same time, as this could result in spark, and is therefore a fire risk.
- If the car still fails to start, there may be a fault with the starter motor.

4 Checking the starter motor

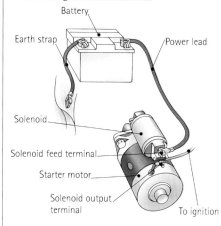

Battery
Earth strap
Power lead
Solenoid
Solenoid feed terminal
Starter motor
Solenoid output terminal
To ignition

- If, when you start the ignition, the engine turns only slowly or not at all, check that the wiring connections between

the battery and the starter motor or solenoid are clean and tight.

- *If there is no click* from the starter motor when you turn on the ignition, check the connections of the wire leading from the ignition to the solenoid.
- *If there is a click* but the engine doesn't turn, hold the ignition key in the starting position and get an assistant to tap the solenoid or starter motor with a spanner or wheelbrace. If the car still fails to start, the starter motor is faulty—seek help.

ENGINE OVERHEATS

If the car temperature gauge stays at a high reading and the engine lacks power, or if steam rises from under the bonnet, the engine is overheating. Pull off the road and stop the car. Either engine coolant (water and antifreeze mixture) is leaking from the cooling system, or coolant isn't circulating because of a faulty alternator belt, electric fan or water pump.

Possible causes

1. Radiator or hoses leaking
2. Engine cooling system leaking, or blown cylinder-head gasket
3. Broken or slack alternator (fan) belt
4. Faulty electric fan or thermoswitch
5. Faulty thermostat valve
6. Leaking water pump

Front-wheel drive engine

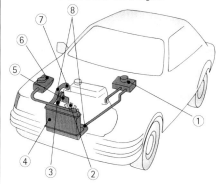

Rear-wheel drive engine

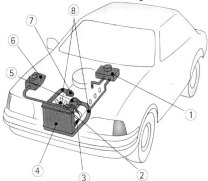

1 Heater	5 Water pump
2 Electric fan	6 Expansion tank
3 Alternator belt	7 Thermostat
4 Radiator	8 Radiator hoses

Cooling system

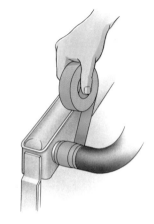

1 Heater blower fan	8 Engine-driven fan
2 Heater	9 Bottom radiator hose
3 Hose from heater	10 Radiator core
4 Hose to heater	11 Bottom tank
from engine block	12 Top tank
5 Core plug	13 Expansion tank and cap
6 Cylinder head	14 Top radiator hose
7 Water pump	15 Thermostat housing

1 Checking for radiator or hose leaks

- Open the bonnet, but don't touch any part of the cooling system for at least 20 minutes, to give the engine time to cool down.
- When the engine has cooled, cover the filler cap on the radiator or expansion tank with a thick cloth and loosen it a quarter turn anticlockwise to let out the steam; then remove the radiator cap.
- When the radiator has cooled enough to touch, top it up with cold water.
- Start the car and switch on the heater to its hot setting so that coolant can circulate and prevent any air locks.
- Once the hoses supplying the heater are hot and the coolant is at the correct level—as marked on the radiator expansion tank—refit the cap tightly and let the engine idle.
- Look for water or steam leaking from the radiator and the top and bottom radiator hoses, and also from the hoses supplying the heater, the water pump (see 6 opposite), the cylinder-head joints, and the core plugs on the cylinder block and head.
- A radiator leak can be slowed down by pressing chewing gum over it. Top up the water level, leave the radiator cap off, keeping it in a safe place, and drive slowly to the nearest garage.

Hose clips

Wire clip   Worm-drive clip

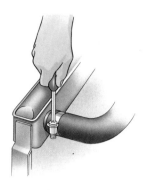

- If water leaks from a hose connection, tighten the hose clips with a screwdriver.

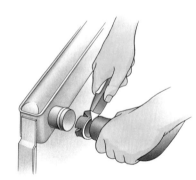

- If the hose has split, bind the affected area with insulating tape or a cloth. This should hold until you get to a garage.

- If the hose end has split, unscrew the hose clip and slide it back. Cut off the split part and reconnect the hose using the hose clip. Wrap tape round the hose end if it has wire clips. Replace the hose.

2 Checking for engine leaks

- Most small leaks can be cured by pouring a tin of radiator sealing compound into the radiator while the engine is warm.
- If coolant gushes out as soon as you top up the radiator, call for assistance.
- If the leak is slow but can't be stopped, loosen the radiator cap and drive slowly to the nearest garage. Every 5 miles (8 km) check and top up the coolant level.
- If the leak is from the cylinder head, call for assistance.
- Check the core plugs, which are on the

side of the engine crankcase or the end of the cylinder head. If you find a hole, insert a small self-tapping screw from the car trim or fascia. Drive to a garage for assistance.
- If there are no leaks, cover the filler cap on the radiator or expansion tank with a thick cloth and remove it. Take great care, as hot water may spurt out at pressure. If large bubbles are rising in the radiator or expansion tank the cylinder-head gasket has blown—call for assistance.
- If there are no bubbles, the alternator (fan) belt may be loose or broken.

3 Checking the alternator belt

- The alternator belt drives both the water pump and alternator, and sometimes the fan—it is often known as the fan belt. If the belt is broken, don't drive the car, as this will damage the engine. If you don't have a spare belt, call for assistance.
- If you have a spare belt, slacken the two bolts holding the alternator to the engine and the bolt on the adjuster arm below the alternator (see 5 page 462). Push the alternator towards the engine so that it pivots on its bolts. Fit the new belt over the alternator, water pump and crankshaft pulleys, making sure it is not twisted.
- To set the tension on a new belt, or to tighten the existing belt, pull the alternator away from the engine until the belt, on its longest run between two pulleys, has no more than ½ in (13 mm) of play at its halfway point (see page 462). Then tighten the adjuster bolt and alternator mounting bolts.
- If the belt isn't loose, check the electric fan.

4 Checking the electric fan

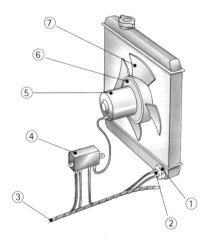

1 Thermoswitch	4 Relay supplying current
2 Thermoswitch	to fan motor
terminals	5 Fan motor
3 Supply from ignition	6 Fan assembly
	7 Fan

- When the engine coolant reaches a certain temperature, a thermoswitch on the radiator turns on the fan. Run the engine until the needle or bar on the temperature gauge nears the hot (red) sector. This may take 10-15 minutes.

• If the fan fails to work, the thermoswitch may be faulty. Remove the two terminals from the thermoswitch, which is located at the bottom rear of the radiator, and use a piece of wire and insulating tape to join them together.

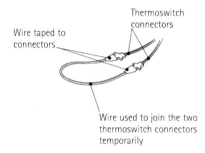

Thermoswitch connectors

Wire taped to connectors

Wire used to join the two thermoswitch connectors temporarily

• If the fan now works, the thermoswitch is faulty. You can drive the car a short distance, but avoid heavy traffic. Get a new thermoswitch fitted as soon as possible.

• If the fan still doesn't work, either a fuse has blown or the fan is faulty. Replace the fuse if you have one, making sure it is of the same rating; otherwise call for assistance.

• If the fan operates but the engine still overheats, the thermostat valve, which controls the circulation of water between the engine and radiator, may be faulty.

5 Checking the thermostat valve

• Feel carefully the temperature of the top and bottom radiator hoses. If the top hose feels cooler than the bottom one, the thermostat is faulty.

• Turn off the engine and let it cool for at least 30 minutes. Check the water level in the radiator. If no water has been lost, you can drive a short distance—about 2 miles (3 km)—to a garage.

• If there is no temperature difference in the radiator hoses, the water pump may be faulty.

6 Checking the water pump

• Find the water pump, which is at the front of the engine behind the top alternator-belt pulley.

• Look for leaks from the joint where the pump is bolted to the engine, and from the shaft behind the pulley.

• If there is a small leak, tighten the bolts that secure the pump to the engine. Then carefully remove the radiator cap and drive slowly to the nearest garage to get the water pump replaced.

• If the leak is bad, don't attempt to drive the car; call for assistance.

NOISY OR ROUGH RUNNING

A sudden, unusual engine noise may mean a serious problem: investigate it straight away. First ensure that the noise—especially if it is intermittent and not in rhythm with the engine or wheels—is not caused by something rolling around in the boot, a loose door or bonnet, or the car's underside scraping the ground under a full load.

Front-wheel drive engine

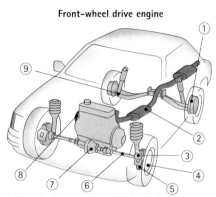

1 Drum brakes	6 Drive shaft
2 Exhaust system	7 Gearbox
3 Wheel bearings	8 Alternator belt
4 Wheel bolts or nuts	9 Suspension joints
5 Disc brakes	

Rear-wheel drive engine

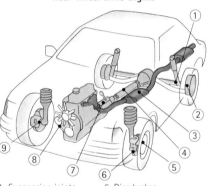

1 Suspension joints	6 Disc brakes
2 Drum brakes	7 Gearbox
3 Exhaust system	8 Alternator belt
4 Drive shaft	9 Wheel bearings
5 Wheel bolts or nuts	

• *Screeching from the engine during hard acceleration* The alternator belt may be slack. Check the belt tension and tighten (see page 462).

• *Screeching from near the radiator* The bearings in the water pump or alternator may be dry. If you suspect this, drive slowly to the nearest garage, keeping an eye on the engine temperature gauge or warning light.

• *Loud knocking from the engine, particularly when accelerating* Check immediately, or the engine may be severely damaged. If the oil-pressure gauge reading is low (or the warning light is lit) and the oil level is low—check using the engine dipstick (see page 470)—stop at once and get assistance.

• *Heavy knocking from the engine* The big-end bearings may be worn,

or, if there is a heavy rumbling noise, the main bearings could be worn. Call for assistance.

• *Light tapping in the top of the engine* The valve clearances are excessive. It is safe to drive, but have the clearances adjusted as soon as possible.

• *Light, tinkling noise—'pinking'—from the engine when accelerating* Either the ignition timing is incorrect, there is a build-up of carbon in the combustion chambers, or the grade of fuel is too low. It is safe to drive, but don't accelerate hard or drive too fast until the fault has been remedied by a garage.

• *Crunching when you change gear* The synchromesh unit inside the gearbox is worn, or the clutch plate is faulty. Get it replaced as soon as possible.

• *Moaning whine in the gearbox* A lack of oil may have caused a bearing to become worn. Drive the car to the nearest garage.

• *Rhythmic knocking or ticking in time with the wheels, especially when cornering tightly* The drive-shaft constant-velocity (CV) joints on the front wheel bearings are worn. Jack up the front of the car, turn the wheels slowly and feel for any resistance or roughness. If the wheels grab or stick, don't drive the car. Call for breakdown assistance.

• *Squealing from the clutch when you change gear* The clutch-release bearing may be worn. Get the bearing replaced as soon as possible.

• *Dry, squawking noise that varies in intensity when the clutch pedal is fully depressed* The spigot bearing that supports the gearbox input shaft is worn or dry. This is not serious, but get the bearing replaced quickly.

• *Squeal or judder when you brake* There may be dirt in the brakes, or the brake discs may be distorted. A stone lodged against a disc brake can also cause squealing. Harsh grinding when you brake indicates worn brake pads or linings. These noises could indicate serious brake failure or damage. Call for assistance or drive the car slowly to a garage.

• *Knocking and vibration from under the car when decelerating* The drive shaft or centre support bearing may be worn. Drive carefully to the nearest garage.

• *Splutterings and vibrations from under the car* The exhaust system may be at fault. Check the exhaust-support brackets under the car. If they have cracked, the exhaust may be touching the car body. Check also for a broken exhaust pipe or a hole in the silencer. Get the exhaust repaired or replaced as soon as possible.

• *Knocking from the wheels or vibration in the steering* The suspension joints may be worn. Call for assistance.

- *Clanking when moving slowly forwards* Wheel bolts or nuts may be slack. Check that they are tight, and that nuts are fitted the right way round—with the bevelled edge towards the wheel.
- *Rough running or misfiring, with an apparent loss of power* There may be a fault in the ignition system. If your car is fitted with a catalytic converter, rectify any misfire as soon as possible, otherwise the converter will be damaged. A lack of acceleration or a sense that the car is being held back may be due to the brakes binding. Check whether the car rolls freely when the handbrake has been released. If it doesn't, get the brakes adjusted as soon as possible.

KEEPING YOUR CAR IN GOOD CONDITION

To reduce the likelihood of a breakdown and ensure that the car is efficient and economic, have it serviced regularly by experienced mechanics. Carry out the following regular checks yourself, and make any necessary adjustments.

Checking before a journey
Before a long journey, and if you use the car for short journeys every day, carry out the following checks at least once a month.

1 *Oil* Remove the engine dipstick and check the oil level; wipe the stick with a clean rag or absorbent paper, replace it and check again. The level should fall between the minimum and maximum. If the oil level is near or below the minimum marked, remove the oil-filler cap and top up. Keep a supply of the engine oil recommended by the manufacturer; it is more economical to buy a 5 litre bottle than a 1 litre bottle.

2 *Coolant* Check the coolant level in the radiator or expansion tank attached, and top up if necessary. If the engine is hot, wait for it to cool down first. Fill up to the level marked on the side of the expansion tank, or on older models to about 1 in (25 mm) below the filler hole in the radiator. In winter top up the radiator and windscreen-washer reservoirs with antifreeze mixture in the correct proportions—check in your handbook or consult a garage.

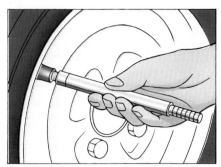

3 *Tyre pressures*
Use a pressure gauge to check that the air pressure in all tyres, including the spare, is as recommended in the car handbook. To get an accurate reading, do this when tyres are cold.

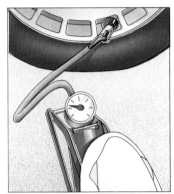

Use a foot pump to put more air in the tyres; most have a gauge registering tyre pressure.

4 *Tyre treads*
Use a tyre-tread tool to measure the depth of the tread on all tyres, and ensure that all have a good depth; the law requires that the depth all round the tyre and across its whole width should be not less than 1.6 mm. Most modern tyres have wear bars, which stand proud of the bottom of the tread grooves. If wear bars are flush with the top of the tread, the tyre must be changed. Check that there are no deep cuts. Remove stones or other debris from the tread with a penknife.

5 *Lights and horn* Check that all lights and indicators are working and clean. Replace any spent bulbs (see page 461). Ensure that the battery terminals are clean and secure.

6 *Windscreen* Keep the windscreen, mirrors and windows clean, and keep the windscreen and rear screen washer reservoirs topped up. In cold, misty or foggy weather check that the windscreen demister works.

7 *Brakes* Test the brakes to make sure they are efficient and not spongy. Don't drive the car if they are not working well.

8 *Mirrors and belts* Ensure that all mirrors, and seat belts are adjusted correctly. With head restraints, keep the top at or above eye level and close to the back of the head.

Additional regular checks
- Check the windscreen wipers—replace them if the rubbers deteriorate.
- Make sure that number plates are clean and firmly attached.
- Check the alternator belt for wear, and ensure that the tension is correct.
- Check the exhaust system for holes and loose mountings.
- Check fluid levels in the brake and clutch reservoirs. If you have power-assisted steering, check the steering-fluid level.
- Check that seat belts run freely and are not frayed or damaged. If there is a child seat, check that mountings and fastenings are secure and in good condition.

CAR TOOL KIT

A simple collection of tools and equipment will help you to deal with an emergency or breakdown. Most can be stowed in a boot.

Accidents and breakdowns
- First-aid kit
- Warning triangle
- Towrope

Wheel-changing
- Foot pump
- Jack
- Tyre-pressure gauge
- Tyre-tread tool
- Wheelbrace

Simple repairs and checks
- Alternator belt
- Cloths/paper roll
- Electrical wire
- Emery paper
- Engine oil
- Feeler gauge
- Insulating tape
- Penknife/Stanley knife
- Pen or pencil
- Pliers
- Screwdrivers
- Set of spanners
- Small paintbrush
- Spare fuses and bulbs
- Spark-plug spanner
- Tape measure/small ruler
- Torch
- Water
- Wire brush

INDEX OF PLACES IN THE BRITISH ISLES
A gazetteer of nearly 30 000 entries

THIS GAZETTEER OF CITIES, towns, suburbs and villages in the United Kingdom and the Republic of Ireland is an index to the maps on pages 33-352. The reference after each name gives the map page number and the letter code of the grid square in which the place appears. If two or more placenames are spelt the same way they are distinguished by their county or administrative area. A list of counties and administrative areas is given below, together with the abbreviated forms used in the gazetteer

ENGLAND

Avon	Avon	Hereford & Worcester	H & W	Sussex, East	E Ssx
Bedfordshire	Beds	Hertfordshire	Herts	Sussex, West	W Ssx
Berkshire	Berks	Humberside	Humb	Tyne and Wear	T & W
Buckinghamshire	Bucks	Isle of Wight	IOW	Warwickshire	Warks
Cambridgeshire	Cambs	Kent	Kent	West Midlands	W Mids
Cheshire	Ches	Lancashire	Lancs	Wiltshire	Wilts
Cleveland	Clev	Leicestershire	Leics	Yorkshire, North	N Yorks
Cornwall	Corn	Lincolnshire	Lincs	Yorkshire, South	S Yorks
Cumbria	Cumb	Merseyside	Mers	Yorkshire, West	W Yorks
Derbyshire	Derbs	Norfolk	Nflk		
Devon	Devon	Northamptonshire	Northants	**WALES**	
Dorset	Dors	Northumberland	Northld	Aberconwy & Colwyn	A & C
Durham	Dur	Nottinghamshire	Notts	Anglesey	Anglsy
Essex	Esx	Oxfordshire	Oxon	Blaenau Gwent	BG
Gloucestershire	Glos	Shropshire	Shrops	Bridgend	Brid
Greater London	GL	Somerset	Som	Caernarfonshire & Merionethshire	C & M
Greater Manchester	GM	Staffordshire	Staffs	Caerphilly	Caer
Hampshire	Hants	Suffolk	Sflk	Cardiff	Crdff
		Surrey	Sry		

Cardiganshire	Card	East Dunbartonshire	E Dun	Fermanagh	Ferm
Carmarthenshire	Carm	Edinburgh, City of	C of Edin	Londonderry	Londy
Denbighshire	Denb	Falkirk	Falk	Tyrone	Tyr
Flintshire	Flint	Fife	Fife		
Merthyr Tydfil	MT	Glasgow, City of	C of Glas	**REPUBLIC OF IRELAND**	
Monmouthshire	Mon	Highland	Hghld	Carlow	Carl
Neath & Port Talbot	N & PT	Inverclyde	Invclyd	Cavan	Cav
Newport	Nwprt	Lanarkshire, North	N Lan	Clare	Clare
Pembrokeshire	Pemb	Lanarkshire, South	S Lan	Cork	Cork
Powys	Pwys	Lothian, East	E Loth	Donegal	Dngl
Rhondda Cyon Taff	RCT	Lothian, West	W Loth	Dublin	Dub
Swansea	Swan	Midlothian	Midln	Galway	Gal
Torfaen	Trfn	Moray	Moray	Kerry	Kerry
Vale of Glamorgan	V of G	Orkney Islands	Ork	Kildare	Kild
Wrexham	Wrex	Perthshire & Kinross	P & K	Kilkenny	Kilk
		Renfrewshire	Ren	Laois	Laois
SCOTLAND		Renfrewshire, East	E Ren	Leitrim	Leit
Aberdeen, City of	C of Aber	Shetland Islands	Shet	Limerick	Lim
Aberdeenshire	Aber	Stirling	Stir	Longford	Long
Angus	Angus	Western Isles	W Is	Louth	Louth
Argyll & Bute	A & B			Mayo	Mayo
Ayrshire, East	E Ayr	**SELF-GOVERNING ISLANDS**		Meath	Meath
Ayrshire, North	N Ayr	Channel Islands	Ch Is	Monaghan	Mongh
Ayrshire, South	S Ayr	Isle of Man	IOM	Offaly	Ofly
Borders	Bdrs	Isles of Scilly	Is OS	Roscommon	Rosc
Clackmannan	Clmnn			Sligo	Sligo
Dumbarton & Clydebank	D & C	**NORTHERN IRELAND**		Tipperary	Tipp
Dumfries & Galloway	D & G	Antrim	Ant	Waterford	Wat
Dundee, City of	C of Dun	Armagh	Arm	Westmeath	Wmth
		Down	Down	Wexford	Wex
				Wicklow	Wklw

A

Name	Page	Grid
Abbas Combe	72	Bc
Abberley	140	Bc
Abberton Esx	128	Dc
Abberton H & W	140	Cc
Abberwick	261	Fd
Abbess Roding	125	Gc
Abbey Devon	68	Db
Abbey Gal	333	Ph
Abbeycwmhir	136	Cd
Abbeydale	192	Ae
Abbey Dore	116	Ae
Abbeydorney	325	Kk
Abbeyfeale	325	Nk
Abbey Hulton	189	Ea
Abbeylara	344	Bc
Abbeyleix	336	Ef
Abbey St Bathans	272	Dd
Abbeyshrule	344	Cb
Abbeystead	213	Fc
Abbeytown	244	Ac
Abbey Wood	101	Fc
Abbotrule	260	Ad
Abbots Bickington	64	Db
Abbots Bromley	165	Ed
Abbotsbury	52	Bc
Abbotsford	272	Aa
Abbotsham	65	Ec
Abbotskerswell	48	Ca
Abbots Langley	124	Bb
Abbots Leigh	92	Cc
Abbotsley	148	Ab
Abbots Morton	141	Eb
Abbots Ripton	148	Ad
Abbot's Salford	141	Eb
Abbotts Ann	73	He
Abbottswood	73	Hc
Abdon	137	He
Aber	133	Ea
Aberaeron	133	Ec
Aberaman	113	Fb
Aberangell	160	Ab
Aber-Arad	132	Da
Aberarder	304	Ec
Aberargie	284	Dd
Aberarth	133	Ec
Aberavon	88	Ce
Aber-banc	132	Da
Aberbeeg	113	Hb
Aberbowlan	112	Be
Abercanaid	113	Fb
Abercarn	89	He
Abercastle	108	Be
Abercegir	160	Ab
Aberchalder	304	Ba
Aberchirder	308	Df
Abercraf	112	Dc
Abercrombie	285	Hc
Abercwmboi	89	Fe
Abercych	132	Ca
Abercynafon	113	Fc
Abercynon	89	Fe
Aber-Cywarch	160	Ac
Aberdalgie	284	Ce
Aberdare	113	Fb
Aberdaron	156	Bd
Aberdeen	308	Gd
Aberdour	284	Da
Aberdulais	88	Ce
Aberdulais Falls	88	Cf
Aberdyfi	157	Ga
Aberedw	136	Ca
Abereiddy	108	Ae
Abererch	156	De
Aber Falls	181	Hc
Aberfan	113	Fb
Aberfeldy	293	Jb
Aberffraw	181	Ec
Aberffrwd	133	Gd
Aberford	217	Ga
Aberfoyle	281	Fc
Abergarw	89	Gd
Abergavenny	113	Hc
Abergeldie Castle	296	Bg
Abergele	184	Cd
Aber-Giâr	133	Fa
Abergorlech	112	Ae
Abergwesyn	136	Ab
Abergwili	109	Hd
Abergwydol	157	Hb
Abergwynant	157	Gc
Abergwynfi	88	De
Abergwyngregyn	181	Hd
Abergynolwyn	157	Gb
Aberhosan	160	Aa
Aberkenfig	88	Dd
Aberlady	272	Ae
Aberlemno	296	Ec
Aberllefenni	157	Hb
Abermeurig	133	Fb
Abermule	160	Da
Aber-naint	160	Dc
Abernant Carm	109	Gd
Abernant RCT	113	Fb
Abernethy	284	Dd
Abernethy Forest	305	Hb
Abernyte	296	Ba
Aberporth	132	Cb
Aberscross	313	Kd
Abersoch	156	Dd
Abersychan	113	Hb
Abertillery	113	Hb
Abertridwr Caer	89	Gd
Abertridwr Pwys	160	Cc
Abertysswg	113	Gb
Aberuthven	284	Bd
Aber Village	113	Gd
Aberyscir	113	Ed
Aberystwyth	133	Fe
Abhainn Suidhe	317	Vm
Abingdon	96	De
Abinger Common	77	He
Abington Lim	333	Pc
Abington S Lan	256	Be
Abington Pigotts	148	Ba
Abingworth	77	Hb
Ab Kettleby	168	Dd
Ablington	120	Ab
Abney	189	Gd
Aboyne	296	Eg
Abram	201	Fc
Abriachan	304	Dd
Abridge	101	Fe
Abson	93	Ec
Abthorpe	144	Ca
Aby	196	Dd
Acaster Malbis	217	Hb
Acaster Selby	217	Hb
Accrington	201	Ge
Acha	288	Cc
Achachork	300	De
Achafour	264	De
Achahoish	316	Jh
Achallader	292	Db
Acha Mor	317	Yp
Achanalt	304	Ag
Achandunie	313	Ja
Ach' an Todhair	292	Ae
Achany	312	Hd
Achaphubuil	292	Ae
Acharacle	289	Hd
Acharn Hghld	289	Jc
Acharn P & K	293	Hb
Acharonich	289	Fa
Achavanich	313	Ph
Achduart	312	Cd
Achentoul	313	Lg
Achfary	312	Eg
Achgarve	312	Ac
Achiemore Hghld	312	Fj
Achiemore Hghld	313	Li
A'Chill	288	Dh
Achill Island	340	Cg
Achill Sound	340	Df
Achiltibuie	312	Cd
Achina	313	Kj
Achinduich	312	Hc
Achindun	289	Ka
Achingills	313	Pj
Achintee	301	Je
Achintee House	292	Be
Achintraid	301	Hd
Achleck	288	Fb
Achleek	289	Jc
Achluachrach	292	Cf
Achlyness	312	Ei
Achmelvich	312	Cf
Achmore Hghld	301	Hd
Achmore Stir	293	Fa
Achnaba	289	La
Achnacarnin	312	Cg
Achnacarry	292	Bf
Achnacloich A & B	289	La
Achnacloich Hghld	300	Ea
Achnaconeran	304	Cb
Achnacroish	289	Kb
Achnadrish	288	Fc
Achnafalnich	280	Ce
Achnagarron	313	Ja
Achnaha Hghld	289	Fd
Achnaha Hghld	289	Hb
Achnahanat	312	Hc
Achnahannet	305	Hc
Achnairn	312	He
Achnalea	289	Kd
Achnaluachrach	313	Jd
Achnamara	277	Fa
Achnasaul	292	Bf
Achnasheen	301	Lf
Achnashelloch	277	Gb
Achnastank	305	Ld
Achosnich	288	Fd
Achranich	289	Jb
Achreamie	313	Nj
Achriabhach	292	Bd
Achriesgill	312	Ei
Achuirghill	312	Gd
Achurch	145	Ge
Achuvoldrach	312	Hi
Achvaich	313	Kc
Achvarasdal	313	Mj
Ackergill	313	Ri
Acklam Clev	229	Hd
Acklam N Yorks	220	Bd
Ackleton	164	Ba
Acklington	261	Gc
Ackton	205	Fe
Ackworth Moor Top	205	Fd
Aclare	341	Lh
Acle	176	Cc
Acock's Green	141	Fe
Acol	105	Gb
Aconbury	116	Cc
Acre	201	Ge
Acrefair	185	Fa
Acrise Place	84	Be
Acton Arm	345	Lk
Acton Ches	188	Bb
Acton GL	100	Dd
Acton H & W	140	Cc
Acton Sflk	149	Ga
Acton Shrops	137	Fe
Acton Beauchamp	140	Ab
Acton Bridge	188	Ad
Acton Burnell	161	Hb
Acton Green	140	Ab
Acton Pigott	161	Hb
Acton Round	164	Aa
Acton Scott	137	Ge
Acton Trussell	164	Dc
Acton Turville	93	Fd
Adamhill	265	Ga
Adamstown	329	Pk
Adare	333	Lb
Adbaston	164	Bd
Adber	69	Hc
Adderbury	120	De
Adderley	164	Ae
Adderstone	273	Ha
Addiewell	268	Dd
Addingham	216	Cb
Addington Bucks	121	Gd
Addington GL	101	Eb
Addington Kent	101	Ha
Addlestone	100	Bb
Addlethorpe	197	Ec
Adel	217	Eb
Adeney	164	Bc
Aden Park	308	Ge
Adfa	160	Cb
Adforton	137	Gd
Adisham	105	Fa
Adlestrop	120	Bd
Adlingfleet	208	Be
Adlington Ches	189	Ee
Adlington Lancs	201	Fd
Admaston Shrops	164	Ac
Admaston Staffs	165	Ed
Admington	141	Fa
Adrigole	325	Kd
Adsborough	69	Ec
Adstock	121	Ge

472 Adstone–Ardfield

Adstone 144 Bb
Adversane 77 Gc
Advie 305 Kd
Adwell 97 Fe
Adwick le Street 205 Gc
Adwick upon Dearne 205 Fc
Ae 256 Ba
Affleck 308 Fc
Affpuddle 53 Ed
Afon-wen 185 Ed
Afton Bridgend 253 Gd
Agglethorpe 228 Da
Aghaboe 336 Df
Aghabullogue 325 Rf
Aghada 328 De
Aghadowey 349 Rh
Aghagallon 352 Ub
Aghagower 340 Ge
Aghalee 352 Ub
Aghamore *Leit* 341 Sf
Aghamore *Mayo* 341 Le
Aghavas 344 Bg
Aghern 328 Dh
Aghleam 340 Ci
Aghnacliff 344 Ce
Aghnamullen 344 Gh
Aglish 333 Rg
Aglish *Wat* 328 Gh
Ahakista 325 Kc
Ahascragh 333 Pk
Aherla 325 Se
Ahoghill 352 Tf
Aike 221 Eb
Aikerness 320 Dk
Aikers 320 De
Aiketgate 244 Db
Aikton 244 Bc
Ailey 137 Fa
Ailsa Craig 252 Ab
Ailsworth 169 Ha
Ainderby Quernhow 229 Ga
Ainderby Steeple 229 Gb
Aingers Green 129 Ed
Ainsdale 200 Cd
Ainsdale Dunes 200 Bd
Ainstable 245 Eb
Ainsworth 201 Gd
Ainthorpe 232 Cc
Aintree 200 Cb
Aird *A & B* 277 Fc
Aird *D & G* 237 Fd
Aird, The 300 Cf
Aird a Mhulaidh 317 Wn
Aird Asaig 317 Wm
Aird Mhighe 317 Wl
Aird of Sleat 300 Ea
Airdrie 268 Bd
Airdriehill 268 Bd
Airds Moss 253 Fe
Aird Uig 317 Vq
Airedale 216 Cb
Airidh a Bhruaich 317 Xn
Airieland 241 Ec
Airlie Castle 296 Bc
Airmyn 208 Ae
Airntully 293 La
Airor 301 Ga
Airth 284 Aa
Airton 216 Bc
Airyhassen 240 Ab
Aisby *Lincs* 169 Ge
Aisby *Lincs* 208 Bb
Aiskew 229 Fa
Aislaby *Clev* 229 Hd
Aislaby *N Yorks* 232 Ca
Aislaby *N Yorks* 232 Dc
Aisthorpe 193 Gd
Aith *Ork* 320 Bg
Aith *Ork* 320 Fh
Aith *Shet* 321 Le
Aith *Shet* 321 Pi
Aithsetter 321 Mc
Aitnoch 305 Hd
Akeld 260 De
Akeley 121 Ge
Akenham 152 Ba
A la Ronde 49 Ec
Albaston 45 Gb
Alberbury 161 Fc
Albourne 80 Ab
Albrighton *Shrops* 161 Gc
Albrighton *Shrops* 164 Cb
Alburgh 152 Ce
Albury *Herts* 125 Fd
Albury *Sry* 77 Ge
Alby Hill 176 Be
Alcaig 304 Df
Alcaston 137 Ge
Alcester 141 Eb
Alciston 61 Fe
Alconbury 145 Hd
Alconbury Weston 145 Hd
Aldborough *Nflk* 176 Be
Aldborough *N Yorks* 217 Gd
Aldbourne 96 Bc
Aldbrough 221 Ga
Aldbrough St John 229 Fd
Aldbury 124 Ac
Aldclune 293 Kd
Aldeburgh 153 Eb
Aldeby 177 Ea
Aldenham 100 Ce
Alderbury 73 Fc
Alderford 176 Bc
Aldergrove 352 Uc
Alderholt 73 Fb
Alderley 93 Ee
Alderley Edge 188 Dd
Alderman's Green 141 He
Aldermaston 97 Eb
Aldermaston Soke 97 Fb
Aldermaston Wharf 97 Fb
Alderminster 141 Ga
Aldersey Green 185 Hb
Aldershot 97 Ha
Alderton *Glos* 117 He
Alderton *Northants* 144 Da
Alderton *Sflk* 152 Da
Alderton *Shrops* 161 Gd
Alderton *Wilts* 93 Fd
Alderwasley 192 Ab
Aldfield 217 Ed
Aldford 185 Hb
Aldham *Esx* 128 Cd
Aldham *Sflk* 152 Aa
Aldingbourne 57 He
Aldingham 212 Ce
Aldington *H & W* 141 Ea
Aldington *Kent* 84 Ad
Aldington Frith 84 Ad
Aldochlay 280 Db
Aldreth 148 Cd
Aldridge 165 Eb
Aldringham 153 Ec
Aldsworth 120 Ab
Aldunie 308 Ac
Aldwark *Derbs* 189 Hb
Aldwark *N Yorks* 217 Gd
Aldwick 57 Hd
Aldwincle 145 Ge
Aldworth 97 Ec
Alexandria 265 Fe
Alfardisworthy 64 Cb
Alfington 49 Fd
Alfold 77 Gd
Alfold Crossways 77 Gd
Alford *Aber* 308 Cb
Alford *Lincs* 196 Dd
Alford *Som* 72 Ad
Alfreton 192 Bb
Alfrick 140 Bb
Alfriston 61 Fe
Algakirk 172 Ae
Alhampton 72 Ad
Alkborough 208 Be
Alkerton 141 Ha
Alkham 84 Ce
Alkington 161 He
Alkmonton 165 Fe
Alladale Lodge 312 Gb
Allaleigh 41 Ge
Allanaquoich 293 Mg
Allangrange Mains 304 Ef
Allanton *Bdrs* 273 Ec
Allanton *D & G* 256 Ba
Allanton *N Lan* 268 Cc
Allanton *S Lan* 268 Bc
Allardice 297 He
All Cannings 93 Hb
Allen 336 Hj
Allen Banks 245 Gd
Allendale Town 245 Hc
Allenheads 245 Hb
Allensford 248 Bc
Allen's Green 125 Fc
Allensmore 116 Be
Allenwood 336 Hj
Aller 69 Gc
Allerby 241 Ha
Allerford *Devon* 45 Gc
Allerford *Som* 68 Be
Allerston 232 Da
Allerthorpe 220 Bb
Allerton 185 Ge
Allerton Bywater 205 Fe
Allesley 141 Ge
Allestree 165 He
Allexton 169 Eb
Allgreave 189 Ec
Allhallows 104 Bc
Allhallows-on-Sea 104 Bc
Alligin Shuas 301 Hf
Allihies 324 Gc
Allimore Green 164 Cc
Allington *Lincs* 193 Fa
Allington *Wilts* 73 Gd
Allington *Wilts* 93 Fc
Allington *Wilts* 93 Hb
Allistragh 344 Jk
Allithwaite 212 De
Allnabad 312 Gh
Alloa 284 Ab
Allonby 241 Hb
Alloway 252 Dd
All Saints South Elmham 152 De
Allscot 164 Ba
All Stretton 161 Ga
Alltforgan 160 Bd
Alltmawr 136 Ca
Alltnacaillich 312 Gh
Allt-nan-sùgh 301 Jc
Alltwalis 109 He
Alltwen 112 Cb
Alltyblaca 133 Fa
Allweston 72 Ab
Almeley 137 Fb
Almer 53 Fd
Almington 164 Be
Alminstone Cross 64 Dc
Almondbank 284 Ce
Almondbury 204 Cd
Almondell 269 Ed
Almondsbury 92 Dd
Alne 217 Gd
Alness 304 Eg
Alnham 260 Dd
Alnmouth 261 Gd
Alnwick 261 Fd
Alphamstone 128 Be
Alpheton 149 Gb
Alphington 48 Dd
Alport 189 Hc
Alpraham 188 Ab
Alresford 128 Dd
Alrewas 165 Fc
Alsager 188 Cb
Alsagers Bank 188 Da
Alsop en le Dale 189 Gb
Alston 245 Gb
Alstone 117 Ge
Alstonefield 189 Gb
Alswear 65 Hc
Altandhu 312 Be
Altanduin 313 Lf
Altarnun 45 Ec
Altass 312 Hd
Alterwall 313 Qj
Altgaltraig 264 Ce
Altham 213 Ha
Althorne 104 Ce
Althorp 144 Cc
Althorpe 208 Bc
Alticry 237 Hb
Altnabreac Station 313 Nh
Altnafeadh 292 Cc
Altnaharra 312 Hg
Altnapaste 348 He
Altofts 205 Ee
Alton *Derbs* 192 Ac
Alton *Hants* 76 Dd
Alton *Staffs* 189 Fa
Alton Pancras 52 Ce
Alton Priors 96 Ab
Altrincham 188 Ce
Altrua 292 Cg
Alva 284 Ab
Alvanley 185 Hd
Alvaston 165 He
Alvechurch 141 Ed
Alvecote 165 Gb
Alvediston 73 Dc
Alveley 140 Be
Alverdiscott 65 Fc
Alverstoke 57 Ed
Alverstone 56 Dc
Alverton 193 Ea
Alvescot 120 Bb
Alveston *Avon* 92 Dd
Alveston *Warks* 141 Gb
Alvie 305 Ga
Alvingham 196 Cf
Alvington 116 Db
Alwalton 169 Ha
Alwinton 260 Dc
Alwoodley 217 Fb
Alyth 296 Bb
Amalebra 36 Cc
Amatnatua 312 Gc
Ambergate 192 Ab
Amber Hill 196 Ba
Amberley *Glos* 117 Fb
Amberley *W Ssx* 77 Gb
Amble-by-the-Sea 261 Gc
Amblecote 140 Ce
Ambleside 225 Ec
Ambleston 108 Dd
Ambrismore 264 Cc
Ambrosden 121 Fc
Amcotts 208 Bd
Amersham 100 Ae
Amesbury 73 Fe
Amington 165 Gb
Amisfield 256 Ca
Amlwch 181 Ff
Amlwch Port 181 Ff
Ammanford 112 Bc
Amotherby 220 Be
Ampfield 73 Hc
Ampleforth 217 He
Ampleforth College 217 He
Ampney Crucis 117 Hb
Ampney St Mary 117 Hb
Ampney St Peter 117 Hb
Amport 73 Ge
Ampthill 124 Be
Ampton 149 Gd
Amroth 109 Eb
Amulree 293 Ja
Anaheilt 289 Kd
Anancaun 301 Kg
An Ard 301 Hh
Anascaul 324 Gi
An Caol 300 Ff
Ancaster 193 Ga
An Cheathru Rua 332 Fj
Anchor 136 De
An Cnoc 317 Zq
Ancroft 273 Fb
Ancrum 260 Ae
Ancton 57 He
Anderby 197 Ed
Anderby Creek 197 Ed
Anderson 53 Ed
Anderton 188 Bd
Andover 73 He
Andover Down 73 He
Andoversford 117 Hc
Andreas 236 Dd
An Fhairche 340 Gb
Angarrack 36 Dc
Angersleigh 68 Db
Angerton 244 Bc
Angle 108 Bb
Anglesey Abbey 148 Dc
Angmering 60 Ae
Angram *N Yorks* 217 Hb
Angram *N Yorks* 228 Bb
Anie 281 Fd
Ankerville 313 La
Anlaby 208 De
An Lionán 340 Ec
Anlore 344 Fi
Anmer 173 Fd
Annacarty 333 Rb
Annaclone 345 Mk
Annacloy 345 Qk
Annacotty 333 Nc
Annacurragh 337 Me
Annadorn 345 Qk
Annagary 348 Eg
Annagassan 345 Lf
Annagh 341 Nd
Annahilt 352 Va
Annalong 345 Ph
Annamoe 337 Mg
Annan 244 Ad
Annaside 224 Ba
Annat *A & B* 277 Je
Annat *Hghld* 301 Hf
Annathill 268 Be
Anna Valley 73 He
Annayalla 344 Hi
Annbank 253 Ee
Anne's Grove 328 Bi
Annesley 192 Cb
Annesley Woodhouse 192 Bb
Annestown 329 Kh
Annfield 333 Sd
Annfield Plain 248 Cc
Annochie 308 Ge
Annsborough 345 Pj
Annscroft 161 Gb
Ansdell 200 Ce
Ansley 165 Ga
Anslow 165 Gd
Anslow Gate 165 Fd
An Spidéal 332 Hj
Anstey *Herts* 125 Fe
Anstey *Leics* 168 Bb
Anstruther 285 Hc
Ansty *Dors* 52 De
Ansty *Warks* 141 He
Ansty *Wilts* 73 Dc
Ansty *W Ssx* 80 Ac
An Teach Doite 340 Fa
Anthill Common 76 Cb
Anthorn 244 Ac
Antingham 176 Ce
An t-ob 317 Vk
Antony 40 Be
Antony House 40 Ce
Antrim 352 Ud
Antrobus 188 Bd
Anvil Corner 45 Fe
Anwick 196 Ab
Anwoth 240 Cc
Apes Hall 172 Da
Apethorpe 169 Ga
Apley 196 Ad
Apperknowle 192 Ad
Apperley 117 Fd
Appersett 228 Bb
Appin 289 Lb
Appin House 289 Lb
Appleby 208 Cd
Appleby-in-Westmorland 225 He
Appleby Magna 165 Hc
Appleby Parva 165 Hb
Applecross 301 Ge
Applecross House 301 Ge
Appledore *Devon* 65 Ed
Appledore *Devon* 68 Cb
Appledore *Kent* 81 Hc
Appleford 97 Ee
Appleshaw 73 He
Applethwaite 224 De
Appleton 120 Db
Appleton-le-Moors 232 Ca
Appleton-le-Street 220 Be
Appleton Park 188 Be
Appleton Roebuck 217 Hb
Appleton Thorn 188 Be
Appleton Wiske 229 Gc
Appletreehall 257 Hd
Appletreewick 216 Cd
Appley 68 Cc
Appley Bridge 201 Ec
Apse Heath 56 Dc
Apsley End 124 Ce
Apuldram 57 Ge
Aqualate Hall 164 Bc
Arabella 313 La
Araglin 328 Ei
Aran Islands 332 Eh
Arbeadie 296 Fg
Arbigland 241 Gc
Arbirlot 296 Fb
Arborfield 97 Gb
Arborfield Cross 97 Gb
Arborfield Garrison 97 Gb
Arbor Low 189 Gc
Arbroath 296 Fb
Arbury Hall 141 He
Arbuthnott 297 He
Archiestown 305 Le
Arclid Green 188 Cc
Ardachearanbeg 277 Ja
Ardachoil 289 Ja
Ardachu 313 Jd
Ardachuple 264 Ce
Ardagh *Lim* 333 Ja
Ardagh *Long* 344 Cc
Ardagh *Meath* 344 Jf
Ardalanish 276 Bd
Ardanaiseig 280 Ae
Ardaneaskan 301 Hd
Ardara 348 Ee
Ardargie House Hotel 284 Cd
Ardarroch 301 Hd
Ardattin 336 Jd
Ardbeg *A & B* 280 Ba
Ardbeg *A & B* 316 Fe
Ardcath 345 Lc
Ardcharnich 312 Db
Ardchattan Priory 289 La
Ardchiavaig 276 Bd
Ardchonnell 277 Hd
Ardchullarie More 281 Fd
Ardchyle 281 Fe
Ardcrony 333 Qf
Ard-dhubh 301 Ge
Arddleen 161 Ec
Ardechive 292 Bg
Ardee 345 Kf
Ardeley 125 Ed
Ardelve 301 Hc
Arden 280 Da
Ardens Grafton 141 Fb
Ardentallan House 277 Ge
Ardentinny 280 Ba
Ardeonaig 293 Ga
Ardersier 305 Ff
Ardery 289 Jd
Ardessie 312 Cb
Ardfern 277 Gc
Ardfert 325 Jk
Ardfield 325 Qb

474 Avon–Balminnoch

Avon 53 Hd
Avonbridge 268 De
Avon Castle 53 He
Avondale Park 337 Mf
Avon Dassett 144 Ab
Avon Gorge 92 Cc
Avonmouth 92 Cc
Avonwick 41 Fe
Awbridge 73 Hc
Awhirk 237 Fc
Awkley 92 Cd
Awliscombe 49 Fe
Awre 117 Eb
Awsworth 192 Ba
Axbridge 92 Ba
Axe Edge 189 Fd
Axford *Hants* 76 Ce
Axford *Wilts* 96 Bb
Axminster 49 Hd
Axmouth 49 Gd
Aydon 248 Bd
Aylburton 116 Db
Ayle 245 Gb
Aylesbeare 49 Ed
Aylesbury 121 Hc
Aylesby 209 Fc
Aylesford 104 Aa
Aylesham 105 Fa
Aylestone 168 Bb
Aylmerton 176 Be
Aylsham 176 Bd
Aylton 116 De
Aymestrey 137 Gc
Aynho 121 Ee
Ayot St Lawrence 124 Cc
Ayot St Peter 124 Dc
Ayr 252 De
Aysgarth 228 Da
Ayshford 68 Cb
Ayside 225 Ea
Ayston 169 Eb
Aythorpe Roding 125 Gc
Ayton *Bdrs* 273 Fd
Ayton *N Yorks* 233 Ea
Aywick 321 Nh
Azerley 217 Ee

B

Babbacombe 48 Da
Babbinswood 161 Fd
Babcary 69 Hc
Babel 112 De
Babell 185 Ed
Babeny 48 Ab
Babraham 148 Db
Babworth 192 De
Bac 317 Zr
Backaland 320 Ei
Backaskaill 320 Dk
Backbarrow 225 Ea
Backburn 297 Hg
Backfolds 309 Hf
Backford 185 Gd
Backhill of Trustach 296 Fg
Backies 313 Ld
Backlass 313 Qi
Backmuir of New Gilston 285 Gc
Back of Keppoch 289 Hf
Backwell 92 Bb
Backworth 248 De
Bacon End 125 Hc
Baconsthorpe 176 Be
Baconstown 344 Ha
Bacton *H & W* 116 Ae
Bacton *Nflk* 176 De
Bacton *Sflk* 152 Ac
Bacup 201 He
Badachro 301 Gh
Badanloch Lodge 313 Kg
Badavanich 301 Lf
Badbury 96 Ad
Badbury Rings 53 Fe
Badby 144 Bb
Badcall *Hghld* 312 Dh
Badcall *Hghld* 312 Ei
Badcaul 312 Cc
Baddeley Green 189 Eb
Baddesley Clinton 141 Gd
Baddesley Ensor 165 Ga
Baddidarach 312 Cf
Baddoch 293 Mf
Badenoch 293 Hg
Badenscoth 308 Ed
Badenyon 305 Mb
Badger 164 Ba
Badgers Mount 101 Gb
Badgeworth 117 Gc
Badgworth 92 Aa
Badgworthy Water 65 He
Badicaul 301 Gc
Badingham 152 Dc
Badlesmere 104 Da
Badlipster 313 Qh
Badluarach 312 Bc
Badminton 93 Fd
Badninish 313 Kc
Badrallach 312 Cc
Badsey 141 Ea
Badshot Lea 77 Ee
Badsworth 205 Fd
Badwell Ash 149 Hc
Badyo 293 Kd
Bagby 229 Ha
Bage, The 137 Ea
Bagenalstown 336 Hd
Bag Enderby 196 Cd
Bagendon 117 Hb
Baggrave Hall 168 Cb
Baggrow 244 Ab
Bagillt 185 Fd
Baginton 141 Hd
Baglan 88 Ce
Bagley 161 Gd
Bagmore 76 Ce
Bagnall 189 Eb
Bagnor 96 Db
Bagshot *Sry* 100 Ab
Bagshot *Wilts* 96 Cb
Bagstone 92 Dd
Bagthorpe *Nflk* 173 Fe
Bagthorpe *Notts* 192 Bb
Bagworth 168 Ab
Bagwyllydiart 116 Bd
Baildon 216 Da
Baile Ailein 317 Xp
Baile an Truiseil 317 Ys
Baile Atha Cliath 337 Mk
Bailebeag 304 Db
Baile Chláir 333 Kk
Baile Mór 276 Ae
Bailey Head 245 Ee
Baileysmill 352 Wa
Bailieborough 344 Gf
Baillieston 268 Ad
Bailliesward 308 Bd
Bail' Ur Tholastaidh 317 Ar
Bainbridge 228 Cb
Bainton *Cambs* 169 Gb
Bainton *Humb* 220 Dc
Bairnkine 260 Ad
Bakers End 125 Ec
Baker Street 101 Hd
Bakewell 189 Hc
Bala 160 Be
Balachairn 300 Ee
Balaglas 317 Th
Balbeg 304 Cc
Balbeggie 284 De
Balbithan 308 Eb
Balblair 304 Fg
Balbriggan 345 Nc
Balcary Point 241 Fb
Balcherry 313 Lb
Balchladich 312 Cg
Balchraggan 304 De
Balchrick 312 Dj
Balcombe 80 Bd
Balcomie 285 Jc
Balcurvie 285 Fc
Baldersby 217 Fe
Balderstone 213 Ga
Balderton 193 Fb
Baldhu 36 Fd
Baldinnie 285 Gd
Baldock 124 De
Baldovie 296 Da
Baldrine 236 Dc
Baldslow 81 Gb
Baldwin 236 Cc
Baldwinholme 244 Cc
Baldwin's Gate 164 Be
Bale 176 Ae
Balemartine 288 Ab
Balephuil 288 Ab
Balerno 269 Fd
Balevulin 276 Ce
Balevullin 288 Ab
Balfield 296 Ed
Balfron 281 Fa
Balgaveny 308 De
Balgavies 296 Ec
Balgedie 284 Dc
Balgonar 284 Cb
Balgove 308 Fd
Balgowan 293 Gg
Balgown 300 Cg
Balgrochan 265 Je
Balgy 301 Hf
Balhaldie 281 Jc
Balhary 296 Bb
Balhelvie 285 Fe
Baligill 313 Lj
Baligrundle 289 Kb
Balintore *Angus* 296 Bc
Balintore *Hghld* 313 La
Balintraid 313 Ka
Balivanich 317 Sh
Balkeerie 296 Cb
Balkholme 208 Ae
Balkissock 252 Ba
Ball 161 Fd
Balla 341 Je
Ballabeg 236 Bb
Ballacannell 236 Dc
Ballacarnane Beg 236 Cc
Ballachulish 292 Ac
Balladoole 236 Ba
Ballagh *Lim* 325 Pk
Ballagh *Rosc* 341 Rb
Ballagh *Rosc* 341 Rd
Ballagh *Tipp* 333 Sb
Ballaghaderreen 341 Nf
Ballaghkeen 337 La
Ballagyr 236 Bc
Ballajora 236 Dd
Ballakilpheric 236 Bb
Ballamodha 236 Bb
Ballantrae 252 Aa
Ballasalla *IOM* 236 Bb
Ballasalla *IOM* 236 Cd
Ballater 296 Cg
Ballaugh 236 Cd
Ballechin 293 Kc
Balleen 336 Dd
Balleigh 313 Kb
Ballencrieff 272 Ae
Ball Haye Green 189 Eb
Ball Hill 96 Db
Balliasta 321 Pj
Ballickmoyler 336 Gf
Ballidon 189 Hb
Balliekine 264 Aa
Balliemore *A & B* 277 Ge
Balliemore *A & B* 280 Aa
Ballig 236 Bc
Balliggan 352 Zb
Ballikinrain Castle 281 Fa
Ballimeanoch 277 Jd
Ballimore *A & B* 277 Ha
Ballimore *Stir* 281 Fd
Ballina *Mayo* 341 Jh
Ballina *Tipp* 333 Pe
Ballinabrackey 344 Fa
Ballinabranagh 336 Ge
Ballinaby 316 Dg
Ballinaclash 337 Mf
Ballinadee 328 Ad
Ballinafad 341 Pg
Ballinagar 336 Ej
Ballinagleragh 341 Ri
Ballinakill 336 Ef
Ballinalack 344 Dc
Ballinalee 344 Ce
Ballinamallard 349 Ka
Ballinameen 341 Qf
Ballinamore 344 Bh
Ballinascarty 325 Rc
Ballinasloe 333 Qk
Ballinclashet 328 Bd
Ballincollig 328 Af
Ballincrea 329 Mj
Ballindaggan 336 Jb
Ballindean 285 Ee
Ballinderreen 333 Ki
Ballinderry 333 Qg
Ballindine 341 Kc
Ballindrait 349 Le
Ballineen 325 Qd
Ballingarrane 333 Kb
Ballingarry *Lim* 333 La
Ballingarry *Tipp* 333 Rg
Ballingarry *Tipp* 336 Db
Ballingdon 149 Ga
Ballingeary 325 Ne
Ballinger Common 124 Ab
Ballingham 116 Ce
Ballingry 284 Db
Ballingurteen 325 Pc
Ballinhassig 328 Be
Ballinkillin 336 Hc
Ballinleeny 333 La
Ballinlick 293 Kb
Ballinlough *Meath* 344 Gd
Ballinlough *Rosc* 341 Md
Ballinluig 293 Kc
Ballinmuck 344 Bf
Ballinrobe 340 Hc
Ballinskelligs 324 Fe
Ballinspittle 328 Ac
Ballintober *Rosc* 341 Pd
Ballintober Abbey *Mayo* 340 Hd
Ballintober Castle *Rosc* 341 Pd
Ballintogher 341 Pi
Ballintra 348 Gb
Ballintubbert 336 Gg
Ballintuim 293 Mc
Ballinunty 336 Cb
Ballinure 336 Bb
Ballitore 336 Hg
Ballivor 344 Gb
Balloch *Angus* 296 Cc
Balloch *D & C* 280 Da
Balloch *S Ayr* 252 Db
Balloch, The 281 Jd
Ballochan 296 Eg
Balloch Castle 280 Da
Ballochford 308 Ad
Ballochmorrie 252 Ca
Ballochyle 280 Ba
Ballogie 296 Eg
Ballon 336 Jd
Balloo 352 Yb
Balls Cross 77 Fc
Ballsmill 345 Kh
Ballure 348 Fb
Ballyagran 325 Rk
Ballyarnet 349 Mh
Ballybay 344 Hi
Ballybeg 328 Gj
Ballyboden 337 Mj
Ballybofey 349 Je
Ballyboghil 345 Mb
Ballybogy 349 Si
Ballybornia 344 Ba
Ballyboy 336 Ci
Ballybrittas 336 Fh
Ballybrood 333 Nb
Ballybrophy 336 Cf
Ballybunnion 332 Eb
Ballycahill 336 Ad
Ballycallar 336 Ec
Ballycanew 337 Mc
Ballycarney 337 Kb
Ballycarra 340 He
Ballycarry 352 Xe
Ballycastle *Ant* 352 Uj
Ballycastle *Mayo* 340 Hj
Ballyclare 352 Ve
Ballyclerahan 328 Gk
Ballyclogh 325 Ri
Ballycolla 336 Df
Ballyconneely 340 Ca
Ballyconnell 344 Ch
Ballycotton 328 Ee
Ballycrossaun 333 Qj
Ballycroy 340 Eh
Ballycumber 336 Ck
Ballycurrane 328 Gg
Ballydangan 333 Rk
Ballydavid *Gal* 333 Ni
Ballydavid *Kerry* 324 Ei
Ballydehob 325 Lb
Ballydesmond 325 Ni
Ballydonegan 324 Gc
Ballydrenid 341 Nj
Ballyduff *Kerry* 332 Ea
Ballyduff *Wat* 328 Eh
Ballyduff *Wat* 329 Li
Ballyeaston 352 Ve
Ballyfarnan 341 Qh
Ballyferriter 324 Ei
Ballyfin 336 Dh
Ballyforan 341 Qa
Ballyfore 336 Fk
Bally Foyle 336 Fd
Ballygalley 352 Wf
Ballygar 341 Pb
Ballygarrett 337 Mb
Ballygarvan 328 Be
Ballygawley *Sligo* 341 Pi
Ballygawley *Tyr* 349 Pa
Ballyglass 341 Jd
Ballygorey 329 Lj
Ballygowan 352 Xb
Ballygown 288 Fb
Ballygrady 325 Ri
Ballygrant 316 Eg
Ballygub 336 Ga
Ballyhaght 328 Ak
Ballyhahill 332 Hb
Ballyhaise 344 Eh
Ballyhalbert 352 Zb
Ballyhale 336 Fa
Ballyhar 325 Lh
Ballyhaugh 288 Cc
Ballyhaunis 341 Md
Ballyhean 340 He
Ballyheelan 344 Ee
Ballyheige 325 Jk
Ballyhooly 328 Ch
Ballyjamesduff 344 Ff
Ballykeel 352 Va
Ballykeeran 344 Aa
Ballykelly 349 Ph
Ballyknockan 337 Li
Ballylanders 328 Ck
Ballylaneen 329 Ki
Ballyleny 345 Kk
Ballylesson 352 Wb
Ballyliffin 349 Lj
Ballyline 336 Db
Ballylintagh 349 Rh
Ballylongford 332 Gb
Ballylooby 328 Fj
Ballylynan 336 Gf
Ballymacarbry 328 Gj
Ballymacaw 328 Mh
Ballymachugh 344 Ee
Ballymackey 333 Rf
Ballymacoda 328 Ff
Ballymacurly 341 Qd
Ballymacward 333 Nk
Ballymagan 349 Li
Ballymagaraghy 349 Pj
Ballymagorry 349 Lf
Ballymahon 344 Bb
Ballymakeery 325 Pf
Ballymakenny 345 Le
Ballymartin 345 Ph
Ballymartle 328 Bd
Ballymeanoch 277 Gb
Ballymena 352 Uf
Ballymichael 264 Ba
Ballymoe 341 Nd
Ballymoney 352 Sh
Ballymore *Dngl* 348 Hi
Ballymore *Wmth* 344 Ca
Ballymore Eustace 337 Ki
Ballymorris 329 Li
Ballymote 341 Nh
Ballymount 336 Jh
Ballymurphy 336 Hb
Ballymurray 341 Rc
Ballynabola 329 Nk
Ballynacally 333 Jd
Ballynacarriga 325 Pd
Ballynacarrigy 344 Db
Ballynacarrow 341 Ni
Ballynacorra 328 Df
Ballynacourty 328 Jh
Ballynacree 344 Fe
Ballynadrummy 344 Ga
Ballynafid 344 Ec
Ballynagaul 328 Jg
Ballynagore 336 Dk
Ballynagree 325 Qg
Ballynaguilkee 328 Gi
Ballynahinch *Down* 352 Wa
Ballynahinch *Tipp* 333 Pd
Ballynahow 324 Ee
Ballynahown 336 Bk
Ballynakill 344 Aa
Ballynamallaght 349 Me
Ballynamona 328 Ah
Ballynamult 328 Gi
Ballynana 324 Fi
Ballynarry 344 Ee
Ballynaskreena 332 Ea
Ballyneety 333 Nb
Ballyneill 328 Jk
Ballynoe 328 Eg
Ballynure 352 We
Ballyorgan 328 Bj
Ballyoughter 337 Mc
Ballypatrick 328 Jk
Ballyphilip 328 Fg
Ballyporeen 328 Ej
Ballyquin 329 Kj
Ballyragget 336 Ee
Ballyrashane 349 Ri
Ballyreagh 349 Pa
Ballyroan 336 Ef
Ballyroebuck 337 Kc
Ballyronan 349 Sd
Ballyroney 345 Nj
Ballysadare 341 Ni
Ballyshannon 348 Fb
Ballysloe 336 Cc
Ballysteen 333 Kc
Ballyvaghan 333 Jh
Ballyvoge 325 Pf
Ballyvourney 325 Pf
Ballyvoy 352 Uj
Ballywalter 352 Zb
Ballyward 345 Nj
Balmacara 301 Hc
Balmacara Square 301 Hc
Balmaclellan 240 De
Balmacneil 293 Kc
Balmacqueen 300 Dh
Balmae 240 Db
Balmaha 280 Eb
Balmalcolm 285 Fc
Balmartin 317 Sj
Balmeanach *A & B* 289 Hb
Balmeanach *Hghld* 300 Ee
Balmedie 308 Gb
Balmerino 285 Fe
Balmerlawn 56 Be
Balminnoch 237 Hd

Balmoral Castle–Beeley 475

Balmoral Castle 296 Bg
Balmore *E Dun* 265 Je
Balmore *P & K* 293 Hc
Balmullo 285 Ge
Balmungie 304 Ff
Balmurrie 237 Hd
Balnaboth 296 Cd
Balnacoil 313 Le
Balnacra 301 Je
Balnafoich 304 Ed
Balnaglaic 304 Cd
Balnagown Castle 313 Ka
Balnaguard 293 Kc
Balnaguisich 313 Ja
Balnahard *A & B* 276 Cb
Balnahard *A & B* 288 Fa
Balnain 304 Cd
Balnakeil 312 Fj
Balnaknock 300 Dg
Balnamoon 296 Ed
Balnamore 349 Sh
Balnapaling 305 Fg
Balne 205 Gd
Balnespick 305 Ga
Balquhidder 281 Fe
Balrath 345 Lc
Balrothery 345 Nc
Balsall 141 Gd
Balsall Common 141 Gd
Balscaddan 345 Mc
Balscote 141 Ha
Balsham 148 Db
Baltasound 321 Pj
Balterley 188 Cb
Baltersan 240 Bd
Balthangie 308 Ff
Balthayock 284 De
Baltimore 325 Ma
Baltinglass 336 Jf
Baltonsborough 69 Hd
Baltray 345 Md
Baluachraig 277 Gb
Balvaird 304 Df
Balvarran 293 Ld
Balvicar 277 Fd
Balvraid 305 Gd
Bamber Bridge 201 Ee
Bamber's Green 125 Gd
Bamburgh 273 Ha
Bamff 296 Bc
Bamford 189 He
Bampton *Cumb* 225 Gd
Bampton *Devon* 68 Bc
Bampton *Oxon* 120 Cb
Banada 341 Lh
Banagher 333 Si
Banavie 292 Be
Banbridge 345 Mk
Banbury 120 Df
Bancffosfelen 109 Hc
Banchory 296 Fg
Bancyfelin 109 Gc
Bancyfford 109 He
Bandirran House 296 Aa
Bandon 325 Rd
Banff 308 Dg
Bangor *Down* 352 Yd
Bangor *C & M* 181 Gd
Bangor *Mayo* 340 Ei
Bangor-is-y-coed 185 Ga
Banham 152 Ae
Bank 56 Ae
Bankend *D & G* 241 Hd
Bankend *S Lan* 268 Ca
Bankfoot 293 La
Bankglen 253 Fd
Bankhead *Aber* 308 Da
Bankhead *Aber* 308 Db
Bankhead *C of Aber* 308 Fb
Bankhead *S Lan* 268 Cb
Bank Newton 216 Bc
Banknock 268 Be
Banks *Cumb* 245 Ed
Banks *Lancs* 200 Ce
Bankshill 256 Da
Bank Street 140 Ac
Banna 325 Jk
Bannfoot 352 Sb
Banningham 176 Cd
Bannister Green 125 Hd
Bannockburn 281 Jb
Bansha 333 Ra
Banstead 100 Da
Banteer 325 Qh
Bantham 41 Ed
Banton 268 Be
Bantry 325 Mc
Banwell 92 Aa
Bapchild 104 Cb
Bapton 73 Dd
Barabhas 317 Yr
Barachander 277 Je
Baramore 289 He
Baranailt 349 Pg
Barassie 265 Fa
Barbaraville 313 Ka
Barber Booth 189 Ge
Barbon 225 Ha
Barbridge 188 Bb
Barbrook 65 He
Barby 144 Bd
Barcaldine 289 Lb
Barcaple 240 Dc
Barcheston 120 Be
Barclose 244 Dd
Barcloy 241 Ec
Barcombe 80 Cb
Barcombe Cross 80 Cb
Barden 229 Eb
Bardennoch 253 Fb
Bardfield End Green 125 He
Bardfield Saling 125 Hd
Bardister 321 Lg
Bardney 196 Ac
Bardon 168 Ac
Bardon Mill 245 Gd
Bardowie 265 He
Bardrainney 265 Fe
Bardsea 212 De
Bardsea Country Park 212 Ce
Bardsey 217 Fb
Bardsey Island 156 Bd
Bardsley 204 Ac
Bardwell 149 Hd
Barefield 333 Kf
Barewood 137 Fb
Barford *Nflk* 176 Bb
Barford *Warks* 141 Gc
Barford St John 120 De
Barford St Martin 73 Ed
Barford St Michael 120 De
Barfrestone 84 Cf
Bargate 192 Aa
Bargoed 89 Ge
Bargrennan 240 Ae
Barham *Cambs* 145 Hd
Barham *Kent* 105 Fa
Barham *Sflk* 152 Bb
Barharrow 240 Dc
Bar Hill 148 Bc
Barholm 169 Gc
Barkby 168 Cb
Barkby Thorpe 168 Cb
Barkestone-le-Vale 168 De
Barkham 97 Gb
Barking *Sflk* 152 Ab
Barking and Dagenham 101 Fd
Barkingside 101 Fd
Barkisland 204 Bd
Barkston 193 Ga
Barkston Ash 217 Ga
Barkway 125 Ee
Barlae 237 Hd
Barlaston 164 Ce
Barlavington 77 Fb
Barlborough 192 Bd
Barlby 220 Aa
Barlestone 168 Ab
Barley *Herts* 125 Ee
Barley *Lancs* 216 Ab
Barleycroft End 125 Fd
Barleyhill 248 Bc
Barleythorpe 169 Eb
Barling 104 Cd
Barlow *Derbs* 192 Ad
Barlow *N Yorks* 205 He
Barlow *T & W* 248 Cd
Barmby Moor 220 Bb
Barmby on the Marsh 205 He
Barmer 173 Ge
Barmoor Castle 273 Fa
Barmoor Lane End 273 Ga
Barmouth 157 Gc
Barmpton 229 Gd
Barmston 221 Fc
Barna *Gal* 333 Jj
Barna *Lim* 333 Pb
Barna *Ofly* 333 Sf
Barnacarry 277 Jb
Barnack 169 Gb
Barnacle 141 He
Barnaderg 341 Ma
Barnalisheen 336 Bd
Barnalyra 341 Lf
Barnard Castle 228 Dd
Barnard Gate 120 Dc
Barnardiston 149 Fa
Barnatra 340 Eg
Barnbarroch *D & G* 241 Fc
Barnburgh 205 Fc
Barnby 153 Ee
Barnby Dun 205 Hc
Barnby in the Willows 193 Fb
Barnby Moor 192 De
Barndennoch 256 Aa
Barnes 100 Dc
Barnet 100 De
Barnetby le Wold 208 Dc
Barney 173 He
Barnham *Sflk* 149 Gd
Barnham *W Ssx* 57 He
Barnham Broom 176 Ab
Barnhead 296 Fc
Barnhill *Moray* 305 Kf
Barnhill *Northld* 261 Ea
Barnhills 237 Ee
Barningham *Dur* 228 Dd
Barningham *Sflk* 149 Hd
Barnmeen 345 Mj
Barnoldby le Beck 209 Fc
Barnoldswick 216 Ab
Barns Green 77 Hc
Barnsley *Glos* 117 Hb
Barnsley *S Yorks* 205 Ec
Barnstaple 65 Fd
Barnston *Esx* 125 Hc
Barnston *Mers* 185 Fe
Barnstone 168 De
Barnt Green 141 Ed
Barnton 188 Bd
Barnwell 145 Ge
Barnwood 117 Fc
Barochreal 277 Ge
Barony, The 320 Bh
Barr 252 Cb
Barra 317 Rc
Barra Castle 308 Ec
Barrachan 240 Ab
Barrack Village 336 Ed
Barraduff 325 Mh
Barraer 240 Ad
Barras *Aber* 297 Hf
Barras *Cumb* 228 Bd
Barrasford 248 Ae
Barravullin 277 Fc
Barregarrow 236 Cc
Barr Hall 128 Ae
Barrhead 265 Hc
Barrhill 252 Ca
Barrigone 333 Jc
Barrington *Cambs* 148 Ba
Barrington *Som* 69 Fb
Barripper 36 Ec
Barrmill 265 Fc
Barrock 313 Qk
Barrow *Kerry* 325 Jj
Barrow *Lancs* 213 Ha
Barrow *Leics* 169 Ec
Barrow *Sflk* 149 Fc
Barrow *Shrops* 164 Ab
Barrowby 169 Ee
Barrowden 169 Fb
Barrowford 216 Aa
Barrow Gurney 92 Cb
Barrow Haven 208 De
Barrow-in-Furness 212 Bd
Barrow Nook 200 Dc
Barrow Street 72 Cd
Barrow upon Humber 208 De
Barrow upon Soar 168 Bc
Barrow upon Trent 165 Hd
Barry *Angus* 296 Ea
Barry *Long* 344 Bc
Barry *V of G* 89 Gb
Barry Island 89 Gb
Barry Links Station 296 Ea
Barryroe 325 Rb
Barsby 168 Cc
Barsham 152 De
Barston 141 Gd
Bartestree 137 Ha
Barthol Chapel 308 Fd
Barthomley 188 Cb
Bartley 73 Hb
Bartlow 148 Da
Barton *Cambs* 148 Cb
Barton *Ches* 185 Hb
Barton *Devon* 48 Da
Barton *Glos* 117 Hd
Barton *Lancs* 200 Cc
Barton *Lancs* 213 Fa
Barton *N Yorks* 229 Fc
Barton *Warks* 141 Fb
Barton Bendish 173 Fb
Barton End 93 Fe
Barton Hartshorn 121 Fe
Barton in Fabis 168 Be
Barton in the Beans 165 Hb
Barton-le-Clay 124 Be
Barton-le-Street 220 Be
Barton-le-Willows 220 Bd
Barton Mills 149 Fd
Barton on Sea 56 Ad
Barton-on-the-Heath 120 Be
Barton St David 69 Hd
Barton Seagrave 145 Ed
Barton Stacey 76 Ae
Barton Turf 176 Dd
Barton-under-Needwood 165 Fc
Barton-upon-Humber 208 De
Barway 148 Dd
Barwell 168 Aa
Barwhillanty 241 Ee
Barwick 69 Hb
Barwick in Elmet 217 Fa
Baschurch 161 Gd
Bascote 144 Ac
Basford Green 189 Eb
Bashall Eaves 213 Gb
Bashall Town 213 Hb
Bashley 56 Ad
Basildon *Berks* 97 Fc
Basildon *Esx* 104 Ad
Basingstoke 97 Fa
Baslow 189 Hd
Bason Bridge 69 Fe
Bassenthwaite 244 Ba
Bassett 76 Ab
Bassingbourn 148 Ba
Bassingfield 168 Ce
Bassingham 193 Gb
Bassingthorpe 169 Fd
Bass Rock 272 Cf
Basta 321 Ni
Baston 169 Hc
Bastwick 177 Ec
Batchcott 137 Gd
Batchworth 100 Be
Batchworth Heath 100 Be
Batcombe *Dors* 52 Ce
Batcombe *Som* 72 Ad
Bate Heath 188 Bd
Bateman's 81 Ec
Bath 93 Eb
Bathampton 93 Eb
Bathealton 68 Cc
Batheaston 93 Eb
Bathford 93 Eb
Bathgate 268 Dd
Bathley 193 Eb
Bathpool *Corn* 45 Eb
Bathpool *Som* 69 Ec
Batley 204 De
Batsford 120 Ae
Battersby 232 Ac
Battersea 100 Dc
Batterstown 345 Ka
Battisborough Cross 40 Dd
Battisford 152 Ab
Battisford Tye 152 Ab
Battle *E Ssx* 81 Fb
Battle *Pwys* 113 Fe
Battlefield 161 Hc
Battlehill 244 Bd
Battlesbridge 104 Ae
Battlesden 124 Ad
Battleton 68 Bc
Battramsley 56 Bd
Batt's Corner 77 Ee
Bauds of Cullen 308 Bg
Baughton 140 Ca
Baughurst 97 Ea
Baulking 96 Ce
Baumber 196 Bd
Baunton 117 Hb
Baveney Wood 140 Ad
Baverstock 73 Ed
Bawburgh 176 Bb
Bawdeswell 176 Ad
Bawdrip 69 Fd
Bawdsey 152 Da
Bawnboy 344 Ch
Bawtry 205 Hb
Baxenden 201 Ge
Baxterley 165 Ga
Bay 300 Bf
Baycliff 212 Ce
Baydon 96 Bc
Bayford *Herts* 125 Eb
Bayford *Som* 72 Bc
Bayhead 317 Si
Bayles 245 Gb
Baylham 152 Bb
Baynard's Green 121 Ed
Baysham 116 Cd
Bayston Hill 161 Gb
Baythorn End 149 Fa
Bayton 140 Ad
Beachampton 121 Ge
Beachborough 84 Bd
Beachley 92 Ce
Beachy Head 61 Fd
Beacon 49 Fe
Beacon End 128 Cd
Beacon Fell 213 Fb
Beacon's Bottom 97 Ge
Beaconsfield 100 Ae
Beacontree 101 Fd
Beadlam 232 Ba
Beadnell 261 Ge
Beaford 65 Fb
Beal *Northld* 273 Gb
Beal *N Yorks* 205 Ge
Bealach Ratagain 301 Hb
Bealaclugga 333 Jh
Bealaha 332 Fd
Béal an Mhuirthead 340 Dj
Bealin 336 Bl
Bealnablath 325 Re
Beamhurst 165 Ee
Beaminster 52 Ae
Beamish 248 Dc
Beamsley 216 Cc
Bean 101 Gc
Beanacre 93 Gb
Beanley 261 Ed
Beara peninsula 324 Hd
Beare Green 77 He
Bearley 141 Fc
Bearna 333 Jj
Bearpark 248 Db
Bearsbridge 245 Gc
Bearsden 265 He
Bearsted 104 Ba
Bearwood 53 Gd
Beattock 256 Cc
Beauchamp Roding 125 Gb
Beauchief 192 Ae
Beaufort *BG* 113 Gc
Beaufort *Kerry* 325 Kh
Beaulieu 56 Be
Beaulieu Abbey 56 Be
Beauly 304 De
Beaumaris 181 Hd
Beaumont *Cumb* 244 Cc
Beaumont *Esx* 129 Ed
Beausale 141 Gd
Beauworth 76 Bc
Beaworthy 45 Gd
Beazley End 128 Ad
Bebington 185 Ge
Bebside 261 Ga
Beccles 153 Ef
Becconsall 200 De
Beckbury 164 Bb
Beckenham 101 Eb
Beckermet 224 Bc
Beckermonds 228 Ba
Beck Foot 225 Hb
Beckfoot *Cumb* 224 Cc
Beckfoot *Cumb* 241 Hb
Beckford 117 Ge
Beckhampton 93 Hb
Beck Hole 232 Dc
Beckingham *Lincs* 193 Fb
Beckingham *Notts* 208 Ab
Beckington 93 Fa
Beckley *E Ssx* 81 Gc
Beckley *Oxon* 121 Ec
Beck Row 149 Ed
Beck Side 224 Da
Beckton 101 Fd
Beckwithshaw 217 Ec
Bective 344 Jb
Bective Abbey 344 Jc
Bedale 229 Fa
Bedburn 248 Ca
Bedchester 72 Cb
Beddau 89 Fd
Beddgelert 181 Ga
Beddingham 61 Ee
Beddington 101 Eb
Bedfield 152 Cc
Bedford 145 Ga
Bedhampton 57 Ee
Bedingfield 152 Bc
Bedlington 261 Ga
Bedlinog 113 Fb
Bedmond 124 Bb
Bednall 164 Dc
Bedrule 260 Ad
Bedruthan Steps 44 Aa
Bedstone 137 Fd
Bedwas 89 Gd
Bedworth 141 He
Beeby 168 Cb
Beech *Hants* 76 Cd
Beech *Staffs* 164 Ce
Beechamwell 173 Fb
Beech Hill 97 Fb
Beechingstoke 93 Ha
Beecraigs 268 De
Beedon 96 Dc
Beeford 221 Fc
Beeley 189 Hc

Brims–Burgh St Margaret 479

Brims 320 Bd
Brims Ness 320 Bd
Brimstage 185 Ge
Brinacory 289 Jg
Brind 220 Ba
Brindister *Shet* 321 Ke
Brindister *Shet* 321 Mc
Brindle 201 Ee
Brindley Ford 188 Db
Brineton 164 Cc
Bringhurst 169 Ea
Brington 145 Gd
Briningham 176 Ae
Brinkburn Priory 261 Fb
Brinkhill 196 Cd
Brinkley 149 Eb
Brinklow 144 Ad
Brinkworth 93 Hd
Brinscall 201 Fe
Brinsley 192 Ba
Brinsop 137 Ga
Brinsworth 205 Fb
Brinton 176 Ae
Brisco 244 Dc
Briska 328 Ji
Brisley 173 Hd
Brislington 92 Dc
Bristol 92 Cc
Briston 176 Ae
Britannia 201 He
Britford 73 Fc
Briton Ferry 88 Ce
Brittas 337 Lj
Britway 328 Dg
Britwell Salome 97 Fe
Brixham 41 He
Brixton *Devon* 40 De
Brixton *GL* 101 Ec
Brixton Deverill 72 Cd
Brixworth 144 Dd
Brize Norton 120 Bb
Broad Blunsdon 96 Ae
Broadbottom 204 Ab
Broadbridge 57 Ge
Broadbridge Heath 77 Hd
Broad Campden 120 Ae
Broad Chalke 73 Ec
Broadclyst 48 Dd
Broadford *Clare* 333 Me
Broadford *Hghld* 300 Fc
Broadford *Lim* 325 Qk
Broadford Bridge 77 Gc
Broad Green *Beds* 145 Fa
Broad Green *Cambs* 149 Eb
Broad Green *Esx* 128 Bd
Broad Green *H & W* 140 Bb
Broadhaugh 257 Gc
Broad Haven 108 Bc
Broadheath *GM* 188 Ce
Broadheath *H & W* 140 Ac
Broadheath *H & W* 140 Cb
Broadhembury 49 Fe
Broadhempston 48 Ca
Broad Hill 148 Dd
Broad Hinton 96 Ac
Broadholme 193 Fd
Broadland Row 81 Gb
Broadlands 73 Hc
Broadlay 109 Gb
Broad Laying 96 Db
Broadley *GM* 201 Hd
Broadley *Moray* 308 Bg
Broadley Common 125 Fb
Broad Marston 141 Fb
Broadmayne 52 Dc
Broadmeadows 269 Ja
Broadmere 76 Ce
Broadnymett 48 Be
Broadoak *Dors* 52 Ad
Broadoak *E Ssx* 81 Ec
Broadoak *Kent* 105 Eb
Broad Oak *Carm* 112 Ad
Broad Oak *Cumb* 224 Cb
Broad Oak *E Ssx* 81 Gc
Broad Oak *H & W* 116 Bd
Broadstairs 105 Gb
Broadstone *Dors* 53 Gd
Broadstone *Shrops* 137 He
Broad Street 104 Ba
Broadstreet Common 92 Ad
Broad Street Green 128 Bb
Broad Town 93 Hc
Broadwas 140 Bb
Broadwater 60 Be
Broadway *Carm* 109 Fc
Broadway *Carm* 109 Gb
Broadway *H & W* 117 He
Broadway *Sflk* 152 Dd
Broadway *Som* 69 Fb
Broadway *Wex* 329 Si
Broadwell *Glos* 116 Cc
Broadwell *Glos* 120 Bd
Broadwell *Oxon* 120 Bb
Broadwell *Warks* 144 Ac
Broadwell House 248 Ac
Broadwey 52 Cc
Broadwindsor 52 Ae
Broadwood-Kelly 48 Ae
Broadwoodwidger 45 Gc
Brobury 137 Fa
Brochel 300 Ee
Brochloch 253 Fb
Brockbridge 76 Cb
Brockdish 152 Cd
Brockenhurst 56 Be
Brocketsbrae 268 Ca
Brockford Street 152 Bc
Brockhall 144 Cc
Brockham 80 Ae
Brockhampton *Glos* 117 Hd
Brockhampton *H & W* 116 Ce
Brockhole 225 Ec
Brockholes 204 Cd
Brockhurst 80 Cd
Brocklesby 209 Ed
Brockley 92 Bb
Brockley Green 149 Gb
Brock of Gurness 320 Ch
Brockton *Shrops* 137 Fe
Brockton *Shrops* 161 Fb
Brockton *Shrops* 161 Ha
Brockton *Shrops* 164 Bb
Brockweir 116 Cb
Brockwood Park 76 Cc
Brockworth 117 Fc
Brocton 164 Dc
Brodick 264 Ca
Brodie Castle 305 Hf
Brodsworth 205 Gc
Brogborough 124 Ae
Brokenborough 93 Gd
Broken Cross *Ches* 188 Bd
Broken Cross *Ches* 188 Dd
Bromborough 185 Ge
Brome 152 Bd
Brome Street 152 Bd
Bromeswell 152 Db
Bromfield *Cumb* 244 Ab
Bromfield *Shrops* 137 Gd
Bromham *Beds* 145 Gb
Bromham *Wilts* 93 Gb
Bromley 101 Fb
Bromley Green 81 Hd
Brompton *Kent* 104 Ab
Brompton *N Yorks* 229 Gb
Brompton *N Yorks* 233 Ea
Brompton-on-Swale 229 Fb
Brompton Ralph 68 Cd
Brompton Regis 68 Bd
Bromsash 116 Dd
Bromsberrow Heath 117 Ee
Bromsgrove 140 Dd
Bromstead Heath 164 Bc
Bromyard 140 Ab
Bromyard Downs 140 Ab
Bronaber 157 He
Brongest 132 Da
Bronington 161 Ge
Bronllys 113 Ge
Bronnant 133 Gc
Bronwydd Arms 109 Hd
Bronydd 137 Ea
Bron-y-gaer 109 Gc
Bronygarth 161 Ee
Brook *Carm* 109 Fb
Brook *Hants* 73 Gb
Brook *Hants* 73 Hc
Brook *IOW* 56 Bc
Brook *Kent* 84 Ae
Brook *Sry* 77 Fd
Brooke *Leics* 169 Eb
Brooke *Nflk* 176 Ca
Brookeborough 344 Dk
Brookfield 265 Gd
Brookhouse *Ches* 189 Ed
Brookhouse *Lancs* 213 Fd
Brookhouse Green 188 Dc
Brookland 81 Hc
Brooklands 241 Fe
Brookmans Park 124 Db
Brooks 160 Da
Brooks Green 77 Hc
Brook Street *Esx* 101 Ge
Brook Street *Sflk* 149 Ga
Brook Street *W Ssx* 80 Bc
Brookthorpe 117 Fc
Brookville 173 Fa
Brookwood 100 Aa
Broom *Beds* 145 Ha
Broom *Warks* 141 Eb
Broomcroft 161 Hb
Broome *H & W* 140 Dd
Broome *Nflk* 176 Da
Broome *Shrops* 137 Fe
Broomedge 188 Ce
Broome Park 261 Fd
Broomer's Corner 77 Hc
Broomfield *Aber* 308 Gd
Broomfield *Esx* 128 Ab
Broomfield *Kent* 104 Ba
Broomfield *Kent* 105 Fb
Broomfield *Som* 69 Ed
Broomfleet 208 Be
Broom Hill *Dors* 53 Ge
Broomhill *Northld* 261 Gc
Broom of Dalreoch 284 Cd
Broom's Green 117 Ee
Broomy Lodge 73 Gb
Brora 313 Md
Broseley 164 Ab
Brosna *Kerry* 325 Nj
Brosna *Ofly* 336 Ag
Brothertoft 196 Ba
Brotherton 205 Fe
Brotton 232 Bd
Broubster 313 Nj
Brough 321 Mg
Brough *Cumb* 228 Ad
Brough *Derbs* 189 Ge
Brough *Hghld* 313 Qk
Brough *Humb* 208 Ce
Brough *Notts* 193 Fb
Brough *Shet* 321 Nf
Broughal 336 Bi
Broughall 188 Aa
Brough Head *Ork* 320 Bh
Brough Ness 320 Dd
Broughshane 352 Uf
Brough Sowerby 228 Ad
Broughton *Bdrs* 269 Fa
Broughton *Bucks* 145 Ea
Broughton *Cambs* 148 Ad
Broughton *Cumb* 241 Ha
Broughton *Flint* 185 Gc
Broughton *GM* 201 Hc
Broughton *Hants* 73 Hd
Broughton *Humb* 208 Cc
Broughton *Lancs* 213 Fa
Broughton *Northants* 145 Ed
Broughton *N Yorks* 216 Bc
Broughton *N Yorks* 220 Be
Broughton *Oxon* 120 De
Broughton *V of G* 89 Ec
Broughton Astley 168 Ba
Broughton Beck 224 Da
Broughton Gifford 93 Fb
Broughton Hackett 140 Db
Broughton in Furness 224 Da
Broughton Mills 224 Db
Broughton Moor 241 Ha
Broughton Park 201 Hc
Broughton Poggs 120 Bb
Broughtown 320 Fj
Broughty Ferry 296 Da
Browland 321 Ke
Brown Candover 76 Bd
Brown Carrick Hill 252 Cd
Brown Clee Hill 137 He
Brown Edge *Lancs* 200 Cd
Brown Edge *Staffs* 189 Eb
Brownhill *Aber* 308 Fe
Brownhill *Lancs* 212 Dd
Brownhills *Fife* 285 Hd
Brownhills *W Mids* 165 Eb
Brownieside 261 Fe
Brownlow Heath 188 Dc
Brownmuir 297 Ge
Brownsea Island 53 Gc
Brownshill Green 141 He
Brownston 41 Ee
Brownstown *Kild* 336 Hi
Brownstown *Wat* 328 Mh
Brown Willy 44 Db
Brow Top 213 Fc
Broxa 233 Eb
Broxbourne 125 Eb
Broxburn *E Loth* 272 Ce
Broxburn *W Loth* 269 Ee
Broxholme 193 Gd
Broxted 125 Gd
Broxwood 137 Fb
Broyle Side 80 Cb
Bru 317 Yr
Bruan 313 Rg
Bruar Lodge 293 Je
Bruera 185 Hc
Bruern Abbey 120 Bd
Bruernish 317 Sc
Bruff 333 Na
Bruichladdich 316 Dg
Bruisyard 152 Dc
Brumby 208 Bc
Brund 189 Gc
Brundall 176 Db
Brundish 152 Cc
Brundish Street 152 Cd
Brunswick Village 248 De
Bruntingthorpe 168 Ca
Brunton *Fife* 285 Fe
Brunton *Northld* 261 Ge
Bruray 321 Pg
Bruree 333 Ma
Brushford 68 Bc
Brushford Barton 48 Ae
Bruton 72 Ad
Bryansford 345 Pj
Bryanston 52 Ee
Brydekirk 244 Ae
Brymbo 185 Fb
Bryn *Carm* 112 Ab
Bryn *GM* 201 Ec
Bryn *N & PT* 88 De
Bryn *Shrops* 137 Ee
Bryn, The 116 Ab
Brynamman 112 Cc
Brynberian 109 Ee
Bryncae 93 Gd
Bryncethin 89 Ed
Bryncir 181 Fa
Bryn-côch 88 Ce
Bryncroes 156 Ce
Bryncrug 157 Gb
Bryneglwys 185 Ea
Brynford 185 Ed
Bryn Gates 201 Ec
Bryngwran 181 Ed
Bryngwyn 136 Da
Bryn-henllan 108 De
Brynhoffnant 132 Db
Brynithel 113 Hb
Brynmawr 113 Gc
Brynmenyn 89 Ed
Brynna 89 Ed
Brynog 133 Fb
Brynrefail 181 Fe
Brynsadler 89 Fd
Brynsiencyn 181 Fc
Brynteg 181 Fe
Bryn-y-maen 184 Bd
Bualintur 300 Dc
Bualnaluib 312 Ac
Bubbenhall 141 Hd
Bubwith 220 Ba
Buccleuch 257 Fd
Buchan 308 Ge
Buchanan Smithy 281 Ea
Buchanty 284 Be
Buchlyvie 281 Fb
Buckabank 244 Cb
Buckden *Cambs* 145 Hc
Buckden *N Yorks* 216 Be
Buckenham 176 Db
Buckerell 49 Fe
Buckfast 48 Ba
Buckfastleigh 48 Ba
Buckhaven 285 Fb
Buckholm 272 Aa
Buckhorn Weston 72 Bc
Buckhurst Hill 101 Fe
Buckie 308 Bg
Buckies 313 Pj
Buckingham 121 Fe
Buckland *Bucks* 121 Hc
Buckland *Devon* 41 Ed
Buckland *Glos* 117 He
Buckland *Herts* 125 Ee
Buckland *Kent* 84 Ce
Buckland *Oxon* 96 Ce
Buckland *Sry* 100 Da
Buckland Abbey 45 Ga
Buckland Brewer 65 Ec
Buckland Common 124 Ab
Buckland Dinham 93 Ea
Buckland Filleigh 45 Ge
Buckland in the Moor 48 Bb
Buckland Monachorum 45 Ga
Buckland Newton 52 Ce
Buckland St Mary 69 Eb
Buckland-tout-Saints 41 Fd
Bucklebury 97 Ec
Bucklerheads 296 Da
Bucklers Hard 56 Cd
Bucklesham 152 Ca
Buckley 185 Fc
Bucklow Hill *Ches* 188 Ce
Buckminster 169 Ed
Buckna 352 Vf
Bucknall *Lincs* 196 Ac
Bucknall *Staffs* 189 Ea
Bucknell *Oxon* 121 Ed
Bucknell *Shrops* 137 Fd
Bucksburn 308 Fa
Buck's Cross 64 Dc
Bucks Green 77 Gd
Bucks Hill 124 Bb
Bucks Horn Oak 77 Ee
Buck's Mills 64 Dc
Buckspool 108 Ca
Buckton *H & W* 137 Fd
Buckton *Humb* 221 Fe
Buckton *Northld* 273 Ga
Buckworth 145 Hd
Budbrooke 141 Gc
Budby 192 Dc
Bude 45 Ee
Budlake 48 De
Budle 273 Ha
Budleigh Salterton 49 Ec
Budock Water 36 Fc
Buerton 188 Ba
Bugbrooke 144 Cb
Bugle 37 Je
Bugthorpe 220 Bc
Buildwas 164 Ab
Builth Road 136 Cb
Builth Wells 136 Cb
Buirgh 317 Vl
Bulby 169 Gd
Buldoo 313 Mj
Bulford 73 Fe
Bulford Camp 73 Fe
Bulgaden 328 Bk
Bulkeley 188 Ab
Bulkington *Warks* 141 He
Bulkington *Wilts* 93 Ga
Bulkworthy 64 Db
Bullaun 333 Nj
Bull Bay 181 Ff
Bullers of Buchan 309 Jd
Bulley 117 Ec
Bullpot Farm 225 Ha
Bull's Green 124 Dc
Bullwood 264 De
Bulmer *Esx* 149 Ga
Bulmer *N Yorks* 220 Ad
Bulmer Tye 128 Be
Bulphan 101 Hd
Bulverhythe 61 He
Bulwark 308 Ge
Bulwell 192 Ca
Bulwick 169 Fa
Bumble's Green 125 Fb
Bun Abhainn Eadarra 317 Wm
Bunacaimb 289 Hf
Bunacurry 340 Dg
Bunarkaig 292 Bf
Bunbeg 348 Fh
Bunbrosna 344 Dc
Bunbury 188 Ab
Bunclody 337 Kc
Buncrana 349 Li
Buncton 77 Hb
Bundalloch 301 Hc
Bundoran 348 Fa
Bunessan 276 Be
Bungay 152 De
Bunlahy 344 Ce
Bun Loyne 301 Ma
Bunmahon 329 Kh
Bunnahabhainn 316 Fh
Bunnanaddan 341 Nh
Bunny 168 Bd
Bunnyconnellan 341 Kh
Bunratty 333 Ld
Buntait 304 Bd
Buntingford 125 Ed
Bunwell 176 Ba
Burbage *Derbs* 189 Fd
Burbage *Leics* 168 Aa
Burbage *Wilts* 96 Bb
Burchett's Green 97 Hd
Burcombe 73 Ed
Burcot 97 Ee
Burcott 121 Hd
Bures 128 Ce
Bures Green 128 Ce
Burf, The 140 Cc
Burford *Oxon* 120 Bc
Burford *Shrops* 137 Hc
Burg 288 Eb
Burgate 152 Ad
Burgess Hill 80 Bb
Burgh 152 Cb
Burgh by Sands 244 Cc
Burgh Castle 177 Eb
Burghclere 96 Db
Burghead 305 Kg
Burghfield 97 Fb
Burghfield Common 97 Fb
Burghfield Hill 97 Fb
Burgh Heath 100 Da
Burghill 137 Ga
Burgh le Marsh 197 Ec
Burghley House 169 Gb
Burgh next Aylsham 176 Cd
Burgh on Bain 196 Be
Burgh St Margaret 177 Ec

490 Euxton—Five Oaks

Euxton 201 Ed
Evanton 304 Eg
Evedon 193 Ha
Evelix 313 Kc
Evenjobb 137 Ec
Evenley 121 Ee
Evenlode 120 Bd
Eventide Home 308 Gb
Evenwood 229 Ee
Everbay 320 Fh
Evercreech 72 Ad
Everdon 144 Bb
Everingham 220 Cb
Everleigh 96 Aa
Everley 233 Ea
Eversholt 124 Ae
Evershot 52 Be
Eversley 97 Gb
Eversley Cross 97 Gb
Everthorpe 220 Da
Everton *Beds* 148 Ab
Everton *Hants* 56 Ad
Everton *Notts* 205 Hb
Evertown 244 Ce
Evesbatch 140 Aa
Evesham 117 Hf
Evington 168 Cb
Ewart Newtown 273 Fa
Ewden Village 204 Db
Ewell 100 Db
Ewell Minnis 84 Ce
Ewelme 97 Fe
Ewen 93 He
Ewenny 89 Ec
Ewerby 196 Aa
Ewerby Thorpe 196 Aa
Ewes 257 Fb
Ewhurst *E Ssx* 81 Fc
Ewhurst *Sry* 77 Ge
Ewhurst Green 77 Gd
Ewloe 185 Gc
Ewood 201 Fe
Eworthy 45 Gd
Ewshot 77 Ee
Ewyas Harold 116 Ad
Exbourne 48 Ae
Exbury 56 Ce
Exebridge 68 Bc
Exelby 229 Fa
Exeter 48 Dd
Exford 68 Ad
Exhall 141 Fb
Exlade Street 97 Fd
Exminster 48 Dc
Exmoor 65 He
Exmouth 49 Ec
Exnaboe 321 La
Exning 149 Ec
Exton *Devon* 48 Dc
Exton *Hants* 76 Cc
Exton *Leics* 169 Fc
Exton *Som* 68 Bd
Exwick 48 Dd
Eyam 189 Hd
Eye *Cambs* 172 Ab
Eye *H & W* 137 Gc
Eye *Sflk* 152 Bd
Eye Green 172 Ab
Eyemouth 273 Fd
Eyeries 324 Hd
Eyeworth 148 Aa
Eyhorne Street 104 Ba
Eyke 152 Db
Eynesbury 145 Hb
Eynort 300 Cc
Eynsford 101 Gb
Eynsham 120 Db
Eype 52 Ad
Eype's Mouth 52 Ad
Eyre 300 Df
Eyrecourt 333 Ri
Eythorne 84 Ce
Eyton *Shrops* 137 Fe
Eyton *Wrex* 185 Ga
Eyton upon the Weald Moors 164 Ac

F

Faccombe 96 Ca
Faceby 229 Hc
Faddiley 188 Ab
Fadmoor 232 Ba
Faerdre 112 Bb
Faha Glen 328 Ji
Fahamore 324 Hj
Fahan *Dngl* 349 Lh
Fahan *Kerry* 324 Eh
Faifley 265 He
Failand 92 Cc
Failford 253 Ee
Failsworth 204 Ac
Fairbourne 157 Gc
Fairburn 205 Fe
Fairfield 140 Dd
Fairford 120 Ab
Fairgirth 241 Fc
Fairlie 264 Ec
Fairlight 81 Gb
Fairmile 49 Ed
Fairmilehead 269 Gd
Fairnington 260 Ae
Fair Oak *Hants* 76 Ab
Fairoak *Staffs* 164 Be
Fair Oak Green 97 Fb
Fairseat 101 Hb
Fairstead 128 Ac
Fairwarp 80 Cc
Fairy Cross 65 Ec
Fairyhill 85 He
Faither, The 321 Kh
Fakenham 173 Hd
Fala 269 Jd
Fala Dam 269 Jd
Falahill 269 Hc
Falcarragh 348 Gi
Faldingworth 193 He
Falfield *Avon* 92 De
Falfield *Fife* 285 Gc
Falkenham 129 Fe
Falkirk 268 Cf
Falkland 285 Ec
Falla 260 Bd
Fallin 281 Jb
Falling Foss 232 Dc
Fall of Glomach 301 Kc
Fall of Warness 320 Eh
Falls of Bruar 293 Jd
Falmer 60 De
Falmouth 37 Gc
Falsgrave 233 Fa
Falstone 260 Ba
Fanagmore 312 Di
Fancott 124 Bd
Fangdale Beck 232 Ab
Fangfoss 220 Bc
Fankerton 281 Ha
Fanmore 288 Fb
Fannich Lodge 301 Mg
Fans 272 Cb
Fara 320 Ce
Faray 320 Ei
Farcet 172 Aa
Far Cotton 144 Db
Farden 137 Hd
Fardrum 336 Ak
Fareham 56 De
Farewell 165 Ec
Far Forest 140 Bd
Far Gearstones 228 Aa
Faringdon 96 Be
Farington 201 Ee
Farlam 245 Ec
Farlary 313 Kd
Farleigh *Avon* 92 Bb
Farleigh *Sry* 101 Eb
Farleigh Hungerford 93 Ea
Farleigh Wallop 76 Ce
Farlesthorpe 196 Dd
Farleton *Cumb* 225 Ga
Farleton *Lancs* 213 Fd
Farley *Shrops* 161 Fb
Farley *Staffs* 189 Fa
Farley *Wilts* 73 Gc
Farley Green 77 Ge
Farley Hill 97 Gb
Farleys End 117 Ec
Farlington 220 Ad
Farlow 140 Ae
Farmborough 92 Db
Farmcote 117 Hd
Farmers 133 Ga
Farmington 120 Ac
Farmoor 120 Db
Farmtown 308 Cf
Farnagh 336 Bk
Farnaght 344 Bf
Farnborough *Berks* 96 Dd
Farnborough *GL* 101 Fb
Farnborough *Hants* 97 Ha
Farnborough *Warks* 144 Aa
Farncombe 100 Aa
Farndish 145 Fc
Farndon *Ches* 185 Hb
Farndon *Notts* 193 Eb
Farne Islands 273 Ja
Farnell 296 Fc
Farnham *Dors* 73 Db
Farnham *Esx* 125 Fd
Farnham *N Yorks* 217 Fd
Farnham *Sflk* 152 Dc
Farnham *Sry* 77 Ee
Farnham Common 100 Ad
Farnham Green 125 Fd
Farnham Royal 100 Ad
Farnhill 216 Cb
Farningham 101 Gb
Farnley 217 Eb
Farnley Tyas 204 Cd
Farnsfield 192 Db
Farnworth *Ches* 188 Ae
Farnworth *GM* 201 Gc
Farr *Hghld* 304 Ed
Farr *Hghld* 305 Ga
Farr *Hghld* 313 Kj
Farran 325 Re
Farranfore 325 Li
Farr House 304 Ed
Farringdon 49 Ed
Farrington Gurney 92 Da
Farsley 217 Ea
Farthinghoe 121 Ee
Farthingloe 84 Ce
Farthingstone 144 Cb
Farway 49 Fd
Fascadale 289 Ge
Fasnacloich 289 Mb
Fasnakyle House 304 Bc
Fasque 296 Fe
Fassfern 289 Me
Fatfield 249 Ec
Fattahead 308 Df
Faugh 245 Ec
Fauldhouse 268 Dd
Faulkbourne 128 Ac
Faulkland 93 Ea
Fauls 161 He
Faversham 104 Db
Favillar 305 Ld
Fawdington 217 Ge
Fawdon 248 Dd
Fawfieldhead 189 Fc
Fawkham Green 101 Gb
Fawler 120 Cc
Fawley *Berks* 96 Cd
Fawley *Bucks* 97 Gd
Fawley *Hants* 56 Ce
Fawley Chapel 116 Cd
Fawsyde 297 He
Faxfleet 208 Be
Faygate 80 Ad
Fazeley 165 Gb
Feakle 333 Mf
Fearby 229 Ea
Fearn Abbey 313 La
Fearnan 293 Hb
Fearnbeg 301 Gf
Fearnhead 201 Fb
Fearnmore 301 Gg
Featherstone *Staffs* 164 Db
Featherstone *W Yorks* 205 Fe
Featherstone Castle 245 Fd
Feckenham 141 Ec
Fedamore 333 Mb
Feeard 332 Dc
Feenagh 325 Rk
Feeny 349 Pf
Feering 128 Bd
Feetham 228 Cb
Feizor 213 Hd
Felbridge 80 Bd
Felbrigg 176 Ce
Felbrigg Hall 176 Be
Felcourt 80 Be
Felden 124 Bb
Felindre *Carm* 109 Ge
Felindre *Carm* 112 Ad
Felindre *Carm* 112 Cd
Felindre *Pwys* 136 De
Felindre *Swan* 112 Bb
Felindre Farchog 109 Ee
Felinfach 113 Fe
Felinfoel 112 Ab
Felingwm Uchaf 112 Ad
Felixkirk 229 Ha
Felixstowe 129 Ge
Felkington 273 Fb
Felldownhead 45 Fc
Felling 248 Dd
Fell Side 244 Ca
Felmersham 145 Fb
Felmingham 176 Cd
Felpham 57 Hd
Felsham 149 Hb
Felsted 125 Hd
Feltham 100 Cc
Felthorpe 176 Bc
Felton *Avon* 92 Cb
Felton *H & W* 137 Ha
Felton *Northld* 261 Fc
Felton Butler 161 Fc
Feltwell 173 Fa
Fenagh 344 Bg
Fence 216 Aa
Fence Houses 249 Ec
Fencote 229 Fb
Fencott 121 Ec
Fen Ditton 148 Cc
Fen Drayton 148 Bc
Fen End 141 Gd
Fenhouses 196 Ba
Feniscowles 201 Fe
Fenit 325 Jj
Feniton 49 Fd
Fennagh 336 Hd
Fennor *Wat* 329 Li
Fennor *Wmth* 344 Fc
Fenny Bentley 189 Gb
Fenny Bridges 49 Fd
Fenny Compton 144 Ab
Fenny Drayton 165 Ha
Fenny Stratford 121 He
Fenrother 261 Fb
Fenstanton 148 Bc
Fenton *Cambs* 148 Bd
Fenton *Lincs* 193 Fb
Fenton *Lincs* 193 Fd
Fenton *Northld* 273 Fa
Fenton *Staffs* 188 Da
Fenwick *E Ayr* 265 Gb
Fenwick *Northld* 248 Be
Fenwick *Northld* 273 Ga
Fenwick *S Yorks* 205 Gd
Feochaig 316 Jb
Feock 37 Gc
Feohanagh *Kerry* 324 Ei
Feohanagh *Lim* 325 Qk
Feolin Ferry 316 Fg
Ferbane 336 Bj
Fermoy 328 Dh
Fern 296 Dd
Ferndale 89 Ee
Ferndown 53 Ge
Ferness 305 He
Fernham 96 Be
Fernhill Heath 140 Cb
Fernhurst 77 Fc
Fernie 285 Fd
Fernilea 300 Cd
Fernilee 189 Fd
Ferns 337 Lc
Ferrensby 217 Fd
Ferrindonald 300 Fa
Ferring 60 Ae
Ferrybridge 205 Fe
Ferryden 297 Gc
Ferryhill 248 Da
Ferryside 109 Gc
Fersfield 152 Ae
Fersit 292 De
Fers Ness 320 Ei
Ferwig 132 Ba
Feshiebridge 305 Ga
Fetcham 100 Ca
Fethard *Tipp* 336 Ca
Fethard *Wex* 329 Ni
Fetlar 321 Pi
Fetterangus 308 Gf
Fettercairn 296 Fe
Fews 328 Ji
Fewston 216 Dc
Ffairfach 112 Bd
Ffair-Rhos 133 Hc
Ffaldybrenin 133 Ga
Ffawyddog 113 Hc
Ffestiniog 184 Aa
Ffordd-las 185 Ec
Fforest 112 Ab
Fforest-fach 88 Be
Ffostrasol 132 Da
Ffos-y-ffin 133 Ec
Ffridd Uchaf 181 Gb
Ffrith 185 Fb
Ffynnon-ddrain 109 Hd
Ffynnongroyw 185 Ee
Fiag Lodge 312 Gf
Fidden 276 Be
Fiddes 297 Hf
Fiddington *Glos* 117 Ge
Fiddington *Som* 69 Ee
Fiddleford 72 Cb
Fiddlers Hamlet 125 Fb
Fiddown 329 Kk
Field 165 Ee
Field Broughton 225 Ea
Field Dalling 176 Ae
Field Head 168 Ab
Fieries 325 Li
Fifehead Magdalen 72 Bc
Fifehead Neville 72 Bb
Fifield *Berks* 100 Ac
Fifield *Oxon* 120 Bc
Fifield Bavant 73 Ec
Figheldean 73 Fe
Filby 177 Ec
Filey 221 Ff
Filgrave 145 Ea
Filkins 120 Bb
Filleigh *Devon* 65 Gc
Filleigh *Devon* 65 Hb
Fillingham 193 Ge
Fillongley 141 Ge
Filmore Hill 76 Cc
Filton 92 Dc
Fimber 220 Cd
Finavon 296 Dc
Finavon Castle 296 Dc
Finchale Priory 248 Db
Fincham 173 Eb
Finchampstead 97 Gb
Fincharn 277 Hc
Finchdean 76 Db
Finchingfield 125 He
Finchley 100 De
Findern 165 He
Findhorn 305 Jg
Findochty 308 Bg
Findo Gask 284 Ce
Findon *Aber* 297 Jg
Findon *W Ssx* 60 Be
Findon Mains 304 Eg
Finedon 145 Fd
Fingal's Cave 288 Ea
Fingal Street 152 Cc
Fingask 308 Ec
Fingest 97 Ge
Finghall 229 Ea
Fingland *Cumb* 244 Bc
Fingland *D & G* 253 Hd
Fingland *D & G* 257 Ec
Finglesham 105 Ga
Fingringhoe 128 Dd
Fingringhoe Wick 128 Dc
Finlaggan Castle 316 Eg
Finlarig 292 Fa
Finmere 121 Fe
Finnart 292 Fc
Finnea 344 Ee
Finningham 152 Ac
Finningley 205 Hb
Finnis 345 Nk
Finnygaud 308 Df
Finsbury 101 Ed
Finstall 140 Dc
Finsthwaite 225 Ea
Finstock 120 Cc
Finstown 320 Cg
Fintona 349 Mb
Fintry *Aber* 308 Ef
Fintry *Stir* 281 Ga
Finuge 332 Fa
Finvoy 352 Sg
Finzean 296 Eg
Fionnphort 276 Ae
Fionnsbhagh 317 Vk
Firbank 225 Hb
Firbeck 192 Ce
Firgrove 204 Ad
Firsby 196 Dc
Firth 321 Mg
Firth of Forth 234 Cd
Firth of Tay 285 Fe
Fir Tree 248 Ca
Fishbourne *IOW* 56 Dd
Fishbourne *W Ssx* 57 Ge
Fishbourne Roman Palace 57 Ge
Fishburn 249 Ea
Fishcross 284 Ab
Fisherford 308 Dd
Fisher's Pond 76 Ac
Fisherstreet 77 Fd
Fisherton *Hghld* 304 Ff
Fisherton *S Ayr* 252 Cd
Fisherton de la Mere 73 Ed
Fishguard 108 Ce
Fishlake 205 Hd
Fishleigh Barton 65 Fc
Fishpond Bottom 49 Hd
Fishtoft 196 Ca
Fishtoft Drove 196 Ca
Fishtown of Usan 297 Gc
Fishwick 273 Fc
Fiskavaig 300 Cd
Fiskerton *Lincs* 193 Hd
Fiskerton *Notts* 193 Eb
Fitful Head 321 La
Fittleton 73 Fe
Fittleworth 77 Gb
Fitton End 172 Cc
Fitty Hill 320 Dj
Fitz 161 Gc
Fitzhead 68 Dc
Fitzwilliam 205 Fd
Fiunary 289 Hb
Fivealley 336 Bi
Five Ashes 80 Dc
Five Bridges 140 Aa
Fivehead 69 Fc
Fivelanes 45 Ec
Fivemilebourne 341 Pj
Fivemiletown 344 Ek
Five Oak Green 81 Ee
Five Oaks 77 Gc

Five Roads–Garden 491

Five Roads	109	Hb
Flack's Green	128	Ac
Flackwell Heath	97	He
Fladbury	140	Da
Fladdabister	321	Mc
Flagg	189	Gc
Flamborough	221	Ge
Flamstead	124	Bc
Flansham	57	He
Flasby	216	Bc
Flash	189	Fc
Flashader	300	Cf
Flatford Mill	128	De
Flaunden	124	Bb
Flawborough	193	Ea
Flawith	217	Gd
Flax Bourton	92	Cb
Flaxby	217	Fc
Flaxley	116	Dc
Flaxpool	68	Dd
Flaxton	220	Ad
Fleckney	168	Ca
Flecknoe	144	Bc
Fleet *Dors*	52	Cc
Fleet *Hants*	97	Ha
Fleet *Lincs*	172	Bd
Fleet Hargate	172	Bd
Fleetwood	212	Db
Flemingston	89	Fc
Flemington	268	Ac
Flempton	149	Gc
Fletchertown	244	Bb
Fletching	80	Cc
Fleur-de-lis	89	Ge
Flexford	100	Aa
Flimby	241	Ha
Flimwell	81	Fd
Flint	185	Fd
Flintham	193	Ea
Flint Mountain	185	Fc
Flinton	221	Ga
Flitcham	173	Fd
Flitton	124	Be
Flitwick	124	Be
Flixborough	208	Bd
Flixton *GM*	201	Gb
Flixton *N Yorks*	221	Ee
Flixton *Sflk*	152	De
Flockton	204	Dd
Flockton Green	204	Dd
Flodda	317	Th
Flodden	273	Fa
Flodigarry	300	Dh
Flookburgh	212	De
Floors *Moray*	308	Bf
Floors Castle *Bdrs*	272	Da
Flordon	176	Ba
Flore	144	Cc
Florence Court	344	Bj
Flotta *Ork*	320	Ce
Flotterton	260	Dc
Flowton	152	Aa
Flurrybridge	345	Lh
Flush House	204	Cc
Flushing *Aber*	309	He
Flushing *Corn*	37	Gc
Flyford Flavell	140	Db
Fobbing	104	Ad
Fochabers	308	Af
Fochriw	113	Gb
Fockerby	208	Bd
Fodderty	304	Df
Foel	160	Bc
Foffarty	296	Db
Foggathorpe	220	Ba
Fogo	272	Db
Fogorig	272	Db
Foindle	312	Dh
Folda	296	Ad
Fole	165	Ee
Foleshill	141	He
Folke	72	Ab
Folkestone	84	Cd
Folkingham	169	Ge
Folkington	61	Fe
Folksworth	169	Ha
Folkton	221	Ee
Folla Rule	308	Ed
Follifoot	217	Fc
Folly	108	Cd
Folly Gate	45	Hd
Fonthill Bishop	73	Dd
Fonthill Gifford	73	Dd
Fontmell Magna	72	Cb
Fontstown	336	Hh
Fontwell	57	He
Foolow	189	Gd
Foots Cray	101	Fc
Force Forge	225	Eb
Forcett	229	Ed
Ford *A & B*	277	Gc
Ford *Bucks*	121	Gb
Ford *Devon*	41	Ee
Ford *Devon*	41	Fd
Ford *Devon*	65	Ec
Ford *Glos*	117	Hd
Ford *Mers*	200	Cb
Ford *Northld*	273	Fa
Ford *Shrops*	161	Gc
Ford *Som*	68	Cc
Ford *Staffs*	189	Fb
Ford *Wilts*	73	Fd
Ford *Wilts*	93	Fc
Ford *W Ssx*	60	Ae
Fordcombe	80	De
Forde Abbey	49	He
Fordell	284	Da
Forden	161	Eb
Ford End	125	Hc
Forder Green	48	Ba
Fordham *Cambs*	149	Ed
Fordham *Esx*	128	Cd
Fordham *Nflk*	173	Ea
Fordingbridge	73	Fb
Fordon	221	Ee
Fordoun	297	Ge
Fordstown	344	Hc
Fordstreet *Esx*	128	Cd
Ford Street *Som*	68	Db
Fordwells	120	Cc
Fordwich	105	Ea
Fordyce	308	Cg
Fore	344	Fd
Forebrae	284	Be
Foreland Point	88	Ca
Foremark	165	Hd
Forestburn Gate	261	Eb
Forest Coal Pit	113	Hd
Forest Gate	101	Fd
Forest Green	77	He
Forest Hall	225	Gc
Forest Head	245	Ec
Forest Hill	121	Eb
Forest-in-Teesdale	228	Be
Forest Lodge *A & B*	292	Cb
Forest Lodge *Angus*	293	Ke
Forest Lodge *Hghld*	305	Jb
Forest Mill	284	Bb
Forest of Ae	256	Bb
Forest of Bowland	213	Gc
Forest of Dean	116	Dc
Forest Row	80	Cd
Forestside	76	Db
Forest Town	192	Cc
Forfar	296	Dc
Forgandenny	284	Cd
Forgie	308	Af
Forkill	345	Lh
Formby	200	Cc
Forncett End	176	Ba
Forncett St Mary	176	Ba
Forncett St Peter	176	Ba
Forneth	293	Lb
Fornham All Saints	149	Gc
Fornham St Martin	149	Gc
Forres	305	Jf
Forrest Lodge	253	Fa
Forsbrook	189	Ea
Forse	313	Qg
Forsie	313	Nj
Forsinain	313	Mh
Forsinard	313	Lh
Forsinard Station	313	Lh
Forstal, The	81	Ge
Forston	52	Cd
Fort Augustus	304	Ba
Forter	296	Ad
Forteviot	284	Dd
Fort George	304	Ff
Forth	268	Dc
Forthampton	117	Fe
Forthill	344	Ab
Fortingall	293	Hb
Forton *Hants*	76	Ae
Forton *Lancs*	213	Ec
Forton *Shrops*	161	Gc
Forton *Som*	49	He
Forton *Staffs*	164	Bd
Fortrie	308	De
Fortrose	304	Ff
Fortuneswell	52	Cb
Fort William	292	Be
Forty Green	100	Ae
Forty Hill	101	Ee
Forward Green	152	Ab
Fosbury	96	Ca
Foscot	120	Bd
Fosdyke	172	Be
Foss	293	Hc
Fossebridge	117	Hc
Foster Street	125	Fb
Foston *Derbs*	165	Fe
Foston *Lincs*	193	Fa
Foston *N Yorks*	220	Ad
Foston on the Wolds	221	Fc
Fota	328	Cf
Fotherby	209	Gb
Fotheringhay	169	Ga
Foubister	320	Ef
Foulden *Bdrs*	273	Fc
Foulden *Nflk*	173	Fa
Foulkesmill	329	Pj
Foul Mile	81	Eb
Foulridge	216	Ab
Foulsham	176	Ad
Fountainhall	269	Jb
Fountains Abbey	217	Ed
Four Ashes	152	Ad
Four Crosses *Denb*	184	Da
Four Crosses *Pwys*	160	Cb
Four Crosses *Pwys*	161	Ec
Four Crosses *Staffs*	164	Db
Four Elms	80	Ce
Four Forks	69	Ed
Four Gotes	172	Cc
Fourlane Ends	192	Ab
Four Lanes	36	Ec
Fourlanes End	188	Db
Four Marks	76	Cd
Four Mile Bridge	180	Dd
Four Mile House	341	Qd
Four Oaks *E Ssx*	81	Gc
Four Oaks *W Mids*	141	Ge
Four Oaks *W Mids*	165	Fa
Fourpenny	313	Lc
Four Roads	341	Qb
Fourstones	245	Hd
Four Throws	81	Fc
Fovant	73	Ec
Foveran	308	Gc
Fowberry Tower	261	Ee
Fowey	37	Ke
Fowlis Easter	296	Ca
Fowlis Wester	284	Be
Fowlmere	148	Ca
Fowlsheugh	297	He
Fownhope	116	Ce
Foxcote	117	Hc
Foxdale	236	Bb
Foxearth	149	Ga
Foxfield *Cumb*	224	Da
Foxfield *Leit*	344	Ag
Foxford	341	Jg
Foxham	93	Gc
Foxhole	37	He
Foxholes	221	Ee
Foxhunt Green	80	Db
Fox Lane	97	Ha
Foxley *Nflk*	176	Ad
Foxley *Northants*	144	Cb
Foxley *Wilts*	93	Fd
Fox Street	128	Dd
Foxt	189	Fa
Foxton *Cambs*	148	Ca
Foxton *Dur*	229	Ge
Foxton *Leics*	144	Df
Foxup	216	Ae
Foxwist Green	188	Bc
Foy	116	Cd
Foyers	304	Cc
Foynes	333	Jc
Fraddon	37	He
Fradley	165	Fc
Fradswell	164	De
Fraisthorpe	221	Fd
Framfield	80	Cc
Framingham Earl	176	Cb
Framingham Pigot	176	Cb
Framlingham	152	Cc
Frampton *Dors*	52	Cd
Frampton *Lincs*	172	Be
Frampton Cotterell	92	Dd
Frampton Mansell	117	Gb
Frampton on Severn	117	Eb
Frampton West End	196	Ca
Framsden	152	Bb
Framwellgate Moor	248	Db
Franche	140	Cd
Frankby	185	Fe
Frankford	336	Bi
Frankley	140	De
Frankton	144	Ad
Frant	80	Dd
Fraserburgh	308	Gg
Frating Green	128	Dd
Fratton	57	Ee
Freathy	40	Be
Freckenham	149	Ed
Freckleton	200	De
Freeby	169	Ed
Freefolk	76	Ae
Freeland	120	Dc
Freemount	325	Qj
Freester	321	Me
Freethorpe	177	Eb
Freiston	196	Ca
Freiston Shore	196	Ca
Fremington *Devon*	65	Fd
Fremington *N Yorks*	228	Db
Frenchay	92	Dc
Frenchbeer	48	Ac
Frenchpark	341	Pf
Frenich	280	Ec
Frensham	77	Ee
Fresgoe	313	Mj
Freshfield	200	Bc
Freshford *Avon*	93	Ea
Freshford *Kilk*	336	Ed
Freshwater	56	Bc
Freshwater East	108	Da
Fressingfield	152	Cd
Freston	129	Ee
Freswick	313	Rj
Fretherne	117	Eb
Frettenham	176	Cc
Freuchie	285	Ec
Freystrop	108	Cc
Friars Carse	256	Ba
Friar's Gate	80	Cd
Friday Bridge	172	Cb
Friday Street *E Ssx*	61	Ge
Friday Street *Sry*	77	He
Fridaythorpe	220	Cc
Friern Barnet	100	De
Friesland	288	Cc
Friesthorpe	193	He
Frieth	97	Ge
Frilford	96	De
Frilsham	97	Ec
Frimley	97	Ha
Frimley Green	97	Ha
Frindsbury	104	Ab
Fring	173	Fe
Fringford	121	Fd
Frinsted	104	Ba
Frinton-on-Sea	129	Fc
Friockheim	296	Eb
Friog	157	Gc
Frisby on the Wreake	168	Cc
Friskney	196	Db
Friskney Eaudyke	196	Db
Friskney Flats	197	Eb
Friston *Sflk*	153	Ec
Friston *W Ssx*	61	Fd
Fritchley	192	Ab
Fritham	73	Gb
Frith Bank	196	Ca
Frith Common	140	Ac
Frithelstock	65	Eb
Frithville	196	Cb
Frittenden	81	Ge
Fritton *Nflk*	176	Ca
Fritton *Nflk*	177	Eb
Fritwell	121	Ed
Frizington	224	Bd
Frocester	117	Eb
Frochas	161	Ec
Frodesley	161	Hb
Frodsham	188	Ad
Frog End	148	Cb
Froggatt	189	Hd
Froghall	189	Fa
Frogham	73	Fb
Frogmore *Hants*	97	Hb
Frogmore *Herts*	124	Cb
Frogmore House	100	Ac
Frog Pool	140	Bc
Frolesworth	168	Ba
Frome	72	Be
Frome St Quintin	52	Be
Fromes Hill	140	Aa
Fron *C & M*	156	De
Fron *Pwys*	136	Cc
Froncysyllte	185	Fa
Frongoch	160	Be
Frosses	348	Fd
Frosterley	248	Ba
Froxfield	96	Bb
Froxfield Green	76	Dc
Fryerning	125	Hb
Fryton	220	Ae
Fuerty	341	Qc
Fugglestone St Peter	73	Fd
Fulbeck	193	Gb
Fulbourn	148	Db
Fulbrook	120	Bc
Fulford *N Yorks*	220	Ab
Fulford *Som*	69	Ec
Fulford *Staffs*	164	De
Fulham	100	Dc
Fulking	80	Ab
Fuller's Moor	185	Hb
Fuller Street	128	Ac
Fullerton	73	Hd
Fulletby	196	Bd
Fullready	141	Ga
Full Sutton	220	Bc
Fullwood	265	Gc
Fulmer	100	Ad
Fulmodeston	173	He
Fulnetby	193	Hd
Fulstow	209	Gb
Fulwell *Oxon*	120	Cd
Fulwell *T & W*	249	Ec
Fulwood *Lancs*	213	Fa
Fulwood *S Yorks*	192	Ae
Fundenhall	176	Ba
Funtington	57	Fe
Funtley	56	De
Funzie	321	Ph
Furley	49	Ge
Furnace	277	Jc
Furness Abbey	212	Ce
Furneux Pelham	125	Fd
Furraleigh	328	Ji
Furzehill	65	He
Fyfett	69	Eb
Fyfield *Esx*	125	Gb
Fyfield *Glos*	120	Bb
Fyfield *Hants*	73	Ge
Fyfield *Oxon*	96	De
Fyfield *Wilts*	96	Ab
Fylingdales Moor	233	Eb
Fylingthorpe	233	Ec
Fyvie	308	Ed

G

Gabhsann	317	Zs
Gablon	313	Kc
Gabroc Hill	265	Gc
Gaddesby	168	Cc
Gaer	113	Gd
Gaer-fawr	92	Be
Gaerllwyd	92	Be
Gaerwen	181	Fd
Gagingwell	120	Dd
Gaick Lodge	293	Hf
Gailey	164	Dc
Gainestown	344	Ea
Gainford	229	Ed
Gainsborough	193	Fe
Gainsford End	128	Ae
Gairloch	301	Hh
Gairlochy	292	Bf
Gairney Bank	284	Db
Gairnshiel Lodge	305	La
Gairsay	320	Dh
Gaisgill	201	Fc
Gaitsgill	244	Cb
Galabank	269	Jb
Galashiels	272	Aa
Galbally *Lim*	328	Dk
Galbally *Wex*	329	Qk
Galby	168	Cb
Galgate	213	Ec
Galgorm	352	Tf
Galhampton	72	Ac
Gallanach	277	Ge
Gallarus Oratory	324	Ei
Gallatown	285	Eb
Gallchoille	277	Fb
Galley Common	165	Ha
Galleyend	128	Ab
Galleywood	128	Ab
Galloway Forest Park	240	Be
Gallowfauld	296	Db
Gallowstree Common	97	Fd
Galltair	301	Hc
Galmisdale	289	Ff
Galmoy	336	Ce
Galmpton *Devon*	41	Ed
Galmpton *Devon*	41	Ge
Galphay	217	Ee
Galston	265	Ha
Galtrigill	300	Af
Galway	333	Jj
Gamblesby	245	Fa
Gamlingay	148	Ab
Gammaton	65	Ec
Gamrie	308	Eg
Gamston *Notts*	168	Ce
Gamston *Notts*	193	Ed
Ganarew	116	Cc
Ganavan	289	Ka
Ganllwyd	157	Hd
Gannochy	296	Ee
Ganstead	221	Fa
Ganthorpe	220	Ae
Ganton	220	De
Gaodhail	289	Ha
Gaoth Sáile	340	Dh
Gap of Dunloe	325	Kg
Garadice	344	Ja
Garbally	333	Qk
Garbat	304	Cg
Garbhallt	277	Jb
Garboldisham	152	Ae
Garden	281	Fb

Harkstead—Hermon 495

Harkstead 129 Ee
Harlaston 165 Gc
Harlaxton 169 Ee
Harlech 157 Fe
Harlesden 100 Dd
Harleston *Devon* 41 Fd
Harleston *Nflk* 152 Ce
Harleston *Sflk* 152 Ac
Harlestone 144 Dc
Harle Syke 216 Aa
Harley 161 Hb
Harling Road Station 149 He
Harlington 124 Be
Harlosh 300 Be
Harlow 125 Fc
Harlow Hill 248 Bd
Harlthorpe 220 Ba
Harlton 148 Bb
Harman's Cross 53 Fc
Harmby 229 Ea
Harmer Green 124 Dc
Harmer Hill 161 Gd
Harmondsworth 100 Bc
Harmston 193 Gc
Harnham 73 Fc
Harnhill 117 Hb
Harold Hill 101 Ge
Haroldston West 108 Bc
Haroldswick 321 Pk
Harold Wood 101 Ge
Harome 232 Ba
Harpenden 124 Cc
Harpford 49 Ed
Harpham 221 Ed
Harpley *H & W* 140 Ac
Harpley *Nflk* 173 Fd
Harpole 144 Cc
Harpsdale 313 Pi
Harpsden 97 Gd
Harpswell 193 Ge
Harpurhey 201 Hc
Harpur Hill 189 Fd
Harrapool 301 Fc
Harrietfield 284 Be
Harrietsham 104 Ba
Harrington *Cumb* 224 Ae
Harrington *Lincs* 196 Cd
Harrington *Northants* 144 De
Harrington Hall 196 Cd
Harringworth 169 Fa
Harris 288 Eg
Harriseahead 188 Db
Harrogate 217 Fc
Harrold 145 Fb
Harrow 100 Cd
Harrow, The 337 Lb
Harrowbarrow 45 Fa
Harrowden 145 Ga
Harrow on the Hill 100 Cd
Harston *Cambs* 148 Cb
Harston *Leics* 169 Ee
Hart 249 Fa
Hartburn 261 Ea
Hartest 149 Gb
Hartfield *A & B* 280 Ca
Hartfield *E Ssx* 80 Cd
Hartford *Cambs* 148 Ad
Hartford *Ches* 188 Bd
Hartfordbridge 97 Ga
Hartford End 125 Hc
Hartforth 229 Ec
Harthill *Ches* 185 Hb
Harthill *S Yorks* 192 Be
Harthill *W Loth* 268 Dd
Hartington 189 Gc
Hartland 64 Cc
Hartland Quay 64 Cc
Hartlebury 140 Cd
Hartlepool 249 Ga
Hartley *Cumb* 228 Ac
Hartley *Kent* 81 Fd
Hartley *Kent* 101 Hb
Hartley *Northld* 249 Ee
Hartley Wespall 97 Fa
Hartley Wintney 97 Ga
Hartlip 104 Bb
Harton *N Yorks* 220 Bd
Harton *Shrops* 137 Ge
Harton *T & W* 249 Ed
Hartpury 117 Ed
Hartshill 165 Ha
Hartshorne 165 Hd
Hartsop 225 Fd
Hartwell 144 Db
Hartwood 268 Cc
Harvel 101 Hb
Harvington *H & W* 140 Cd
Harvington *H & W* 141 Ea
Harvington Cross 141 Ea
Harwell 96 Dd
Harwich 129 Fe
Harwood *Dur* 245 Ha
Harwood *GM* 201 Gd
Harwood Dale 233 Eb
Harworth 205 Hb
Hascombe 77 Gd
Haselbech 144 Dd
Haselbury Plucknett 69 Gb
Haseley 141 Gc
Haselor 141 Fb
Hasfield 117 Fd
Hasguard 108 Bb
Haskayne 200 Cc
Hasketon 152 Cb
Hasland 192 Ac
Haslemere 77 Ed
Haslingden 201 Ge
Haslingden Grane 201 Ge
Haslingfield 148 Cb
Haslington 188 Cb
Hassall 188 Cb
Hassall Green 188 Cb
Hassell Street 84 Ae
Hassendean 257 He
Hassingham 176 Db
Hassocks 80 Bb
Hassop 189 Hd
Hastigrow 313 Qj
Hastingleigh 84 Ae
Hastings 81 Ga
Hastingwood 125 Fb
Hastoe 124 Ab
Haswell 249 Eb
Hatch *Beds* 145 Ha
Hatch *Hants* 97 Fa
Hatch *Wilts* 73 Dc
Hatch Beauchamp 69 Fc
Hatch End 100 Ce
Hatching Green 124 Cc
Hatchmere 188 Ad
Hatcliffe 209 Fc
Hatfield *H & W* 137 Hb
Hatfield *Herts* 124 Db
Hatfield *S Yorks* 205 Hc
Hatfield Broad Oak 125 Gc
Hatfield Forest 125 Gd
Hatfield Heath 125 Gc
Hatfield Peverel 128 Ac
Hatfield Woodhouse 205 Hc
Hatford 96 Ce
Hatherden 96 Ca
Hatherleigh 45 He
Hathern 168 Bd
Hatherop 120 Ab
Hathersage 189 He
Hatherton *Ches* 188 Ba
Hatherton *Staffs* 164 Dc
Hatley St George 148 Ab
Hatt 45 Fa
Hattingley 76 Cd
Hatton *Aber* 309 Hd
Hatton *Ches* 188 Ae
Hatton *Derbs* 165 Ge
Hatton *GL* 100 Cc
Hatton *Lincs* 196 Ad
Hatton *Shrops* 161 Ga
Hatton *Warks* 141 Gc
Hattoncrook 308 Fc
Hatton Heath 185 Hc
Hatton of Fintray 308 Fb
Haugham 196 Ce
Haughhead *E Dun* 265 Je
Haugh Head *Northld* 261 Ee
Haughley 152 Ac
Haughley Green 152 Ac
Haughley New Street 152 Ac
Haugh of Glass 308 Bd
Haugh of Urr 241 Fd
Haughs 308 Ce
Haughton *Notts* 192 Dd
Haughton *Shrops* 161 Fd
Haughton *Shrops* 161 Hc
Haughton *Shrops* 164 Aa
Haughton *Staffs* 164 Cd
Haughton Green 204 Ab
Haughton Le Skerne 229 Gd
Haughton Moss 188 Ab
Haultwick 125 Ed
Haun 317 Sd
Haunton 165 Gc
Hauxton 148 Cb
Havant 57 Fe
Haven 137 Gb
Haven, The 77 Gd
Havenstreet 56 Dd
Haverfordwest 108 Cc
Haverhill 149 Ea
Haverigg 212 Be
Havering 101 Gd
Havering-atte-Bower 101 Ge
Haversham 145 Ea
Haverthwaite 225 Ea
Hawarden 185 Gc
Hawbridge 140 Da
Hawcoat 212 Ce
Hawen 132 Da
Hawes 228 Ba
Hawford 140 Cc
Hawick 257 Hd
Hawkchurch 49 He
Hawkedon 149 Fb
Hawkeridge 93 Fa
Hawkerland 49 Ec
Hawkesbury 93 Ed
Hawkesbury Upton 93 Ed
Hawkes End 141 Ge
Hawkhill 261 Gd
Hawkhurst 81 Fd
Hawkinge 84 Cd
Hawkley 76 Dc
Hawkridge 68 Ad
Hawkshead 225 Eb
Hawksland 268 Ca
Hawkstone 161 He
Hawkswick 216 Be
Hawksworth *Notts* 193 Ea
Hawksworth *W Yorks* 216 Db
Hawkwell *Esx* 104 Be
Hawkwell *Northld* 248 Be
Hawley *Hants* 97 Ha
Hawley *Kent* 101 Gc
Hawling 117 Hd
Hawnby 232 Aa
Haworth 216 Ca
Hawsker 233 Ec
Hawstead 149 Gb
Hawthorn *Dur* 249 Fb
Hawthorn *Wilts* 93 Fb
Hawthorn Hill *Berks* 97 Hc
Hawthorn Hill *Lincs* 196 Bb
Hawthorpe 169 Gd
Hawton 193 Eb
Haxby 220 Ac
Haxey 208 Ab
Haxted 80 Ce
Haydock 201 Eb
Haydon 72 Ab
Haydon Bridge 245 Hd
Haydon Wick 96 Ad
Haye 45 Fb
Hayes *GL* 100 Bd
Hayes *GL* 101 Fb
Hayfield *Derbs* 189 Fe
Hayhillock 296 Eb
Haylands 56 Dd
Hayle 36 Dc
Hayling Island 57 Fe
Hay Mills 141 Fe
Haynes 145 Ga
Haynes Church End 145 Ga
Hay-on-Wye 113 Hf
Hays 345 Kd
Hayscastle 108 Bd
Hayscastle Cross 108 Cd
Hay Street 125 Ed
Hayton *Cumb* 244 Ab
Hayton *Cumb* 245 Ec
Hayton *Humb* 220 Cb
Hayton *Notts* 193 Ee
Hayton's Bent 137 He
Haytor Vale 48 Bb
Haywards Heath 80 Bc
Haywood Oaks 192 Db
Hazelbank 268 Cb
Hazelbury Bryan 52 De
Hazeleigh 128 Bb
Hazel End 125 Fd
Hazeley 97 Ga
Hazel Grove 189 Ee
Hazelside 256 Ae
Hazelslade 165 Ec
Hazelton Walls 285 Fe
Hazelwood 192 Aa
Hazlemere 97 He
Hazlerigg 248 De
Hazleton 117 Hc
Heacham 173 Ee
Headbourne Worthy 76 Ad
Headcorn 81 Ge
Headford 341 Ja
Headington 121 Eb
Headlam 229 Ed
Headless Cross 141 Ec
Headley *Hants* 77 Ed
Headley *Hants* 97 Eb
Headley *Sry* 100 Da
Head of Moclett 320 Dj
Head of Muir 281 Ja
Headon 193 Ed
Heads Nook 244 Dc
Heage 192 Ab
Healaugh *N Yorks* 217 Gb
Healaugh *N Yorks* 228 Db
Heald Green 188 De
Heale 65 Ge
Healey *GM* 201 Hd
Healey *Northld* 248 Bc
Healey *N Yorks* 229 Ea
Healey Dell 201 Hd
Healeyfield 248 Bb
Healing 209 Fd
Heamoor 36 Cc
Heanish 288 Bb
Heanor 192 Ba
Heanton Punchardon 65 Fd
Heapham 193 Fe
Hearthstane 256 De
Heasley Mill 65 Hd
Heast 300 Fb
Heath 192 Bc
Heath, The 149 Ha
Heath and Reach 124 Ad
Heathcote 189 Gc
Heath End *Hants* 97 Eb
Heather 165 Hc
Heathfield *Devon* 48 Cb
Heathfield *E Ssx* 80 Dc
Heathfield *Som* 68 Dc
Heathfield *Strath* 265 Fd
Heath Hayes 165 Ec
Heath Hill 164 Bc
Heath House 69 Ge
Heathrow Airport 100 Bc
Heathton 164 Ca
Heatley 188 Be
Heaton *Lancs* 213 Ed
Heaton *Staffs* 189 Ec
Heaton *T & W* 248 Dd
Heaton Hall *GM* 201 Hc
Heaton Moor 201 Hb
Heaverham 101 Ga
Heaviley 189 Ee
Heavitree 48 Dd
Hebburn 249 Ed
Hebden 216 Cd
Hebden Bridge 204 Ae
Hebden Green 188 Bc
Hebing End 125 Ed
Hebron *Carm* 109 Ed
Hebron *Northld* 261 Fa
Heck 256 Ca
Heckfield 97 Gb
Heckfield Green 152 Bd
Heckfordbridge 128 Cd
Heckington 196 Aa
Heckmondwike 204 De
Heddington 93 Gb
Heddle 320 Cg
Heddon-on-the-Wall 248 Cd
Heddon's Mouth 65 Ge
Hedenham 176 Da
Hedge End 76 Ab
Hedgerley 100 Ad
Hedging 69 Fc
Hedley on the Hill 248 Bc
Hednesford 165 Ec
Hedon 209 Ee
Hedsor 100 Ad
Heeley 192 Ae
Hegdon Hill 137 Hb
Heggerscales 228 Bd
Heglibister 321 Le
Heighington *Dur* 229 Fe
Heighington *Lincs* 193 Hc
Heights of Brae 304 Dg
Heights of Kinlochewe 301 Kg
Heilam 312 Gi
Heiton 272 Da
Hele *Devon* 48 De
Hele *Devon* 65 Fe
Hele Lane 65 Hb
Helen's Bay 352 Xd
Helensburgh 265 Ff
Helford 36 Fb
Helford River 36 Fb
Helhoughton 173 Gd
Helions Bumpstead 149 Ea
Helland 44 Cb
Hellesdon 176 Bc
Hellifield 216 Ac
Helli Ness 321 Mb
Hellingly 80 Db
Hellington 176 Db
Helmdon 144 Ba
Helmingham 152 Bb
Helmsdale 313 Ne
Helmshore 201 Ge
Helmsley 232 Ba
Helperby 217 Gd
Helperthorpe 220 De
Helpringham 196 Aa
Helpston 169 Hb
Helsby 185 Hd
Helston 36 Eb
Helstone 44 Cc
Helton 225 Ge
Helvellyn 225 Ed
Helwith Bridge 216 Ad
Hemblington 176 Dc
Hemel Hempstead 124 Bb
Hemingbrough 220 Aa
Hemingby 196 Bd
Hemingford Abbots 148 Ad
Hemingford Grey 148 Ad
Hemingstone 152 Bb
Hemington *Leics* 168 Ad
Hemington *Northants* 145 Ge
Hemington *Som* 93 Ea
Hemley 152 Ca
Hempholme 221 Ec
Hempnall 176 Ca
Hempnall Green 176 Ca
Hempriggs 305 Kg
Hempstead *Esx* 125 He
Hempstead *Nflk* 176 Be
Hempstead *Nflk* 177 Ed
Hempsted *Glos* 117 Fc
Hempton *Nflk* 173 Hd
Hempton *Oxon* 120 De
Hemsby 177 Ec
Hemswell 208 Cb
Hemswell Cliff 193 Ge
Hemsworth 205 Fd
Hemyock 68 Db
Henbury *Avon* 92 Cc
Henbury *Ches* 188 Dd
Henderland 241 Fe
Hendersyde Park 272 Da
Hendon *GL* 100 Dd
Hendon *T & W* 249 Fc
Hendre 185 Ec
Hendy 112 Ab
Heneglwys 181 Fd
Henfield 80 Ab
Henford 45 Fd
Henghurst 81 Hd
Hengoed *Caer* 89 Ge
Hengoed *Pwys* 137 Eb
Hengoed *Shrops* 161 Ee
Hengrave 149 Gc
Henham 125 Gd
Heniarth 160 Db
Henlade 69 Ec
Henley *Sflk* 152 Bb
Henley *Shrops* 137 Hd
Henley *Som* 69 Gd
Henley *W Ssx* 77 Ec
Henley-in-Arden 141 Fc
Henley-on-Thames 97 Gd
Henley Park 100 Aa
Henley's Down 81 Fb
Henllan *Card* 132 Da
Henllan *Denb* 184 Dc
Henllan Amgoed 109 Ed
Henllys 89 He
Henlow 124 Ce
Hennock 48 Cc
Henny Street 128 Be
Henryd 184 Ad
Henry's Moat 108 Dd
Hensall 205 Ge
Henshaw 245 Gd
Henstead 153 Ee
Henstridge 72 Bb
Henstridge Marsh 72 Bc
Henton *Oxon* 121 Gb
Henton *Som* 69 Ge
Henwick 140 Cb
Henwood 45 Eb
Heogan 321 Md
Heolgerrig 113 Fb
Heol Senni 113 Ed
Heol-y-Cyw 89 Ed
Hepburn 261 Ee
Hepple 260 Dc
Hepscott 261 Ga
Heptonstall 204 Ae
Hepworth *Sflk* 149 Hd
Hepworth *W Yorks* 204 Cc
Herbertstown 333 Nb
Herbrandston 108 Bb
Herdicott 45 Fd
Hereford 116 Cf
Hergest 137 Eb
Heriot 269 Hc
Herma Ness 321 Pk
Hermitage *Bdrs* 257 Hb
Hermitage *Berks* 97 Ec
Hermitage *D & G* 241 Fd
Hermitage *Dors* 52 Ce
Hermitage *Hants* 57 Fe
Hermitage, The 100 Da
Hermitage Castle 257 Gb
Hermon *Anglsy* 181 Ec
Hermon *Carm* 109 Ge
Hermon *Pemb* 109 Fe

500 Kinnadie–Langenhoe

Kinnadie 308 Ge
Kinnaird 284 Ee
Kinnaird Castle 296 Fc
Kinneff 297 He
Kinnegad 344 Fa
Kinnelhead 256 Cc
Kinnell 296 Fc
Kinnerley 161 Fd
Kinnersley *H & W* 137 Fa
Kinnersley *H & W* 140 Ca
Kinnerton 137 Ec
Kinnesswood 284 Dc
Kinninvie 228 De
Kinnitty 336 Bh
Kinnordy 296 Cc
Kinoulton 168 Ce
Kinross 284 Dc
Kinrossie 296 Aa
Kinsale 328 Bd
Kinsalebeg 328 Gg
Kinsaley 345 Na
Kinsbourne Green 124 Cc
Kinsham 137 Fc
Kinsley 205 Fd
Kinson 53 Gd
Kintail Forest 301 Jb
Kintbury 96 Cb
Kintessack 305 Jg
Kintillo 284 Dd
Kintocher 308 Ca
Kinton *H & W* 137 Gd
Kinton *Shrops* 161 Fc
Kintore 308 Eb
Kintour 316 Ff
Kintra 316 Ee
Kintraw 277 Gc
Kintyre 316 Jd
Kinuachdrach 277 Fb
Kinvarra 333 Ki
Kinveachy 305 Hb
Kinver 140 Ce
Kiplin Hall 229 Fb
Kippax 217 Ga
Kippen 281 Gb
Kippenross House 281 Hc
Kippford or Scaur 241 Fc
Kipping's Cross 81 Ee
Kirbuster 320 Fh
Kirby Bedon 176 Cb
Kirby Bellars 168 Dc
Kirby Cane 176 Da
Kirby Corner 141 Gd
Kirby Cross 129 Fd
Kirby Grindalythe 220 Dd
Kirby Hall 145 Ff
Kirby Hill *N Yorks* 217 Fd
Kirby Hill *N Yorks* 229 Ec
Kirby Knowle 229 Ha
Kirby le Soken 129 Fd
Kirby Misperton 220 Be
Kirby Muxloe 168 Bb
Kirby Row 176 Da
Kirby Sigston 229 Hb
Kirby Underdale 220 Cc
Kirby Wiske 229 Ga
Kircubbin 352 Zb
Kirdford 77 Gc
Kirk 313 Qi
Kirkabister 321 Mc
Kirkandrews 240 Db
Kirkandrews-on-Eden 244 Cc
Kirkbampton 244 Cc
Kirkbean 241 Gc
Kirk Bramwith 205 Hd
Kirkbride 244 Bc
Kirkbuddo 296 Eb
Kirkburn *Bdrs* 269 Ga
Kirkburn *Humb* 220 Dc
Kirkburton 204 Cd
Kirkby *Lincs* 208 Db
Kirkby *Mers* 200 Db
Kirkby *N Yorks* 232 Ac
Kirkby Fleetham 229 Fb
Kirkby Green 193 Hb
Kirkby-in-Ashfield 192 Bb
Kirkby-in-Furness 224 Da
Kirkby la Thorpe 193 Ha
Kirkby Lonsdale 213 Ge
Kirkby Malham 216 Ad
Kirkby Mallory 168 Ab
Kirkby Malzeard 217 Ee
Kirkby Mills 232 Ca
Kirkbymoorside 232 Ba
Kirkby on Bain 196 Bc
Kirkby Overblow 217 Fb
Kirkby Stephen 228 Ac
Kirkby Thore 225 He
Kirkby Underwood 169 Gd
Kirkby Wharfe 217 Hb
Kirkcaldy 285 Eb
Kirkcambeck 245 Ed
Kirkcarswell 241 Eb
Kirkcolm 237 Fd
Kirkconnel *D & G* 253 Hd
Kirkconnell *D & G* 241 Gd
Kirkcowan 240 Ad
Kirkcudbright 240 Dc
Kirkdean 269 Fb
Kirk Deighton 217 Fc
Kirk Ella 208 De
Kirkfieldbank 268 Cb
Kirkgunzeon 241 Fd
Kirk Hallam 192 Ba
Kirkham *Lancs* 213 Ea
Kirkham *N Yorks* 220 Bd
Kirkhamgate 204 De
Kirk Hammerton 217 Gc
Kirkharle 261 Ea
Kirkheaton *Northld* 248 Be
Kirkheaton *W Yorks* 204 Cd
Kirkhill *Angus* 296 Fd
Kirkhill *Hghld* 304 De
Kirkhills 352 Sh
Kirkhope 257 Fe
Kirkhouse 269 Ha
Kirkibost 300 Eb
Kirkinch 296 Cb
Kirkinner 240 Bc
Kirkintilloch 268 Ae
Kirk Ireton 189 Hb
Kirkistown 352 Za
Kirkland *Cumb* 245 Fa
Kirkland *D & G* 224 Bd
Kirkland *D & G* 253 Hd
Kirkland *D & G* 256 Ab
Kirk Langley 165 Ge
Kirkleatham 232 Ae
Kirklevington 229 Hc
Kirkley 177 Fa
Kirklington *Notts* 192 Db
Kirklington *N Yorks* 229 Ga
Kirklinton 244 Dd
Kirkliston 269 Fe
Kirkmadrine 237 Fb
Kirkmaiden 237 Ga
Kirk Merrington 248 Da
Kirk Michael 236 Cd
Kirkmichael *P & K* 293 Ld
Kirkmichael *S Ayr* 252 Dc
Kirkmond le Mire 209 Eb
Kirkmuirhill 268 Bb
Kirknewton *Loth* 269 Fd
Kirknewton *Northld* 273 Fa
Kirk of Shotts 268 Cd
Kirkoswald *Cumb* 245 Eb
Kirkoswald *S Ayr* 252 Cc
Kirkpatrick Durham 241 Ee
Kirkpatrick-Fleming 244 Be
Kirk Sandall 205 Hc
Kirksanton 224 Ca
Kirk Smeaton 205 Gd
Kirkstall 217 Ea
Kirkstile 308 Cd
Kirkton 296 Da
Kirkton *A & B* 277 Fc
Kirkton *Aber* 308 Db
Kirkton *Aber* 308 Dc
Kirkton *Aber* 308 Fe
Kirkton *Aber* 309 Jf
Kirkton *Angus* 296 Db
Kirkton *Bdrs* 257 Hd
Kirkton *D & G* 256 Ba
Kirkton *Fife* 285 Fe
Kirkton *Hghld* 301 Hc
Kirkton *Hghld* 301 Je
Kirkton *Hghld* 313 Kc
Kirkton *P & K* 284 Bd
Kirkton *S Lan* 256 Be
Kirktonhill 296 Fd
Kirkton Manor 269 Ga
Kirkton of Airlie 296 Cc
Kirkton of Auchterhouse 296 Ca
Kirkton of Barevan 305 Ge
Kirkton of Collace 296 Aa
Kirkton of Craig 297 Gc
Kirkton of Culsalmond 308 Dd
Kirkton of Durris 297 Gg
Kirkton of Glenbuchat 308 Ab
Kirkton of Glenisla 296 Bd
Kirkton of Kingoldrum 296 Cc
Kirkton of Largo 285 Gc
Kirkton of Lethendy 293 Mb
Kirkton of Logie Buchan 308 Gc
Kirkton of Maryculter 297 Hg
Kirkton of Menmuir 296 Ed
Kirkton of Monikie 296 Ea
Kirkton of Skene 308 Fa
Kirkton of Strathmartine 296 Ca
Kirktown 309 Hf
Kirktown of Alvah 308 Dg
Kirktown of Auchterless 308 Ee
Kirktown of Deskford 308 Cg
Kirktown of Fetteresso 297 Hf
Kirkwall 320 Dg
Kirkwall Aerodrome 320 Df
Kirkwhelpington 260 Da
Kirk Yetholm 260 Ce
Kirmington 209 Ed
Kirn 264 De
Kirriemuir 296 Cc
Kirstead Green 176 Ca
Kirtlebridge 244 Be
Kirtling 149 Eb
Kirtling Green 149 Eb
Kirtlington 120 Dc
Kirtomy 313 Kj
Kirton *Lincs* 172 Be
Kirton *Notts* 192 Dc
Kirton *Sflk* 129 Fe
Kirton End 196 Ba
Kirton Holme 196 Ba
Kirton in Lindsey 208 Cb
Kisdon Gorge 228 Bc
Kishkeam 325 Pi
Kislingbury 144 Cb
Kites Hardwick 144 Ac
Kitley Caves 40 De
Kitwood 76 Cd
Kiveton Park 192 Be
Klibreck 312 Hg
Knabbygates 308 Cf
Knaith 193 Fe
Knap Corner 72 Cc
Knaphill 100 Aa
Knapp *P & K* 296 Ba
Knapp *Som* 69 Fc
Knappogue Castle 333 Le
Knapton *Nflk* 176 De
Knapton *N Yorks* 217 Hc
Knapton *N Yorks* 220 Ce
Knapton Green 137 Gb
Knapwell 148 Bc
Knaresborough 217 Fc
Knarsdale 245 Fc
Knaven 308 Fe
Knayton 229 Ha
Knebworth 124 Dd
Knedlington 208 Ae
Kneesall 193 Ec
Kneesworth 148 Ba
Kneeton 193 Ea
Knelston 85 Hd
Knettishall 149 He
Knightacott 65 Gd
Knightcote 141 Hb
Knighton *Devon* 40 Dd
Knighton *Leics* 168 Cb
Knighton *Pwys* 137 Ed
Knighton *Staffs* 164 Bd
Knighton *Staffs* 188 Ca
Knights Town 324 Ff
Knightwick 140 Bb
Knill 137 Ec
Knipoch 277 Ge
Knipton 169 Ee
Knitsley 248 Cb
Kniveton 189 Hb
Knock *A & B* 289 Ga
Knock *Clare* 332 Gc
Knock *Cumb* 225 He
Knock *Mayo* 341 Ke
Knock *Moray* 308 Cf
Knockaderry 333 Ka
Knockaholet 352 Th
Knockainy 333 Na
Knockally 313 Pf
Knockan 312 Ee
Knockananna 337 Lf
Knockan Cliff 312 Dd
Knockandhu 305 Lc
Knockando 305 Ke
Knockanevin 328 Cj
Knockanure 332 Ga
Knockaunroe 324 Jh
Knockboy 328 Hi
Knockbrack 349 Kf
Knockbreak 300 Bg
Knockbrex 240 Cb
Knockbride 344 Gg
Knockbridge 345 Kg
Knockbrit 336 Ba
Knock Castle 264 Dd
Knockcloghrim 349 Re
Knockcoid 237 Fd
Knockcroghery 341 Rb
Knockdee 313 Pj
Knockdolian Castle 252 Ba
Knockdow 264 De
Knockdown 93 Fd
Knockenkelly 252 Ae
Knockentiber 265 Fa
Knockholt 101 Fa
Knockholt Pound 101 Fa
Knockin 161 Fd
Knocklearn 241 Ee
Knocklofty 328 Gk
Knocklong 333 Pa
Knockmore 341 Jg
Knocknagashel 325 Mk
Knocknagree 325 Nh
Knocknain 237 Ed
Knocknalina 340 Dj
Knocknalling 253 Fa
Knocknalower 340 Ej
Knockraha 328 Cf
Knockrome 316 Gh
Knocksharry 236 Bc
Knocktopher 336 Fa
Knodishall 153 Ec
Knole 101 Ga
Knolls Green 188 Dd
Knolton 161 Fe
Knook 73 De
Knossington 169 Eb
Knott End-on-Sea 212 Db
Knotting 145 Gc
Knotting Green 145 Ge
Knottingley 205 Ge
Knotty Green 100 Ae
Knowbury 137 Hd
Knowe 240 Ae
Knowehead 253 Gb
Knowesgate 260 Da
Knoweside 252 Cd
Knowetownhead 257 Hd
Knowhead 308 Gf
Knowle *Avon* 92 Dc
Knowle *Devon* 48 Be
Knowle *Devon* 65 Ed
Knowle *Dors* 49 Ec
Knowle *Shrops* 137 Hd
Knowle *Som* 69 Fd
Knowle *W Mids* 141 Fd
Knowle Green 213 Ga
Knowl Hill 97 Hc
Knowlton *Dors* 53 Ge
Knowlton *Kent* 105 Fa
Knowl Wall 164 Ce
Knowsley 200 Db
Knowsley Hall 200 Db
Knowsley Industrial Estate 200 Db
Knowstone 68 Ac
Knucklas 137 Ed
Knutsford 188 Cd
Knypersley 188 Db
Kuggar 36 Fa
Kyleakin 301 Gc
Kylemore Abbey 340 Db
Kyle of Lochalsh 301 Gc
Kylerhea 301 Gc
Kylesbeg 289 He
Kylesku 312 Eg
Kylesmorar 289 Kg
Kylestrome 312 Eg
Kyllachy House 305 Fc
Kynance Cove 36 Ea
Kynnersley 164 Ac
Kyre Park 140 Ac

L

Labasheeda 332 Hc
Labost 317 Xr
Lacasaigh 317 Yp
Laceby 209 Fc
Lacey Green 121 Hb
Lach Dennis 188 Cd
Lack 349 Kb
Lackan 344 Dc
Lackford 149 Fd
Lacock 93 Gb
Ladbroke 144 Ab
Laddingford 81 Ee
Lade Bank 196 Cb
Ladock 37 Ge
Ladybank *Fife* 285 Fc
Ladybank *S Ayr* 252 Cc
Ladycross 45 Fc
Ladykirk 273 Eb
Ladysbridge 328 Ef
Ladysford 308 Gg
Lady's Green 149 Fb
Laga 289 Hd
Lagavulin 316 Fe
Lagg *A & B* 316 Gh
Lagg *N Ayr* 249 He
Lagg *S Ayr* 252 Cd
Laggan *A & B* 316 Df
Laggan *Hghld* 292 Cg
Laggan *Hghld* 293 Gg
Laggan *S Ayr* 252 Ca
Laggan Lodge 276 Ee
Lagganulva 288 Fb
Laghey Corner 349 Rb
Laghy 348 Gc
Laglingarten 280 Bc
Lagrae 253 Hd
Lahardaun 340 Hg
Laide 312 Ac
Laide 312 Bc
Laindon 101 Hd
Lair 301 Ke
Lairg 312 Hd
Lairgmore 304 Dd
Laithes 244 Da
Lake 73 Fd
Lake Cottage 237 Fb
Lakenham 176 Cb
Lakenheath 149 Fe
Lake of Menteith 281 Fc
Lakesend 172 Da
Lakeside 225 Ea
Lake Vyrnwy 160 Bd
Laleham 100 Bb
Laleston 88 Dc
Lamarsh 128 Be
Lamas 176 Cd
Lamb Corner 128 De
Lambden 272 Db
Lambeg 352 Vb
Lamberhurst 81 Ed
Lamberton 273 Fc
Lambeth 101 Ec
Lambfell Moar 236 Bc
Lamb Head 320 Fh
Lambley *Northld* 245 Fc
Lambley *Notts* 192 Da
Lambourn 96 Cc
Lambourne End 101 Fe
Lambs Green 80 Ad
Lambston 108 Cc
Lamerton 45 Gb
Lamesley 248 Dc
Lamington *Hghld* 313 Ka
Lamington *S Lan* 268 Da
Lamlash 264 Ca
Lamloch 253 Fb
Lamoge 336 Ea
Lamonby 244 Da
Lamorna 36 Cb
Lamorran 37 Gd
Lampeter 133 Fa
Lampeter Velfrey 109 Ec
Lamphey 108 Db
Lamplugh 224 Be
Lamport 144 Dd
Lamyatt 72 Ad
Lana 45 Fd
Lanark 268 Cb
Lancaster 213 Ed
Lanchester 248 Cb
L'Ancress *Ch Is* 52 Db
Landbeach 148 Cc
Landcross 65 Ec
Landerberry 308 Ea
Landford 73 Gb
Landford Manor 73 Gc
Landimore 85 He
Landkey 65 Fd
Landore 88 Be
Landrake 45 Fa
Landscove 48 Ba
Land's End 33 Bb
Landshipping 108 Dc
Landulph 45 Ga
Landwade 149 Ec
Landywood 164 Db
Laneast 45 Ec
Lane End *Bucks* 97 He
Lane-end *Corn* 44 Ca
Lane End *Cumb* 224 Cb
Lane End *Derbs* 192 Bc
Lane End *Dors* 53 Ed
Lane Green 164 Cb
Laneham 193 Fd
Lane Head *Dur* 229 Ed
Lane Head *GM* 201 Fb
Lane Head *W Yorks* 204 Cc
Lanesborough 341 Sc
Laneshaw Bridge 216 Bb
Langar 168 De
Langbank 265 Fe
Langbar 216 Cc
Langcliffe 216 Ad
Langdale End 233 Eb
Langdon Beck 245 Ha
Langdon Cliffs 84 De
Langdon Cross 45 Fc
Langdon Hills 101 Hd
Langdyke 285 Fc
Langenhoe 128 Dc

510 Old Goole–Pelutho

Old Goole 208 Ae
Old Gore 116 Dd
Old Hall, The 209 Fd
Oldham 204 Ac
Oldhamstocks 272 De
Old Head 328 Bc
Old Heath 128 Dd
Old Hurst 148 Bd
Old Hutton 225 Ga
Old Kea 37 Gd
Old Kilcullen 336 Jh
Old Kildimo 333 Lc
Old Kilpatrick 265 Ge
Old Knebworth 124 Dd
Oldland 92 Dc
Old Leake 196 Db
Oldleighlin 336 Gd
Old Malton 220 Be
Old Man of Hoy 320 Af
Oldmeldrum 308 Fc
Old Micklefield 217 Ga
Old Milverton 141 Gc
Old Monkland 268 Bd
Old Newton 152 Ac
Oldpark 164 Ab
Old Philpstoun 269 Ee
Old Radnor 137 Eb
Old Rattray 309 Hf
Old Rayne 308 Dc
Old Romney 84 Ac
Old Ross 329 Nk
Old Sarum 73 Fd
Old Scone 284 De
Old Shields 268 Ce
Oldshore Beg 312 Di
Oldshoremore 312 Ei
Old Slains Castle 309 Hc
Old Sodbury 93 Ed
Old Somerby 169 Fe
Oldstead 232 Aa
Old Stratford 144 Da
Old Swarland 261 Fc
Old Town *Cumb* 225 Ga
Oldtown *Dub* 345 Mb
Old Town *Laois* 336 Ef
Old Town *Northld* 260 Cb
Old Town *Rosc* 333 Rj
Oldtown of Ord 308 Df
Oldwalls 85 He
Old Warden 145 Ha
Oldways End 68 Ac
Old Weston 145 Gd
Oldwhat 308 Ff
Old Winchester Hill 76 Cc
Old Windsor 100 Ac
Old Wives Lees 104 Da
Old Wolverton 145 Ea
Olgrinmore 313 Ni
Oliver 256 Ce
Oliver's Battery 76 Ac
Ollaberry 321 Lh
Ollach 300 Ed
Ollerton *Ches* 188 Cd
Ollerton *Notts* 192 Dc
Ollerton *Shrops* 164 Ad
Olney 145 Eb
Olveston 92 Dd
Omagh 349 Mc
Ombersley 140 Cc
Omeath 345 Mh
Omeath 345 Mh
Ompton 192 Dc
Onaght 332 Ei
Onchan 236 Db
Onecote 189 Fb
Ongar Hill 172 Dd
Ongar Street 137 Fc
Onibury 137 Gd
Onich 292 Ad
Onllwyn 112 Dc
Onneley 188 Ca
Onslow Village 77 Fe
Oola 333 Qb
Opinan *Hghld* 301 Gh
Opinan *Hghld* 312 Ac
Orange Lane 272 Db
Oranmore 333 Kj
Orasaigh 317 Yn
Orbost 300 Be
Orby 196 Dc
Orchard 72 Cb
Orchard Portman 69 Ec
Orcheston 73 Ee
Orcop 116 Bd
Orcop Hill 116 Bd
Ord 300 Fb
Ordhead 308 Db
Ordie 308 Ba
Ore 81 Gb
Oreham Common 80 Ab
Oreston 40 De
Oreton 140 Ae
Orford *Lancs* 201 Fb
Orford *Sflk* 153 Eb
Orford Ness 153 Ea
Orgreave 165 Fc
Orielton 108 Ca
Oristown 344 Hd
Orlestone 84 Ad
Orleton *H & W* 137 Gc
Orleton *H & W* 140 Ac
Orlingbury 145 Ed
Ormesby 232 Ad
Ormesby St Margaret 177 Ec
Ormesby St Michael 177 Ec
Ormiclate Castle 317 Sf
Ormiston 269 Jd
Ormsaigmore 289 Fd
Ormskirk 200 Dc
Orpington 101 Fb
Orrell 201 Ec
Orritor 349 Qc
Orroland 241 Eb
Orsett 101 Hd
Orslow 164 Cc
Orston 193 Ea
Orton 305 Mf
Orton *Cumb* 225 Hc
Orton *Northants* 145 Ed
Orton Longueville 169 Ha
Orton-on-the-Hill 165 Hb
Orton Waterville 169 Ha
Orwell 148 Bb
Osbaldeston 213 Ga
Osbaldwick 220 Ac
Osbaston *Leics* 168 Ab
Osbaston *Shrops* 164 Ac
Osborne House 56 Dd
Osbournby 169 Ge
Oscroft 188 Ac
Ose 300 Ce
Osgathorpe 168 Ac
Osgodby *Lincs* 208 Db
Osgodby *N Yorks* 220 Aa
Osgodby *N Yorks* 233 Fa
Oskaig 300 Ed
Oskamull 288 Fb
Osmaston 189 Ga
Osmington 52 Dc
Osmington Mills 52 Dc
Osmotherley 229 Hb
Osnaburgh or Dairsie 285 Gd
Ospisdale 313 Kb
Ospringe 104 Cb
Ossett 204 De
Ossington 193 Ec
Ostend 104 Ce
Oswaldkirk 220 Ae
Oswaldtwistle 201 Ge
Oswestry 161 Ed
Otford 101 Ga
Otham 104 Aa
Othery 69 Fd
Otley *Sflk* 152 Cb
Otley *W Yorks* 217 Eb
Otterbourne 76 Ac
Otterburn *Northld* 260 Cb
Otterburn *N Yorks* 216 Ac
Otterburn Camp 260 Cb
Otter Ferry 277 Ha
Otterham 44 Dd
Otterhampton 69 Ee
Ottershaw 100 Bb
Otterswick 321 Nh
Otterton 49 Ec
Ottery St Mary 49 Fd
Ottinge 84 Be
Ottringham 209 Fe
Oughterard 340 Ha
Oughterby 244 Bc
Oughtershaw 228 Ba
Oughtibridge 205 Eb
Oulart 337 Lb
Oulston 217 He
Oulton *Cumb* 244 Bc
Oulton *Nflk* 176 Bd
Oulton *Sflk* 177 Fa
Oulton *Staffs* 164 De
Oulton *W Yorks* 205 Ee
Oulton Broad 177 Fa
Oulton Street 176 Bd
Oundle 145 Ge
Ousby 245 Fa
Ousdale 313 Nf
Ousden 149 Fb
Ousefleet 208 Be
Ouse Washes 148 Ce
Ouston *Dur* 248 Dc
Ouston *Northld* 248 Be
Outeragh 328 Fk
Outgate 225 Eb
Outhgill 228 Ac
Outlands 164 Be
Outlane 204 Bd
Out Newton 209 Ge
Out Rawcliffe 213 Eb
Out Skerries 321 Pg
Outwell 172 Db
Outwood *Sry* 80 Be
Outwood *W Yorks* 205 Ee
Oval, The 93 Eb
Ovenden 204 Be
Ovens 325 Sf
Over *Avon* 92 Cd
Over *Cambs* 148 Bd
Over *Ches* 188 Bc
Overbister 320 Fj
Overbury 117 Ge
Over Compton 69 Hb
Over Haddon 189 Hc
Over Kellet 213 Fd
Over Kiddington 120 Dd
Overleigh 69 Gd
Over Norton 120 Cd
Overseal 165 Gc
Over Silton 229 Hb
Oversland 104 Da
Oversley Green 141 Eb
Overstone 145 Ec
Overstrand 176 Cf
Over Stratton 69 Gb
Overthorpe 144 Aa
Overton *C of Aber* 308 Fb
Overton *D & G* 241 Gd
Overton *Hants* 76 Be
Overton *Lancs* 213 Ec
Overton *Shrops* 137 Gd
Overton *Swan* 85 Hd
Overton *Wrex* 185 Ga
Overtown 268 Cc
Over Wallop 73 Gd
Over Whitacre 165 Ga
Over Worton 120 Dd
Oving *Bucks* 121 Gd
Oving *W Ssx* 57 He
Ovingdean 60 De
Ovingham 248 Bd
Ovington *Esx* 149 Fa
Ovington *Hants* 76 Bd
Ovington *Nflk* 173 Hb
Ovington *Northld* 248 Bd
Ovington *N Yorks* 229 Ed
Owenbeg 341 Kj
Ower 73 Hb
Owermoigne 52 Dc
Owlswick 121 Gb
Owmby 208 Dc
Owmby-by-Spital 193 He
Owning 329 Kk
Owslebury 76 Bc
Owston 168 Db
Owston Ferry 208 Bc
Owstwick 221 Ga
Owthorpe 168 Ce
Oxborough 173 Fb
Oxburgh Hall 172 Cb
Oxcombe 196 Cd
Oxen End 125 Hd
Oxenfoord Castle 269 Hd
Oxenholme 225 Gb
Oxenhope 216 Ca
Oxen Park 225 Ea
Oxenton 117 Ge
Oxenwood 96 Ca
Oxford 121 Eb
Oxhill 141 Ha
Oxley 164 Db
Oxley's Green 81 Ec
Oxnam 260 Bd
Oxney Green 125 Hb
Oxshott 100 Cb
Oxspring 204 Dc
Oxted 101 Ea
Oxton *Bdrs* 272 Ac
Oxton *Notts* 192 Db
Oxwich 85 Hd
Oxwich Green 85 Hd
Oxwick 173 Hd
Oykel Bridge 312 Fd
Oyne 308 Dc
Oystermouth 88 Bd
Ozleworth 93 Ee

P

Pabail 317 AAq
Packington 165 Hc
Padanaram 296 Dc
Padbury 121 Ge
Paddington 100 Dd
Paddlesworth 84 Bd
Paddockhaugh 305 Lf
Paddockhole 257 Ea
Paddock Wood 81 Ee
Paddolgreen 161 He
Padeswood 185 Fc
Padiham 213 Ha
Padside 216 Dc
Padstow 44 Bb
Pagham 57 Gd
Paglesham Churchend 104 Ce
Paglesham Eastend 104 Ce
Paible 317 Si
Paignton 48 Ca
Pailton 144 Ae
Painscastle 136 Da
Painshawfield 248 Bd
Painswick 117 Fb
Paisley 265 Gd
Pakefield 177 Fa
Pakenham 149 Hc
Palatine 336 He
Pale 160 Be
Palestine 73 Ge
Paley Street 97 Hc
Palgowan 252 Da
Palgrave 152 Bd
Pallas Grean (New) 333 Pb
Pallaskenry 333 Lc
Pallinsburn House 273 Ea
Palmerstown 89 Gb
Palnackie 241 Fc
Palnure 240 Bd
Palterton 192 Bc
Pamber End 97 Fa
Pamber Green 97 Fa
Pamber Heath 97 Fb
Pamington 117 Ge
Pamphill 53 Fe
Pampisford 148 Ca
Panborough 69 Ge
Panbride 296 Ea
Pancrasweek 45 Ee
Pandy *C & M* 157 Gb
Pandy *Mon* 116 Ad
Pandy *Pwys* 160 Bb
Pandy *Wrex* 160 De
Pandy Tudur 184 Bc
Panfield 128 Ad
Pangbourne 97 Fc
Pannal 217 Fc
Pant 161 Ed
Pantasaph 185 Ed
Panteg 108 Ce
Pant Glâs *C & M* 181 Fa
Pant-glâs *Pwys* 157 Ha
Pantglas Hall 112 Ad
Pantgwyn 132 Ca
Pant-lasau 112 Bb
Pant Mawr 136 Ae
Panton 196 Ad
Pant-pastynog 184 Dc
Pantperthog 157 Hb
Pant-y-dwr 136 Bd
Pant-y-ffridd 160 Db
Pantyffynnon 112 Bc
Panxworth 176 Dc
Papa Stour 321 Jf
Papa Stronsay 320 Fh
Papa Westray 320 Dk
Papcastle 244 Aa
Papple 272 Be
Papplewick 192 Cb
Papworth Everard 148 Ac
Papworth St Agnes 148 Ac
Par 37 Je
Parbold 200 Dd
Parbrook 69 Hd
Parcllyn 132 Cb
Parc-Seymour 92 Be
Pardshaw 224 Be
Parham 152 Dc
Parham House 60 Af
Parish Holm 253 He
Park 349 Nf
Park Corner 97 Fd
Parkend *Glos* 116 Db
Park End *Northld* 245 He
Parkeston 129 Fe
Parkford 296 Dc
Parkgate *Ant* 352 Vd
Parkgate *Ches* 185 Fd
Parkgate *Ches* 188 Cd
Parkgate *D & G* 256 Ca
Park Gate *Hants* 56 De
Parkgate *Sry* 80 Ae
Parkham 64 Dc
Parkham Ash 64 Dc
Parkhill 296 Ab
Parkhouse 116 Cb
Parkhurst 56 Cd
Park Lane 161 Ge
Parkmill 88 Ad
Parkneuk 297 Ge
Parkstone 53 Gd
Park Street 124 Cb
Parley Cross 53 Gd
Parracombe 65 Ge
Parrog 108 De
Parsonby 244 Aa
Parson Cross 205 Eb
Parson Drove 172 Bb
Partick 265 Hd
Partington 201 Gb
Partney 196 Dc
Parton *Cumb* 224 Ae
Parton *D & G* 240 De
Partridge Green 77 Hb
Partrishow 113 Hd
Partry 340 Hd
Parwich 189 Gb
Passage East 329 Mj
Passage West 328 Ce
Passenham 121 Ge
Passfield 77 Ed
Passingford Bridge 101 Ge
Paston 176 De
Patcham 60 De
Patching 60 Ae
Patchole 65 Ge
Patchway 92 Dd
Pateley Bridge 216 Dd
Pathe 69 Fd
Pathfinder Village 48 Cd
Pathhead *E Ayr* 253 Gd
Pathhead *Fife* 285 Eb
Pathhead *Midln* 269 Hd
Path of Condie 284 Cd
Patmore Heath 125 Fd
Patna 253 Ed
Patney 93 Ha
Patrick 236 Bc
Patrick Brompton 229 Fb
Patrickswell 333 Mb
Patrington 209 Ge
Patrixbourne 105 Ea
Patshull Hall 164 Cb
Patterdale 225 Ed
Patterton Station 265 Hc
Pattingham 164 Ca
Pattishall 144 Cb
Pattiswick 128 Bd
Patton Bridge 225 Gb
Paul 36 Cb
Paulerspury 144 Da
Paull 209 Ee
Paulstown or Whitehall 336 Gc
Paulton 92 Da
Pauperhaugh 261 Fb
Pavenham 145 Fb
Pawlett 69 Ee
Pawston 273 Ea
Paxford 120 Ae
Paxton 273 Fc
Paxton's Tower 112 Ac
Payhembury 49 Ee
Paythorne 216 Ac
Peacehaven 61 Ee
Peak Dale 189 Fd
Peak District National Park 189 Ge
Peak Forest 189 Gd
Peakirk 169 Hb
Pean Hill 105 Eb
Peanmeanach 289 Jf
Pearsie 296 Cc
Peasdown St John 93 Ea
Peasemore 96 Dc
Peasenhall 152 Dc
Pease Pottage 80 Ad
Peaslake 77 Ge
Peasmarsh 81 Gc
Peaston 269 Jd
Peaston Bank 269 Jd
Peathill 308 Gg
Peat Inn 285 Gc
Peatling Magna 168 Ba
Peatling Parva 144 Be
Peaton 137 He
Pebmarsh 128 Be
Pebworth 141 Fa
Pecket Well 204 Ae
Peckforton 188 Ab
Peckleton 168 Ab
Pedmore 140 De
Pedwell 69 Gd
Peebles 269 Gb
Peel 236 Bc
Pegswood 261 Ga
Peinchorran 300 Ed
Peinlich 300 Df
Pelaw 248 Dd
Pelcomb Bridge 108 Cc
Pelcomb Cross 108 Cc
Peldon 128 Cc
Pelsall 165 Eb
Pelton 248 Dc
Pelutho 244 Ab

514 Ringstead–St Bees

Ringstead *Nflk* 173 Ff
Ringstead *Northants* 145 Fd
Ringville 328 Hg
Ringwood 53 He
Ringwould 84 De
Rinmore 308 Bb
Rinsey 36 Db
Ripe 80 Db
Ripley *Derbs* 192 Ab
Ripley *Hants* 53 Hd
Ripley *N Yorks* 217 Ed
Ripley *Sry* 100 Ba
Riplingham 220 Da
Ripon 217 Fe
Rippingale 169 Gd
Ripple *H & W* 117 Fe
Ripple *Kent* 105 Ga
Ripponden 204 Bd
Rireavach 312 Cc
Risbury 137 Hb
Risby 149 Fc
Risca 89 He
Rise 221 Fb
Risegate 172 Ad
Riseley *Beds* 145 Gc
Riseley *Berks* 97 Gb
Rishangles 152 Bc
Rishton 201 Ge
Rishworth 204 Bd
Rising Bridge 201 Ge
Risley *Ches* 201 Fb
Risley *Derbs* 168 Ae
Risplith 217 Ed
Rispond 312 Gj
Rivar 96 Cb
Rivenhall 128 Bc
Rivenhall End 128 Bc
River 77 Fc
River Bank 148 Dc
Riverchapel 337 Mc
Riverhead 101 Ga
Riverstick 328 Bd
Riverstown *Cork* 328 Cf
Riverstown *Sligo* 341 Pi
Riverstown *Tipp* 333 Sh
Rivington 201 Fd
Roachill 68 Ac
Roade 144 Db
Roadmeetings 268 Cb
Roadside 313 Pj
Roadside of Catterline 297 He
Roadside of Kinneff 297 He
Roadwater 68 Cd
Roag 300 Be
Roa Island 212 Cd
Roath 89 Gc
Roberton *Bdrs* 257 Gd
Roberton *S Lan* 256 Be
Robertsbridge 81 Fc
Robertstown 305 Le
Roberttown 204 Ce
Robeston Cross 108 Bb
Robeston Wathen 108 Dc
Robin Hood *Derbs* 189 Hd
Robin Hood *W Yorks* 205 Ee
Robin Hood's Bay 233 Ec
Robins 77 Ec
Robinstown 344 Jc
Roborough *Devon* 45 Ha
Roborough *Devon* 65 Fb
Rob Roy's House 280 Bd
Roby Mill 201 Ec
Rocester 165 Fe
Roch 108 Bd
Rochallie 296 Ac
Rochdale 201 Hd
Roche 44 Ba
Rochester *Kent* 104 Ab
Rochester *Northld* 260 Cb
Rochford *Esx* 104 Be
Rochford *H & W* 140 Ac
Rochfortbridge 344 Ea
Rochsoles 268 Bd
Rock *Caer* 89 Ge
Rock *Corn* 44 Bb
Rock *H & W* 140 Bd
Rock *Northld* 261 Ge
Rock, The 349 Qc
Rockbeare 49 Ed
Rockbourne 73 Fb
Rockchapel 325 Pj
Rockcliffe *Cumb* 244 Cd
Rockcliffe *D & G* 241 Fc
Rockcorry 344 Gh
Rock Ferry 185 Ge
Rockfield *Gwent* 116 Bc
Rockfield *Hghld* 313 Mb
Rockhampton 92 De
Rockhill 333 Ma
Rockingham 169 Ea
Rockland All Saints 173 Ha
Rockland St Mary 176 Db
Rockland St Peter 173 Ha
Rockley 96 Ac
Rockmills 328 Ci
Rockwell End 97 Gd
Rodbourne 93 Gd
Rodd 137 Fc
Roddam 261 Ee
Rodden 52 Cc
Rode 93 Fa
Rode Heath *Ches* 188 Db
Rodeheath *Ches* 188 Dc
Rodel 317 Vk
Roden 161 Hc
Rodhuish 68 Cd
Rodington 161 Hc
Rodington Heath 161 Hc
Rodley 117 Ec
Rodmarton 93 Ge
Rodmell 61 Ee
Rodmersham 104 Cb
Rodney Stoke 69 Ge
Rodono Hotel 257 Ee
Rodsley 189 Ha
Roecliffe 217 Fd
Roe Green 125 Ee
Roehampton 100 Dc
Roesound 321 Lf
Roffey 77 Hd
Rogart 313 Kd
Rogart Halt 313 Kd
Rogate 77 Ec
Rogerstone 89 Hd
Rogerton 265 Jc
Roghadal 317 Vk
Rogiet 92 Bd
Roker 249 Fc
Rollesby 177 Ec
Rolleston *Leics* 168 Db
Rolleston *Notts* 193 Eb
Rolleston *Staffs* 165 Gd
Rolston 221 Gb
Rolvenden 81 Gd
Rolvenden Layne 81 Gd
Romaldkirk 228 Ce
Romanby 229 Gb
Romannobridge 269 Fb
Romansleigh 65 Hc
Romford *Dors* 53 Ge
Romford *GL* 101 Gd
Romiley 204 Ab
Romney Marsh 84 Ad
Romsey 73 Hc
Romsley *H & W* 140 Dd
Romsley *Shrops* 140 Be
Ronague 236 Bb
Rookby 228 Bd
Rookhope 248 Ab
Rookley 56 Dc
Rooks Bridge 92 Aa
Roonah Quay 340 De
Roos 221 Ga
Roosebeck 212 Cd
Roosecote 212 Cd
Roosky *Mayo* 341 Mg
Roosky *Rosc* 341 Se
Rootpark 268 Dc
Ropley 76 Cd
Ropley Dean 76 Cd
Ropsley 169 Fe
Rora 309 Hf
Rora Head 320 Ae
Rorrington 161 Fb
Roscommon 341 Qc
Roscrea 336 Bf
Rose 36 Fe
Roseacre 213 Ea
Rose Ash 65 Hc
Rosebank 268 Cb
Rosebrough 261 Fe
Rosebush 108 Dd
Rose Cottage 289 Gd
Rosedale Abbey 232 Cb
Roseden 261 Ee
Rosefield 305 Gf
Rosegreen 336 Ba
Rosehaugh Mains 304 Ef
Rosehearty 308 Gg
Rosehill *Aber* 296 Eg
Rosehill *Shrops* 164 Ae
Roseisle 305 Kg
Rosemarket 108 Cb
Rosemarkie 304 Ff
Rosemary Lane 68 Db
Rosemount 296 Ab
Rosemount *P & K* 296 Bb
Rosemount *S Ayr* 252 De
Rosenallis 336 Dh
Rosenannon 44 Ba
Rosepool 108 Bc
Rosewarne 36 Ec
Rosewell 269 Gd
Roseworthy 36 Ec
Rosgill 225 Gd
Roshven 289 Je
Roskhill 300 Be
Rosley 244 Cb
Roslin 269 Gd
Rosliston 165 Gc
Rosmult 333 Sc
Rosnakill 349 Ji
Rosneath 280 Ca
Ross *D & G* 240 Db
Ross *Meath* 344 Ee
Ross *Northld* 273 Ha
Ross *P & K* 281 He
Rossbrin 325 Lb
Ross Carbery 325 Pb
Rossett 185 Gb
Rossie Farm School 296 Fc
Rossie Ochill 284 Cd
Rossie Priory 296 Ba
Rossington 205 Hb
Rossinver 341 Rk
Rosskeen 304 Eg
Rossland 265 Ge
Rosslare 329 Sj
Rosslare Harbour 329 Sj
Rosslea 344 Fj
Rossmore 325 Qc
Ross-on-Wye 116 Dd
Ross Port 340 Ej
Ross Priory 280 Ea
Rostellan 328 De
Roster 313 Qg
Rostherne 188 Ce
Rosthwaite 224 Dd
Roston 189 Ga
Rostrevor 345 Mh
Rosyth 284 Da
Rothbury 261 Ec
Rotherby 168 Cc
Rotherfield 80 Dc
Rotherfield Greys 97 Gd
Rotherfield Peppard 97 Gd
Rotherham 205 Fb
Rothersthorpe 144 Db
Rotherwick 97 Ga
Rothes 305 Le
Rothesay 264 Cd
Rothienorman 308 Ed
Rothiesholm 320 Fh
Rothley *Leics* 168 Bc
Rothley *Northld* 261 Ea
Rothmaise 308 Dd
Rothwell *Lincs* 209 Eb
Rothwell *Northants* 145 Ee
Rothwell *W Yorks* 205 Ee
Rotsea 221 Ec
Rottal 296 Cd
Rottingdean 60 De
Rottington 224 Ad
Roud 56 Dc
Roudham 149 He
Rougham *Nflk* 173 Gd
Rougham *Sflk* 149 Hc
Rougham Green 149 Hc
Roughburn 292 Df
Rough Close 164 De
Rough Common 105 Ea
Roughlee 216 Ab
Roughley 165 Fa
Roughsike 245 Ee
Roughton *Lincs* 196 Bc
Roughton *Nflk* 176 Ce
Roughton *Shrops* 164 Ba
Roundbush Green 125 Gc
Roundhay 217 Fa
Roundstone 340 Da
Roundstreet Common 77 Gc
Roundway 93 Hb
Roundwood 337 Mh
Rounton 229 Hc
Rousay 320 Di
Rousdon 49 Gd
Rousham 120 Dd
Rousky 349 Nd
Rous Lench 141 Eb
Routenburn 264 Dd
Routh 221 Eb
Row *Corn* 44 Cb
Row *Cumb* 225 Fa
Rowallane 352 Xa
Rowanburn 244 De
Rowberrow 92 Ba
Rowde 93 Gb
Rowen 184 Ad
Rower, The 336 Ha
Rowfoot 245 Fd
Rowhedge 128 Dd
Rowhook 77 Hd
Rowington 141 Gc
Rowington Green 141 Gd
Rowland 189 Hd
Rowland's Castle 76 Db
Rowlands Gill 248 Cc
Rowledge 77 Ee
Rowley *Devon* 65 Hb
Rowley *Dur* 248 Bb
Rowley *Humb* 220 Da
Rowley *Shrops* 161 Fb
Rowley Regis 140 De
Rowlstone 116 Ad
Rowly 77 Ge
Rowney Green 141 Ed
Rownhams 73 Hb
Rowrah 224 Bd
Rowsham 121 Hc
Rowsley 189 Hc
Rowston 193 Hb
Rowthorne 192 Bc
Rowton *Ches* 185 Hc
Rowton *Shrops* 164 Ac
Rowton Castle 161 Fc
Roxburgh 272 Ca
Roxby *Humb* 208 Cd
Roxby *N Yorks* 232 Cd
Roxton 145 Hb
Roxwell 125 Hb
Royal British Legion Village 104 Aa
Royal Leamington Spa 141 Hc
Royal Military Canal 81 Hd
Royal Tunbridge Wells 80 Dd
Roybridge 292 Cf
Roydon *Esx* 125 Fb
Roydon *Nflk* 152 Ae
Roydon *Nflk* 173 Fd
Royston *Herts* 125 Ef
Royston *S Yorks* 205 Ed
Royton 204 Ac
Rozel 53 Ga
Ruabon 185 Ga
Ruan Lanihorne 37 Gd
Ruan Major 36 Fa
Ruan Minor 36 Fa
Ruardean 116 Dc
Ruardean Woodside 116 Dc
Rubane 352 Zb
Rubery 140 Dd
Ruckcroft 245 Eb
Ruckhall 116 Be
Ruckinge 84 Ad
Ruckland 196 Cd
Rucklers Lane 124 Bb
Ruckley 161 Hb
Rudbaxton 108 Cd
Rudby 229 Hc
Ruddington 168 Be
Rudford 117 Ed
Rudge 93 Fa
Rudgeway 92 Dd
Rudgwick 77 Gd
Rudhall 116 Dd
Rudley Green 128 Bb
Rudry 89 Gd
Rudston 221 Ed
Rudyard 189 Eb
Rufford 200 Dd
Rufforth 217 Hc
Rugby 144 Bd
Rugeley 165 Ec
Ruilick 304 De
Ruisgarry 317 Uk
Ruishton 69 Ec
Ruislip 100 Bd
Rùm 288 Eg
Rumbling Bridge 284 Cb
Rumburgh 152 De
Rumford *Corn* 44 Ab
Rumford *Falk* 268 De
Rumney 89 Hc
Runacraig 281 Fd
Runcorn 188 Ae
Runcton 57 Ge
Runcton Holme 173 Eb
Runfold 77 Ee
Runhall 176 Ab
Runham 177 Ec
Runnington 68 Dc
Runsell Green 128 Ab
Runswick Bay 232 Dd
Runtaleave 296 Bd
Runwell 104 Ae
Rushall *H & W* 116 De
Rushall *Nflk* 152 Be
Rushall *Staffs* 165 Eb
Rushall *Wilts* 96 Aa
Rushbrooke 149 Gc
Rushbury 161 Ha
Rushden *Herts* 125 Ee
Rushden *Northants* 145 Fc
Rushford 149 He
Rush Green 101 Gd
Rushlake Green 81 Eb
Rushmere 153 Ee
Rushmere St Andrew 152 Ca
Rushmoor 77 Ee
Rushock 140 Cd
Rusholme 201 Hb
Rushton *Ches* 188 Ac
Rushton *Northants* 145 Ee
Rushton *Shrops* 164 Ab
Rushton Spencer 189 Ec
Rushwick 140 Cb
Rushyford 229 Fe
Ruskie 281 Gc
Ruskington 193 Hb
Rusko 240 Cc
Rusland 225 Ea
Rusper 80 Ad
Ruspidge 116 Dc
Russell's Water 97 Gd
Rustington 60 Ae
Ruston 233 Ea
Ruston Parva 221 Ed
Ruswarp 232 Dc
Rutherend 268 Ab
Rutherford 272 Ca
Rutherglen 265 Jd
Ruthernbridge 44 Ca
Ruthin 185 Eb
Ruthrieston 308 Ga
Ruthven *Aber* 308 Ce
Ruthven *Angus* 296 Bb
Ruthven *Hghld* 305 Gd
Ruthven House 296 Cb
Ruthvoes 44 Ba
Ruthwell 244 Ad
Rutland Water 169 Fb
Ruyton-XI-Towns 161 Fd
Ryal 248 Be
Ryal Fold 201 Fe
Ryall *Dors* 96 De
Ryall *H & W* 140 Ca
Ryarsh 101 Ha
Rydal 225 Ec
Ryde 56 Dd
Rye 81 Hc
Rye Foreign 81 Gc
Rye Harbour 81 Hb
Ryehill 333 Mk
Ryhall 169 Gc
Ryhill 205 Ed
Ryhope 249 Fc
Rylane Cross 325 Rg
Rylstone 216 Bc
Ryme Intrinseca 69 Hb
Ryther 217 Ha
Ryton *Glos* 117 Ee
Ryton *N Yorks* 220 Be
Ryton *Shrops* 164 Bb
Ryton *T & W* 248 Cd
Ryton-on-Dunsmore 141 Hd

S

Saasaig 300 Fa
Sabden 213 Ha
Sackers Green 128 Ce
Sacombe 125 Ec
Sacquoy Head 320 Ci
Sacriston 248 Db
Sadberge 229 Gd
Saddell 316 Jd
Saddington 168 Ca
Saddle Bow 173 Ec
Sadgill 225 Fc
Saffron Walden 125 Ge
Saggart 337 Lj
Saham Toney 173 Hb
Saighton 185 Hc
St Abbs 273 Fd
St Agnes 36 Fe
St Albans 124 Cb
St Allen 37 Ge
St Andrews 285 Hd
St Andrews Major 89 Gc
St Anne 53 Ha
St Anne's 200 Ce
St Ann's 256 Cb
St Ann's Chapel *Devon* 41 Ed
St Ann's Chapel *Devon* 45 Gb
St Anthony-in-Meneage 36 Fb
St Arvans 92 Ce
St Asaph 184 Dd
St Athan 89 Fb
St Aubin 53 Fa
St Austell 37 Je
St Bees 224 Ad

St Benet's Abbey–Scottow 515

St Benet's Abbey	176	Dc
St Blazey	37	Je
St Blazey Gate	37	Je
St Boswells	272	Ba
St Brelade's	53	Fa
St Breock	44	Bb
St Breward	44	Cb
St Briavels	116	Cb
St Brides	108	Bc
St Brides Major	88	Dc
St Brides Netherwent	92	Bd
St Brides-super-Ely	89	Gc
St Bride's Wentlooge	89	Hd
St Budeaux	40	Ce
Saintbury	120	Ae
St Buryan	36	Cb
St Catherine	93	Ec
St Catherines	280	Bc
St Clears	109	Fc
St Cleer	45	Ea
St Clement	37	Gd
St Clether	45	Ec
St Colmac	264	Cd
St Colme House	284	Da
St Columb Major	44	Ba
St Columb Minor	44	Aa
St Columb Road	37	He
St Combs	309	Hg
St Cross South Elmham	152	Ce
St Cyrus	297	Gd
St Davids *Fife*	284	Da
St David's *P & K*	284	Be
St David's *Pemb*	108	Ad
St Day	36	Fd
St Decumans	68	Ce
St Dennis	37	He
St Dogmaels	132	Ba
St Dominick	45	Fa
St Donats	89	Eb
St Endellion	44	Bb
St Enoder	37	Ge
St Erme	37	Gd
St Erth	36	Dc
St Erth Praze	36	Dc
St Ervan	44	Ab
St Ewe	37	Hd
St Fagans	89	Gc
St Fergus	309	Hf
Saintfield	352	Xa
St Fillans	281	Ge
St Florence	108	Db
St Gennys	44	Dd
St George	184	Cd
St George's	89	Fc
St Germans	40	Be
St Giles in the Wood	65	Fb
St Giles on the Heath	45	Fd
St Govan's Head	108	Ca
St Harmon	136	Bd
St Helen Auckland	229	Ee
St Helens *IOW*	57	Ec
St Helens *Mers*	201	Eb
St Helier	53	Ga
St Hilary *Corn*	36	Dc
St Hilary *V of G*	89	Fc
Saint Hill	80	Bd
St Illtyd	113	Hb
St Ippollitts	124	Cd
St Ishmael	109	Gb
St Ishmael's	108	Bb
St Issey	44	Bb
St Ive	45	Fa
St Ives *Cambs*	148	Bd
St Ives *Corn*	36	Dd
St Ives *Dors*	53	He
St James South Elmham	152	De
St John *Ch Is*	53	Fb
St John *Corn*	40	Ce
St John's *Dur*	248	Ba
St Johns *H & W*	140	Cb
St John's *IOM*	236	Bc
St John's Chapel *Devon*	65	Fc
St John's Chapel *Dur*	245	Ha
St John's Fen End	172	Dc
St John's Head	320	Af
St John's Highway	172	Dc
St Johnstown	349	Lf
St John's Town of Dalry	253	Ga
St Jude's	236	Cd
St Just	33	Bc
St Just-in-Roseland	37	Gc
St Katherines	308	Ed
St Keverne	36	Fb
St Kew	44	Cb
St Kew Highway	44	Cb
St Keyne	45	Ea
St Lawrence *Corn*	44	Ca
St Lawrence *Esx*	128	Cb
St Lawrence *IOW*	56	Db
St Leonards *Bucks*	124	Ab
St Leonards *Dors*	53	He
St Leonards *E Ssx*	81	Ga
St Levan	33	Bb
St Lythans	89	Gc
St Mabyn	44	Cb
St Madoes	284	De
St Magnus Bay	321	Kf
St Margaret's *Dub*	345	Ma
St Margarets *H & W*	116	Ae
St Margarets *Herts*	125	Ec
St Margaret's at Cliffe	84	De
St Margaret's Hope	320	De
St Margaret South Elmham	152	De
St Mark's	236	Bb
St Martin *Ch Is*	52	Da
St Martin *Corn*	36	Fb
St Martin *Corn*	40	Ae
St Martins *P & K*	296	Aa
St Martin's *Shrops*	161	Fe
St Mary Bourne	96	Da
St Mary Church	89	Fc
St Mary Cray	101	Fb
St Mary Hill	89	Ec
St Mary in the Marsh	84	Ac
St Mary's	320	Df
St Mary's Bay	84	Ac
St Mary's Croft	237	Fd
St Mary's Grove	92	Bb
St Mary's Hoo	104	Bc
St Mary's Loch	257	Ee
St Mawes	37	Gc
St Mawgan	44	Aa
St Mellion	45	Fa
St Mellons	89	Hd
St Merryn	44	Ab
St Mewan	37	He
St Michael Caerhays	37	Hd
St Michael Penkevil	37	Gd
St Michaels *H & W*	137	Hc
St Michaels *Kent*	81	Gd
St Michael's Mount	36	Db
St Michael's on Wyre	213	Eb
St Michael South Elmham	152	De
St Minver	44	Bb
St Monance	285	Hc
St Nectan's Glen	44	Cc
St Neot	44	Da
St Neots	145	Hc
St Newlyn East	37	Ge
St Nicholas *Pemb*	108	Ce
St Nicholas *V of G*	89	Fc
St Nicholas at Wade	105	Fb
St Ninians	281	Hb
St Ninian's Isle	321	Lb
St Osyth	129	Ec
St Owen's Cross	116	Cd
St Pauls Cray	101	Fb
St Paul's Walden	124	Cd
St Peter Port	52	Da
St Peter's	105	Gb
St Petrox	108	Ca
St Pinnock	45	Ea
St Quivox	252	De
St Sampson	52	Da
St Stephen	37	He
St Stephens *Corn*	40	Ce
St Stephens *Corn*	45	Fc
St Stephens *Herts*	124	Cb
St Teath	44	Cc
St Thomas	48	Dd
St Tudy	44	Cb
St Twynnells	108	Ca
St Veep	37	Ke
St Vigeans	296	Fb
St Wenn	44	Ba
St Weonards	116	Bd
St Winnow	37	Ke
Salcombe	41	Fc
Salcombe Regis	49	Fc
Salcott	128	Cc
Sale	201	Gb
Saleby	196	Dd
Sale Green	140	Db
Salehurst	81	Fc
Salem *C & M*	181	Gb
Salem *Card*	133	Ge
Salem *Carm*	112	Bd
Salen *A & B*	289	Gb
Salen *Hghld*	289	Hd
Salesbury	213	Ga
Salford *Beds*	124	Ae
Salford *GM*	201	Gb
Salford *Oxon*	120	Bd
Salford Priors	141	Eb
Salfords	80	Ae
Salhouse	176	Dc
Saline	284	Cb
Salisbury	73	Fc
Salisbury Plain	73	Ee
Salkeld Dykes	245	Ea
Sallachy *Hghld*	301	Jd
Sallachy *Hghld*	312	Hd
Sallahig	324	Gf
Salle	176	Bd
Sallins	336	Jj
Sallybrook	328	Cf
Sallypark	333	Re
Salmonby	196	Cd
Salmond's Muir	296	Ea
Salperton	117	Hd
Salph End	145	Gb
Salsburgh	268	Cd
Salt	164	Dd
Saltaire	216	Da
Saltash	40	Ce
Saltburn	304	Fg
Saltburn-by-the-Sea	232	Be
Saltby	169	Ed
Saltcoats	264	Eb
Saltdean	60	De
Saltee Islands	328	Qh
Salter	213	Gd
Salterforth	216	Ab
Salterswall	188	Bc
Saltfleet	209	Hb
Saltfleetby All Saints	209	Hb
Saltfleetby St Clement	209	Hb
Saltfleetby St Peter	196	De
Saltford	92	Db
Salthaugh Grange	209	Fe
Salt Hill	100	Ad
Salthouse	176	Af
Saltley	141	Ee
Saltmarshe	208	Ae
Saltmills	329	Ni
Saltney	185	Gc
Salton	232	Ca
Saltram House	40	De
Saltwick	261	Fa
Saltwood	84	Bd
Salum	288	Bb
Salwarpe	140	Cc
Salwayash	52	Ad
Salwick Station	213	Ea
Samala	317	Si
Sambourne	141	Ec
Sambrook	164	Bd
Samlesbury	213	Fa
Samlesbury Bottoms	201	Fe
Sampford Arundel	68	Db
Sampford Brett	68	Ce
Sampford Courtenay	48	Ae
Sampford Peverell	68	Cb
Sampford Spiney	45	Hb
Samuelston	272	Ae
Sanachan	301	He
Sanaigmore	316	Dh
Sancreed	36	Cb
Sancton	220	Ca
Sand *Hghld*	312	Bc
Sand *Shet*	321	Ld
Sandaig *Hghld*	301	Ga
Sandaig *Hghld*	301	Gb
Sandal	205	Ed
Sandall Beat Wood	205	Hc
Sanday	320	Gj
Sandbach	188	Cc
Sandbank	280	Ba
Sandbanks	53	Gc
Sandend	308	Cg
Sanderstead	101	Eb
Sandford *Avon*	92	Ba
Sandford *Cumb*	228	Ad
Sandford *Devon*	48	Ce
Sandford *Dors*	53	Fc
Sandford *IOW*	56	Dc
Sandford *S Ayr*	268	Bb
Sandfordhill	309	Je
Sandford-on-Thames	121	Eb
Sandford Orcas	72	Ac
Sandford St Martin	120	Dd
Sandgate	84	Cd
Sandgreen	240	Cc
Sandhaven	308	Gg
Sandhead	237	Fb
Sandhoe	248	Ad
Sand Hole	220	Ca
Sandholes	349	Qc
Sandholme *Humb*	220	Ca
Sandholme *Lincs*	172	Be
Sandhurst *Berks*	97	Hb
Sandhurst *Glos*	117	Fd
Sandhurst *Kent*	81	Gc
Sand Hutton *N Yorks*	220	Ac
Sandhutton *N Yorks*	229	Ga
Sandiacre	168	Ae
Sandilands	197	Ee
Sandiway	188	Bd
Sandleheath	73	Fb
Sandleigh	120	Db
Sandling	104	Aa
Sandness	321	Je
Sandon *Esx*	128	Ab
Sandon *Herts*	125	Ee
Sandon *Staffs*	164	Dd
Sandown	56	Dc
Sandplace	40	Ae
Sandridge *Herts*	124	Cc
Sandridge *Wilts*	93	Gb
Sandringham	173	Ed
Sandsend	232	Dd
Sand Side	224	Da
Sands of Forvie	309	Hc
Sandsound	321	Ld
Sandtoft	208	Ac
Sandway	104	Ba
Sandwich	105	Ga
Sandwick *Cumb*	225	Fd
Sandwick *Shet*	321	Mb
Sandwick *W Is*	317	Tg
Sandwick *Shet*	321	Mb
Sandwith	224	Ad
Sandy	145	Ha
Sandycroft	185	Gc
Sandyford	337	Mj
Sandygate *Devon*	48	Cb
Sandygate *IOM*	236	Cd
Sandy Haven	108	Bb
Sandyhills	241	Fc
Sandy Lane	93	Gb
Sangobeg	312	Gj
Sanna	288	Fd
Sanquhar	253	Hc
Santon	208	Cd
Santon Bridge	224	Cc
Santon Downham	149	Ge
Sapcote	168	Aa
Sapey Common	140	Bc
Sapiston	149	Hd
Sapperton *Glos*	117	Gb
Sapperton *Lincs*	169	Ge
Saracen's Head	172	Bd
Sarclet	313	Rh
Sardis	108	Cb
Sarisbury	56	De
Sarn *Brid*	89	Ed
Sarn *Pwys*	160	Ea
Sarnau *C & M*	160	Be
Sarnau *Card*	132	Db
Sarnau *Carm*	109	Gc
Sarnau *Pwys*	161	Ec
Sarn Bach	156	Dd
Sarnesfield	137	Fb
Sarn Helen	133	Gb
Sarn Meyllteyrn	156	Ce
Saron *C & M*	181	Gc
Saron *Carm*	109	Ge
Saron *Carm*	112	Bc
Sarratt	100	Be
Sarre	105	Fb
Sarsden	120	Bd
Sarsgrum	312	Fj
Satley	248	Cb
Satterleigh	65	Gc
Satterthwaite	225	Eb
Saucher	296	Aa
Sauchieburn	296	Fd
Sauchrie	252	Dd
Saughall	185	Gd
Saughtree	257	Hb
Saul *Down*	345	Rk
Saul *Glos*	117	Eb
Saundby	193	Ee
Saundersfoot	109	Eb
Saunderton	121	Gb
Saunton	65	Ed
Sausthorpe	196	Cc
Saval	312	Hd
Savary	289	Hb
Sawbridge	144	Bc
Sawbridgeworth	125	Fc
Sawdon	233	Ea
Sawley *Derbs*	168	Ae
Sawley *Lancs*	213	Hb
Sawley *N Yorks*	217	Ed
Sawrey	225	Eb
Sawston	148	Ca
Sawtry	145	He
Saxby *Leics*	169	Ed
Saxby *Lincs*	193	He
Saxby All Saints	208	Cd
Saxelbye	168	Cd
Saxilby	193	Fd
Saxlingham	176	Ae
Saxlingham Green	176	Ca
Saxlingham Nethergate	176	Ca
Saxlingham Thorpe	176	Ca
Saxmundham	152	Dc
Saxondale	168	Ce
Saxon Street	149	Eb
Saxtead	152	Cc
Saxtead Green	152	Cc
Saxthorpe	176	Be
Saxton	217	Ga
Sayers Common	80	Ab
Scackleton	220	Ae
Scafell	224	Dc
Scaftworth	205	Hb
Scagglethorpe	220	Ce
Scalasaig	276	Bb
Scalby *Humb*	208	Be
Scalby *N Yorks*	233	Fb
Scaldwell	144	Dd
Scaleby	244	Dd
Scaleby Hill	244	Dd
Scale Houses	245	Eb
Scales *Cumb*	212	Ce
Scales *Cumb*	225	Ee
Scalford	168	Dd
Scaling	232	Cd
Scallastle	289	Ha
Scalloway	321	Mc
Scalpay House	300	Fc
Scamblesby	196	Bd
Scamodale	289	Ke
Scampston	220	Ce
Scampton	193	Gd
Scapa	320	Df
Scar	320	Fj
Scarborough	233	Fa
Scarcewater	37	He
Scarcliffe	192	Bc
Scarcroft	217	Fb
Scardaun	341	Qb
Scardroy	301	Mf
Scarff	321	Kh
Scarfskerry	313	Qk
Scargill	228	Dd
Scarinish	288	Bb
Scarisbrick	200	Cd
Scarning	173	Hc
Scarriff	333	Nf
Scarrington	193	Ea
Scartaglin	325	Mi
Scarth Hill	200	Dc
Scartho	209	Fc
Scarva	345	Lk
Scatsta	321	Lg
Scawby	208	Cc
Scawton	232	Aa
Scayne's Hill	80	Bc
Scethrog	113	Gd
Schaw	253	Ee
Scholar Green	188	Db
Scholes *W Yorks*	204	Cc
Scholes *W Yorks*	217	Fa
Schoolhill	308	Ea
Scleddau	108	Ce
Scofton	192	De
Scole	152	Bd
Scolpaig	317	Sj
Scolt Head	173	Gf
Scolton	108	Cd
Scone Palace	284	De
Sconser	300	Ed
Scoor	276	Cd
Scopwick	193	Hb
Scoraig	312	Cc
Scorborough	221	Eb
Scorrier	36	Fd
Scorton *Lancs*	213	Fb
Scorton *N Yorks*	229	Fc
Sco Ruston	176	Cd
Scotby	244	Dc
Scotch Corner	229	Fc
Scotch Street	349	Sa
Scotforth	213	Ec
Scothern	193	Hd
Scotland Gate	261	Ga
Scotlandwell	284	Dc
Scotsburn	313	Ka
Scotscalder Station	313	Ni
Scotscraig	285	Ge
Scot's Gap	261	Ea
Scotshouse	344	Eh
Scotstarvit Tower	285	Fd
Scotston	293	Kb
Scotstown *Hghld*	289	Kd
Scotstown *Mongh*	344	Gj
Scotter	208	Bc
Scotterthorpe	208	Bc
Scotton *Lincs*	208	Bb
Scotton *N Yorks*	217	Fc
Scotton *N Yorks*	229	Eb
Scottow	176	Cd

Sidlesham—South Willingham 517

Sidlesham 57 Gd
Sidley 61 He
Sidlow 80 Ae
Sidmouth 49 Fc
Sigford 48 Bb
Sigglesthorne 221 Fb
Sigingstone 89 Ec
Silbury Hill 93 Hb
Silchester 97 Fb
Sileby 168 Cc
Silecroft 224 Ca
Silfield 176 Ba
Silian 133 Fb
Silkstone 204 Dc
Silkstone Common 204 Dc
Silksworth 249 Ec
Silk Willoughby 193 Ha
Sillerhole 285 Fc
Silloth 244 Ac
Sills 260 Cc
Siloh 112 Ce
Silpho 233 Eb
Silsden 216 Cb
Silsoe 124 Be
Silton 72 Bc
Silver Bridge 345 Kh
Silverburn 269 Gd
Silverdale *Lancs* 213 Ee
Silverdale *Staffs* 188 Da
Silver End 128 Bc
Silver Hill 81 Fc
Silverley's Green 152 Cd
Silvermines 333 Qe
Silverstone 144 Ca
Silverton 48 De
Silvington 140 Ad
Silwick 321 Kd
Simonburn 245 He
Simonsbath 65 Hd
Simonstone 213 Ha
Simprim 273 Eb
Simpson 121 He
Simpson Cross 108 Bc
Sinclairston 253 Ed
Sinderby 229 Ga
Sinderhope 245 Hc
Sindlesham 97 Gb
Sinfin 165 He
Sinfin Moor 165 He
Singdean 257 Hc
Singleton *Lancs* 212 Da
Singleton *W Ssx* 77 Eb
Singlewell 101 Hc
Sinnahard 308 Bb
Sinnington 232 Ca
Sinton Green 140 Cc
Sion Mills 349 Le
Sipson 100 Bc
Sirhowy 113 Gc
Sisland 176 Da
Sissinghurst 81 Fd
Sissinghurst Garden 81 Gd
Siston 92 Dc
Sithney 36 Eb
Sittingbourne 104 Cb
Six Ashes 140 Be
Sixhills 196 Ae
Sixmile 84 Be
Six Mile Bottom 148 Db
Sixmilebridge 333 Ld
Sixmilecross 349 Nb
Sixpenny Handley 73 Db
Sizergh Castle 225 Fa
Sizewell 153 Ec
Skail 313 Kh
Skaill 320 Ef
Skara Brae 320 Bg
Skares 253 Fd
Skarpigarth 321 Jd
Skateraw 272 De
Skaw 321 Nf
Skeabost 300 De
Skeagh 344 Cb
Skea Skerries 320 Dj
Skeeby 229 Ec
Skeffington 168 Db
Skeffling 209 Gd
Skegby 192 Bc
Skegness 197 Ec
Skehanagh 341 Ma
Skelberry 321 La
Skelbo 313 Kc
Skeldyke 172 Be
Skelligs, The 324 De
Skellingthorpe 193 Gd
Skellister 321 Me
Skellow 205 Gd
Skelmanthorpe 204 Dd
Skelmersdale 200 Dc
Skelmonae 308 Fd
Skelmorlie 264 Dd
Skelmuir 308 Ge
Skelpick 313 Ki
Skelton *Cumb* 244 Da
Skelton *Humb* 208 Ae
Skelton *N Yorks* 217 Fd
Skelton *N Yorks* 217 Hc
Skelton *N Yorks* 228 Dc
Skelton *N Yorks* 232 Bd
Skelwick 320 Dj
Skelwith Bridge 225 Ec
Skendleby 196 Dc
Skenfrith 116 Bd
Skerne 221 Ec
Skerray 313 Jj
Skerries 345 Nc
Sketty 88 Be
Skewen 88 Ce
Skewsby 220 Ae
Skeyton 176 Cd
Skibbereen 325 Nb
Skidbrooke 209 Hb
Skidby 221 Ea
Skiddaw 224 De
Skilgate 68 Bc
Skillington 169 Ed
Skinburness 244 Ac
Skinflats 284 Ba
Skinidin 300 Be
Skinningrove 232 Cd
Skipness 264 Ac
Skipsea 221 Fc
Skipton 216 Bc
Skipton-on-Swale 217 Fe
Skipwith 220 Aa
Skirlaugh 221 Fa
Skirling 269 Ea
Skirmett 97 Gd
Skirpenbeck 220 Bc
Skirwith 245 Fa
Skirza 313 Rj
Skomer Island 108 Ab
Skreen *Meath* 345 Kc
Skreen *Sligo* 341 Mj
Skulamus 301 Fc
Skull 325 Lb
Skullomie 312 Jj
Skye, Island of 300 Dc
Skye Folk Museum 300 Ec
Skye of Curr 305 Hc
Slack 204 Ae
Slackhall 189 Fe
Slackhead 308 Bg
Slacks of
Cairnbanno 308 Fe
Slad 117 Fb
Slade 65 Fe
Slade Green 101 Gc
Slaggyford 245 Fc
Slaidburn 213 Hc
Slaithwaite 204 Bd
Slaley 248 Ac
Slamannan 268 Ce
Slane 345 Kd
Slapton *Bucks* 124 Ad
Slapton *Devon* 41 Gd
Slapton *Northants* 144 Ca
Slapton Ley 41 Gd
Slattocks 201 Hc
Slaugham 80 Ac
Slaughterford 93 Fc
Slawston 168 Da
Sleaford *Hants* 77 Ed
Sleaford *Lincs* 193 Ha
Sleagill 225 Gd
Sleapford 164 Ac
Sledge Green 117 Fe
Sledmere 220 Dd
Sleightholme 228 Cd
Sleights 232 Dc
Slepe 53 Fd
Slickly 313 Qj
Sliddery 249 He
Sliemore 305 Jc
Slieve Donard 345 Pi
Slieveroe 329 Mj
Sligachan 300 Dc
Sligo 341 Nj
Sligrachan 280 Bb
Slimbridge 117 Eb
Slindon *Staffs* 164 Ce
Slindon *W Ssx* 57 He
Slinfold 77 Hd
Slingsby 220 Ae
Slioch 308 Cd
Slip End 124 Bc
Slipton 145 Fd
Slochd 305 Gc
Slockavullin 277 Gb
Sloley 176 Cd
Sloothby 196 Dd
Slough *Berks* 100 Ac
Slough *Pwys* 137 Fc
Slyne 213 Ed
Smailholm 272 Ca
Smallbridge 204 Ad
Smallburgh 176 Dd
Smallburn *Aber* 309 He
Smallburn *E Ayr* 253 Ge
Small Dole 80 Ab
Smalley 192 Ba
Smallfield 80 Be
Small Hythe 81 Gd
Smallridge 49 He
Smannell 73 He
Smardale 228 Ac
Smarden 81 Ge
Smeatharpe 68 Db
Smeeth 84 Ad
Smeeton Westerby 168 Ca
Smerclate 317 Sd
Smerral 313 Pg
Smerwick 324 Ei
Smethwick 141 Ee
Smirisary 289 He
Smisby 165 Hc
Smithborough 344 Fj
Smith End Green 140 Bb
Smithfield 244 Dd
Smithincott 68 Cb
Smith's End 125 Ee
Smithstown 336 Fe
Smithton 304 Fe
Smithy Green 188 Cd
Smoo Cave 312 Gj
Snaefell 236 Cc
Snaigow House 293 Lb
Snailbeach 161 Fb
Snailwell 149 Ec
Snainton 233 Ea
Snaith 205 He
Snape *N Yorks* 229 Fa
Snape *Sflk* 152 Db
Snape Green 200 Cd
Snarestone 165 Hb
Snarford 193 He
Snargate 81 Hc
Snave 84 Ad
Sneachill 140 Db
Snead 161 Fa
Sneaton 232 Dc
Sneatonthorpe 233 Ec
Sneem 324 He
Snelland 193 He
Snelston 189 Ga
Snetterton 173 Ha
Snettisham 173 Ee
Snig's End 117 Ed
Snipe Dales Park 196 Cc
Snishival 317 Sf
Snitter 261 Ec
Snitterby 208 Cb
Snitterfield 141 Gb
Snitton 137 Hd
Snodhill 137 Fa
Snodland 104 Ab
Snowdon 181 Hb
Snowdonia National
Park 181 Gb
Snowshill 117 He
Soberton 76 Cb
Soberton Heath 76 Cb
Sockburn 229 Gc
Sodylt Bank 161 Fe
Soham 148 Dd
Soldon Cross 64 Db
Soldridge 76 Cd
Solent, The 56 Cd
Sole Street *Kent* 84 Ae
Sole Street *Kent* 101 Hb
Solihull 141 Fd
Sollas 317 Tj
Sollers Dilwyn 137 Gb
Sollers Hope 116 De
Sollom 200 Dd
Solva 108 Bd
Solwaybank 244 Ce
Solway Firth 241 Hc
Somerby 168 Dc
Somercotes 192 Bb
Somerford Keynes 93 He
Somerley 57 Gd
Somerleyton 177 Ea
Somersal Herbert 165 Fe
Somersby 196 Cd
Somersham *Cambs* 148 Bd
Somersham *Sflk* 152 Aa
Somerton *Nflk* 177 Ec
Somerton *Oxon* 120 Dd
Somerton *Som* 69 Gc
Sompting 60 Be
Sonning 97 Gc
Sonning Common 97 Gd
Sopley 53 Hd
Sopworth 93 Fd
Sorbie 240 Bb
Sordale 313 Pj
Sorisdale 288 Dd
Sorn 253 Fe
Sornhill 265 Ha
Sortat 313 Qj
Sotby 196 Bd
Sots Hole 196 Ac
Sotterly 153 Ee
Soughton 185 Fc
Soulbury 121 Hd
Soulby 228 Ad
Souldern 121 Ee
Souldrop 145 Fc
Sound *Shet* 321 Le
Sound *Shet* 321 Md
Sound, The 40 Ce
Soundwell 92 Dc
Sourhope 260 Ce
Sourin 320 Di
Sourton 45 Hd
Soutergate 224 Da
South Acre 173 Gc
Southall 100 Cd
South Allington 41 Fc
South Alloa 284 Ab
Southam *Glos* 117 Gd
Southam *Warks* 144 Ac
South Ambersham 77 Fc
Southampton 56 Cf
South Anston 192 Ce
South Ballachulish 292 Ac
South Bank 232 Ae
Southbar 265 Gd
South Barrow 72 Ac
South Beddington 100 Db
South Benfleet 104 Ad
South Bersted 57 He
Southborough 80 De
Southbourne *Dors* 53 Hd
Southbourne *W Ssx* 57 Fe
South Bowood 52 Ad
South Brent 48 Aa
South Brewham 72 Bd
South Broomhill 261 Gb
Southburgh 176 Ab
South Burlingham 176 Db
Southburn 220 Dc
South Cadbury 72 Ac
South Cairn 237 Ed
South Carlton 193 Gd
South Cave 220 Da
South Cerney 93 He
South Chard 49 He
South Charlton 261 Fe
South Cheriton 72 Ac
Southchurch 104 Cd
South Cliffe 220 Ca
South Clifton 193 Fd
South Cockerington 196 Ce
South Cornelly 88 Dd
South Cove 153 Fe
South Creake 173 Ge
South Croxton 168 Cc
South Dalton 220 Db
South Darenth 101 Gb
Southdean 260 Ac
South Duffield 220 Aa
Southease 61 Ee
South Elkington 196 Be
South Elmsall 205 Fd
Southend *A & B* 316 Ha
South End *Berks* 97 Ec
South End *Bucks* 121 Hd
South End *Cumb* 212 Cd
South End *Humb* 209 Ee
Southend-on-Sea 104 Bd
Southerndown 88 Dc
Southerness 241 Gc
South Erradale 301 Gh
Southery 173 Ea
South Fambridge 104 Be
South Fawley 96 Cc
South Ferriby 208 Ce
Southfleet 101 Hc
South Garvan 289 Le
Southgate *GL* 101 Ee
Southgate *Nflk* 173 Ee
Southgate *Nflk* 176 Bd
Southgate *Swan* 92 Cd
South Godstone 80 Be
South Gorley 73 Fb
South Green 101 He
South-haa 321 Lh
South Hall 264 Ce
South Hanningfield 104 Ae
South Harting 76 Db
South Hayling 57 Fd
South Hazelrigg 273 Ga
South Heath 124 Ab
South Heighton 61 Ee
South Hetton 249 Eb
South Hiendley 205 Ed
South Hill 45 Fb
South Hole 64 Cb
South Holmwood 77 He
South Hornchurch 101 Gd
South Hourat 265 Ec
South Hykeham 193 Gc
South Hylton 249 Ec
Southill 145 Ha
Southington 76 Be
South Kelsey 208 Db
South Killingholme 209 Ed
South Kilvington 229 Ha
South Kilworth 144 Ce
South Kirkby 205 Fd
South Kirkton 308 Ea
South Kyme 196 Aa
South Lancing 60 Be
South Ledaig 289 La
Southleigh *Devon* 49 Gd
South Leigh *Oxon* 120 Cb
South Leverton 193 Ee
South Littleton 141 Ea
South Lopham 152 Ae
South Luffenham 169 Fb
South Malling 80 Cb
South Marston 96 Ad
South Middleton 260 De
South Milford 217 Ga
South Milton 41 Fd
South Mimms 124 Db
Southminster 104 Ce
South Molton 65 Hc
South Moor 248 Cc
South Moreton 97 Ed
South Mundham 57 Ge
South Muskham 193 Eb
South Newbald 220 Da
South Newington 120 De
South Newton 73 Ed
South Normanton 192 Bb
South Norwood 101 Eb
South Nutfield 80 Be
South Ockendon 101 Gd
Southoe 145 Hc
Southolt 152 Bc
South Ormsby 196 Cd
Southorpe 169 Gb
South Otterington 229 Ga
Southowram 204 Ce
South Oxhey 100 Ce
South Perrott 52 Ae
South Petherton 69 Gb
South Petherwin 45 Fc
South Pickenham 173 Gb
South Pool 41 Fd
Southport 200 Cd
South Radworthy 65 Hd
South Rauceby 193 Ha
South Raynham 173 Gd
Southrepps 176 Ce
South Reston 196 De
Southrey 196 Ac
South Ronaldsay 320 Dd
Southrop 120 Ab
Southrope 76 Ce
South Runcton 173 Eb
South Scarle 193 Fc
Southsea 57 Ed
South Shian 289 Lb
South Shields 249 Ed
South Shore 212 Da
South Somercotes 209 Hb
South Stainley 217 Fd
South Stainmore 228 Bd
South Stoke *Avon* 93 Eb
South Stoke *Oxon* 97 Fd
South Stoke *W Ssx* 77 Gb
South Street *E Ssx* 80 Bb
South Street *Kent* 101 Hb
South Swale Nature
Reserve 104 Db
South Tawton 48 Ad
South Thoresby 196 Dd
South Tidworth 73 Ge
South Town 76 Cd
South Tullich 280 Ad
South Uist 317 Se
Southwaite 244 Db
South Walls 320 Cd
South Walsham 176 Dc
Southwark 101 Ec
South Warnborough 76 De
Southwater 77 Hc
Southway 69 He
South Weald 101 Ge
Southwell *Dors* 52 Cb
Southwell *Notts* 193 Eb
South Weston 97 Ge
South Wheatley 45 Ed
Southwick *Hants* 57 Ee
Southwick
Northants 169 Ga
Southwick *T & W* 249 Ec
Southwick *Wilts* 93 Fa
Southwick *W Ssx* 60 Ce
South Widcombe 92 Ca
South Wigston 168 Ba
South Willingham 196 Ae

520 Swinscoe–Thorpe Satchville

Swinscoe	189	Ga
Swinside Hall	260	Bd
Swinstead	169	Gd
Swinton *Bdrs*	272	Eb
Swinton *GM*	201	Gc
Swinton *N Yorks*	217	Ee
Swinton *N Yorks*	220	Be
Swinton *S Yorks*	205	Fb
Swintonmill	272	Eb
Switha	320	Ce
Swithland	168	Bc
Swona	320	Cd
Swordale	304	Dg
Swordland	289	Jg
Swordly	313	Kj
Swords	345	Ma
Sworton Heath	188	Be
Swyddffynnon	133	Gc
Swynnerton	164	Ce
Swyre	52	Bc
Syde	117	Gc
Sydenham *GL*	101	Ec
Sydenham *Oxon*	121	Gb
Sydenham Damerel	45	Gb
Syderstone	173	Ge
Sydling St Nicholas	52	Cd
Sydmonton	96	Da
Syerston	193	Ea
Syke	201	Hd
Sykehouse	205	Hd
Sykes	213	Gc
Syleham	152	Cd
Sylen	112	Ab
Symbister	321	Nf
Symington *S Ayr*	265	Fa
Symington *S Lan*	268	Da
Symondsbury	52	Ad
Symonds Yat	116	Cc
Synod Inn	133	Eb
Syre	313	Jh
Syreford	117	Hd
Syresham	144	Ca
Syston *Leics*	168	Cc
Syston *Lincs*	193	Ga
Sytchampton	140	Cc
Sywell	145	Ec

T

Tackley	120	Dd
Tacolneston	176	Ba
Tacumshin Lake	329	Ri
Tadcaster	217	Gb
Tadden	53	Fe
Taddington	189	Gd
Taddiport	65	Eb
Tadley	97	Fb
Tadlow	148	Aa
Tadmarton	120	Ce
Tadworth	100	Da
Tafarnaubach	113	Gc
Tafarn-y-bwlch	108	De
Tafarn-y-Gelyn	185	Ec
Taff's Well	89	Gd
Tafolwern	160	Ab
Taghmon	329	Qk
Taghshinny	344	Cc
Tagoat	329	Sj
Taibach *N & PT*	88	Cd
Tai-bach *Pwys*	160	Dd
Tain *Hghld*	313	Kb
Tain *Hghld*	313	Qj
Tai'n Lôn	181	Fb
Tairbeart	317	Wm
Tairlaw	253	Ec
Takeley	125	Gd
Takeley Street	125	Gd
Talachddu	113	Fe
Talacre	185	Ee
Talaton	49	Ed
Talbenny	108	Bc
Tale	49	Ee
Talerddig	160	Bb
Talgarreg	133	Eb
Talgarth	113	Ge
Talisker	300	Cd
Talke	188	Db
Talkin	245	Ec
Talladale	312	Ba
Tallaght	337	Lj
Talla Linnfoots	256	De
Tallanstown	345	Kf
Tallantire	244	Aa
Tallarn Green	185	Ha
Talley	112	Be
Tallington	169	Gb
Tallow	328	Eh
Tallowbridge	328	Eh
Talmine	312	Hj
Talog	109	Gd
Tal-sarn	133	Fb
Talsarnau	157	Ge
Talskiddy	44	Ba
Talwrn *Anglsy*	181	Fd
Talwrn *Wrex*	185	Fa
Tal-y-bont *A & C*	181	Hd
Tal-y-bont *C & M*	157	Fd
Tal-y-Bont *C & M*	184	Ac
Tal-y-bont *Card*	133	Ge
Talybont *Pwys*	113	Gd
Tal-y-cafn	184	Ad
Tal-y-llyn *C & M*	157	Hb
Talyllyn *Pwys*	113	Gd
Talysarn	181	Fb
Tal-y-Wern	160	Ab
Tamavoid	281	Fb
Tamerton Foliot	45	Ga
Tamlaght *Ferm*	344	Ck
Tamlaght *Londy*	349	Sf
Tamworth	165	Gb
Tandragee	345	Lk
Tandridge	101	Ea
Tanerdy	109	Hd
Tanfield	248	Cc
Tangiers	108	Cc
Tangley	96	Ca
Tangmere	57	He
Tangwick	321	Kg
Tan Hill	228	Cc
Tankerness	320	Ef
Tankersley	205	Eb
Tan-lan	181	Ha
Tannach	313	Rh
Tannachie	297	Gf
Tannadice	296	Dc
Tannington	152	Cc
Tansley	192	Ab
Tansor	169	Ga
Tantallon Castle	272	Bf
Tantobie	248	Cc
Tanton	232	Ad
Tanworth in Arden	141	Fd
Tan-y-fron	184	Cc
Tanygrisiau	181	Ha
Tan-y-groes	132	Ca
Taobh Tuath	317	Uk
Tapeley Park	65	Ec
Taplow	100	Ad
Tap o' Noth	308	Bc
Tarbert *A & B*	264	Ad
Tarbert *A & B*	276	Ea
Tarbert *Kerry*	332	Gb
Tarbert *W Is*	317	Wm
Tarbet *A & B*	280	Dc
Tarbet *Hghld*	289	Jg
Tarbet *Hghld*	312	Dh
Tarbock Green	185	He
Tarbolton	253	Ee
Tarbrax	268	Ec
Tardy Gate	201	Ee
Tarfside	296	De
Tarland	308	Ba
Tarleton	200	De
Tarlogie	313	Kb
Tarlscough	200	Dd
Tarlton	93	Ge
Tarnbrook	213	Fc
Tarnock	92	Aa
Tarporley	188	Ac
Tarr	68	Dd
Tarrant Crawford	53	Fe
Tarrant Gunville	73	Db
Tarrant Hinton	73	Db
Tarrant Keyneston	53	Fe
Tarrant Launceston	53	Fe
Tarrant Monkton	53	Fe
Tarrant Rawston	53	Fe
Tarrant Rushton	53	Fe
Tarrel	313	Lb
Tarring Neville	61	Ee
Tarrington	140	Aa
Tarrnacraig	264	Ba
Tarsappie	284	De
Tarskavaig	300	Eb
Tarves	308	Fd
Tarvie *Hghld*	304	Cf
Tarvie *P & K*	293	Ld
Tarvin	185	Hc
Tarvin Sands	185	Hc
Tasburgh	176	Ca
Tasley	164	Aa
Taston	120	Cd
Tatenhill	165	Gd
Tatham	213	Gd
Tathwell	196	Ce
Tatsfield	101	Fa
Tattenhall	185	Hb
Tattenham Corner Station	100	Da
Tatterford	173	Gd
Tattersett	173	Gd
Tattershall	196	Bb
Tattershall Bridge	196	Ab
Tattershall Thorpe	196	Bb
Tattingstone	129	Ee
Tatton Park	188	Ce
Tatworth	49	He
Taunton	69	Ec
Taverham	176	Bc
Tavernspite	109	Ec
Tavistock	45	Gb
Tavool House	276	Ce
Taw Green	48	Ad
Tawny	349	Ji
Tawnyin	341	Lf
Tawstock	65	Fc
Taxal	189	Fd
Tayinloan	316	He
Taymouth Castle	293	Hb
Taynafaed	280	Ad
Taynish	277	Fa
Taynton *Glos*	117	Ed
Taynton *Oxon*	120	Bc
Taynuilt	289	Ma
Tayport	285	Ge
Tayvallich	277	Fa
Tealby	209	Eb
Tealing	296	Da
Teangue	300	Fa
Tebay	225	Hc
Tebworth	124	Ad
Tedavnet	344	Gj
Tedburn St Mary	48	Cd
Tedd	349	Kb
Teddington *GL*	100	Cc
Teddington *Glos*	117	Ge
Tedstone Delamere	140	Ab
Tedstone Wafre	140	Ab
Teemore	344	Di
Teeranearagh	324	Ff
Teerelton	325	Qe
Tees-Side Airport	229	Gd
Teeton	144	Cd
Teevurcher	344	Hf
Teffont Evias	73	Dd
Teffont Magna	73	Dd
Tegryn	109	Fe
Teigh	169	Ec
Teigngrace	48	Cb
Teignmouth	48	Db
Telford	164	Ac
Telham	81	Fb
Tellisford	93	Fa
Telscombe	61	Ee
Templand	256	Ca
Temple *C of Glas*	265	Hd
Temple *Corn*	44	Db
Temple *Midln*	269	Hc
Temple, The	352	Wb
Temple Bar	133	Fb
Templeboy	341	Lj
Temple Cloud	92	Da
Templecombe	72	Bc
Templederry	333	Rd
Templeetney	328	Hk
Temple Ewell	84	Ce
Temple Grafton	141	Fb
Temple Guiting	117	Hd
Temple Hirst	205	He
Templemartin	325	Re
Templemore	336	Be
Temple Newsam	217	Fa
Templenoe	325	Ke
Temple Normanton	192	Bc
Templeshanbo	336	Jb
Temple Sowerby	225	He
Templeton *Devon*	68	Ab
Templeton *Pemb*	109	Ec
Templeton Bridge	68	Ab
Templetouhy	336	Be
Templetown	329	Ni
Tempo	344	Dk
Tempsford	145	Hb
Tenbury Wells	137	Hc
Tenby	109	Eb
Tendring	129	Ed
Ten Mile Bank	173	Ea
Tenterden	81	Gd
Tentsmuir Point	285	Ge
Terally	237	Gb
Terling	128	Ac
Termonbarry	341	Sd
Termonfeckin	345	Me
Termon Rock	349	Pc
Ternhill	164	Ae
Terregles	241	Ge
Terrington	220	Ae
Terrington St Clement	172	Dd
Terrington St John	172	Dc
Terryglass	333	Qh
Teston	104	Aa
Testwood	73	Hb
Tetbury	93	Fe
Tetbury Upton	93	Fe
Tetchill	161	Fe
Tetcott	45	Fd
Tetford	196	Cd
Tetney	209	Gc
Tetney Haven	209	Gc
Tetney Lock	209	Gc
Tetsworth	121	Fb
Tettenhall	164	Cb
Tetworth	148	Ab
Teuchan	309	Hd
Teversal	192	Bc
Teversham	148	Cb
Teviothead	257	Gc
Tewel	297	Hf
Tewin	124	Dc
Tewkesbury	117	Fe
Teynham	104	Cb
Thakeham	77	Hb
Thame	121	Gb
Thames Ditton	100	Cb
Thames Haven	104	Ad
Thamesmead	101	Fd
Thaneston	296	Fe
Thanington	105	Ea
Thankerton	268	Da
Tharston	176	Ba
Thatcham	97	Eb
Thatto Heath	201	Eb
Thaxted	125	He
Theakston	229	Ga
Thealby	208	Bd
Theale *Berks*	97	Fc
Theale *Som*	69	Ge
Thearne	221	Ea
Theberton	153	Ec
Thedden Grange	76	Cd
Theddingworth	144	Ce
Theddlethorpe All Saints	196	De
Theddlethorpe St Helen	196	De
Thelbridge Barton	65	Hb
The Lhen	236	Ce
Thelnetham	152	Ad
Thelveton	152	Be
Thelwall	188	Be
Themelthorpe	176	Ad
Thenford	144	Ba
Therfield	125	Ee
Thetford	149	Ge
Theydon Bois	101	Fe
Thickwood	93	Fc
Thimbleby *Lincs*	196	Bc
Thimbleby *N Yorks*	229	Hb
Thirkleby	217	Ge
Thirlby	229	Ha
Thirlestane	272	Bb
Thirn	229	Fa
Thirsk	229	Ha
Thistleton *Lancs*	213	Ea
Thistleton *Leics*	169	Fc
Thistley Green	149	Ed
Thixendale	220	Cd
Thockrington	248	Ae
Tholomas Drove	172	Cb
Tholthorpe	217	Gd
Thomas Chapel	109	Eb
Thomas Street	341	Qa
Thomastown *Kilk*	336	Fb
Thomastown *Meath*	344	He
Thomastown *Tipp*	333	Ra
Thompson	173	Ha
Thomshill	305	Lf
Thong	101	Hc
Thongsbridge	204	Cc
Thoor Ballylee	333	Lh
Thoralby	228	Da
Thoresby	192	Dd
Thoresway	209	Eb
Thorganby *Lincs*	209	Fb
Thorganby *N Yorks*	220	Ab
Thorgill	232	Cb
Thorington	153	Ed
Thorington Street	128	De
Thorlby	216	Bc
Thorley	125	Fc
Thorley Street	56	Bc
Thormanby	217	Ge
Thornaby-on-Tees	229	Hd
Thornage	176	Ae
Thornborough *Bucks*	121	Ge
Thornborough *N Yorks*	217	Ee
Thornbury *Avon*	92	Dd
Thornbury *Devon*	45	Ge
Thornbury *H & W*	140	Ab
Thornby	144	Cd
Thorncliff	189	Fb
Thorncombe	49	He
Thorncombe Street	77	Ge
Thorncote Green	145	Ha
Thorndon	152	Bc
Thorndon Cross	45	Hd
Thorne	205	Hd
Thorner	217	Fb
Thorne St Margaret	68	Cc
Thorney *Cambs*	172	Ab
Thorney *Notts*	193	Fd
Thorney *Som*	69	Gc
Thorney Hill	56	Ad
Thornfalcon	69	Ec
Thornford	72	Ab
Thorngumbald	209	Fe
Thornham	173	Ff
Thornham Magna	152	Bd
Thornham Parva	152	Bd
Thornhaugh	169	Gb
Thornhill *Crdff*	89	Gd
Thornhill *D & G*	256	Ab
Thornhill *Derbs*	189	Ge
Thornhill *Hants*	76	Ab
Thornhill *Stir*	281	Gb
Thornhill Edge	204	Dd
Thornholme	221	Fd
Thornicombe	52	Ee
Thornley *Dur*	248	Ca
Thornley *Dur*	249	Ea
Thornliebank	265	Hc
Thorns	149	Fb
Thornsett	189	Fe
Thornthwaite *Cumb*	224	De
Thornthwaite *N Yorks*	216	Dc
Thornton *Angus*	296	Cb
Thornton *Bucks*	121	Ge
Thornton *Clev*	229	Hd
Thornton *Fife*	285	Eb
Thornton *Humb*	220	Bb
Thornton *Lancs*	212	Db
Thornton *Leics*	168	Ab
Thornton *Lincs*	196	Bc
Thornton *Mers*	200	Cc
Thornton *Northld*	273	Fb
Thornton *W Yorks*	216	Da
Thornton Abbey	209	Ed
Thornton Castle	296	Fe
Thornton Curtis	208	Dd
Thorntonhall	265	Hc
Thornton Hough	185	Ge
Thornton-in-Craven	216	Bb
Thornton-le-Beans	229	Gb
Thornton-le-Clay	220	Ad
Thornton-le-Dale	232	Da
Thornton le Moor *Lincs*	208	Db
Thornton-le-Moor *N Yorks*	229	Ga
Thornton-le-Moors	185	Hd
Thornton-le-Street	229	Ha
Thorntonloch	272	De
Thornton Park	273	Fb
Thornton Rust	228	Ca
Thornton Steward	229	Ea
Thornton Watlass	229	Fa
Thornwood Common	125	Fb
Thornylee	269	Ja
Thoroton	193	Ea
Thorp Arch	217	Gb
Thorpe *Derbs*	189	Gb
Thorpe *Humb*	220	Db
Thorpe *Lincs*	196	De
Thorpe *Nflk*	177	Ea
Thorpe *Notts*	193	Ea
Thorpe *N Yorks*	216	Cd
Thorpe *Sry*	100	Bb
Thorpe Abbotts	152	Bd
Thorpe Acre	168	Bd
Thorpe Arnold	168	Dd
Thorpe Audlin	205	Fd
Thorpe Bassett	220	Ce
Thorpe Bay	104	Cd
Thorpe by Water	169	Ea
Thorpe Constantine	165	Gb
Thorpe Culvert	196	Dc
Thorpe End Garden Village	176	Cc
Thorpe Fendykes	196	Dc
Thorpe Green	149	Hb
Thorpe Hall	217	He
Thorpe Hesley	205	Eb
Thorpe in Balne	205	Gd
Thorpe Langton	168	Da
Thorpe Larches	229	Ge
Thorpe le Fallows	193	Ge
Thorpe-le-Soken	129	Ed
Thorpe le Street	220	Cb
Thorpe Malsor	145	Ed
Thorpe Mandeville	144	Ba
Thorpe Market	176	Ce
Thorpe Morieux	149	Hb
Thorpeness	153	Eb
Thorpe on the Hill	193	Gc
Thorpe St Andrew	176	Cb
Thorpe St Peter	196	Dc
Thorpe Salvin	192	Ce
Thorpe Satchville	168	Dc

Thorpe Thewles–Tregoyd 521

Thorpe Thewles 229 He
Thorpe Underwood 217 Gc
Thorpe Waterville 145 Ge
Thorpe Willoughby 217 Ha
Thorpland 173 Eb
Thorrington 128 Dd
Thorverton 48 De
Thrandeston 152 Bd
Thrapston 145 Fd
Threapland 216 Bd
Threapwood 185 Ha
Threave Castle 241 Ed
Three Bridges 80 Ad
Three Chimneys 81 Gd
Three Cocks 113 Ge
Three Crosses 88 Ae
Three Cups Corner 81 Ec
Three Holes 172 Db
Threekingham 169 Ge
Three Legged Cross *Dors* 53 Ge
Three Legged Cross *Kent* 81 Ed
Three Mile Cross 97 Gb
Threemilestone 36 Fd
Threlkeld 225 Ee
Threshers Bush 125 Gb
Threshfield 216 Bd
Threxton Hill 173 Ga
Thrigby 177 Ec
Thringarth 228 Ce
Thringstone 168 Ac
Thrintoft 229 Gb
Thriplow 148 Ca
Throcking 125 Ee
Throckley 248 Cd
Throckmorton 140 Da
Throphill 261 Fa
Thropton 261 Ec
Throsk 284 Ab
Throwleigh 48 Ad
Throwley 104 Ca
Thrumpton 168 Be
Thrumster 313 Rh
Thrunton 261 Ed
Thrupp *Glos* 117 Fb
Thrupp *Oxon* 120 Dc
Thrushelton 45 Gc
Thrushgill 213 Gd
Thrussington 168 Cc
Thruxton *H & W* 116 Be
Thruxton *Hants* 73 Ge
Thrybergh 205 Fb
Thulston 168 Ae
Thundersley 104 Ad
Thurcaston 168 Bc
Thurcroft 192 Be
Thurgarton *Nflk* 176 Be
Thurgarton *Notts* 192 Da
Thurgoland 204 Dc
Thurlaston *Leics* 168 Ba
Thurlaston *Warks* 144 Ad
Thurlbear 69 Ec
Thurlby *Lincs* 169 Hc
Thurlby *Lincs* 193 Gc
Thurleigh 145 Gb
Thurles 336 Bc
Thurlestone 41 Ed
Thurlow 149 Eb
Thurloxton 69 Ec
Thurlstone 204 Dc
Thurlton 177 Ea
Thurmaston 168 Cb
Thurnby 168 Cb
Thurne 177 Ec
Thurnham *Kent* 104 Ba
Thurnham *Lancs* 213 Ec
Thurning *Nflk* 176 Ad
Thurning *Northants* 145 Ge
Thurnscoe 205 Fc
Thursby 244 Cc
Thursford 173 He
Thursford Green 173 He
Thursley 77 Fd
Thurso 313 Pj
Thurstaston 185 Fe
Thurston 149 Hc
Thurstonfield 244 Cc
Thurstonland 204 Cd
Thurton 176 Db
Thurvaston 165 Ge
Thuxton 176 Ab
Thwaite 152 Bc
Thwaite Head 225 Eb
Thwaite St Mary 176 Da
Thwing 221 Ee
Tibbermore 284 Ce
Tibberton *Glos* 117 Ed
Tibberton *H & W* 140 Db
Tibberton *Shrops* 164 Ad
Tibbie Shiels Inn 257 Ee
Tibenham 152 Be
Tibohine 341 Nf
Tibshelf 192 Bc
Tibthorpe 220 Dc
Ticehurst 81 Ed
Tichborne 76 Bd
Tickencote 169 Fb
Tickenham 92 Bc
Tickhill 205 Gb
Ticklerton 161 Ga
Ticknall 165 Hd
Tickton 221 Eb
Tidcombe 96 Ba
Tiddington *Oxon* 121 Fb
Tiddington *Warks* 141 Gb
Tidebrook 81 Ed
Tideford 40 Be
Tidenham 92 Ce
Tideswell 189 Gd
Tidmarsh 97 Fc
Tidmington 120 Be
Tidpit 73 Eb
Tiers Cross 108 Cc
Tiffield 144 Cb
Tifty 308 Ee
Tigerton 296 Ed
Tigharry 317 Sj
Tighnablair 281 Hd
Tighnabruaich 264 Be
Tighnafiline 312 Ab
Tigley 48 Ba
Tikincor 328 Hk
Tilbrook 145 Gc
Tilbury 101 Hc
Tile Cross 141 Fe
Tile Hill 141 Gd
Tilehurst 97 Fc
Tilford 77 Ee
Tillathrowie 308 Bd
Tillers Green 116 De
Tilley 161 Hd
Tillicoultry 284 Bb
Tillingham 128 Cb
Tillington *H & W* 137 Ga
Tillington *W Ssx* 77 Fc
Tillington Common 137 Ga
Tillyarblet 296 Ed
Tillyfour 308 Cb
Tillygarmond 296 Fg
Tillygreig 308 Fc
Tilmanstone 105 Ga
Tilney All Saints 172 Dc
Tilney High End 172 Dc
Tilney St Lawrence 172 Dc
Tilshead 73 Ee
Tilstock 161 He
Tilston 185 Hb
Tilstone Fearnall 188 Ac
Tilsworth 124 Ad
Tilton on the Hill 168 Db
Tiltups End 93 Fe
Timahoe *Kild* 336 Hk
Timahoe *Laois* 336 Fg
Timberland 196 Ab
Timbersbrook 188 Dc
Timberscombe 68 Be
Timble 216 Dc
Timoleague 325 Rc
Timolin 336 Hg
Timperley 188 Ce
Timsbury *Avon* 92 Da
Timsbury *Hants* 73 Hc
Timsgearraidh 317 Vq
Timworth 149 Gc
Timworth Green 149 Gc
Tinahely 337 Le
Tincleton 52 Dd
Tindale 245 Fc
Tingewick 121 Fe
Tingley 204 De
Tingrith 124 Be
Tinhay 45 Gc
Tinshill 217 Eb
Tinsley 205 Eb
Tinsley Green 80 Ad
Tintagel 44 Cc
Tintern Abbey 92 Cf
Tintern Parva 116 Cb
Tintinhull 69 Hb
Tintwistle 204 Bb
Tinwald 256 Ca
Tinwell 169 Gb
Tipperary 333 Qa
Tipperty *Aber* 297 Gf
Tipperty *Aber* 308 Gc
Tips End 172 Da
Tiptoe 56 Ad
Tipton 164 Da
Tipton St John 49 Ed
Tiptree 128 Bc
Tiptree Heath 128 Bc
Tirabad 112 Df
Tiree 288 Ab
Tirkane 349 Rf
Tirley 117 Fd
Tirphil 113 Gb
Tirril 225 Ge
Tir-y-dail 112 Bc
Tisbury 73 Dc
Tissington 189 Gb
Titchberry 64 Cc
Titchfield 56 De
Titchmarsh 145 Gd
Titchwell 173 Ff
Titley 137 Fc
Titlington 261 Fd
Titson 45 Ee
Tittensor 164 Ce
Titterstone Clee Hill 137 Hd
Tittleshall 173 Gd
Tiverton *Ches* 188 Ac
Tiverton *Devon* 68 Bb
Tivetshall St Margaret 152 Be
Tivetshall St Mary 152 Be
Tixall 164 Dd
Tixover 169 Fb
Toab 320 Ef
Toab 321 La
Toadmoor 192 Ab
Toames 325 Qe
Tober 336 Ck
Tobercurry 341 Mh
Tobermore 349 Re
Tobermory 289 Gc
Toberonochy 277 Fc
Toberscanavan 341 Ni
Tocher 308 Dd
Tockenham 93 Hc
Tockenham Wick 93 Hd
Tockholes 201 Fe
Tockington 92 Dd
Tockwith 217 Gc
Todber 72 Cc
Toddington *Beds* 124 Bd
Toddington *Glos* 117 He
Toddington *W Ssx* 60 Ae
Todenham 120 Be
Todhills *Angus* 296 Da
Todhills *Cumb* 244 Cd
Todmorden 204 Ae
Todwick 192 Be
Toem 333 Qb
Toft *Cambs* 148 Bb
Toft *Lincs* 169 Gc
Toft Monks 177 Ea
Toft next Newton 193 He
Toftrees 173 Gd
Tofts Ness 320 Gj
Toftwood 173 Hc
Togher *Cork* 325 Pd
Togher *Louth* 345 Me
Togher *Meath* 344 Ha
Togher *Wklw* 337 Mh
Togston 261 Gc
Tokavaig 300 Fb
Tokers Green 97 Gc
Tolastadh a'Chaolais 317 Wq
Tolastadh bho Thuath 317 AAr
Tolland 68 Dd
Tollard Royal 73 Db
Toll Bar 205 Gc
Toller Fratrum 52 Bd
Toller Porcorum 52 Bd
Tollerton *Notts* 168 Ce
Tollerton *N Yorks* 217 Hd
Toller Whelme 52 Be
Tollesbury 128 Cc
Tolleshunt D'Arcy 128 Cc
Tolleshunt Knights 128 Cc
Tolleshunt Major 128 Cc
Toll of Birness 309 Hd
Tolpuddle 52 Dd
Tolquhon Castle 308 Fc
Tolworth 100 Cb
Tomatin 305 Gc
Tombreck 304 Ed
Tomcrasky 304 Ab
Tomdoun 301 La
Tomdow 305 Je
Tomen-y-Mur 157 He
Tomhaggard 329 Ri
Tomich 313 Ka
Tomich House 304 De
Tomintoul *Aber* 296 Ag
Tomintoul *Moray* 305 Kb
Tomnaven 308 Bd
Tomnavoulin 305 Lc
Tomsléibhe 289 Ha
Tonbridge 80 De
Tondu 88 Dd
Tong 164 Bb
Tonge 168 Ad
Tongham 77 Ee
Tongland 240 Dc
Tongue 312 Hi
Tongwynlais 89 Gd
Tonna 88 Ce
Ton Pentre 89 Ee
Tonwell 125 Ec
Tonyduff 344 Gg
Tonypandy 89 Ee
Tonyrefail 89 Fd
Toome 349 Se
Toomyvara 333 Re
Tooraneena 328 Gi
Tooraree 332 Hb
Toormakeady 340 Gc
Toormore 325 Kb
Toot Baldon 121 Eb
Toot Hill *Esx* 125 Gb
Toothill *Hants* 73 Hb
Topcliffe 217 Fe
Topcroft 176 Ca
Topcroft Street 176 Ca
Top End 145 Gc
Toppesfield 128 Ae
Toppings 201 Gd
Topsham 48 Dc
Torbay 48 Da
Torbeg *Aber* 305 Ma
Torbeg *N Ayr* 249 Ge
Torboll Farm 313 Kc
Torbryan 48 Ca
Torcastle 292 Be
Torcross 41 Gd
Tore 304 Ef
Torksey 193 Fd
Torlum 317 Sh
Torlundy 292 Be
Tormarton 93 Ec
Tormisdale 316 Cf
Tormitchell 252 Cb
Tormore 264 Aa
Tornagrain 304 Fe
Tornahaish 305 La
Tornaveen 308 Da
Torness 304 Dc
Torosay Castle 289 Ja
Torpenhow 244 Ba
Torphichen 268 De
Torphins 308 Da
Torpoint 40 Ce
Torquay 48 Da
Torque 336 Dk
Torquhan 269 Jb
Torran *A & B* 277 Gc
Torran *Hghld* 300 Ee
Torrance *E Dun* 265 Je
Torrance *Strath* 268 Ac
Torrans 276 Ce
Torridon 301 Jf
Torridon House 301 Hf
Torrin 300 Ec
Torrisdale 313 Jj
Torrish 313 Me
Torrisholme 213 Ed
Torroble 312 Hd
Torry 308 Bd
Torryburn 284 Ca
Torrylin 249 He
Torsonce 272 Ab
Torterston 309 He
Torthorwald 241 He
Tortington 60 Ae
Tortworth 92 De
Torvaig 300 De
Torver 224 Db
Torwood 281 Ja
Torworth 192 De
Tosberry 64 Cc
Toscaig 301 Gd
Toseland 148 Ac
Tosside 213 Hc
Tostock 149 Hc
Totaig 300 Af
Tote 300 De
Totegan 313 Lj
Totford 76 Bd
Tothill 196 De
Totland 56 Bc
Totley 192 Ad
Totnes 41 Gf
Toton 168 Be
Totscore 300 Cg
Tottenham 101 Ee
Tottenhill 173 Ec
Totteridge 100 De
Totternhoe 124 Ad
Tottington 201 Gd
Totton 73 Hb
Touchen-end 97 Hc
Tournaig 312 Ab
Toux *Aber* 308 Gf
Toux *Moray* 308 Cf
Tovil 104 Aa
Toward 264 Dd
Towcester 144 Ca
Towednack 36 Cc
Tower Hamlets 101 Ed
Towersey 121 Gb
Towie 308 Bb
Towiemore 308 Ae
Tow Law 248 Ca
Towneley Hall 216 Aa
Town End *Cambs* 172 Ca
Town End *Cumb* 225 Fa
Townend *Cumb* 225 Fc
Townfield 248 Ab
Townhead *Cumb* 245 Fa
Townhead *D & G* 240 Db
Townhead of Greenlaw 241 Ed
Townhill 284 Da
Town Row 80 Dd
Townshend 36 Dc
Town Yetholm 260 Ce
Towthorpe 220 Ac
Towton 217 Ga
Towyn 184 Cd
Toynton All Saints 196 Cc
Toynton Fen Side 196 Cc
Toynton St Peter 196 Dc
Toy's Hill 101 Fa
Trabboch 253 Ee
Trabbochburn 253 Ee
Traboe 36 Fb
Tracton 328 Cd
Tradespark 305 Gf
Trafford Park 201 Gb
Tralee 325 Kj
Trallong 113 Ed
Tramore 329 Li
Tranent 269 Je
Trantlemore 313 Li
Tranwell 261 Fa
Trapp 112 Bc
Traprain 272 Be
Traquair 269 Ha
Trawden 216 Ba
Trawsfynydd 157 He
Trealaw 89 Ee
Treales 213 Ea
Treantagh 349 Jg
Trearddur 180 Dd
Treaslane 300 Cf
Trebanos 112 Cb
Trebarrow 45 Ed
Trebartha 45 Eb
Trebarwith 44 Cc
Trebetherick 44 Bb
Treborough 68 Cd
Trebudannon 44 Aa
Trebullett 45 Fb
Treburley 45 Fb
Trecastle 112 Dd
Trecwn 108 Ce
Trecynon 113 Eb
Tredavoe 36 Cb
Tredegar 113 Gb
Tredington *Glos* 117 Gd
Tredington *Warks* 141 Ga
Tredinnick *Corn* 40 Ae
Tredinnick *Corn* 44 Bb
Tredomen 113 Ge
Tredrizzick 44 Bb
Tredunnock 92 Ae
Treen 33 Bb
Treeton 192 Be
Trefasser 108 Be
Trefdraeth 181 Fd
Trefecca 113 Ge
Trefeglwys 160 Ba
Trefenter 133 Gc
Treffgarne 108 Cd
Treffynnon 108 Bd
Trefil 113 Gc
Trefilan 133 Fb
Treflach 161 Ed
Trefnanney 161 Ec
Trefnant 184 Dd
Trefonen 161 Ed
Trefor *Anglsy* 181 Ed
Trefor *C & M* 181 Ea
Treforest Industrial Estate 89 Gd
Trefriw 184 Ac
Tregadillett 45 Ec
Tregaian 181 Fd
Tregare 116 Bc
Tregaron 133 Gb
Tregarth 181 Hc
Tregear 37 Ge
Tregeare 45 Ec
Tregeiriog 160 De
Tregele 181 Ef
Tregidden 36 Fb
Treglemais 108 Bd
Tregolds 44 Ab
Tregole 44 Dd
Tregonetha 44 Ba
Tregony 37 Hd
Tregoyd 113 Ge

526 Wing–Wycoller

Wing *Bucks* 121 Hd
Wing *Leics* 169 Eb
Wingate 249 Fa
Wingates *GM* 201 Fc
Wingates *Northld* 261 Eb
Wingerworth 192 Ac
Wingfield *Beds* 124 Ad
Wingfield *Sflk* 152 Cd
Wingfield *Wilts* 93 Fa
Wingham 105 Fa
Wingmore 84 Be
Wingrave 121 Hc
Winkburn 193 Eb
Winkfield 100 Ac
Winkfield Row 100 Ac
Winkhill 189 Fb
Winkleigh 48 Ae
Winksley 217 Ee
Winkton 53 Hd
Winkworth Arboretum 77 Fe
Winlaton 248 Cd
Winless 313 Ri
Winmarleigh 213 Eb
Winnard's Perch 44 Ba
Winnersh 97 Gc
Winscales 224 Be
Winscombe 92 Ba
Winsford *Ches* 188 Bc
Winsford *Som* 68 Bd
Winsham 49 He
Winshill 165 Gd
Winskill 245 Ea
Winslade 76 Ce
Winsley 93 Eb
Winslow 121 Gd
Winson 117 Hb
Winster *Cumb* 225 Fb
Winster *Derbs* 189 Hc
Winston *Dur* 229 Ed
Winston *Sflk* 152 Bc
Winstone 117 Gb
Winswell 65 Eb
Winterborne Came 52 Dc
Winterborne Clenston 52 Ee
Winterborne Herringston 52 Cc
Winterborne Houghton 52 Ee
Winterborne Kingston 53 Ed
Winterborne Monkton 52 Cc
Winterborne Stickland 52 Ee
Winterborne Whitechurch 53 Ed
Winterborne Zelston 53 Ed
Winterbourne *Avon* 92 Dd
Winterbourne *Berks* 96 Dc
Winterbourne Abbas 52 Cd
Winterbourne Bassett 96 Ac
Winterbourne Dauntsey 73 Fd
Winterbourne Earls 73 Fd
Winterbourne Gunner 73 Fd
Winterbourne Monkton 93 Hc
Winterbourne Steepleton 52 Cc
Winterbourne Stoke 73 Ee
Winterburn 216 Bc
Winteringham 208 Ce
Winterley 188 Cb
Wintersett 205 Ed
Wintershill 76 Bb
Winterslow 73 Gd
Winterton 208 Cd
Winterton-on-Sea 177 Ec
Winthorpe *Lincs* 197 Ec
Winthorpe *Notts* 193 Fb
Winton *Cumb* 228 Ad
Winton *Dors* 53 Gd
Wintringham 220 Ce
Winwick *Cambs* 145 He
Winwick *Mers* 201 Fb
Winwick *Northants* 144 Cd
Wirksworth 189 Hb
Wirral 185 Ge
Wirswall 188 Aa
Wisbech 172 Cb
Wisbech St Mary 172 Cb
Wisborough Green 77 Gc
Wiseton 193 Ee
Wishaw *N Lan* 268 Bc
Wishaw *Warks* 165 Fa
Wisley 100 Ba
Wispington 196 Bd
Wissett 152 Dd
Wissington 128 Ce
Wistanstow 137 Ge
Wistanswick 164 Ad
Wistaston 188 Bb
Wiston *Pemb* 108 Dc
Wiston *S Lan* 268 Da
Wiston *W Ssx* 77 Hb
Wiston Park 77 Hb
Wistow *Cambs* 148 Ae
Wistow *N Yorks* 217 Ha
Wiswell 213 Ha
Witcham 148 Ce
Witchampton 53 Fe
Witchford 148 Dd
Witcombe 69 Gc
Witham 128 Bc
Witham Friary 72 Be
Witham on the Hill 169 Gc
Witherenden Hill 81 Ec
Witheridge 68 Ab
Witherley 165 Ha
Withern 196 De
Withernsea 209 Ge
Withernwick 221 Fb
Withersdale Street 152 Ce
Withersfield 149 Ea
Witherslack 225 Fa
Witherslack Hall 225 Fa
Withiel 44 Ba
Withiel Florey 68 Bd
Withington *Ches* 188 Dd
Withington *Glos* 117 Hc
Withington *GM* 201 Hb
Withington *H & W* 137 Ha
Withington *Shrops* 161 Hc
Withington *Staffs* 165 Ee
Withington Green 188 Dd
Withleigh 68 Bb
Withnell 201 Fe
Withybrook 144 Ae
Withycombe 68 Ce
Withycombe Raleigh 49 Ec
Withyham 80 Cd
Withypool 68 Ad
Witley 77 Fd
Witley Court 140 Bc
Witnesham 152 Bb
Witney 120 Cb
Wittering 169 Gb
Wittersham 81 Gc
Witton 296 Ee
Witton Bridge 176 De
Witton Gilbert 248 Db
Witton le Wear 248 Ca
Witton Park 248 Ca
Wiveliscombe 68 Cc
Wivelsfield 80 Bc
Wivelsfield Green 80 Bb
Wivenhoe 128 Dd
Wivenhoe Cross 128 Dd
Wiveton 176 Af
Wix 129 Ed
Wixford 141 Eb
Wixoe 149 Fa
Woburn 124 Ae
Woburn Sands 124 Ae
Wokefield Park 97 Fb
Woking 100 Ba
Wokingham 97 Hb
Wolborough 48 Cb
Woldingham 101 Ea
Wold Newton *Humb* 209 Fb
Wold Newton *N Yorks* 221 Ee
Wolferlow 140 Ac
Wolferton 173 Ed
Wolfhill *Laois* 336 Ff
Wolfhill *P & K* 296 Aa
Wolf's Castle 108 Cd
Wolfsdale 108 Cd
Woll 257 Ge
Wollaston *Northants* 145 Fc
Wollaston *Shrops* 161 Fc
Wollaston *W Mids* 140 Ce
Wollaton Hall 168 Be
Wollerton 164 Ad
Wolsingham 248 Ba
Wolston 144 Ad
Wolvercote 120 Db
Wolverhampton 164 Da
Wolverley *H & W* 140 Cd
Wolverley *Shrops* 161 Ge
Wolverton *Bucks* 145 Ea
Wolverton *Hants* 97 Ea
Wolverton *Warks* 141 Gc
Wolvesnewton 92 Be
Wolvey 144 Ae
Wolviston 229 He
Wombleton 232 Ba
Wombourne 164 Ca
Wombwell 205 Ec
Womenswold 105 Fa
Womersley 205 Gd
Wonastow 116 Bc
Wonersh 77 Ge
Wonson 48 Ac
Wonston *Dors* 52 De
Wonston *Hants* 76 Ad
Wooburn 100 Ad
Wooburn Green 100 Ad
Woodale 216 Ce
Woodbastwick 176 Dc
Woodbeck 193 Ed
Woodborough *Notts* 192 Da
Woodborough *Wilts* 96 Aa
Woodbridge 152 Ca
Wood Burcote 144 Ca
Woodburn 352 Wd
Woodbury 49 Ec
Woodbury Salterton 49 Ec
Woodchester 117 Fb
Woodchurch 81 Hd
Woodcote *Oxon* 97 Fd
Woodcote *Shrops* 164 Bc
Woodcroft 92 Ce
Woodcutts 73 Db
Wood Dalling 176 Ad
Woodditton 149 Eb
Woodeaton 121 Ec
Woodenbridge 337 Me
Wood End *Beds* 145 Ga
Woodend *Cumb* 224 Cb
Wood End *Herts* 125 Ed
Woodend *Hghld* 289 Jd
Woodend *Northants* 144 Ca
Wood End *Warks* 141 Fd
Wood End *Warks* 165 Ga
Woodend *W Ssx* 57 Ge
Wood Enderby 196 Bc
Woodfalls 73 Fc
Woodford *Corn* 64 Cb
Woodford *Devon* 41 Fe
Woodford *Gal* 333 Ph
Woodford *GL* 101 Ee
Woodford *GM* 188 De
Woodford *Northants* 145 Fd
Woodford Bridge 101 Fe
Woodford Green 101 Fe
Woodgate *H & W* 140 Dc
Woodgate *H & W* 140 De
Woodgate *Nflk* 176 Ac
Woodgate *W Ssx* 57 He
Woodgreen *Ant* 352 Ue
Wood Green *GL* 101 Ee
Woodgreen *Hants* 73 Fb
Woodhall 228 Cb
Woodhall Spa 196 Ac
Woodham 100 Bb
Woodham Ferrers 104 Ae
Woodham Mortimer 128 Bb
Woodham Walter 128 Bb
Woodhaven 285 Ge
Wood Hayes 164 Db
Woodhead 308 Ed
Woodhill 140 Be
Woodhorn 261 Ga
Woodhouse *Cumb* 225 Ga
Woodhouse *Leics* 168 Bc
Woodhouse *S Yorks* 192 Be
Woodhouse Eaves 168 Bc
Woodhouselee 269 Gd
Woodhouses 165 Fc
Woodhurst 148 Bd
Woodingdean 60 De
Woodland *Devon* 48 Ba
Woodland *Dur* 228 De
Woodlands *Aber* 297 Gg
Woodlands *Dors* 53 Ge
Woodlands *Hants* 73 Hb
Woodlands Park 97 Hc
Wood Lanes 189 Ee
Woodleigh 41 Fd
Woodlesford 205 Ee
Woodley 97 Gc
Woodmancote *Glos* 117 Gd
Woodmancote *Glos* 117 Hb
Woodmancote *W Ssx* 57 Fe
Woodmancote *W Ssx* 80 Ab
Woodmancott 76 Be
Woodmansey 221 Ea
Woodmansterne 100 Db
Woodminton 73 Ec
Woodnesborough 105 Ga
Woodnewton 169 Ga
Wood Norton 176 Ad
Woodplumpton 213 Ea
Woodrising 173 Hb
Woodseaves *Shrops* 164 Ae
Woodseaves *Staffs* 164 Bd
Woodsend 96 Bc
Woodsetts 192 Ce
Woodsford 52 Dd
Woodside *Berks* 100 Ac
Woodside *Herts* 124 Db
Woodside *N Ayr* 265 Fc
Woodside *P & K* 296 Ba
Woodside *Shrops* 137 Fe
Woodstock 120 Dc
Woodstown 329 Mi
Wood Street 77 Ff
Woodthorpe *Derbs* 192 Bd
Woodthorpe *Leics* 168 Bc
Woodton 176 Ca
Woodtown 65 Ec
Woodville 165 Hc
Woodwalton 148 Ae
Woodyates 73 Eb
Woofferton 137 Hc
Wookey 69 He
Wookey Hole 69 He
Wool 53 Ec
Woolacombe 65 Ee
Woolage Green 84 Ce
Woolaston 92 Ce
Woolavington 69 Fe
Woolbeding 77 Ec
Wooler 260 De
Woolfardisworthy *Devon* 48 Ce
Woolfardisworthy *Devon* 64 Dc
Woolfords Cottages 268 Ec
Woolhampton 97 Eb
Woolhope 116 De
Woolland 52 De
Woollaton 65 Eb
Woolley *Avon* 93 Eb
Woolley *Cambs* 145 Hd
Woolley *S Yorks* 205 Ed
Woolley House 96 Dc
Woolmere Green 140 Dc
Woolmer Green 124 Dc
Woolmersdon 69 Ed
Woolpit 149 Hc
Woolscott 144 Ac
Woolstaston 161 Ga
Woolsthorpe *Lincs* 169 Ee
Woolsthorpe-by-Colsterworth 169 Fd
Woolston *Ches* 188 Be
Woolston *Devon* 41 Fd
Woolston *Hants* 76 Ab
Woolston *Shrops* 137 Ge
Woolston *Shrops* 161 Fd
Woolstone *Bucks* 96 Bd
Woolstone *Oxon* 96 Bd
Woolston Green 48 Ba
Woolton 185 He
Woolton Hill 96 Db
Woolverstone 129 Ee
Woolverton 93 Ea
Woolwich 101 Fc
Woonton 137 Fb
Wooperton 261 Ee
Woore 188 Ca
Wootton *Beds* 145 Ga
Wootton *Hants* 56 Ad
Wootton *Humb* 208 Dd
Wootton *Kent* 84 Ce
Wootton *Northants* 144 Db
Wootton *Oxon* 120 Db
Wootton *Oxon* 120 Dc
Wootton *Shrops* 137 Gd
Wootton *Staffs* 164 Cd
Wootton *Staffs* 189 Ga
Wootton Bassett 93 Hd
Wootton Bridge 56 Dd
Wootton Common 56 Dd
Wootton Courtenay 68 Be
Wootton Fitzpaine 49 Hd
Wootton Rivers 96 Ab
Wootton St Lawrence 97 Ea
Wootton Wawen 141 Fc
Worcester 140 Cb
Worcester Park 100 Db
Wordsley 140 Ce
Wordwell 149 Gd
Worfield 164 Ba
Workington 224 Ae
Worksop 192 Cd
Worlaby 208 Dd
World's End *Berks* 96 Dc
Worlds End *Hants* 76 Cb
Worle 92 Ab
Worleston 188 Bb
Worlingham 153 Ee
Worlington 149 Ed
Worlingworth 152 Cc
Wormbridge 116 Be
Wormegay 173 Ec
Wormelow Tump 116 Be
Wormhill 189 Gd
Wormiehills 296 Fa
Wormingford 128 Ce
Worminghall 121 Fb
Wormington 117 He
Worminster 69 He
Wormit 285 Fe
Wormleighton 144 Ab
Wormley *Herts* 125 Eb
Wormley *Sry* 77 Fd
Wormleybury 125 Eb
Worms Head 85 Hd
Wormshill 104 Ba
Wormsley 137 Ga
Worplesdon 100 Aa
Worrall 205 Eb
Worsbrough 205 Ec
Worsley 201 Gc
Worstead 176 Dd
Worsthorne 216 Aa
Worston 213 Hb
Worth *Kent* 105 Ga
Worth *W Ssx* 80 Bd
Wortham 152 Ad
Worthen 161 Fb
Worthenbury 185 Ha
Worthing *Nflk* 173 Hc
Worthing *W Ssx* 60 Be
Worthington 168 Ad
Worth Matravers 53 Fb
Wortley *Glos* 93 Ee
Wortley *W Yorks* 205 Eb
Worton 93 Ga
Wortwell 152 Ce
Wotherton 161 Eb
Wotter 45 Ha
Wotton 77 He
Wotton-under-Edge 93 Ee
Wotton Underwood 121 Fc
Woughton on the Green 121 He
Wouldham 104 Ab
Wrabness 129 Ee
Wrafton 65 Ed
Wragby 196 Ad
Wragholme 209 Gb
Wramplingham 176 Bb
Wrangham 308 Dd
Wrangle 196 Db
Wrangle Bank 196 Db
Wrangle Lowgate 196 Db
Wrangway 68 Db
Wrantage 69 Fc
Wrawby 208 Dc
Wraxall *Avon* 92 Bc
Wraxall *Som* 69 Hd
Wray 213 Gd
Wraysbury 100 Bc
Wrea Green 212 Da
Wreay *Cumb* 225 Fe
Wreay *Cumb* 244 Db
Wrecclesham 77 Ee
Wrekenton 248 Dc
Wrekin, The 164 Ab
Wrelton 232 Ca
Wrenbury 188 Aa
Wreningham 176 Ba
Wrentham 153 Ee
Wrenthorpe 205 Ee
Wressle 220 Ba
Wrestlingworth 148 Aa
Wretham 173 Ha
Wretton 173 Ea
Wrexham 185 Gb
Wrexham Industrial Estate 185 Ga
Wribbenhall 140 Bd
Wrightington Bar 201 Ed
Wrinehill 188 Ca
Wrington 92 Bb
Writtle 125 Hb
Wrockwardine 164 Ac
Wroot 208 Ac
Wrotham 101 Ha
Wrotham Heath 101 Ha
Wroughton 96 Ad
Wroxall 56 Db
Wroxeter 161 Hb
Wroxhall 141 Gd
Wroxham 176 Dc
Wroxton 144 Aa
Wyaston 189 Ga
Wyberton 196 Ca
Wyboston 145 Hb
Wybunbury 188 Ba
Wychbold 140 Dc
Wych Cross 80 Cd
Wyck 76 Dd
Wycliffe 229 Ed
Wycoller 216 Ba

ACKNOWLEDGMENTS

Sources of information and illustrations in *Book of the Road* are listed below

Our thanks to the following for their help in producing this book: An Oige; Assn of Railway Preservation Societies; Assn of Chief Police Officers (Traffic Committee); BBC Engineering; Stefanie Blake; Bord Luthchleas na h Eireann; British Amateur Athletic Board; British Aviation Authority; British Canoe Union; British Gliding Assn; BP Oil UK Ltd; British Railways Board; British Showjumping Assn; British Tourist Authority; British Water Ski Federation; Cadw Welsh Historic Monuments; Civil Aviation Authority; Conoco Ltd; Countryside Commission; Department of the Environment; Department of Transport; English Heritage; Esso Petroleum Co Ltd; Eurotunnel; Football League; Forest Enterprises; Margaret Fotheringham; Gaelic Athletic Assn; David Green LLB; Green Flag National Breakdown; HM Coastguard; Historic Scotland; Hunting Aerofilms Ltd; Hull Town Docks Museum; Hurlingham Polo Assn; Irish Greyhound Board; Irish Water Ski Federation; Manx National Heritage; Manx National Trust; Metropolitan Police; Mobil Oil Co Ltd; Murco Petroleum Ltd; National Maritime Museum; National Remote Sensing Centre (Airphoto Group); *National Tourist Boards:* English, Irish (Bord Failte), Isle of Man, Jersey, Northern Ireland, Scottish, States of Guernsey, Wales; National Trust; National Trust for Scotland; Nature Conservancy Council; New Forest DC; Office of Public Works, Dublin; Jeremy Plummer; Gillian Pope; Racecourse Assn; Royal Automobile Club; Royal Irish Automobile Club; RoSPA; RSPB; Royal Yachting Assn; Rugby Football Union; Rugby League Yearbook; Save Service Stations Ltd; Scottish Games Assn; Scottish Natural Heritage; Scottish Nature Conservancy; Scottish Office; Scottish Wildlife Trust; Shell UK Ltd; Ski Club of Great Britain; South Country Secrets; Speedway Controls Board; Test and County Cricket Board; Texaco Ltd; The Golf Course Guide; The Meteorological Office; The Radio Authority; Total Oil GB Ltd; *Regional Tourist Boards:* Cumbria, East Anglia, East Midlands, Heart of England, London, North West, Northumbria, Southern, South East England, Thames and Chilterns, West Country, Yorkshire and Humberside; Waterford Glass; Welsh Office; Western Isles Council; William Morris Gallery; Yorkshire Dales National Park; Youth Hostels Assn.

The photographs in this book were provided by the following photographers and agencies.
The position of photographs on each page is indicated by letters in parentheses after the page number: T = top; B = bottom; L = left; C = centre; R = right. The following short forms have been used: BL = Permission of the Board of the British Library; BM = Permission of the Trustees of the British Museum; Co = Collections; HD = Hulton Deutsch Collection; JC = John Cleare/Mountain Camera; ME = Mary Evans Picture Library; NP = National Portrait Gallery, London; NT = The National Trust Photograph Library; RH = Robert Harding Picture Library; SiF = Scotland in Focus; TB = Tourist Board; TW = Tim Woodcock; V & A = By Courtesy of the Board of the Victoria and Albert Museum.

38 (BL inset) (BL) HD; (BR) JC. **39** (T) Arcaid/Richard Bryant; (CR) Co/Paul Watts; (BL) HD; (BR) NT/Rob Matheson. **42** (TL) NP; (BL) ME; (BC) JC; (BR) Co. **43** (L) ME; (TC) (TR) NT/John Bethell; (BC) RH/Girts Gailans. **46** (TL) The Royal Institution of Cornwall; (BR) Peter Kent. **47** (TL) RH/Adam Woolfitt; (TC) Plymouth City Museum; (CL) HD; (C) Images/Colour Library; (CR) Co/Paul Watts; (B) NT/Andreas von Einsiedel. **50** (TL) Tate Gallery, London. **51** (T) TW; (TR) Images Colour Library; (CL) (CR) ME; (BL) NP; (B inset) Arcaid/Lucinda Lambton. **54** (TL) Christie's Colour Library; (BL) NP; (BR) NT/Eric Crichton. **55** (BL) RH/Adam Woolfitt; (BR) NT/Joe Cornish. **58** (TL) BL Ms.Roy20A II f.6; (TR) Bruce Coleman Ltd/Peter Terry; (BL) Neil Holmes; (BR) Mike Read. **59** (Inset) Michael Holford; (CL) ET Archive, London; (CR) Andrew Lawson; (BL) Images Colour Library; (BR) Fishbourne Roman Palace. **62** (CL) HD; (C) RH; (CR) RH/Ruth Tomlinson. **63** (TL) Arcaid/Richard Bryant; (TC) (TR) (C) NP; (CL) (CR) Co/David Bowie; (BR) RH/Ron Oulds. **66** (TL) ME; (CL) The Penguin Group/Artist, Charles Tunnicliffe; (CR) TW; (BR) Comstock Photofile Limited/Simon McBride. **67** (T) NT; (CL) RH/Larsen-Collinge; (CR) Stanley Gibbons; (BC) Arcaid/Lucinda Lambton. **70** (TL) TW; (B) Somerset County Council. **71** (TC) Skyscan; (C) ME/Jeffrey Morgan; (BL) Institute of Agricultural History and Museum of English Rural Life. **74** (TL) The Bridgeman Art Library, London/V & A; (BL) Comstock Photophile Limited/Georg Gerster. **75** (TR) RH/Adam Woolfitt; (C) Neil Holmes; (BL) TW. **78** (TL) BL/954G1-24 pl 138-George Shaw-Naturalist Misc; (TC) The Zoological Society of London from Thomas Pennant's book *The British Zoology* Class I quadrupeds, II birds; (BC) (BR) *Old West Surrey* by Gertrude Jekyll. **79** (I) JC; (CL) ME; (C) NT/Nicholas Sapieha; (BL) Jane Austen Memorial Trust; (BC) Jarrold & Sons Ltd. **82** (TL) Co/Alain Le Garsmeur; (CR) (hop machine) HD (oast-house) Arcaid/Martin Jones; (BL) (BR) HD. **83** (T) Sheila & Oliver Mathews; (TR) Images Colour Library/Derry Brabbs; (CL) BL; (C) NP; (CR) Bruce Coleman Ltd/Jennifer Fry; (B) NT/Stephen Robson. **86** (TL) ME; (CR) Derek Pratt; (BL) Julian Cotton; (BR) HD. **87** (T) Images Colour Library; (CL) Bruce Coleman Ltd/Peter Terry; (C) Co/Alain Le Garsmeur; (CR) Bruce Coleman Ltd/Gordon Langsbury; (BR) ME. **90** (CL) HD; (C) ME/Henry Grant; (B) Rhondda Heritage Park. **91** (TL) Camera Press; (TR) NT/Joe Cornish; (CL) TW; (CR) (BL) Cadw: Welsh Historic Monuments. Crown Copyright. **94** (TL) TW; (CL) NT/Nick Carter; (CR) RH/Christopher Nicholson; (BR) Andrew Lawson. **95** (T) RH/Lesley Burridge; (C) HD; (CR) V & A; (BC) NP; (BR) The Garden Picture Library/John Bethell. **98** (CR) The Image Bank/Trevor Wood; (BL) RH/Jenny Pate; (BR) Comstock Photofile Limited/Georg Gerster. **99** (T) Neil Holmes; (CL) Arcaid/Clay Perry; (C) Sonia Halliday; (CR) The Image Bank/Derek Redfearn; (BC) ME. **102** (T) (CL) All-Sport (UK); (CR) (BL) (BR) The William Morris Gallery, Walthamstow, London; (BC) HD. **103** (TL) Popperfoto; (TR) Skyscan; (CL) (Ham House) NT/Nick Meers; (CR) Arcaid/Lark Gilmer; (BL) NT/Bill Batten; (BC) London Transport Museum; (BR) Andrew Lawson. **106** (TL) ME; (BL) HD; (BC) NHPA/David Woodfall; (BR) Arcaid/Barbara Godzikowska. **107** (coin, private collection); (CL) Arcaid/Martin Jones; (C) ME; (CR) Arcaid/Lucinda Lambton. **110** (T) Popperfoto; (C) TW; (B) Arcaid/Mark Fiennes. **111** (T) The Image Bank; (C) HD; (CR) Arcaid/Mark Fiennes; (BC) RH/David Beatty; (BR) HD. **114** (TL) BL 10825.ee.21; (CL) Wales Tourist Board; (C) (CR) Merthyr Tydfil Borough Council Library Service; (B) Wales TB. **115** (CL) Wales TB; (C) JC; (B) NT/David Noton. **118** (TL) Peter Clayton; (CL) JC. **119** (TC) NT/Andreas von Einsiedel; (TR) TW; (C) Robert Opie; (CR) Andrew Lawson; (BR) NT/Ian Shaw. **122** (TL) ME; (C) TW; (BL) (BC) Sheila & Oliver Mathews; (BR) Andrew Lawson. **123** (TL) Sheila & Oliver Mathews; (TC) (TR) (CL) Andrew Lawson; (C) NT/Nick Meers; (CR) ME. **128** (TL) TW; (CL) (C) Hertfordshire Publications; (CR) Dr Mervyn Miller. **129** (TL) (CR) (BL) TW; (Inset) Camera Press; (BR) RH/Adam Woolfitt. **130** (CR) NT/Colin R. Chalmers; (BR) The National Gallery, London. **131** (TR) NT/Nick Meers; (CR) NT. **134** (TL) Mick Sharp; (B) The Welsh Pony & Cob Society. **135** (TL) TW; (TC) RH; (CL) By permission of the National Library of Wales; (B) Heather's Picture Workshop. **138** (TL) ME. **139** (T) (BL) TW; (CR) JC. **142** (TL) (CL) NP; (CR) (BR) Andrew Lawson. **143** (TL) NT/Stephen Robson; (BL) Co/McQuillan & Brown; (B) NT/Joe Cornish. **146** (TL) ME; (TR) NP; (BL) NT/Oliver Benn. **147** (TL) Northampton Museums; (lodge) Neil Holmes; (C) (cross) Andrew Lawson; (CR) Co; (BL) ME; (BC) TW. **150** (TL) ME; (CL) (B) Neil Holmes; (BR) NT/Ray Hallett. **151** (TL) Julian Cotton; (CL) (BR) TW. **154** (TL) Sonia Halliday; (TR) HD; (CL) BM; (CR) (BL) (BR) Michael Holford. **155** (T) Co/Robert Hallman; (CL) Sean Leahy; (CR) Co; (B) NT/Joe Cornish. **158** (Patrick McGoohan) PolyGram Video; (TL) ME; (CL) Mick Sharp; (CR) Sheila & Oliver Mathews; (BR) PolyGram Video. **159** (TR) JC; (B) Sheila & Oliver Mathews. **162** (TL) (C) HD; (CR) Mick Sharp; (B) Neil Holmes. **163** (TL) Cadw: Welsh Historic Monuments. Crown Copyright; (TR) NT/Joe Cornish; (CL) NT/Charlie Waite; (B) Mick Sharp. **166** (BL) Science & Society Picture Library; (BR) Skyscan. **167** (T) NT/Andrew Haslam; (TR) NT; (CL) Arcaid/Martin Jones; (C) NP; (BR) RH; (B) Neil Holmes. **170** (TL) Universiteitsbibliotheek Gent/HS.236,FOL.2; (C) (BC) (BR) NT/Tessa Musgrave; (BL) NP. **171** (T) Arcaid/Martine Hamilton Knight; (C) Neil Holmes; (BR) Mick Sharp; (rest) Jacqui Hurst. **174** (TL) HD; (CL) (C) Sheila & Oliver Mathews; (B) TW. **175** (T) (CL) (BR) TW; (CR) Jacqui Hurst. **178** (TL) BM; (CL) (C) RH/G.M. Wilkins; (BR) The Anthony Blake Photo Library/Jonathan Topps. **179** (TR) Neil Holmes; (CL) Co/Barbara West; (C) Neil Holmes; (Mustard shop) (BL) Co/Liz Stares; (Cley) Sheila & Oliver Mathews. **182** (TL) Science & Society Picture Library; (CL) HD; (CR) Popperfoto; (BR) Co/Liz Stares. **183** (TL) JC; (C) Mick Sharp; (CR) Science & Society Picture Library/National Railway Museum; (B) RH/Adam Woolfitt. **186** (TL) Popperfoto; (C) (BR) NT/Andreas von Einsiedel; (BL) NT/John Hammond. **187** (T) NT/Oliver Benn; (CR) Mick Sharp. **190** (TL) Sonia Halliday; (CL) (CR) by courtesy of the Wedgwood Museum Trustees, Barlaston, Stoke-on-Trent, Staffordshire; (BL) Co/McQuillan & Brown; (BR) Bryan & Cherry Alexander. **191** (T) NT/Rupert Truman; (CL) Quadrant/Philip Talbot; (Eyam cottages) Mick Sharp; (BL) RH. **194** (TL) (TC) NT/Geoffrey Frosh; (CL) TW; (CR) NT/Nick Meers; (B) NT/Angelo Hornak. **195** (T) HD; (TC) Co/Robin Weaver; (TR) NP; (CL) Neil Holmes; (C) ME; (CR) Andrew Lawson; (BL) Co/Liz Stares; (BR) Mick Sharp. **198** (T) NP; (C) Sheila & Oliver Mathews; (CR) Co/Liz Stares; (B) From the Tennyson Research Centre, Lincoln, by permission of Lincolnshire County Council. **199** (TL) TW; (TR) Co/Liz Stares; (C) The Bridgeman Art Library, London/V & A; (BL) Mick Sharp; (BR) BM. **202** (T) (CL) HD; (CR) (BR) ME. **203** (TC) Co/Jonathan Hodson; (CL) Pictorial Press; (CL) Co/Simon Matthews; (C) ME; (BR) ET Archive, London/Reproduced by courtesy of Mrs Carol Ann Danes. **206** (TL) HD. **207** (TR) Images Colour Library; (CL) Co/Dorothy Burrows; (CR) NT/Mark Fiennes. **210** (TL) HD. **211** (T) Images Colour Library; (CL) (Queen of Holderness) (CR) (BL) Co/Gary R. Smith; (BR) Joe Cornish. **214** (T) (C) The Kobal Collection; (CR) HD; (BL) (BR) Images Colour Library; (BC) Co/Kevin Walsh. **215** (T) The Garden Picture Library/Nick Meers; (B) RH/Linda Proud. **218** (TL) Co/Dorothy Burrows; (C) HD. **219** (T) NT/Matthew Antrobus; (CL) (Leeds) Arcaid/Richard Waite (Brontës) NP; (C) Images Colour Library; (CR) Robert Thompson's Craftsmen Ltd; (B) David Tarn. **222** (TL) From the Winifred Holtby Collection, Hull Central Library; (CL) David Tarn. **223** (TR) Co/Gary R. Smith; (C) Derek Forss; (BL) David Tarn. **226** (TL) RH/Ellen Rodney; (CL) NP; (C) Copyright © F. Warnes & Co. 1902, 1987; (BL) Copyright © F. Warnes & Co. 1907, 1987; (BR) Copyright © F. Warnes & Co./courtesy Warne Archive. **227** (T) (CL) (CR) Images Colour Library; (C) Co; (BL) TW. **230** (TL) Derek Forss; (TC) NP; (CL) (BL) David Tarn; (BR) JC. **231** (TL) JC; (C) Images Colour Library; (BL) David Tarn; (BR) Co/Gary R. Smith. **235** (T) RH; (C) (BL) David Tarn. **238** (TL) Don Morley; (CR) SiF/G. Thomson; (B) TW. **239** (TL) Island Photographics; (CL) Stamps reproduced courtesy of the Isle of Man Post Office. For further information on Manx stamps contact IOM Philatelic Bureau; (C) (CR) Images Colour Library; (BL) courtesy of Manx National Heritage. **242** (T) HD; (CL) Douglas Botting; (BC) Camera Press/Terence Spencer; (BR) SiF/J. Howard. **243** (TL) NT Scotland; (TC) SiF/David Tarn; (CL) SiF; (CR) SiF/H. Cheek; (BL) TW; (BR) Scottish TB/Paul Tomkins. **246** (T) NP; (CL) JC; (CR) NT/Paul Wakefield; (BC) Neil Holmes. **247** (TR) Co/Graeme Peacock; (CL) Co/Roy Stedall-Humphreys; (C) Co/Graeme Peacock; (BR) David Tarn. **250** (TL) RH/Michael Jenner; (TR) BM; (BL) RH; (BC) (BR) Arcaid/Colin Dixon. **251** (T) (BL) Co/Graeme Peacock; (CL) Co/Philip Nixon; (C) Neil Holmes; (BR) David Tarn. **254** (TL) The Mansell Collection; (BL) (BR) SiF/A.G. Firth. **255** (TL) (BL) SiF/A.G. Firth; (CL) Mick Sharp; (BR) SiF/W.S. Paton. **258** (T) HD; (CR) ME; (BL) SiF/G. Stevenson. **259** (T) SiF/R. Weir; (BR) SiF/G. Satterley. **262** (TL) ET Archive, London; (BR) SiF/H. Cheek. **263** (TR) (CL) (BL) Images Colour Library. **266** (TL) Science & Society Picture Library; (CL) (BR) SiF/A.G. Firth; (C) T & R Annan & Sons Ltd. **267** (T) SiF/R. Weir; (C) © Glasgow Museum & Art Galleries; (BR) SiF/J. Weir. **270** (T) National Galleries of Scotland; (BL) Bruce Coleman Ltd. **271** (T) (B) SiF; (C) SiF/B. Lawson. **274** (TL) SiF/B. Lawson; (CL) The Royal Collection © Her Majesty The Queen; (C) Neil Holmes; (BL) (private collection); (BR) SiF/J. Hunt. **275** (T) Arcaid/Colin Dixon; (C) Neil Holmes; (CR) Scottish TB/Paul Tomkins; (BL) David Tarn. **278** (TL) Popperfoto; (CL) (BL) (BR) Mick Sharp. **279** (CR) Mick Sharp; (BL) SiF/J & PM Clarke. **282** (T) (BR) Alastair Scott; (C) The Mansell Collection; (BL) SiF/R. Purcell. **283** (T) SiF/R. Weir; (CL) Scottish TB; (C) (CR) Alastair Scott. **286** (TL) Scottish National Portrait Gallery; (TC) Perth & Kinross District Libraries; (B) SiF/R. Weir. **287** (TL) SiF/ J. Guidi; (TR) SiF/W.S. Paton; (CL) Alastair Scott; (B) SiF/J. McPake. **290** (T) Mick Sharp/Jean Williamson; (BL) Alastair Scott; (BR) HD. **291** (T) Bruce Coleman Ltd/Geoff Dore; (inset) Alastair Scott; (CR) Mick Sharp. **294** (TL) HD; (CL) SiF; (B) The Burrell Collection. **295** (TR) (C) (B) SiF. **298** (TL) ME; (CL) Scottish TB; (C) Popperfoto; (CR) Scottish TB; (B) SiF/B. Chapple. **299** (T) Alastair Scott; (TL) SiF/E.D. Lee; (TR) Alastair Scott; (BL) SiF/G. Thomson. **302** (TL) Scottish National Portrait Gallery; (CL) Mick Sharp; (BL) SiF/R.G. Elliott; (BR) Mick Sharp/Jean Williamson. **303** (TL) SiF; (C) SiF/R. Weir; (B) SiF/R.G. Elliott. **306** (TL) HD; (B) The Royal Collection © Her Majesty The Queen. **307** (TL) SiF/Willbir; (TR) (CR) SiF/R. Weir; (BR) Robert Estall/Alastair Scott. **310** (TL) SiF/Willbir; (C) Norsk Teknisk Museum/The Ronald Grant Archive; (BL) Popperfoto; (BR) Norsk Teknisk Museum. **311** (T) (B) SiF/Jason Smalley; (CL) SiF/J. Stephen; (CR) SiF/Don McKinnell. **314** (TL) © Glasgow Museum & Art Galleries/The Mitchell Library; (CL) (CR) (B) Laidhay Croft Museum. **315** (TL) (BR) SiF/R. Weir; (C) SiF/ J. MacPherson. **318** (T) SiF/L. Campbell; (C) (B) Phipps Public Relations Ltd. **319** (TR) SiF/L. Campbell; (CL) SiF/D. Burrows; (CR) Mick Sharp/Jean Williamson; (B) SiF/R.G. Elliott. **322** (TL) SiF/J & PM Clarke; (CL) © The Trustees of the National Museums of Scotland; (BL) (BR) Charles Tait. **323** (T) (CL) (BL) Charles Tait; (C) SiF/D. Houghton; (BR) SiF/J.G. Corbett. **326** (TL) Slide File. **327** (CL) Bord Failte Photo/Pat Odea. **330** (TL) Slide File; (BR) V & A/Daniel McGrath. **331** (T) (CR) (BR) Slide File. **334** (TL) Bord Failte Photo/ Pat Odea; (CL) Co/Alain Le Garsmeur; (CR) Slide File; (BL) Hugh Lane Municipal Gallery of Modern Art, Dublin/Sarah Purser; (BR) Hugh Lane Municipal Gallery of Modern Art, Dublin/Antonio Mancini. **335** (TL) (C) (BR) Slide File; (TR) Paul Wakefield. **338** (TL) (CL) (BL) Slide File. **339** (TL) (CR) (BR) Slide File; (BL) The Board of Trinity College, Dublin, fol 27v. **342** (TL) Vickers plc; (BL) Slide File; (BR) Sligo County Museum & Art Gallery/Photo John Searle. **343** (T) (BL) Slide File. **346** (TL) HD; (BR) Slide File. **347** (T) (B) Slide File; (CR) HD. **350** (CL) (C) (BL) Christopher Hill Photographic. **351** (TL) Slide File; (B) Christopher Hill Photographic.

40/439/01

ROAD DISTANCES IN IRELAND

	ATHLONE	BALLYMENA	BANGOR	BELFAST	COLERAINE	CORK	DONEGAL	DUBLIN	ENNIS	ENNISKILLEN	GALWAY	KILKENNY	KILLARNEY
ARMAGH	99	54	54	40	61	236	78	82	168	50	148	150	240
ATHLONE		153	153	140	153	134	113	77	68	79	57	75	142
BALLYMENA			41	28	28	286	90	131	221	81	201	199	295
BANGOR				14	71	272	124	118	222	97	202	186	282
BELFAST					57	259	110	104	209	84	189	172	268
COLERAINE						297	77	142	222	92	206	218	294
CORK							250	161	86	212	128	92	55
DONEGAL								144	165	36	129	188	255
DUBLIN									145	109	136	74	191
ENNIS										148	43	94	91
ENNISKILLEN											119	151	220
GALWAY												105	133
KILKENNY													122
KILLARNEY													
LA													

ROAD DISTANCES IN GREA

	LONDON	ABERDEEN	ABERYSTWYTH	AYR	BARNSTAPLE	BERWICK	BIRMINGHAM	BLACKPOOL	BOURNEMOUTH	BRIGHTON	BRISTOL	CAMBRIDGE	CARDIFF	CARLISLE	DOVER	EDINBURGH	EXETER	FISHGUARD	FORT WILLIAM	GLASGOW	GLOUCESTER	HARWICH	HOLYHEAD	INVERNESS	KENDAL	KINGSTON UPON HULL	LEEDS	LINCOLN	LIVERPOOL	MANCHESTER	MIDDLES	N
ABERDEEN	548																															
ABERYSTWYTH	238	470																														
AYR	419	190	341																													
BARNSTAPLE	216	606	222	477																												
BERWICK	351	187	323	130	435																											
BIRMINGHAM	120	433	123	304	178	273																										
BLACKPOOL	245	336	167	207	303	189	130																									
BOURNEMOUTH	108	578	213	449	121	417	161	274																								
BRIGHTON	59	608	290	479	202	415	170	304	95																							
BRISTOL	120	516	132	387	100	364	88	212	82	169																						
CAMBRIDGE	61	464	215	364	267	296	98	229	158	120	171																					
CARDIFF	155	536	118	407	137	384	108	232	128	205	48	205																				
CARLISLE	314	234	236	105	372	87	199	102	344	374	282	259	302																			
DOVER	78	589	325	506	272	420	208	332	179	81	206	124	241	401																		
EDINBURGH	413	125	335	82	471	57	298	201	443	474	381	336	401	99	461																	
EXETER	200	589	206	460	55	448	161	286	84	172	83	250	121	355	244	454																
FISHGUARD	261	526	56	397	243	379	177	223	233	310	153	310	112	292	347	391	227															
FORT WILLIAM	524	157	446	136	582	192	409	312	554	585	492	469	512	210	611	133	566	502														
GLASGOW	412	148	334	35	469	105	296	199	441	472	379	356	399	97	499	46	454	390	102													
GLOUCESTER	103	481	110	352	126	330	53	178	101	155	36	150	65	247	192	346	110	171	458	344												
HARWICH	82	548	309	448	312	380	192	316	206	132	218	69	251	343	136	420	297	357	553	440	191											
HOLYHEAD	283	462	105	333	341	315	168	159	313	344	251	260	206	228	370	327	325	161	439	325	216	355										
INVERNESS	574	106	496	216	632	219	459	362	604	634	542	519	561	259	661	157	616	552	65	174	507	603	487									
KENDAL	268	281	190	152	326	134	153	56	298	328	236	253	256	47	355	146	310	246	258	144	201	340	181	307								
KINGSTON UPON HULL	188	360	228	276	322	187	141	142	284	282	232	140	252	171	264	232	306	285	382	268	197	224	220	431	165							
LEEDS	199	328	174	228	302	160	121	87	264	262	212	148	231	123	272	200	286	230	333	220	177	232	165	383	72	60						
LINCOLN	142	389	199	288	274	221	88	154	240	215	185	94	204	183	219	261	259	254	394	280	150	179	205	443	177	48	73					
LIVERPOOL	216	360	111	231	274	213	101	56	246	277	184	193	204	126	303	225	258	167	336	223	149	288	102	386	79	129	74	141				
MANCHESTER	204	355	131	226	261	211	89	51	234	264	172	161	191	121	291	220	246	187	331	218	137	245	122	380	74	99	44	85	35			
MIDDLES	256	275	244	199	359	102	178	133	321	320	269	200	289	94	325	147	344	300	280	191	235	284	235	307	83	89	64	125	145	115		
N	288	236	277	161	392	63	211	152	354	352	302	233	322	59	357	108	376	333	240	153	267	317	268	267	92	145	97	157	177	147	39	
	115	488	277	388	329	320	159	253	220	169	233	63	266	283	173	360	313	372	493	380	212	74	305	543	277	151	173	103	241	185	224	257
	131	394	160	294	235	226	54	126	197	195	145	87	165	189	218	266	219	215	399	286	110	171	174	449	149	93	74	36	108	71	130	163
	514	182	436	126	571	181	398	301	543	574	481	458	501	199	601	123	556	492	50	92	447	542	427	115	246	371	322	383	325	320	269	230
	56	505	159	376	170	323	68	201	93	109	74	100	109	271	146	370	154	215	482	368	48	145	239	532	225	190	171	128	173	160	228	260
	309	699	316	570	109	548	271	396	196	283	194	361	231	465	356	564	109	337	676	562	219	406	433	725	419	415	395	368	367	355	452	484
	462	86	384	104	520	104	347	250	492	522	430	381	459	147	549	42	504	440	103	62	395	465	375	114	195	277	245	306	273	268	191	153
	86	435	205	335	264	267	87	200	184	158	158	38	194	230	162	307	248	300	440	327	140	122	225	490	224	111	120	50	188	132	171	204
	241	631	247	502	61	479	203	327	127	215	125	292	162	397	287	496	45	268	607	494	151	338	365	657	351	346	327	299	299	286	384	41
	75	591	245	461	161	418	153	287	53	49	97	135	160	356	141	456	133	266	567	453	119	168	324	616	310	284	265	217	258	246	322	35
	169	364	167	276	272	196	91	101	235	233	183	123	202	171	256	236	257	223	381	268	148	207	158	431	125	66	36	47	80	38	100	13
	163	415	74	286	221	268	48	111	193	224	131	140	110	181	251	280	205	128	391	278	97	235	104	441	134	163	118	125	66	70	189	22
	80	572	226	442	140	390	134	268	32	63	76	131	141	337	152	437	112	247	548	434	100	179	305	597	291	257	237	213	239	227	294	32
	44	536	272	453	275	368	155	279	163	90	179	71	214	348	94	408	229	320	559	445	154	63	316	608	302	211	220	166	250	238	272	30
	163	389	115	260	221	242	48	86	193	224	131	140	151	155	251	254	206	171	366	252	97	235	123	415	109	130	93	92	57	45	163	19
	422	240	344	52	479	171	307	210	452	482	390	367	409	107	509	132	464	400	186	85	355	451	335	266	154	279	230	291	233	228	202	16
	191	571	78	442	173	420	143	268	163	240	83	240	42	337	277	436	157	72	548	434	100	287	182	597	291	287	277	240	176	227	324	35
	629	161	551	271	687	274	514	417	659	689	597	574	616	314	716	212	671	607	112	229	562	658	542	57	362	486	438	498	440	435	361	32
	677	210	599	319	735	322	562	465	707	738	645	622	665	363	765	261	719	655	168	277	611	706	590	105	410	535	486	546	489	484	410	37
	212	321	200	221	315	153	134	114	278	276	226	157	245	116	281	193	300	256	326	213	191	241	191	376	91	38	24	81	101	71	50	90